REGNUM EDINBURGH CENTENARY SERIES
Volume 22

The Lausanne Movement: A Range of Perspectives

REGNUM EDINBURGH CENTENARY SERIES

The centenary of the World Missionary Conference of 1910, held in Edinburgh, was a suggestive moment for many people seeking direction for Christian mission in the 21st century. Several different constituencies within world Christianity held significant events around 2010. From 2005, an international group worked collaboratively to develop an intercontinental and multi-denominational project, known as Edinburgh 2010, and based at New College, University of Edinburgh. This initiative brought together representatives of twenty different global Christian bodies, representing all major Christian denominations and confessions, and many different strands of mission and church life, to mark the centenary.

Essential to the work of the Edinburgh 1910 Conference, and of abiding value, were the findings of the eight think-tanks or 'commissions'. These inspired the idea of a new round of collaborative reflection on Christian mission – but now focused on nine themes identified as being key to mission in the 21st century. The study process was polycentric, open-ended, and as inclusive as possible of the different genders, regions of the world, and theological and confessional perspectives in today's church. It was overseen by the Study Process Monitoring Group: Miss Maria Aranzazu Aguado (Spain, The Vatican), Dr Daryl Balia (South Africa, Edinburgh 2010), Mrs Rosemary Dowsett (UK, World Evangelical Alliance), Dr Knud Jørgensen (Norway, Areopagos), Rev John Kafwanka (Zambia, Anglican Communion), Rev Dr Jooseop Keum (Korea, World Council of Churches), Dr Wonsuk Ma (Korea, Oxford Centre for Mission Studies), Rev Dr Kenneth R. Ross (UK, Church of Scotland), Dr Petros Vassiliadis (Greece, Aristotle University of Thessalonikki), and co-ordinated by Dr Kirsteen Kim (UK, Edinburgh 2010).

These publications reflect the ethos of Edinburgh 2010 and will make a significant contribution to ongoing studies in mission. It should be clear that material published in this series will inevitably reflect a diverse range of views and positions. These will not necessarily represent those of the series' editors or of the Edinburgh 2010 General Council, but in publishing them the leadership of Edinburgh 2010 hopes to encourage conversation between Christians and collaboration in mission. All the series' volumes are commended for study and reflection in both church and academy.

Series Editors

Knud Jørgensen	Areopagos, Norway, MF Norwegian School of Theology & the Lutheran School of Theology, Hong Kong. Former Chair of Edinburgh 2010 Study Process Monitoring Group
Kirsteen Kim	Leeds Trinity University and former Edinburgh 2010 Research Co-ordinator, UK
Wonsuk Ma	Oxford Centre for Mission Studies, Oxford, UK
Tony Gray	Words by Design, Bicester, UK

REGNUM EDINBURGH CENTENARY SERIES
Volume 22

The Lausanne Movement: A Range of Perspectives

Edited by
Lars Dahle
Margunn Serigstad Dahle,
and Knud Jørgensen

First published 2014 by Regnum Books International

Regnum is an imprint of the Oxford Centre for Mission Studies
St Philip and St James Church
Woodstock Road
Oxford OX2 6HR, UK
www.ocms.ac.uk/regnum

09 08 07 06 05 04 03 7 6 5 4 3 2 1

British Library Cataloguing in Publication Data
A catalogue record for this book is available from the British Library

ISBN: 978-1-506476-40-7

Typeset by Words by Design

The publication of this title is made possible through the generous financial assistance of Normisjon (Norway), Norwegian Lutheran Mission, Norwegian Council on Mission and Evangelism and the Lausanne Committee on World Evangelization.

Distributed by 1517 Media in the US and Canada

Contents

CONCLUSION

FOREWORD

This volume sets out a range of perspectives on the Lausanne Movement, the third Lausanne Congress (Cape Town 2010), and Lausanne's work to serve the global church. I am grateful to all the contributors, and not least to the editors.

In the opening section, we find helpful 'personal preludes'. They remind us of how the Lausanne Movement, now a global, multi-cultural and multi-lingual network of networks – a wonderful work of God, in the hands of fallen men and women – began with individual conversations, small private meetings, phone calls, letters, personal prayers, and friendship. There has long been a culture of friendship in Lausanne, as we seek to model what has become known as 'the spirit of Lausanne'. These values of prayer, study, partnership, hope and humility, a legacy of Billy Graham and John Stott, remain at our core. Chris Wright's address included here, taking forward their application in the three words 'Humility, Integrity, Simplicity', was one of the most-viewed Congress addresses.

The editors invite us to use Lausanne as a lens as we explore missiological thinking and practice in the twentieth and twenty-first centuries. Essays cover their historical, theological, and contemporary aspects.

We then encounter fine thinkers and practitioners in world evangelization offering fresh and biblically-grounded approaches to Jewish evangelization, pneumatology, theodicy, and religious pluralism. The critical self-examination they bring adds *gravitas* to Lausanne's desire to call the whole church back to a biblical humility and integrity; to social responsibility, and to reconciliation. It is a call that longs for the church to be whole, in all her beauty and brokenness.

The writers approach issues from a variety of perspectives and cultural contexts. Some have long and deep involvement at the heart of the Movement; others write from outside looking in. Some bring a measured, weighed, and objective style to their writing; others a more journalistic approach, expressing their emotion and sometimes personal frustration. Most contributions here are well-researched, conveying helpful background. Lausanne wants to be open to criticism, and there is much to learn from criticisms levied in this volume. Where such criticism is based on an informed reading of events, and expressed in a constructive spirit , it demands to be heard.

It was a surprising development (even to me) for the Lausanne board to choose a relatively young leader and an Asian leader to serve as Executive Director / CEO. My own development and vision have been profoundly impacted by the Lausanne Movement. My first involvement was at the 2004 Forum in Pattaya, Thailand, then I helped to plan the 2006 Lausanne Younger Leaders' Gathering, at which I delivered the keynote address; for me this was a life-changing experience. Being a part of the Cape Town Congress was an unforgettable blessing. The Lausanne Movement strives to help younger leaders face the road ahead with faith in God, with a global perspective, and with thankfulness for what previous generations have done. We will always need to be a movement that embraces younger leaders and seeks an ever more diverse set of global voices with a unified purpose.

Let me reiterate my thanks to the editors and contributors for bringing us the fruits of their international collaboration. As we look forward, we have much to *celebrate* as we participate in the mission of God, for we are Christ's ambassadors, entrusted with the message of reconciliation (2 Corinthians 5:18-20). This volume will, I trust, enrich its readers' sense of gratitude for how God has made, and is making, his appeal through his people, in every sphere of society.

It is our calling, as the people of God, to engage our world in ways that are paradoxical and powerful, courageous and creative, yet marked by humility, integrity, and simplicity. There is much here to help stimulate thinking, planning and initiatives to that end. Share your discoveries at www.lausanne.org as part of the wider, global conversations taking place in the Lausanne Movement community.

Dr Michael Oh
Executive Director / CEO
The Lausanne Movement

ABBREVIATIONS

BGC	Billy Graham Center
BGEA	Billy Graham Evangelistic Association
CCC	Campus Crusade for Christ
CEVAA	Communauté d'Églises en mission, Community of Churches in Mission
CFO	Church for Others
CICCU	Cambridge Inter-Collegiate Christian Union
CLADE I	Latin American Congress of Evangelization (First)
CLADE II	Latin American Congress of Evangelization (Second)
COWE	Consultation on World Evangelization
CRESR	Consultation on the Relationship between Evangelism and Social Responsibility (CRESR)
CT 2010	Cape Town 2010
CTC	Cape Town Commitment
CTICC	The Cape Town International Convention Centre
CWG	Communications Working Group
CWM	Council for World Mission
CWME	Commission on World Mission and Evangelism in the WCC
DUFE	Deliver Us from Evil Consultation
EA	Evangelical Alliance
EPSA	English and Portuguese Speaking Africa
ERCDOM	Evangelical-Roman Catholic Dialogue on Mission
ESF	Evangelical Student Fellowship
GLF	Global Leadership Forum
HIS	*Humility*, *Integrity* and *Simplicity*
IDD	International Deputy Directors
IFES	International Fellowship of Evangelical Students
IMC	International Missionary Council
INFEMIT	International Fellowship of Evangelical Mission Theologians
IVF	Inter-Varsity Fellowship
IVP	Inter-Varsity Press
KCEN	Korea Campus Evangelization Network (KCEN)
LCJE	Lausanne Consultation on Jewish Evangelism
LCWE	Lausanne Committee for World Evangelization
LIWG	Lausanne Intercession Working Group
LM	Lausanne Movement
LOP	Lausanne Occasional Papers
LTEG	Lausanne Theology and Education Group
MM	Manila Manifesto

OCMS	Oxford Centre for Mission Studies
PCID	Pontifical Council for Inter-religious Dialogue
SFC	Students For Christ
TEF	Theological Education Fund
TWG	Theology Working Group (formerly the Lausanne Theology and Education Group, or LTEG)
UBF	University Bible Fellowship
UCCF	Universities and Colleges Christian Fellowship
UN	United Nations
WCC	World Council of Churches
WEA	World Evangelical Alliance
WEF	World Evangelical Fellowship
YLG	Younger Leaders' Gathering
YWAM	Youth With A Mission

Introductory Chapter
Evangelical Perspectives on Mission: From Lausanne to Cape Town

Lars Dahle, Margunn Serigstad Dahle
and Knud Jørgensen

This book is one of the volumes in the Regnum Edinburgh Centenary Series, a series that has grown out of the celebration of the Edinburgh 1910 World Missionary Conference and a series that eventually will include about thirty volumes on mission in the 21st century. Most of the titles relate to the nine themes of the Edinburgh 2010 study process while other titles explore missiological thinking within the major confessions and key Christian communities. In addition there are titles on significant missional topics, such as mission and the next generation, mission at and from the margins, Bible in mission, and mission and Diasporas. The series also includes volumes reflecting on the major 2010 events in Edinburgh, Tokyo and Cape Town.

The Cape Town 2010 event was the third Lausanne Congress on World Evangelization. The current volume reflects on this major event, on the wider historical context of the Lausanne Movement, as well as on the theological and missiological characteristics and contributions of that evangelical Movement.

The Rationale: Why a Volume on the Lausanne Movement?

The Regnum Edinburgh Centenary Series explores the continuing heritage of and challenge from Edinburgh 1910. In their concluding essay in the volume on the 1910 study commissions, missiologists David A. Kerr and Kenneth R. Ross point out the significant link between the 1910 conference and the Lausanne Movement: 'Though in strictly institutional terms it is the World Council of Churches which is the heir of Edinburgh 1910, in terms of promoting the agenda of world evangelization the Lausanne Movement might be seen as standing in direct continuity.'[1]

Since its beginning in 1974, the Lausanne Movement has had an ambivalent relationship to the heritage from the 1910 conference. Whereas

[1] K. R. Ross and D. A. Kerr, 'Conclusion: The Commissions after a Century', in K. R. Ross and D. A. Kerr (eds), *Edinburgh 2010: Mission Then and Now* (Oxford, UK: Regnum Books International, 2009), 315.

Lausanne always has affirmed the great global missionary endeavours coming out of that historic event, key leaders in the Movement have also consistently expressed deep theological concerns about the 1910 event and the subsequent WCC story. Thus, the leading Lausanne theologian John Stott claimed in 1996 that 'theologically, the fatal flaw at Edinburgh was not so much doctrinal disagreement as apparent doctrinal indifference, since doctrine was not on the agenda. Vital themes like the content of the gospel, the theology of evangelism, and the nature of the church were not discussed'.[2] However, on the contemporary scene, as documented in this volume, key leaders in the ecumenical movement have been more open to listening to – and often integrating – central evangelical theological concerns. There has also been a growing appreciation among the Lausanne leadership of the need to build appropriate relationships with the wider global church – beyond the evangelical communities.[3]

It is interesting to note that the only mentioning of Edinburgh 1910 in the *Cape Town Commitment* – which came out of the Cape Town Congress – is related to the global nature of today's world Christianity:

> At least two thirds of all the world's Christians now live in the continents of the global south and east. The composition of our Cape Town Congress reflected this enormous shift in world Christianity in the century since the Edinburgh Missionary Conference in 1910. We rejoice in the amazing growth of the Church in Africa, and we rejoice that our African sisters and brothers in Christ hosted this Congress.[4]

This quote also illustrates the strong relational dimension of the Lausanne Movement. Whereas the emphasis in WCC is on 'church ecumenism' between leading representatives from different confessions and member churches, the Lausanne Movement is characterized by 'alliance ecumenism' between individual leaders united by common evangelical convictions and a shared commitment to world evangelization. Hence, Lausanne has recently been officially introduced as 'a network of

---

[2] J. R. W. Stott, 'An Historical Introduction', in Stott (ed), *Making Christ Known: Historic Mission Documents from the Lausanne Movement 1974-1989* (Carlisle, UK: Paternoster Press, 1996), xii.

[3] It should also be mentioned that leading church ecumenicals have expressed key theological concerns in relation to Lausanne, especially regarding (a) the strong emphasis on church growth during the first Lausanne decade, (b) the lack of clarity on holistic Christian ministry, especially in the earlier years of Lausanne, and (c) the fact that the sacraments are not mentioned anywhere in the official Lausanne statements or in the Lausanne Occasional Papers (LOP).

[4] *The Cape Town Commitment: A Confession of Faith and a Call to Action* (Peabody, MA: Hendrickson, 2011) [often referred to below as *CTC*], 7.

evangelical leaders, thinkers, and reflective practitioners, [with the] purpose to strengthen the church for world evangelization'.[5]

Against the background of such structural, theological and missiological characteristics, this volume seeks to expound and explore the distinctive contributions of the Lausanne Movement. This also includes critical reflections and discussions. Before outlining the content of the various sections in this volume, it is natural to include a brief overview both of the Lausanne history and of evangelical theological convictions.

The Prelude: The Pivotal Role of Billy Graham

From about 1950 and onwards, American Baptist pastor Billy Graham gradually emerged as an evangelist of international significance and influence. This enabled Graham to play a vital role in the process leading up to the first Lausanne global congress in 1974.

In 1966, *The World Congress on Evangelism* was held in Berlin. It was jointly organized and funded by *Christianity Today* and The Billy Graham Evangelistic Association (BGEA), with Billy Graham as honorary chair and a central keynote speaker. Even though this congress 'was overwhelmingly American planned, led and financed … [the] reports and papers at the congress helped to illustrate the shift of Christianity's centre of gravity from Europe and North America to Africa, Asia and Latin America'.[6] The Berlin Congress is usually considered as the predecessor to Lausanne 1974. This is illustrated by the fact that it is included as a fourth global congress on the official Lausanne website.[7]

But how did the process move from Berlin in 1966 to Lausanne in 1974? Brian Stanley tells the story in his *The Global Diffusion of Evangelicalism: The Age of Billy Graham and John Stott*:

> The Berlin Congress in 1966 had been conceived as a singular event that would not be repeated …
>
> In January 1970 the Billy Graham Evangelistic Association convened a small international group of advisors in Washington to advice whether a sequel to Berlin would be desirable; the unanimous view, at least among the overseas members of the group, was that it would not. However, when Graham invited a similar group of sixteen to a meeting at White Sculpture Springs at the end of November 1971 to reconsider the question, he found a much more favourable response …

[5] 'The Lausanne Movement', in J. E. M. Cameron (ed), *Christ Our Reconciler: Gospel / Church / World. The Third Lausanne Congress on World Evangelization* (Nottingham, UK, and Downers Grove, IL: IVP, 2012), 9.

[6] 'Historical Introduction', www2.wheaton.edu/bgc/archives/berlin66.htm.

[7] www.lausanne.org/en/gatherings/global-congress/berlin-1966.html.

> It was agreed to consider planning a second world congress to take place in the summer of 1974 with the aim 'To unite all evangelicals in the common task of total evangelization of the world'.[8]

The focus of the second world congress would be broader than in Berlin. Sydney Bishop A. Jack Dain, who had been personally asked by Graham at the December 1971 meeting to be Chairman of the steering committee (later known as the planning or executive committee),[9] expressed the following overall aim in February 1972: "We ought to be looking again at the whole mission of the Church, bearing in mind that this involves making disciples, baptising and teaching."[10]

From December 1971 and onwards, Billy Graham and his organization (BGEA) 'were committed to bringing this vision to reality'.[11] With an awareness of the emerging global nature of evangelicalism and world mission, with deep concerns for recent developments in the World Council of Churches and out of a deep vision for co-operation among evangelicals, Billy Graham therefore invited evangelical leaders from all over the world to the ground-breaking congress on world evangelization in Lausanne in 1974. Graham and his organization played a significant role in providing funding and organizational support for the congress.

As in Berlin in 1966, Billy Graham was one of the most influential keynote speakers also in Lausanne. His opening speech 'Why Lausanne?' set the course for the whole congress – and for the subsequent Movement, whereas his closing address 'The King is Coming' provided a conclusion to the congress from an evangelist's more personal perspective.[12]

In view of the above, we may conclude that the Lausanne 1974 congress would never have taken place without Billy Graham's vision, initiative, support and networks.[13] This unique contribution does not in any way diminish the role of other essential contributors, such as Jack Dain and

---

[8] B. Stanley, *The Global Diffusion of Evangelicalism: The Age of Billy Graham and John Stott* [A History of Evangelicalism, Vol. 5 (1940s-1990s) (Nottingham, UK: IVP, 2013), 155-156. See also Lausanne's own account at www.lausanne.org/en/gatherings/global-congress/lausanne-1974/historical-background.html.

[9] Stanley, *The Global Diffusion of Evangelicalism*, 157.

[10] Wheaton College, Billy Graham Center Archives, Collection 46, LCWE, Box 30/1, A. J. Dain to Charles Troutman, 17th Feb 1972.

[11] Stanley, *The Global Diffusion of Evangelicalism*, 157.

[12] It should be mentioned that the concluding chapter of this volume uses Graham's opening speech as a grid for understanding the global impact of the Lausanne Movement.

[13] 'The first Congress in 1974 was actually convened through the vision of Billy Graham together with the strong leadership of Bishop Jack Dain who served as the chairman of ICOWE in Lausanne in 1974. Interestingly, John Stott was ambivalent about the Congress and only agreed to participate after Graham and Dain both met with him on two separate occasions.' (Previous CEO / Executive Director Doug Birdsall in an email to Lars Dahle on 28th Jan 2014.)

John Stott, to the process leading up to and including the congress itself in 1974.

The dynamic between Billy Graham and John Stott in the Lausanne context is well expressed by Doug Birdsall:

> As it turned out, Stott emerged as the most influential person in the Lausanne Congress and in the Lausanne Movement because of his primary role as the architect of the *Lausanne Covenant*, his prominence as a Bible expositor at Berlin 66, Lausanne 74, and Lausanne II in Manila, and his leadership role as the Chair of the Theology Working Group for many years. However, John Stott always deferred to Billy Graham and consistently stated that the Lausanne Movement would not have happened without Graham's vision and global stature. When we asked each of them to write a letter of greeting for Cape Town, John Stott said that he wanted to see Billy Graham's letter first. He said, "Billy should have the first word, and then I will write what I think would be appropriate to complement his letter." It was a very interesting dynamic between them. They were the luminaries of the Lausanne Movement and exemplary leaders for global evangelicalism.[14]

The Story: From Lausanne 1974 to Cape Town 2010 and Beyond

The global congress on evangelization in Lausanne in 1974 was the start of the fascinating Lausanne story, which may be explored at various interconnected levels.[15]

First, it is a story on *the structural level* of key Lausanne-related events. The three global congresses in Lausanne (1974), Manila (1989) and Cape Town (2010) stand out as the most decisive events. The three global leadership forums in Pattaya (1980 and 2004) and in Bangalore (2013) should also be mentioned, along with a long series of influential global consultations. Among the more important Lausanne events are also the global conferences with younger leaders held in Singapore (1987) and in Kuala Lumpur (2006).

---

[14] Doug Birdsall in an email to Lars Dahle on 28th Jan 2014. The letters of greeting from Graham and Stott to the Cape Town Congress are published in Cameron, *Christ Our Reconciler*, 14-16. It should be added that Billy Graham's long-term involvement in the Lausanne Movement has been less extensive and influential than in this early phase, despite his continuing role in the international advisory leadership as 'Founder' (cf. www.lausanne.org/en/about/leadership/advisory-leadership.html).

[15] For informative introductions to these issues, see e.g. J. Scherer, *Gospel, Church and Kingdom: Comparative Studies in World Mission Theology* (Augsburg Publishing House, 1987), C. Ott, S. J. Strauss and T. C. Tennent, *Encountering Theology of Mission: Biblical Foundations, Historical Developments and Contemporary Issues* (Grand Rapids, MI: Baker Academic, 2010), and T. C. Tennent, *Invitation to World Missions: A Trinitarian Missiology for the Twenty-first Century* (Grand Rapids, MI: Kregel Publications, 2010).

Secondly, it is a story on *the resource level* of key Lausanne-related publications coming out of Lausanne events. This includes the three seminal congress documents (i.e. the *Lausanne Covenant*, the *Manila Manifesto*, and the *Cape Town Commitment*), all the *Lausanne Occasional Papers* from global forums and consultations, many influential books, and a wealth of available online material from the whole Lausanne history.

Thirdly, it is a story on *the catalyst level* of key Lausanne-related convictions and ideas that have been influential both within and beyond the Movement itself. This includes connecting and convening evangelical (and other interested Christian) leaders, communicating ideas and strategies, and hosting discussion and resource-sharing. And it also includes influencing the wider Christian world with foundational evangelical theological and missiological convictions.

Fourthly, it is a story on *the relational level* of key Lausanne-related formal and informal networks. It is significant to note how many contributors in this volume express a deep appreciation of the personal significance of Lausanne-related networks, partnerships and friendships.

The Foundations: Evangelical Perspectives

In the words of International Director Lindsay Brown in the final address to the Cape Town Congress, 'Lausanne is an unashamedly evangelical movement.' He claimed therefore the need 'to have clarity on four things: (i) the exclusive claims of Christ, (ii) the meaning of Christ's death; (iii) the necessity of conversion; and (iv) the lostness of humankind. The *Cape Town Commitment* seeks to give this clarity.'[16]

This statement on central evangelical convictions is closely related to influential current definitions and descriptions of 'evangelicalism'.[17] In the midst of the huge theological, ecclesiological and sociological variety within today's evangelical world, historian David W. Bebbington has proposed four key evangelical priorities which have gained wide support:

> *conversionism*, the belief that lives need to be changed;
> *activism*, the expression of the gospel in effort;
> *Biblicism*, a particular regard for the Bible;
> and what may be called *cruci-centrism*, a stress on the sacrifice of Christ on the Cross.[18]

---

[16] Lindsay Brown's final address is published as a chapter in this volume.

[17] 'Evangelicalism' should not be understood as an organized movement *per se*, but rather as (a) a cluster of a wide variety of churches, missions, para-church organizations, institutions, and individuals, (b) a set of shared theological and missiological convictions and passions, and (c) local, national and global networks associated with WEA and/or the Lausanne Movement.

[18] D. W. Bebbington, *Evangelicalism in Modern Britain: A History from the 1930s to the 1980s* (London: Unwin Hyman, 1989), 3. It should be noted that Bebbington's four terms have not been as influential as his analysis.

Even though Bebbington's summary is based primarily on an historical analysis of British evangelicalism, the correspondence seems clear to 'the cluster of six controlling convictions' in global evangelicalism offered by influential theologian and historian of ideas Alister E. McGrath:

> 1. The supreme authority of Scripture as a source of knowledge of God, and a guide to Christian living.
> 2. The majesty of Jesus Christ, both as incarnate God and Lord, and as Saviour of sinful humanity.
> 3. The lordship of the Holy Spirit.
> 4. The need for personal conversion.
> 5. The priority of evangelism for both individual Christians and the church as a whole.
> 6. The importance of the Christian community for spiritual nourishment, fellowship and growth.[19]

This central cluster of key doctrinal and existential evangelical convictions is a natural link to the summary offered by John Stott in his *Evangelical Truth: A Personal Plea for Unity*. According to Stott, the evangelical faith has a Trinitarian emphasis – on the Word, the Cross and the Spirit. These are

> the three essentials to which evangelical people are determined to bear witness. They concern the gracious initiative of God the Father in revealing himself to us, in redeeming us through Christ crucified, and in transforming us through the indwelling Spirit.[20]

This evangelical commitment to Trinitarian faith and to the threefold emphasis of the Word, the Cross and the Spirit may be viewed as defining theological characteristics of the Lausanne Movement. The first emphasis is found in the focus on the authority and the centrality of the Scripture. The second emphasis is found in the focus on the uniqueness and the redemptive work of Christ. The third emphasis is found in the focus on the presence and power of the Spirit enabling the whole church to do integral mission in the whole world.[21]

It is important to realize that Lausanne's commitment to world evangelization flows out of these fundamental theological convictions and emphases. As expressed in the section on 'We love the mission of God' – i.e. the *missio Dei* – in the *Cape Town Commitment*:

> We are committed to world mission, because it is central to our understanding of God, the Bible, the Church, human history and the ultimate future …

---

[19] A. E. McGrath, *Evangelicalism and the Future Christianity* (London: Hodder & Stoughton, 1988).

[20] (Leicester, UK: IVP, 1999), 38.

[21] The centrality of this threefold theological emphasis in the Lausanne Movement may be illustrated with a reference to the *Cape Town Commitment* and to the six plenary Bible expositions in Cape Town by a global team of Bible teachers. These six expositions are published in Cameron, *Christ Our Reconciler*.

… We commit ourselves to the integral and dynamic exercise of all dimensions of mission to which God calls his Church.

- God commands us to make known to all nations the truth of God's revelation and the gospel of God's saving grace through Jesus Christ, calling all people to repentance, faith, baptism and obedient discipleship.
- God commands us to reflect his own character through compassionate care for the needy, and to demonstrate the values and the power of the kingdom of God in striving for justice and peace and in caring for God's creation.[22]

These central theological concerns should be kept in mind, when reading the various contributions from our global team of writers. This is especially important, since a key intention behind our volume is to give a broad perspective on the missiological development and thinking among evangelicals in general, with a particular focus on the Lausanne Movement.[23]

Introducing the Four Sections

The first section of this volume is an overall introduction to the Lausanne Movement, both historically, theologically and missiologically. This includes three chapters on the Lausanne story offering personal perspectives, two chapters on the theological and missiological contributions of Lausanne, two chapters on the Lausanne Movement in relation both to communications and to the news media, a chapter on the formative influence of John Stott, and finally a chapter on available Lausanne resources. Thus, this first section illustrates the above-mentioned fact that the history of Lausanne may be explored at various levels.

The second section explores key issues and concepts of Lausanne as they have emerged in thematic consultations over the years. The selected central topics are:

- The Holy Spirit and the Gospel
- Deliver Us From Evil Consultation
- Faith and Truth in a Pluralistic, Globalized World
- Gospel and Culture

---

[22] *CTC*, 27, 29 .

[23] This section on evangelical foundations should not be seen as exhaustive – but rather as indicative – in terms of key theological foci in classical evangelicalism as represented by The Lausanne Movement. The very heart of classical evangelical identity – as traditionally understood – has recently been succinctly expressed by well-known Lausanne speaker Os Guinness: 'Evangelicals are those who define themselves and their faith by the "good news" of the kingdom announced by Jesus' (O. Guinness, 'Found Faithful: Standing Fast in Faith in the Advanced Modern Era', in R. Lints (ed), *Renewing the Evangelical Mission* (Grand Rapids, MI: Eerdmans, 2013), 104.

- Evangelism and Social Responsibility: The Making of a Transformational Vision
- Jewish Evangelism
- A Case Study: The Influence of the Lausanne Movement on Korean Younger Christian Leaders
- Strategy in Mission – 21st Century Style
- Calling the Church of Christ Back to Humility and Integrity
- Poverty, Prosperity and the Gospel
- The Church and the Message of Reconciliation
- History of the Partnership of Men and Women in the Lausanne Movement

The third section introduces the Cape Town Congress. The introductory chapter in this section explores the mission statement of the Lausanne III congress: 'Its goal? To bring a fresh challenge to the global Church to bear witness to Jesus Christ and all his teaching – in every nation, in every sphere of society, and in the realm of ideas.'[24] This is followed by a chapter on Cape Town 2010 as process and event and a chapter with the closing address at the congress. The final part of this third section contains a number of regional evangelical perspectives offering significant reflections on Lausanne III – from Latin-America, Asia, Middle East, and the west.[25]

The fourth section of this volume contains critical reflections and discussions on Lausanne and Cape Town from key representatives from within the Movement and from other major mission communities.[26] The introductory chapter in this section sets the scene for subsequent chapters by comparing and contrasting the three major 2010 events in Tokyo, Edinburgh, and Cape Town. This is followed by appreciative yet critical reflections on Lausanne from representatives of the World Evangelical Alliance, the World Council of Churches, the Roman Catholic Church, and the Pentecostal movement. These are set within the context of a chapter on Lausanne in critical contemporary dialogue with the whole church, a chapter comparing the views on dialogue and mission in Lausanne and in WCC, and a final chapter reflecting on the *Cape Town Commitment* from an evangelical perspective in terms of both continuity and change.

---

[24] Foreword, *Cape Town Commitment*, 4. This significant mission statement was articulated and communicated by International Director Lindsay Brown at The Cape Town Congress and subsequently included in the signed foreword to the *Cape Town Commitment*. 'It was chosen because we wanted to highlight the application of the Gospel, the Lordship of Christ, and Biblical truth to every area of life.' (Lindsay Brown in an email to Lars Dahle on 28th Jan 2014.)

[25] In spite of wholehearted attempts, we were not able to secure a specific African reflection. As a feeble compensation, we have as editors tried to highlight African perspectives where relevant.

[26] This is also in line with the ethos of the whole Regnum Edinburgh Centenary Series.

Our concluding chapter focuses on the Lausanne Movement as it moves forward from Cape Town and beyond the 40th anniversary in 2014. In this chapter, we seek to identify key missiological contributions from Lausanne, to describe essential elements of a Lausanne identity, and to summarize the current status of the Movement by focusing on a new series of global consultations and other key initiatives, networks and strategies.

It should be mentioned that we are grateful for the insightful and engaging foreword by Michael Oh as the new Executive Director and CEO of the Lausanne Movement. As an Appendix, we have also included the helpful summary of the *Cape Town Commitment* by Kevin Smith, which we acknowledge with gratitude.

This book is the result of the work of a global team of more than thirty contributors – from a wide variety of contexts, traditions and ministries – but united in the appreciation of the Lausanne Movement as a key contributor to contemporary missiology and missions. The team of peer reviewers should also be mentioned for its significant effort. We want to thank our many collaborators and colleagues for inspiring partnership in this project. It is our hope and prayer that this volume may be of real and enduring value to the Lausanne Movement, other missional communities in the global church, and beyond.

Lars Dahle, Margunn Serigstad Dahle and Knud Jørgensen
April 2014

SECTION ONE

INTRODUCING THE LAUSANNE MOVEMENT

THE LAUSANNE STORY: A PERSONAL PRELUDE

Knud Jørgensen

In 1974 I attended Lausanne as a young journalist. In 2010 I attended Cape Town as a senior statesman. The decades between these two events contain the life of an 'evangelical ecumenical'. I was sent to the Lausanne Congress on World Evangelization in 1974 by one of the major Geneva-based ecumenical organizations to report on events and themes for Radio Voice of the Gospel in Ethiopia. At the end of Lausanne 1974 I signed the *Lausanne Covenant* – and returned to Geneva and Ethiopia.

The word 'evangelization' was new to me; it had an American tone and smelled of effectiveness. I knew what 'evangelism' was from my days within Christian youth work and the Intervarsity movement in Denmark. But 'evangelization' meant more than witnessing to a neighbour. It had to do with 'unreached' people groups, church growth theory, the need for *sodalities* (go-structures) and not just *modalities* (come-structures). And there was a professor (Ralph Winter) from Fuller Theological Seminary who talked about various types of evangelism: E-1, E-2, and E-3. I understood that I probably was an E-3 evangelist in my radio ministry in Africa.

My job at Lausanne 74 was to make radio programmes. So I pulled key people into my small home-made studio: Billy Graham, John Stott, Peter Beyerhaus, Samuel Escobar, René Padilla, Ralph Winter, etc. I did not know that they were 'famous'. I asked questions, listened – and sensed that what they said echoed the tones of revival and radical discipleship of my Intervarsity days.

'Radical discipleship' was something I had learned from reading Dietrich Bonhoeffer's *The Cost of Discipleship.*[1] At Lausanne I heard the same tone, first in the desire to bind together evangelism and socio-political involvement, as expressed in the *Lausanne Covenant*, but even more in the insistent call from the Latin Americans to 'repudiate as demonic the attempt to drive a wedge between evangelism and social action'.[2] I came from a church[3] in Ethiopia whose guiding light was 'Serving the Whole Human Being', so I was in tune with what they said, that there is no dichotomy in the Bible between the Word spoken and the Word made visible in the lives of God's people. I understood that there was a tension

---

[1] Dietrich Bonhoeffer, *The Cost of Discipleship* (New York: Macmillan, 1966).

[2] James A. Scherer, *Gospel, Church & Kingdom. Comparative Studies in World Mission Theology* (Minneapolis, MN: Augsburg Publishing House, 1987), 174f.

[3] The Ethiopian Evangelical Church Mekane Yesus (EECMY).

here between the 'evangelization' people and the 'holistic' people. I sided with those who said that those who proclaim the Cross must be marked by the Cross.

While studying at Fuller Theological Seminary shortly after Lausanne 1974, I felt rather alone with my holistic view. Church growth, à la Fuller professor Donald McGavran,[4] the name of the game, and his focus was 'redemption and social lift': disciple people and then the Spirit will change their lives and they will be change-makers in society. I was therefore relieved when the very first *Lausanne Occasional Paper* (LOP) dealt with the 'homogeneous unit principle',[5] and when one of the most important subsequent LOPs was a report from the consultation in Grand Rapids about *Evangelism and Social Responsibility*,[6] both of them were edited by 'Uncle John' (John Stott). I taught regularly at his London Institute for Contemporary Christianity and was therefore included in his extended 'family'.

On my bookshelves I have found 25 books and booklets directly related to Lausanne. A fair number are the LOPs which have followed me and inspired me throughout my life – and which I would love to see revived. Here was a format easily accessible and requiring clarity in form. Among the books are three volumes that grew out of consultations and study processes of which I had the privilege of being part. The first volume is a book on *God the Evangelist*[7] which grew out of a consultation on the 'Work of the Holy Spirit and Evangelization' held in Oslo in May 1985. The co-ordinator was my close friend, Dr Tormod Engelsviken. The purpose of the consultation was to take the Holy Spirit seriously in connection with evangelism. All of us had prepared solid and learned papers on the topic; my paper was on 'The Use of Electronic Media in Evangelization'. As we discussed and deliberated on these papers, we realised on the second-to-last day that we were stuck. We simply did not know how to proceed. Here was a group of top missiologists and evangelical leaders from around the globe, including John Wimber from the Vineyard movement in California, and we did not know where to go. Then someone suggested that perhaps we should wait for the Holy Spirit; for a whole hour we sat still, praying and letting the Spirit talk. To me that was the most memorable part of the consultation. The Holy Spirit was present

[4] Let me add that I learned a lot from McGavran and his colleagues about church growth, culture, contextual theology and the biblical base for mission. Fuller is my *alma mater* and a place that has impacted my life.

[5] LCWE, *The Pasadena Consultation – Homogeneous Unit Principle* (Wheaton, IL: IL: LCWE, 1978).

[6] LCWE and the World Evangelical Fellowship, *Evangelism and Social Responsibility. An Evangelical Commitment* (Wheaton, IL: LCWE and WEF, 1982).

[7] David F. Wells, *God the Evangelist: How the Holy Spirit Works to Bring Men and and Women to Faith* (Grand Rapids, MI: William B. Eerdmans, 1987).

in a strong and quiet manner, and rather than pass a number of resolutions (which Bruce Nichols from the World Evangelical Fellowship and I actually had worked the whole night to formulate!), we agreed to hand over our papers and the input of our discussions to David Wells who then pulled all of it together in his book on *God the Evangelist.*

The second book to which I contributed was on *Faith and Modernity.*[8] Also at that time (in 1993) I wrote on media ('Modernity, information technology and Christian faith'). It was Os Guinness that had inspired us to hold a consultation in Uppsala on Faith and Modernity. He had given a paper in Manila in 1989 on the same topic – a paper which provoked great interest and which was so well delivered that all of us got up and applauded. The Uppsala consultation did not get under my skin as the Oslo event (1985), but it represented an honest and biblically based attempt to set up signposts for our encounter with modernity and post-modernity. We struggled, we sweated, and we discussed and listened to one another – Lesslie Newbigin, David Wells, Harold Netland, Vinay Samuel and Os Guinness. I was 43 years of age but felt like a teenager in this solemn company. What impressed me then and now is how Lausanne people have been concerned not only for unreached people, but also for searching for inroads for the Gospel into contemporary society in the Global North. The role this search played in Cape Town in 2010 is a good illustration (where Os Guinness once again played a key role).

The third book is about 'an uneasy frontier in Christian mission' as we called it. My field of study had by then shifted from information society to missiology. Within missiology at that time a major controversy had erupted around the concept 'spiritual warfare'. I was then chair of the Lausanne Theology Working Group, and we decided to bring together a group of key players in August 2000 outside Nairobi. 'We' included Scott Moreau, Tormod Engelsviken, Tokunboh Adeyemo, Birger Nygaard and me. We agreed to replace the word 'warfare' with 'conflict' (to take the military hot air out of the balloon), and we managed to put together a statement on 'Deliver Us From Evil'. As a moderator, I have seldom felt so 'successful' in terms of having achieved something essential for the understanding of the Gospel and the understanding of the adversary Satan and his forces. This echoed Luther's hymn, 'A mighty fortress is our God', and my own experiences in Ethiopia and the East African Revival: 'You must live in the light so that the devil doesn't catch you in the dark,' the African leaders had taught me. A key text is Col 2:13ff about how Christ cancelled my record of debts on his Cross and freed me from the power of the spiritual rulers and authorities: 'He made a public spectacle of them by leading them as captives in his victory procession.' Hallelujah! This tone can still make me weep and laugh at one and the same time. In Danish and Norwegian we

---

[8] Philip Sampson, Vinay Samuel and Chris Sugden (eds), (Oxford, UK: Regnum Books, 1994).

have a hymn about this: 'God's Son has set me free from Satan's tyranny.' The outcome of the consultation was an LOP written by Tormod Engelsviken[9] and a book edited primarily by Scott Moreau about *Deliver Us From Evil*[10] – a book which reflects a meeting of sisters and brothers where we managed to talk together about a most controversial topic at that time. My own paper was on 'Spiritual Conflict in the Socio-Political Context' – a topic which brought together my African experiences and spiritual conflict in political and economic arenas. It was at this consultation I came to know Hwa Yung from Malaysia who since then has been a good friend. Also my doctoral mentor Charles H. Kraft from Fuller and his wife Marguerite were there with their warmth and wise input.

The modernity and the spiritual conflict consultations took place after the second Lausanne Congress on World Evangelization in Manila in 1989. My role in Manila was information and communication. Prior to Manila I had for a couple of years been part of the Communication Working Group headed by Warwick Olson. At the last hour before the congress, the group had to become operational and take over the running of the information service.[11] My job became to lead some of the press conferences. One of them featured a man I had met already in Oslo in 1985, John Wimber. 'Signs and Wonders' was his trademark. Having lived in Ethiopia and encountered the stark reality of evil spirits, I was open for what Wimber had to share. Already in Oslo in 1985 he had talked about 'demonizing powers over Oslo' – strong words for a non-charismatic Lutheran. But prior to 1989 in Manila I had experienced renewal through meeting with the charismatic movement Oase in Norway, and had become personally acquainted with Wimber. In Manila the focus on signs and wonders – and on Pentecostalism – was highly controversial, and therefore the press conference became quite 'excited'. But in the *Manila Manifesto* it was clearly affirmed 'that spiritual warfare demands spiritual weapons, and that we must both preach the words in the power of the Spirit, and pray constantly that we may enter into Christ's victory over the principalities and powers of evil'.[12]

Manila inspired me deeply with its clarion call: 'Proclaim Christ until He Comes'. Here was the focus that since then has become the watchword for the Movement: 'Calling the Whole Church to Take the Whole Gospel to

---

[9] Tormod Engelsviken, *Spiritual Conflict in Today's Mission* (Monrovia, CA: Marc Publications, 2001).

[10] A. Scott Moreau, Tokunboh Adeyemo, David G. Burnett, Bryant L. Myers and Hwa Yung, *Deliver Us From Evil. An Uneasy Frontier in Christian Mission* (Monrovia, CA: Marc Publications, 2002).

[11] See Kåre Melhus' chapter in this volume on 'The three global Lausanne congresses as influential media events'.

[12] LCWE, *Manila Manifesto. An elaboration of the Lausanne Covenant fifteen years later* (Pasadena, CA: LCWE, 1989), 5-6.

the Whole World'.[13] While in Manila, the Communication Working Group, of which I was a member, there and then brought to completion a book on the last day of the congress with the title *The Whole Gospel for the Whole World.*[14] The editor was Australian Alan Nichols who managed to get all of us to write and give input. How exciting and exhausting to write a book while the congress was still in session. The congress also gave birth to a small book in Danish which I have cherished and often used when telling about Manila.[15] If we want to make Lausanne appeal to people at the grass roots, we need such popular books in different languages.

Upon my return from Manila, I wondered how to put into action and find expression for my deep-felt inspiration. The result was a list of topics and headlines which I shared with my friend Ole Christian Kvarme, then General Secretary of the Norwegian Bible Society and today Bishop of the Church of Norway in Oslo. "Why don't we write a book?" I asked Ole Christian. He suggested that I join hands with two missiologists, Jan-Martin Berentsen and Tormod Engelsviken. We took the challenge and worked together for several years. The outcome was a major textbook on *Missiology Today.*[16] This is, as far as I know, the only textbook based on the *Lausanne Covenant* and the *Manila Manifesto.* The textbook (500 pages!) is, twenty years after the first edition, still the major textbook on missiology in Scandinavia. Here is a major legacy of Lausanne and Manila. May Cape Town inspire younger missiologists to set in motion similar endeavours! Why? Because such an endeavour like *Missiology Today* will influence students of theology, missiology and Christian faith in the next decade. We sorely need this in the midst of a theological universe in the Global North where mission has lost its cutting edge.

Another outcome of Manila 1989 was a booklet which in Norwegian was called *Vitner i arbeid og fritid* – 'Witnesses in work and leisure time: Tentmaking Ministry to the Ends of the World'. J. Christy Wilson's book *Today's Tentmakers* (1979) had been available for quite some time, but was first brought to my attention in Manila by a very persuasive Norwegian lady called Berit Helgøy Kloster. The *Manila Manifesto* had emphasized that 'the priesthood of all believers' also meant 'the ministry of all believers': "We repent of our share in discouraging the ministry of the laity, especially of women and young people. We determine in the future to encourage all Christ's followers to take their place, rightfully and naturally,

---

[13] J. D. Douglas (ed), *Proclaim Christ until He Comes: Calling the Whole Church to Take the Whole Gospel to the Whole World* (Minneapolis, MN: World Wide Publications, 1990).

[14] Alan Nichols (ed), *The Whole Gospel for the Whole World* (Charlotte, NC: LCWE and Regal Books, 1989).

[15] Kai Kjær-Hansen and Bodil F. Skjøtt, *Forkynd Kristus indtil han kommer* (Århus: OKAY-BOG, 1989).

[16] Jan-Martin Berentsen, Tormod Engelsviken & Knud Jørgensen (eds), *Missiologi i dag* (Oslo: Universitetsforlaget, 1994 and 2004).

as his witnesses."[17] The workplace was in particular focus in the *Manila Manifesto*. Here was Berit's entry point: If the workplace is a primary arena of witnessing about the Lord, then the tentmaking mission strategy of Paul and the Early Church had to be rediscovered fully. The track on tentmaking at the congress developed a list of challenges about the possibilities for cross-cultural positions as a means for spreading the Kingdom, and for churches and mission agencies to acknowledge tentmaking as a ministry, and therefore to recruit tentmakers. My friend Berit got me hooked and we co-authored a Norwegian booklet[18] and developed a full-scale training programme for tentmakers. Today, 24 years later, Berit is still the torchbearer (and the senior associate) for tentmaking in Lausanne circles. She is in my view one of the best illustrations of what Lausanne is all about: a Movement 'staffed' by committed and persevering people. *A propos* witness in the workplace, this challenge and concern is still high on the Lausanne agenda. The latest illustration was the Global Leadership Forum in Bangalore in June 2013 where a whole day in the programme was devoted to 'Influence in and through the workplace as people of simplicity'. The Forum, three short years after Cape Town 2010, was for me and many a time for taking stock and for looking ahead: how may we, through old and new partnerships, chart the course into our broken world as messengers of a wounded God? And then it was, once again, a blessed time of basking in the 'spirit of Lausanne'.

For several years from 2000 onwards I was a member of the Lausanne Administrative Committee under the gracious leadership of Paul Cedar. We met regularly for teleconferences, we struggled to find the way ahead in the midst of (and in competition with) Luis Bush's dynamic push for 'Towards 2000 and beyond', and we finally ended up calling the Lausanne family and all its 'relatives' together in Pattaya in 2004. The 2004 Forum for World Evangelization was held 29th September-5th October, co-ordinated and steered by David Claydon from Australia (married to Robyn Claydon; this couple has for decades incarnated the Lausanne spirit and been an inspiration to me and many others). Pattaya 2004 brought together more than 1,500 Christian leaders from around the world to focus on the task of global evangelism. Through a comprehensive worldwide research effort, 31 specific issues were identified as roadblocks to evangelism, and issue groups were formed around each issue. These issue groups each prepared a paper concerning their issue that included a strategic action plan for addressing the concern. I was part of a group led by Ryan Bolger, a young missiologist from Fuller Theological Seminary. We worked together, both while in Pattaya and afterwards, on an LOP entitled *The Local Church in Mission: Becoming a Missional Congregation in the Twenty-First Century*

---

[17] *Manila Manifesto* (1989), 20f.

[18] Knud Jørgensen & Berit Helgøy Kloster, *Vitner i arbeid og fritid. Teltmakertjeneste til jordens ender* (Oslo: Credo, 1991).

Global Context.[19] This was my first meeting with the concept 'emerging churches'.[20] Together with my earlier discovery of the concept 'missional church', as an expression of what the church *is* before it *does*, 'emerging church' has changed my view of the church and mission, a view which in turn is reflected in what I contributed to the Edinburgh 2010 study group on Forms of Missionary Engagement.[21]

That takes me to one of the last books in my Lausanne library. It is entitled *Transforming Mission – Misjon til forandring*,[22] a title borrowed from David Bosch's magisterial volume with the same title.[23] I got the idea while listening to an evening plenary in Cape Town on 'The Church on the Move'. Sitting with my table group (a major personal experience that I cherish from Cape Town), I started making notes about possible chapters: God's footsteps in the world, Christian mission in a changing world, Bringing Christ to people of another faith, Reconciliation in a divided world, Mission and migration, Media messages matter. The end-result in early 2011 was a book in Norwegian about Lausanne and Cape Town – a book where we as participants from Norway wanted to share what we experienced in Cape Town as challenges for mission in the 21st century.

Included in the book was also a translation into Norwegian of the *Cape Town Commitment*.

It was a lot of work to get the book off the ground. Why spend so much time on Cape Town – and earlier on Lausanne, Pattaya and Manila? Because Lausanne 74 changed my life. It opened my windows to see the whole world, it challenged me to costly discipleship and a simple lifestyle, and it gave me a solid and lifelong foundation in Scripture, in the uniqueness of Christ, and in *diakonia* (Christian social responsibility). It has helped me significantly to clarify theological issues in mission, and to understand the importance of strategies and contextual approaches to cross-cultural mission. In my evangelical-ecumenical life[24] it has blended

---

[19] www.lausanne.org/en/documents/lops/854-lop-39.html.

[20] Eddie Gibbs and Ryan Bolger, *Emerging Churches: Creating Christian Community in Postmodern Cultures* (Grand Rapids, MI: Baker Academic, 2005).

[21] Daryl Balia and Kirsteen Kim (eds), *Edinburgh 2010: Witnessing to Christ Today* (Oxford, UK: Regnum Books International, 2010), 116-147.

[22] Rolf Ekenes, Tormod Engelsviken, Knud Jørgensen and Rolf Kjøde (eds), *Misjon til forandring. Refleksjoner og visjoner fra Lausanne III* (Skjetten: Hermon Forlag, 2011).

[23] David J. Bosch, *Transforming Mission: Paradigm Shifts in Theology of Mission* (Maryknoll, NY: Orbis Books, 1991).

[24] I refer to my chapter in this book *Edinburgh, Tokyo and Cape Town: Comparing and Contrasting on the Way to 2110* where I deal with some of the different views among conciliars/ecumenicals and evangelicals on some key theological and ecclesiological issues. Most important among these issues are the uniqueness of Christ, the view of revelation in other living faiths, the understanding of Scripture as the sole source of and norm for faith and praxis, the radical nature of sin, and the role of the *magisterium* (pastoral office) vis-à-vis the priesthood of all believers.

evangelical tradition with modernity/post-modernity and made me yearn for renewal, similar to the Vatican II focus on *aggiornamento.*[25] It has provided me with a critical reflection on the meaning of culture[26] and a fresh view of conversion.

Above all – or in the midst of it all – Lausanne has become my network, even a family, of friends, contacts and mentors around the world with whom I walk on the road to Emmaus, to share a meal with the risen Lord.

Lausanne transformed my life and continues to make my heart tick.

---

[25] A new agenda and beginning. Pope John XXIII used this word to describe what he wanted from Vatican II: to bring about an internal renewal of the church in faithfulness to the Gospel.

[26] *Willowbank Report – Consultation on Gospel and Culture:* www.lausanne.org/en/documents/lops/73-lop-2.html.

The Lausanne Story: A Personal Prelude

Robyn Claydon

Lausanne II in 89 in Manila was life-changing for me in a variety of ways, not least as a catalyst for an occupation change! But let me go back a few years.

One day in 1985 I was sitting in my office at a Sydney Girls' School where I was the Vice-Principal, when I received an unexpected phone call. It was from Dr Bill Hogue in America inviting me to be on the Planning Committee for the next Lausanne Congress to be held in Manila in 1989. He said that they had divided the world into ten geographic areas and were looking for a person to represent each region. His invitation to me was to represent Oceania, i.e. Australia, New Zealand and the South Pacific. It was his next sentence that particularly grabbed my attention: "We already have nine men and need a woman on the committee," he said. They were the days of token women in business and in the church! I was strongly inclined to say "Yes", but there was a difficulty. He said that starting early in 1986 there would be a number of planning meetings in different parts of the world for the next three years in preparation for the Congress. I explained that it would be very difficult for me to leave my role in education to travel so would have to reluctantly decline.

This problem was readily dismissed as he said that they had already considered that and would plan the meetings in my school holidays. So, for the next three years, I met with nine Christian leaders several times a year in different parts of the world and we planned the congress. I came to appreciate each of these men and they became my very good friends.

These were the days when international phone calls were very expensive, mobile phones didn't exist, and emails were a novelty! I remember one significant meeting when we needed a logo for Lausanne, and Graham Wade from Australia was asked to submit a suggested design.[1] He faxed his sketch through to our committee, we agreed on it almost immediately, and soon the "fish" bringing light to the darkness of the world became the very well-known logo for the Lausanne Movement.

Although I had not been at Lausanne 74, I knew that, of the 2,000 who attended, only about 100 were women and that the involvement of women in the conference leadership was virtually non-existent. I was determined that this would change in 89 and was very encouraged that the rest of the Planning Committee agreed. We worked closely with the Selection

[1] Alan Nichols (ed), *The Whole Gospel for The Whole World* (California: Regal Books and LCWE, 1989), 5.

Committee to urge each country to seek 25% of their delegation women. This was very nearly achieved since, of the 4,000 participants, 900 were women. This was despite some countries saying they didn't know any women leaders to invite. We told them to go and look because they were there!

At the Manila Congress, Dr Roberta Hestenes preached at the concluding Communion Service,[2] I was invited to give one of the plenary Biblical expositions on *Co-operation in Evangelism,*[3] and many women chaired plenary sessions, led workshops and shared about their ministries.

There were a number of 'tracks' at the conference and participants chose to be involved in one track for the whole week. One of the tracks was on *Women in Evangelism,*[4] and the number of people who came – both men and women – was so large that we were given the ballroom for our workshops for the entire time! I allotted each two-hour session to a different country and asked the women from that country or region to present a programme that included testimonies, dance, drama and highlights of the various ministries women were involved in. I also asked them to share about the obstacles and difficulties they faced. The recurring obstacle they highlighted was the limitations placed on them by the church and/or culture to use the gifts God had given them as they sought to fulfil the Great Commission. The women's track was informative, challenging and creatively presented, and resulted in women being affirmed and prayed for by their brothers and sisters at the conference.

So what contributed to my 'occupation change'? I had been involved in education for thirty years and had no intention of retiring for several more years. Yet, when the invitation came at the end of the Congress from Dr Leighton Ford asking me to consider becoming the *Lausanne Senior Associate for Women in World Evangelization* I faced a dilemma. I asked for time to think and pray about it. At Manila I had met 900 wonderful women leaders from all over the world and, in overseeing the meetings of the Women's Track each day, had heard their testimonies and discovered some of the amazing ministries they were exercising in their own countries and beyond. I had also heard of the limitations many of them faced in their countries and churches restricting them in the use of their gifts in Christian ministry. Their faces were etched in my memory and their stories had touched my heart.[5]

One of the strengths of the Lausanne Movement since 74 had been the appointment of *Senior Associates*, men and women who have a particular ministry such as Urban Mission, Tentmaking, Jewish Evangelism, Youth and Children's Ministries, Church Research, Other Religions, etc. and

---

[2] J. D. Douglas (ed), *Proclaim Christ Until He Comes* (Minneapolis, MN: World Wide Publications, 1990), 199.

[3] J. D. Douglas, 212.

[4] J. D. Douglas, 396.

[5] Alan Nichols, 66-70.

whose ministries had been strengthened by involvement with the Lausanne Movement and/or whose ministries could enhance Lausanne's commitment to world evangelization. However, there had never been a Senior Associate for Women. My husband David and I prayed about it and decided that the need was great, that I was already fairly well-known by those who had been in Manila and that, as a result, I had contacts with women leaders in many parts of the world. So in 1991 I 'retired' from teaching and began a new, exciting and somewhat daunting ministry. No longer did I have a salary; I wasn't quite sure where to start; or how I would raise money for my travel from Australia and the finances that would be needed for this new ministry. God provided for me over and over again from the gifts of Christian friends.

I decided to go first to Russia and then to Nepal, since both those countries had sent no women as delegates to Manila 89. I was committed, not only to encouraging the women I had met in Manila, but to finding women leaders with a passion for evangelization who had not had the opportunity to share with us all at the conference. As this new ministry began to unfold, I met wonderfully gifted women all over the world and in the last 22 years have been to over sixty countries ministering alongside hundreds of Christian women. I have preached in churches, spoken at evangelistic rallies, taught at theological colleges, expounded the Scriptures at conferences, mentored young women who are just starting out in their ministries, and sat one-on-one with secret believers in the Middle East.

Lausanne provided many opportunities for women leaders to be identified and encouraged, and my own life has been enriched by the women I have ministered with. These have included Nexhimija from Albania whose grandmother whispered to her, "There is a God who loves you," while the communist youth group to which she was forced to belong kept telling her, "There is no God"! It was many years later, after her grandmother had died, that a group of tourists visiting the capital city answered her question, "Can anyone tell me about the God who loves me?" Another woman, Olga, who has had a vibrant ministry for a number of years in Moldova had, with her husband and children, experienced persecution because of her Christian faith, but persevered and today leads women's Bible studies and has started a Christian magazine.

Evangeline from India is part of the Lausanne younger women leaders' network and started a school under a tree for children from the slums of Hyderabad sixteen years ago. Today she is the Principal of a school for 600 children. She has also set up a school and a church in the leper village and has planted seven churches. Evangeline participated in the 2004 Forum in Pattaya and was a delegate at Lausanne III in Cape Town. D from the Central Asian Republics was attacked by her family when she changed her religion and became a Christian. She was befriended by a local woman pastor, went to Bible College in Moscow, studied theology and has returned to her country in the hope of planting a church! Hilda was a secretary in a church office in Africa, came to one of the Lausanne young women's leadership meetings, was sponsored by a group of German Christian women to go to theological college, gained a Master's Degree in Theology and now teaches in a Bible school in Tanzania. Saane, Mele and Theresa are Tongan Christian leaders whose varied ministries touch women all over the South Pacific.

This is just a fraction of the women in whose ministries I have had the privilege of sharing in my Lausanne journey, and I have been able to write their stories, and the stories of so many others I have met around the world, so that their courage, hopes, challenges and ministries can be an encouragement to others.

One of my passions has been to identify young women who have a desire to serve God, but are not sure how to accomplish this and who need encouragement and, in some instances, need new and creative ideas as to how this can happen. Through the *Lausanne Younger Women Leaders' Network* we have been able to provide opportunities for young women from a number of different countries to go away for a week at a time for mentoring in Christian leadership. These young women are not only now in vibrant ministries both within the church and in the marketplace, but are also encouraging each other and travelling to each other's countries to share in ministry.

Lausanne has contributed in a number of ways to the encouragement and training of young leaders, and the *Lausanne Younger Leaders' Gathering* (YLG)[6] held in 2006 in Malaysia brought together 550 young leaders from over 112 countries. The participants were between the ages of 25 and 35 and were joined by 150 older Christian leaders who were mentors. Those of us privileged to be part of that conference found ourselves being mentored and encouraged as much by the young as, we hope, they were by us. Some of the young women in the *Lausanne Women's Network* were part of that conference. Among the participants were 65% young men and women from Africa, Latin America and Asia, 7% from Eastern Europe and 28% from the west. One of the young leaders from that conference is Michael Oh, the newly appointed Executive Director of the Lausanne Movement!

The *Forum* in Pattaya, Thailand in 2004 was a significant milestone for me and 1,500 others in our personal journey and in the journey of Lausanne. It brought together missiologists, evangelists, teachers and practitioners in 31 Issue Groups. I had the privilege of chairing the Program Committee, and my husband David, who was at the time the Lausanne International Director, was the Director of the Forum. One of the outstanding, and somewhat different, aspects of the conference was that people had to commit to a particular issue related to evangelization six months beforehand and work together (via email and Skype) on an issue

[6] Judson Birdsall (ed), *Living & Leading like Jesus: Plenary Addresses from the 2006 Younger Leaders Gathering* (Pasadena, CA: William Carey Library, 2007).

that was of particular interest to them. Then they continued working together during conference, committing themselves to a written report at the conclusion. Out of this came the three volumes: *A New Heart, A New Vision, A Renewed Call* and 31 new *Lausanne Occasional Papers.*[7] One of the Issue Groups at the Forum was on Men and Women Ministering Together, and from that came a new Lausanne Special Interest Group Alliance *2, 29* and a new Senior Associate role currently held by dynamic young missiologists Leslie and Chad Segraves.

The 2004 *Forum* was a working conference, and the small groups worked so well that at Cape Town 2010 the idea was taken a step further with the setting up of 'table' groups for reflection and discussion throughout the conference. Lausanne III in Cape Town provided an opportunity for women leaders from different countries to set up a café – open to men and women – where women presented aspects of the ministries they were involved in. This was a rich, colourful, challenging and encouraging time each day. Women were involved in Cape Town at every level from plenary presentations and Biblical exposition to overall administration of the Congress, and the modelling of the partnership of men and women in ministry was evident throughout the Congress.

It has been an enormous privilege to be involved in the Lausanne Movement and I have been enriched by a journey which began in 1985 as a member of the Programme Committee for Manila 89, to being appointed as the Lausanne Senior Associate for Women, becoming a member of the Lausanne International Committee, Vice-Chair of Lausanne for a number years, a mentor at the YLG to now being a Lausanne Senior Advisor! Age catches up with us all as evidenced by my now august title!

One of the responsibilities – and joys – of being a mentor is being ready to hand the baton on to the next generation of leaders, and I have been delighted to hand the leadership of the *Lausanne Women's Network* to Elke Werner from Germany. Elke is now the *Lausanne Senior Associate for Women* and, as an outstanding woman leader, preacher, evangelist, author and pastor, and a member of the Lausanne International Board, is making a significant contribution to the ministry of Lausanne.

The Lausanne Movement has enriched my life in so many ways: challenging me to a renewed commitment to Jesus and a revitalized commitment to take the Gospel to the world, and it has given me wonderful travelling companions from many nations as together we reflect Christ in our lives so that others might see Jesus.

---

[7] David Claydon (ed), *A New Vision, A New Heart, A Renewed Call* (Pasadena, CA: William Carey Library, 2005), 3 vols.

The Role of the Lausanne Movement in Modern Christian Mission

Tormod Engelsviken

Introduction

"Missions and ecumenism are inseparable. Revival, missions, Christian unity, is an inevitable series." This famous quote of the historian of the ecumenical movement, Ruth Rouse, taken from her chapter on the role of voluntary movements, and in particular mission movements, highlights the fact that the Lausanne Movement (LM) also stands in this long 'series' dating back to the great revivals in the 18th and 19th centuries.[1] These were the pietistic revivals in Germany and Scandinavia, primarily Methodism in Britain, and the Great Awakening in North America. If the modern Christian mission includes the last 200 years or so, the LM obviously has only played a part for the last forty years, since 1974. Still, one might say that the LM has taken over roles that others had before it, or that the LM has had a role as a Movement furthering concerns that go far back in the modern mission history, to the great revivals and the mission and ecumenism that resulted from them. In addition, the LM has also played new roles in the mission history of the post-colonial and post-modern period.

We understand the term 'role' in this chapter quite loosely to mean something like 'function', 'significance' and 'influence'. In discussing this role we have to make some limitations. Fortunately, this book will in other chapters raise many questions and explore several issues that have been important in the history and the contemporary situation of the LM. Some of these will be only briefly touched upon in order to understand the role of the LM, while I refer to other chapters for a deeper understanding.

When discussing the role of the LM in modern Christian mission, I have decided to do so in a primarily historical, theological and contextual perspective. The reason for the *historical* perspective is first and foremost that the LM arose out of a specific historical situation in 1974 with roots far back in modern mission history. Hence, it cannot be understood apart from that history. Secondly, although the LM truly is and has always been a global Movement, no one author, it seems to me, would be able to cover the role of the Lausanne Movement in all parts of the world. This role is far greater and far more complex than a short chapter can cover. Yet it is

[1] Rouse 1967. 310.

possible to outline this role particularly with regard to the *theological* and *ecumenical context* in which the LM emerged.

As a person who has followed the LM closely since my first experience of it at the Willowbank Consultation on Gospel and Culture in 1978, and who has benefitted enormously from it in many ways, I find it appropriate also at points to have a more *personal* perspective, not least since I retire from my position as Professor of Missiology at MF Norwegian School of Theology this year (2013) and want to look back and reflect on some of the events and influences that have shaped me and my ministry for the last 35 years.

A Short Historical Perspective on the Evangelical-Ecumenical Mission Movement

The breakthrough of modern mission in the churches of western Europe and North America happened subsequent to William Carey's booklet *Enquiry* (1792) and his going to India as a missionary in 1793.[2] The mission work, mainly carried out by evangelicals, was often organized in voluntary mission societies, especially in Europe where the large folk and state churches were unwilling or unable to engage in any work beyond the borders of their nations. Some of these organizations were interdenominational, others strictly denominational or confessional. The passion for evangelism at home and mission to the ends of the earth sprang out of the revivals. It also included work of charity and an engagement for social reform.[3]

Although these organizations were not formed with Christian unity as their main purpose, they created 'a consciousness of that unity', a 'sense of togetherness' amongst Christians of different Churches,[4] and, we may add, different nations. A strong interest in Christian unity arose particularly in the 1830s and 1840s, and led eventually to the formation of the Evangelical Alliance (EA) in 1846, an international and interdenominational organization. The term 'alliance ecumenism' denotes a kind of ecumenism where Christian individuals of different churches with common convictions come together to create instruments for expressing and furthering their spiritual unity.[5] The basis of the Evangelical Alliance was 'the great evangelical principles held in common by them', and included nine affirmations on such doctrines as the authority of the Scriptures, the depravity of human nature, Christ's work of atonement, justification by

---

[2] Stephen Neill rightly points out that it is a misunderstanding to see Carey as 'the father of modern missions' as there were many Protestant missionaries before him. Yet he represents a turning point, especially with regard to the English-speaking world. Neill 1964, 261.

[3] Rouse 1967, 310.

[4] Rouse 1967, 310.

[5] Rouse1967, 319.

faith alone, and eternal blessedness and punishment.[6] We cannot describe the history of the Evangelical Alliance here, but only underline its importance as an international organization of evangelical unity in the nineteenth century.[7] After a difficult period; when the Evangelical Alliance was kept alive by national alliances, sporadic conferences and an annual week of prayer, it was revived in 1951 under the name of World Evangelical Fellowship (WEF).[8] The WEF/WEA has existed parallel to the LM, and shares many of the same concerns and convictions. WEF/WEA has a broader agenda than LM and has today also another structure with a different membership base. The LM and the WEA have worked closely together and co-sponsored many conferences and consultations. The two bodies are the most representative expressions of evangelical Christianity in today's Christian world. They should therefore be seen together.[9]

Later in the nineteenth century and in the beginning of the twentieth, the initiative in the work for unity in Christian mission was taken over by others under the leadership of men like the Methodist student leader John R. Mott. An important factor was still prayer for Christian unity. New ideas about the form of ecumenical work were promoted, replacing the former Alliance ecumenism with 'church ecumenism' where official representatives of churches could come together and contribute to unity and co-operation in mission without giving up their confessional identity. The international student movement that had arisen in the 1880s gave new impetus to the ecumenical movement. In 1900 John R. Mott published his book *The Evangelization of the World in this Generation.* This was the slogan of the student mission movement and expressed the strong optimism that characterized the mission movement about the turn of that century. This again led up to the great missionary conference in Edinburgh 1910. The story of this conference and the following development belongs elsewhere. Here we would only state that Edinburgh 1910 gave impetus to the establishment of the ecumenical organizations that eventually formed the World Council of Churches (WCC) in 1948, and the International Missionary Council which was integrated into the WCC in 1961. Structurally, the WCC is the heir to the Edinburgh 1910 conference, but the missionary passion and the strategic vision of the conference are equally embodied in the evangelical mission movement represented by the

---

[6] Quotes of the actual text is found in Rouse 1967:320 .

[7] A popular account of the founding of the Evangelical Alliance is found in Fuller 1996:14ff.

[8] Fuller 1996:27-28. WEF has recently changed its name back to the World Evangelical Alliance (WEA).

[9] It is significant that in Norway both the Norwegian Evangelical Alliance and the Norwegian Lausanne Committee in 2000 were integrated in the new Norwegian Council for Mission and Evangelism together with the former Norwegian Missionary Council.

Lausanne Movement. This shared heritage and ownership were demonstrated by the celebration of the centenary in 2010 in Edinburgh.[10]

The Role of the Lausanne Movement in the Missiological Debate

The Context: The Missiological Development in the World Council of Churches

Although the *Lausanne Covenant* is not a strongly polemical document, it reflects a situation in which there were deep concerns among evangelicals with regard to the doctrinal and missiological developments in the World Council of Churches.[11] This historical context should not be ignored in looking at the role of the LM. In 1948 the two ecumenical organizations that grew out of the Edinburgh 1910 conference, Faith & Order and Life & Work, merged to form the World Council of Churches. The International Missionary Council (IMC), that was also a result of the Edinburgh conference and was established in 1921, held several international conferences, the most important being Jerusalem 1928, Tambaram 1938, Whitby 1947, and Willingen 1952.

The enthusiasm and optimism of the Edinburgh 1910 conference met four years later with the catastrophe in the 'Christian' world: the First World War. The twenty-year period between the First and the Second World War was quite different from the somewhat triumphalist period before the First World War. It also became obvious that the Edinburgh 1910 conference had serious shortcomings. John Stott points out that "the fatal flaw of Edinburgh was not so much doctrinal disagreement as apparent doctrinal indifference, since doctrine was not on the agenda". This meant that "the theological challenges of the day were not faced".[12] This again opened the door for theological liberalism to find its way not only into the churches but also into the mission movement. The so-called 'social gospel movement', growing out of liberal theology at the turn of the century, had gained influence in some mission circles and the German theologian Ernst Troeltsch's views of the relationship between Christianity and other religions was followed up in America through the so-called *Hocking Report* which questioned the salvific uniqueness of Christianity

---

[10] See e.g. Knud Jørgensen's chapter in Section 4 in this volume.

[11] There had been a World Congress on Evangelism in Berlin in 1966 co-sponsored by Billy Graham and *Christianity Today* (Stott 1996, xiii) and another smaller conference in German in Frankfurt in 1970 that produced the *Frankfurt Declaration on the Foundational Crisis (Grundlagenkrise) in Mission*, drafted by Peter Beyerhaus. See Beyerhaus 1970.

[12] Stott 1996, xii.

and emphasized the common elements in the different religions, primarily the ethical aspects of the Kingdom of God and Jesus as an example.[13]

The liberal mission thinking was forcefully countered by Karl Barth and his followers, among them the Dutch missiologist Hendrik Kraemer. His book *The Christian Message in a Non-Christian World* would dominate the meeting of the IMC in Tambaram, India, in 1938. This meeting was soon followed by the Second World War. The meetings of the IMC in Whitby 1947 and in Willingen 1952 were still characterized by a classical understanding of mission. After Willingen, the term *missio Dei* (God's mission) became dominant as an overall perspective on mission, emphasizing that mission is not a merely human endeavour but originates in God and implies the Father's sending of the Son and the Holy Spirit who in turn send the church into the world with the message of the Gospel.[14]

In 1961 the IMC was integrated into the WCC at the WCC Assembly in New Delhi and became the Commission on World Mission and Evangelism in the WCC (CWME).[15] The aim of the Commission was "to further the proclamation to the whole world of the Gospel of Jesus Christ to the end that men may believe in him and be saved". The 'aim' was revised during the Assembly in Nairobi 1975 to read "to assist the Christian community in the proclamation of the Gospel of Jesus Christ, by word and deed, to the whole world and to the end that all may believe in him and be saved".[16] This aim was clear and pointed but the reality of the role of mission within the WCC during the first years after integration was an entirely different matter. In his evaluation of the results of the integration, the American Lutheran missiologist James Scherer claims that:

> ... the entire agenda of the world church in all six continents suddenly seemed to invade the serene world of mission with its former priority of completing the unfinished task ... The distinction between a specific missionary *intention* and a broader missionary *dimension*, and the claim that crossing the frontier between faith and unbelief constituted the unique *differentium* of mission activity, proved incapable of being maintained in practice.[17]

The result was a broadening of the concept of mission to include everything the church does, above all its most important priority tasks. Scherer, who himself was no 'card-carrying' evangelical, did not mince

[13] Hocking 1932, 56-59, cf. Berentsen 1994, 18-19.

[14] See Engelsviken 2003.

[15] Scherer 1987, 105ff. The Norwegian Missionary Council (NMC), as the only national mission council, decided not to join the CWME. This was the result of a growing scepticism towards the WCC in evangelical circles in Norway. This decision by the NMC however left the mission movement in Norway without an international ecumenical fellowship in the years to come. This lack was not overcome until the formation of the LM.

[16] Scherer 1987, 105.

[17] Scherer 1987, 106-7.

words when he wrote that "some of the consequences (of the integration) was potentially disastrous for mission work in the ensuing period".[18]

The theological and missiological development in the WCC after New Delhi 1961 was closely tied up with the programme 'The Missionary Structure of the Congregation' which changed the understanding of mission radically within the dominant structures of the WCC.

The Dutch missiologist J. C. Hoekendijk's radical new interpretation of mission which had been rejected in Willingen now came to the fore. Hoekendijk considered a church-centred understanding of mission illegitimate and argued that God was primarily at work in the *world* to create *shalom* (peace). Hoekendijk's missiology was largely taken up by two study groups under the auspices of the WCC whose reports were later published in the book *Church for Others.* A western European group focused on the work of God outside the church, *extra muros ecclesiae.* God sends us into the world, and to participate in God's mission is to enter into co-operation with God in the world and its history. The primary focus of *missio Dei* is the world. The order is therefore not as in a more classical understanding of mission, God-church-world, but rather God-world-*shalom*, or as an American group would argue, God-world-humanization. In his sharp analysis and evaluation, Scherer says, "For Hoekendijk, it appeared *missio Dei* had become identified with a process of theological transformation whereby humankind would achieve the goals of the messianic kingdom through the process of secular history."[19] Therefore, the world and its most burning issues would set the agenda for the church in mission, not God's revelation or the biblical Gospel. Scherer concludes, "Hoekendijk's reflections went far beyond the challenge to church parochialism and self-sufficiency; they implied a quite new, unhistorical and methodologically unclear model for Christian mission."[20] The Norwegian missiologist Jan-Martin Berentsen says that in the 1960s *missio Dei* became a comprehensive term for God's work in general, where God's redemptive work is integrated into his creative and preserving work in the historical process.[21]

Underlying this new view of mission is a new view of the world and world history. Mission in the classical sense is not necessary in order for human beings to be saved; the whole world is already redeemed through Christ's death and resurrection and on its way to final salvation. The primary locus of God's work is therefore the world, not the church. The distinction between general history and salvation history is abandoned. There is only one history on the way to God's goal. It is God's work in the

[18] Scherer 1987, 107.
[19] Scherer 1987, 113.
[20] Scherer 1987, 114.
[21] Berentsen 1983, 6.

secular world that is mission. God does not use missionaries; he is himself the missionary.[22]

Although the views expressed in *The Church for Others* were moderated somewhat in the WCC Assembly in Uppsala, Sweden, in 1968, the central focus was still the world and its many problems and challenges. 'Humanization' of society, rather than Christianization, was presented as the goal of mission, and struggle for social justice had priority over proclamation of the Gospel. Scherer claims that the "radical worldliness of the Uppsala report on mission is found … in its strategic proposals".[23] He points out that: "Uppsala foreshadowed the growing rift with the evangelicals, epitomized in Donald MacGavran's question: Will Uppsala betray the two billions?"[24]

We shall take a look at one more conference that took place shortly before the Lausanne Congress. In its second major conference, the CWME wanted to explore the meaning of the term salvation. The conference which was held in Bangkok, Thailand, had as its theme 'Salvation Today'. The method of the conference was to gather 'salvation testimonies' from around the world. There was no biblical exposition of salvation as a basis. Scherer criticizes the conference committee for its practice of "associating biblical salvation more or less indiscriminately with salvific themes and personalities in contemporary social and political movements and in other religions".[25]

Between Uppsala 1968 and Bangkok 1973, the issues of interreligious dialogue had risen to a prominent position. There had been Christian-Muslim-Buddhist-Hindu dialogue in Ajaltoun in 1970, and at the meeting of the WCC Central Committee in Addis Ababa, the Orthodox theologian Georges Khodr had argued for the saving presence of Christ in other religions. A special emphasis was laid on the economy of the Spirit: "The Spirit is present everywhere and fills everything by virtue of an economy distinct from that of the Son." He further argued that "all who are visited by the Spirit are the people of God". Mission is then to awaken the Christ who sleeps in the night of the religions.[26] This was not the official position of the WCC, but this theology influenced the Bangkok conference and its understanding of salvation.

The Bangkok conference and the process that led up to it challenged the evangelical mission movement in two ways: first, by understanding salvation primarily in socio-economic and political terms as liberation. As Scherer says, "The real significance of Bangkok is that it marked the

---

[22] *The Church for Others* 1968, 15, 107.

[23] Scherer 1987, 119.

[24] Scherer 1987, 121, In footnote 112 on 254 Scherer also refers to John R. W. Stott, 'a leading Anglican evangelical', criticizing the draft for its lack of reference to the millions who are perishing without Christ. See also *The Uppsala Report* 1968, 26.

[25] Scherer 1987, 121-122.

[26] Khodr 1971, 37-49.

emergence of the liberation theme as the dominant motif in ecumenical mission."[27] Secondly, by viewing other religions as possible ways of salvation and carrying on interreligious dialogue on theological terms that threatened the classical Christian understanding of the uniqueness of Christ.

It is important to note that in the WCC and CWME conferences there are reports from sections as well as speeches that may reflect different theological positions. It is therefore always dangerous to claim that these conciliar ecumenical organizations promote only one view of mission and evangelism. There are always statements that evangelical Christians may agree with and support. In this context, however, we have primarily highlighted the controversial and radical views that most severely challenged a classical understanding of mission, since it was these views that the *Lausanne Covenant* later on would be dealing with.

We have devoted some space to the ecumenical mission movement and the conferences and documents that led up to Lausanne 1974. Much more could be said, but this may suffice to explain part of the missiological background for the content of the *Lausanne Covenant*, its positive reception by evangelicals around the world, and the important role it has played from its first presentation until today.

The basically new and world-orientated missiology that dominated the WCC in the 1960s and early 1970s had consequences and implications in many different areas of missiology, not all of them immediately obvious. Instead of presenting them here and having to repeat them as we look at the *Lausanne Covenant*, we will point out some of the most serious challenges to classical mission as they are dealt with in the Covenant.

In his introduction to the historic mission document of the LM, John Stott very briefly confirms that one of the backgrounds of the *Lausanne Covenant* was a development within the WCC:

> It was said when the IMC became the missionary arm of the WCC, mission would be at the heart of the Council's concern and so of its member churches. In the event, however, mission became marginalized by being largely reinterpreted in socio-political terms. Thus the vision of Edinburgh 1910 suffered an almost total eclipse.[28]

Stott does, however, give an even broader background, including the important political events of the 1960s on a global scale, the Second Vatican Council, the spread of liberation theology, and the growth of the charismatic movement.[29] This was the historical global context in which the

---

[27] Scherer 1987, 124. Scherer also adds that Bangkok marked "the transition from Western mission agency dominance to Two Thirds World leadership in the CWME". This change of leadership reflecting a new situation in the global church would also be an issue in the Lausanne Movement. It is important to note that one of the first leaders in the LCWE was Gottfried Osei-Mensah from Ghana.

[28] Stott 1996, xii.

[29] Stott 1996, xiii.

Lausanne Congress took place and the *Lausanne Covenant* was composed and signed.

The Lausanne Congress and Covenant: The Evangelical Affirmations and Responses

The American evangelist and sponsor of the Lausanne Congress in 1974, Billy Graham, held the opening speech on the theme: 'Why Lausanne?' In this he recognized the conference as a 'conference of evangelicals' in the tradition of many movements of evangelism throughout the history of the church, and that it was concentrating on one task, namely evangelization. Graham declared that he hoped the Congress would "frame a biblical declaration on evangelism", and that it would "re-emphasize those biblical concepts which are essential to evangelism". Among them were the authority of Scripture, the lostness of human beings apart from Christ, salvation in Jesus alone, Christian witness by both word and deed, and the necessity of evangelism. Graham also expressed the hope that the Congress would help to develop "a new 'koinonia' or fellowship among evangelicals of all persuasions ... throughout the world", and the need for prayer and being filled with the Holy Spirit.[30]

When we now turn to the *Lausanne Covenant*, we shall see that Graham's programme was followed up in several ways. We shall highlight some aspects of the *Lausanne Covenant* that we deem especially important for the role the LM has played.

Paragraph 1: *The Purpose of God* affirms the classical Christian understanding of the Triune God and attributes to this God the 'calling out from the world a people for himself and sending his people back into his world to be his servants and his witnesses for the extension of his kingdom, the building up of Christ's body, and the glory of his name'. Although the term *missio Dei* is not used explicitly, the statement is clearly compatible with the classical understanding of *missio Dei* emphasizing that mission has its origin in the Triune God and involves a sending of the church to the world to witness in word and deed.

Paragraph 2: *The Authority and Power of the Bible* is a crucial paragraph in at least two respects. First, the paragraph reiterates the fundamental evangelical (and traditionally Protestant) conviction that the Scriptures are the sole authority for Christian faith and practice (*sola scriptura*). This view would stand in contrast to Roman Catholic and Orthodox views of the Scriptures in relation to church tradition, but it also represents a difference from modern Protestant views where critical and liberal theology questions the authority of the Bible or adds other contemporary sources of authority in the church.

[30] Graham's speech is found in Douglas 1975, 22-36, cp. also Stott 1996, xiii-xiv.

Secondly, it deals with a divisive question in the evangelical movement between fundamentalists and other evangelicals, namely the question of the inerrancy of Scripture. By its formulation that the Scriptures is 'without error in all that it affirms, and the only infallible rule of faith and practice', both sides could be satisfied depending upon how 'in all that it affirms' is interpreted. Especially among many evangelical academics, it was welcomed that one could be a part of the LM and still recognize that there might be 'errors' in the Bible in areas that did not impinge on Christian doctrine and ethics. It was also possible for evangelicals to use the historico-critical method in their studies of the Bible. It is noteworthy that it has not been deemed necessary or advisable to have a special Lausanne consultation to deal with the view of the Scriptures in Paragraph 2!

Paragraph 3: *The Uniqueness and Universality of Christ* also deals with an issue that is close to the heart of the evangelical movement. It strongly emphasizes that there is salvation only in Jesus Christ. This is the first paragraph that explicitly rejects views that are contrary to evangelical convictions and which have been voiced especially within the WCC. One such view is that one could be saved by general revelation (by implication: without knowing Christ). What is also rejected is 'every kind of syncretism and dialogue which implies that Christ speaks equally through all religions and ideologies'. The *Lausanne Covenant* takes a clear exclusivist stance in its evaluation of other religions, referring to Acts 4:12. In line with this, it also emphasizes the lostness of those who reject Christ and extends that to 'eternal separation from God'. Universalism and the so-called inclusivity position in the theology of religions are explicitly rejected when the *Lausanne Covenant* says: "To proclaim Jesus as 'the Savior of the world' is not to affirm that all men are either automatically or ultimately saved, still less to affirm that all religions offer salvation in Christ." Salvation is dependent upon 'personal commitment of repentance and faith'.[31] The uniqueness of Christ in relation to salvation and the eternal lostness of humans apart from Christ belong together in this foundational paragraph.

Paragraph 4: *The Nature of Evangelism* emphasizes the nature and importance of evangelization and understands it as spreading the Gospel of the specific saving work of Christ on the Cross and in the Resurrection. Salvation is described here with the word forgiveness of sins and the liberating gift of the Holy Spirit. Again there is an indirect critique of views within the WCC: although both Christian presence and dialogue with the purpose 'to listen sensitively in order to understand' are indispensable to evangelism, these are not evangelism itself, 'which is the proclamation of the historical, biblical Christ as Savior and Lord, with a view to persuading people to come to him personally and so be reconciled to God'.

---

[31] The same emphasis on repentance and faith as a condition for salvation is also found in Paragraph 4.

The results of evangelism should also include 'obedience to Christ, incorporation into his church and responsible service in the world".

Paragraph 5: *Christian Social Responsibility* deals with the topic in a way that addresses both people outside the LM and people within it. In my opinion, this paragraph and the following consultation in 1982 on *Evangelism and Social Responsibility* have had the most impact on the evangelical mission movement since it represented a new way of thinking about the issue.

The main author of the *Lausanne Covenant*, John Stott, says that he had gone through a 'conversion' with regard to the relationship between evangelism and social action. In his opinion, the Great Commission must be understood to include social and evangelistic responsibility. Especially the commission as expressed in John 20:21 makes Jesus' 'mission the model of ours'. Jesus as a model sends the church to the world to be a serving church. "It is in our servant role that we can find the right synthesis of evangelism and social action."[32] Based on theological arguments that include both creation and redemption, the paragraph concludes that both "evangelism and socio-political involvement ... are necessary expressions of our doctrines of God and man, our love for our neighbour and our obedience to Jesus Christ". Although the paragraph contains a humble expression of penitence "for our neglect and for having sometimes regarded evangelism and social concern as mutually exclusive", it has a clear polemical address to WCC mission theology and liberation theology when it says that "reconciliation with man is not reconciliation with God, nor is social action evangelism, nor is political liberation salvation". There has been a steady development in the LM towards a more comprehensive and holistic understanding of mission, reaching a climax in the *Cape Town Commitment*. Yet, the LM has also insisted that there is a certain priority for proclamation, primarily based on the fact that it relates to people's eternal destiny. "The supreme and ultimate need of all humankind is the saving grace of Jesus Christ, and ... therefore a person's eternal, spiritual salvation is of greater importance than his or her temporal and material well-being."

There are also several other paragraphs in the *Lausanne Covenant* that have been important both in drawing the profile of LM in the larger Christian world and which also have served to overcome tensions and divisions within the evangelical movement itself. We could mention Paragraph 10: *Evangelism and culture* and the consultation in Willowbank, Bermuda, in 1978 with its statement on Gospel and Culture,[33] Paragraph 12: *Spiritual Conflict* and the consultation in Nairobi 2000 named *Deliver Us From Evil*,[34] Paragraph 14 *The Power of the Holy Spirit* and the

[32] Stott 1975, 23-27.

[33] Stott 1996, 73-114.

[34] Moreau 2002, Engelsviken 2001.

consultation on the Work of the Holy Spirit and Evangelization in Oslo in 1985.[35] All these paragraphs and the consultations and writings that followed them have contributed to defining the position and role of the LM and the evangelical movement within the larger global bodies of churches and movements.

The Influence of the Lausanne Movement on the Ecumenical Mission Movement

One role that the LM has had is that of an explicit or implicit conversation partner with the ecumenical mission movement. Through this, it has exerted missiological influence on the ecumenical mission movement. Already in the WCC Assembly in Nairobi in 1975 this was obvious when John Stott applauded Bishop Mortimer Arias' plea for evangelism, but also observed that it was "not typical of recent ecumenical utterances". Then Stott added five things that the WCC needed to recover:

> (1) recognition of the lostness of humans; (2) confidence in the truth, relevance and power of the gospel; (3) conviction about the uniqueness of Christ; (4) a sense of urgency about evangelism; (5) and a personal experience of Jesus Christ.[36]

In the history of the LM there have been differing views of the WCC, from those who see the ecumenical movement as a seduction of the church and a betrayal of the Gospel to those who have a more positive attitude and want to work for Christian unity also within the structures of the WCC. Regardless of this, there have been contacts and attempts at overcoming some of the differences. Stott pleaded in Nairobi that evangelical and ecumenical leaders take steps to overcome "the wide gap of confidence and credibility which exists today". Scherer concludes that "the WCC at Nairobi was making efforts to promote reconciliation, overcome polarization, and build bridges towards evangelicals, Roman Catholics and the Orthodox".[37]

Signs of a growing convergence[38] can be seen already in the official mission document of the WCC from 1982: *Mission and Evangelism: An Ecumenical Affirmation.*[39] This document attempts to avoid any one-sidedness. Mission is seen as having a Trinitarian point of departure with a 'Christological concentration'. The church again receives a central position and the view that the Kingdom of God will be realized in this world is rejected. There is place for conversion, for church planting and for the sending of missionaries. Yet some of the old problems remain as the

---

[35] Wells 1987.

[36] Referred to in Scherer 1987, 129, see also Stott 1976, 30.

[37] Scherer 1987, 129.

[38] See to this my article on convergence or divergence, Engelsviken 2001.

[39] See World Council of Churches, 1982.

Ecumenical Affirmation e.g. does not affirm the uniqueness of Christ but simply states, "Among Christians there are still differences of understanding as to how salvation in Christ is available to people of diverse religious persuasions. But all agree that witness should be rendered to all."[40]

The story of the historical development of the relationship between the LM and the WCC, and how various theological and missiological positions as well as missionary practices have been changed and modified through mutual influence cannot be discussed fully here. Suffice it to say that there is no doubt that the evangelical movement has exerted a considerable influence on the WCC and CWME,[41] and that the WCC also has had influence on the LM, particularly with the insistence that holistic mission also includes a socio-political struggle for peace, justice and liberation, care for creation and advocacy on behalf for the oppressed, poor and marginalized.

The Role of the Lausanne Covenant as a Missiological Confession in Our Time

The *Lausanne Covenant* was never intended to be a confession in the classical sense, yet it has many of the same characteristics as the important confessions of the Reformation. Let me point out five characteristics that in my opinion make it justifiable to call the *Lausanne Covenant* a confession in a somewhat loose sense.

First, the *Lausanne Covenant* was an answer to a serious threat to biblical, classical Christian doctrine with particular reference to mission. It was composed in a situation which may be called a *status confessionis* (a state in which a confession of faith is required) with regard to mission. That is why we have taken pains to emphasize how the Covenant dealt with some burning issues at the time of its production. In the answers to those

[40] World Council of Churches, 1982, 29. In 1989, prior to the Manila Congress, a consultation was held in Stuttgart, Germany, with five representatives each from the CWME, WEF and Lausanne, with Bishop David Gitari from Kenya and Vinay Samuel from India as joint moderators. The aim was to explore the theological relationship between the ecumenical and the evangelical mission movements. The secretary of the CWME, Eugene Stockwell, concluded after the consultation that, in spite of agreement in some areas, there were still very significant differences between the movements.

[41] The WCC Commission on World Mission and Evangelism has from before the turn of the century had official representatives of evangelicals, Pentecostals and Roman Catholics as full members. When I was one of three evangelical members of CWME from 1999 to 2005 I experienced a Commission that was open to different traditions, including the evangelical. Some of the documents that were produced and the mission conference in Athens 2005 reflect this – see World Council of Churches, 2005, 90-162.

threats the author(s) chose to express their deep convictions primarily in positive terms as affirmations of what they believed, and only secondarily identified what they did not believe, or rejected as false.

Secondly, although the *Lausanne Covenant* was mainly the work of one man, John Stott, it was also contributed to by many during the process of its composition, and was in its final form affirmed by an overwhelming majority of those present at the Lausanne Congress through an official signing process. As such, the Covenant is not the private opinions of one person, but represents a broad consensus on mission among mission and church leaders from around the world.

Thirdly, the *Lausanne Covenant* is not only a theological document but it also invites personal acceptance, endorsement and commitment. As such, it also has a spiritual function.

Fourthly, the *Lausanne Covenant* with its irenic evangelical and ecumenical form has served as a theological basis for many ecumenical organizations and institutions all over the world, and in that capacity is similar to many of the more particular confessions that are the basis for denominations or denominational institutions, e.g. the Lutheran Confessions.

Fifthly, the *Lausanne Covenant* has stood the test of time. Forty years after its composition it is still relevant. Although, like all texts, it is contextual both in terms of its origin, its language, its main focus, etc. it still is one of the most universally accepted texts and seems to speak in a meaningful and relevant way to Christians in all contexts.

So in conclusion, we may say that one of the major roles of the LM was to give to the Christian church the *Lausanne Covenant*, and one of its continuing roles is to preserve and spread this covenant to new generations of mission and church leaders.

The Role of the Structure of the Lausanne Movement

The role of the LM is also closely tied to the *structure* of the Movement. The Lausanne Congress in 1974 represented the ecumenical model of 'alliance ecumenism' which meant that the participants were *individual Christians* united by common interests, convictions and visions. The WCC represents the model of 'church ecumenism' which means that the WCC is a fellowship of *churches.* The leaders who come together in the WCC are elected representatives of their churches. One important consequence of this structural difference is that the WCC and the LM are not organizational alternatives in the sense that participation in one excludes participation in the other. It is possible to belong to a church that is a member of the WCC and at the same time be engaged in the LM. Especially in large, theologically pluralistic churches, this fact was and still is important.

This could be seen very clearly e. g. in Norway. While the Norwegian Evangelical Alliance had appealed mostly to the free churches and was a very small movement in Norway, the LM had a much wider constituency and a more narrow focus on mission. It attracted several top leaders in the Lutheran Church of Norway (a national church) as well as leaders of the smaller free churches. Several of the leaders of the Lausanne Movement in Norway were bishops or top leaders in other positions in church and academia who saw no problem in engaging actively in the LM while their church was a member of the WCC. Some leaders were active both in the WCC and in the LM, while most who joined the LM kept a critical distance from the WCC. The same situation existed to a large extent also in the other European countries, such as the Nordic countries and Germany.

To say that the LM was made up only of individuals can, however, be misleading. Participants at Lausanne events and in Lausanne committees both on the national and international level were often chosen after a process of nomination and election that involved both churches and mission organizations. As such, they were representatives of large segments of the evangelical movement within the churches. When they spoke and acted, it was not only on behalf of themselves but of those who had elected them to leadership positions and as their representatives in the international Lausanne Movement.

The LM structure with its congresses, conferences, consultations, working groups, senior associates – and not least the publications that have come out of the LM – has served to provide evangelical mission leaders around the world with strong links to the global evangelical missionary community with all that implies in terms of prayer,[42] factual information, spiritual inspiration, international networking and co-operation.

The Role of the Lausanne Movement as a Catalyst for Missionary Thinking and Strategy

As a Movement made up of individuals representing a broad spectrum of churches and organizations, the LM has had no missionary programmes of its own. It does not 'do mission'; that is left to the churches and organizations of its constituency. Yet the LM is not only an instrument for Christian fellowship and conversation; it has served as an important *catalyst* for both missionary thinking and missionary practice.

It could have been a danger for the LM to become a merely reactive Movement, reacting against what it found wrong or wanting in the mission thinking and practice of the ecumenical movement in the 1960s and 70s. Ruth Rouse points out that one of the reasons for the loss of support for the

[42] The LM has had its own Intercessory Working Group, and only God knows what that has meant for world evangelization. So often prayer is not included or is marginalized when we do historical studies of Christian movements. I apologize for not placing more emphasis on prayer and its enormous importance when discussing the role of the LM.

Evangelical Alliance in the nineteenth century was a lack of programme for the future.[43] The LM was from the beginning both a re-active and a *pro-active* Movement. I believe one of the main reasons for this was its combination of concern both for mission thinking and mission practice. I do personally remember how forcefully John Stott instructed the leaders of the various so-called mini-consultations during the conference in Pattaya, Thailand, in 1980, that mission theologians and mission practitioners should work together and supplement each other. The theme for the conference was 'How shall they hear?' and the main emphasis of all the *Lausanne Occasional Papers* (LOPs) that came out of this conference was on mission strategies to reach various target groups with the Gospel. Yet undergirding it all was an evangelical theological understanding of mission. As a catalyst, the Lausanne Movement inspired both theological reflection and innovative mission practice. Instruments for this catalytic function were often the 'working groups' that were established after the Lausanne Congress in 1974. They included working groups on theology and education, strategy, communication and prayer. I believe that these groups and their consultations together with the large conferences, Lausanne I in 1974, Lausanne II in Manila 1989 and Lausanne III in Cape Town 2010, have contributed most significantly to the role of the LM. I want to expand this a little with regard to the Lausanne II Congress in Manila in 1989 and two of the working groups.

Lausanne II in Manila

Lausanne II in Manila brought the missiological development in the LM a significant step further forward. Although Lausanne II was a huge conference with 4,300 people present from 173 countries and addressing a large number of issues,[44] we will focus on the *Manila Manifesto* (MM) that resulted from the conference as its major document.[45] It explicitly builds on the *Lausanne Covenant* and adds some perspectives that come out of the missiological work that had been done during the 15 years since 1974. The Manifesto consists of 21 short 'Affirmations' and twelve 'Articles'. John Stott was the main drafter but Professor David Wells and Bishop John Reid made significant contributions and drafted parts of the Manifesto. I want briefly to highlight four areas.

First, the MM repeats, emphasizes and develops further some of the basic evangelical convictions concerning the human predicament, the content of the Gospel and the uniqueness of Christ, all in a way of humility and with repentance of former sins or neglects.

---

[43] Rouse 1967, 323.

[44] See Douglas 1980, 11 (Foreword by Leighton Ford).

[45] *Manila Manifesto* is found in Douglas 1980, 25-38.

Secondly, with regard to the Gospel and social responsibility, the MM includes the views of the Grand Rapids consultation in 1982. Yet the socio-ethical obligation is formulated more sharply in the MM than before:

> We affirm that the proclamation of God's kingdom of justice and peace demands the denunciation of all injustice and oppression, both personal and structural; we will not shrink from this prophetic witness (Affirmation 9).

The stand taken here both with regard to *structural* evil as well as personal evil, and the *prophetic witness* represents a more comprehensive view and a stronger urgency with regard to social issues in the evangelical mission movement.

Thirdly, the Manila Congress and the MM make it clear (if there were still doubts) that the *Pentecostal and Charismatic movements* belong in the evangelical mission movement. Pentecostals played a prominent part in the programme, and the MM affirms the gifts of the Spirit given to all God's people and their partnership in evangelization (Affirmation 14). The MM wants to strike a balance between extremes, echoing the Oslo Consultation in 1985 and Wells' book *God the Evangelist*:

> We reject both the scepticism which denies miracles and the presumption which demands them, both the timidity which shrinks from the fullness of the Spirit and the triumphalism which shrinks from the weakness in which Christ's power is made perfect (Article 5).

I see it as one of the most significant roles of the LM today to include, serve, and maybe even to guide theologically and missiologically, the great variety of Pentecostal and Charismatic mission movements, which are the most dynamic and fastest-growing mission movements in the global church today.

Fourthly, the MM explicitly affirms that the Jewish people need to acknowledge Jesus as their Messiah, and rejects the view that Jews have their own covenant which renders faith in Jesus unnecessary. In this way, it affirms the Messianic Jews and goes as far as saying that "it would be a form of anti-Semitism, as well as being disloyal to Christ, to depart from the New Testament pattern of taking the gospel to 'the Jew first'" (Art. 3: The Uniqueness of Jesus Christ).

In the aftermath of Manila 1989, the LM met with some severe problems both financially and structurally that resulted in a weakened Movement for more than ten years. However, around 2000 a process of reconciliation and co-operation with other movements such as AD 2000 & Beyond and the World Evangelical Fellowship resulted in renewed vision and influence leading up the Lausanne III Congress in Cape Town in 2010. The role of the LM in light of the Cape Town Congress and the *Cape Town Commitment* I believe is better dealt with in other chapters in this volume.

The Theology Working Group

We have already several times mentioned the role of the *Lausanne Covenant*. The *Lausanne Covenant* was, as we have seen, a short and concise expression of evangelical convictions with regard to several missiological issues. It was in need of further elaboration and exploration. Part of this task was taken up by individuals, but the Lausanne Movement chose to establish a Theology Working Group (TWG – formerly the Lausanne Theology and Education Group, or LTEG) that would work as a team arranging consultations on the various topics dealt with in the covenant as well as other burning issues in world evangelization. There is no space here for enumerating or discussing all the consultations and conferences arranged by the TWG,[46] often in co-operation with the World Evangelical Fellowship Mission Commission. In a separate article, I have characterized the Lausanne Movement as a powerful centre for missiological literature.[47] Although the LM is a Movement of individuals, the work of the TWG has given the consultation documents (books and LOPs) a theological and spiritual authority that in part derives from a consensus reached by representative leaders from across the evangelical spectrum. In addition to specialists in the issues being discussed who had signed the *Lausanne Covenant*, the consultations have also brought in missiological experts who were 'in general sympathy with the *Lausanne Covenant*' without having signed it. This means that the contributions to these consultations have come from a wider circle than those personally committed to the *Lausanne Covenant*.[48]

The Strategy Working Group

One of the plenary papers at the Lausanne Congress in 1974 that has had the greatest impact was that of the American missiologist Ralph Winter on 'The Highest Priority: Cross-Cultural Evangelism'.[49] From this paper and the work of the Strategy Working Group the concept of 'hidden' or 'unreached' people groups was developed. A large part of the Lausanne congresses and conferences have been devoted to developing strategies to reach different groups of people. Although there has been controversy within the LM about definitions, and the use of statistics and concrete strategies, the LM has functioned as a platform where this discussion has gone on and where mission strategists around the world have been challenged with regard to priorities and methods in mission. There is no

---

[46] All the consultations up to the Lausanne II Congress in Manila in 1989 are dealt with in Stott 1996. See also several of the chapters in this book.

[47] Engelsviken 1997.

[48] This was e.g. the case at the Willowbank consultation on Gospel and Culture – see Stott 1996, 112.

[49] Douglas 1975, 213-258.

doubt that the catalytic function of the LM in this regard has produced new inspiration and motivation for mission and has changed strategic mission priorities in the direction of reaching the least engaged.

Conclusion

Much more could be said about the ministry of different Lausanne-related individuals and groups such as the important work of the *Lausanne senior associates*, and the groups for special concerns such as the *Consultation for Jewish Evangelism*. The LM has played such a significant role in so many contexts that it would be impossible to enumerate them all or offer them justice in a short chapter. However, I will conclude by stating that I pray, hope and believe that by God's grace the LM will continue to play a significant role as a global force in world evangelization and contribute to mobilizing God's people for mission to the ends of the world and to the end of time.

Lausanne and Global Evangelicalism: Theological Distinctives and Missiological Impact

Timothy C. Tennent

The Lausanne Committee for World Evangelization (LCWE), known popularly as the Lausanne Movement, is a global evangelical Movement that emerged as a part of the International Congress on World Evangelization in 1974. This event was attended by about 2,700 delegates from over 150 countries in Lausanne. Organized by Billy Graham and John Stott, the Lausanne Movement is responsible for several strategic global consultations including the 1974 event in Lausanne, as well as major events in Manila (1989) and in Cape Town, South Africa (2010). The purpose of this chapter is to explore the key theological distinctives of the Lausanne Movement as well as its missiological impact. The chapter will begin with a discussion of the key theological distinctives, followed by an exploration of the larger missiological impact of the Movement as a whole.

Theological Distinctives of the Lausanne Covenant

One of the most enduring theological legacies of the Lausanne Movement has been the documents, the *Lausanne Covenant*, the *Manila Manifesto* and the *Cape Town Commitment* which sets forth the central theological distinctives of the Movement.[1] The *Lausanne Covenant* is widely regarded as one of the most important theological documents in the evangelical movement. In a moving ceremony at the end of the Lausanne Congress on World Evangelization in 1974, Billy Graham, along with key leaders from the global church, signed the document which quickly spread around the world. Within a few years the document had become the guiding statement of faith of countless churches, new Christian movements, seminaries and mission organizations around the world.

The *Lausanne Covenant* contains fifteen Articles which set forth the central theological distinctives. Each of the central affirmations of the document will now be explored.

---

[1] The three foundational documents of the Lausanne Movement can be found at www.lausanne.org. All quotations in this chapter are from the three documents, the *Lausanne Covenant, Manila Manifesto* and *Cape Town Commitment* unless otherwise noted.

The Purpose of God (Article 1)

The first Article, entitled The Purpose of God, affirms that the Triune God is a missionary God who has called us to joyfully participate in His redemptive mission in the world. It seeks to clarify that mission is first and foremost about God and his redemptive purpose and initiative in the world, quite apart from any actions or tasks or strategies or initiatives which the church undertakes. To put it plainly, mission is more about God and who He is, than about us and what we do. In short, mission is not primarily a subset of the doctrine of the church which is seeking to grow and extend its reach and influence around the world. Rather, it is the story of God's redemptive action in the world which precedes the life of the church. The document declares that: "God has been calling out from the world a people for himself, and sending his people back into the world to be his servants and his witnesses, for the extension of his kingdom, the building up of Christ's body, and the glory of his name." Of course, we recognize that God has called his church to fully participate in his mission in specific acts of obedience, proclamation and service in the world, but this must arise within the larger frame of God's mission. This enables the church to avoid triumphalism and keeps our witness God-centered.

The Authority and Power of the Bible (Article 2)

The second Article highlights another major theological distinctive of the Lausanne Movement; namely, the central role of Scripture in world evangelization. The Lausanne Movement affirms the divine inspiration, truthfulness and authority of both the Old and New Testament Scriptures in their entirety as the Word of God, "without error in all that it affirms, and the only infallible rule of faith and practice."[2] The beauty of this affirmation is that it avoids two potential problems which have sometimes negatively influenced how the church has understood Scripture. On the one hand, the Lausanne Movement stands firmly within the great stream of historic Christian faith in affirming the power and efficacy of God's word. The failure to remain firm on the authority of Scripture is the root cause of much of the decline in many branches of the church. On the other hand, it is important to recognize that the power of Scripture is ultimately rooted in God himself. This does not erode the fact that God's Word as we have

---

[2] For more on an evangelical understanding of the authority of the Bible, see John R. W. Stott, *The Authority of the Bible* (Grand Rapids, MI: InterVarsity Press, 1999). The Lausanne Movement has embraced both those who understand "without error" as inerrancy in every detail as well as those who affirm a limited inerrancy which acknowledges that the Bible is wholly trustworthy even if the writers were not always technically accurate on certain minor historical or scientific facts, or when different details or broad summary statements emerge from multiple witnesses to the same event.

received it is without error and is propositionally true. But, we also must remember that we read and proclaim the Scripture in the presence of the risen Christ himself and in continuity with the living church through the ages. The Scriptures are 'God-breathed' and therefore always flow forth from his divine authority as the Lord of the world and of the church, which is his body.

The Uniqueness and Universality of Christ (Article 3)

The third major theological distinctive of the Lausanne Movement is the centrality of Jesus Christ who is the 'only ransom for sinners', and is the 'only mediator between God and people'. Lausanne affirms the uniqueness of Jesus Christ who alone has died for our sins.[3] The *Lausanne Covenant* rejects the notion that God speaks equally through all religions or that other religions can extend salvation anonymously through Christ. Rather, the church is called to proclaim to the entire human race the power of Christ, and call all men and women to repent of their sins and explicitly place their faith and trust in Jesus Christ. The Lausanne Movement, therefore, rejects both traditional universalism as well as various Christocentric forms of universalism (such as inclusivism) by insisting not only on the supremacy of Jesus Christ, but also the importance of the call to explicit repentance and faith in Jesus Christ for salvation.

The Nature of Evangelism / Church and Evangelism (Articles 4 and 6)

The Lausanne Movement is fundamentally a network of Christians committed to world evangelization. This does not mean that we expect every person in the world to respond to the Gospel, but that it is our sacred duty to make sure that every people group in the world has the opportunity to hear the Gospel and to see the living witness of the Gospel lived out through the witness of the church. While the fourth Article focuses on evangelism, the sixth Article makes it clear that the task of world evangelization is church-centered. Indeed, the document proclaims that "the church is at the very center of God's cosmic purpose and is his appointed means of spreading the gospel". Sometimes the church is seen as having only an instrumental purpose in the world, i.e. the work of proclaiming the Gospel. However, the Lausanne Movement envisions that the church has a deeper ontological purpose and is integrally related to the final consummation of the Kingdom.[4] In other words, it is not merely that the church is the instrument through which God proclaims the Gospel;

---

[3] See John R. W. Stott, *The Cross of Christ*, study edition (Grand Rapids, MI: InterVarsity Press, 2010).

[4] For more discussion on the relationship between ecclesiology and the nature of evangelism see Simon Chan, *Liturgical Theology* (Grand Rapids, MI: IVP, 2006).

rather, the church *is* what God is building in the world. The church is not to be equated with the Kingdom, but the Kingdom is not consummated in isolation from the redeemed people of God who have been called out of a life of sin into the joyful fellowship of the church, the company of the redeemed. The church does not only proclaim the power of the cross, it is called to be itself 'marked by the cross'. The Gospel is not merely an independent message of words, it is a message which is actually embodied in a living community of faith around the world. Thus, the church is not merely the aggregate collection of redeemed individuals or, even less, the sum of all the various church institutions around the world, but is, more fundamentally, 'the community of God's people' which transcends all cultures, social or political systems and ideologies.

Christian Social Responsibility / Freedom and Persecution (Articles 5 and 13)

The Lausanne Movement led the global evangelical movement in listening to the voices of many Christians around the world who felt that the church had not demonstrated sufficient solidarity with those who have been denied justice and have been marginalized in various ways. Thus, the Lausanne Movement affirms God's concern for justice and liberation from all forms of oppression. The church has sometimes had difficulty articulating the relationship of evangelism to social action in the world. The commitment to proclaim the Gospel has sometimes been reduced to evangelistic campaigns without a concomitant concern for the poor, the homeless and the disenfranchised. The church has recognized the vibrant witness of both Billy Graham and Mother Teresa, for example, but has not always known how the two witnesses relate one to another. Some evangelicals see social action as a *bridge* to evangelism. Others conceptualize it as a natural *consequence* of evangelism. Still others try to see the two as *complementary* partners.[5]

There are three key features of the Lausanne Movement which deserve to be highlighted. First, it properly places social action in a theological context, linking it to the doctrines of God, reconciliation, righteousness and the fact that all men and women are created in the image of God. Second, the statement affirms that evangelism and social action are not 'mutually exclusive', thereby laying the groundwork for an integrated view of how the person and work of Christ are reflected in the life and witness of the church. Finally, at the heart of the *Lausanne Covenant* is an expression of *metanoia,* or repentance, for the church's failure to live consistently with

[5] For a more detailed discussion of the evangelical discussions around the relationship between evangelism and social action see Timothy C. Tennent, *Invitation to World Missions: A Trinitarian Missiology for the 21st Century* (Grand Rapids, MI: Kregel, 2009), 387-406.

the biblical witness to social action and the struggle for justice on behalf of the oppressed.

The Lausanne Movement has also aligned itself theologically with the Universal Declaration of Human Rights. It is important to recognize that social action is not only needed for the unbelieving world, but also for millions of Christians who are unjustly imprisoned and who are suffering persecution. The *Lausanne Covenant* affirms the importance of addressing both personal expressions of evil as well as structural evils which deny religious freedom for millions of people.

Co-operation in Evangelism and Churches in Evangelistic Partnership (Articles 7 and 8)

One of the great hallmarks of the Lausanne Movement is its desire to transcend issues which have divided the church and find our deeper unity in the core Gospel message. The Lausanne Movement is simultaneously an evangelical movement as well as a profoundly ecumenical one. As part of the ecumenical movement, Lausanne stands in the tradition of the World Evangelical Alliance and the World Council of Churches, but Lausanne has flourished, in part, because it is a movement rather than an organization *per se*. There is no official Lausanne 'headquarters' and the network is sustained by a small paid staff, supported by dozens of volunteers scattered all over the world. The Lausanne Movement has provided a common platform for a stunning array of Christians from hundreds of cultures and languages, all sharing a common evangelical commitment to the evangelization of the world. Precisely because the Lausanne Movement is not an organization or an institution in the formal sense, it finds its deepest joy in helping to grow fruit on the trees of countless other Christian bodies. It boldly affirms that those "who share the same biblical faith should be closely united in fellowship, work and witness". The Lausanne Movement has provided a global platform upon which often neglected Christian movements from around the world could meet together and form viable partnerships in global evangelization. The Movement, while church-centered, has also helped to link a host of para-church organizations committed to Bible translation, theological education, distribution of literature and evangelism, to name but a few.

The Urgency of the Evangelistic Task (Article 9)

The Lausanne Movement has fostered a greater realization of just how many people groups do not have sufficient access to the Gospel message or viable expressions of the church. Thus, the Lausanne Movement has helped to foster a whole wave of research in understanding the social, linguistic, cultural and caste barriers which often keep people from hearing the Gospel in a way which is understandable and culturally applicable. Different criteria have emerged in defining what exactly an 'unreached people group' is and exactly what percentage of a given group needs to be Christian before a group can be declared 'reached'. This has led to various numbers ranging from 4,000 to over 6,000 distinct unreached groups.[6] However, the Lausanne Movement is known for its theological emphasis on the urgency of the task and the importance of the church making certain that every people group in the world has access to the Gospel. The *Lausanne Covenant* goes so far as to call Christians from more affluent countries to adopt simpler lifestyles and to contribute more generously to the work of global evangelism. It is also crucial that this work be seen not as a 'West reaching the rest' initiative, but rather a shared responsibility by all Christians on every continent to both send and receive missionaries and cross-cultural witnesses for the sake of Christ.

Evangelism and Culture (Article 10)

Another theological distinctive of the Lausanne Movement has been an affirmation of human culture. While every culture manifests evidence of the power of sin, it is also true that every culture is 'rich in beauty and goodness'. The Lausanne Movement affirms that God is the source and sustainer of both physical and social culture. By virtue of his Triune reality, God is inherently relational, and human relationships, endowed by him at creation, represent a reflection of his presence in creation itself. The Christian belief that God is beyond all human cultures and yet has chosen to reveal himself within all the particularities of human cultures is a distinctive affirmation of Lausanne. God has chosen to reveal himself within the context of human cultures and therefore we must resist attitudes which presuppose that one culture is superior to another. The Gospel has the power to elevate every culture and all the realities of the in-breaking New Creation can be expressed in the full, multi-faceted particularities of every culture.

In communicating the Gospel, the church has a long history of contextualizing the message so that the unchanging truths of the Gospel can be understood and received. The historic deposit of the Gospel is unchanging, but contextualization acknowledges the need to 'translate' the message into forms which are "meaningful and applicable to peoples in their separate cultural settings such that the original message and impact of the

---

[6] There are different criteria which are used by mission organizations in defining a 'people group' and then determining whether it has been 'reached' or 'unreached' with the Gospel. The three most important public databases (all using different criteria) can be found at www.joshuaproject.net and http://imb.org/ globalresearch/ and http://worldchristiandatabase.org/wcd. For a full discussion of the Lausanne role in the discussion about unreached people groups and how this theme has undergone development over the last forty years, see Timothy C. Tennent, *Invitation to World Missions*, 354-386.

Gospel is communicated".[7] The commitment to appropriate contextualization protects the Gospel from being communicated only through a monocultural lens as well as an undue separation from real history. The truths of the Gospel are unchanging and not culturally determined, but those truths cannot be experienced, celebrated or communicated without being culturally embodied. All Gospel communication, including the New Testament itself, is a contextual event. Even a statement as simple as 'Jesus is Lord' must be communicated in a particular language to some particular cultural setting. Contextualization, therefore, assures that the objective and subjective dimensions of revelation are not allowed to drift apart.

Education and Leadership (Article 11)

The Lausanne Movement has led the way in helping the church to understand that evangelism cannot be theologically isolated to 'decisions for Christ' or any reductionistic view of salvation which is equated with the doctrine of justification. Instead, evangelism fundamentally includes the raising up of discipled believers and a whole new generation of theologically educated Christian leaders. The role of the church, seminaries and organizations committed to discipleship is crucial for the long-term growth and sustainability of the church in the world. Every nation and culture should also have access to theological education, and every Christian should be given opportunities to grow in discipleship and service. This does not mean exporting western forms of theological education around the world, but discovering a whole range of effective strategies for training the whole people of God, ordained and lay.

Spiritual Conflict (Article 12)

One of the most important theological distinctives which arises out of placing missions within the larger work of God's mission in the world is the recognition that the advance of the church is ultimately not a logistical or institutional task, but is rooted in a cosmic spiritual conflict which must be faced by prayer and the recognition of the nature of spiritual warfare. The church is not simply fighting forces of liberal theology or dangerous ideologies or non-Christian religious expressions. Ultimately, we are engaged in spiritual warfare against principalities and powers of evil which seek to thwart the church and to impede the progress of world evangelization. Thus, the Lausanne Movement has embraced the importance of calling for purity in the church, faithfulness in prayer and the recognition of the spiritual forces arrayed against us. Ultimately, Jesus

---

[7] Bruce J. Nicholls and David Hesselgrave, *Communicating Christ Cross-Culturally*, 143, 144.

Christ, the Word of God and a faithful, prayerful church are the most important features of world evangelization.

The Power of the Holy Spirit (Article 14)

Some expressions of the church have been thoroughly Christocentric, but have not always embraced the centrality of the Triune God in the larger work of evangelism and world evangelization. The Lausanne Movement affirms that the Father is the great initiator, sender and goal of all missions. The Son is the redemptive embodiment of God's mission. The Holy Spirit is the empowering presence of God in his unfolding mission in the world. Without the power and witness of the Holy Spirit then no one will be convicted of sin, be enabled to place their faith in Christ, or grow in the Christian faith. It is the Spirit who renews the church and empowers and enables us to be his effective witnesses in the world. The Spirit also enables the church to manifest all the realities of the New Creation in the midst of a world in bondage to sin and death. The gifts and fruits of the Spirit are essential to the life and witness of the church.

The Return of Christ (Article 15)

Finally, the *Lausanne Covenant* embraces a strong Christian view of history which is framed by an eschatological perspective where the glorious and visible return of Jesus Christ will bring an end to human history, consummate his salvific plan, judge the world and consummate his eternal kingdom. Thus, the mission of the church has been framed by God as occurring between the ascension and the return of Christ. Lausanne does not envision the emergence of a global utopia or that the Kingdom of God will become fully consummated apart from his final intervention at the end of time. Ultimately, the full manifestation of righteousness and peace will be the result of God's final initiative and action. This is a constant reminder that all our actions and acts of obedience in the world must finally be framed within his initiative to initiate the plan of redemption as well as to bring it to its final consummation. Indeed, our effective ministry in the world cannot be fully comprehended apart from this larger theological frame in which the church serves and obeys.

It was at the end of the 1974 Congress that Ralph Winter, a noted missiologist, explained publicly for the first time how, even if the entire church was engaged in effective evangelism, it would only lead to approximately one billion new Christians. There would still remain an additional two billion who were out of reach of the Gospel without an intentional cross-cultural witness.[8] This led, as will be explored later, to a far greater effort to cross cultural boundaries with the Gospel of Jesus Christ.

Theological Distinctives of the *Manila Manifesto* and *Cape Town Commitment*

The Manila Manifesto

The second International Congress on World Evangelization took place in Manila, Philippines in 1989. It is sometimes called 'Lausanne II'. Over 4,000 Christian leaders gathered from all over the world to discuss the progress of world evangelization and to reflect on how the world and context of missions had changed since the 1974 Congress. Like the first Congress, the Manila gathering culminated in the release of what has become known as the *Manila Manifesto*. It is important to understand that both the *Manila Manifesto* in 1989 as well as the *Cape Town Commitment* in 2010 were not conceptualized as replacing the *Lausanne Covenant* or initiating major changes in the historic theological distinctives of the Lausanne Movement. Rather, the purpose of these documents is to build on the foundation of the *Lausanne Covenant* and to highlight new challenges which the church was facing, or theological themes which required greater clarification based on further reflection on the *Lausanne Covenant.*

The *Manila Manifesto* is organized round 21 opening Affirmations which largely reaffirm the substance of the *Lausanne Covenant.* This is followed by twelve Articles and a final conclusion which go into more depth concerning particular theological, cultural and ecclesiastical challenges which impede global evangelization. In the opening Affirmations there are two distinctives which were not explicitly present in the *Lausanne Covenant.* First, there is the Affirmation that the Jesus of history is the same as the Christ of glory (Affirmation 5). This statement deepens Lausanne's concern about various theological attempts to separate the saving work of Christ from his historical manifestation in the Incarnation as revealed in history. The idea that Christ can be experienced implicitly through other religions or through various cultural movements is not embraced by the Lausanne Movement. This point is further expounded in Article 3 which explicitly renounces the view that the Jewish people can be saved through a separate covenant apart from their personal response to Jesus Christ. By implication, this would clearly apply also to Muslims, Hindus and Buddhist, among others.

[8] The entire text of Ralph Winter's address, including the paper sent to all the delegates in advance of the 1974 Congress, as well as the actual address given by Winter at Lausanne, is available at www.lausanne.org/documents.

The second theological distinctive of the *Manila Manifesto*, found in Affirmation 18, is the call to invest more time in studying society to better understand its 'structures, values and needs' as a part of the larger work of developing mission strategy. This *Affirmation* implies a more robust embrace of the work of cultural and social anthropology in helping the church to better fulfil its mission.

Further theological distinctives that arose out of the *Manila Manifesto* included an explicit *Affirmation* of the role of apologetics in world evangelization. The congress was more conscious of a rising tide of intellectual challenges to the Christian Gospel which require a more concerted evangelical response. The declaration also built upon the *Lausanne Covenant's* affirmation of the Universal Declaration of Human Rights by explicitly affirming the importance of standing up for religious freedom throughout the world. Finally, in Article 8 the *Manila Manifesto* devotes far more attention to the importance of training, equipping and empowering the laity for world evangelization.

While it does not appear in the *Manila Manifesto*, it was at the 1989 Congress that Luis Bush introduced the concept which in 1990 was described as the '10/40 window'. This refers to the area of the world 10 degrees to 40 degrees north of the equator where two thirds of the world lives and which is marked by the highest levels of poverty and the least access to the Gospel. This has resulted in dozens of mission agencies and churches targeting missionary work in that particular region of the world which represents the heart of the Islamic, Hindu and Buddhist world.

The Cape Town Commitment

In 2010 the third Lausanne Congress on World Evangelization was held in Cape Town, South Africa. Over 4,200 evangelical leaders from 198 countries gathered to reflect on the progress of world evangelization. The Congress was preceded by three years of study and listening to the global church in order to discern what were the key theological and cultural issues which needed to be addressed by the global church. The resulting document, the *Cape Town Commitment* represents, on the one hand, a clear affirmation of all the theological distinctives of the *Lausanne Covenant* while, on the other hand, offering a complete reframing of how the Gospel might be more effectively proclaimed to the world. Rather than issue new theological distinctives, the *Cape Town Commitment* seeks to reframe the discussion in a way which can be carried out and applied in a myriad of new global contexts. The meeting in Cape Town was the first congress which was attended by more 'Majority World' Christians than Christians from the western world. It was undoubtedly one of the most diverse gathering of Christians ever held in the history of the world.

The *Cape Town Commitment* reorganized the basic affirmations of the *Lausanne Covenant* and the *Manila Manifesto* round the theme of the love of God. Without taking away from the monumental achievement of the *Lausanne Covenant* to set forth the central theological distinctives of the Movement, the love of God was only mentioned once in the entire document. It became increasingly clear that the truths of the *Lausanne Covenant* needed to be retained, but released within the larger context of the love of God. The *Cape Town Commitment* reframes the entire theological work of the Movement round the love of God. The document is divided into two main parts. The first portion is organized round ten central themes such as 'We love because God first loved us' which is a new presentation of Article 1 of the *Lausanne Covenant*. The document follows with Articles affirming that we "love the living God, we love the Father, we love the Son, we love the Holy Spirit, we love God's Word, we love God's world, we love the gospel of God, we love the people of God and, finally, we love the mission of God". This is the most important theological distinctive of the *Cape Town Commitment*.

The second part of the document identifies six key themes which, again, restate many of the classic themes of the Lausanne Movement. Several new features were emphasized in the *Cape Town Commitment*, including caring for creation (Part II, II,5) and a strong critique of the idolatry of the prosperity gospel (Part V, 4). The document is a clarion call for the church to remain faithful even in the midst of a broken world which is increasingly hostile to the Gospel. The document is also more consciously aware of the growing diversity of the church and the need for even greater levels of collaboration and true partnership which will enable the church to fulfil the original theme of the Lausanne Congress in Lausanne; namely 'the Whole Church, bringing the Whole Gospel, to the Whole World'.

Missiological Impact

The second part of this chapter seeks to explore the wider missiological impact of the Lausanne Movement. This will be explored under five themes.

The Reclaiming of Trinitarian Missiology and the 'Missio Dei': The God of Mission and the Church of Missions

As noted in Articles 1 and 14 of the *Lausanne Covenant* and made even more explicit in the subsequent documents, Lausanne has brought the evangelical global mission movement into a more fully Trinitarian frame. It is not enough to simply proclaim Christ. Our central proclamation must be reconceptualized within the larger frame of God's mission (*missio Dei*) and with the empowering work of the Holy Spirit. This defining phrase, *missio Dei* (the mission of God) as a way of conceptualizing mission was originally coined by German missiologist Karl Hartenstein in 1934. Later, in 1952, at a major conference sponsored by the International Missionary

Council held in Willingen, Germany, the theological emphasis that God's redemptive action precedes the church was set forth, even though they did not explicitly use the phrase *missio Dei*. The phrase was later popularized by Georg Vicedom as a key concept in missions with the publication of his 1963 landmark book, *The Mission of God: An Introduction to the Theology of Mission*. Vicedom insightfully conceptualized mission as our participation in the Father's mission of 'sending the Son'. Vicedom declared that "the missionary movement of which we are a part has its source in the Triune God Himself".[9] However, the application of this concept increasingly disconnected the church from the mission of God. The result was a focus on the world as the stage of God's redemptive activity which marginalized the church and her redemptive proclamation. The church's role, at best, was merely to point out where society was struggling for humanization or where God's *shalom* was emerging in the world.

There was a significant period where evangelical Christians avoided the phrase *missio Dei* because it became associated with the separation of God's work from the life and witness of the church. The Lausanne Movement helped to reintroduce the concept of *missio dei* and to re-connect the theology of *missio dei* with the clear understanding that the church is central to how God's mission is unfolded in the world and, indeed, that the church is God's redemptive goal. To be fair, this re-connection of *missio dei* to ecclesiology was probably not intended by the Lausanne leaders, but it became the logical result of hundreds of church leaders gathering together regularly to discuss missions in the regional meetings and issue-based consultations which have been the backbone of the Lausanne Movement.

The Emphasis on Access to the Gospel: From People Groups to Global Immigration Patterns

The most important missiological breakthrough of the twentieth century was the awareness that the Great Commission texts were about discipling entire nations and bringing the Gospel to every people group on the earth. The word 'nations' in the New Testament is a translation of the Greek word *ethne* meaning 'people groups' or 'ethnic groups.' The work of Ralph Winter in pioneering the concept of an unreached people's group and Luis Bush with the 10/40 window are two vital insights which were widely embraced by churches within the Lausanne Movement and thereby helped to make these emphases a part of the legacy of Lausanne.

This has resulted, not merely in a deeper theological basis for global missions, but has translated into millions of new Christians and tens of

---

[9] Georg Vicedom, *The Mission of God: An Introduction to the Theology of Mission*; translated by Gilbert A. Thiele and Dennis Hilgendorf (Saint Louis, MO: Concordia Publishing House, 1965), 5. Vicedom is quoting Hans Hartenstein.

thousands of new churches in people groups who heretofore had no viable access to the Christian Gospel. At the turn of the twentieth century, only 10% of the world's Protestants were located outside the west, and the vast majority of all Christians were located in the west. Today, the church of Jesus Christ is the most diverse movement in the history of the world. More people in more countries using more languages confess the name of Jesus than at any time in history. The Lausanne Movement played an important role in unleashing so many new church-planting movements around the world, including new ones in the west, many of which use the *Lausanne Covenant* as their statement of faith.

The remarkable work of the Joshua Project, the Adopt-a-People initiative, AD 2000 & Beyond, the extensive research of the International Missions Board of the Southern Baptists, the World Christian Database, among others, would not be where they are today without the work of Lausanne.

As someone who has followed Lausanne from the beginning of the Movement, it is probably fair to observe that Lausanne has become more focused on the praxis of missions, sometimes to the detriment of good theological and missiological reflection. In the formative period, John Stott and Billy Graham represented a unique partnership of theological clarity and ministry praxis. Both deeply understood the important role each played in the success and sustainability of the wider movement. As time progressed, the Lausanne Movement became more globalized, more diverse, and less centralized. Indeed, it is only in the last ten years that Lausanne could really claim to be a globally representative Movement. Yet, in the process, the focus has increasingly been on the practice of mission and the general value of building cross-cultural relationships in the global Christian movement. However, if Lausanne is to continue as a vibrant force, the theological foundations of the Movement and the call for deeper missiological reflection must remain at the forefront.

The Emergence of a New Ecumenism: The Changing Face of Global Christianity and the Collapse of the "West Reaches the Rest Paradigm"

As late as the year 1990 when *Christian History* magazine listed the one hundred most significant events in the history of Christianity, there was not a single reference to any event taking place in the Majority World or initiated by Majority World Christians. We sometimes forget from today's vantage-point how slow the church has been in recognizing the dramatic global developments in the Christian church throughout Africa, Asia and Latin America. Missions practice remained largely framed within a paradigm which assumed a vital western church being mobilized to reach the non-western world with the Gospel. It was the Lausanne Movement which gave voice and, quite literally, the platform to dozens of new voices in world Christianity. The Lausanne Movement has sponsored several major conferences dedicated to identifying emerging global leaders. It was at the 2004 consultation in Pattaya, Thailand, which brought together 1,500 leaders from around the world that Lausanne really began to become more intentionally global in terms of its leadership, representation at meetings, and serious grappling with many of the structural, linguistic and cultural challenges which seeks to keep the Movement from being fully globalized.[10]

The growth of independent, indigenous Christian movements from only eight million at the turn of the twentieth century to 423 million by the close of the century was finally being recognized as one of the most significant demographic shifts in Christian affiliation in history. The writings of Philip Jenkins in such books as *The Next Christendom*, the *New Faces of Christianity* and *God's Continent* popularized what had become a reality in the Lausanne Movement. In a relatively short period of time, the western church finally began to recognize that it was situated in a newly emerging mission field, and that many of the most vibrant and growing Christian movements in the world were located in places which for centuries had been regarded as the mission field. Today it is unthinkable that the evangelization of the world is even possible without the full collaboration of the 'Whole Church bringing the Whole Gospel to the Whole World'.

The Rediscovery of a Larger Gospel: A Holistic Gospel for the Whole World

The evangelical movement in the opening decades of the twentieth century was dangerously isolated from recognizing our broader commitment to serve the poor, to fight against injustices, and to address the larger structural evils which trap and disenfranchise people. A more holistic Gospel was, of course, always the legacy of evangelicalism and few were as committed to it as those in the missionary movement. However, the fundamentalist-modernist controversy in the late nineteenth and early twentieth centuries tended to polarize evangelism from social action in ways which were historically alien to the life of the church. Broadly speaking, fundamentalism tended to truncate the Gospel, reducing it to a message of personal salvation. In contrast, the modernist tended to equate the Gospel with our broader, corporate, social witness with less of an emphasis on personal repentance and faith in Jesus Christ. The Gospel, of course, involves both. It was the Lausanne Movement which helped to shape and galvanize the church around a broader redemptive mission. The 1982 Lausanne consultation on the relationship between evangelism and

10 All the papers from the working groups which met in Pattaya have been published in three volumes. See David Claydon (ed), *A New Vision, A New Heart, A Renewed Call* (Pasadena, CA: William Carey Library, 2005). Many of these papers are also available at www.lausanne.org/documents.

social action was one of several events which helped to reframe this issue for the church. Today, millions of Christians who have been shaped by the Lausanne Movement are addressing issues from human trafficking, to poverty, to creation care. In fact, the Lausanne Movement has sponsored dozens of consultations throughout the years on hundreds of issues which have allowed Christians to think better about issues which were the rightful legacy of Christian witness.

Deeper Collaboration with the Whole Church: A New Understanding of Partnership

One of the themes which unite all the major Lausanne documents explored earlier is the call to deeper collaboration with the global church, especially in bringing together the broader 'evangelical family' of the global church. The Lausanne Movement, especially in the early decades of the Movement, tended to avoid collaboration with large conciliar bodies of Christians. However, as time progressed, the Lausanne Movement opened up meaningful points of dialogue between Roman Catholic, Eastern Orthodox and mainline Protestant churches, especially when it became clear that these movements contained many vibrant Christians who shared Lausanne's core commitment to world evangelization. Lausanne has also struggled to keep itself as a 'movement' rather than an 'organization'. As a movement, it provides a unique platform for a wide variety of groups to meet and collaborate around a common commitment to world evangelization. As an organization, Lausanne can create confusion *vis à vis* other longstanding organizations such as the World Evangelical Alliance. Lausanne must work hard to remain a 'platform' for a host of other organizations, Christian sodalities and church movements.

Lausanne is at its best when it helps to facilitate partnerships in the practical working out of missions at the grassroots level around the world. The Lausanne Movement facilitated key discussions which focused specifically on new understandings of partnership. For example, at the 2004 Forum for World Evangelization held in Pattaya, Thailand, more than 1,500 global leaders gathered to discuss 31 issues which had been identified as roadblocks to evangelism. One of the most important issues discussed in Pattaya was the issue of healthy partnerships. It became clear that much of what was being described as partnership still retained unhealthy relationships due to power differentials which inevitably arise when power and money are involved. Candid and open conversations took place which had a significant impact on the actual practice of missions throughout the world. It was finally recognized that those churches found in the poorest regions of the world bring substantial assets to the global church which cannot be quantified in financial ways.

Conclusion

The Lausanne Movement remains a strong and vibrant force contributing to world evangelization. The original convenors of Lausanne back in 1974 could scarcely have imagined the remarkable global movement which they were unleashing. The theological legacy of Lausanne has been one of its most enduring contributions to the global church. Undoubtedly, the historic Christian faith which so clearly sounds forth from the Lausanne Movement is, in fact, the very basis of its equally powerful missiological impact. Thus, the theological distinctives and the missiological impact are not two separate things, but one thing understood from two perspectives. It is clear that all glory and honour goes to God for calling such a movement forth which, despite its many shortcomings, has nevertheless given untold blessings to millions of new Christians around the world. It is difficult to imagine that the global church could meet in such remarkable venues for worship and discussion, and collaborate on so many global initiatives with such remarkable fruit, without the Lausanne platform. In the end, Lausanne is not about documents or global gatherings. Lausanne is about Christians working and praying together in a shared commitment that we might live to see, in our generation, 'the whole Gospel brought by the whole church to the whole world'.[11]

[11] The well-known Lausanne phrase, 'the Whole Church, Taking the Whole Gospel, to the Whole World' refers to the great missiological mandate of the global church. This mandate cannot be achieved only by those who are connected with the Lausanne Movement, or any denomination, organization or movement. Rather, this is a visionary phrase pointing to that great corporate goal of the people of God from all times and ages which will only be fully consummated at the return of Christ.

John Stott and the Lausanne Movement: A Formative Influence

Julia Cameron

John Stott died on the afternoon of 27th July 2011, in the College of St Barnabas, a home for retired clergy in Surrey, England. Obituaries appeared in all four leading UK newspapers on 29th July, where he was afforded more space than is given to most cabinet ministers.

Few clergy become the subject of doctoral theses. John Stott's life and work had, in his lifetime, already attracted over a dozen such theses; there will be more, and doubtless a stream of further biographies. As decades pass, history will unfold the extent of his influence on theological thinking, on preaching, on the tensions between the Gospel and culture, on the development of a Christian mind, on evangelical commitment to social justice, and supremely on world evangelization.

The calling, gifting, *métier*, of this unusually able man was unique. He had no peer and, as Archbishop Peter Jensen said in the thanksgiving service in Sydney Cathedral, we should not look for a successor. In Vancouver, Prof Jim Packer paid tribute to 'a fifteen talent man', and so he was.[1]

If we were to abstract two major foci of John Stott's ministry, consistently served through seven decades, they would be the student world[2] and the training of pastors;[3] but to this must be added his

[1] Both thanksgiving addresses are available on www.johnstottmemorial.org

[2] From his undergraduate days in CICCU (Cambridge Inter-Collegiate Christian Union), John Stott maintained a close friendship with Oliver Barclay. He regarded Douglas Johnson, founding General Secretary of the Inter-Varsity Fellowship (now UCCF), as the greatest single influence on UK evangelicalism, and was deeply committed to the global ministry of the International Fellowship of Evangelical Students (IFES), developing strong links with its first General Secretary, Australian Stacey Woods. Starting and ending in his Alma Mater, the University of Cambridge (1952, 1977), John Stott led many university missions in the UK and around the world. The IFES goal to make Christ known in every university in the world was, he said, 'the most strategic work imaginable'.

[3] The Langham Partnership, founded in 2001, drew together earlier initiatives of the Evangelical Literature Trust and a scholarship fund for the (largely post-doctoral) training of non-westerners who would return to teach in seminaries in their home countries. To this was added 'Langham Preaching' which now trains preachers globally.

contributions to Scripture Union,[4] Tearfund, the World Evangelical Alliance; his founding of the National Evangelical Anglican Council (NEAC) and the London Institute for Contemporary Christianity; his concern that Christians speak into contemporary issues, including ecological questions; his model of preaching; and his extensive writing which merited its own published bibliography.[5] Alongside these lay his expert knowledge of ornithology, having personally sighted 2,500 of the world's 6,000 bird species.

John Stott's relationship with Lausanne,[6] particularly in the period 1974-96 could well be described as reciprocal, even symbiotic. His multi-faceted ministry fitted the multi-faceted Lausanne aspirations which he had played no small part in fashioning. Lausanne channels and networks would become a major means through which he brought influence to the church globally.

In 2006, Doug Birdsall, Lausanne Movement Executive Chair, invited John Stott to accept a lifetime title of Honorary Chairman, which he did, with a sense of pleasure. It had been a consistent pattern to accept honorary titles only if he could maintain a lively link with the endeavour,[7] and he followed news of planning for the third Lausanne Congress with eager interest. Lindsay Brown,[8] who was appointed as Lausanne Movement International Director in 2007, and Chris Wright,[9] who followed in John Stott's own stead as chair of the Lausanne Theology Working Group,[10] were both old friends.[11]

---

[4] John Stott served as President of Scripture Union England and Wales 1965-73. While not listing offices for each ministry, special mention must be made of Scripture Union (SU). EJH Nash of SU staff (more commonly known as 'Bash') ran the Iwerne Minster camps for public schoolboys, and it was through Bash that John Stott was converted to Christ and nurtured as a young Christian. He always maintained that the greatest spiritual influences on his life had been 'Iwerne and the CICCU'.

[5] Timothy Dudley-Smith (Nottingham, UK: IVP), 1995.

[6] Often used as shorthand in speech and writing for the Lausanne Movement, formerly known and still registered as the LCWE (LCWE). It took its name from the Swiss city which hosted the 1974 International Congress on World Evangelization, out of which the Movement grew.

[7] John Stott was also lifetime Honorary President of Langham Partnership and of CICCU.

[8] Former General Secretary of IFES, of which UCCF is the British affiliate and a founding member.

[9] International Director of Langham Partnership.

[10] Chris Wright also chaired the statement working group which brought together the *Cape Town Commitment*. He consulted with John Stott about the way it would be crafted.

[11] While senior staff and board members of Christian endeavours often move, or are seconded, from one ministry to another, this is no more clearly illustrated than by Langham Partnership International, IFES, and the Lausanne Movement. Each owes a significant debt of gratitude to 'Uncle John'; and their common values, not least

Friendship featured highly in all John Stott's ministry and dealings; he worked and he networked through friendship. This gift of friendship, combined with his interdisciplinary and enquiring mind, equipped him 'to bring traditional Christianity to bear on science, medicine, contemporary thinking about war and nuclear deterrence, and such large questions. He was perhaps uniquely able to convene that largely private discussion [among] the upper echelons of science and medicine and the armed forces … as he laboured mightily to bridge the Christian faith community and the hottest of emerging issues'.[12]

Billy Graham and John Stott served together on a CICCU[13] mission in 1955, John as Billy's chief assistant missioner. Three years earlier, John Stott had himself been the missioner. The story is told of how they would go round and round in the revolving door of Cambridge's University Arms Hotel, where they were both staying, each deferring to the other, neither wanting to get out first! This well-rooted friendship drew John Stott into the early stages of planning for the 1974 International Congress on World Evangelization, held in Lausanne, and from which city the Movement would take its name. Lausanne was soon to have a lion's share of his time.

Edinburgh 1910 – Learning from History

The major missions' conference in Edinburgh, in June 1910, convened by John R. Mott, a visionary from the U.S. Mid-West with a deep passion for evangelism, was a remarkable gathering by any criteria. But from the outset it was flawed through a well-intentioned decision. In a move to gain the participation of the then Archbishop of Canterbury, Randall Thomas Davidson, and John Mott agreed that matters of doctrine would not be discussed. This was a costly error of judgement. Mott opened his final address: "The end of the congress is the beginning of the conquest", and participants streamed out on this stirring note, resolved to give their best energy to the glory of Christ in world evangelization. The two world wars would have a huge bearing on mission strategy. But the decision to include the Archbishop on the terms required was regarded by Stott as of more profound and longer-lasting significance.[14]

---

of building and strengthening indigenous Christian leadership, has forged strong synergy among them around the world. In Lausanne 1974, according to the church historian Ian Rennie, over fifty percent of platform speakers had a background in an IFES movement. In 2010 the proportion was equally high.

[12] Prof Nigel Cameron in *The Times* (8th Aug 2011). He added: "It struck me then [in the 1970s], and does more forcefully now, how his network of personal friendships, which snaked across the face of the planet, was both embedded in his character, and was more than anything else the key to his astonishing influence."

[13] Cambridge Inter-Collegiate Christian Union.

[14] See Foreword to *Making Christ Known: Historic mission documents from the Lausanne Movement, 1974-1989*. John Stott (ed), Paternoster, 1996.

Central questions on the content of the Gospel, the theology of evangelism, and the nature of the church, were conspicuous by their absence. As a result, Edinburgh 1910 proved a lost opportunity to engage with the critical theological challenges of the day. Theological liberalism was to dominate in university faculties and in seminaries for the next several decades. As a result, mission became sidelined in the church.[15]

The World Council of Churches, constituted in 1948, traces its roots back to Edinburgh 1910. But there is a sense in which the Lausanne Movement is the 'spiritual legacy' of that conference, taking forward John Mott's true aspirations.

In 1974 clear action was taken in the formation of the programme to reclaim what had been intended. This can be seen in the strength of the speaker list, and also in John Stott's first plenary address, on 'The biblical basis of evangelism'.[16] Thirty five years later, in 2009, the matter was still clearly on his mind. Doug Birdsall and Lindsay Brown conferred with him on several occasions as the Congress was being planned. He said he felt ashamed that leaders in his own communion refused to discuss doctrinal issues for fear of division. It had rendered John Mott's rallying cry as delegates left Edinburgh severely weakened. "You cannot speak of the gospel of Christ and the mission of the church without reflecting on biblical truth," he said.

Lindsay Brown's closing address in Cape Town would leave no doubt about the clarity of vision and hope for Lausanne.[17] The Congress was to sound 'a ringing reaffirmation of the uniqueness of Christ and the truth of the biblical gospel and a crystal-clear statement on the mission of the church – all rooted in Scripture'. To launch a movement without biblical consensus was, he said, 'folly'. The *Cape Town Commitment* drew evangelicals together around its biblical indicatives before moving on to its

[15] In 1919 we See by contrast, the resolve of undergraduates in Cambridge to maintain the centrality of the Atonement in their definition of the Gospel. This led Norman Grubb and fellow CICCU leaders to sever the CICCU's links with the nationally-respected Student Christian Movement. Their firmness led within ten years to the birth of the IVF [now UCCF] in 1928, and to the founding of the InterVarsity Press (IVP) in 1936. This publishing house has, through the endeavours of evangelical graduates, given rise to sister publishers in over thirty nations, covering much of the world. The founding of Tyndale House, Cambridge, in 1944 is another direct outcome of the 1919 resolve. Under God, we now see evangelicals teaching in university theology faculties and departments across the UK and around the world. A further part of the 1919 CICCU legacy was the forming in 1947 of IFES, with affiliated evangelical student ministries now in over 150 nations.

[16] Much material is available online at www.lausanne.org. All papers and responses appear in the compendium *Let the Earth Hear His Voice*, J. D. Douglas (ed), World Wide Publications, 1975.

[17] See full text in final section of *Christ our Reconciler*, J. E. M. Cameron (ed).

Gospel imperatives. John Stott was actively engaged with Chris Wright on the way those biblical indicatives were crafted.[18] But let us not rush ahead.

1974 – A Congress and a Covenant

From the 1974 Congress a winsome phrase – 'the spirit of Lausanne' – emerged. No one could be precise about its provenance, whether from Billy Graham (who himself was not sure), or simply as a phrase that was mused on by someone, repeated, liked and then adopted. The 'spirit' was exemplified by (i) prayer, (ii) study, (iii) partnership, (iv) hope and (v) humility. One could say that John Stott embodied it. He often referred to the phrase, and used it as a reference point for the Movement as it developed. Each of its components was, for him, of personal concern. To borrow Peter Kuzmic's quip in 2007, John Stott 'war ein Lausanner'.

John Stott's reputation for clear theological thinking, his breadth of sympathy within the evangelical tradition,[19] and his gracious dealings with those of different persuasions, made him an obvious first choice to lead the process of crafting the *Lausanne Covenant*, which issued from the 1974 Congress.

The *Lausanne Covenant* was adopted as a basis for hundreds of collaborative ventures over the rest of the century, and came to be regarded as one of the most significant documents in modern church history.[20] Social justice, too long identified as a concern only for adherents to a 'social gospel' was now declared a biblical responsibility for evangelical Christians. This proved a watershed moment for the church. Realizing the seriousness of the *Lausanne Covenant*, John Stott worked on an exposition and commentary, published in 1975. It would, he sensed, be critical for the Covenant to be read and studied by individuals and groups.[21] His Preface is modestly written, and does not record the intense pressure of working through nights to ensure that all comments received from the participants were read and given proper consideration. It was a mammoth operation to

---

[18] Part I of the *Cape Town Commitment* (entitled *The Cape Town Confession of Faith*) is formed around an expression of God's covenantal love.

[19] Evangelical 'breadth within boundaries' continues to be a value of Lausanne.

[20] You can listen to John Stott's presentation of *The Covenant* on the last full day of the 1974 Congress at Lausanne.org (archive recordings). He and his drafting team, of Samuel Escobar and Hudson Armerding, assisted by J. D. Douglas and Leighton Ford, invited comments at each stage of the process. They received hundreds, from individuals and from national or regional groups. These were translated and all carefully considered – some, as he explains, cancelling others out. It was a finely-tuned and meticulous process. The *Covenant* truly reflected the mood of the Lausanne Congress as well as any single document could.

[21] This exposition and commentary has been republished in the *Didasko Files* series, 2009 (www.didaskofiles.com).

translate them in a timely manner, but vital for the voices of the whole evangelical Church to be heard.

The name 'Covenant' was carefully chosen. This was a covenant with God himself, and a covenant between those who wanted to adopt it. The banner on the stage, in six languages, had proclaimed 'Let the Earth hear His Voice', and for that to happen, the whole evangelical church needed to work together.

The Covenant, in the words of Chris Wright, was 'prophetic in the sense of speaking in a way which applied the Word of God to the realities of the hour. And it retains its relevance and challenge now and indeed for generations to come'.[22] He concluded: 'May these creative combinations of confidence and humility, of human energy and trust in God, of vision and realism, of joy in the Lord's doings and grief over our human failures, of strategic thinking and the Spirit's leading, of global vision and local action, of words and works – always remain characteristic of the Lausanne Movement as they are of its Covenant.'

In July 1989 John Stott led the crafting team for the *Manila Manifesto* in the second Lausanne Congress (Lausanne II in Manila, as it became known). Its 31 clauses built on and elaborated the *Lausanne Covenant.* This second Congress took place a month after what the Chinese government termed the 'Tiananmen Incident', and just three months before the dismantling of the Berlin Wall. It drew 3,000 participants from 170 countries including Eastern Europe and the Soviet Union, but sadly none from China. This gathering was the catalyst for over 300 strategic partnerships and new initiatives, in the developing world and elsewhere.

In 1984, five years before Lausanne II, John Stott published a new and ground-breaking book, *Issues Facing Christians Today.* This covered nuclear issues, pluralism, human rights, industrialization, sexual issues … It became a handbook for pastors and thinking church members. It was, Stott said, his contribution to the 'catching-up process' since the Church was 'recovering from its temporarily mislaid social conscience'. The *Lausanne Covenant* was continuing to create waves in the 1980s, reawakening a social conscience which had lain dormant in many quarters for perhaps two generations. The Lord Jesus had commissioned the apostles to teach new disciples 'everything' he had commanded them. This had plainly not been done. Indeed, the Great Commission seemed, in evangelical circles, to have eclipsed the Great Commandment. In God's grace, John Stott and the Lausanne Movement would become a means of re-establishing this significant aspect of Christian duty.

[22] From the Foreword to the 2009 *Didasko Files* edition.

Establishing a Movement from a Congress

After the 1974 Congress, 70% of participants urged that a Continuation Committee be established, to build on what had been achieved. In January 1975 this group, appointed by the Congress, met in Mexico City with Bishop Jack Dain in the chair. There was considerable support for Billy Graham to become President of the new Lausanne Committee for World Evangelization (LCWE), as it was then named. John Stott urged that this not happen or that there be several Co-Presidents. Billy Graham had already articulated his preference that the Movement adopt a narrower brief of what we could call 'proclamation evangelism'. If this were followed, the Movement would reflect neither the scriptural mandate of the church to be salt and light, nor its historical roots. On the strength of their twenty-year friendship, John Stott, hating discord, felt the need to speak. Jack Dain was in agreement with him, while others could not bring themselves to voice anything other than blind allegiance to Billy Graham, given his worldwide stature. Some saw the disagreement as a power struggle between these two global leaders. But when John Stott spoke with Billy Graham in his room before breakfast the following day, Billy Graham immediately acknowledged his mistake in yielding to pressure to accept the role.

John Stott was asked to be on the drafting committee to prepare a statement on the progress of the meetings, which was accepted with only minor amendments. He described this in his diary as 'a helpful note of unanimity on which to conclude a rather traumatic conference'.[23]

When the Committee met the following year in Atlanta, four functions were identified to achieve the Movement's aim: Intercession, Theology and Education, Strategy, and Communication. A working group for each was set up, and all four of these groups remain to this day. John Stott became Chairman of the Theology and Education Working Group (later called the Theology Working Group).

As a backdrop to his preparation of *Issues Facing Christians Today*, Stott continued to make Lausanne consultations a priority. Not only was he present, but frequently in the chair. He edited the papers from all the consultations up to Lausanne II, published in 1996 under the title *Making Christ Known: Historic Mission Documents from the Lausanne Movement 1974-1989.* As is clear from the contributors, Lausanne had the standing (helped, no doubt, by Stott's own presence) to draw the sharpest evangelical thinkers globally.

The book opened with the *Lausanne Covenant* (1974) and finished with the *Manila Manifesto* (1989). Some papers, such as the 1977 *Pasadena Statement on the Homogeneous Unit Principle* (*i.e.* of church growth and

---

[23] See the full story in Timothy Dudley-Smith, *John Stott: A Global Ministry,* Chapter 7. John Stott always maintained that evangelism be primary, but that the need to make a choice was very rare. Blair Carlson has now been appointed in the newly-created Lausanne role of Ambassador for Proclamation Evangelism.

evangelization) and the 1980 *Evangelical Commitment to Simple Lifestyle,* gained considerable traction. Shortly before his 87th birthday, John Stott surveyed his years in Lausanne, and looked forward in anticipation to what Cape Town 2010 would bring. He said he felt the 1978 *Willowbank Report on Gospel and Culture* merited more attention than it had been afforded.[24] This perceptive, urbane and erudite pastor, living just a few minutes from Oxford Circus, strove, as had his mentor the apostle Paul, with all the energy God mightily inspired within him, to preach relevantly, to apply the eternal to the temporal with skill, and to grasp what lay *behind* people's responses to the Gospel. He worked to be anchored in the eternal Gospel, and, for each decade and each context, to apply it with intellectual and theological rigour, with perceptiveness, with cultural sensitivity – and with an eye to the future.

For as long as the Lausanne Movement was characterized by 'the spirit of Lausanne', John Stott sensed it was critically placed. Humility would always be needful. It was often said of Lausanne that its fruit 'grew on other peoples' trees' and that it acted most effectively as a catalyst. It drew, and draws, from across the divides of secondary issues, so gathers the whole evangelical church. Within that, Lausanne can host smaller meetings for specialized mission agencies with expert knowledge in their fields – Christians in the public arenas of government, business, academia – to shake salt and shine light – believers North and South, rich and poor, in nominally Christian cultures and as minority groups under oppressive regimes … Through such consultations, as leaders met face-to-face and got to know one another as friends, Lausanne would offer a unique means to share freely in the gifts Christ gives to his church.

A Pastor-Theologian

John Stott was one of the few true pastor-theologians. People mattered to him. We cannot strategize with integrity about world evangelization if we do not care about the people in our own town. John Stott was an integrated man. While a schoolboy at Rugby, he had founded the ABC Club as a way to provide a bath for vagrants. As a curate, he had taken boys from the poorer families in the parish for their first experience of camping. As a rector, he sometimes gave up his bed to homeless men, and slept on a camp bed in his study.

The term 'glocal', not coined until the 1980s, describes the way John Stott had lived since the 1930s. It was a core value for him. As one of the world's most effective global public evangelists, he cared for individuals locally, whatever their status. While Lausanne would always function at a strategic level, among theological thinkers, it would be of no more worth

[24] Personal conversation with the present writer Feb 2008. These papers are all available on www.lausanne.org.

than a resounding gong or clanging cymbal if the benefit of its networking did not touch down in real-life situations. At John's funeral at All Souls' on 8th August 2011, Toby Howarth, a former study assistant, related how he never tired of people wanting to talk with him, even after full days of ministry. When Toby broached this with him, wanting, as it were, to protect him, the reply came, "Toby, I remember that God made them, Christ died for them and the Holy Spirit lives in them. How can I not give them my full attention?"

Four decades before 'Fresh expressions of church' appeared on the curricula of theological colleges,[25] John Stott was already practising it. In 1958 the All Souls' Clubhouse in Cleveland Street was opened, to welcome poorer families from the parish who would not feel comfortable in a church building. It was an inner-city church without pews, and a kind of forerunner of Chicagoland's wealthier Willow Creek as a 'church' for the unchurched.

A Leader of Seminal Influence

Forming the influencers of the next generation is a serious obligation for the church. Pulpits in reach of major universities will always be strategic places for the Gospel. In London in the 1970s hundreds of evangelical students poured into All Souls', including growing numbers from overseas, especially the former British colonies. Here they imbibed Scripture – and a model for the way it should be handled.

John Stott's gifting as an expositor and writer with wide intellectual reach fitted precisely with Billy Graham's aspiration for the 1974 Congress.[26] Invitations to speak at this Congress included some of the most able evangelical thinkers: Francis Schaeffer, Jim Packer, Samuel Escobar, Henri Blocher, the young Os Guinness, and the recent convert Malcolm Muggeridge. John Stott's name had already become a byword for the

---

[25] This term was coined by the Archbishops' Council. See *Mission-Shaped Church* (Chair of the working group: Graham Cray. London: Church House Publishing, 2004). In recognition of massive changes in British culture, new-look 'churches' were beginning to spring up for sub-cultures with no means of engaging with mainstream churches or expressions of faith.

[26] At John Stott's funeral, His Honour, Judge David Turner, a long-time friend and advisor, spoke of John Stott kneeling to pray before he preached 'in the scarlet cassock of a Queen's Chaplain under a gleaming white surplice'. He continued, "This was expository preaching of exceptional clarity and authority such as I had never heard. John treated us as intelligent people. He trained us in 'thoughtful allegiance' to scripture. He moved us by his passion. He taught us 'double listening' – the need to 'hear' the Word and the world, and to find the connections. He abhorred in equal measure 'undevotional theology' [mind without heart] and 'untheological devotion' [heart without mind]. He was, as he liked to say, 'An impenitent believer in the importance of biblical preaching.' We loved it!" See *John Stott: Pastor, leader and friend. A man who embodied 'the spirit of Lausanne'*, 25 (Chris Wright et al. Didasko Files series 2012).

diligent handling of Scripture and for a doctrine of Scripture as a touchstone for all human experience and enterprise. His seminal address on the biblical basis for evangelism, opening with the dialogue on meaning between Alice in Wonderland and Humpty Dumpty, established itself as a classic treatment of core Christian thinking.

In Manila in 1989, John Stott gave the first three expositions, covering Romans 1-5, on 'Eagerness to preach the gospel', 'The world's guilt', and 'Amazing Grace'. (He loved the Pauline epistles, and friends joked that he understood Paul better than the apostle understood himself!) Like the apostle Paul, he was 'obsessed by the Cross'.

A Humble Disciple

John was a humble disciple of Christ. Each morning he would greet the three Persons of the Trinity in turn, seeking genuinely to live as a son of his heavenly Father, as a sinner saved by grace, and in the power of the Holy Spirit, his advocate and counsellor. He always said *The Cross of Christ* (1986) was his most important book. As he prepared for his death, he asked that the words on his headstone, following his name and years of service at All Souls' should read: 'Who resolved, both as the ground of his salvation and as the subject of his ministry, to know nothing except JESUS CHRIST and him crucified (1 Corinthians 2:2).'[27]

In 2007, in an interview to mark the 25th anniversary of the London Institute for Contemporary Christianity, he was asked by Brian Draper how he would most like to be remembered. He was by this stage starting to speak slowly, and occasionally faltering, but there was no hesitation in the content of his response. "As an ordinary Christian, who has struggled to understand, expound, relate and apply the Word of God," he said.

For over fifty years he read the whole Bible through annually, using Robert Murray McCheyne's reading plan. "Nothing has helped me more than this," he said, "to grasp the grand themes of the Bible." It became his pattern to rise early to read and pray, and to listen to the BBC World Service news. Listening to God through Scripture should not be removed from world events. We must practise 'double-listening', he would say, so we can apply the Word to the world.

---

[27] In the churchyard in Dale, Pembrokeshire, close to his writing retreat, The Hookses. The quotation echoed the inscription on the memorial plaque in Holy Trinity Church, Cambridge, for his mentor, Charles Simeon (1759-1836). See *Silhouettes and Skeletons* (J. E. M. Cameron (ed), Didasko Publishing, 2013) for the 150-year trajectory of Simeon's influence on John Stott and into the Lausanne Movement.

Dialogue with Roman Catholic and Other Traditions

John Stott was probably the widest-connected evangelical statesman in the twentieth century. In a personal capacity he regularly participated in dialogues, brokered discussions and attended major gatherings such as those of the World Council of Churches (WCC), either as an invited observer or as a responder. He was always prepared to learn from others, and was keen that the evangelical faith be both clearly represented and clearly grasped.[28]

When the Lausanne Movement was founded, John Stott had already engaged with the WCC in Uppsala (1968) as an observer and adviser, and in the same personal capacity, he took part in the WCC gathering in Nairobi (1975) as a responder.

Again in a personal capacity, he initiated the idea of formulating the Evangelical-Roman Catholic Dialogue on Mission (ERCDOM), which he co-chaired with Monsignor Basil Meeking of the Secretariat for Promoting Christian Unity. This dialogue took place in three meetings (1977-84). The text of the papers was published in a booklet,[29] and a report from the meetings appeared in the *International Bulletin of Missionary Research* (January 1986).

To act in a personal capacity gave John Stott freedom. His name and profile naturally drew wide public attention to dialogues, unless they were held privately, but the distinction was always noted. ERCDOM's existence was not confidential. In part, it was this which, at the 1980 World Evangelical Fellowship General Assembly, led to the surfacing of potential divisions among WEF members over links with Roman Catholics. In response, as a parallel endeavour, a task force was convened, to make an in-depth assessment of the *de facto* state of the Roman Catholic Church, its tenets of faith and the beliefs of its members across the continents.

In the early 1980s, at the invitation of a senior Anglican, David L. Edwards, John Stott agreed to a published dialogue between the two of them to explore the essentials of the Christian faith from both their perspectives.[30] Each of Stott's responses, chapter by chapter, begins 'My Dear David' and is written in a consistently gracious style. Graciousness and a willingness to listen always marked his engagement with leaders of other Christian traditions.

---

[28]The *Lausanne Movement* from its early days made a careful distinction between public and personal participation in dialogues with bodies which are not evangelical. John Stott was one of the voices to advocate this distinction. Where Lausanne itself hosts dialogues with those from other Christian traditions or from other faiths, these are still largely held privately – at least, in their initial stages.

[29] Basil Meeking and John Stott (eds), *The Evangelical-Roman Catholic Dialogue on Mission* (Grand Rapids, MI: Eerdmans, 1986).

[30] David L. Edwards and John Stott, *Essentials* (London: Hodder and Stoughton, 1986).

Cape Town 2010

John Stott and Billy Graham both sent greetings to the third Lausanne Congress. John would have loved to be there, and briefly considered the possibility, despite his advancing frailty. He wrote:

> I shall be very sorry to miss being with you in Cape Town. But I will be with you all each day in prayer, expectation and confidence as you plan to make known the uniqueness of Jesus Christ all over the world.

He continued his greeting with a reflection on the Movement since 1974, the growth of the church, his particular delight that the Congress was hosted in Africa, and then concluded: "As you will be studying Ephesians together, my encouragement to you echoes the Apostle Paul. 'I urge you to live a life worthy of the calling you have received. Be completely humble and gentle; be patient, bearing with one another in love. Make every effort to keep the unity of the Spirit in the bond of peace.'"[31]

The Congress Programme Committee commissioned a special video tribute, reflecting his lifelong focus on Christ, from his conversion aged 16 at Rugby School through the legendary public schools' evangelist, E. J. H. Nash, better known as Bash, a story he never tired of telling.

In late March 2011, around a month before John Stott's 90th birthday, Doug Birdsall called him. By this stage, his eyesight was failing badly, and he had not been able to read for several months, and was very frail. Doug was in Boston, and had just received his advance copy of the newly-printed *Cape Town Commitment*. Frances Whitehead had received John Stott's copy two or three days earlier, and had begun to read it to him.[32] When Doug Birdsall called, a friend, Phillip Herbert, picked up the phone. At John's request Phillip was at that moment reading it aloud, section by section, picking up from where Frances had left off.

In the historic line of the *Lausanne Covenant*, evangelical leaders in 198 nations were working to discern what the Holy Spirit was saying to the Church now on each continent, and the evangelical faith was being articulated for the current generation. It would be widely adopted, as the Covenant had been, and no one knew more clearly than John Stott the critical importance of getting it right. He had been praying for the planning, for the Congress itself, and for the writing of the *Commitment*. His words on that call with Doug Birdsall were halting, but his heart was full. The

---

[31] For the full text of the greetings from both John Stott and Billy Graham, see the opening section of *Christ our Reconciler*, J. E. M. Cameron (ed).

[32] Frances Whitehead served as John Stott's Secretary for 55 years, from 1956 until his death. She was honoured by the Archbishop of Canterbury with a Lambeth MA in 2001, in recognition of her 'energetic and enthusiastic ministry to God's Church through her dedicated support of Dr John Stott'. She combined personal warmth and humour with being fast, focused and exacting, and is widely regarded as having known Stott's mind better than anyone else. The present writer is her authorized biographer.

Commitment was in his view 'profound and beautiful'. He went on, "And in it, you seem to have achieved an astonishing degree of unity."

There was a sense of the baton being passed on. As he had struggled over writing *Issues Facing Christians Today*, he had felt 'caught between two worlds' with the text of Scripture on one hand, and 'space probes and micro-processors' on the other. "They are centuries apart," he wrote in the Foreword. "Yet I have sought to resist the temptation to withdraw from either world by capitulation to the other." The *Commitment*, he sensed, stood with him, urging the evangelical church to fill the breach.

Each of the ministries and endeavours with which John Stott had been closely associated was part of the Cape Town Congress. All his concerns, in which he had yearned for evangelicals to engage, were clearly laid out – not just in a document but in a 'Commitment', firmly rooted in God's covenantal love. He had heard plans for global consultations on major areas in the *Commitment* to take matters forward. No doubt there was a sense of completion as he listened to it being read, while sensing he himself would soon be with Christ.

Continuing the Vision from Lausanne 1974: A Personal Perspective

Ramez Atallah

Preamble

The following notes are some of my personal memoirs of my involvement in Lausanne since the 1974 Congress. *This is not a history of the Lausanne Movement.* I am neither qualified nor able to write such a history. What I record below are some selective personal reflections and insights of nearly forty years of involvement in this remarkable Movement. Many important and significant Lausanne leaders are *not* mentioned below. This should in no way be seen as a judgement by me on their contribution but simply the reality, for which I apologize, that I couldn't write about everyone.

Discipled by Committee Meetings

As a young 28-year-old, the Lausanne Congress of 1974 had a distinct impact on my Christian thinking, my *vision*, and my whole life. In preparation for the Congress, I read the preparatory papers in depth and responded enthusiastically, realizing that several of these talks were presenting earth-breaking radical thoughts compared with what I had known to date in the evangelical world.

At the Congress itself I was struck by the breadth and depth of the church worldwide and was impressed by Christian leaders of stature from the four corners of the earth. But the greatest impression I still carry from that historic Congress was the small prayer group which met every night in our hotel lounge to reflect on the day's proceedings and to pray together. As we introduced each other the first night, each one tried to impress the group by his great credentials (president of a seminary, pastor of a large church, leader of a significant Christian ministry etc.). An African man just introduced himself as a 'pastor from Kenya'. During the week he shared how, when he was a school teacher, he was a very hard and unforgiving man who treated his wife and children badly. As a result of the East African Revival, his life was radically transformed as Jesus met him powerfully, and transformed not only the direction of his life but his very character. He said that the five children he had before his conversion were always envious of the five children he had after his conversion who were treated much better than themselves!

As we came to leave on the last day, we all exchanged business cards and I put them in my pocket to read later. On the flight back to Canada, where I was living at the time, I looked through these cards and I came across the simple card this African pastor had given me. I nearly did not read it, assuming that all I would see would be his name and address, but I was struck beyond words to read 'Festo Olang, Archbishop of Kenya'! Here was the man with the highest credentials in the group and we all thought he was simply a pastor of a small rural church in Kenya! I remember this because he had such a strong impact on my life, making me yearn to be much more like him than the rest of us who were trying to impress people by our position or ministry.

The Lausanne Continuation Committee

Probably because I was the youngest seminar presenter at the Congress, I was chosen as the 'youth' representative on the Continuation Committee which met in Mexico City in January 1975. That meeting had a great impact on my life as I began getting a much fuller picture than I had previously had about the evangelical world, and the challenges evangelicals faced in the world and among one another. *Forward from Lausanne* (Appendix IX of the minutes of that meeting) clearly summarizes the direction the first meeting set for the Lausanne Movement.

I was especially impressed by the humility, graciousness and statesmanship of Billy Graham and John Stott who agreed to disagree with one another on the parameters of the mission of Lausanne, while maintaining their deep friendship. This was a wonderful example to me of how Christian leaders do not have to agree on every point to co-operate effectively together!

The fact that I was invited to lead one of the devotions for the first Committee meeting – even though I was only 28 years old – was a true indication that the leadership of Lausanne at that time wanted to include younger leaders in an active way. (At that time, a 'youth' representative was under 30, but as the years passed and I grew older, the committee graciously adjusted that definition upward every five years to keep me on!)

At that meeting in Mexico City in January 1975, Bishop Jack Dain, who had chaired the 74 Congress and was one of the architects of the Movement, tendered his resignation as Chairman.

So the first task of the next meeting in January 1976 was to elect a new Chairman. Each of the six regional groups met together to nominate their candidate for Chairman. I remember Armin Hoppler, the Chairman of the nominations committee, confiding in me that he was very afraid that Lausanne would be terribly divided by each region desiring a different Chairman! A few hours later he was elated and on the verge of tears as he informed me that the top name of every list was the same person – Leighton Ford!

Leighton asked me if I would assist him with his new responsibilities, and I agreed to assist him on a part-time basis. So I travelled down from my home in Montreal, Quebec, to Charlotte, North Carolina (where he lived), several times a year to prepare Lausanne meetings, and in between corresponding and phoning each other frequently.

The impact of Leighton on my life was very significant as he mentored me into Christian leadership. Leighton became my model of a humble, visionary, sacrificial, genuine, transparent, Kingdom-minded, Christian bridge-builder. He had the uncanny ability to bring people into the Lausanne fold through persistently reaching out to those who could easily have been excluded. He became known for his 'reconciliation walks': when someone was upset or disagreed with something, Leighton would invite him/her for a walk, and by the time they came back, everything had been resolved!

The distinctive of the Lausanne Movement at that time was its focus on *'evangelization'* as distinct from simply *'evangelism'*. That new term encompassed both the evangelistic mandate of the Gospel as well as the holistic (called then 'socio-political') responsibility of Christians living in this fallen world.

Lausanne soon convened several small consultations of evangelical leaders on 'burning topics' of the day:

The Homogeneous Unit Principle Consultation in Pasadena, 1977; the Willowbank or Gospel and Culture Consultation in Bermuda, 1978; the North American Conference on Muslim Evangelization in Glen Eyrie, Colorado, 1978; the U.S. Simple Lifestyle Consultation in Ventnor, NJ, 1979, and the International Simple Lifestyle Consultation in London, 1980; the Consultation on the Relationship between Evangelism and Social Responsibility (CRESR) in Grand Rapids, 1982; the Consultation on the Work of the Holy Spirit and World Evangelization in Oslo, 1985; and the Consultation on Jewish Evangelism in Easneye, England, 1986. Other meetings were also held, such as national consultations in Brazil and Canada, and the International Prayer Assembly for World Evangelization in Seoul in 1984.

Each consultation brought together the best minds in the evangelical world related to that topic, and pains were taken to include as broad a range of perspectives and positions as possible. The conclusions were published as *Lausanne Occasional Papers* and served to share the findings worldwide.

The Consultation on World Evangelization (COWE) 1980

During that time a larger gathering was held in June 1980 in Thailand under the theme 'How Shall They Hear?' It gathered together 650 practitioners meeting in fifteen smaller 'consultations', each of which focused on different groups needing to be evangelized.

I was part of a small committee involved in planning the event. The committee was chaired by David Howard, who was Executive Director of Lausanne, with Gordon MacDonald, John Stott, Peter Wagner and me as members. Most of the time of the committee consisted of heated discussions between John and Peter, with the other three of us listening in! I firmly believe that, more than planning the consultation, that committee's greater usefulness was giving a first opportunity for John and Peter to work through their deep disagreements. And though they did not resolve their differences, yet they certainly deepened their mutual respect and understanding for each other's positions and helped us to develop a programme that encompassed their divergent views, particularly related to church growth and the mission of the church.

Gottfried Osei-Mensah, the Lausanne International Director, and John Howell, his Executive Assistant and COWE Director of Operations, were also involved in the planning and preparations for the meeting from their office in Nairobi.

At the consultation itself, I remember one evening sitting beside Arthur Johnstone while John Stott gave his presentation on the 'Bible and World Evangelization'. Arthur had written a book entitled *The Battle for World Evangelism* in which he claimed that among others, Stott was leading the evangelical movement away from a firm belief in the Bible. As he listened to John that night, Arthur leaned over to me and said in amazement, *"He seems to really believe in the Bible!"* This was Lausanne at its best, allowing people who had strong positions against others the unique opportunity to listen and dialogue with one another.

By far the most impactful consultation at COWE was that led by Ray Bakke on megacities. Ray had visited nearly 200 cities in preparation for the Consultation and started a movement within Lausanne that gave evangelicals worldwide a much greater concern for and appreciation of the need to reach out to the megacities of the world.

The Younger Leaders' Consultation 1987 in Singapore

Following the tragic death of his son Sandy, Leighton began to focus much of his ministry on equipping younger leaders. It was out of that vision that 300 key younger leaders (aged under 45) from around the world gathered together for ten days in Singapore in the summer of 1987.

Brian Stiller chaired the planning committee, Steve Hoke was consultation director, and I was responsible for the programme. The committee was made up for the most part of dynamic, opinionated, entrepreneur-type younger leaders. Trying to make them listen to one another and come up with joint decisions was a tremendous challenge, and Brian struggled to lead this unwieldy group.

A turning-point took place during one of our meetings when we couldn't agree on anything. Brian did not know how to lead us out of that impasse.

After a very long period of awkward silence, a softly-spoken young Chinese woman from Hong Kong, Ellie Lau, challenged us – in her own unusual way – to look beyond ourselves to God's Kingdom and be willing to have the humility to work together in a way different form the 'older leaders' whom we criticized for their divisiveness! Ellie's intervention broke the ice, and from then on we began listening to one another rather than just trying to get across our opinion or position.

I firmly believed that one of the main reasons the consultation was a remarkable success was because of what God did in each of us in the planning group. Many of the counter-cultural issues and approaches we tried to integrate into the programme were effective, and most participants felt this was not 'just another conference'! Many of the speakers and participants have, since then, become well-known Christian leaders worldwide. Many of them have affirmed that this consultation was a key turning-point in their lives and ministries. Among them was Doug Birdsall who eventually became Lausanne Chairman and revived the Movement for the 21st century.

To me it was proof that a well-chosen group of 300 younger leaders can impact the worldwide church.

The Second Lausanne Congress 1989 in Manila

Two years later, the Lausanne Movement put on its most ambitious event since Lausanne 74. More than 4,000 leaders from around the world met in Manila for the second Lausanne Congress.

Planning it was extremely painful and challenging …

- Some members of the committee, including myself, were not convinced that we had the resources to undertake such a large event without the financial and logistical help of the Billy Graham Evangelistic Association which had funded and organized the 74 Congress.
- Lausanne had very few full-time staff so it was a real challenge to recruit so many people to help put on the Congress.
- It was difficult to get complete consensus on the focus and vision of the Congress.

Nevertheless, God blessed his people as they gathered in his name …

- Roger Parrott, a young, little-known Nazarene pastor, nearly single-handedly raised the eight million dollars needed to fund the Congress. He was strongly supported in this task by Leighton and Tom Zimmerman (General Superintendent of the Assemblies of God). This made it clear that Lausanne could 'stand on its own' without BGEA support.
- Key planners were Paul McKaughan, Saphir Athyal and Ed Dayton. They planned an excellent programme and steered it through many rough seas.

- This was the first time ever that a significant number of Christians from the Soviet/Eastern bloc had ever attended such an event.
- There was some struggle between charismatic/non-charismatic participants, but a real breakthrough took place under Leighton and the planners' leadership, resulting in a joint statement reconciling the two strongest protagonists – Jack Hayford and Jim Packer!
- One of the greatest impacts of the Congress was the bringing together of all Bible publishing agencies to co-operate under the Lausanne banner. *The Forum of Bible Agencies*, birthed in Manila, continues to this day to help Bible agencies co-operate in their task of communicating God's Word. Fergus Macdonald who eventually became Lausanne Chairman was key in promoting this Forum.

The Manila Manifesto

That carefully written document, bringing together the various strands of the Congress and pointing towards the future, did not receive enough attention worldwide, probably due to the lack of infrastructure available to Lausanne to follow up many of the great achievements of the Congress.

In addition to Leighton, the other most influential Lausanne leader in my life was John Stott. In spite of his British reserve, he never hesitated to give me counsel, advice, reprimand and guidance. As Leighton's assistant, I worked with John on many Lausanne consultations, and in each learned a tremendous amount both theologically and in terms of Christian character. But the most memorable time was working as his typist for the *Manila Manifesto*. It was late on the last night of the Congress when he realized he would have to stay up all night finalizing the Manifesto. The only typists available were women, and he could not have a woman working with him in his bedroom all night. So, in spite of my limited typing abilities, I worked with him through the night typing out each small sheet of the final draft as he gave it to me. It was an incredibly bonding experience and I thank God for that opportunity.

Sadly, the limited resources of Lausanne after the Congress made the follow-up task extremely difficult, and Tom Houston as the new leader struggled to keep the Lausanne boat afloat. But, by God's grace, the Movement survived.

Lausanne was there to help evangelicals co-operate in the task of world evangelization with integrity, realism, Biblical *depth*, and an open and loving spirit. I served on that Committee from the Mexico meeting in January 1975 until 1994, by which time I was Deputy Chairman.

Lausanne Reinvented

In 1980 I returned with my family to my native Egypt, in great part as a result of the impact of the Lausanne Movement on my life. In 1994 I concluded twenty years as a member of the Lausanne leadership believing that I had nothing else to contribute and that Lausanne might have had its day. But, like many times before, I was wrong!

In early 2006, Doug Birdsall – the new Lausanne Executive Chairman – and I were visiting Tom Houston in Oxford, and Doug asked me to consider being the International Director of Lausanne. I declined, explaining to him why I believe most people from the Majority World, including myself, do not have a worldwide vision for the church.

As he described what he wanted in an International Director, I felt that Lindsay Brown – who had just completed sixteen remarkable years as General Secretary of IFES – would be the ideal person. Lindsay had a passion for evangelism, was astute theologically, personally knew Christian leaders in most countries, and had an uncanny ability to befriend them. Lindsay has filled that responsibility admirably since then!

Having convinced Doug that Lindsay was the better candidate, he somehow convinced me to accept being Program Chairman for the 2010 Cape Town Congress. To this day I have no idea how he was able to convince me!

Younger Leaders' Gathering 2006

This gathering drew together 550 young leaders from over 100 countries. As these younger leaders met together with 80 mentors, they brought a new, young and dynamic profile to the ageing Lausanne. In a real sense, this was the worldwide 'kick off' for the new Lausanne under Doug Birdsall's leadership.

At that meeting I introduced Doug to an Egyptian Christian leader who told me later: "Your friend is an unusual American!" "What do you mean?" I asked. His response was quick and to the point: "He is humble!"

Like what Leighton did for his generation, Doug was able to put Lausanne on the map for the 21st century. He did this by incredible effort and very hard work, travelling around the world and recruiting the best Christian leaders worldwide – in his own humble yet very convincing manner – to embrace the Lausanne Movement's vision of world evangelization.

As I observed him do this, I frankly doubted that he could mobilize the human and material resources needed to put on the Cape Town 2010 Congress. But one man with God on his side is a majority, and Doug was able by God's grace, and the many volunteers he recruited, to accomplish this superhuman task to God's glory, but at great expense to his own personal health.

Looking Towards the Future

As I look to the future of Lausanne after the 2010 Congress, I realize that the same unique factors of the original Lausanne vision are still valid and needed in today's world. Evangelicals need more than ever before to co-operate in the task of world evangelization, leave their differences behind, and work together to bring the glorious message of the Gospel to the whole world. The more we *co-operate* together and strengthen one another, the better our own ministries flourish and the greater the impact for the Kingdom of God.

However, we need to do this with an open spirit, willing to frankly share together our disagreements as we face one another with Christian love, responsible scholarship and an open mind.

The evangelical world has changed since the 1974 Lausanne Congress but many of the issues among evangelicals remain quite similar.

Some of the major emphases of Lausanne from 1974 which are more than ever needed today are:

Grappling with Thorny or Controversial Issues

The Cape Town Congress was living proof of the fact that Lausanne is still challenging evangelicals to grapple with issues with which they may disagree internally and on which they may be challenged from the outside. The six major issues presented in plenary sessions at the 2010 Lausanne Congress and the 24 other issues handled in 'multiplexes' during the afternoons all reflected a deep concern to grapple openly with issues that either divide evangelicals internally or challenge evangelicals externally. The maturity, depth and openness with which these topics were handled in Cape Town show how much the evangelical movement has matured since 1974. Cutting edge presentations were made by some of the best thinkers in the world on each of these thirty major issues. This, to me, is living proof that the Lausanne Movement is continuing to help evangelicals co-operate together in the task of world evangelization in an open and yet biblically rooted approach.

One of my major concerns at this point is that the wealth of resources which came out of Cape Town – which are now available on the Lausanne website – need to be widely propagated to encourage and challenge evangelicals who did not have access to them at the Congress. I do not believe this has been done sufficiently, and one of the great challenges that the Lausanne Movement now faces is how to unpack and disseminate this information in a way that would impact the church worldwide.

One way to do this would be to find an effective means by which these rich resources are propagated worldwide through the social media. We are in an age where many people are accessing information electronically and remotely rather than through the printed page. So one of the challenges Lausanne faces is how to aggressively and creatively unpack the gems that are on their website – to feed, stimulate, encourage and act as a catalyst for Christian work worldwide.

Another way to do this, of course, is to continue consultations on some of the more controversial issues where the time at Cape Town was too short to give the topic its needed attention. Some of the consultations that are planned for the future are:

1. The Gospel & Identity & Ethnicity (EPSA & Francophone Africa)
2. The Gospel & Media (North America)
3. The Gospel & Nominalism (Europe)
4. The Gospel & Prosperity Theology (Latin America)
5. The Gospel & Truth in the Public Sphere
6. The Gospel & Work
7. The Gospel & Megacities
8. The Gospel & the Image of Man
9. The Gospel & Partnership
10. The Gospel & Globalization
11. The Gospel & Human Sexuality

The uniqueness of Lausanne is that it can bring together for these consultations people who otherwise would not work together or meet together if it were not for the Lausanne 'umbrella'.

Co-operating Rather than Competing

One of the greatest challenges which faced the Movement in its early days was convincing evangelicals of the value of co-operating rather than competing. This was especially hard for people of entrepreneur-like spirit and who came from cultures that had a desire for world conquest! But as Christian leaders from different cultures, organizations and ministries worked together, they were able to see the value of this emphasis on co-operation. One striking example of this was the way evangelical youth ministries such as the Navigators, Campus Crusade and InterVarsity were brought closer together as their leaders, who were in the Lausanne Movement, began to appreciate one another's ministries. Another example would be the co-operation which developed between Youth with a Mission and Operation Mobilization, two very different movements theologically and culturally, but both of which encourage young people for mission work. In an unprecedented generous move, Youth with a Mission, upon hearing that Operation Mobilization's ship had been put out of service; contributed money they had raised for a ship – but had not yet used – to Operation Mobilization!

In the present global scene, Christian churches, para-church organizations and movements have multiplied tremendously since that first Lausanne Congress. This is both a blessing and a curse. How can all these people work together without falling over one another, competing with one another or discrediting one another? *The need for co-operation is more essential now than it was in the late seventies* and the new Lausanne leadership needs to work hard to challenge a new generation of evangelicals to work together rather than compete with one another. The Cape Town Congress was a wonderful example of this, particularly the 1,000 volunteers who helped with the running of the Congress, most of whom were loaned by different Christian organizations and who would otherwise have never had a chance to meet colleagues from sister organizations whom they did not know and would not naturally work with. This kind of cross-organization and cross-church co-operation is needed to break down barriers and to strengthen the evangelical movement worldwide.

Remaining a Movement Rather than an Institution

There were many pressures over the years to institutionalize Lausanne. This was especially true when Lausanne leaders felt in competition with the World Evangelical Alliance. But over the years Lausanne leaders continued to insist that they remain a movement and were minimally institutionalized. The two times where this concept was endangered was in preparation for both the 1989 and 2010 Congresses. These Congresses had to be run in an organized way and created large infrastructures in order to operate. The temptation would then be to have continued with these structures after the Congress. But in both cases, fortunately, the infrastructures built for the Congress were quickly dismantled while the Movement continued.

The question facing Lausanne's new leadership was whether the challenges of creating visibility, impact and usefulness for Lausanne could be done without being forced, consciously or unconsciously, to build up a large infrastructure. It is extremely difficult to resist the temptation of doing so, particularly when there are many people who would be available as staff and resource people, seconded or supported by their own organizations. Instead, what Lausanne needs to think of doing is to use the resources within the different parts of the evangelical movement worldwide so as to accomplish these goals.

Relating to Roman Catholic and Orthodox Believers

In addition to having the broadest spectrum of evangelicals worldwide, Lausanne is reaching out to evangelicals within the Catholic and Orthodox communities. This is delicate, complex and sensitive. But it is essential if we are to look at the reality of a world where the majority of conservative Christians are to be found today within the Catholic and Orthodox constituencies which have been less affected than Protestants by modernity. The allies for many of the issues which Lausanne and evangelicals want to promote are found by the hundreds of thousands within these constituencies, and Lausanne needs to find a creative, sensitive and theologically sound way of relating to them.

Lausanne has had a long history of dialogue with the mainline Protestant churches, and this is continuing and should deepen. The participation of Olav Fykse Tveit, the General Secretary of the WCC, at the Cape Town Congress was like an outstretched hand, and thus reflected a new era of appreciation by the ecumenical movement of the Lausanne Movement, and more openness in Lausanne for such relationships. Since 1995 the WCC and its Commission on World Mission and Evangelism have invited and included Lausanne representation in all major events.

The new initiative with the Orthodox Churches is just beginning with a first Consultation between some key Lausanne leaders and representatives of both Eastern and Oriental Orthodox Churches in Albania in September 2013.

While such dialogue is very important, I am convinced that the real change Lausanne can foster and encourage is for there to be more local initiatives by evangelicals worldwide to relate positively to Catholic and Orthodox believers in their area.

Maybe the publication of the results of the above-mentioned dialogues can open the way to better relate locally.

Remaining Truly Representative of all Evangelicals Worldwide

At the beginning, as was to be expected, Lausanne was dominated by western leaders. They had the money, the vision and the connections to establish and maintain such a Movement. But over the years, as the Evangelical Movement matured worldwide, African, Asians, Latin American, and Eastern European voices began speaking loudly, increasingly being heard. The danger still lurks in the background whenever Lausanne has moved into areas that require large infrastructures and much money such as a world congress. It has been then that western dominance has been most at risk of taking over the Movement. But from personal experience in the Cape Town 2010 Congress, though much of the help came from the developed world, the platform at Cape Town was fairly representative of the broad spectrum of evangelicals worldwide. Keeping this balance in the future will also remain a great challenge for the Movement.

Another important aspect of Lausanne's inclusiveness is being sure to include in the Movement people from the broadest possible evangelical theological spectrum. Men and women, older and younger, all need to be heard. In the early days of Lausanne the struggle was whether to include charismatic Christians in the Movement. Today this is a non-issue but there are other segments of evangelicals worldwide that may be unintentionally neglected. The Movement needs to seek out and make sure that all segments of evangelicals feel comfortable and are welcomed as part of the

Movement. This needs special attention when choosing participants in consultations and gatherings. So often we are tempted to choose those we know, and yet the strength of Lausanne has been to bring to the world scene 'unknown' Christian leaders from around the world who over the years have become known and had a much wider impact than they would have had if it were not for Lausanne.

New Leadership for a New Age

The choice of Michael Oh as the new CEO of Lausanne bodes good for the future. Michael, in addition to incarnating the vision of Lausanne, is young, visionary, Korean, and a missionary in Japan.

Michael has the right profile for post-Cape Town 2010 Lausanne. The challenges facing him and his small staff – and a large group of volunteers – are enormous, but so are the opportunities. Following the 2010 Congress there was great goodwill and potential ready to be tapped for world evangelization. Michael and his team will need to work hard on tapping this potential before it peters out. We all need to pray for them and lend them a hand.

Hope for the Future

In spite of all the challenges around us today, evangelicals still have a great contribution to make and a glorious message to proclaim.

The world we live in has changed radically since 1974 but the need for the life-transforming Gospel of Jesus Christ has increased rather than decreased since then.

As I look to the future of the Lausanne Movement, I am excited and encouraged that the Lausanne Movement will continue to help evangelicals to co-operate together in all ways possible in the mission of world evangelization.

To Tell the Whole World: Three Lausanne Congresses Seen from the Press Centre

Kåre Melhus

In this chapter I will recount my experience as the Press Centre Manager at Manila in 1989 and at Cape Town in 2010. Since I was not present at Lausanne in 1974, I have asked three journalists who were there to give their impressions from the birth of the Lausanne Movement. The view of the congresses from the press centre and a discussion of the relationship between LCWE and the press have not been published in official Lausanne literature.[1] Thus I am attempting to do this now. I will also reflect on the changing conditions under which the congresses were held, and on the attitudes the LCWE leadership displayed towards the media.

Lausanne III in Cape Town

CT 2010 is about to start. A small army of leaders, volunteers, IT experts and stewards have worked gruelling hours for longer than they care to remember. More than sixty journalists from all over the world are seated in the main assembly hall at Cape Town International Convention Centre, or watching a screen in the press centre, laptops and cameras at the ready.

Behind the convention centre, a small town of converted containers, broadcast vans and trucks with satellite disks, connected with miles and miles of cables, are lined up and manned by the best and brightest IT minds the world Christian community could muster.

As Press Centre Manager, I had explained to the journalists that they would not be allowed to take photos during the opening session, but that CT 2010 had its own photographers whose work would be available online minutes after the conclusion of the opening ceremony, as would the scripts of the speeches delivered. The press centre was there to give the world press service second to none.

And then … nothing. None of the IT services worked. The IT system, which was supposed to occupy more bandwidth than the FIFA World Cup,[2]

---

[1] See J. D. Douglas (ed), *Let the Earth hear His Voice* (Minneapolis, MN: World Wide Publications, 1975); J. D. Douglas (ed), *Proclaiming Christ Until He Comes* (Minneapolis, MN: World Wide Publications, 1989); and Julia E. M. Cameron (ed), *Christ Our Reconciler.* See also www.lausanne.org/en.

[2] www.lausanne.org/en/about/news-releases/1296-cape-town-2010-congress-using-more-internet-bandwidth-than-the-world-cup.html.

organized in South Africa a few months earlier, was down. The journalists did not get the service we had promised, and the IT people in the village behind the convention centre were powerless to serve ambitious projects like the Lausanne Global Conversation and GlobaLink, in which people at 700 sites in some 95 countries were waiting for video feeds from Lausanne III.[3]

The opening ceremony went as scheduled while IT people and other officials gathered backstage to find out what had gone wrong. Among the IT stewards were two young men from India: Vijay Kumar, an employee of Unisys Global Services, and Daniel Singh, a pastor with a doctorate in computational biology, had volunteered to hook up computers and printers and do other menial tasks. They now modestly stepped forward and suggested that they might be able to help.[4] They found out that our congress was under cyber attack. The technical term for this kind of attack is Denial of Service. It means that malicious, computer-generated requests to access a website causes a traffic jam which slows everything down and essentially denies access to the site. Kumar and Singh determined that the attacks came from 66 servers in China, totally overwhelming our systems. They also located an internal virus or worm, which knowingly or possibly unknowingly, had been introduced into our IT systems. These two problems caused what was described as a 'perfect storm'.

The communications team went into a low-tech mode and passed on photos to the media using flash drives. They also shared files outside the regular channels that had been established.

It took most of the next day to sort things out and get our announced services back online. An official Lausanne press release went out, where the attack was described, but where LCWE was careful not to name the country the attack came from.[5] I, on the other hand, saw it as my duty to make sure the stories the journalists in the newsroom produced were as detailed as possible, so I confirmed, off the record, that our IT people had located the transmitting servers in China.

The attack obviously sparked a lot of speculation as to the motivation Chinese officials might have had. Most of the comments offered in the halls of the Cape Town Convention Centre leaned in the direction of Chinese anger at the way the CT 2010 leadership had handled the invitations to the Chinese evangelical leaders.

As it turned out, the Chinese story was a blessing for the press centre: it became global news. Papers such as New York Times[6] and South China

---

[3] www.lausanne.org/en/about/news-releases/1309-cyber-attack-hits-global-church-gathering.html.

[4] www.lausanne.org/en/about/news-releases/1309-cyber-attack-hits-global-church-gathering.html.

[5] www.lausanne.org/en/about/news-releases/1309-cyber-attack-hits-global-church-gathering.html.

[6] 'Chinese Christians barred from conference', *New York Times*, 15th Oct 2010.

Morning Post[7] wrote about it. We could not possibly have organized a wider coverage of the opening of Cape Town 2010!

During the following days, the business in the newsroom assumed some degree of normality, and daily press conferences were staged. The Lausanne viewpoints on issues like the call for a return to humility, integrity and simplicity; the church and poverty, ethnicity and climate change, and specific African issues like church growth and leadership, interfaith harmony, and environment and food security were communicated. In addition to the attending journalists, we had our own correspondents producing stories and sending them out to a mailing-list of some 460 media outlets worldwide. During the period from 1st April to 8th December 2010, the UK-based clippings service Meltwater registered 429 articles in 28 countries.[8] This number included only material published online. Many other articles appeared in printed publications.

Media Terms

As I see it, my main contribution to the CT 2010 press service came about six months before the congress. While I was talking to the CT 2010 communication management who had offered me the position of Press Centre Manager, a Norwegian journalist friend who had applied for press credentials at CT 2010 told me that he had received a document defining the terms under which the media were expected to work at the congress. He was surprised, and I read the document with increasing alarm.

The media terms required that the journalists had to accept that stewards, armed with recorders and microphones, would be present at interviews to document what was said. The journalists would only be allowed access to participants during the morning coffee break. The only way they could get in touch with speakers and the Lausanne leadership would be to request interviews through a service office at the press centre. Some of the more sensitive afternoon multiplex sessions would be closed to the press. These sessions dealt with topics such as Islam and homosexuality.

The media terms almost gave the impression that CT 2010 demanded total control of the contact between the press and congress people. This is remarkable, particularly since most of the journalists in attendance represented Christian media.

As politely as I could, I told my superiors at Lausanne communications that I would not accept any of these points in a news operation headed by me. I did not use much energy on trying to find out who authored the media terms, but I got the impression that some members of the communication

---

[7] 'House churches insist on end to travel ban', *South China Morning Post*, 17th Oct 2010.

[8] S. Woodworth (Chair), *Lausanne Communications Working Group Report*, 29th Dec 2010, 27.

team had little experience with the press or journalistic thinking. They accepted my arguments and the media terms were dropped.

CT 2010 Press Releases

An ambitious scheme whereby writers from various parts of the world wrote press releases and articles especially tailored to home audiences, worked only partially. Despite much effort before the congress, we had managed to recruit only a few writers. Some of them did a fine job of reporting, but the production process was slowed down by a cumbersome editorial process. Some of the thinking behind the media terms seemed to live on. Overburdened and overworked Lausanne officials had to read the scripts before they were released, a process which held the stories back for a whole day, if not more.

The CT 2010 leadership was deeply worried that a multiplex session, dealing with the question of homosexuality, would cause the well-known homosexual community in Cape Town to riot outside the convention centre. Some people were in favor of refusing the press entry to this session. Val Pauquet, a leading South African journalist, responsible for the contact with local media, and I explained that this would only make the press more interested, and that they would learn the content of the meeting, even if they were not allowed inside. We also pointed out that it was hardly news that many evangelicals were against homosexual practice. And finally: So what if some people carried banners outside the convention hall? As it turned out, the session went off without incident.

In hindsight, I think that the most important communication in connection with CT 2010 took place on the internet.[9] Initiatives such as Global Conversation and GlobaLink were crucial and effective. The Lausanne Communications Working Group report states that the plenary sessions and multiplex videos registered 500,000 views. The congress web site logged some 68,000 unique visits from 189 countries and territories, 2,800 people followed the congress on Twitter and 8,000 on Facebook.[10] The future of Lausanne communications lies here. Traditional media like newspapers, magazines, radio and TV will play an important role in the years to come, but fibre-optic cables are now put in the ground all over the world, and many communities are skipping several stages in their communications development and embracing the digital age. Secondly, I think that the various attending journalists, filing stories for newspapers, magazines, radio and TV, contributed greatly to the spreading of the message from CT 2010. The massive pre-congress publication effort created awareness and interest in CT 2010 which helped the post-congress

---

[9] See the article by J. Cameron and L. Dahle on 'Communicating Lausanne – Yesterday, Today and Tomorrow' in this volume.

[10] Woodworth, *LCWG Report*, 8.

communications effort. Some 117 magazines and journals carried regular monthly articles leading up to the congress in a wide range of languages.

As I had managed to get away from the press centre and sat in the back of the plenary hall and observed the Closing Ceremony, I reflected a bit on what had happened during the last few days. A large gathering of people from all over the world had made a huge joint effort. They had a variety of reasons for doing it the way they did. But in the end we came together in a worship session we will remember for the rest of our lives. Under the leadership of Archbishop of the Church of Uganda, Henry Luke Orombi, we bowed in fellowship before the Lord, whom we all serve, and gave him glory.

Lausanne II in Manila

The summer of 1989 was a turbulent time in East Asia. The Chinese crackdown on demonstrators in Tiananmen Square on 3rd-4th June prevented the Chinese delegation from travelling to the Lausanne II World Congress, 11th-20th July. Also contributing to a tense atmosphere was the fact that the former Filipino dictator Ferdinand Marcos, exiled to Honolulu, was seriously ill and could die at any time. Although Corazon Aquino had taken over as President in 1986, Marcos still had many followers in the Philippines, and it was feared that they would cause unrest when the former President died. Security was therefore tight in and around the Philippine International Convention Center.

Thus, an abandoned briefcase in the press centre triggered a swift response from the convention centre security, which called in the Manila Police bomb squad. They came and carefully carried the briefcase outside and blew it up. It contained only papers and personal items. The owner of the briefcase was not happy when he later came to collect his stuff, but got no sympathy from the security guards or the press centre staff.

As the Press Centre Manager, I worked under the leadership of Congress Media Director Jim Newton, an American Southern Baptist. I led a staff of 38 people; about half of them were reporters. We produced stories in English, German, French and Spanish. Each language group was managed by an editor, who had two to six reporters.

We all attended a morning editorial meeting where we gave out assignments for the day. The editing was done by congress media staff. The stories were not sent to the congress leadership for approval. This meant that the finished articles were send by FedEx courier service overnight to a mailing-list of about 1,500 media. This was a huge and very expensive operation.

One of the hottest theological issues raised in Manila was how to deal with the charismatic movement. The distinguished theologian James I. Packer and Foursquare pastor Jack Hayford presented differing viewpoints on how to utilize the charismatic movement in world evangelization.

Reporter Lloyd Mackey found deep emotions and strong viewpoints among the participants. Some thought that the charismatic movement and the Pentecostals were about to hijack the Lausanne Movement and evangelicalism in general. A rumour floating round the Philippine International Convention Center in Manila had it that the reason why Billy Graham had at the last minute decided not to attend Manila II was that his advisors had convinced him that the charismatics would take over the congress. Lloyd Mackey reported that Leighton Ford used all his diplomatic skills to keep the Lausanne ship steady in choppy waters and wrote that Ford "to resounding applause suggested that perhaps one of the historic marks of Lausanne II in Manila will be that here, in a new way, Pentecostals or charismatic evangelicals and non-Pentecostals or non-charismatic evangelicals came together in Christ and covenanted together to advance His Gospel as never before".[11]

The issue of women in ministry was another very hot topic. Sharon Mumper reported that nearly a quarter of the 3,500 participants at Lausanne II in Manila were women, as were four of the forty plenary speakers. "This is a step in the right direction compared with Lausanne 74, where none of the plenary speakers were women, and only a few hundred women participated," Robyn Claydon, of Australia, was quoted as saying. She went on to say that the national selection committees had had a hard time locating capable women in their countries. "This highlights the fact that, until recently, women's ministries have not been recognized as fully as they should be," Claydon said.[12] That some Lausanne II participants in Manila still had a hard time recognizing and accepting women's ministries was evidenced by the walkout during the communion service led by Roberta Hestenes. At the press centre we decided not to report the incident.

The journalistic and possibly also the spiritual highlight for me at Manila was an evening spent with John Stott, just him and me. I had been asked to write an official Lausanne portrait of the man who wrote the *Lausanne Covenant*, and who now led the editorial committee producing the *Manila Manifesto*. The mild-mannered English gentleman, aged 69 at the time, was quite frustrated. Prior to Manila he had sent out a draft manifest, and now hundreds of suggested revisions were pouring in. "Many suggestions are mutually excluding each other," he said with a sigh. "Some of them are also quite rude," he added with a sad expression in his eyes. Even so, a *Manila Manifesto* did emerge after much hard work.

We talked about the original *Lausanne Covenant*, and Stott admitted that he, in 1974, had had no idea that this piece of writing would end up as possibly one of the most important Christian documents in the twentieth

---

[11] L. Mackey, 'Participants discuss charismatic question', *LCWE press release*, Manila, July, 1989.

[12] S. E. Mumper, 'Gift of women considered at Congress', *LCWE press release*, Manila, July, 1989. See also paper by Robyn Claydon on 'The Lausanne Story: A personal Prelude' in this volume.

century, forming the theological platform for a host of Christian initiatives and ministries.

I drew Stott's attention to the issues under debate in Manila and asked him to predict which topics would be hottest at the turn of the century, then eleven years away. I thought that he might decline the opportunity to answer this question, but, to my surprise, he answered without hesitation: "The most controversial issue in the year 2000 will be the uniqueness of Christ!" He said that an increasing number of liberal theologians would encourage the evangelicals to give up their naïve idea of the uniqueness of Christ. "They will do this partly to preserve the unity of the Church and partly because they do not believe in it themselves," Stott said. "Their viewpoint is that it is impossible to dismiss other religions by saying that Christianity is the only true religion. I think such a voice will sound louder and louder," he said with worried look on his face. Since 2000 I have often thought about this, and marvelled at how right he was.

The portrait caused a bit of a stir in evangelical circles because Stott spoke about why he had never married. I had not planned to ask about it, but all of a sudden he introduced the subject into our conversation when I asked if he wished to be young again and participate in the upcoming battles. "Yes and no", he answered. He went on to say that he had made three sacrifices in his life; even though he loved Cambridge and academic life, he obeyed his calling to the priesthood. In his ministry he refused to climb the career ladder and end up as a bishop. His third sacrifice surprised evangelical circles: "Even though I had many female friends, when it came to the moment of proposal, I did not get a confirmation from God to proceed. So I backed off, and after a while I started to believe that God had called to me to a single life. It has been difficult and lonely. I have always loved children, but I do not doubt that I have been in the ministry God called me to, and that these three sacrifices has been right for me," he said with a smile. Then he added: "I have hundreds of spiritual children, and thousands of nieces and nephews in Christ, who call me Uncle John!"[13]

Before I went to Manila, I had agreed to make a radio report from the congress for the Norwegian Broadcasting Corporation. It was to be aired on Sunday, and to be transferred to the NRK studios in Oslo on Saturday. I had been too busy running the press centre to think about this until Friday. When I started planning my report, I realized that there was no way I could contact the members of the Norwegian delegation, or any other people for that matter. This was long before mobile phones and email, and the congress centre with the 3,500 participants was the size of a small Norwegian town. I made a list of about ten people I wanted to interview. I prayed to the Lord, told him my predicament, and asked him to lead me to the people I needed to interview, and started walking. About 100 metres down a corridor, I ran into the person on top of my list, the Bishop of

[13] Kåre Melhus, 'John Stott, the listener', LCWE press release, Manila, July 1989.

Stavanger, Bjørn Bue. After having made my interview with him, and shared how I found him, I prayed again, and within about 90 minutes, I had made contact with all the names on my list!

Lausanne I in 1974

As I wasn't present at Lausanne I in 1974, I have asked three friends and colleagues, who did attend, to recall their experiences.

Knud Jørgensen, who has been involved with LCWE since the beginning,[14] attended Lausanne 1974 as a reporter:

> I was sent to Lausanne by Radio Voice of the Gospel in Ethiopia to bring back as much material for programming as possible. Prior to Lausanne, I had done something similar at the Commission on World Mission and Evangelism conference on Salvation Today in Bangkok (1972). On my way to Lausanne, I visited the Ecumenical Centre in Geneva and the Lutheran World Federation, the owner of Radio Voice of the Gospel. I remember the communication people at the Ecumenical Centre questioning whether I belonged to 'Geneva or Lausanne' and asking me to send them stories on 'Lausanne against Geneva', etc.
>
> In Lausanne I found my desk in the press room. After a few hours I discovered the journalist Helge Kjøllesdal, whom I had never met before, but have known and appreciated since. The communications director was a dynamic Australian by the name of Warrick Olson. My interest was in obtaining as many interviews with key people as possible. I asked Warrick and his soldiers to help me, but realized soon that the only way forward was for me to grab hold of the VIPs and tag them along to a small room I had made into my own radio studio. It took a lot of hard work and a lot of persuasion – and preparation, but I got them in: Billy Graham, John Stott, Peter Beyerhaus, Leighton Ford, René Padilla, Samuel Escobar, Donald McGavran, Ralph Winter, etc. The number of tapes (old-fashioned, no cassettes) kept growing. When I later returned to Addis Ababa, I had material for months and months for various programs. And very good material. These people were open and frank and took plenty of time with this young novice in evangelical waters. Particularly John Stott gave me many hours for recording a whole series on 'You and the Bible'. It was only later that I realized that he was an evangelical guru.
>
> I quickly sensed that also evangelicals were divided. One faction consisted of the church growth people from Fuller Theological Seminary: Donald McGavran, Ralph Winter, Peter Wagner and Art Glasser. Glasser I knew already from the Bangkok conference; he was trying to bridge the gap to the 'radical Latinos', Escobar and Padilla. Winter focused on E-1, E-2 and E-3 evangelism and on 'the two structures of mission' – sodality and modality he called them – unknown words to me and most others. Escobar and Padilla criticized the church growth theory for transforming mission into a marketing

---

[14] See the paper by Knud Jørgensen on 'The Lausanne Story: A Personal Prelude' in this volume.

> strategy. And they insisted on lifting high the social responsibility of Christians and of churches. McGavran focused on what he called 'redemption and social lift': disciple people and then the concern for a better society will come 'automatically'. Focus on homogeneous units, the Fuller people said. Escobar and Padilla claimed that apartheid in South Africa also was a homogeneous unit. Towards the end of the congress the tension was out in the open. And behind the scenes, John Stott and his small team worked to find formulations that could bridge the gap and become a common platform.
>
> Someone told me that Stott was working on some sort of 'covenant'. The only covenant I had heard about was Yahweh's covenant with Israel. A Danish bishop (Thorkild Græsholt) and a German theologian (Peter Beyerhaus) tried to enlighten me. And when the Covenant was presented to the floor, I remember the feeling: "Yes, here is the sort of stuff I believe in; here is both the zeal for bringing people to the foot of the cross and the concern to give an account for the hope within me." We were told that the participants would be asked to literally sign the Covenant on the last day, but first they were encouraged to submit proposals and suggestions for revising the Covenant – there were numerous, hundreds of small and large pieces of paper lying around on the tables in Stott's drafting room. Later Uncle John told me what a gruesome job it had been to review and adjust the text. When it was presented in its final form, people nodded. And the large majority signed the Covenant. I liked it a lot, except for the pledge to a simple lifestyle. Art Glasser challenged me and said, "Why don't you also sign?" "But I am here as a journalist." "Well, if you agree with and can identify with the content, even a journalist may sign." And so I did – with a strange solemn feeling that I would be part of something great, and a pledge and conviction that might change my life. And that is what happened: The Covenant became the bottom floor in my life with the Lord, the rock of my trust in Scripture, and the blessed framework for my life in mission. And it still is.

Helge Kjøllesdal, a Norwegian journalist was sent to Lausanne by the Christian daily, *Vårt Land*:

> It was primarily Christian newspapers and magazines that covered Lausanne 74. The congress had attracted a lot of journalists. People from *Christianity Today*, and from other leading American publications. I remember that *Time* magazine had its religion reporter there. There were also British and German reporters there. The Swedish newspaper *Dagen* was there as well as the Danish newspaper *Kristeligt Dagblad*.
>
> My impression is that secular media during the congress discovered what was happening in Lausanne and started to contact sources. Billy Graham played a strong and central role. So did Leighton Ford. John Stott's efforts in creating a balanced covenant, was noted not only in the Christian media.
>
> The press realized that the evangelicals sharpened their views on evangelization, that people who do not know Christ must be led to him, and that the Church's responsibility also includes creation theology, consisting of the fight for justice, against poverty and repression. Those who had thought that the *Lausanne Covenant* would be a one-sided frontal attack on the theology dominating the World Council of Churches had to revise their opinion.

> It is wrong to say that the Lausanne Movement got a breakthrough in the secular media, but what happened in Lausanne in 1974 was noted. The Christian media emphasized the enormous geographical and denominational breadth in what is recognized as the evangelical world and that there were nuances in the way the movement acted when it came to the global challenges. Not only the Americans spoke, but also strong voices from the global south, not the least from Latin America. The press noted that conversations normally heard during WCC meetings also were heard at Lausanne.

Odd Sverre Hove represented the Norwegian daily *Sunnmørsposten*:

> Billy Graham's opening address made a strong impression on me. I wrote in *Sunnmørsposten* that he with this speech emerged as a global leader. Several of the speeches on cross-cultural, rather than intra-cultural evangelism, left a strong impression. But I was worried about a 'hole' I saw in the otherwise marvellous *Lausanne Covenant* draft. It did not clearly confront WCC's signals on a moratorium on world mission (Bangkok 1973). Even so, I signed the *Lausanne Covenant* with enthusiasm on the last day of the congress.

Journalism vs. Public Relations

Journalism is fundamentally based on Christian principles such as truth, transparency, integrity, justice and human rights. Sometimes it hurts when the news media uncover the truth. There are also times when the media are telling lies, or at least they angle the stories in such a way that they paint a distorted picture. Some media outlets make their money by telling lies. But major, serious news organizations foster a culture of serious truth-seeking, even though one can find examples where they fall short of their ideals. Major news organizations are guided by code of ethics, such as the one adopted by the Norwegian Press Association. I am quoting from relevant paragraphs:

> 3.7. It is the duty of the press to report the intended meaning in quotes from an interview. Direct quotes must be accurate
> 4.1. Make a point of fairness and thoughtfulness in contents and presentation.
> 4.2. Make plain what is factual information and what is comment.
> 4.3. Always respect a person's character and identity, privacy, race, nationality and belief. Never draw attention to personal or private aspects if they are irrelevant.
> 4.4. Make sure that headlines, introductions and leads do not go beyond what is being related in the text. It is considered good press conduct to reveal your source when the information is quoted from other media.[15]

Public relations work, on the other hand, is preoccupied with the idea of showing the best side of an organization, cause or person. James E. Grunig defines public relations as 'management of communications between an

[15] http://presse.no/Saker/code-of-ethics-of-the-norwegian-press.

organization and its publics'.[16] Good public relations does not communicate lies, but the whole story may not be told either. There is nothing wrong or illegitimate with public relations. It is important and necessary. Sometimes public relations people need to set the record straight when journalists have done a poor job.

But good public relations work demands as much integrity as good journalism. Christian organizations should be leading the way. But this is not always the case. Arnhild Helgesen, a Norwegian doctoral candidate at the School of Mission and Theology in Stavanger, Norway, is, as part of her dissertation,[17] asking if Christian organizations and churches in Latin America present themselves differently depending on whom they are talking to or directing the information at. From what I understand, the answer is Yes, they often communicate strategically and in a way that serves specific purposes. I do not think that this practice is limited to Latin America. If communication is done this way, an encounter with a probing journalist can be uncomfortable, but whose problem is that?

I am not at all suggesting that LCWE is guilty of this practice, but I am saying that my experience at CT 2010 gave me the impression that some of the people which came together to form the CT 2010 team came from organizations where fear of the news media prevails.

The solution to this problem is that people in Christian organizations, such as LCWE, must recognize the role of journalism. When the journalists are invited to a conference, they must be allowed to do their job according to their own professional codes. LCWE has full control over the material it sends out through its own press service, but not over the material produced by the journalists covering the event. To attempt such control communicates that the LCWE staff does not recognize fundamental democratic principles such as free speech, and thus exposes the organization to potential scandal.

It goes without saying that the leaders of organizations must make sure that they have nothing to hide in terms of unethical behaviour. If this is the case, they have nothing to fear from the press. If the organizations hold unpopular views on topics such as homosexuality, these views should be openly stated and argued for in the marketplace of ideas. To state them only in closed forums is unwise.

The Media Revolution

In 1974, the typewriter ruled the day and the reporters read their texts to tape recorders in their home newsrooms from phone booths. At Manila in

---

16 J. E. Grunig (ed), *Excellence in Public Relations and Communications Management* (Lawrence Erlbaum Associates, Inc., Publishers, New Jersey, 1992), 4.

17 The title of the PhD project is *Diakonia in context: Models of praxis, reflection and communication in diaconal work with indigenous people in Latin America.*

1989, the computer age was dawning. Odd Sverre Hove, who at that time worked for the Christian daily *Dagen*, brought a small PC with a five-line LCD screen and a cable for phone connection. This equipment generated a lot of interest in the press centre. Hove was happy to share his cable with colleagues at Manila II. It was widely used for communicating the first electronic messages from a Lausanne congress to the world.

At Cape Town in 2010, it was all happening online, and thus the game changed completely. Earlier we had to depend on outside journalists to tell the congress story. At CT 2010 Lausanne basically told its own story to the world. The outside reporters were still there, and they reached a lot of people with their stories. But CT 2010 communicated to a huge audience online.

Talking to Ourselves?

It might be tempting to think that the internet audience out there is all we need. Large numbers of hits may mislead us to think that we are reaching further than we actually do. The vast majority of people who seek us out on the internet is probably Christian, actively involved in ministry and mission. It is of course of primary importance for LCWE to communicate with them, but the Lausanne Movement also needs to communicate with the secular audience. One important channel for this communication is the mainstream news media. It is in LCWE's interests to maintain a professional relationship with secular media. In this context, it is most unhelpful to view these media with suspicion and distrust because it backfires on the Movement itself. It creates the impression that LCWE has something to hide.

Religion has not been a priority for the secular media over the past decades, but this has now changed. Two Norwegian researchers, Cora Alexa Døving and Siv Ellen Kraft, in a book recently published by the University of Oslo Press, says that "from being absent from public debate, religion has become an increasingly visual topic. Even if society has become more secularized, the number of stories related to religion has increased significantly since the turn of the century, in Norwegian as well as in international media".[18]

A *Time* magazine cover story published on 15th April 2013, featuring the Latino evangelicals' impact on U.S. protestant churches, is an example of this new trend.[19] The reason for the new trend is probably that news organizations notice what Timothy Samuel Shah and Monica Duffy Toft point out in their essay: 'God is Winning: Religion in Global Politics': "Far from stamping out religion, modernization has spawned a new generation

[18] C. A. Døving and S. E. Kraft, *Religion i pressen* (Oslo: Universitetsforlaget, 2013), 9. (The translation is my own.)

[19] E. Dias, 'Evangélicos!' *Time*, 15 April, 2013, 18-25.

of savvy, activist, organizationally sophisticated and technologically adept religious movements."[20] As this is happening, the secular media are covering this trend, applying the same investigative techniques here as they use when covering politics and economics. Christian and other religious ministries are taken seriously, because they have real impact on society. This gives Christian organizations an opportunity to reach out beyond its membership. But it also exposes them to scrutiny from the press.

On 4th August 2003, the same *Time* magazine devoted its cover to a picture of a hand holding a golden cross and the text 'Onward, Christian Soldiers?'[21] It questioned the wisdom of evangelical mission to Islamic countries in the wake of 9/11 and the U.S. invasion of Iraq. At that time, I was a member of the LCWE Executive Committee and I remember the discussion we had after some of us had been contacted by journalists from *Time* magazine working on the story. Several people said that we should refuse to talk to them. I was among those who voiced the opposite view. As it turned out, the article asked critical questions and mentioned unhelpful behaviour and attitudes among some evangelicals, but overall the article was a balanced and not at all hostile story on how evangelicals try to live up to the great commandment in difficult terrain.

Outsiders have a legitimate right to ask evangelicals to account for their actions, especially if their actions could put outsiders' lives at risk. LCWE and evangelicals in general should give thoughtful and logic answers to the hard questions asked, instead of hiding or circling their wagons. Such defensive behaviour hurts world evangelization.

[20] Marshall, L. Gilbert, R. Green-Ahmanson (eds), *Blind Spot: When Journalists Don't Get Religion* (New York: OUP, 2009), 24.
[21] David van Biema, "Missionaries under cover", 4th Aug 2003, 34-41.

COMMUNICATING LAUSANNE – YESTERDAY, TODAY AND TOMORROW

Julia Cameron and Lars Dahle

Strategic communication is central to any institution or movement. The Lausanne Movement is no exception. In the published record of the third Lausanne Congress, we note the emphasis on the Movement's role in 'connecting and convening evangelical leaders, communicating ideas and strategy, and hosting discussion and resource sharing'.[1]

This chapter has three foci.[2] Part 1 presents an overview of communication within the Lausanne Movement up to 2007. Part 2 documents Cape Town 2010 as a communications event, with an emphasis on philosophy, strategy and process.[3] Part 3 contains brief reflections on the subsequent task of communicating Lausanne convictions, ideas and strategies today and tomorrow, with the *Cape Town Commitment* as the foundation.[4]

Communicating Lausanne Yesterday: Context and Historical Background

Lausanne Communications Working Group

Following the 1974 International Congress on World Evangelization in Lausanne, a Lausanne Continuation Committee was formed. At its first meeting, in Mexico City in 1975, it confirmed the focus on world evangelization within the wider context of the *Lausanne Covenant*. John Stott explains:

---

[1] 'The Lausanne Movement', in J. E. M. Cameron (ed), *Christ Our Reconciler: Gospel / Church / World. The Third Lausanne Congress on World Evangelization* (Nottingham, UK: InterVarsity Press, 2012), 9-10.

[2] Whereas both authors are co-authors of the whole chapter, Lars Dahle is the major contributor for Parts 1 and 3, and Julia Cameron for Part 2.

[3] By its nature, the communications operation spilled into all areas of Congress planning with a public interface.

[4] The papers by Lars Dahle and Margunn Serigstad Dahle on 'Resourcing the Global Church' and by Kåre Melhus on 'To Tell the Whole World: Three Lausanne Congresses Seen from the Press Centre' in this volume should be seen as supplementary to this chapter.

> Any topic contained in the Covenant came within the Committee's mandate (whether culture or simple lifestyle or social responsibility or freedom and persecution), provided that it was handled in relation to world evangelization.
>
> When the Committee met the following year in Atlanta, its defined aim was broken down into four functions (intercession, theology, strategy and communication), and four working groups were established to concentrate on them.[5]

A clause in The *Lausanne Covenant* formed the foundation for establishing the working groups:

> We pledge ourselves to seek a deeper unity in truth, worship, holiness and mission. We urge the development of regional and functional co-operation for the furtherance of the church's mission, for strategic planning, for mutual encouragement, and for the sharing of resources and experience.[6]

The Lausanne Communications Working Group (CWG) was set up in 1976, with Thomas Zimmerman as the first Chair.[7] The Lausanne Continuation Committee formulated the wide-ranging CWG mandate as follows, under the title 'Communication and pooling of resources':

1. To maintain contact with and encourage co-operation among churches and evangelical bodies committed to world evangelization.
2. To disseminate continuing information on evangelism today and to challenge churches, organizations and Christians everywhere to fulfil their evangelistic task, to highlight the need for full-time ministries in monocultural and cross-cultural evangelization, and to promote worldwide united efforts such as a worldwide day of witness.
3. To help bring together such human, spiritual and material resources as are available for the achievement of evangelistic goals.
4. To encourage and assist regions in formulating plans for co-operation, and where it seems advisable, in forming geographical and functional committees on world evangelization; to encourage the appointment of a convenor or a co-ordinator or any other workers, as required to serve each region.
5. To encourage and assist in the convening consultations, conferences and congresses on world evangelization.[8]

---

[5] J. R. W. Stott, 'Historical Introduction', in J. R. W. Stott, *Making Christ Known: Historical Mission Documents from the Lausanne Movement 1974-1989* (Carlisle, UK: Paternoster Press, 1996).

[6] Excerpt from *Lausanne Covenant*, § 7 'Cooperation in Evangelism'.

[7] Thus, the CWG became one of the four 'classical' Lausanne Working Groups. Later CWG Chairs include Horst Marquardt, Warwick Olsen, Wingtai Leung and Steve Woodworth.

[8] Billy Graham Center Archives, Collection 46, Box 21; received in an email from BGC Archives to Lars Dahle on 26th Sept 2013.

Moving from Lausanne I to Lausanne II

One of the key initiatives in the first decade of the Lausanne history was the establishing of an international newsletter, the *Information Bulletin of the Lausanne Continuation Committee for World Evangelization.* The first issue came out in April 1975. Its front page featured an article on 'To pray, to plan and to work together for the evangelization of the whole world', which ended with the above quote on 'regional and functional co-operation'. Alongside was a news story on the appointment of Gottfried Osei-Mensah (Ghana) as the first Executive Secretary.

The news bulletin ran for 81 issues until 1985, when it was replaced with *World Evangelization Magazine.*[9] Former Lausanne International Director Tom Houston tells the story of the magazine in the period leading up to the Lausanne II Congress in Manila:

> In the period to January 1990, the issues of the magazine were approximately bi-monthly. These were largely produced by Thomas Wang, to begin with from Singapore, and are very creditable productions. Their highest title to fame is that they really launched the AD 2000 movement. Thomas wrote an article in June 1987 with the title: 'By the year 2000, is God telling us something?' He had 700 responses and that stimulated the activities that led to the movement.[10]

This focus on 'AD 2000 and beyond' was central at the Manila Congress and is documented in the *Manila Manifesto.*[11]

At the last minute before the Manila Congress, the CWG was informed about a crisis situation in the area of communications. Knud Jørgensen, a CWG member at the time, recalls the huge challenge suddenly facing chair Warrick Olsen[12] and the whole working group:

> Our task was to take part in planning the communication strategy and activities at Manila 89. A communication director was recruited in late 1988. When we came together for a meeting in late spring 1989, we realized that the plans for the congress had not been implemented and were not now realistic. That was when we decided to take over the show. One of us, Jim Newton, was made director. I recommended that we asked Kåre Melhus to take charge of the newsroom. The rest of us filled in and assisted as best we could.[13]

---

[9] Thanks to Paul Ericksen, The BGC Archives, for detailed information on the bulletin and the magazine in an email to Lars Dahle on 19th Oct 2013.

[10] Tom Houston in an email to Lars Dahle on 14th Oct 2013. Thomas Wang is also a former International Director of Lausanne.

[11] *Manila Manifesto*, Section 11.

[12] Warrick Olsen had been Communications Director at Lausanne 1974.

[13] Knud Jørgensen in an email to Lars Dahle on 3rd Oct 2013. For more information, readers are referred to Kåre Melhus' paper in this volume on 'To Tell the Whole World: Three Lausanne Congresses Seen from the Press Centre'.

Moving from Lausanne II to Pattaya 2004

In 1993, a communications centre was established in Oslo, Norway. This centre produced *World Evangelization Magazine* as a quarterly publication, did editorial work on *Lausanne Occasional Papers* (LOP), and also produced a quarterly Lausanne newsletter in Spanish. The new Oslo team created high-quality productions until 1998, with many in-depth articles and a professional layout, including many pictures.[14]

It was decided at this stage to move to online publications. This included establishing a website and transforming the magazine into an electronic newsletter. Arne Fjeldstad was central in the first of these tasks:

> During the fall of 1995 Pamela Melhus and I started working on getting the Lausanne Movement on the internet. We asked the various national and regional committees to provide translated copies of the *Lausanne Covenant* and the *Manila Manifesto* and received the documents also as picture files – in Chinese, French, Korean, Spanish as well as in several other languages. We selected articles from *World Evangelization Magazine* together with other useful material and got the website Lausanne.org up and running in early 1996.[15]

The communications centre in Oslo was disestablished in 1998, due to lack of financial resources. Kåre Melhus, who took over as editor from Arne Fjeldstad in 1996, carried responsibility for the electronic newsletter, which was moved to Gimlekollen School of Journalism and Communication, Norway, in 1999. Responsibility was later transferred to Naomi Frizzell, based in the USA.[16]

In 1999, Wingtai Leung (Hong Kong) took over as chair of the CWG:

> My mandate as a CWG Chair was to recruit a group of evangelical communication leaders to explore issues on communication and to facilitate Lausanne conferences. Most Christian views on communication were instrumental or utilitarian, without cultural and ethical reflections. We therefore examined the role of communication in social development, poverty, prophetic mission, and in other key areas. This led to deeper explorations in the wider issue group on Media & Technology at the Pattaya

---

[14] Information provided by Kåre Melhus and Arne Fjeldstad in emails to Lars Dahle on 3rd and 7th Oct 2013. Editor was Arne Fjeldstad, whereas Kåre Melhus served as Deputy Editor and Pamela Melhus as Editorial Assistant. Members of the Editorial Committee were Arne Fjeldstad, Knud Jørgensen, Tormod Engelsviken, Ingrid Eskilt and Kåre Melhus. Members of the Advisory Committee for the magazine were Hay-Him Chan, Robyn Claydon, Jim Newton and Valdir Steuernagel. It should be added that the Spanish newsletter was produced with the help of the General Secretary of the Spanish Bible Society.

[15] Arne Fjeldstad in an email to Lars Dahle on 10th Oct 2013.

[16] Reference should be made to *World Pulse Online* (www. lausanneworldpulse. com/worldpulse, 2001-04), later called *Lausanne World Pulse* (www.lausanneworld pulse.com/archives.php, 2005-11).

Forum 2004. These explorations were documented in *LOP 48 Media and Technology – The Rainbow, the Ark & the Cross.*[17]

In 2004, David Claydon convened the ambitious 2004 Forum in Pattaya, Thailand, which was to prove critical to the continuing viability of Lausanne. The 2004 Forum bore testimony to the Movement's ability to draw from a rich pool of leading thinkers and practitioners. Working groups on 31 major issues stimulated progress in each of their areas, and *Lausanne Occasional Papers* issuing from Pattaya were to be widely appreciated. The 2004 Forum was essentially the runway on which the third Lausanne Congress could be launched.

Two years later, in 2006, Steve Woodworth[18] was invited by the newly-installed Lausanne Executive Chair and CEO Doug Birdsall to re-establish a CWG in preparation for Cape Town 2010.[19] Whereas the 2004 Forum had proved the credibility of Lausanne, if it were in doubt, the event itself did not create wider waves. So when the communications effort began for the third Lausanne Congress, comparatively few people under forty were aware of the Movement. Much work needed to be done.

Preparing for the Third Lausanne Congress

The role of this newly-formed CWG would be to engender a sense of anticipation around the world for the third Lausanne Congress. Its central task before the Congress would be to communicate the message of the Congress to the local church, to mission agencies, to seminaries, and to Christians in the public arenas: in the post-modern West and the modern and pre-modern Majority World; in hi-tech urban cultures and in rural underdeveloped cultures. The CWG would, in essence, shape this message. In addition, it would work to ensure that news of the Congress reached as many stripes of evangelicalism as was possible (and beyond, to the wider Christian world). A phrase later used to describe the span of evangelical convictions within Lausanne was 'breadth within boundaries' where the boundaries were clearly defined.[20]

By late 2007, two Communications Directors were appointed for the Congress, serving under the CWG: Naomi Frizzell and Julia Cameron.[21] The demanding task stretched way beyond the capacity of two westerners, but the reach of the CWG effort, leading up to the Congress and on-site,

---

[17] Wingtai Leung in an email to Lars Dahle on 3rd Oct 2013.

[18] CEO of Masterworks, a US marketing agency working with the voluntary sector.

[19] The Lausanne Executive Committee ratified the re-established CWG in Jan 2007.

[20] See D. Birdsall and L. Brown, Preface, *Cape Town Commitment.*

[21] Naomi Frizzell (Internal Communications and Digital Media) had served as Lausanne Movement Director of Communications since 2004, and previously with Mission America Coalition. Julia Cameron (External Relations, Print Media and Radio) had formerly served as Head of Communications for OMF International (UK) and then for the International Fellowship of Evangelical Students.

was greater than anyone could have imagined. That was due in no small part to the gifts and the dogged dedication of many, many volunteers. We will name only a handful here, in order to illustrate with particular stories.[22]

Cape Town 2010 as a Communications Event[23]

Engaging the Whole Evangelical Church

Budgetary constraints led the CWG to focus on the internet as our major means of communication. But the internet would not reach the church in the rural expanses of the Majority World. And neither would print media, even in the major languages, had the necessary financial resources been available for production and distribution. Some printed materials were produced for Africa in English, but while English is widely used across the continent, as across India, it remains the third or fourth language for most people, not their mother tongue.

By midway through 2010, the Congress website would become operational in all the Congress languages (English, French, Spanish, Chinese, Portuguese, Russian, Arabic), enabling the first issues-based multi-lingual discourse of its kind. As the Congress approached, this was complemented by a bloggers' network, a Facebook page and Twitter feed.[24]

---

[22] The full list of names may be found at the back of *The Congress Handbook* which was published in seven languages and distributed to all participants. (The handbook is archived in the BGC Archives at Wheaton College.)

[23] A critical self-appraisal of the communication efforts, compiled within two months of the Cape Town Congress, appears in a detailed 100+ page report, archived in the BGC Archives, Wheaton College. This detailed report gives careful appraisal of the effectiveness of each operation insofar as that could be judged within two months of the Congress. The report is constructed particularly for those preparing for a future Fourth Lausanne Congress. Our thanks are due to Steve Woodworth (Chair, Lausanne Communication Working Group, 2006-present) and Naomi Frizzell (Lausanne Chief Communications Officer to 2013) for their help in compiling this section of this chapter.

[24] Up to and including the Congress there were 68,024 unique visits recorded (jointly to *lausanne.org* and *capetown 2010.com*) from 189 countries/ territories. During the Congress there were 500,000 views of the 200 plenary sessions in English. (Figures for other languages are not available.) A network of bloggers re-posted the content with their own stories and responses. This network, based at home, came from the Americas, Africa, Asia, Australia and Europe. The Facebook page drew 8,000 fans (60% male; 39% female, mainly from, in descending order: USA, South Africa, UK, Brazil, Canada and India.) We had 2,800 Twitter followers.

The Lausanne Global Conversation

From early 2008, as the communications effort gained pace, the Congress programme was being developed, layer by layer, in wide consultation around the world. In October 2009, the U.S. magazine *Christianity Today* published the first of a series of twelve major articles in partnership with Lausanne, each engaging an issue to be pursued in the Congress. Lausanne and *Christianity Today* featured the articles on their respective websites and invited readers to discuss them as part of what became known as the Lausanne Global Conversation. Each article had two commissioned responses by reflective practitioners from different parts of the world. Some articles were accompanied by a short video. This material formed a substantial body, and commanded good attention, at least in the global North.

But how could the mighty churches of the global south be properly engaged through the Global Conversation? It could hardly be deemed 'global' in any meaningful sense if these significant churches were not engaged, and swathes of territories were not online.

The Global Conversation articles were made available at no charge to any media wishing to use them.[25] But at 2,500 words, they were over-long for most magazines and journals. So they were edited down to 1,200 words as a shorter option, and uploaded with images. Some 120 magazines and journals sought permission to download the articles, for use in whole or in part, in English or in translation, in print or online, as best served their readers. Here was Lausanne at its most distinctive: offering fine content from some of the sharpest evangelical thinkers one could find, and sharing it among key influencers around the world. As John Stott never tired of pointing out, Christ gave gifts to his church to *share*; he then rather beautifully described Lausanne gatherings as 'an exchange of gifts'.[26]

As 2010 progressed, advance papers for the Congress multiplex sessions,[27] in English and in translation, were uploaded to the Lausanne Global Conversation website. These and the *Christianity Today* articles formed a strong backbone for robust online discussion. The Lausanne Global Conversation attracted 50,000 unique visitors from 172 countries or territories.

---

[25] This series of articles were jointly copyrighted to *Christianity Today* and the *Lausanne Movement.*

[26] See the paper by Julia Cameron on 'John Stott and The Lausanne Movement: A Formative Influence' in this volume.

[27] The multiplex sessions were electives, held in the afternoons during Lausanne III, which fed into *The Cape Town Call to Action.* See also Lars Dahle's chapter on 'Mission in 3D: A Key Lausanne Theme'.

'Divine serendipities'

Reflecting back on the communication task for Lausanne III, we trace a clear pattern of divine guidance. Connections and networks emerged in unexpected places and unforeseen ways. Julia Cameron recalls:

> We were dependent on God's superintendence. Here are no more than a few vignettes, to illustrate the Lord's hand of providence. A conversation struck up over dinner at a meeting in Seoul, between Naomi Frizzell and Steve Evans of the International Missions Board, led to the provision of a cohort of photographers and videographers for the Congress;[28] a friendship from his days with World Vision years earlier led Ken Moy of Masterworks to invite Rick Krekel of Biblesoft Inc. to handle print management on-site. Competence built from years of technical experience would be needed for the tight turnaround of writing, translating and designing a daily four-page newssheet, to be printed overnight in eight languages, and a commemorative magazine to be handed out after the final session, plus some 30-50 *ad hoc* jobs daily. Each on-site operation delegated to a manager was in itself huge. One wrong choice of person could have serious consequences.
>
> Shortly before the first *Christianity Today* article appeared, we received serendipitous approaches from Joe Nimi, a South Asian living in Korea, and Rudolf Kabutz from South Africa. Both brought high energy, a passion for the gospel, and deep knowledge of their regions. By working long and dogged hours, they were to extend the reach of our communications efforts in ways we could not have planned.
>
> Joe Nimi's approach to us lay in a divine serendipity via Facebook. Through a common friend, he noticed I was in Seoul for a few days, where he was living at that time; he asked if we could meet and we had an unhurried meal together at the airport, before I flew home. As we parted, I handed him a copy of Ajith Fernando's searching booklet *An Authentic Servant.*[29] This meeting had unexpected outcomes. *First*, Joe drove through the printing of thousands of 'partnership bookmarks', thus planting a grassroots Lausanne presence in languages we would otherwise not have reached. His idea was simple: to contact mission agencies or churches and ask if they would print a bookmark for their members, which would carry their logo and the Congress logo, with some brief text.[30] *Secondly*, he contacted several European and Asian publishing houses, inviting them to publish the *Didasko Files*.[31] It was this

[28] Some 30,000 images were shot and 1,000 edited and captioned for release. Between 1.5-2.0 terrabytes of video images were recorded.

[29] Published 2008 in *The Didasko Files Series.*

[30] The text and design were handled by the Communications team, and printed with mission-minded churches, IFES national movements and mission agencies in Bangladesh, India, Iraq, Korea, Lebanon, Nepal, Philippines, Sri Lanka, UK and USA.

[31] A series of titles written by friends of Lausanne, and published to support the movement. They are now serving the church in the heartlands of the Islamic, Buddhist and Hindu worlds, in 24 languages at the time of publication. Joe resolved not to come to Cape Town as a member of the onsite Communications effort.

initial drive which took them around the world, serving readers with fine content, and acting, in Doug Birdsall's words, as 'foot soldiers for Lausanne'.

> Rudolf Kabutz of Transworld Radio would open the way for us to link radio programmes into the Lausanne Global Conversation, to extend its reach into groups who did not use the internet. To this he brought ambitious ideas, and the capacity and networks to shape a strategy. Together with the 'Africa by Radio' coalition of producers and broadcasters, he was able to create and air a series of programmes across the continent, in English and in some major African languages, under the title *Down to Earth*.[32] These programmes, focused around the Global Conversation issues and contextualised, invited listeners to phone in responses. In this way, vast numbers of African evangelicals were encompassed, and it became possible for two-way interaction. The contributions of rural leaders were fed into the online Conversation, and the programme makers allowed the online Conversation to inform the programme content.[33]

Reflecting back on the whole process, CWG chair Steve Woodworth expresses both its high demands and its great rewards:

> The task given to the CWG to prepare for the Lausanne III Congress was huge, simply immensely challenging. This was partly due to lack of human and financial resources. But it was also due to the constant need to balance and negotiate between different opinions and perspectives. But in the midst of it all, we had the immense joy of seeing what God was doing beyond all human expectations and from very humble beginnings. What started [in 2007] with just two people, Naomi Frizzell as Lausanne Communications Director and myself, became – through God's many interventions – a little army of highly capable people coming out of nowhere to fulfil many key roles.[34]

Communications On-site

The total communications team on-site was 150-strong, from over 25 nations, with scores more working in remote locations around the world. For each role, there had been layers of preparation, including a refining of organizational charts and job descriptions followed by a drive for recruitment. This last process involved several stages, as we looked for proven technical competence together with theological awareness (for writers and broadcasters), and a clear commitment to the ethos of Lausanne. Volunteers brought high-level experience, and over weekly

---

Instead he invested the money it would have cost him in covering translation and production expenses of a Didasko File for a Eurasian publishing house.

[32] Rudolf Kabutz brought a team onsite to create programmes, and to gather content for further programmes to be aired for several months after the Congress.

[33] For other accounts of divine presence and guidance at the Lausanne congresses, see the essay by Kåre Melhus on 'To Tell the Whole World: Three Lausanne Congresses Seen from the Press Centre' in this volume.

[34] Steve Woodworth in an email to Lars Dahle on 10th Oct 2013.

Skype calls, teams were formed, roles defined, and friendships begun. On 15 October 2010, when the Communications team assembled in Cape Town for orientation, people felt they already knew their immediate colleagues. This was needed, as pressure from the outset was considerable.[35]

GlobaLink and Data-Mining

The reach and extent of the digital communications effort was extraordinary. Through the Cape Town GlobaLink,[36] the discussions were extended to over 600 registered remote sites in some ninety countries.[37] While plans were derailed for two days by a cyber attack, GlobaLink marked a significant step in extending the reach of participation. A data-mining team of 60 people, with 19 on-site, formed the Communications 'listening' team, providing summaries of sessions and tracing trends and responses.[38] The data this team collected was fed into the Lausanne Global Conversation so those participating around the world could also contribute to the discussions.

TV and Radio

Arnold Enns (Paraguay), a member of the CWG, built a substantial network of radio and television stations, mainly across Latin America and Europe.[39] Some twenty programmes in English and Spanish were aired throughout the world prior to the Congress. From trucks in the Convention Centre marshalling yard, he oversaw the production of seven television feature stories and 69 stories for radio. These were aired by over 160 radio and television stations. From partway through the week, his team interviewed

---

[35] For example, the first daily newssheet *Cape Town Today* had to be compiled, translated and designed in eight languages and sent to print by 6pm that same day.

[36] While organizationally separate in the Congress structure from the communications team effort, GlobaLink is included here for its significant reach. GlobaLink sites were developed in 93 countries, under the chairmanship of Zimbabwean Victor Nakah, Africa Director for the Overseas Council.

[37] Each of the GlobaLink sites arranged its own meetings. Congress sessions were to be broken into segments, with a synopsis in multiple languages, and uploaded to servers based in the USA. Remote participation hinged on a robust internet connection to receive material, and the successful uploading of that material. The cyber-attack foiled plans for the first two days. For more, see Day 6 Endnote 1 in *Christ our Reconciler* (J. E. M. Cameron (ed), IVP 2012).

[38] Led by Filipino Terry Casino. The feedback report from each of 42 substantial Congress events was modelled on that used by the Global Economic Forum. (Full data in Appendices 9-12, The Communications Report.)

[39] Arnold Enns is President of COICOM (La Confederación Iberoamericana de Comunicadores y Medios Masivos Cristianos).

all the main speakers as they came off-stage, gaining strong material for broadcast.

The work to service TV and radio was largely with Christian networks. One exception was BBC Radio 4's *Sunday Worship* broadcast on 17th October (the first full day of the Congress) from All Souls' Church, Langham Place, London. The service was led in London by the Rector, Hugh Palmer, with Chris Wright preaching from Cape Town, and including an interview with Archbishop Henry Orombi. The Cape Town segments were recorded on the Friday evening in the marshalling yard. This BBC programme *Sunday Worship* typically draws an audience of between 1.5 and 1.75 million listeners, thus giving a measure of status to the Congress in the wider public eye.

The Newsroom

The newsroom was led by Kåre Melhus. He was assisted by two South Africans, Val Pauquet managing African media and Miles Giljam managing non-African media. Val Pauquet's role among the media on the host continent began a year before the Congress.[40]

Kåre Melhus, Val Pauquet, Rosemary Grier and Julia Cameron worked on the credentialling and allocation process for on-site media places. The space was limited, and we wanted a global spread with a careful apportioning of space to each continent.[41] It was expensive to send a journalist, given the cost of hotels in the vicinity, as well as an air fare; some publications and news agencies opted instead for off-site credentialling, which gave a full press kit and privileged access to material in advance of its public availability. In the event, IT difficulties meant off-site media were redirected to a Flickr stream for photos and for posted news releases.

The news conferences were set up early in the day, based on the Congress themes. As the senior news team was short-staffed, and not able to get into the plenary sessions, the team missed some of the most memorable platform moments, which may have reshaped the press conferences. This loss was assuaged in part by having dedicated newsroom staff to arrange interviews for the journalists, so the journalists could create their own stories.

The two-day cyber attack described elsewhere could not have been foreseen. As cyber warfare grows, it will be a 'known-unknown' for all future Congresses.

---

[40] Val Pauquet's 'doyenne status' in African media brought significant benefit to the Communications Team.

[41] Places were apportioned by region (cf. detailed listing in Communications Report Appendix 22). Of the 100 credentialled media, 69 came, as finance proved a problem for some in the end and they accessed news remotely. The notable thinly-covered areas onsite were Latin America, Africa outside South Africa, and Eurasia.

Alongside the credentialled journalists, Lausanne had a small team of experienced writers to generate news releases. More such writers could have been used. In total, 21 English-language news releases were sent out, which were later tracked into a total of 1,067 publications online.[42] Several items were translated into at least one additional Congress language. The team included a writer from Hong Kong who sent out news only in Chinese.

A team of spokespeople were selected several months in advance, from different regions of the world. For a multi-disciplinary Congress, rich in theological and intellectual content, no spokespeople could adequately handle all anticipated questions on their own. The plan was for experts in a range of disciplines each to prepare questions which were likely to be asked by the media, and to fashion answers to them. In this way, there would be consistency of voice for the spokespeople, and contentful responses. These questions related to Congress content and to major issues of Lausanne theology and policy.[43]

A new feature of news reporting was introduced in Cape Town, through a team of Special Correspondents. This initiative created capacity to parcel news for regional audiences, or audiences with particular interests. Each Special Correspondent worked in the months before the Congress to build a network of mission agencies, publications and news agencies to receive his/her targeted news reports. For example, a team of Special Correspondents wrote and blogged for the student world, another for Indian journals, another for those serving with mission agencies, while a freelance journalist gained commissions from the secular media.

The Cape Town Commitment

The outcomes of the Congress were captured in the *Cape Town Commitment*. This two-part publication reflects the voices of evangelicals in 198 nations. Its title was chosen with care: it is not a declaration or a manifesto, but a *commitment* for the Lausanne Movement to fulfil. This document, now the road map for the Movement, is being published in an increasing number of languages.[44]

The central aim of the Congress and the *Commitment* is summarized by Doug Birdsall in his preface to the formal published record of the Congress:

---

[42] The clippings service could not track journals on the African and Asian continents which did not have any online presence. The communications team is confident that such journals carried articles, some with wide distribution.

[43] Unexpected circumstances meant the preparation of answers was severely delayed. We were grateful to Mark Russell of Russell Media for stepping in at the eleventh hour to produce questions and answers for a range of topics.

[44] At the time of publication, the *Cape Town Commitment* is available in 25 languages, with plans for 20 African languages in place.

> The purpose of the third Lausanne Congress was to strengthen the church for world evangelization. To this end we were joined on-site by participants from 198 nations, selected from local churches, agencies, national and international movements, and including senior leaders in the public arenas. Through our GlobaLink we were able to extend our discussions; we had over 600 registered remote sites in some ninety countries. We received interactive responses from GlobaLink, and from television and radio programmes created on-site, through our blogger network, and from news reports filed by nearly a hundred reporters and crew.
>
> Our aim? To discern what the Holy Spirit is saying to the churches now, and the outcome of our work is contained in the *Cape Town Commitment*. I would urge you, your church, your student fellowship on campus, your Christian fellowship at the office or in the lab, to study it carefully before God, and to find your place in its outworking.[45]

This illustrates the theological basis, the missional focus and the personal nature of Lausanne's communication efforts, both from the Congress, and as a Movement.

Communicating Lausanne Today and Tomorrow

This final section considers the task of taking Lausanne's convictions, ideas and strategies, and applying them in an increasingly global context of missional challenges, opportunities and communities.

The backdrop for these reflections is the mandate given to the CWG following the Cape Town Congress:

> Assure maximum exposure of Lausanne – its thinking, activities, events and outputs – to leaders of world evangelization.
>
> 1. Build networks of various audiences – mission organizations, denominations, publishers, media outlets, digital best practitioners.
> 2. Ensure coverage of all regions.
> 3. Enlist a key leader who has deep reach into each of these audiences across all regions.
> 4. Disseminate Lausanne information.
> 5. Listen and bring feedback to Lausanne leadership.
> 6. Plan long term strategy to maximize reach of Lausanne.[46]

Lausanne is essentially a global network of networks, focused on world evangelization, and with a commitment to integral mission. This unique branding leads to the intentional sharing of theological convictions and key

---

[45] Doug Birdsall, 'Foreword', in Cameron, *Christ Our Reconciler*, 11-12.

[46] This is the *first* of the two mandates given in the document 'Vision for CWG' (received by Lars Dahle in an email from CWG Chair Steve Woodworth on 2nd July 2013). The *second* mandate, expressed as 'thought leadership on how all disciplines of communications can serve the cause of world evangelization', was in June 2013 transferred to the new role of Senior Associate for Media Engagement. Lars Dahle was appointed to this position in Oct 2013.

missiological ideas, strategies and tasks. Communication is vital to keep this network connected, and to keep it growing, and the need for reflective communication strategists and practitioners will always be central.

The Lausanne Movement is inviting churches, agencies and individual Christians in the public arenas to find their place in fulfilling the *Cape Town Commitment.* To undergird this work, Lausanne is hosting a series of Global Consultations to engage with critical issues identified in *The Cape Town Call to Action.* A new book publishing imprint, *The Lausanne Library,* was established in 2010, which serves alongside the online *Lausanne Global Analysis*, regular newsletters, blogs and other social media.

Lausanne's serving of evangelical leaders includes being a bridge-builder between mission leaders, thought leaders and reflective practitioners. Increasingly the focus is on connecting with younger, emergent leaders globally. Further, the Movement is committed to facilitating dialogue between evangelical leaders, and the building of collaborative partnerships.

All leaders must engage in the hard work of 'double listening', to the Word and the world. To help equip leaders for this, Lausanne is building an online resource bank.

Final Reflections

The unique Lausanne brand of *a global evangelical movement focused on world evangelization, with a commitment to integral mission*, needs to be communicated clearly, consistently and creatively, internally to its own constituencies and externally through news media. The Movement has a missional contribution to the evangelical church and to the wider church. Conversely, it needs to guard against any theological, strategic or political attempts to change its nature, focus and task.

When moving forward, all appropriate means of communication need to be used in promoting, sharing and justifying the Movement's theological convictions, its missional ideas, and its global strategies for evangelization, especially as expressed in the *Cape Town Commitment.*

Resourcing the Global Church: A Guide to Key Lausanne Resources 1974-2013

Lars Dahle and Margunn Serigstad Dahle

Throughout its history, resourcing the global church for evangelization and mission has been a central task for the Lausanne Movement. The challenge was formulated in the *Lausanne Covenant*, in the context of 'Co-operation in Evangelism': 'We urge the development of regional and functional co-operation for the furtherance of the Church's mission, for strategic planning, for mutual encouragement, and for the sharing of resources and experience.'[1]

This vital task of sharing resources is recently expressed in an official self-presentation in the authorized volume from the Cape Town Congress:

> Lausanne is a network of evangelical leaders, thinkers and reflective practitioners. Its purpose is to strengthen the church for world evangelization. To this end, it serves the body of Christ as a catalyst for engaging major issues by:
>
> - *Connecting and convening evangelical leaders* (in Christian ministry, and in the secular professions) for focused discussion, prayer and strategic action on issues which impact the church and God's world;
> - *Communicating ideas and strategy* by, for example, publishing books and occasional papers (hard copy and online), and using social media and targeted communication to inform, persuade and stimulate ideas and action;
> - *Hosting discussion and resource sharing* through the online Lausanne Global Conversation, which provides a forum for ideas and strategy on mission and evangelization.[2]

In this chapter, we seek to document and explore this strategic global resourcing role, by providing an overview of significant historical and contemporary Lausanne resources. This includes showing how the current Lausanne leadership are exploring various ways to make the rich storehouse of Lausanne resources more available through all the regions and to emerging generations of leaders, especially online. The final part of

---

[1] *Lausanne Covenant*, paragraph 7: 'Co-operation in Evangelism'.

[2] 'The Lausanne Movement', in J. E. M. Cameron (ed), *Christ Our Reconciler*, 9.

this chapter contains some critical reflections on the interpretative, educational and formative dimensions of such key Lausanne resources.[3]

Overview of Key Lausanne Resources[4]

The Three Foundational Lausanne Documents

The official declarations from the three global Lausanne congresses play a unique and constitutive role within the Lausanne Movement. Therefore, the *Lausanne Covenant* (1974), the *Manila Manifesto* (1989) and the *Cape Town Commitment* (2010) deserve a special focus in this chapter.

The *Cape Town Commitment* emphasizes that 'among [the major gifts from the first Lausanne Congress] to the world church were: (i) the *Lausanne Covenant*; (ii) a new awareness of the number of unreached people groups; and (iii) a fresh discovery of the holistic nature of the biblical gospel and of Christian mission'.[5] Alongside the affirmation of classical biblical, Trinitarian and evangelical beliefs and their relation to evangelization, the *Lausanne Covenant* may be characterized by 'seven major emphases ... the authority of Scripture, the nature of evangelism, the grounds of Christian social responsibility, the costliness and the urgency of world mission, the problems of culture and the reality of spiritual warfare'.[6] The fifteen paragraphs of this foundational document are explained in John Stott's *Commentary and Exposition of the Covenant* (1975).[7]

The *Manila Manifesto* 'is essentially an elaboration of the *Lausanne Covenant* fifteen years later'.[8] The *Manila Manifesto* contains (a) an explanatory preamble, (b) twenty-one theological *Affirmation*s which are distilled from the Covenant, followed by (c) the second major part with three sections on the whole Gospel, the whole Church and the whole world. The first of these sections ('The Whole Gospel') has paragraphs on 'our human predicament', 'good news for today', 'the uniqueness of Jesus

---

[3] The paper by Julia Cameron and Lars Dahle on 'Communicating Lausanne – Yesterday, Today and Tomorrow' in this volume should be seen as supplementary to this chapter.

[4] The official Lausanne documents from international congresses, consultations and conferences are made available at www.lausanne.org/en/documents/all.html. Reference should also be made to http://ecumenism.net/docu/lcwe.htm.

[5] Preamble, *The Cape Town Commitment: A Confession of Faith and a Call to Action* (Hendrickson: Peabody, MA, 2011; The Didasko Files), 4. (Often referred to as *CTC*.)

[6] J. R. W. Stott, 'An Historical Introduction', J. R. W. Stott (ed), *Making Christ Known: Historic Mission Documents from the Lausanne Movement 1974-1989* (Carlisle, UK: LCWE / Paternoster Press, 1996), xv.

[7] This publication currently exists both as a Lausanne Occasional Paper (LOP) 3 and as a booklet in *The Didasko Files* (with a new study guide);

[8] Stott, 'An Historical Introduction', xx.

Christ', and 'the Gospel and social responsibility', whereas the paragraphs in the second section ('The Whole Church') deals with 'God the evangelist', 'the human witnesses', 'the integrity of the witnesses', 'the local church' and 'co-operation in evangelism'. The final section ('The Whole World') contains paragraphs on 'the modern world', 'the challenge of AD 2000 and beyond', and 'difficult situations'. Finally, the motto of Lausanne II ('Proclaim Christ until He Comes') constitutes the conclusion of the *Manila Manifesto*.

Whereas *Let the Earth Hear His Voice* was the motto of Lausanne I and *Proclaim Christ until He Comes* was the overall theme for Lausanne II, *God in Christ, Reconciling the World to Himself* was the official theme for Lausanne III in Cape Town. This motto clearly shaped the *Cape Town Commitment* with its overall emphasis on covenant love, together with the significant Congress mission statement of 'bearing witness to Jesus Christ and all his teaching – in every nation, in every sphere of society, and in the realm of ideas'.[9]

The *Cape Town Commitment* consists of two parts: 'Part I sets out biblical convictions, passed down to us in the Scriptures, and Part II sounds the call to action.'[10] The first part, entitled 'A Confession of Faith', was distributed at the Congress, whereas the second part, which was called 'A Call to Action', was completed after the Congress. Whereas John Stott had been the key author of both the *Lausanne Covenant* and the *Manila Manifesto*, this role was taken over by Chris Wright in relation to the *Cape Town Commitment.* Both parts of this document were results of a global, comprehensive process starting years before the 2010 Congress:[11]

> How was Part I shaped? It was first discussed in Minneapolis in December 2009, at a gathering of 18 invited theologians and evangelical leaders, drawn from all continents. A smaller group, led by Dr Christopher J. H. Wright, chair of the Lausanne Theology Working Group, was asked to prepare a final document, ready to be presented to the Congress.
>
> How was Part II shaped? An extensive listening process began more than three years before the Congress. The Lausanne Movement's International Deputy Directors each arranged consultations in their regions, where Christian leaders were asked to identify major challenges facing the Church. Six key issues emerged. These (i) defined the Congress programme and (ii) formed the framework for the call to action. This listening process continued on through the Congress, as Chris Wright and the Statement Working Group worked to record all contributions faithfully. It was a herculean and monumental effort.[12]

---

[9] 'Foreword', *CTC*, 4. See also the paper by Lars Dahle on 'Mission in 3D: A key Lausanne III theme' in this volume.

[10] 'Foreword', *CTC*, xi.

[11] See also www.lausanne.org/en/gatherings/global-congress/cape-town-2010/ road-to-cape-town.html.

[12] 'Foreword', *CTC*, xi.

The comprehensive process related to producing Part I is documented in a number of significant papers produced by the Theology Working Group (TWG), including three *Lausanne Occasional Papers* and a summary document.[13]

It should be noticed that a number of educational resources directly related to the *Cape Town Commitment* have been developed since Lausanne III, including the following:[14]

- A summary statement.[15]
- A study edition for general use.[16]
- Bibliographical resources, especially aimed at higher education.[17]
- Curriculum resources for small groups in churches, as a combined book /DVD-publication.[18]
- Curriculum resources for women, primarily intended for North American women's groups.[19]

Efforts are currently being made to translate the *Cape Town Commitment* into an increasing number of languages.[20] The expressed intention is to utilize the document as a 'blueprint for the Lausanne Movement over the next ten years', uniting evangelicals globally and offering it to a wide spectrum of Christians globally for consideration:

> We trust that it will be talked about, discussed, and afforded weight as a united statement from evangelicals globally; that it will shape agendas in

---

[13] See LOP 63: 'The Whole Gospel', LOP 64 'The Whole Church', LOP 65 'The Whole World', and *TWG Three Wholes Statement.* The latter is published at www.lausanne.org/en/documents/all/twg/1234-twg-2007-2010.html. It should also be mentioned that the TWG currently is producing a theological commentary to the *CTC*.

[14] See also www.lausanne.org/en/documents/books.html. *Ephesians: Studying with the Global Church* (2013), which is a study guide / DVD for church fellowship groups with Lausanne Senior Associate for Scripture Engagement Lindsay Olesberg as the lead author, is the only new Lausanne publication that is not related to the *CTC*.

[15] The summary statement is published as an Appendix to this volume. It is also online, see www.lausanne.org/en/documents/ctcommitment/ctc-summary.html.

[16] R. Dowsett, *The Cape Town Commitment Study Edition: A Confession of Faith and a Call to Action* (Peabody, MA: Hendrickson, 2012).

[17] D. Bock (ed), *Bibliographical Resources for The Cape Town Commitment: A Confession of Faith, A Call to Action* (Eugene, OR: Wipf & Stock, 2013).

[18] S. Singleton and M. Ristuccia (eds) *The Cape Town Commitment: A Call to Action. A Study Guide for Small Groups* (Peabody, MA: Hendrickson, 2013).

[19] Bennett (ed), *The Cape Town Commitment: 12 Group Studies with Homework*, available for free download at www.lausanne.org/en/documents/ctcommitment/womens-curriculum.html.

[20] At the time of publication, the *CTC* is available in 25 languages, with plans for twenty African languages in place.

Christian ministry; that it will strengthen thought-leaders in the public arena, and that bold initiatives and partnerships will issue from it.[21]

Publications and Online Resources from the Three Congresses[22]

Official Lausanne volumes have been published from all the three global congresses. The papers from Lausanne I were collected in *Let the Earth Hear His Voice,*[23] whereas key Lausanne II contributions were made available in *Proclaim Christ until He Comes: Calling the Whole Church to Take the Whole Gospel to the Whole World.*[24] A selection of significant presentations from Lausanne III has recently been published in *Christ Our Reconciler.*[25]

There is also a wealth of available material – both in text, audio and video formats – from the three global congresses on the Lausanne website.[26] This includes significant plenary sessions, papers and presentations, interviews, news releases and much supplementary material. Space does not permit to interact with the entire material, but some of the most significant and influential resources will be highlighted in the following.

In terms of *Lausanne I*, Billy Graham's opening speech (entitled 'Why Lausanne?') provides an introduction to the Congress's 'four basic presuppositions':[27]

1. "The Congress stands in the tradition of many movements of evangelism throughout the history of the church", while being itself "a conference of evangelicals".
2. The Congress convenes "as one body, obeying one Lord, facing one world, with one task", namely evangelization.
3. The Congress convenes "to re-emphasize those biblical concepts which are essential to evangelism", especially five, namely –
    (a) commitment to the authority of Scripture,
    (b) the lostness of human beings apart from Christ,
    (c) salvation in Jesus Christ alone,

---

[21] 'Foreword', CTC, xi-xii.

[22] It should also be mentioned that a section on the preceding Congress on evangelism in Berlin 1966 is included on the Lausanne website, see www.lausanne.org/en/gatherings/global-congress/berlin-1966.html.

[23] J. D. Douglas (ed) (Minneapolis, MN: World Wide Publications, 1975).

[24] J. D. Douglas (ed), (Minneapolis, MN: World Wide Publications, 1990). Reference should also be made to A. Nichols (ed), *The Whole Gospel for the Whole World* (Charlotte, NC: LCWE and Regal Books, 1989).

[25] J. E. M. Cameron (ed) *Christ Our Reconciler.*

[26] See www.lausanne.org/en/gatherings/global-congress.html.

[27] An overview of multimedia resources is found at www.lausanne.org/en/gatherings/global-congress/lausanne-1974/multimedia-archives.html. Graham's opening speech is found at www2.wheaton.edu/bgc/archives/docs/Lausanne/704/graham.htm.

(d) Christian witness "by both word and deed" (neither denying Christian social responsibility, nor making it "our all-consuming mission"), and
(e) the necessity of evangelism for the salvation of souls.

4. "The Congress convenes to consider honestly and carefully both the unevangelized world and the church's resources to evangelize the world."[28]

The *Lausanne Covenant* reflects these four basic presuppositions of Lausanne I, while at the same time seeking to be sensitive to the wide spectrum of theological concerns, missiological emphases and cultural perspectives represented at this global congress. This wide-ranging variety was illustrated by John Stott in his speech 'Comments on the final draft of the *Lausanne Covenant*'.[29] The theological focus and the personal challenge of the Covenant were expressed in Bishop Festo Kivengere's final address 'The Cross and World Evangelization'.[30]

Most of the papers from *Lausanne II* are found in the rich collection of online material.[31] This includes some of the most well-known and influential presentations in Manila:

- The plenary Bible studies by John Stott on chapters 1-5 in the book of Romans were received as an appropriate and challenging summary of 'the Whole Gospel'.[32]
- The papers on the mandate of the laity resulted in an emphasis in the *Manila Manifesto* on 'the ministry (as well as the priesthood) of all believers', thus shaping the understanding of 'the whole church' and laying the foundation for a subsequent holistic emphasis on spiritual gifts, tentmaking and the workplace.[33]
- The paper by Os Guinness on 'The Impact of Modernization' raised the issue whether evangelicals properly understood, critiqued and engaged 'the whole world'.[34]

---

[28] Summary in Stott, 'An Historical Introduction', xiv. See also Douglas, *Let the Earth Hear His Voice*, 22-36. For further reference to Graham's keynote address, see the concluding chapter in this volume.

[29] This speech is found at www2.wheaton.edu/bgc/archives/docs/Lausanne/704/stott.htm.

[30] The speech is found at www2.wheaton.edu/bgc/archives/docs/Lausanne/704/kivengere.htm. See also Douglas, *Let the Earth Hear His Voice*, 400-404.

[31] See www.lausanne.org/en/documents/all/manila-1989/86-manila-1989-documents.html.

[32] Key elements of these Bible studies are found in Stott's later commentary *The Message of Romans: God's Good News for the World* (Leicester, UK: IVP, 1994), 45-166.

[33] The three papers on 'the mandate of the laity' were presented by Pete Hammond, Lee Yih and Ford Madison.

[34] The discussion generated by this influential paper resulted later in *The Uppsala Consultation on Faith and Modernity* (1993). The papers from this consultation was published in Sampson, V. Samuel and C. Sugden (eds), *Faith and Modernity* (Oxford, UK: Regnum Books, 1994).

A section in Leighton Ford's 'Foreword' to the official Manila documents provides a succinct summary of the theological and missiological emphases of this second Lausanne Congress:

> Lausanne II in Manila has played a significant role in [the Lausanne] Movement.
>
> It was significant in its *purpose*: to focus the whole church of Jesus Christ in a fresh way on the task of taking the whole gospel to the whole world.
>
> It was significant in its *representation*: 4,300 in attendance from 173 countries, including the Soviet Union and Eastern Europe, and with a larger proportion of women, lay persons and younger leaders than at previous conferences.
>
> It was significant in its *timeliness*: building on the foundation of Lausanne 74, on the work which has taken place since then, and leading into the final decade of this century.
>
> It was significant in its *breadth*: consideration was given to scores of important topics, ranging from the AD 2000 movement, to the work of the Holy Spirit, to liberating lay people, to the heart-cry of the poor of our world – and all related to Christ's global cause.
>
> Ultimately, however, the significance of [the Lausanne Movement] will be judged not by the event, but by significant advances in world evangelization which will follow in the decade ahead.[35]

In retrospect, in addition to the *Manila Manifesto*, the major significance of Lausanne II seemed to have been the fact that this second Congress 'gave birth to more than 300 strategic partnerships in world evangelization, including many that involved co-operation between nations in all parts of the globe'.[36]

When it comes to the *Lausanne III* Congress in Cape Town, this is too recent an event to properly estimate its influence and significance, also in terms of the various resources which have been generated. We have already mentioned the published educational resources related to the *Cape Town Commitment*. There is also a vast amount of available and relevant online resources related to the Congress programme:

- The introductory page to the Cape Town Congress material provides an overview of the available online material.[37]
- There are videos (and accompanying material) from every plenary and multiplex session, published as resources on the Lausanne Global Conversation.[38]

---

[35] 'The Foreword' by Leighton Ford is published at www.lausanne.org/en/documents/all/manila-1989/88-foreword.html.

[36] 'Preamble', *CTC*, 6.

[37] See www.lausanne.org/en/gatherings/global-congress/event/8-cape-town-2010-the-third-lausanne-congress-on-world-evangelization.html.

[38] See www.lausanne.org/en/multimedia/videos/ct2010-session-videos.html.

- There are available advance papers for all the multiplex sessions. Those papers were foundational for the various topical areas in 'Part II: A Call to Action' in the *Cape Town Commitment*. The advance papers are published as resources on the Lausanne Global Conversation.[39]
- In addition to the above-mentioned videos and advance papers, the Lausanne Global Conversation also contains articles, blog posts and ongoing discussions on all the themes and topics of Lausanne III.[40]

The Lausanne Occasional Papers and Related Documents

Many would point to the *Lausanne Occasional Papers* (LOP) as some of the most influential resources in the history of Lausanne, being 'historically important documents that have emerged from global consultations involving widely recognized evangelical leaders'.[41] These consultations were often initiated and sponsored by the TWG, in some cases in partnership with the WEA Theological Commission or other equivalent associations. It is natural to divide the LOPs into various groups related to their date, place of origin and/or theme.

LOPs 1-4 are key documents from the first phase in the Lausanne history (1975-79):

- The first Lausanne consultation in Pasadena, California, in 1977 on 'The Homogenous Unit Principle' produced LOP 1.
- The second Lausanne consultation was held at Willowbank in Bermuda in 1978. The theme was Gospel and Culture and resulted in LOP 2.
- As mentioned above, *The Lausanne Covenant with Exposition and Commentary* by John Stott was published in 1975 and became later LOP 3.
- The Glen Eyrie conference on Muslim evangelization in Colorado Springs in 1978 produced LOP 4 on Muslim Evangelization.

Most of LOPs 5-24 originate from the major Lausanne Consultation on World Evangelization (COWE) in Pattaya, Thailand, in 1980, where almost 900 leaders gathered:

> The COWE divided for five of its ten days into seventeen 'mini-consultations'. These focused on how to reach particular peoples for Christ. Each produced a report, which was published as a *Lausanne Occasional Paper*. The major part of each report went through a draft and a revised draft,

---

[39] See http://conversation.lausanne.org/en/pages/advance-papers.

[40] The home page for the Lausanne Global Conversation is http://conversation.lausanne.org/en.

[41] The LOPs are published at www.lausanne.org/en/documents/lops.html. This overview contains a list with hyperlinks to LOP 1-65, but with no reference to any LOPs 25, 28, 29 or 61.

> which involved all members of the mini-consultation. It was also submitted to a wider 'sub-plenary' group for comment, but the responsibility for the final text rests with the mini-consultation and its chairman. The documents are highly valuable and informative reports of the mini-consultations.[42]

In addition to these influential LOPs on Christian witness to various groups, the COWE also produced 'The Thailand Statement'[43] and LOP 24 on 'Co-operating in World Evangelization', which focuses on how to handle church / para-church relationships.

The 1980 High Leigh Consultation in UK resulted in LOP 20 on 'An Evangelical Commitment to Simple Lifestyle', which is an exposition and application of the challenging and controversial paragraph 9 clause in the *Lausanne Covenant* on 'our duty to develop a simple lifestyle'.[44]

The 1982 'Grand Rapids Report on Evangelism and Social Responsibility: An Evangelical Commitment' (LOP 21) is a highly significant and influential Lausanne document. Stott, who again was a key author, summarizes how the crucial fourth chapter in 'The Grand Rapids Report'

> spells out a threefold relationship between evangelism and social responsibility. Social activity is a *consequence* of evangelism (since evangelism brings people to new birth, and their new life manifests itself in the service of others), a *bridge* to evangelism (since it breaks down suspicion and gains a hearing for the gospel), and a *partner* of evangelism (words and works belonging together, 'like the two blades of a pair of scissors or the two wings of a bird').[45]

Most of the remaining LOPs have their origin from the 2004 Forum for World Evangelization in Pattaya, Thailand. But before introducing these resources, three other preceding LOPs need to be mentioned. Whereas LOP 26 explores 'Radio in Mission' (1989), being based on a joint venture between the Lausanne Movement and major evangelical international broadcasters, LOP 27 on 'Modern, Postmodern and Christian' summarizes and applies the papers from The Uppsala Consultation on Modernity (1993).[46] LOP 29, available from MARC Publications, deals with 'Spiritual Conflict in Today's Mission'.[47]

More than 1,500 evangelical leaders were invited to The Global Leadership Forum in Pattaya in 2004 to explore key contemporary issues in world evangelization, under the leadership of David Claydon:

---

[42] www.lausanne.org/en/documents/all/pattaya-1980.html.

[43] This statement is found at www.lausanne.org/en/documents/all/pattaya-1980/49-thailand-statement.html.

[44] See e.g. R. Steer, *Inside Story: The Life of John Stott* (Nottingham, UK: IVP, 2009), 162-163.

[45] Stott, 'An Historical Introduction', xix-xx.

[46] See the above reference to Simpson et al., *Faith and Modernity*.

[47] See references at http://ecumenism.net/docu/lcwe.htm and in A. Scott Moreau's chapter in this volume.

> Through a comprehensive worldwide research effort, thirty one specific issues were identified as roadblocks to evangelism and Issue Groups were formed around each issue. These Issue Groups each prepared a paper concerning their issue that includes a strategic action plan for addressing the concern. The 31 papers are now LOPs number 30-61.[48]

It should also be mentioned that presentations and papers from Pattaya 2004 are published in *A New Vision, A New Heart, A New Call.*[49]

LOP 62, entitled 'Following Jesus in our Broken World', was the result of the 2007 Limuru Consultation in Nairobi. 'It was deliberately conceived as an agenda-setting conference [for the TWG], in which we attempted to identify and discuss some of the most urgent matters confronting the church of Christ in its mission in the 21st century.'[50] As already mentioned, LOPs 63-65 emerged as subsequent explorations in the Theology Working Group of the central Lausanne motto: 'The Whole Church with the Whole Gospel to the Whole World', in order to prepare for the *Cape Town Commitment.*

Book Publications from Lausanne Consultations[51]

Some of the most influential consultations resulted not in LOPs but in publications of significant books. This includes the following events and titles:

- 'The International Prayer Assembly for World Evangelization' in Seoul, Korea, in 1984, resulted in *Unleashing the Power of Prayer*.[52]
- 'The Consultation on the Work of the Holy Spirit and Evangelization' in Oslo, Norway, in 1985, resulted in *God the Evangelist: How the Holy Spirit Works to Bring Men and Women to Faith.*[53]

---

48 The quote is from www.lausanne.org/en/documents/all/2004-forum.html. Reference is also made to (a) the publication of the LOPs at www.lausanne.org/en/documents/lops.html and (b) 'The 2004 Forum Summary Affirmations' published at www.lausanne.org/en/documents/all/2004-forum/94-2004-forum-summary-affirmations.html.

49 D. Claydon (ed), (Pasadena, CA: William Carey Library, 2005), 3 volumes.

50 C. Wright, 'Editorial: Following Jesus in Our Broken World', *Evangelical Review of Theology*, 31:4, 291, published at www.lausanne.org/docs/ TWG/LOP62-2007Limuru-Kenya.pdf.

51 It should also be mentioned that at the time of writing, plans are being set in place for publishing on different platforms from a series of global consultations, covering major issues identified in the *Cape Town Commitment.* A tentative list of these consultations is provided in the concluding chapter by L. Dahle, M. S. Dahle and K. Jørgensen on 'Moving on from Cape Town – Beyond the 40th Lausanne Anniversary' in this volume.

52 V. Bright and B. A. Jennings (eds), (Chicago, IL: Moody Press, 1989).

53 D. Wells (ed), (Grand Rapids, MI: Wm. B. Eerdmans, 1987).

- 'The Consultation on Conversion and World Evangelization' in Hong Kong, in 1988, resulted in *Turning to God: Biblical Conversion in the Modern World.*[54]
- As mentioned above, 'The Uppsala Consultation on Faith and Modernity' in 1993, resulted in *Faith and Modernity.*[55]
- 'The Deliver Us From Evil Consultation' on spiritual conflict and warfare in Nairobi in 2000 resulted in *Deliver Us From Evil: An Uneasy Frontier in Christian Mission.*[56]

The Seoul event was co-sponsored by the Lausanne Intercessory Working Group and the Korean Evangelical Fellowship, whereas the Oslo and the Hong Kong events were co-sponsored by the Lausanne Theology Working Group and the WEF Theological Commission.

The Lausanne Library and The Didasko Files

There is currently a growing number of Lausanne book publications. We have already mentioned a number of the current titles in *The Lausanne Library*, including *Christ Our Reconciler, The Cape Town Commitment: Bibliographic Resources, The Cape Town Commitment Study Edition,* and *Ephesians: Studying with the Global Church.* There is also a series of booklets entitled The Didasko Files, with Julia Cameron as Series Editor. This series, which is introduced as 'biblical, pastoral, [and] incisive', include the following titles:[57]

- *The Cape Town Commitment: A Confession of Faith and A Call to Action*
- *The Lausanne Covenant: Complete Text and Study Guide* by John Stott
- *More Precious than Gold* by Robert Murray M'Cheyne.
- *An Authentic Servant: The Marks of a Spiritual Leader* by Ajith Fernando.
- *The Glory of the Cross: Exploring the meaning of the death of Christ* by James Philip.
- *John Stott. Pastor, Leader and Friend: A man who embodied 'the spirit of Lausanne'* by a team of international authors who knew him well.

---

[54] D. Wells (Grand Rapids, MI: Baker Book House, 1989).

[55] Reference is made to footnote 34 above.

[56] S. Moreau et al. (eds), (Uxbridge, UK: World Vision International, 2002). See the presentations and papers published at www.lausanne.org/en/documents/all/nairobi-2000.html. Reference should also be made to LOP 29 'Spiritual Conflicts in Today's Mission' (MARC Publications).

[57] Reference is made to www.lausanne.org/en/documents/books.html and www.didaskofiles.com.

- *Charles Simeon of Cambridge: Silhouettes and Skeletons* by Julia Cameron, John Benton and Michael Rees.

Other Online Resources from the Lausanne Movement

In November 2012, *Lausanne Global Analysis* (LGA) was launched, as a new online publication with six issues per year and integrated into the Global Conversation.[58] The purpose of this new publication was to 'deliver strategic and credible information and insight from an international network of evangelical analysts so that Christian leaders will be equipped for the task of world evangelization'.[59] In his Publisher's Memo to the first issue, Doug Birdsall claimed that the LGA has a distinct role to play:

> What makes the LGA unique is our intentional focus on globally representative, thoughtfully written articles that provide timely analysis and policy recommendations that respond to our ever-changing political, social, and religious climate. We seek to serve leaders who are faced with major decisions about the deployment of personnel and other resources because of political unrest, natural disaster and other circumstances. We seek to serve leaders who need to be well-informed and conversant on the issues today – and their implications for ministry in 2, 3 or even 10 years.[60]

The first issues of the LGA have included such themes as the Arab Spring (November 2012), freedom of conscience (January 2013), religious freedom (March 2013), global trends (June 2013), and the persecution of Christians (September 2013).

Three other types of online resources should also be mentioned in this survey.[61] *First*, there are various documents from other significant Lausanne events. This includes The Younger Leaders' Gatherings in Singapore (1987) and in Malaysia (2006), the meeting in Haslev (Denmark) in 1997 on 'Gospel Contextualization Revisited', and the recent 'Global Consultation on Creation Care and the Gospel' in Jamaica (2012). *Secondly*, there is a wide-ranging collection of various consultation statements, illustrating the breadth of themes, communities and locations within Lausanne. *Thirdly*, there is a set of standards or principles to facilitate international funding relationships in Christian mission contexts. These principles are called *The Lausanne Standards* and should be seen as a set of global guiding affirmations and agreements for effective giving and receiving in mission.

---

[58] Reference should be made to the significant predecessor, first called *World Pulse Online* (2001-04; see archive at www.lausanneworldpulse.com/worldpulse) and thereafter called *Lausanne World Pulse* (2005-11; see archive at www.lausanneworldpulse.com/archives.php), with Naomi Frizzell as editor.

[59] The quarterly issues are published at www.lausanne.org/en/analysis, with David Taylor as editor.

[60] www.lausanne.org/en/documents/global-analysis/2012-11/publishers-memo.html.

[61] See www.lausanne.org/en/documents/all.html.

Critical reflections

The preceding survey of available Lausanne resources was primarily descriptive by nature. It is not the intention of this chapter to offer a comprehensive theological and missiological assessment of these influential resources. However, we will introduce the three categories of interpretative, educational and formative resources as a helpful analytical grid for understanding the global significance of these Lausanne resources.[62]

Interpretative Resources: Providing Essential Material for Evangelical Identity, Partnership and Mission

The *Lausanne Covenant* has had a formative role globally for evangelical leaders, organizations and churches in at least three key areas. First, the actual statements in the covenant have proved to contain essential elements for a theological identity as an evangelical. Secondly, the covenant has functioned as a unique organizational resource, both as a faith basis for many evangelical organizations and agencies, and as a theological platform for evangelical partnerships. Thirdly, the concept of evangelization in the covenant combines a clear focus on evangelism with a holistic approach and emphasis. Thus, the *Lausanne Covenant* 'eloquently expressed a balanced understanding of mission, which has remained unsurpassed as a rallying-point and basis of co-operation in mission among very diverse evangelical groups'.[63]

In an account of the story of the covenant, Tom Houston expresses this interpretative function as follows:

> Clearly, the *Lausanne Covenant* gave evangelicals a bigger worldview within which they could work together in the work of evangelization. Co-operation requires that people operate from within compatible worldviews and that the obstacles to effective co-operation can arise from a clash of worldviews. The challenge is to be ready, in the cause of co-operation, to compare, reconsider and perhaps amend or expand our worldviews. If our mission is to mobilize the whole church to take the whole gospel to the whole world, then surely such a radical approach is justified.[64]

We expect that the *Cape Town Commitment* will have an equivalent function, especially related to the wide-ranging task of bearing witness 'to

---

[62] For the threefold emphasis on interpretative, educational and formative perspectives, reference is made to M. S. Dahle, 'Forskningsprosjektet "10-25" – i religionspedagogisk perspektiv", *Theofilos*, 4:2 (2012), 28-48.

[63] C. Ott, S. J. Strauss and T. C. Tennent, *Encountering Theology of Mission: Biblical Foundations, Historical Developments, and Contemporary Issues* (Grand Rapids, MI: Baker Academic, 2010), xxvii.

[64] www.lausanne.org/en/gatherings/global-congress/lausanne-1974/story-of-the-covenant.html. Tom Houston served as Lausanne International Director 1989-93 and as Lausanne Minister-at-Large 1994-98.

Jesus Christ and all his teaching – in every nation, in every sphere of society, and in the realm of ideas'. In view of this task, it is helpful to consider the central Lausanne resources – such as the three Congress documents – as providing an interpretative worldview perspective on evangelism and mission.[65]

Educational Resources: Providing Essential Material for Teaching on Evangelization and Integral Mission

Central Lausanne documents, such as the *Lausanne Covenant* and the *Manila Manifesto*, have had a key role in the teaching on evangelism and missiology in evangelical and ecumenical seminaries and missionary training colleges (and beyond), whether as foundational historical documents or as foundational resources for textbooks, articles, lectures and sermons. It is helpful to consider the educational role of these resources in view of a four-dimensional New Testament-based approach to preaching, teaching and sharing the Gospel of Jesus Christ.[66]

First, central Lausanne resources (such as the three primary Congress documents) paint a rich picture of the biblical *kerygma*. The heart of this Gospel is expressed in the *Lausanne Covenant*: 'Jesus Christ, being himself the only God-man, who gave himself as the only ransom for sinners, is the only mediator between God and people.'[67] The meaning and significance of this biblical Gospel is underlined in the *Cape Town Commitment*: 'We love the good news in a world of bad news … We love the story the gospel tells … We love the assurance the gospel brings … We love the transformation the gospel produces.'[68]

Secondly, a number of Lausanne resources contribute significantly towards the understanding of teaching (*didache*) a whole biblical Gospel. The *Lausanne Covenant* defines evangelization as 'the Whole Church

[65] In this context, we use 'worldview' as 'a commitment, a fundamental orientation of the heart, that can be expressed as a story or in a set of presuppositions (assumptions which may be true, partially true, or entirely false) which we hold (consciously or subconsciously, consistently or inconsistently) about the basic construction of reality, and that provides the foundation on which we live and move and have our being' (J. W. Sire, *The Universe Next Door: A Basic Worldview Catalog* (Downers Grove, IL: IVP, 2005), 15-16). See also G. Hiebert, *Transforming Worldviews: An Anthropological Understanding of How People Change* (Grand Rapids, MI: Baker Academic, 2008).

[66] The first three dimensions – represented by *kerygma*, *didache* and *paraklese* – are proposed by Professor Emeritus in Homiletics and Bishop Emeritus Olav Skjevesland in *Det skapende ordet: En prekenlære* (Oslo: Universitetsforlaget, 1995). We have added *apologia* as a fourth dimension; cf. L. Dahle, 'Truth, Christian Mission and Apologetics: A Response and A Proposal', *Norwegian Journal of Missiology*, 67:1 (2013), 21-38.

[67] *LC*, paragraph 3: 'The Uniqueness and Universality of Christ'.

[68] *CTC*, I8: 'We love the gospel of God'.

Taking the Whole Gospel to the Whole World'. The same emphasis is clear in the *Manila Manifesto*: 'We are committed to preaching the whole gospel, that is, the biblical gospel in its fullness.' This is illustrated in Part I of the *Cape Town Commitment*, where a theological foundation is provided for teaching on evangelization within a holistic view of *missio Dei* (God's mission). This leads in Part II of the *Cape Town Commitment* to missiological applications 'in every nation, in every sphere of society and in the realm of ideas', thus again a rich resource for wholesome biblical teaching.

Thirdly, following established patterns in the New Testament, many Lausanne resources explicitly admonish Christian believers to live lives worthy of their calling as disciples, witnesses, and leaders. This strong emphasis on *paraklese* (exhortations) is an integrated part of the formative function of these resources, which we will come to shortly.

Fourthly, the emphasis on *apologia* has gradually been strengthened in the primary documents throughout the history of the Lausanne Movement. Whereas the *Lausanne Covenant* points to truth as a defining feature of God's revelation in the Bible, the *Manila Manifesto* affirms 'that apologetics, namely "the defence and confirmation of the Gospel" is integral to the biblical understanding of mission and essential for effective witness in the modern world'.[69] This is re-emphasized in the *Cape Town Commitment*: 'We long to see greater commitment to the hard work of robust apologetics.'[70] Thus includes communicating the *kerygma*, the *didache* and the *paraklese* as truth, i.e. teaching the whole Gospel in all its fullness as truth. 'Because Jesus *is* truth, truth in Christ is (i) personal as well as propositional; (ii) universal as well as contextual; (iii) ultimate as well as present.'[71]

Formative Resources: Providing Essential Material for Personal, Leadership and Organizational Developments

The formative aspect of the Lausanne resources is evident from many of the contributors to this volume. An extended engagement with these Lausanne resources has been a decisive factor in shaping many evangelical leaders' theological and missiological convictions, their personal ministries and callings, as well as the mission strategies of their churches, organizations or institutions.

The formative influence of significant Lausanne resources may thus be seen at different levels:

- Personal formation, in terms of shaping convictions, informing strategic thinking and challenging to integrity and the cost of

[69] *Manila Manifesto*, Section A2: 'Good News for Today'.
[70] *CTC*, IIA1: 'Truth and the Person of Christ'.
[71] *CTC*, IIA1: 'Truth and the Person of Christ'.

commitment, as a result of being exposed to the resources through reading, attending, discussing and participating.

- Leadership formation, in terms of formal leadership programmes for younger leaders and other target groups.
- Organizational formation, in terms of shaping organizational cultures and mission strategies in evangelical organizations, through leaders who have been exposed to and influenced by key Lausanne events and resources.

Concluding Reflections

We started this chapter by referring to a recent official presentation, where the Lausanne Movement was introduced as 'a catalyst for engaging major issues by connecting and convening evangelical leaders, communicating ideas and strategy, and hosting discussion and resource sharing'. The above discussion has validated this claim.

The intention of this chapter is to make the wealth of available Lausanne resources more accessible for missiological, strategic and practical interactions, whether this happens in the contexts of practical missions, formal and informal education, or research and development projects. It is our hope and prayer that this survey will serve this purpose.

Our own interactions with various Lausanne resources throughout the writing of this paper have resulted in a number of new and illuminating discoveries combined with fascinating and challenging applications. This is especially related to the areas of apologetics, media and youth ministry. But that is another story.

Section Two

Introducing Major Lausanne Concerns

THE HOLY SPIRIT AND THE GOSPEL

David F. Wells

The most important missiological contribution the Lausanne networks and Congresses have made is, in one important respect, to make no theological contribution at all. Lausanne has been deliberate about staying within the biblical parameters. It, therefore, has never seen its task as being inventive and it has been quite content to make no new contribution on the Holy Spirit.[1]

Early in the Church's life, Tertullian observed that his first principle was that 'Christ laid down one definite system of truth which the world must believe without qualification.'[2] It was this truth that the Church immediately sought to define and protect and, in time, it produced its classic creeds like Nicea and Chalcedon. Behind each word in these creeds

---

[1] There have been three Lausanne Congresses. They were held in Lausanne (1974), Manila (1989), and Cape Town (2010). Each produced a formal document in which there are some sections which deal with the Holy Spirit. They are as follows: *Lausanne Covenant,* Sections 4 and 14; the *Manila Manifesto,* Section 5. These two statements are published together as *Manila Manifesto: An Elaboration of the Lausanne Covenant Fifteen Years Later* (Pasadena, CA: The LCWE, 1989); and the *Cape Town Commitment,* Section 5. This was published as Chris Wright (ed), *The Cape Town Commitment: A Confession of Faith and a Call to Action* (Peabody, MA: Hendrickson Publishers, 2011). Each of these Congresses also published volumes containing the papers and addresses that had been given. In addition, in 1985, the Theology Working Group from Lausanne joined with the Theology Unit of the World Evangelical Fellowship to explore the work of the Holy Spirit in evangelism. David Wells was asked by those present to put the papers and discussions into publishable form and this appeared as *God the Evangelist: How the Holy Spirit Works to Bring Men and Women to Faith* (Grand Rapids, MI: William B. Eerdmans, 1987). A second Consultation, originally planned along with the first, was held in Hong Kong in 1988. Again Wells was asked to get the materials ready for publication and this resulted in *Turning to God: Biblical Conversion in the Modern World* (Grand Rapids, MI: Baker Book House, 1989). Finally, important conversations were carried on with Roman Catholicism through the Secretariat for Promoting Christian Unity. These conversations included discussions on the Holy Spirit and were published in Basil Meeking and John Stott (eds), *The Evangelical-Roman Catholic Dialogue on Mission 1977-1984: A Report* (Grand Rapids, MI: William B. Eerdmans, 1986).

[2] Tertullian, *Prescription Against Heretics,* 9. The classic examination of the way in which this orthodoxy emerged is probably still H. E. W. Turner's Bampton Lectures published as *The Pattern of Christian Truth: A Study in the Relations between Orthodoxy and Heresy in the Early Church* (London: A. R. Mowbray, 1954).

lay conflict and debate but the church was determined to speak out of a common understanding on the core doctrinal issues such as the Trinity, the person of Christ, and of the Holy Spirit.

With respect to the Holy Spirit, this early consensus is what was heard, for example, in Basil's *De Spiritu Sancto* where, after some initial hesitations, he came to a full Nicene view of the deity of the Holy Spirit within the Trinitarian framework. This understanding was carried forward. In the sixteenth century, the Protestant reformers reaffirmed it. And it was these same truths that informed the great, nineteenth-century missionary conferences that finally led up to Edinburgh 1910. Lausanne deliberately stands in this tradition with respect to the doctrines of the Trinity, Christ, and the Holy Spirit.

At the same time, Lausanne has had to articulate this understanding in a theological context today of considerable diversity. Furthermore, we live in a world which, in the west and parts of Asia especially, is highly modernized. The challenge that Lausanne has taken up, then, is how to affirm and practise historic orthodoxy while, at the same time, interfacing with the many different contexts in which it seeks to make known the Christian Gospel. It is these connections that I wish to explore a little in this essay.

First, though, I need to summarize the position Lausanne has stated with respect to the Holy Spirit and this will lead into a brief consideration of the other religions. Then, second, I will review the rather extraordinary discussions that took place in the 1970s and 1980s between representatives of Lausanne and of the Vatican as these related to the Holy Spirit. Finally, I need to make some observations about Lausanne's reckoning with modernity.

Biblical Affirmation

The three Lausanne Congresses assume, and briefly state, the church's historic understanding of the Trinity and Christ's incarnation. They further state what is a Protestant understanding of his substitutionary death on the Cross. This is the theological setting for understanding the person and work of the Holy Spirit.

The most complete summary of the Holy Spirit's work came from Manila. It is interesting to note that it appears under the heading, 'God the Evangelist'. This was, in fact, the title of the book that had just been published and which contained the substance of the deliberations of Lausanne's Theological Working Group's Consultation on the Holy Spirit. This Consultation was held in Oslo in 1985. Under the book title's heading, the Manila Congress stated:

> For the Holy Spirit of God is the Spirit of truth, love, holiness, and power, and evangelism is impossible without him. It is he who anoints the messenger, confirms the word, prepares the hearer, convicts the sinful,

> enlightens the blind, gives life to the dead, enables us to repent and believe, unites us to the body of Christ, assures us that we are God's children, leads us into Christ-like character and service, and sends us out in turn to be Christ's witnesses. In all this the Holy Spirit's main preoccupation is to glorify Jesus by showing him to us and forming him in us.[3]

Statements from Lausanne Congresses, like this one, are brief summaries. They are only intended to give the doctrinal basis for the evangelistic action which they want to focus and spur. However, at the Oslo Consultation that preceded the Manila Congress, time was given to exploring the person and work of the Holy Spirit.

It was the Incarnation of the Son and the giving of the Holy Spirit that made the fact of the Trinity inescapable. The Old Testament contains material that certainly points in this direction but after the Incarnation and the giving of the Spirit, this truth was made explicit and unmistakable. Indeed, it would be true to say that the Trinitarian nature of God is the presupposition of all New Testament soteriology.[4] The Father, after all, 'sent' the Son into the world (John 4:34; 5:23-4) and 'sent' the Holy Spirit to bring conviction about sin (John 16:8-10), to point men and women to Christ and, upon belief in the Gospel, to take up residence in their hearts (Gal 4:4-6). The key point to note here is that the missions of the Son and that of the Spirit are linked together.

This is the important transition that occurred as the Old Testament ended and the apostolic period began. In the Old Testament, there are almost a hundred explicit references to the Holy Spirit. They speak to the fact that the Spirit was active in creation, in history, in giving gifts, in teaching God's will and ways, and in giving prophetic utterance. However, none of this was explicitly related to Christ except, of course, for the prophecies. How could it have been? Christ had not yet come.

After the Incarnation, this changes. Now, what Scripture tells us about the Holy Spirit's power and work is all directly related to Christ. Indeed, this is now the exclusive focus. Undoubtedly, as the agent of creation (Gen 1:2), the Holy Spirit continues to be present to all of life, but once the Incarnation had occurred, it is his linkage to Christ that is to the fore. The reason for this is that their respective work is correlated and co-ordinated.

This gave, in the post-resurrection period, a structured Trinitarian shape to Christian life. Believers are reconciled to the Father, through the substitutionary death of the Son, by the work of the Holy Spirit who imparts the will and ability to believe. More than that, it is the Holy Spirit who imparts a new nature in regeneration and thus applies to sinners what Christ had secured on the Cross.[5]

---

[3] *Manila Manifesto,* Section 5.

[4] Wells, *God the Evangelist,* 6.

[5] This was the theme of the second of the two related Consultations which in 1989 was published as *Turning to God: Biblical Conversion in the Modern World.*

So it is that this Holy Spirit is given to abide with those who are Christ's. He is 'the Spirit of your Father' (Matt 10:20) even as he is also 'the Spirit of his Son', (Gal 4:4). He is the 'Spirit of life' (Rom 8:2) who has set us free in Christ from sin and death. He is, therefore, the 'Spirit of grace' (Heb 10:29). This 'Spirit of truth' is the possession of believers but, Jesus said, 'the world cannot receive' him because it does not know him (John 14:17).[6] In fact, he is known only in and through Christ, and Christ is known only because of the Spirit's work.

This is why, in the New Testament, the work of the Son and of the Spirit are correlated, not only theologically, but also linguistically. Father, Son and Spirit are seen as working together in a single plan of grace (e.g. Eph 1:3-13; 4:4-6; 2 Thess 2:13-4; 1 Pet 1:2). And this correlation is made plain in the fact that the Spirit is the Spirit *of* Christ. He who is the 'Spirit of God' (Rom 8:9) is also 'the Spirit of Christ' (1 Pet 1:11), 'the Spirit of his Son' (Gal 4:6), and 'the Spirit of Jesus Christ' (Phil 1:19).

The *Cape Town Commitment* reiterated these same truths within a larger summary of the many different aspects of the Holy Spirit's work. This was placed within a fully Trinitarian framework, and the soteriological connections between the work of the Son and that of the Spirit were declared. The statement then went on to say that our 'engagement in mission, then, is pointless and fruitless without the presence, guidance and power of the Holy Spirit.'[7] Indeed, it said that there is 'no authentic biblical mission, without the Person, work and power of the Holy Spirit.'[8]

This linkage is of enormous missiological consequence today. The unmistakable implication is that there is no legitimate claim to the saving presence of the Holy Spirit in the world today unless that presence has produced trust in Christ's substitutionary work on the Cross. The first Lausanne Congress had asserted this.[9] And Manila built upon it recognizing that in the New Testament period there were 'many gods and many lords' so religious pluralism, such as we know today, is no novelty. Yet it noted that the apostles boldly 'affirmed the uniqueness, indispensability, and centrality of Christ'. We, it said, must do likewise. Its reasoning was that since there is only one incarnate Christ, only one Cross, only one work of divine salvation, there is only one Gospel. We, therefore, must reject the relativism that accepts as valid other religions and spiritualities as well as the syncretism that is content to add other beliefs to those that are biblical.[10]

The fundamental insight here is that, contrary to what much modern theology has asserted in different ways, the Holy Spirit cannot be said to be at work in Hinduism, Buddhism, Islam or any other religion. The Holy

---

[6] Wells, *God the Evangelist,* 8.

[7] *Cape Town Commitment,* Section 13.

[8] Ibid.

[9] *Lausanne Covenant*, Section 3.

[10] *Manila Manifesto,* Section 3. This position was also affirmed in Cape Town. See *Cape Town Commitment,* Section 4.

Spirit does not validate other religions, is not present to them in redemptive ways, and does not create in them alternative paths to the Father. There is only one path and it goes through Christ. It is, therefore, only to Christ that the Spirit points men and women that they might be regenerated, converted, justified, and accepted by the Father.

In the nineteenth century, Protestant theology in Europe was dominated by the thought of Schleiermacher, Ritschl, and Harnack. It had turned away from the orthodoxy of the Reformation period and, instead, made its peace with Kant. Often, as with Schleiermacher, this peace came way of a kind of pantheism. Schleiermacher claimed that religion consisted in the 'immediate feeling of absolute dependence.'[11] This feeling was at the base of all religions.[12] The divine was to be found in the depths of human beings where it gave to all a kind of Godward direction. In time, of course, this produced the 'history of religions' school which looked for divine reality in all religions. Nor were they alone. Later in the century, on the Catholic side, the Modernists made much the same argument. George Tyrrell, for example, the leader among the English Modernists, said that religions are 'but the languages in which men hold converse with God. And these languages are of one family and one origin, human and divine; the work of God through man, and of man under God'.[13] It was a viewpoint he pursued relentlessly until his excommunication.

The period of neo-orthodoxy on the Protestant side that was dominant from roughly 1920 to 1960 put an end to this liberal outlook. And in Rome, the encyclical *Pascendi Gregis* in 1907 put a stop to Modernism. It was followed, in 1910, by the institution of the Oath Against Modernism that every priest was obliged to swear.

There matters stood for a while. But on both sides of the equation, the question has been revisited more recently. On the Protestant side, the door has been opened wide to the other religions, notably by John Hick.[14] The cause has been taken up by many in the World Council of Churches. On the Catholic side, the Second Vatican Council also revisited this issue. The result was a rather different attitude than had been traditional as we shall see.

Although this is an enormously complex story, we can at least see where the distinctiveness of Lausanne's position lies. It is that natural revelation is not supernatural and it is not saving. Furthermore, the work of the Holy

---

[11] Friedrich Schleiermacher, *The Christian Faith,* trans. H. R. Mackintosh and J. S. Stewart (Edinburgh: T. & T. Clark, 1928).

[12] Ibid., 47.

[13] George Tyrrell, *Through Scylla and Charybdis or the Old Theology and the New* (London: Longmans, Green and Co. 1907), 44.

[14] See especially John Hick's *God and the Universe of Faiths* (London: Macmillan, 1973); *God Has Many Names* (Louisville, KY: Westminster/John Knox Press, 1982); *A Christian Theology of Religions* (Louisville, KY: Westminster/John Knox Press, 1995).

Spirit is not to validate human spirituality but to bring the knowledge that no human striving, no religion, no obedience of a moral kind, can provide the basis for a saving knowledge of God. Other religions, therefore, are not different paths to the same end. The only truth which the Spirit validates which is of a saving kind is that of the uniqueness, centrality, and indispensability of Christ's redemptive work.

Natural revelation cannot provide this basis because there is, in fact, a boundary between God and sinners. This boundary cannot be crossed from below. It can only be crossed from above, by God himself, and that is what he did in the person of the Son. It is in John, in particular that this theme is taken up. The Son, he says repeatedly was 'sent' into the world (John 10:36; cf: John 3:31; 13:3; 12:46; 16:27). He came from 'above' (John 8:23). It is to this unique break-in that the Holy Spirit points men and women. Faith is not about the human spirit questing upwards. It is about the Holy Spirit working to create repentance from sin and trust in Christ as alone the sin-bearer and resurrected Lord of life. The Holy Spirit has no other mission than to apply what the Son achieved on the Cross.

An Opening to Catholicism

The Second Vatican Council concluded in December 1965, committing itself to work toward ecumenical discussion, toward 'that continual reformation of which she always has need',[15] and to a fresh study of Scripture. It was less than a decade later, in 1974, that the first of the Lausanne Congresses also concluded its work. After this Congress, it was clear that there was a fresh, evangelical consensus about evangelism that had emerged. It was shortly after this, then, that the Vatican, through the Secretariat for Promoting Christian Unity, made an approach to the Lausanne Committee. It proposed some meetings to explore afresh differences and similarities between Catholicism and this resurgent evangelicalism. It was a reasonable request but it created a delicate situation for the evangelicals. The Lausanne Committee feared that, were it to engage with the Vatican, there might be a perception among some of its constituents that it was 'negotiating' with Rome. The fear was not without foundation. Later, in 1994, a similar set of meetings in the USA produced the document, *Evangelicals and Catholics Together,* and this caused a firestorm. The Lausanne Committee therefore decided to keep the meetings unofficial. John Stott, the principal drafter of the *Lausanne Covenant*, was asked to lead the dialogue. This took place in three sets of meetings in three locations: Venice (1977), Cambridge (1982), and Landevennec in France (1984).

Although there was a diplomatic tone to these meetings, they were also remarkably frank and the theological differences were never obscured.

[15] *Decree on Ecumenism,* 6.

Common areas of agreement certainly emerged but so, too, did the quite different conceptions of what is entailed in the Gospel mission and hence of the Holy Spirit's role in that mission.

The differences start with the Gospel itself. Evangelicals see Christ doing in his death what he did not do in his life. He 'became sin' for us (2 Cor 5:21) and 'a curse' for us (Gal 3:13), thus propitiating the wrath of God by absorbing our punishment in himself and thus turning God's wrath away from its rightful objects. Christ's death was, in this way, substitutionary. Thus the Gospel is a message of deliverance from sin, punishment, and death. It is so because of Christ's death and hence it is by grace alone. Believing this Gospel and entrusting ourselves to the Christ of this Gospel results in pardon, renewal, and the Spirit's indwelling.

Catholics, on the other hand, see Christ's death as the continuation of his life in the sense that it was his final act of obedience. It was offered to the Father in love. In this sense, he did not do in his death what he had not done in his life. This thought of obedience then lays the conceptual foundation for our doing what Christ did. 'In consequence, we can enter into the sacrifice of Christ and offer ourselves to the Father in and with him.'[16]

The rather deep difference here in the alternative understandings of the Gospel is what also explains the differences over Mary. Evangelicals expressed their dismay over many of the titles and terms used of her like her 'salvific Motherhood' and the Second Vatican Council's statement that 'Mary is rightly seen as co-operating in the work of human salvation through free faith and obedience'. Although the Council did not itself use the term *Mediatrix,* the idea was certainly there. To ascribe an active role to Mary in securing our salvation is, the evangelicals countered, to detract from Christ who, in fact, secured it all. The evangelicals in this dialogue therefore made a counter point. Catholics wanted to see Mary as modelling their understanding of the Gospel. That is, it is a message of human co-operation with the divine through obedience. However, that is not the model we have in Scripture. We co-operate with God in *proclaiming* the Gospel; Mary, Catholics were saying, co-operated with God by *procuring* it.[17] It was that which the evangelicals vigorously disputed. Mary herself, they countered, needed a Saviour and they rejected the idea that she was born sinless.

This has significance for the different conceptions of the role of the Holy Spirit. In Scripture, the evangelicals said, this role 'is to honour Christ the Son, not Mary the mother'.[18] Clearly, the missiological role of the Holy Spirit is shaped entirely by how several other questions are decided. If Christ alone secured our redemption and justification, then to Christ alone

---

[16] Meeking and Stott, 43.
[17] Ibid., 51.
[18] Ibid., 50.

does the Spirit point men and women. If salvation can be secured through co-operation with Christ, or even simply though living a virtuous life, then the Holy Spirit's mission becomes something entirely different.

When the Catholic church emerged after Vatican II, it was flush with the progressive spirit. This is evident in many of the conciliar documents. But a decade later, when this evangelical/Roman Catholic dialogue began, it was rather evident that the Vatican was applying the brakes. The influence of Pope John Paul II and Cardinal Ratzinger, as he then was, was quite clear in this.

In fact, Vatican II had explored the matter of the other religions rather adventurously. Some of what was said at the Council was even reminiscent of what the Modernists had said. This question of the other religions therefore became unavoidable when this evangelical/Catholic dialogue began.

Vatican II declared the church to be 'the sacrament of salvation'. As such, it is the visible representation of God's presence in life and it is, in particular, the dwelling place of his glory and the source of his grace. Christ uses the church 'as an instrument for the redemption of all'.[19] The church both signifies and effects this salvation.

Although the Council did not use Karl Rahner's language of 'anonymous Christians' being present in the other religions, the thought was certainly there. The Council's use of the 'people of God' was quite elastic. It included others who were not Catholic. This was true of the Eastern Orthodox and Protestants though they were both viewed, of course, as being incomplete. But the Council ranged even further into the non-Christian religions, searching for evidences of truth and of the divine presence in them. And it even went to so far as to say that atheists, without rescinding their atheism, are not denied the help they need from God 'for salvation' provided they 'strive to live a good life, thanks to his grace'.[20]

What this means, then, is that the Spirit is present throughout human history working to bring liberation from sin, suffering and oppression, and that this happens sometimes without explicit reference to Christ. This is the only conclusion that can be drawn and the evangelicals rejected it. The 'history of salvation,' they said, is not 'coterminous with the history of the world'.[21]

In contrast to Catholic teaching, then, Lausanne showed itself to have a rather tautly argued view on the Holy Spirit's role in salvation. It is not a redemptive presence in other religions, or liberation movements, nor does he validate earnest moral striving. The Spirit works, instead, to bring that striving, that longing for freedom which is found in human life, to rest by

---

[19] *Dogmatic Constitution on the Church,* 9.

[20] Ibid., 16.

[21] Meeking and Stott, 31.

trusting in the finished, substitutionary work of Christ. That is the Spirit's only role in salvation.

The Modernized World

In the almost four decades between the first Lausanne Congress in 1974 and the third in Cape Town in 2010, there have been staggering changes in the world. Among these, has been the shifting centre of gravity in the Christian world from the global north to the south. This is due, on the one hand, to the effective evangelism that has occurred in the global south and parts of Asia and, on the other hand, to the decline of Christian faith, numerically speaking, throughout the west. On a typical Sunday in Europe, Canada, Australia and New Zealand, attendance at any church at all is only between 2% and 5% of the population. By contrast, in Zambia, for example, about 80% will attend some church. Why is this? Why is Christian faith so hard to sustain in highly modernized contexts, and why is the Christian Gospel apparently also so hard to believe?

The problems created by modernization were beginning to dawn on people when the first Congress was held in 1974. In that Congress, this theme was addressed but nothing was said in its final document. This, though, had changed when Manila took place in 1989 and modernization was given some attention in its statement. Since the world is becoming increasingly modernized, and what the west has long experienced is increasingly the experience of many countries outside the west, one might have expected the Cape Town Congress, in 2010, to have addressed this reality even more intentionally than had Manila. That did not happen. There were a few addresses, only one plenary,[22] on some of the themes of modernization. There was a recognition that truth is one of the chief casualties of what modernization produces. The *Cape Town Commitment,* furthermore, does speak of the reality of technology, of the importance of the media, and of why truth in this kind of world is sometimes hard to find. What is missing in its statement, though, is a coherent understanding of how all of these components of the modern world cohere together, interact with one another, and create a public environment which is really hostile to Christian faith. Manila had, in fact, already gone down this road but in Cape Town, in 2010, it was as if the earlier progress had simply been forgotten.

Modernization, to be sure, is an enormously complex matter. What makes it especially difficult to grasp is that these are global processes which also look a little different in different cultural contexts. The face of

[22] An important aspect of modernization is globalization. This subject was addressed in the Congress and an abbreviated version of the paper from which the addresses came was published. See Os Guinness and David Wells, 'Discipleship and mission in the age of globalization', *Christ Our Reconciler* J. E. M. Cameron (ed) (Nottingham, UK: IVP, 2012), 95-105.

modernization in the west is not quite the same as in Asia. And none of these developments ever stands still. Each is in constant flux.

And yet, while this is true, modernization is also profoundly changing our world. Manila had said that 'we have become concerned about the impact of "modernity", which is an emerging world culture produced by industrialization with its technology and urbanization with its economic order'.[23] It went on to say that these factors combine to produce a cultural and psychological environment 'which significantly shapes the way we see our world'.[24] There are, undoubtedly, enormous benefits that come from modernization but they come with costs attached. As a part of this picture is the fact that where secularism has taken root, belief in God becomes meaningless and unnecessary and where the media dominates our consciousness, truth is devalued. This loss of truth has an enormous impact both on the message which many are preaching as well as on the motivation to evangelize.

The Manila Congress had recognized how slow evangelicals have been to understand these changes. 'We confess,' it said, 'that we have not struggled as we should to understand modernization.' Not understanding it, we do not see its dangers and so, very often, we have 'used its methods and techniques'[25] when doing evangelism and therefore have often done it in worldly ways.

Not long after this Congress in Manila, and well before the Congress in Cape Town, the Theology Working Group took up this theme at a Consultation in Uppsala in 1993.[26] James Hunter set up the theme by saying that "nearly everyone nowadays senses deep within themselves a visceral unease about contemporary life".[27] This is not simply the realization that for Christians this world is not their home. "No, the tension, the dissonance, the emptiness is more unsettling than just that. Something, we sense, is unique about the nature and direction of our personal and collective existence and it is not all agreeable to us."[28] This is the internal signal that we are receiving that something profound is afoot. It speaks to the disintegration of some of our most basic institutions and the disappearance of some of the core ideals of our western civilization. And while this has been going on, Hunter said, evangelicals have been in "a deep but restless and agitated slumber".[29] Unfortunately, this slumber was not really interrupted in Cape Town.

---

[23] *Manila Manifesto,* Section 10.

[24] Ibid.

[25] Ibid.

[26] The papers from this Consultation were later published: Philip Sampson, Vinay Samuel and Chris Sugden (eds), *Faith and Modernity* (Oxford, UK: Regnum Books, 1994).

[27] Samson, Samuel, and Sugden, 12.

[28] Ibid.

[29] Ibid.

All of this may seem to be far removed from the work of the Holy Spirit. There is, though, an important point of connection. It is that technology and the media greatly magnify human powers and foster an illusion about human ability that is simply false when it comes to the Kingdom of God. The point about the historic doctrine of the Spirit is that it underscores human *inability*. The reason that the Gospel does not take root without the work of the Spirit is that we are, by nature, disinclined to hear the Gospel or believe its truth, unwilling to change our ways, incapable of that trust in Christ without which there can be no redemption. All of these things the Spirit enables us to do. By contrast, modernity greatly heightens the sense of human ability.

So it is that some have imagined that the church is but a business, with a product, which simply needs to be sold to customers as any other product might be. We can generate our own success. Christian faith thus is 'produced' with very little reference to truth. Indeed, the fact that so much success has been had in the Christian world without much biblical truth is a testimony to the power, not of the Holy Spirit, but of the tools of the modernized world. This is what Manila had had in mind when it spoke of the worldly techniques which now abound in the evangelical world.

It ought to be impossible to hold the historic view of the Holy Spirit and be unaware of the worldliness inherent within modernity. But it plainly is not. Many of those engaged in the marketing of Christian faith would be shocked to learn that their practices are at odds with such an important doctrine. But they are!

This is a doctrine that functions within a t*heological* framework. Too much of our evangelism, at least in the west, has been carried out within a *non-theological* framework. This is one of the most profound consequences of our prolonged exposure to modernity. Manila plainly put this matter on the agenda. Perhaps, if there is another Congress, it can be taken up once again more intentionally.

The distinctive missiological contribution Lausanne has made, then, has been to reaffirm the Church's longstanding doctrine of the Holy Spirit and to do so in a theological context. Central to this are two considerations. First, it is God who must establish his own Kingdom for we cannot do it by ourselves. We can pray for it, seek it, want it, but it is *God alone* who can establish it. And this he has done in and through Christ.

This leads to the second point. The work of the Holy Spirit, in this Kingdom, is focused on, and linked to, Christ and his saving death on the Cross. The Holy Spirit gives no validation to other religions and is not at work redemptively in them. His sole work is to point men and women to Christ and enable them to trust in his grace alone for their salvation.

DELIVER US FROM EVIL CONSULTATION 16-22 AUGUST, 2000 (NAIROBI, KENYA)

A. Scott Moreau

In providing a very limited perspective about any event that involves several years of co-ordination and planning, one may choose to focus on either the process of the event or the content or perspectives of the event. Since the latter are well documented,[1] I have chosen as my focus an overview of the process of the consultation rather than its content with the anticipation of providing readers with a bit more of the behind-the-scenes activities and thinking that are part of every major international event.

Background of the DUFE Consultation[2]

The felt need among several Lausanne constituents for a consultation on spiritual warfare was initially generated as a result of the surge in interest in spiritual warfare and New Age phenomena in the 1980s and 1990s, notably in North America and several European settings. A very popular and highly attended[3] set of workshops on spiritual warfare at Lausanne II at Manila (1989) generated among several Lausanne leaders a felt need to address spiritual warfare in a more significant way than done previously. In 1993 the Lausanne Intercession Working Group (LIWG) added momentum by hosting a one-day working group meeting on spiritual warfare in London.

---

[1] See A. Scott Moreau, Tokunboh Adeyemo, David G. Burnett, Bryant L. Myers and Hwa Yung (eds), *Deliver Us From Evil* (Monrovia, CA: LCWE and MARC, 2002); Tormod Engelsviken, *Spiritual Conflict in Today's Mission.* Edited by A. Scott Moreau. LOP 29. Monrovia, CA: LCWE and MARC, 2001; and www.lausanne.org/en/ gatherings/event/22-deliver-us-from-evil-consultation.html.

[2] Material for much of this chapter is gleaned from A. Scott Moreau, 'Preface' in A. Scott Moreau, Tokunboh Adeyemo, David G. Burnett, Bryant L. Myers and Hwa Yung (eds), *Deliver Us From Evil* (Monrovia, CA: LCWE and MARC, 2002) and Engelsviken, *Spiritual Conflict in Today's Mission.* I limit footnotes to these two sources to specific quotes; they are the source of all of the specifics unless otherwise noted.

[3] Kraft, Charles A. 2002. 'Contemporary Trends in the Treatment of Spiritual Conflict' in A. Scott Moreau, Tokunboh Adeyemo, David G. Burnett, Bryant L. Myers and Hwa Yung (eds), *Deliver Us From Evil.* (Monrovia, CA: LCWE and MARC, 2002), 187.

The LIWG produced a brief statement[4] from the workshop, noting their concerns:

- To help our Lausanne constituency to stay firmly within the balanced biblical teaching on prayer.
- To provide clarity, reassurance and encouragement to those whom the emphasis is causing confusion and anxiety.
- To harness what is biblical, Christ-exalting and culturally relevant in the new emphasis to the work of evangelization so that it yields lasting fruit.[5]

After the working group meeting, several involved felt that further work needed to be done. Tom Houston embarked on a needs analysis to determine what, if any, further steps a Lausanne group might take. As noted in the preface to *Deliver Us From Evil:*

> Over the next few years an informal group of people who shared a concern about contemporary trends in spiritual warfare and a conviction that the LCWE was in a position to offer guidance discussed the possibility of organising a consultation to address the issues. Eventually, under the direction of the Theology and Strategy Working Group of Lausanne, a planning committee was formally brought together to organize the proposed consultation.[6]

Houston's need analysis after the LIWG Working Group meeting helped frame the planning for the DUFE consultation. For example, given the time constraints and resources likely to be available for the consultation, it was determined that the consultation planners should not attempt a meeting with a purpose of laying out a complete understanding of the nature of the world of the spirits, even though the gathering should seek to be as comprehensive as possible.

> Over the following years, planning committee members engaged in regular teleconferences. In August of 1998 they met together in Oslo, Norway, for three days of planning. There they put together the administrative preparations necessary for the consultation and articulated their concerns which made the consultation necessary.[7]

To Houston's original needs assessment, at the Oslo meeting the DUFE planning committee added that the purpose for the consultation needed to include the response in the life of the church to the struggle against evil as

---

[4] Lausanne Intercession Working Group. 'Statement on Spiritual Warfare (1993): A Working Group Report'. Online: www.lausanne.org/en/documents/ all/consultation-statements/206-statement-on-spiritual-warfare-1993.html; cited 22nd Feb 2013.

[5] Lausanne Intercession Working Group, 'Statement on Spiritual Warfare' (1993).

[6] A. Scott Moreau, 'Preface' in A. Scott Moreau, Tokunboh Adeyemo, David G. Burnett, Bryant L. Myers and Hwa Yung (eds), *Deliver Us from Evil.* (Monrovia, CA: LCWE and MARC, 2002), vii.

[7] Moreau, 'Preface', vii.

well as a biblical understanding of prayer in relation to struggle against evil. Ultimately the reasons for the consultation included the following:[8]

1. A heightened interest in the spiritual warfare among evangelicals, and the growth in numbers and influence of the Pentecostal movement.

2. As the world globalized, Christians in the west experienced ever greater contact with adherents to the major religions of the world as well as the folk religious practices adherents bring with them. Simultaneously, Christians in Majority World settings wrestled with spiritual warfare issues in light of their own worldviews and perspectives. The net result was "fuzzy borders and a variety of interpretations and practices on issues like prayer in spiritual warfare, possession, demonization, and territorial spirits. Among these newer practices and emphases, questions as to what is the biblical, what is extra-biblical and what is non-biblical or even non-Christian have been raised".[9]

3. A flood of books, articles, courses, seminars and workshops were generated around the world, giving prominence to the demonic world.

4. Church responses varied from dismissal with disdain to uncritical acceptance and practice of the newest methods or seminar teachings.

The planning committee expressed concern that spiritual warfare had generated divisiveness among evangelicals which resulted in a significant set of challenges for Lausanne and its focus on world evangelization. Thus, they expressed a need for greater clarity on spiritual warfare, and it was anticipated that the DUFE consultation would help meet that need through 1) the consultation itself,[10] 2) a consultation statement that was anticipated would bring clarity to significant issues related to spiritual warfare,[11] 3) a *Lausanne Occasional Paper*[12] which would put a synopsis into the hands of those who wanted a shorter treatment of the topic, and 4) a compendium of papers from the consultation[13] that would provide the full discussion as a resource for pastors, theologians, missiologists and other Christian leaders.

As Engelsviken noted, "The purpose of this consultation was therefore to develop an understanding of who the Enemy is, how he is working and how we can fight him in order to evangelise all peoples."[14]

---

[8] Moreau, 'Preface', vii-vix.

[9] Moreau, 'Preface', viii.

[10] 'Nairobi 2000 Documents'. Online: www.lausanne.org/en/documents/all/nairobi-2000.html; cited 22nd Feb 2013.

[11] 'Deliver Us from Evil – Consultation Statement.' Online: www.lausanne.org/en/documents/all/nairobi-2000/179-overview.html; cited 22nd Feb 2013.

[12] Tormod Engelsviken, *Spiritual Conflict in Today's Mission.* Lausanne Committee on World Evangelization Occasional Paper 29, A. Scott Moreau (ed). Monrovia, CA: LCWE and MARC, 2001.

[13] A. Scott Moreau, Tokunboh Adeyemo, David G. Burnett, Bryant L. Myers and Hwa Yung (eds), *Deliver Us from Evil* (Monrovia, CA: LCWE and MARC, 2002).

[14] Engelsviken, *Spiritual Conflict in Today's Mission*, 7.

Because of the nature of the consultation topic, it was decided that the consultation would be limited to an invitation-only basis of participants who would represent a diversity of continental origin and ethnicity, theological persuasion, vocation, church ministry and gender. Because so much of spiritual warfare practice and issues are more overtly seen in Majority World settings, the committee chose a venue in such a setting, with the Association of Evangelicals in Africa (AEA) hosting and co-sponsoring the consultation.

Procedure for the DUFE Consultation

After several years of planning and preparation, the DUFE Consultation was convened from August 16th-22nd 2000 in Nairobi, Kenya. DUFE was initiated with a keynote opening address from the Archbishop of Kenya. Over the course of our week together, twelve plenary papers and ten case studies and overviews were delivered. The papers and case studies came from a broad variety of geographic orientations and perspectives. In addition, each day was started with a Bible reading. Almost all of the plenary papers and case studies were made available in advance of the Consultation by being posted on the Lausanne website and through email to the participants.

The Planning Committee notified participants that they were to read all the papers before the presentations, while presenters were strongly encouraged to summarize their papers but to move beyond them during their presentation and open the floor for discussion over the issues raised in the paper. As a result, a significant proportion of our time together was given over to discussion to ensure that all voices were heard.

Additionally, for several hours each day during the consultation a working editorial group met before, in between, and after the presentations with the goal of developing a statement for the consultation. I was given the assignment of serving as the group secretary. It is important to note that we did not go into the consultation with a pre-drafted statement; I literally started our first editorial group meeting with a blank screen!

The Planning Committee's goal was to develop a statement directly from the participants' papers and discussions. Each day the planning committee met, we talked through our impressions of those ideas and issues in which the consultation participants seemed to share a common perspective, then those ideas and issues in which we saw a *lack* of common perspective or outright disagreement, and finally what we felt as an editorial committee accurately captured the important and most significant ideas from the day's proceedings. This required several hours of work as an editorial committee each day. First we listed the salient points we heard, then we talked through each point word by word until we had unanimity among the editorial committee that we had accurately and adequately captured the day's discussion. We repeated this each day of the consultation until the evening before the final day, when (for the first time) we took all the statements and organized them into an outline that made sense to the entire planning committee and through which we would present the Statement to the participations of the consultation for discussion and eventual ratification.

The final day of the consultation was set aside to focus exclusively on the Consultation Statement. Led by the editorial committee, we spent the entire day walking through the Statement point by point as a group with all the participants. Each point was presented, discussed and amended as necessary until we had a unanimous agreement by the participants that the Statement accurately represented the perspective of everyone present. In one case, for example, we were not able to get a unanimous agreement so one of the points that had been under 'Common Ground' section had to be moved to the 'Areas of Tension' section.

As a result, while I was the secretary to the editorial group, it is fair to say that the Statement is not *my* Statement nor the editorial committee's Statement (and thus no 'author' is attached to it). It truly is a document produced by the entire group of forty participants wrestling with significant issues and controversial concerns from a variety of theological, experiential, and cultural perspectives. As I note, "The intention of the Statement is to provide common ground on which all believers may stand as well as elucidate areas of controversy and tension remaining in spiritual conflict."[15]

The Statement itself is divided into six sections. The first two sections introduce the DUFE consultation and the Statement itself, contextualising it by offering a very cursory overview of the consultation and noting prior Lausanne Statements related to spiritual warfare.

The final four sections are the 'meat' of the Statement. 'Common Ground' explores those things on which all consultation participants agreed, including theological affirmations and spiritual conflict practices. 'Warnings' addresses areas of excess in both directions (whether too much spiritual warfare emphasis or too secular of an emphasis which ignores spiritual warfare). 'Areas of Tension' are those areas that the consultation participants could not agree. We felt it important to include this in the statement because we wanted to demonstrate that we could identify these areas and identify them as areas in need of continued discussion. Finally, 'Frontiers that need continuing exploration' are areas which we were not able to directly address but that came up as a result of our week together. Our hope was that this section would provide impetus for ongoing research, dialogue and reflection on ministry practice.

---

[15] Moreau, Preface, x.

Post-Consultation

After the consultation, the Consultation Statement was immediately posted online for dissemination. Within two years, the *Lausanne Occasional Paper* for the consultation and *Deliver Us From Evil* had both been published, further disseminating the discussions and findings. While the LOP is no longer in print, the materials on the consultation remain available on the Lausanne website,[16] providing ongoing resources for this controversial topic.

[16] "Nairobi 2000 Documents."

FAITH AND TRUTH IN A PLURALISTIC, GLOBALIZED WORLD

Stefan Gustavsson

Groucho Marx once famously remarked: "Those are my principles, and if you don't like them … well, I have others." What was once a joke is today a widespread attitude. As Terry Eagleton, 'one of the world's leading literary theorists',[1] writes in his book *After Theory*:

> No idea is more unpopular with contemporary cultural theory than that of absolute truth. The phrase smacks of dogmatism, authoritarianism, a belief in the timeless and universal.[2]

This stands in stark contrast to the repeated affirmation in the Lausanne documents that the Gospel is God's good news *for the whole world.* Again and again the absolute universality, uniqueness and truth are underlined. The *Lausanne Covenant* affirms there is 'only one Saviour and only one gospel',[3] the *Manila Manifesto* that 'Jesus Christ is absolutely unique'[4] and the *Cape Town Commitment* that Jesus is 'the truth of the universe'.[5]

This emphasis on truth has been a hallmark of the Lausanne Movement from its very beginning. At Lausanne 1974 Francis Schaeffer said: "Christianity is a specific body of truth; it is a system and we must not be ashamed of the word *system.* There is truth and we must hold that truth." And he continued: "Christianity is truth, truth that God has told us, and if it is truth, it can answer questions."[6]

One of the must influential messages from Manila was Os Guinness' paper *The Impact of Modernization,* where he wrote: "There are two

---

[1] Paul Vallely, "Terry Eagleton: Class warrior", in *The Independent* (13th Oct 2007). The article is online at: www.independent.co.uk/news/people/profiles/ terry-eagleton-class-warrior-396770.html.

[2] Terry Eagleton, *After Theory* (London: Basic Books, 2003), 103.

[3] The Lausanne Covenant, Article 3: www.lausanne.org/en/documents/lausanne-covenant.html.

[4] *Manila Manifesto*, Affirmation 5: www.lausanne.org/en/documents/manila-manifesto.html.

[5] *Cape Town Commitment*, Part II, Section IIA: *Bearing witness to the truth of Christ in a pluralistic, globalized world:* www.lausanne.org/en/documents/ ctcommitment.html.

[6] Francis Schaeffer, *Form and Freedom in the Church*, Plenary Paper Lausanne 1974; www.lausanne.org/docs/lau1docs/0368.pdf.

dangers in living with modernity. The old fear was that modernity was against religion altogether. Actually, modernity is hostile only to religions that believe in transcendence and truth; and therefore it is hostile to the gospel."[7]

In Cape Town the theme of the first whole day of the conference was *Truth*.[8] Again, Os Guinness gave a clarion call to stand firm on truth. In his message *Why Truth Matters* he gave 'six reasons why truth matters supremely':[9]

> First, only a high view of truth honors the God of Truth.
> Second, only a high view of truth reflects how we come to know and trust God.
> Third, only a high view of truth empowers our best human enterprises.
> Fourth, only a high view of truth can undergird our proclamation and defines of the faith.
> Fifth, only a high view of truth is sufficient for resisting evil and hypocrisy.
> Sixth, only a high view of truth will help our growth and transformation in Christ.

There has from the beginning, as an integral part of the Lausanne Movement, been a strong emphasis on truth. Through the Lausanne conferences and publications we hear constant challenges to ideas that undermine the truth claims of the Gospel. A word count shows that in the *Lausanne Covenant* the word 'truth' appears eight times, in the *Manila Manifesto* nine times, and in the *Cape Town Commitment* 76 times! In an increasingly pluralistic and relativistic culture, Lausanne has called the church to be faithful to the truth.

Now, tensions between a pluralistic culture and the absolute claims of the Gospel are not new; there are many examples in history of similar situations, not least during the first three centuries of the Christian movement. What is new is the globalized world that has resulted in pluralism on a previous unparalleled scale.

I have found it helpful to deal with this tension in three steps, asking for (i) reason, (ii) knowledge and (iii) relationship.

Reason

The easy response to pluralism – the fact of conflicting truth claims around us – is to downplay the whole issue of truth and retort to relativism. Why not say with Mahatma Gandhi: "I believe in the fundamental truth of all

[7] Os Guinness, *The Impact of Modernization.* www.lausanne.org/docs/lau2docs/283.pdf.

[8] Including my own presentation *Dogma and Diversity – Can Evangelical Truth Effectively Face Up to Secularity in a Pluralistic World?* http://conversation.lausanne.org/en/resources/detail/11356#.UtoeRnnnOgQ.

[9] Os Guinness, *Why Truth Matters.* http://conversation.lausanne.org/en/resources/detail/11392#.Utm7aXnnOgQ.

great religions of the world"? Why not say with Muhammad Ali: "Religions all have different names, but they all contain the same truths …"?

The answer is that reason and the principles of logic, like the principle of non-contradiction, have closed that door. Contradictory statements cannot both be true, not in the same sense and at the same time. We cannot, therefore, avoid categories of true and false.

Ravi Zacharias tells this illustrative story from his own experience:

> My philosopher friend went to great lengths to establish the both/and logic as a superior way by which to establish truth.
>
> "So, Dr Zacharias," he said, "when you see one Hindu affirming that God is personal and another insisting that God is not personal, just because it is contradictory you should not see it as a problem. The real problem is that you are seeing that contradiction as a Westerner when you should be approaching it as an Easterner. The both/and is the Eastern way of viewing reality."
>
> After he had belaboured these two ideas of either/or and both/and for some time and carried on his tirade that we ought not to study truth from a Western point of view but rather from an Eastern viewpoint, I finally asked if I could interrupt his unpunctuated train of thought and raise one question. He agreed and put down his pencil.
>
> I said, "Sir, are you telling me that when I am studying Hinduism I *either* use the both/and system of logic *or* nothing else?"
>
> There was pin-drop silence for what seemed an eternity. I repeated my question: "Are you telling me that when I am studying Hinduism I *either* use the both/and logic *or* nothing else? Have I got that right?"
>
> He threw his head back and said, "The either/or does seem to emerge, doesn't it?"
>
> "Indeed, it does emerge," I said. "And as a matter of fact, even in India we look both ways before we cross the street – it is either the bus or me, not both of us."
>
> Do you see the mistake he was making? He was using the either/or logic in order to prove the both/and. The more you try to hammer the law of non-contradiction, the more it hammers you.[10]

Looking at the factual claims of the different great religious traditions of the world, their non-compatibility is obvious. Take their claims about ultimate reality:

> Buddhism: ultimate reality is emptiness.
>
> Hinduism: ultimate reality is oneness.
>
> Judaism: ultimate reality is a personal God.
>
> Islam: ultimate reality is a personal God, who is an absolute unity in his essence.

---

[10] Ravi Zacharias, *Can Man Live Without God?* (Dallas, TX: Word Publishing, 1994), 129.

> Christianity: ultimate reality is a personal God, who is unity and diversity in his essence; he is a triune God of Father, Son and Holy Spirit.

Emptiness, oneness, a personal God, a personal God in absolute unity or a personal God in unity and diversity … it cannot all be true!

Or take another example, what the three Semitic religions say about Jesus. More precisely, what they say about the – according to Christianity – defining events of Jesus' life: his death on a cross and his bodily resurrection from the dead. Again, we are faced with contradictory claims:

> Islam: Jesus did not die and did not rise again, but was taken directly up to heaven.
>
> Judaism: Jesus died but did not rise.
>
> Christianity: Jesus died and rose again.

These claims cannot all be true, since they are mutually exclusive. We cannot reasonable avoid the question of truth.

Knowledge

Even if we agree that reason forces us to accept the distinction between true and false, we have still not solved the real question that pluralism poses. It is one thing to acknowledge that something must be true; it is another thing to claim to have knowledge about that truth. There is a vital distinction between *ontology* (what is) and *epistemology* (what we know). This is the second question we need to deal with, the question of knowledge. Most contemporary suspicion towards truth is anchored here. Even if there is an ultimate truth we cannot, that is the assumption, know that truth. The wisest thing is therefore to ignore the questions altogether or to count every truth claim as an equally good guess.

This has for many become the default position in relation to the ultimate questions of God and meaning. As the American writer Robert A. Heinlein has said:

> Theology is never any help; it is searching in a dark cellar at midnight for a black cat that isn't there. Theologians can persuade themselves of anything.[11]

Many liberal theologians have bought into this train of thought. K G Hammar, for example, former Archbishop of the Lutheran Church in Sweden, writes about the importance of distinguishing GOD from god. GOD with capital letters stands for who God is in himself, which is beyond human knowledge. And god in small letters stands for our picture of God, how we individually or collectively think about God. The Christian faith therefore ends in mysticism. To quote the title of one of the Archbishop's many books: "I do not have the truth, I seek it."[12]

---

[11] Robert A. Heinlein, *Job: A Comedy of Justice* (Del Rey, 1985), 283.

[12] K. G. Hammar & Ami Lönnroth, *Jag har inte sanningen, jag söker den* (Ordfront, 2004).

This is one possibility, that we are excluded from knowledge about the ultimate. But it is not the *only* possibility. Even if we, from our side, cannot break through time and space in order to investigate what is there, God could (if he exists) break into our time and space from his side. And this is precisely what the Judeo-Christian tradition – as well as Islam – is proclaiming. God has revealed himself and made himself known, in many ways.

The Creator's communication with his creation, according to the Christian faith, is rich and includes at least the following aspects:

- *The glory of the created order*, reflecting 'God's invisible qualities – his eternal power and divine nature', as Paul formulates it in Rom 1:20.
- *Human beings*, made in God's image and therefore reflecting aspects of who he is through our creativity, rationality, morality and love.
- *His chosen people Israel*, who received his wonderful promises and witnessed his mighty acts of redemption and judgement.
- *Prophets and Apostles in Old and New Testament times*, who spoke his words and wrote them down for coming generations.
- *The Church*, which is 'the pillar and foundation of the truth'[13] and God's special agent in reaching the world with the good news.
- Above all, *Jesus Christ*, who is God's revelation of himself in his Son.

As John says in the opening chapter of his Gospel: "No one has ever seen God, but the one and only Son, who is himself God and is in closest relationship with the Father, has made him known."[14]

With us as the only source of knowledge, God would be the unseen and unknown, and mysticism the only option. But God has – from his side – made himself known to us, eminently and finally through his Son. Therefore real, even if not exhaustive, knowledge about God is possible.

Relation

If there is a truth and if it is possible to know that truth, what then is the relationship between the truth and us? This is the third question we need to ask. Even with knowledge about the truth, it is still possible to personally be estranged from it – like a son or daughter with knowledge of their father's existence and identity, but still alienated from him.

In Matt 11:27 Jesus makes the most provocative statement imaginable concerning knowledge about God:

---

[13] 1 Tim 3:15.

[14] John 1:18.

> All things have been committed to me by my Father. No one knows the Son except the Father, and no one knows the Father except the Son and those to whom the Son chooses to reveal him.

Michael Green writes this in his commentary:

> Jesus is quietly claiming to be the locus of all revelation. Whatever revelation there may be, dispersed in human intellect and values, in virtuous action, in nature and in the history of humankind, the centre of all God's self-disclosure is Jesus of Nazareth. He fulfils all the hopes of the Old Testament, and is the heart of all revelation. In a dark world lit by candles and lamps, he comes as a searchlight.[15]

The claims are amazing and consist of five distinct aspects. (*i*) All true understanding of God depends on the Son – Jesus – revealing him for us. (*ii*) The Son is sent from the Father as his unique representative. (*iii*) Only the Father fully understands the Son. As Michael Green writes: "It takes God to know God. Only the Father knows the Son."[16] (*iv*) And the reverse, only the Son fully understands the Father. (*v*) The Son, therefore, is the only one who can truly reveal the Father to us.

These five elements go to make up the most astounding claim that has ever been heard on human lips, that the way to know the Father is through Jesus.[17]

So far we have been discussing reason, knowledge and relation to God in a general way. I would like to move on to a New Testament test case, looking into Acts 17.

Paul in Athens

The first generations of Christians, living in the Roman Empire, were challenged by a far-reaching pluralism, and still they were very successful in communicating the Gospel. Through Luke's writing in the book of Acts, we have a window into the work of both Peter and Paul amongst the Gentiles. Of special interest here is Acts 17 and the elaborate presentation of Paul's ministry to the Athenians.

Confronted and stirred by the religious and philosophical diversity in Athens, Paul did not attack them in anger and condemnation, nor did he isolate himself in contempt and fear. Instead he reasoned with people, day by day in the marketplace, discussing, debating and preaching the good news about Jesus. This opened the door to a public presentation at a meeting at the Aeropagos.[18]

---

[15] Green, Michael; *The Message of Matthew – The Bible Speaks Today* (Leicester, UK: IVP, 2001), 140.
[16] Ibid.
[17] Ibid., 141.
[18] Acts 17:16-34.

Tom Wright has helpfully compared Paul's approach in his speech to that of a really good chess player, who

> plays more than one opponent at the same time. Sometimes grand masters will put on a display where they play several different people all at once, walking from one chessboard to the next and making the next move, leaving a string of opponents, with only one game each to concentrate on, baffled and eventually defeated.[19]

In a similar way Paul played simultaneously against polytheistic believers as well as against Epicurean and Stoic philosophers.[20] And he used the three concepts of reason, knowledge and relation.

Paul and Reason

Paul took as his starting point the Athenians' religious beliefs and critiqued their reasoning. Their city was filled with altars and temples and they worshipped many gods. The act of worship indicates by itself that what is worshipped is greater than those who worship. Yet, the whole religious scene in Athens – temples built by humans, images in gold, silver or stone made by human design and skill, and served by human hands – did not make sense. What was worshipped was lower than the worshipper. Reason tells us that if there is a God he must be higher than us and cannot be contained in buildings or stand in need of our services. He is our source and origin; in Athens it was the reverse.

Paul and Knowledge

Paul *affirmed* his audience and some of their knowledge. He mentioned one of their altars and he quoted two of their poets, Epimenides and Aratus. They were not all wrong, but had real insights. Paul could reason with them, without referring to Scripture or any other religious authority, because they all lived in the same created order and shared the same human existence. Therefore Paul took seriously their ability to reflect upon God and upon their place in his world.

At the same time Paul *questioned* his audience. They worshipped what they did not know and they were ignorant. Even when Paul spoke about humans seeking and perhaps finding God, his language was ambivalent with purpose. John Stott writes:

> God's purpose in this has been so that the human beings he has made in his own image might seek him, and perhaps reach out for him, or 'feel after him'

[19] Tom Wright, *Acts for Everyone, Part 2: Chapters 13-28* (London: SPCK, 2008), 86.

[20] See Eckhard J. Schnabel, *Paul the Missionary – Realities, Strategies and Methods* (IVP 2008), 168-183, and Lars Dahle, 'Acts 17:16–34. An Apologetic Model Then and Now? [Diss. Summary]' *Tyndale Bulletin* 53:2 (2002), 313-316.

(RSV), a verb which 'denotes the groping and fumbling of a blind man', and find him. Yet this hope is unfulfilled because of human sin, as the rest of Scripture makes clear. Sin alienates people from God even as, sensing the unnaturalness of their alienation, they grope for him. It would be absurd, however, to blame God for, this alienation, or to regard him as distant, unknowable, uninterested. For he is not far from each one of us. It is we who are far from him. If it were not for sin which separates us from him, he would be readily accessible to us.[21]

Paul and Relation

This leads Paul to a bold – a really bold – challenge. Ultimately, everyone has a problem in relation to God, regardless of our amount of knowledge and how accurate our knowledge is. But God has not abandon us; instead he 'commands all people everywhere to repent'.[22] The reason for this is that God has decided to put the world right again; to judge it and thereby restore it. And it will all happen through *one* man.

Paul moves from the universal and the inclusive – 'all men … every nation of men … the whole earth'[23] – to one unique individual, 'the man he has appointed'.[24] Everyone is created by God, everyone has lost their way and now everyone everywhere must repent and turn to the one. Why? The destiny of all depends on this one individual exclusively. It is through one man – with a unique role as judge of the world – that the door to the future is opened. Only through him can a right relationship with God be restored.

This emphasis on the one – Jesus Christ – comes across, not only in Acts 17, but virtually on every page of the New Testament. Jesus is presented as:

The only way: 'I am the way and the truth and the life. No one comes to the Father except through me.'[25]

The only name: 'Salvation is found in no one else, for there is no other name under heaven given to mankind by which we must be saved.'[26]

The only foundation: 'For no one can lay any foundation other than the one already laid, which is Jesus Christ.'[27]

The only mediator: 'For there is one God and one mediator between God and mankind, the man Christ Jesus, who gave himself as a ransom for all people.'[28]

---

[21] John Stott, *The Message of Acts – The Bible Speaks Today* (Leicester, UK: IVP, 1990), 286.
[22] Acts 17:30.
[23] Acts 17:25-26.
[24] Acts 17:31.
[25] John 14:6.
[26] Acts 4:12.
[27] 1 Cor 3:11.
[28] 1 Tim 2:5-6.

Since the importance of Jesus is so crucial, it is no surprise that God has given public 'proof of this to all men by raising him from the dead'. Paul's proclamation in Athens of Jesus unique role is backed up by the Resurrection as a real historical event. It is proof of the truth proclaimed.

Conclusion

The *Cape Town Commitment* formulates the challenge we have before us very well:

> We urge church leaders, pastors and evangelists to preach and teach the fullness of the biblical gospel as Paul did, in all its cosmic scope and truth. We must present the gospel not merely as offering individual salvation, or a better solution to needs than other gods can provide, but as God's plan for the whole universe in Christ. People sometimes come to Christ to meet a personal need, but they stay with Christ when they find him to be the truth.[29]

And further on:

> We long to see greater commitment to the hard work of robust apologetics. This must be at two levels.
>
> 1. We need to identify, equip and pray for those who can engage at the highest intellectual and public level in arguing for and defending biblical truth in the public arena.
>
> 2. We urge Church leaders and pastors to equip all believers with the courage and the tools to relate the truth with prophetic relevance to everyday public conversation, and so to engage every aspect of the culture we live in.[30]

Or as Paul says in Col 4:4-6:

> Pray that I may proclaim it clearly, as I should. Be wise in the way you act toward outsiders; make the most of every opportunity. Let your conversation be always full of grace, seasoned with salt, so that you may know how to answer everyone.

---

[29] *Cape Town Commitment*, Part II, Section IIA: *Bearing witness to the truth of Christ in a pluralistic, globalized world.*

[30] Ibid.

GOSPEL AND CULTURES IN THE LAUSANNE MOVEMENT

Tite Tiénou

The International Congress on World Evangelization held in Lausanne, in July 1974 was a gathering of Christians 'committed … to the task of world evangelization … despite the diversity of [their] racial and cultural backgrounds' and ecclesial affiliations.[1] In light of this diversity, acknowledged and celebrated at the Congress, it is not surprising that the relationship between the Gospel and human cultures should become one of the 'seven major emphases' of the *Lausanne Covenant*, the document reflecting 'the mind and mood of the Lausanne Congress'.[2] Why and how did the issue of culture occupy such a significant place at the 1974 Congress and in the Lausanne Movement?

The purpose of this essay is to assess how the Lausanne Movement has dealt with culture, one of the perennial issues encountered by Christians in all ages and all places.[3] It will do so by examining the issue of Gospel and culture in the documents produced by the Congress held in Lausanne in 1974 and the Consultation convened in Willowbank in 1978. The

---

[1] 'The Lausanne Covenant, with an exposition and commentary' in *Making Christ Known: Historic Mission Documents from the Lausanne Movement, 1974-1989,* John Stott (ed) (Grand Rapids, MI: William B. Eerdmans Publishing House, 1996), 5, 7. Unless noted otherwise, quotations of documents of the Lausanne Movement of this period will be from the volume indicated above..

[2] 'An Historical Introduction' and 'Preface to the Commentary' in *Making Christ Known*, xv, 5.

[3] The nature and focus of this essay should be understood within the broader context of evangelical discussions of issues related to Christian mission and human cultures. Given its limited scope, no attempt is made to provide either the overall history of the discussions or the nuances of the various positions taken by evangelicals. For succinct treatments of these, one can read the following two chapters in *Appropriate Christianity*, Charles H. Kraft (ed) (Pasadena, CA: William Carey Library, 2005); Charles H. Kraft, 'The Development of Contextualization Theory in Euroamerican Missiology', 15-34; and Wilbert R. Shenk, 'The Missionary Encounter with Culture since the Seventeenth Century', 35-48. Eugene L. Smith's *Mandate for Mission* (New York: Friendship Press, 1968) deserves special mention. According to Smith (73ff), four areas of compromise have plagued the church-in-mission throughout the ages: compromise with the state, with culture, with disunity in the church, and with money.

Congresses of Manila (1989), and Cape Town (2010) will not be considered here because the issue of Gospel and culture was not as central for these two gatherings as it was for the 1974 Congress.[4] We will deal extensively with the 1974 Congress and the *Lausanne Covenant*.

Lausanne 1974[5]

Andrew Walls has observed that "Christianity began the twentieth century as a western religion, and indeed, *the* western religion; it ended the century as a non-western religion, on target to become progressively more so".[6] For worldwide evangelicalism, the de-westernization of the Christian religion was perceptible at the Lausanne Congress where it was noted "with special joy that 50% of the participants, and also of the speakers and the Planning Committee, were from the Third World".[7] In the light of the demographic composition of the Congress and the binary division of the world between mission-sending nations (the west) and mission-receiving nations (the Third World), a view held by many Christians, "culture was a major topic of thought and discussion at Lausanne".[8] In order to clarify the nature of the discussion, we will review the contributions made by McGavran, Padilla and Kato. The ideas expressed by these three speakers at the Congress introduce the discussion of the topic and provide the context for understanding the format and the contents of Paragraph 10 of the *Lausanne Covenant* (Evangelism and Culture).

In his plenary paper entitled 'The Dimensions of World Evangelization', Donald A. McGavran, at the time Senior Professor of Missions at the School of World Mission of Fuller Theological Seminary in Pasadena, California, made several statements relative to evangelization and culture. The most significant ones are:

> A pernicious notion that world evangelism is a concealed form of Eurican imperialism and will destroy the beautiful cultures of Asia, Africa and Latin

[4] This essay is written by one who has been a participant in all three Lausanne Congresses and in the following consultations: Gospel and Culture, Willowbank, Bermuda, 1978; Simple Lifestyle, High Leigh, England, 1980; Consultation on World Evangelization, Pattaya, Thailand, 1980; and Evangelism and Social Responsibility, Grand Rapids, Michigan, 1982.

[5] The reader will note the unusual length of the citations from the documents of the Lausanne Congress. This has been deemed necessary for the purposes of introducing a new generation to the voice and concerns of the speakers.

[6] Andrew F. Walls, *The Cross-Cultural Process in Christian History* (Maryknoll, NY: Orbis Books, and Edinburgh, UK: T. & T. Clark, 2002), 64. Italics in the original.

[7] 'Introduction to the Covenant' in *Making Christ Known,* 7. I have kept 'Third World' for that part of the world that is now commonly referred to as 'Majority World' or 'Two Thirds World'.

[8] 'The Lausanne Covenant', *Making Christ Known,* 40.

> America has recently been retarding world evangelism. The idea is false and must be cleared out of the way. It is not in harmony with the revealed will of God. World evangelism has nothing to do with Eurican imperialism past or present. This Congress does not believe that Eurican culture is God's chosen culture.
>
> According to the Bible, God has no favorites among cultures. He accepts them all.
>
> The cultures as they stand are incredibly varied and rich. Yet every one is a mixture of good and bad components.
>
> Evangelism redeems each culture whose adherents believe the Gospel and *makes each more beautiful while it remains itself.* Evangelization is the greatest benefit possible to confer on any culture. Far from destroying it, evangelization brings out its latent goodness, which Christianity, the world religion, rapidly disseminates to all men.[9]

While many Congress participants agreed with McGavran, others distanced themselves from the ideas he expressed, especially his view that 'world evangelism has nothing to do with Eurican imperialism past or present'. For them, this statement is problematic because McGavran does not acknowledge the long and complex history of the unhappy equation of the Christian faith with the culture of the Gospel proclaimer, a history dating back to Chapter 15 of the book of Acts. Especially troubling is McGavran's quick dismissal of the link between European and American imperialism and world evangelization. McGavran was certainly aware of the link between colonialism and mission. It is therefore surprising that he did not make this link explicit in his address. For many participants from Africa, Asia and Latin America, the continued identification of Christianity with the cultures of Europe and Europeanized societies was, indeed, a significant issue in mission and world evangelization. Padilla's plenary paper at the Congress expressed the sentiment of those participants.

At the time of the Congress, C. René Padilla, based in Buenos Aires, Argentina, was Associate General Secretary for Latin America of the International Fellowship of Evangelical Students. In his paper entitled 'Evangelism and the World', Padilla warned that "we cannot fool ourselves about the actual historic situation of the church in relation to the world", and pointed to the fact that a "form in which worldliness enters the life and mission of the church today is the adaptation of the Gospel to the 'spirit of the times'".[10] Padilla then provides 'two examples' of the church's 'adaptation to the "spirit of the times"': 'secular Christianity' and 'culture Christianity'. Although both forms of adaption distort the Gospel and are

---

[9] Donald A. McGavran, 'The Dimensions of World Evangelization' in *Let the Earth Hear His Voice: International Congress on World Evangelization, Lausanne, Switzerland,* J. D. Douglas (ed) (Minneapolis, MN: World Wide Publications, 1975) 96, 97. Italics in the original. 'Eurican' is the adjective deriving from 'Eurica' meaning Europe and America, one of McGavran's neologisms.

[10] René Padilla, 'Evangelism and the World' in *Let the Earth Hear his Voice,* 123.

cultural, we will focus our attention here on 'culture Christianity'. Padilla defines 'culture Christianity' as 'the identification of Christianity with a culture or cultural expression'[11] and provides the following specific instances:

> In the sixteenth century, Latin America was conquered in the name of the Catholic king and queen of Spain. The conquest was not only military but religious as well. It was concerned with implanting not merely Spanish culture, but a 'Christian culture' … In the nineteenth century, the Christian missionary outreach was so closely connected with European colonialism that in Africa and Asia Christianity would become identified as the white man's religion.
>
> Today [1974], however, there is another form of 'culture Christianity' that has come to dominate the world scene – 'the American Way of Life'.
>
> In light of the powerful influence that this type of Christianity has had in what is known as 'the mission field', the Gospel that is preached today in the majority of countries of the world bears the marks of 'the American Way of Life'.[12]

One may object to Padilla's criticisms by pointing out their un-nuanced over-generalizations. Indeed, these observations could have been more nuanced but they highlight an enduring problem that must be taken seriously in all discussions relative to the issue of Gospel and human cultures.

Contrary to McGavran's claim, and in support of Padilla's warnings, there are numerous examples of cultural superiority in the history of Protestant mission practice since the seventeenth century.[13] This should not be a surprise because we know "that the gospel never comes alone to a culture: it is always brought by someone who is part of some cultural form

[11] René Padilla, 'Evangelism and the World' in *Let the Earth Hear His Voice,* 125.

[12] René Padilla, 'Evangelism and the World' in *Let the Earth Hear His Voice,* 125.

[13] In an essay of this size and nature, it is impossible to take into account the vast and varied literature on colonialism and evangelization and mission. A few titles will suffice: T. O. Beidelman, *Colonial Evangelism: A Socio-Historical Study of an East Africa Mission at the Grassroots* (Bloomington, IN: Indiana University Press, 1982); Orishatukeh Faduma, 'Success and Drawbacks to Missionary Work in Africa' in *Africa and the American Negro: Addresses and Proceedings of the Congress on Africa, Atlanta, 1895,* J. W. E. Bowen (ed) (Atlanta, GA: Gammon Theological Seminary, 1896), 125-136; Ajith Fernando, 'Evangelism – An Extension of Colonialism?' in *World Evangelization,* No. 35 (June 1984), 1-3; Richard V. Pierard, 'The World Missionary Conference, Edinburgh, 1910: Its Shortcomings and Historical Significance' in *Missiongeschichte als Geschichte der Globalisierung von Wissen,* Ulrich van der Heyden and Andreas Feldtkeller (eds), (Stuttgart, Germany: Franz Steiner Verlag, 2012), 299-306; Bernard Salvaing, *Les missionnaires à la rencontre de l'Afrique au XIXe siècle* (Paris, France: Editions l'Harmattan, 1994).

of Christianity".[14] Gospel proclaimers may unwittingly transplant their own 'cultural form of Christianity' but, when they possess an acute sense of cultural superiority, they willingly promote what Ghanaian David Kpobi calls 'cultural mission', a situation "whereby the church seeks to transfer what is perceived as a superior culture to a people through evangelization".[15] It is worth noting that Kpobi is describing the mission practice of the Presbyterian Church of Ghana in Northern Ghana at the end of the twentieth century. Strange as it may seem, this practice coincides with the view expressed in the message of the Imperial German Colonial Office to the Edinburgh 1910 World Missionary Conference: "The German Colonial Office recognizes with satisfaction and gratitude that the endeavours for the spread of the Gospel are followed by the blessings of civilization and culture in all countries."[16] The reproduction of 'cultural forms of Christianity' is, therefore, a more general problem besetting Christians from all continents and from the various cultures of humankind. What should Gospel proclaimers do?

At the Lausanne Congress there was a recognition that Gospel proclaimers must make sure the Gospel is understood by people in their social and cultural situations and that the Christian faith should be expressed in the plurality of human cultures. McGavran proposed the following: "The true goal [of world evangelization] is to multiply, *in every piece of the magnificent mosaic, truly Christian churches which fit that piece*, are closely adapted to its culture, and recognized by its non-Christians as 'our kind of show'."[17] Byang H. Kato, based in Nairobi, Kenya, at the time and General Secretary of the Association of Evangelicals of Africa and Madagascar, took a similar approach in his paper entitled 'The Gospel, Cultural Context and Religious Syncretism'. Kato defined 'contextualization' as 'making concepts or ideals relevant in a given situation' and affirmed that "since the Gospel message is inspired but the mode of its expression is not, contextualization of the modes of expression is not only right but necessary".[18] But Kato was concerned about syncretism and the possibility of the Gospel being 'compromised'. This concern may be the reason for his suggestion that:

---

[14] Robert J. Schreiter, 'Faith and Cultures: Challenges to a World Church' *Theological Studies,* 50 (1989), 745.

[15] David Kpobi, 'The PCG, a Church in Mission in the 21st Century: Renewal and Reformation' in *Akrofi-Christaller Centre News,* No. 25 (July-Dec 1999), 11.

[16] W. H. T. Gairdner, '*Edinburgh 1910': An Account and Interpretation of the World Missionary Conference* (Edinburgh and London: Oliphant, Anderson and Ferrier, 1910), 45.

[17] Donald A. McGavran, 'The Dimensions of World Evangelization', 101. Italics in the original.

[18] Byang H. Kato, 'The Gospel, Cultural Context and Religious Syncretism' in *Let the Earth Hear his Voice,* 1217.

> Contextualization can take place in the area of liturgy, dress, language, church service, and any other form of expression of the Gospel truth … Not only should the message be preached in the language best understood by the congregation, but terminology of theology should be expressed the way common people can understand. But theological meanings must not be sacrificed at the altar of comprehension.[19]

Kato's understanding of contextualization reflects the sentiment of many evangelicals who, in 1974, were cautious in adopting the relative new terminology of "contextualization".

Taken as a whole, the ideas of McGavran, Padilla and Kato indicate the state of evangelical wrestling with contextualization at the time and shed light on the contents, emphasis and formulation of Paragraph 10 of the *Lausanne Covenant*. They also explain why, in his commentary on the covenant, John Stott states that Paragraph 10 ('Evangelism and Culture' and paragraph eleven 'Education and Leadership') 'handle two related subjects, culture and leadership'. "Both," he writes, "have to do with churches which come into being as the fruit of missionary labour."[20]

Regarding the issue of the relationship between the Gospel and human cultures, treated specifically in Paragraph 10,[21] one can make several observations. First, the interest in Gospel and culture seems to focus on "the development of strategies for world evangelization" and on "imaginative pioneering methods". Secondly, such strategies and methods will produce "churches deeply rooted in Christ and closely related to their culture". Thirdly, Paragraph 10 is clear that "culture must always be tested and judged by Scripture". Fourthly, there is acknowledgement that "the Gospel does not presuppose the superiority of any culture to another". Fifthly, there is recognition that "missions have all too frequently exported with the Gospel an alien culture, and churches have sometimes been in bondage to culture rather than to Scripture". Sixthly, Paragraph 10 calls "Christ's evangelists" to "humbly seek to empty themselves of all but their personal authenticity in order to become the servants of others", but falls short of issuing a call for lament, confession and repentance. The absence of a call for lament and confession was noted by some participants, especially so by those who formed an *Ad Hoc Group*, during the Congress.

The *Ad Hoc Group* gave itself the task of probing the 'Theology Implications of Radical Discipleship'. It produced a statement dealing with numerous issues and containing a list of confessions. The following two confessions deal with the issue of Gospel and culture: We confess that "We have often been in bondage to a particular culture and sought to spread it in the name of Jesus"; that "We have not been aware of when we have debased and distorted the Gospel by acceptance of a contrary value

[19] Byang H. Kato, ibid.

[20] John Stott 'The Lausanne Covenant' in *Making Christ Known,* 40.

[21] Paragraph 10 can be found on 39 of *Making Christ Known.*

system".[22] While the *Lausanne Covenant* did not include a statement of confession on matters pertaining to Gospel and culture, confession appeared elsewhere in the document. In Paragraph 7, 'Co-operation in evangelism', one reads: "We confess that our testimony has sometimes been marred by sinful individualism and needless duplication." Perhaps one should not speculate on the reasons for the difference between Paragraphs 7 and 10 (confession in one but not the other), but the difference is striking.

Now, forty years after Lausanne 1974, what should be the overall assessment of its treatment of the relationship between the Gospel and human cultures? I offer a threefold assessment. In the first place, the focus on strategy was too narrow, and this limited the impact of the work done in the Lausanne Movement. Secondly, Lausanne 1974 did not sufficiently extend the discussion on Gospel and culture to all aspects of Christian life, including theology, as the deliberate choice of the word *evangelization* would have encouraged. Bishop Jack Dain, Executive Chairman of the Congress, explained this choice by affirming that "Lausanne is a Congress on evangelization, not a Congress on evangelism", because "we not only need to think of evangelism, that is, the proclamation of the Gospel, but the whole task given to us by the risen Christ. This, I think, is more aptly called evangelization".[23] Thirdly, Lausanne 1974 did not concern itself with matters related to the definition of culture. This is not surprising because "many [Congress participants] were introduced for the first time at Lausanne to the problems raised by culture".[24] In the years following the Congress, the Lausanne Movement would devote time and energy to aspects of this threefold assessment. An example of this is the international consultation on Gospel and Culture convened in Willowbank, Bermuda, in January 1978.

Willowbank 1978

The Willowbank 1978 international consultation on Gospel and Culture was the second of six consultations sponsored by the Lausanne Theology and Education Group between 1977 and 1982.[25] The Lausanne Committee

---

[22] 'Theology Implications of Radical Discipleship' in *Let the Earth Hear His Voice,* 1295. It is noteworthy that the report of the *Ad Hoc Group* was included in the official volume of the Congress proceedings. This illustrates one of the remarkable characteristics of the Lausanne Movement from the very beginning: a genuine desire to foster mutual understanding and co-operation among Evangelicals.

[23] *The Whole Gospel for the Whole Church: Story of Lausanne II Congress on World Evangelization, Manila 1989,* Alan Nichols (ed) (Charlotte, NC: LCWE, and Ventura, CA: Regal Books, 1989), 16.

[24] John Stott, 'An Historical Introduction' in *Making Christ Known,* xv.

[25] Although the Willowbank Consultation was convened by the Lausanne Theology and Education Group (LTEG), it was co-sponsored by the Strategy Working Group (SWG).

for World Evangelization established the Lausanne Theology and Education Group 'to promote theological reflection on issues related to world evangelization and, in particular, to explore the implications of the *Lausanne Covenant*'.[26]

Paragraph 10 of the Covenant, as we have noted above, raised issues needing further exploration. The exploration of these issues was the task given to those assembled at Willowbank for an international consultation on Gospel and Culture. The work of the consultation resulted in the publication of the book containing the papers presented at the event, *Gospel and Culture,* edited by John Stott and Robert Coote (Pasadena, CA: William Carey Library, 1979) as well as the *Willowbank Report – Consultation on Gospel and Culture* (*Lausanne Occasional Paper 2*).

The consultation set four goals. These goals established the framework of the consultation and, ultimately, the drafting of the results were communicated to the public. For the purposes of this essay, I will note only one of the goals: "To develop our understanding of the interrelation of the gospel and culture with special reference to God's revelation, to our interpretation and communication of it, and to the response of the hearers in their conversion, their churches and their lifestyle."[27] Were this and the other three goals reached at the consultation? This question can be answered only after a careful and complete analysis of the *Willowbank Report*, a task beyond the scope of this investigation. In my opinion, Willowbank 1978 has made significant contributions to an evangelical understanding of the relationship between the Gospel and culture in at least three areas: the definition of culture, the emphasis on humility on the part of messengers of the Gospel, and a clear statement on the nature and content of the Gospel. I will make observations on the first and the third.

The definition of culture is found in Section 2 of the *Willowbank Report.* After acknowledging that "culture is a term which is not easily susceptible of definition", the *Report* states: "In the broadest sense, it means simply a patterned way in which people do things together." This is closely related to Paul Hiebert's definition of culture as "the more or less integrated systems of behavior and products shared by a group of people who organize and regulate what they think, feel, and do".[28] This section of the *Willowbank Report* also recognizes the plurality of cultures. "Cultures," we read, "are never static; there is a continuous process of change."[29] This definition of culture offered hope for the possibility of an open and fruitful discussion among evangelicals worldwide.

---

[26] John Stott 'An Historical Introduction' in *Making Christ Known,* xvi.

[27] 'The Willowbank Report on Gospel and Culture' in *Making Christ Known,* 77.

[28] Paul G. Hiebert *Anthropological Insights for Missionaries (Grand* Rapids, MI: Baker Book House, 1985), 30.

[29] 'The Willowbank Report on Gospel and Culture' in *Making Christ Known,* 78, 79.

In Section 5, the *Willowbank Report* considers 'The Content and Communication of the Gospel'. Although there is no definition of the Gospel, stated explicitly as such, the following statement can be taken as defining the Gospel: "The Gospel is to be found in the Bible. In fact, there is a sense in which the whole Bible is Gospel, from Genesis to Revelation."[30] This understanding of the Gospel is accepted today by evangelicals across the spectrum of evangelicalism, from Padilla to Hesselgrave.[31]

John Stott provides this very helpful summary of the contributions of Willowbank 1978. According to him, the *Willowbank Report*

> considers [culture's] influence in six areas – in the writers and the readers of the Bible (since they and we are both culturally conditioned), in the preaching and the receiving of the gospel (contextualization and conversion), in the formation of the church and in ethical behavior.[32]

In many ways Willowbank 1978 represents a high-water mark in the Lausanne Movement in matters pertaining to the relationship between the Gospel and human cultures. It probed the issue with greater depth and it provided the stimulus for further work in this area. It was at this consultation that contextualization acquired greater acceptance in evangelical circles. Overall, though the Willowbank Consultation acknowledged "cultural diversity and the development of a culturally pluriform Church",[33] it did not deal with the full ramifications of this diversity. In the years following Willowbank, in evangelicalism and in the Lausanne Movement, the implications of cultural diversity in Christianity were captured in one word: *contextualization.*

Gospel and Culture in the Lausanne Movement since Willowbank

The Consultation on Gospel and Culture appeared to have created an evangelical consensus regarding the vision of contextualization, a vision whereby "Jesus Christ and his kingdom will find fuller expression in the whole life of people in every culture".[34] Perhaps this is the reason why, in the 1970s and 80s, evangelicals devoted significant energy and resources to the issue of contextualization. The numerous publications on the topic, in these decades, attest to evangelicals' engagement with contextualization. A sampling of these publications is provided in the bibliography below.

---

[30] 'The Willowbank Report' in *Making Christ Known,* 86.

[31] C. René Padilla *Mission between the Times* (Grand Rapids, MI: William B. Eerdmans Publishing House, 1985), 62-82; David J. Hesselgrave in *Paradigms in Conflict* (Grand Rapids, MI: Kregel Publications, 2005), 245.

[32] John Stott 'An Historical Introduction' in *Making Christ Known,* xvii.

[33] Aylward Shorter *Inculturation in Africa: The Way Forward* (Chicago, IL: CCGM Publications, 2005), 7.

[34] 'Gospel contextualization revisited' in *MARC Newsletter,* Number 97-3 (Sept 1997), 6.

In January 1978, soon after the Willowbank Consultation, the journal *Gospel in Context* was launched. In the *Premiere Issue* the publisher stated the purpose of the new journal in these words:

> *Gospel in Context* will be about 'contextualization', the challenges presented by the new awareness of the Church's inevitable incarnation in particular societies and cultures for a faithful proclamation and demonstration of the Gospel of Jesus Christ. It will focus on the critical problem of how the Church can avoid the kind of captivity to particular cultures or class interests which blunts its faithfulness as a messenger of the Gospel while allowing the Gospel to speak meaningfully within particular contexts.[35]

For a brief period, before it ceased publication abruptly, *Gospel in Context* generated a healthy conversation on Gospel and culture among evangelicals. In addition to this journal, articles on contextualization appeared in other evangelical periodicals. Books dealing with contextualization, or Gospel and culture, were published. As the literary output on these related topics increased, evangelical consensus, if it existed, decreased. For evangelicals in the United States, the 1979 publication of Charles H. Kraft's *Christianity in Culture: A Study in Dynamic Biblical Theologizing in Cross-Cultural Perspective* brought to light significant differences among evangelicals.

Evangelicals could agree, in principle, that "historically the Church has taken certain peculiarities from the national and racial traits of those who have composed it".[36] They were less unified on the possibility of extending the influence of "national and racial traits" to theology. Kraft's book suggested the latter and it was met with sharp criticism, in print and in conversations. Some authors portrayed Kraft as an advocate of continuity between the Gospel and culture, a view incompatible with evangelicalism in their judgement. Edward N. Gross, for example, wondered if Kraft could still be considered an evangelical since "he, evidently, does not appreciate the irreconcilable differences between Christianity and anthropology".[37] Carl F. H. Henry is another evangelical who expressed strong disagreement with Kraft. In his 1980 review article of Kraft's book, with the title 'The Cultural Relativizing of Revelation', Henry understood Kraft to suggest the 'normativity of anthropology'. According to Henry, Kraft's view is incompatible with 'Judeo-Christian revelation'. Henry warns that "the normativity of biblical theology cannot survive alongside the normativity of anthropology".[38] In their criticisms of Kraft's book, Gross and Henry

[35] Stephen C. Knapp, 'Introducing "Gospel in Context"' in *Gospel in Context,* Vol. I, No.1 (Jan 1978). No page indicated.

[36] A. W. Tozer, *Let My People Go: The Life of Robert A. Jaffray* (Harrisburg, PA: Christian Publications, 1947), 39.

[37] Edward N. Gross, *Is Charles Kraft an Evangelical? A Critique of Christianity in Culture* (published by the author, 1985), 101.

[38] Carl F. H. Henry, 'The Cultural Relativizing of Revelation' in *Trinity Journal, NS* (1980): 157, 164.

seem to favour the view of radical incompatibility or discontinuity between the Gospel and culture.

Other evangelicals joined Gross and Henry. One example will suffice. In 1988 *Culture and Biblical Hermeneutics,* by William J. Larkin, was published. It was not a direct reply to Kraft but, in this book, Larkin dismisses the idea of accommodation to culture. For him, "the Bible as divine revelation has its source *a priori* outside any given culture".[39] In one of his statements, Larkin disagrees with the idea of the cultural conditioning of the Bible. He writes: "if the message is applicable to all cultures, the language in which it was revealed must not have cultural conditionedness as its basic characteristic."[40]

On the issue of Gospel and culture, Kraft, Gross, Henry and Larkin, evangelicals from the United States, have articulated, as we have seen, viewpoints reminiscent of those attributed to Clement of Alexandria: continuity (Kraft), and Tertullian of Carthage: discontinuity (Gross, Henry, Larkin). One can find a similar pattern among evangelicals of other continents. Though the words continuity and discontinuity are convenient labels, they imply rigidity, and individuals seldom use either one of them to describe their own position. This raises the question: Is there a correct evangelical view of relating the Gospel to human cultures? Attempts to answer that question once and for all may be futile. Given the complexity of the issue, evangelicals should reconcile themselves to the fact that "there is no single correct way to relate to a given culture as a whole, or even to its dominant thrust".[41] Evangelicals have much work to do before they are comfortable with the ambiguity entailed in this suggestion. Many evangelicals seek a clear and definite evangelical position in matters related to Gospel and culture. The debate over contextualization provides an additional illustration.

Evangelicals have recognized the importance of contextualization since the Lausanne Congress. They probed it further at the Willowbank Consultation and in subsequent years. On the topic of contextualization, evangelical positions represent a spectrum similar to the one observed above regarding the relationship between the Gospel and culture.

The word *contextualization* caused uneasiness for evangelicals, in part, because of its perceived link to theological liberalism. In 1999 David Hesselgrave stated that "in the early 1970s liberals coined the word 'contextualization' and infused it with a meaning that detracted from biblical theology and mission. In response, conservatives adopted the word

---

[39] William J. Larkin, *Culture and Biblical Hermeneutics* (Grand Rapids, MI: Baker Book House, 1988), 191-192.

[40] William J. Larkin, *Culture and Biblical Hermeneutics,* 228.

[41] Miroslav Volf, 'When Gospel and Culture Intersect: Notes on the Nature of Christian Difference' in *Pentecostalism in Context: Essays in Honor of William W. Menzies*, Wonsuk Ma and Robert Menzies (eds) (Sheffield, UK: Sheffield Academic Press, 1997), 233.

but redefined it to agree with Scripture and enhance mission".[42] Hesselgrave's statement alludes to the fact that the word *contextualization* originated in the work of the *Theological Education Fund (TEF),* an organization established in 1958 by the International Missionary Council. The *Theological Education Fund* adopted the word *contextualization* as its focus for the years 1970 to 1977, the so-called Third Mandate. But, did the *TEF* "infuse it with a meaning that detracted from biblical theology and mission"? Not everyone would agree with Hesselgrave. After all, as Christine Lienemann-Perrin writes,

> The TEF is … credited with having pioneered the promotion of what came to be known as 'contextualization' – the embodiment of the Gospel in different socio-economic-cultural situations, as a means of releasing its transforming, liberating and reconciling power … But it would be more accurate to say that the TEF gave a name to a dynamic process which was there in the first place, and joined forces with this process.[43]

Evangelicals were familiar with the history of the *Theological Education Fund.* They did agree with the need for 'the embodiment of the Gospel' but some wondered if a new word was required to describe that process. Some evangelicals, such as Bruce Fleming, preferred the word *indigenization* and suggested it as the evangelical alternative to *contextualization.* According to Fleming, "properly speaking, evangelicals do not, and should not, contextualize the gospel. The indigenizing, or more properly, the context-indigenizing of the gospel, should be the method of evangelical work".[44]

Fleming's suggestion did not gain wide acceptance. Most evangelicals in the Lausanne Movement chose to use the word *contextualization.* In 1997 Bryant Myers noted that "contextualization is accepted dogma now. Studying local culture and language is important so we can answer the question, 'How can we best present the gospel in this place or to this people?'".[45] For Myers, and for many evangelicals, contextualization is useful as a method and a strategy.[46] In June 1997, fifty-two evangelical

---

[42] David J. Hesselgrave, 'Redefinng Holism' in *Evangelical Missions Quarterly,* Vol. 35, No. 3 (July 1999), 281.

[43] Christine Lienemann-Perrin, *Training for a Relevant Ministry: Study of the Work of the Theological Education Fund* (Madras, India: The Christian Literature Society, 1981), x.

[44] Bruce C. E. Fleming *Contextualization of Theology: An Evangelical Assessment* (Pasadena, CA: William Carey Library, 1980), 78.

[45] Bryant Myers 'Research? What for?' in *MARC Newsletter,* Number 97-3 (Sept 1997), 3.

[46] In Jan 1978 the *Evangelical Missions Quarterly* devoted an entire issue to contextualization, with several articles focusing on method and strategy. A more recent evangelical focus on method and strategy as it pertains to contextualization is A. Scott Moreau's *Contextualization in World Missions: Mapping and Assessing Evangelical Models* (Grand Rapids, MI: Kregel Academic and Professional, 2011). Interestingly, according to the publisher, the book will 'help readers spread the Gospel more effectively'.

missiologists, theologians and mission practitioners met in Haslev, Denmark, to assess the progress made by evangelicals in the area of contextualization since Willowbank 1978. They expressed "disappointment" and "penitence" over evangelical preoccupation with method and they made a plea to evangelicals to "seek ... a deeper understanding of contextualization by moving from contextualization as a method towards it as a way of life and a way of being more fully human".[47] In my opinion, the assessment made in 1997 is still valid today: evangelicals have much work to do before they reach a comfortable consensus on the implications of contextualization in *discipleship.* Ultimately, contextualization fosters the development of Christian faith with many cultural centres. Accepting the "polycentric nature of Christianity" may cause uneasiness for some people, "nevertheless returning to a Christianity with only one cultural centre is now an impossibility".[48] The Lausanne Movement seems to be moving forward in this direction.

The *Cape Town Commitment* captures the current sentiment in the Lausanne Movement in these words: "We long to see the gospel embodied and embedded in all cultures, redeeming them from within so that they may display the glory of God and the radiant fullness of Christ".[49] This shows the significance of the Lausanne Movement as a major contributor to global evangelical conversations on the issue of Gospel and culture. This issue has not been as central in Lausanne II (Manila 1989) or Lausanne III (Cape Town 2010) as it was in Lausanne I (1974) but the Movement has continued to build on the foundations established in 1974 and 1978.

---

[47] 'Gospel contextualization revisited', *MARC Newsletter,* Number 97-3 (Sept 1997), 6. About the same time, in 1998, Ralph Winter expressed his frustration with contextualization in this pithy statement: "OK, forget the turgid theologies of contextualization." See his 'De-Westernization Tomorrow' in *Mission Frontiers,* Vol. 20, Nos. 9-12 (Sept-Dec 1998), 24.

[48] Tite Tiénou 'Forming Indigenous Theologies' in *Toward the 21st Century in Christian Mission,* by James M. Phillips and Robert T. Coote (eds) (Grand Rapids, MI: William B. Eerdmans Publishing Company, 1993), 248-249.

[49] *The Cape Town Commitment: A Confession of Faith and a Call to Action,* Part I 'Confession of Faith', Paragraph 7.

Evangelism and Social Responsibility: The Making of a Transformational Vision

Al Tizon

Shortly after Ron Sider, one of the pioneers of evangelical holistic mission, returned from Cape Town 2010, he wrote the following reflection: "At Lausanne III ... the biblical obligation to combine evangelism and social action was assumed by almost everyone. A deep powerful longing to share the gospel with everyone who is not a believer pervaded the Congress. But so did the call to seek justice for the poor, care for the environment, combat HIV/AIDS, and work for peace."[1]

For some – I think especially of younger evangelicals who may view the fundamentalist-modernist split that plagued much of the twentieth century as ancient history – this reflection may seem somewhat benign, but as Sider concludes, "Lausanne III ... reflected the huge change that has occurred among evangelicals all around the world. Holistic ministry – combining evangelism and social action – is now part of our spiritual DNA."[2] The very fact that younger evangelicals view the evangelism vs. social concern issue as a curious debate of a less enlightened time attests to the maturing of an evangelical social vision. The Lausanne Movement has been catalytic in this shift.

Indeed, one of the most important developments to have flowed out of the now forty-year-old missionary movement called Lausanne has been the restoration of social responsibility to the evangelical missionary agenda. And because this social vision has been developed by and among evangelicals, it has always been cultivated in the uncompromising soil of world evangelization.

However, as much as the Lausanne Movement itself should be credited for restoring social concern on the evangelical missionary agenda, it was a lesser known but no less potent movement that at once flowed from, and reacted to, the cautious posture that Lausanne leaders often took through the years with regard to evangelical social involvement. This Movement, which emerged primarily out of the Two Thirds World, mined the richness

---

[1] Ron Sider, 'Evangelizing the World: Reflections on Lausanne III,' in *Prism* (Jan-Feb 2011), 48.
[2] Ibid., 48.

of the word 'transformation', thus eventually becoming known as the Transformational Movement or 'Mission as Transformation'.[3]

This Movement took the evangelical social vision to unprecedented heights since the Great Reversal.[4] In order to understand the evangelical journey toward holistic mission, the Transformational vision – what it is, how it came to be, who the chief proponents were/are, etc. – must be in full view. The purpose of this chapter, then, is to focus on the development of the Transformational social vision, and thereby shed light on the holistic thrust within and beyond the Lausanne Movement as a whole.

Affirmation of Socio-Political Involvement at Lausanne I

For much of the twentieth century, evangelicals suffered from a kind of missionary myopia, viewing mission narrowly in terms of verbal proclamation (evangelism) at the expense of social justice. Although this myopia was a consequence of a debate that sizzled most intensely in North America, the disease went global through North America's strong missionary movement.[5] Scholars across disciplines have offered their respective views to explain this myopia, but they share at least one common explanation. They all agree that it largely developed as a reaction to ultra-liberal definitions of mission in the early part of the twentieth century that emphasized social justice at the expense of evangelization (a myopia of another sort).

Lausanne 74 marks the first serious corporate attempt to correct this short-sightedness among evangelicals. Billy Graham – the inspirational figurehead and catalyst of Lausanne I – listed four hopes in his opening address at the Congress, the third of which pertains directly to the social question.[6] He announced at the outset, "I trust we can state ... the

---

[3] I humbly refer you to my book, *Transformation after Lausanne* (Oxford et al.: Regnum, 2008), which is precisely about the Transformational Movement. In fact, this chapter reflects – and sometimes even culls whole sections verbatim – the basic thrust of that book.

[4] In *Transformation after Lausanne,* I define the Great Reversal as, "the move of evangelicals from spearheading social reform in the eighteenth and nineteenth centuries to retreating almost totally from mainstream society by the late 1920s" (22-23). For a much more detailed sociological perspective, see David Moberg's classic, *The Great Reversal: Evangelism Versus Social Concern* (Philadelphia, PA and New York, NY: J. B. Lippincott, 1972).

[5] Tizon, *Transformation after Lausanne,* 24-26.

[6] Billy Graham, 'Why Lausanne?' in James D. Douglas (ed), *Let the Earth Hear His Voice: International Congress on World Evangelization* (Minneapolis, MN: World Wide Publications, 1975), 34. The other three of Graham's stated hopes were: 1. 'I would like to see the Congress frame a biblical declaration on evangelism'; 2. 'I would like to see the church challenged to complete the task of world evangelization'; the third is discussed above; and 4. 'I hope that a new

relationship between evangelism and social responsibility ... [which] disturbs many believers. Perhaps Lausanne can help to clarify it."[7] This opening statement demonstrates that by the time of the Congress, Graham and many others came prepared to settle this issue.

The *Lausanne Covenant*, the official resultant document of the first Congress, includes 'Christian Social Responsibility' as Article 5 (of fifteen key Articles),[8] thereby clearly recognizing and affirming social concern as essential to the task of world evangelization. Article 5, which basically synthesized the papers presented at the Congress by René Padilla, Samuel Escobar and Carl Henry,[9] dealt with the issue most directly.[10] In his analytical treatment of the contents of the Article, Klaus Bockmühl extracts and then comments on the nine 'verbs of action' contained in it, offering a detailed interpretation of the social vision articulated at the Congress.[11]

At least two overall themes emerge from his analysis: 1. To act prophetically in society, denouncing injustices and calling governments to repentance, and 2. To demonstrate and promote the righteousness of the Kingdom of God for and among the oppressed. This summary of the Lausanne social vision points out its two-pronged reactive and pro-active elements. But obviously, these themes only hint at a social ethic; it does not provide one. Article 5 of the *Lausanne Covenant* simply and officially affirmed socio-political involvement, thus validating it among evangelicals as part of the missionary task.

---

koinonia or fellowship among evangelicals of all persuasions will be developed throughout the world'.

[7] Graham, 'Why Lausanne?', 34.

[8] 'The Lausanne Covenant', in John R. W. Stott (ed), *Making Christ Known: Historic Mission Documents from the Lausanne Movement, 1974-1989* (Grand Rapids, MI and Cambridge, UK: Eerdmans, 1996), 24.

[9] Klaus Bockmühl, *Evangelicals and Social Ethics* (trans. David T. Priestly; Downers Grove, IL: InterVarsity, 1979), 8-12. These papers to which Bockmühl refers are available in James D. Douglas (ed), *Let the Earth His Voice* (Minneapolis, MN: World Wide Publications, 1976), the official reference volume of Lausanne I. Padilla's address entitled 'Evangelism and the World' (116-146) and Escobar's 'Evangelism and Man's Search for Freedom, Justice, and Fulfillment' (303-326) were both plenary papers, while Henry's address 'Christian Personal and Social Ethics in Relation to Racism, Poverty, War, and Other Problems' (1163-1182) provided a foundation for the sessions of a special committee on ethics.

[10] C. René Padilla and Chris Sugden (eds), *Texts on Evangelical Social Ethics* (Nottingham, UK: Grove Books, 1985), 5-7. The editors discuss Articles 4 and 10 as also influencing the development of social ethics in evangelical mission.

[11] Bockmühl, *Evangelicals and Social Ethics,* 17ff. The nine 'verbs of action' that Bockmühl extracts from the Covenant are: 1. Share God's concern for justice, 2. Share God's concern for reconciliation, 3. Share God's concern for the liberation of men from every kind of oppression, 4. Respect the dignity of every person, 5. Exploit no one, 6. Serve every person, 7. Denounce evil and injustice, 8. Seek to exhibit the righteousness of the kingdom of Christ, 9. Seek to spread the righteousness of the kingdom of Christ.

The strength of this validation gave evangelical theologians and practitioners alike a new sense of freedom to explore what social responsibility might mean for mission. Athol Gil comments that "in expressing penitence 'for having sometimes regarded evangelism and social concern as mutually exclusive' and in emphasizing that 'evangelism and socio-political involvement are both part of our Christian duty', the *Lausanne Covenant* marked a turning point in evangelical thinking ..."[12] Vinay Samuel and Chris Sugden concur and add, "Evangelical relief and development agencies around the world received fresh energy because they could now appeal to the evangelical constituency as 'family' without the fear of either being rebuked for preaching the 'social gospel' or being charged with compromising on evangelism."[13] Indeed, for both theological reflection and mission practice, the *Lausanne Covenant* – particularly Article 5 – provided new impetus for evangelicals to engage in social ministries.

The Statement on Radical Discipleship: Seeds of Transformation

The Covenant's clear affirmation of social concern, however, did not go unchallenged at the Congress. Many conservatives saw it as a distraction from the original Lausanne vision of what they called cross-cultural evangelism. Others to the right of the conservatives went even further and accused Lausanne's stated social vision as being the old 'social gospel' in evangelical clothing.[14]

For those left of centre, however, the affirmation of socio-political involvement in the *Lausanne Covenant* did not go far enough. They claimed that even though Article 5 repented of past negligence and affirmed the inseparable relationship of social responsibility to evangelism, it did not define that relationship. Moreover, social concern still felt like an

---

[12] Gill, 'Christian Social Responsibility', 89.

[13] Samuel and Sugden, 'Introduction', *The Church in Response to Human Need,* ix.

[14] See Valdir Steuernagel, 'The Theology of Mission in its Relation to Social Responsibility within the Lausanne Movement' (ThD thesis, Lutheran School of Theology at Chicago, 1988), 151-156; Roger Hedlund, *Roots of the Great Debate in Mission* (Bangalore, India: Theological Book Trust, 1997), 294-299, and René Padilla 'Evangelism and Social Responsibility: From Wheaton 66 to Wheaton 83' in *Transformation* 2:3 (1985), 29, to know who had problems with the Covenant's social affirmation. The list included Peter Wagner, Ralph Winter, Donald McGavran, Arthur Johnstone, and Peter Beyerhaus. Hedlund mentions these individuals sympathetically from a 'church growth' perspective, which he shares, while Padilla discusses them from a radical evangelical perspective. Steuernagel attempts a more objective discussion, although he falls decidedly on the radical evangelical side.

appendage to the 'real work' of the Gospel.[15] So a group of about 200 people at the Congress formed an *ad hoc* committee to discuss the shortcomings of the Covenant's social affirmation in the light of the implications of radical discipleship. They drafted an official response to Lausanne aptly titled "Theology [and] Implications of Radical Discipleship".[16]

Divided into four main parts, the official response challenged the Congress to declare more overtly the place of social concern in the mission of the church by affirming the comprehensive scope of the Gospel of the Kingdom of God. "The gospel," the paper read, "is Good News of liberation, of restoration, of wholeness, and of salvation that is personal, social, global and cosmic."[17] It ended with a resolution that affirmed both the spiritual and social dimensions of the task of world evangelization:

> We resolve to submit ourselves afresh to the Word of God and to the leading of his Spirit, to pray and work together for the renewal of his community as the expression of his reign, to participate in God's mission to his world in our generation, showing forth Jesus as Lord and Savior, and calling on all men everywhere to repent, to submit to his Lordship, to know his salvation, to identify in him with the oppressed and work for the liberation of all men and women in his name.[18]

In sum, the Statement on Radical Discipleship repudiated the dichotomy between evangelism and social concern, challenged the language of the primacy of evangelism, and broadened the scope of God's salvific work in the world, all the while remaining wholly committed to biblical authority and world evangelization. Writing over ten years after the issuance of the Statement, René Padilla assessed that it "provided the strongest statement on the basis for holistic mission ever formulated by an evangelical conference up to that date".[19]

Sugden reports that although the Statement did not end up as part of the Covenant, convenor John Stott presented it at the end of the Congress along with the final draft of the Covenant, thus giving prominent place to it.[20] Moreover, almost 500 people, approximately a quarter of the number of official delegates, signed it before leaving the Congress. So between the Covenant's affirmation of socio-political involvement and the inclusion of the Statement on Radical Discipleship among the official papers of the

---

15. Chris Sugden, 'Evangelicals and Wholistic Evangelism', in Vinay Samuel and Albrecht Hauser (eds), *Proclaiming Christ in Christ's Way: Studies in Integral Evangelism* (Oxford, UK: Regnum, 1989), 33.

16 'Theology [and] Implications of Radical Discipleship', in James D. Douglas (ed), in *Let the Earth His Voice* (Minneapolis; MN: World Wide Publications, 1975), 1294-1296.

17 'Theology and Implications of Radical Discipleship', 1294.

18 'Theology and Implications of Radical Discipleship', 1296.

19 Padilla, 'Evangelism and Social Responsibility', 29.

20 Sugden, 'Wholistic Evangelism', 34.

Congress, the status of social concern within the evangelical constituency enjoyed a new level of validation that it had not experienced since the days before the fundamentalist-modernist debacle.

Post-Lausanne Tensions

Predictably, evangelicals went about interpreting and developing the Lausanne social vision according to their respective schools of thought. And as proponents of these various schools encountered one another at conferences, as well as on the mission field, an unprecedented level of tension intensified within the post-Lausanne evangelical missionary community.

This tension came to a head at a large Lausanne follow-up gathering in 1980 in Pattaya, Thailand. Time and space will not allow us to go into detail about it;[21] suffice it to say here that the drafters of the Statement on Radical Discipleship at Lausanne I were not happy with the narrow view of evangelism that won the day in Pattaya. Samuel and Sugden lamented that the consultation organizers seemed, "... painfully unaware of all the developments in the Lausanne Movement in seeking to communicate the whole Gospel to the whole world. The years of slow growth in sensitivity to the social dimensions of the Gospel and to the contexts in which it was proclaimed, seemed to be wiped out."[22] Kwame Bediako described the travesty in terms of theology and strategy, and lamented, "The victory of theology over strategy [won at Lausanne 74] was overturned at Pattaya."[23]

If any hope existed for conservatives and radicals within the evangelical missionary community to find some level of consensus on the social question, it hinged upon the 1982 Consultation on the Relationship between Evangelism and Social Responsibility in Grand Rapids (CRESR). Valdir Steuernagel's description of CRESR as 'the most carefully planned, sensitive, feared, and threatening consultation ever held by the LCWE [Lausanne Committee on World Evangelization]' underscores what was at stake at this consultation – namely, unity or another tragic split of the worldwide evangelical family.[24] Co-sponsored by the LCWE and the World Evangelical Fellowship, CRESR gathered fifty evangelicals from around the world to understand better the relationship between evangelism and social responsibility in biblical, historical, and missiological perspectives.

For a full week, the delegates presented papers and responded to each other with openness and respect as well as with honesty and intensity, in what turned out to be, according to CRESR chairpersons Bong Rin Ro and

---

[21] See Tizon, *Transformation after Lausanne,* 43-48.

[22] Samuel and Sugden cited in Steuernagel, 'The Theology of Mission', 196-197.

[23] Kwame Bediako, 'World Evangelisation, Institutional Evangelicalism and the Future of the Christian World Mission', in Vinay Samuel and Albrecht Hauser (eds), *Proclaiming Christ in Christ's Way* (Oxford, UK: Regnum, 1989), 57.

[24] Steuernagel, 'The Theology of Mission', 199.

Gottfried Osei-Mensah, 'a model of how Christians should approach a ... divisive issue'.[25] CRESR produced a seven-chapter, 64-page document entitled 'The Grand Rapids Report on Evangelism and Social Responsibility: An Evangelical Commitment'.[26]

The strength of the report relied on the fact that it did not arrive at any one conclusion concerning the relationship; instead it offered a range of possibilities that it considered faithful to biblical and historic Christianity. According to the report, social action can be seen as: 1. A *consequence of* evangelism – one of the principle aims of a changed life is to serve others; 2. A *bridge to* evangelism – with no need of manipulation, good deeds naturally create opportunities to share the Gospel; and 3. A *partner with* evangelism – the church must witness Christ in the world by both word and deed.[27]

Due to this range of valid views, delegates for the most part reached an important level of consensus on the subject. Both Peter Wagner and René Padilla, insofar as they represented the conservative and radical constituencies respectively, expressed satisfaction for what CRESR accomplished – namely, recognizing the vital importance of socio-political involvement in the missionary task.[28] In light of the Grand Rapids Report, evangelicals of all persuasions could no longer ignore the church's social responsibility. Those who chose to retain the language of the primacy of evangelism could not allow that language to reduce or, worse, eliminate the mandate of social responsibility – that which makes credible the church's witness to Christ in a needy world – from the missionary task.

As important a level of consensus as CRESR reached, however, it still operated under a North American-nurtured dualism between body and soul, and social and spiritual, separating these two vital realities from each other and then falsely asking which one has priority over the other.[29] Radicals desired the evangelical community to see the falsity of this unbiblical dualism and then to begin to train its thinking, and therefore its doing, in more non-dualistic, i.e. holistic, terms. For the most part, those who adhered to these holistic notions remained somewhat marginalized from the mainstream of the Lausanne Movement. Indeed, the tension surrounding the implications of the social question to the task of world evangelization enjoyed, at best, only temporary relief as a result of CRESR.

---

[25] Bong Rin Ro and Gottfried Osei-Mensah, 'Preface', in Bruce J. Nicholls (ed), *Word and Deed: Evangelism and Social Responsibility* (Grand Rapids, MI: Eerdmans, 1986), 7.

[26] 'The Grand Rapids Report', in John R. W. Stott (ed), *Making Christ Known* (Grand Rapids, MI and Cambridge, UK: Eerdmans, 1996), 167-210.

[27] 'The Grand Rapids Report', *Making Christ Known,* 181-182. Italics mine.

[28] Steuernagel, 'The Theology of Mission', 204-205.

[29] Mark Lau Branson, 'Striving for Obedience, Haunted by Dualism', in *TSF Bulletin* 6.1 (Sept/Oct 1982), 11; Bosch, *Transforming Mission,* 406.

INFEMIT: The Birth of Transformation

In their disappointment for the way the Thailand consultation went, as well as not being wholly satisfied with the results of CRESR, radical evangelicals "resolved to meet … as a Two Thirds World consultation".[30] Making good on their promise, the first consultation – framed and organized for the first time by theologians of evangelical conviction from the Two Thirds World – convened in 1982 at Bangkok. This gathering led to the formation of a loose global network called the International Fellowship of Evangelical Mission Theologians, or INFEMIT.

Although 1987 marks the year when INFEMIT officially formed, 1980 claims its true beginnings when this group of radical evangelicals at Pattaya in 1980 reacted strongly against what they considered a regrettable return to pre-Lausanne mission thinking. They began to come to terms with the fact that the brand of holistic mission theology they espoused would probably never flow into the mainstream of evangelical missionary consciousness as long as 'managerial missiology', as Samuel Escobar described it, dictated the current.[31] Names and institutions associated with this network early on would include Vinay Samuel and Chris Sugden at the Oxford Centre for Mission Studies in the UK, René Padilla, Samuel Escobar and the late Orlandò Costas of the Latin American Theological Fraternity based in Argentina, Ronald Sider of Evangelicals for Social Action in the USA, Melba Maggay of the Institute for Studies in Asian Church and Culture in the Philippines, and David Lim of China Ministries International and the Centre for Community Transformation, also in the Philippines, David Gitari and Kwame Bediako of the African Theological Fraternity based in both Kenya and Ghana, and many others.

Through many gatherings, publications, and collaborative actions, INFEMIT made a significant impact on maturing a Transformational – i.e. holistic and contextual – social vision for evangelicals. Despite stops and, starts, its work continues in and through the next generation of evangelical theologian-practitioners. Now renamed as the International Fellowship for Mission as Transformation, INFEMIT articulates its mission in the following way: "Called and equipped by the Father, Son and Holy Spirit, we are a Gospel-centered fellowship of mission theologian-practitioners that serves local churches and other Christian communities so we together embody the Kingdom of God through transformational engagement, both locally and globally."[32]

---

[30] Sugden, 'Wholistic Evangelism', 38. Incidentally, the 'radical evangelical' label is one I used extensively in *Transformation after Lausanne;* it was not one that they attached to themselves.

[31] Samuel Escobar, 'A Movement Divided', in *Transformation* 8.4 (Oct 1991), 11-13, and 'Evangelical Missiology: Peering into the Future at the Turn of the Century', William Taylor (ed), in *Global Missiology for the 21st Century* (Grand Rapids, MI: Baker Academic, 2000), 109-112.

[32] INFEMIT, http://infemit.org/ (accessed 12th Dec 2012).

Wheaton 83: Transformation Articulated

If Mission as Transformation was born with the formation of INFEMIT in 1980, then it was given a name at the Wheaton Consultation in 1983. Compared with Lausanne 74, the Wheaton 83 Consultation could not boast huge numbers of participants nor monumental worldwide notoriety. But in terms of the evangelical journey toward holistic mission, Wheaton 83 looms large. Organized into three tracks, Track III of Wheaton 83 with the sub-theme, 'The Church in Response to Human Need', took significant strides toward holistic mission by developing a biblical, theological, and practical understanding of the term, 'transformation'. According to the Wheaton 83 Statement, the official document resulting from Track III, "Transformation is the change from a condition of human existence contrary to God's purposes to one in which people are able to enjoy fullness of life in harmony with God."[33]

This particular understanding of Transformation has undergone its own transformations since its inception.[34] It emerged through reflections on social ethics but later expanded into reflections on a holistic missiology – thus, expansion of the name from Transformation to *Mission* as Transformation.[35] This broadening, however, did not reduce the importance of social concern; on the contrary, it made social concern part and parcel of the Gospel and therefore part and parcel of the church's mission. Proponents of Mission as Transformation refuse to understand evangelization without liberation, a change of heart without a change of structures, vertical reconciliation (between God and people) without horizontal reconciliation (between people and people), and church planting without community building. They point to the biblical paradigm of the reign or kingdom of God as the source and driver for this holistic understanding of mission.[36] Vinay Samuel's 1999 articulation of the term sums it up well; he wrote, "Transformation is to enable God's vision of society to be actualized in all relationships – social, economic and

---

[33] 'Wheaton 83: Statement on Transformation', in Vinay Samuel and Chris Sugden (eds), *The Church in Response to Human Need* (Oxford, UK: Regnum and Grand Rapids, MI: Eerdmans, 1987), 257.

[34] For developments on the definition of Transformation since 1983, see Chris Sugden, 'Transformational Development: Current state of understanding and practice', in *Transformation* 20.2 (April 2003), 70-72.

[35] Vinay Samuel, 'Mission as Transformation', in Vinay Samuel and Chris Sugden (eds), *Mission as Transformation* (Oxford, UK et al.: Regnum, 1999), 228.

[36] Some theologians have made a viable case to use the term 'reign' over 'kingdom' on the grounds that 'kingdom' has male, patriarchal overtones that the broader biblical reality of 'kingdom of God' did not necessarily intend to convey. For more on this, see Mortimer Arias, *Announcing the Reign of God* (Minneapolis, MN: Fortress, 1984), xvi. For this study, because the more familiar 'kingdom of God' overwhelms Transformational literature, I have chosen to retain it.

spiritual – so that God's will may be reflected in human society and his love be experienced by all communities, especially the poor."[37]

Many of the same people, who drafted the Statement on Radical Discipleship at Lausanne I and formed INFEMIT, were responsible for Track III of the Wheaton consultation, as well as the drafting of the Wheaton Statement on Transformation. This strongly suggests that the Transformational Movement finds its roots more in the Statement on Radical Discipleship than in the *Lausanne Covenant* itself.[38] To be sure, the drafters understood the Radical Discipleship Statement with reference to the Covenant, and indeed, the Covenant validated the Statement. So the link between the Transformational Movement and the Lausanne Movement remains organically intact. Nevertheless, the convictions, hopes, and spirit of the Statement – viewed by its drafters as both an addendum and a corrective to the Covenant – set a course that was destined not only to go beyond the Covenant in affirming and defining socio-political involvement, but also to go a very different way from the conservative evangelical constituency.

Oxford Centre for Mission Studies: Transformation on the Move

The Transformational Movement matured through a number of channels, including INFEMIT-sponsored consultations, the journal *Transformation*, and book publications by Regnum Books International. But perhaps the most enduring channel through which the Movement has advanced is the Oxford Centre for Mission Studies (OCMS) in Oxford, UK.

The Transformational Movement has always been, at the core, a theological endeavour that involved deep reflection on the service of responsible mission in the world. Pressing missiological issues undoubtedly evoked the questions that shaped Mission as Transformation; but believing that mission finds its vitality and longevity in well-grounded theology, Transformationists have always held up the importance of doing theology – and doing it well, lest "theology take a backseat to strategic initiatives".[39] They knew that solid, research-based, graduate-level, theological education was a key to the success of the Movement. Enter: OCMS. Founded in 1983,

---

[37] Vinay Samuel quoted in Chris Sugden, 'Mission as Transformation – Its Journey Since Lausanne I,' in *Holistic Mission: God's Plan for God's People,* eds. Brian Woolnough and Wonsuk Ma (Oxford et al.: Regnum, 2010), 33.

[38] In light of this, Samuel and Sugden's *Mission as Transformation* should have perhaps included the 'Statement on Radical Discipleship' as an Appendix rather than, or at least in addition to, the Lausanne Covenant. Chris Sugden's *Radical Discipleship* (Hants, UK: Marshall, Morgan and Scott, 1981), in fact, does just that: Appendix 1 is the 'Statement on Radical Discipleship' and Appendix 2 is the Lausanne Covenant.

[39] Vinay Samuel and Chris Sugden, 'Introduction,' Vinay Samuel and Chris Sugden (eds), *Mission as Transformation* (Oxford et al.: Regnum, 1999), xi.

OCMS has sought to provide a viable avenue for quality graduate theological education for the past 25 years, primarily in the service of the church in the Two Thirds World.[40]

I had the privilege of being invited to speak at the 25th anniversary of OCMS in 2008. In my presentation, I celebrated the accomplishments of this institution in advancing the core commitments of Transformation – i.e. holistic mission and contextualization wrapped in deep, thorough theological scholarship.[41] At the risk of over-simplification, while INFEMIT has represented the cultural agenda of the Movement – a constant reminder that an understanding of the whole Gospel must come from the whole church – OCMS has emphasized the theological scholarship needed to advance the Movement. Between the ongoing work of INFEMIT and OCMS, the Transformational social vision – which thoroughly integrates evangelism and social justice – has continued to thrive and mature.

Cape Town 2010: The Necessity of Mission as Transformation

Time and space compel us to fast-forward to Cape Town 2010, and ask an assessment question: 'What is now the state of the relationship between evangelism and social concern?' I began this chapter with a quote from Ron Sider that evangelicals now essentially assume a holistic orientation to mission. I basically agree, and I credit Sider and the other 'Transformationists' whose courageous tenacity restored the social dimension of the Gospel on the evangelical missionary agenda (alongside evangelism, of course), and thus helped evangelicals move toward greater biblical faithfulness these last forty years.

However, the diversity of, and therefore the tension between, evangelical viewpoints regarding the relationship between evangelism and social concern still exists and perhaps always will. All may affirm the whole Gospel, but some are still cautious about placing social justice on a par with evangelism. In other words, the Gospel may be a whole, but one part is still more important than the other. Unfortunately, I sensed the felt need of some of the plenary speakers at Cape Town 2010 to affirm social ministry with a caveat. *It's important, but we should not be distracted from the real work of evangelism. We should alleviate human suffering, but especially eternal suffering.* And so on. To a Transformationist, this kind of prioritizing and qualifying only perpetuates the dichotomy, and therefore doesn't feel integrally and deeply 'holistic'. So even though evangelicals

---

[40] INFEMIT and OCMS as separate institutions are currently redefining their relationship, but I continue in this paper to keep them together as sustaining symbols of Mission as Transformation.

[41] My presentation is available in article form. Al Tizon, 'Mission as Education: A Past-to-Future Look at INFEMIT/OCMS,' in *Transformation* 28/4 (Oct 2011), 253-264.

have come a long way in negotiating evangelism and social responsibility since the first Congress in 1974, I was disappointed that such statements still had to be made almost forty years later.

At least one other occurrence in Cape Town further points to the tension of which I speak. During my long flight home, I read a *Time* magazine article about Desmond Tutu, the celebrated Anglican Archbishop of South Africa, who did his significant part in effectively toppling the evil giant of apartheid.[42] I was once again inspired by the bishop's example of what it means to follow Jesus in the context of injustice, deepened no doubt by spending a week in his country. After reading the article, my embarrassment that apartheid was not acknowledged, much less repented of, at Lausanne III, only intensified. I was not the only one who was pained by the omission. 'A Statement of Lament' about apartheid was circulated among, and signed by, many participants. It read in part, "This Lausanne Congress ... gathered in a land which sixteen years ago stood in the grip of one of the greatest evils of our time – apartheid. We regret that this was not named or confessed at the opening of the Congress."[43] We cannot expect a gathering, even one of this magnitude, to cover everything; but how could we have overlooked such a thing while celebrating Christ's holistic mission in the world?

In light of these things, I believe that the Transformational perspective, which holds together theologically and practically the Gospel of God's reign of peace, justice and salvation, is absolutely crucial, not only for the health of the Lausanne Movement, but for the integrity of our mission in the world.

---

[42] Alex Perry, 'The Laughing Bishop', *Time* (Oct 11, 2010).

[43] 'Statement of Lament for Evangelicals and the Legacy of Apartheid,' http://reconcilers.wordpress.com/2010/10/22/apartheid-legacy-lament/ (accessed 12th Dec 2012).

JEWISH EVANGELISM

Susan Perlman

When the Lausanne Movement held its strategic meeting in Pattaya, Thailand, in 1980, the smallest of the mini-consultation groups to meet as part of that gathering was the group on *Reaching Jewish People*. Our seventeen participants included mission leaders, academics and practitioners in the field of Jewish evangelism. In addition, there was advance input from dozens of practitioners in our field. Eight of those who met in Pattaya have since gone on to glory. As one of the seventeen contributors who put together what is known as *Lausanne Occasional Paper 7* entitled, 'Christian Witness and the Jewish People', I am very encouraged that the Lausanne Movement recognized Jewish evangelism as a concern of global importance back then and has increasingly recognized it to this day. The 1980 document can be read in its entirety on the Lausanne website.[1] However, the opening section which deals with the biblical basis for Jewish evangelism cannot be restated more clearly:

> Scripture gives the rationale for Jewish evangelism in John 14:6 and Acts 4:12, which indicate that salvation is found only in Christ. For Christians to know that Christ is the only way to be saved and then not proclaim the gospel to Jews presumes the exclusion of Jews from the need and possibility of salvation in Jesus Christ. It is a reflection of inadequate biblical and theological understanding. The great commission given in all four gospels makes no exception for Israel. To decline to preach the gospel to Jews, then, calls into question the credibility of all the church's evangelistic activity.
>
> Scripture not only gives the rationale for Jewish evangelism; it also speaks of its priority. Jesus stressed in his ministry that he came first to the 'lost sheep of the house of Israel'. St. Paul in his ministry followed that procedure for evangelism. In every city on his missionary journeys, he went first to the Jews and then subsequently to the Gentiles.
>
> He also stated to the predominately Gentile church in Rome that the gospel is '… the power of God for the salvation of everyone who believes: first for the Jew, then for the Gentile' (Rom 1:16). It might be difficult to be precise about what Paul understood by the phrase, 'to the Jew first'. (Compare Rom 2:9-10 where he uses the same phrase when speaking of future rewards and judgement.) However, it can be argued that Paul does state that the Jewish people, far from being outside the scope of the great commission, should have a special place in the church's evangelistic outreach.

---

[1] www.lausanne.org/en/documents/lops/52-lop-7.html

> First, God has used the Jewish people to give the Christian the way of salvation. Secondly, the Jewish people have a prior and continuing covenant relationship with God (Jer 31:31-34, Isa 49:6). Part of that covenanted responsibility involves their being a light to the world. Jews, however, cannot perfectly fulfil that responsibility without Christ. Thirdly, Paul anticipated the turning of Jews to Christ which would have a life-giving impact on the entire church.
>
> There is, therefore, a great responsibility laid upon the church to share Christ with the Jewish people. This is not to imply that Jewish evangelism is more important in the sight of God, or that those involved in Jewish evangelism have a higher calling. We observe that the practical application of the scriptural priority is difficult to understand and apply. We do not suggest that there should be a radical application of 'to the Jew first' in calling on all the evangelists, missionaries, and Christians to seek out the Jews within their sphere of witness before speaking to non-Jews! Yet we do call the church to restore ministry among this covenanted people of God to its biblical place in its strategy of world evangelization.

The remaining pages of that document go on to assess the global Jewish community as it appeared in 1980 as well as commenting on the obstacles to Jewish evangelism, current methods and practices in our field, the theological and missiological issues to consider and a way forward. That way forward took the form of a proposal to establish a task force on Jewish evangelism with a fivefold purpose:

> (a) To gather and catalogue information useful in Jewish evangelism and to furnish such material in an occasional publication.
> (b) To provide a platform on which Jewish missions can meet to co-ordinate strategies.
> (c) To monitor and report trends in the Jewish community.
> (d) To stimulate theological and missiological research related to Jewish evangelism.
> (e) To arrange for consultations that will be useful to those engaged or interested in Jewish evangelism.

Shortly after the Pattaya meetings, that task force became a reality. The purposes stated above still govern this working group. The Lausanne Consultation on Jewish Evangelism (LCJE) today stands as the longest existing network of the Lausanne Movement. Its members include those in the Jewish missions community, those in academia with a special concern for the Jewish people, those in the messianic congregational movement and other interested individuals.

LOP 7 ends with this statement:

> As we conclude the work of this consultation, we are in agreement as we appeal for Jewish evangelism as a central and unavoidable task for the body of Christ. We regret with sorrow that there are local churches, church leaders, and missionary agencies which deny the need to return the gospel to the Jewish people from whence it first came; and that evangelicals who say they love the Jewish people sometimes lack the will to bring them the gospel.

> Including Jewish people is a test of our willingness to be involved in world evangelization. It is a test of our faith in the one exclusive way of salvation and of our proclamation of Christ as an adequate Saviour for those who are apparently adequate so far as worldly righteousness is concerned.

LCJE has convened nine international conferences since then (its tenth to take place in Israel in 2015) and held more than fifty regional conferences in Europe, North America, Asia, Africa, Oceania and the Middle East since its formation. More importantly, understanding between Jewish missions has been fostered at these meetings and co-operative efforts in Jewish evangelism have been birthed at them as well. The second international conference, held in Newmarket, England, in 1983, included this commendation as part of its statement to the global church:

> We rejoice in the growing co-operation among Jewish missions, as exemplified in the recent 'Messiah has come' evangelistic campaign in London, England.[2] We urge that this spirit of co-operation be emulated elsewhere by those concerned to reach the Jewish people with the gospel.[3]

The information found in LOP 7 was updated and expanded in LOP 60 entitled, 'Reaching the Jewish People With the Gospel'. The more recent LOP was a result of the work of the Jewish Evangelism Working Session (JEWS) issue group meeting at the 2004 Forum for World Evangelization held in Pattaya, Thailand. This group of seven were all long-time members of LCJE and, again, I was one of the contributors.

The rest of this article will address the broader issues covered in both these LOPs as well as take into account changes in demographics and the body of material on the theological and missiological issues germane to this topic. However, this all sits well within the framework of the *Cape Town Commitment* of 2010 and, particularly, the following sentiments found in Section IIB: Building the peace of Christ in our divided and broken world:

> Reconciliation to God is inseparable from reconciliation to one another. Christ, who is our peace, made peace through the cross, and preached peace to the divided world of Jew and Gentile. The unity of the people of God is both a fact ('he made the two one') and a mandate ('make every effort to preserve the unity of the Spirit in the bond of peace'). God's plan for the integration of the whole creation in Christ is modeled in the ethnic reconciliation of God's new humanity. Such is the power of the gospel as promised to Abraham.
>
> We affirm that whereas the Jewish people were not strangers to the covenants and promises of God, in the way that Paul describes the Gentiles, they still stand in need of reconciliation to God through the Messiah Jesus. There is no difference, said Paul, between Jew and Gentile in sin; neither is there any

[2] 'Messiah Has Come' was a joint outreach in London in 1983 of five mission agencies all involved with LCJE.

[3] LCJE 1983 Second International Consultation Newmarket Statement (final paragraph).

> difference in salvation. Only in and through the cross can both have access to God the Father through the one Spirit.
>
> We continue, therefore, strongly to affirm the need for the whole Church to share the good news of Jesus as Messiah, Lord and Saviour with Jewish people. And in the spirit of Romans 14–15, we urge Gentile believers to accept, encourage and pray for Messianic Jewish believers, in their witness among their own people.[4]

The Jewish People and Jewish Evangelism

A look at current demographics shows some significant shifts that have great bearing on the way Jewish evangelism is conducted today and what strategies are needed for the future.

1. Demographics

Much has happened since the early days of LCJE. The shift in Jewish demographics has been dramatic. A 2012 survey of world Jewish population conducted by Sergio Della Pergola, professor emeritus of the Hebrew University of Jerusalem, came up with these results:[5]

A. Jewish Population Growth

The Jewish rate of growth is about half that of the general world population: At the beginning of 2012, the world's Jewish population was estimated at 13,746,100 – an increase of 88,300 (0.65%) over the 2011 estimate. The world's total population increased by 1.26% in 2011.

This growth rate, if looked at through the lens of Israel and the Diaspora Jewish community, tells another story as well. Since 1945 Israel has grown in Jewish population from half a million to 5.9 million, whereas during that same time frame the Diaspora Jews have gone from 10.5 million to 7.8 million.

B. Concentration of Jewish Population

Forty-three per cent of all Jews live in Israel. Thirty-nine per cent of all Jews live in the United States. Sixteen per cent live in sixteen additional countries. And 2% can be found, in very small numbers, in another 75 countries.

Germany has had the fastest-growing Jewish population in Europe, although that may be changing. The former Soviet Union has seen the most significant decrease in Jewish population. France currently has the largest

---

[4] *The Capetown Commitment: A Confession of Faith and a Call to Action,* 39-40. www.lausanne.org/en/documents/ctcommitment.html.

[5] www.jewishdatabank.org/Studies/downloadFile.cfm?FileID=2941.

Jewish population in Europe, and perhaps more emphasis should be given to the evangelization of French Jewry.

C. MIGRATION OF JEWS FROM THE FORMER SOVIET UNION

Since 1989, more than one million Soviet Jews have migrated to Israel, 300,000 to the USA and 225,000 to Germany. The Jewish population in the former Soviet Union continues to decline.

D. RISING RATE OF INTERMARRIAGE TO NON-JEWS

The most frequently mentioned item among open responses in the Second Survey of European Jewish Leaders and Opinion Formers, 2011,[6] was the subject of intermarriage and what Jewish communal policies should be toward such couples and their children. Thirty-one percent of all married Jews are intermarried. Of that number 39% of these marriages are Jewish-Catholic, 23% are Jewish-Protestant and 26% are between a Jewish person and a person who doesn't affiliate with any religion.[7]

E. FASTEST-GROWING SUB-GROUPS ARE THE ULTRA-ORTHODOX JEWS, PARTICULARLY IN MAJOR CITIES LIKE NEW YORK CITY

According to the Jewish Community Study of New York: 2011, 32% of the New York Jewish community is Orthodox. A significant number of those are part of what is called the New Orthodox (55,000 households or 157,000 Jews) and this sub-group is rising due to a much higher birth-rate than the non-Orthodox Jewish community.

Note: Depending on how Jews are being defined or counted, there may be some variation from the sources quoted here.

2. Theological issues related to Jewish evangelism

A. COVENANT

A proper soteriology is key to understanding the need for Jewish evangelism, yet some contemporary thinking on covenant is cause for concern. The following paragraph is from a Section of the *Manila Manifesto* (1989) on the uniqueness of Christ:

> It is sometimes held that in virtue of God's covenant with Abraham, Jewish people do not need to acknowledge Jesus as their Messiah. We affirm, that they need him as much as anyone else, that it would be a form of anti-Semitism, as well as being disloyal to Christ, to depart from the New Testament pattern of taking the Gospel to 'the Jews first ...' We therefore

6 www.jdc-iccd.org/en/article/31/second-european-jewish-leaders-survey-2011.

7 www. interfaithfamily.com/news_and_opinion/synagogues_and_the_jewish_community/Jewish_Intermarriage_Statistics.shtml.

> reject the thesis that Jews have their own covenant which renders faith in Jesus unnecessary.[8]

The issue of covenant was also highlighted in the soteriology section of our LOP 60 in Pattaya (2004):

> A church that is uncertain of its doctrine of Christ is inevitably uncertain of its doctrine of salvation. Those of the church who hold a doctrine of universalism reject Jewish evangelism as a valid or necessary enterprise. The two-covenant theory proclaims two ways of salvation, stating that God has a covenant with Israel distinct from His covenant with the rest of the world. It therefore denies the need for Jewish evangelism. Judaism also proclaims its own way of salvation. It is argued that Jews are exempt from the necessity of a faith-response to Christ. Such statements, however, deprecate the unique salvation offered by God as the only way to be saved from sin.[9]

More and more, churches are being challenged to retreat from Jewish evangelism based on this two-covenant position. Yet Lausanne has stood strong and unwavering on this and we are very grateful.

B. Post-Holocaust

Others are dissuaded from Jewish evangelism by holding to a post-Holocaust theology that says that the church has given up its right to share Jesus with Jewish people. The reasoning goes something like this: During the genocide of the Holocaust, the large majority of the Christian world did nothing and so we have no right to speak today. One of my European-based colleagues in Jewish ministry responds with this challenge to other Christians in post-Holocaust Europe: "To deny the gospel message to Jewish people today is keeping silent a second time. God is giving us a second chance to bring a message of love to Jewish people – don't waste it." It is true that many Christians feel shame as well as insecurity about sharing the Gospel with Jewish people and have replaced that with attempts at interfaith dialogue.

However, as well stated in the *Berlin Declaration* on the Uniqueness of Christ written in August of 2008,

> … genuine love cannot be passive. Jesus taught that authentic love could not be unfeeling when other human beings are in misery and need … Love in action compels all Christians to share the gospel with people everywhere, including the Jewish people of Europe.[10]

C. Supersessionism

Another concern that has been a stumbling-block to Jewish evangelism is the teaching that promotes certain supersessionist theologies. Those who hold to such beliefs often fail to recognize the implications for Jewish

[8] www.lausanne.org/en/documents/manila-manifesto.html.

[9] www.lausanne.org/en/documents/lops/877-lop-60.html.

[10] www.worldevangelicals.org/commissions/tc/berlin.htm.

evangelism. The most extreme form of supersessionism was found in second-century Marcion, who did not believe that Israel's God was identical with the God of the New Testament. The one was the God of vengeance and wrath, whereas the other was portrayed as a loving God. In more moderate forms, the church has been seen as the recipient of Israel's blessing whereas, in contrast, the Jewish people are no longer the recipients of God's good promises outside of faith in Christ. A position more faithful to the biblical text will balance God's continued care for the Jewish nation with the need for Jewish people to come to faith in Christ in order to experience the fullness of his blessings. In this connection, it should be noted that many Reformed theologians have integrated a positive theology of God's current relationship to Israel into a more traditionally Reformed framework.

Today, a 'replacement theology' position, which marginalizes the Jewish people and God's promises to them, can be just as dangerous if it leads to a lesser regard for the Jewish people and their need for Christ.

D. Israel

A fourth theological concern has to do with a theology concerning Israel itself. David Brickner, executive director of Jews for Jesus, in an online dialogue with theologian John Piper, commented:

> Christians often have a great depth of theological understanding regarding Israel in the past. Many also have a keen interest and firm convictions regarding Israel in the future. Yet when it comes to present-day Israel, it seems biblical thinking often takes a back seat to political expedience on both sides of the current conflict. Christians today desperately need an informed theology concerning present-day Israel.[11]

Such a theology would include issues relating to the place of Israel in God's plan, the 'Christian Zionist' movement and the tendency for some to relegate these questions to the realm of dispensationalism where historically these have been relevant issues for Christians of varying persuasions. Particularly problematic has been the extremes of the Christian Zionist movement in which support (often overtly political) for the state of Israel has marginalized concern for Jewish evangelism. Some proponents of this view deem it unnecessary to proclaim the Gospel to Jews. In this way there is some overlap in what we see in supersessionist theology.

E. Reconciliation and the Israeli-Palestinian conflict

In reaction to some of the highly politicized factions of the Christian Zionist movement, there has been a polar opposite move that is highly politicized as well which seeks to promote Palestinian rights under the guise of Christian social actions and justice. As Christians, we need to

---

[11] www.christianitytoday.com/ct/2012/juneweb-only/john-piper-david-brickner-israel-3.html.

distinguish legitimate human rights concerns for all parties from an anti-Israel position that can be borderline anti-Semitic. Such politicized anti-Israel rhetoric on the part of some Christians is not only detrimental to Jewish evangelism but works counter to God's desire for reconciliation.

When Jews and Arabs can say to one another, "I love you" in Jesus' name, the reality of His reconciliation of divergent people to himself is evident to a broken and antagonistic world.

F. Messianic Jews

There is a wide spectrum of belief when it comes to how Messianic Jews should live. With regard to the Law, there are those who see the Law of Moses as no longer valid and actually counter to God's intended purposes. They would argue that any manner of observance rejects the grace of God and the belief in justification by faith alone.

Then there are those who would affirm the cultural aspects of 'Torah observance' such as Sabbath practice, celebrating rites of passage (e.g. *bar mitzvah* and circumcision) following the laws of *kashrut* (dietary laws) but not for religious reasons. They would say that doing so is normative for them as Jews but has no theological merit, and Messianic Jews are free to observe them if they choose.

An approach possibly overlapping with some of the others was expressed in LOP 60:

> It recognises the continuing validity of Jewish tradition as the interpretative context for understanding the biblical Torah of the Old and New Testaments. Jesus, in His teaching and example, and the practice of the early church, defined a new *halacha* (rule of conduct) for the new covenant community. This *halacha* is developed today following the first Christians' example in the book of Acts. They observed Jewish lifestyle and practices, adapted some, abandoned others and applied only a few to the nations. Messianic Jews who observe Torah in this way both acknowledge its value but challenge its interpretation by the main branches of Judaism. They propose a new interpretation of Torah based on the teaching and practice of Jesus and the first disciples.[12]

Another view maintains that it is incumbent upon Messianic Jews to follow the Law according to Orthodox and Conservative traditions, and as a matter of identifying themselves as Jews.

Richard Harvey explains this view in his seminal volume, *Mapping Messianic Jewish Theology, A Constructive Approach*: "Torah observance preserved the Jewish community through its rabbinic leaders over the centuries, and Messianic Jews should accept their normative authority and work within this. This will enable them to develop their primary identity within the Jewish community rather than the mainstream Church. They

---

[12] www.lausanne.org/en/documents/lops/877-lop-60.htm.

should see themselves as members of the community of Israel, even if others do not accept them."[13]

For a more comprehensive look at this subject this writer commends Dr Harvey's volume.

The Lausanne Movement is looking to move forward in this area as evidenced by the formation at the Bangalore Leadership meetings in 2013 of a Lausanne-sponsored working group on reconciliation composed of Jewish believers in Jesus and Palestinian Christian believers. Though in its early stages, theological reflection here can prove very valuable.

In addition to theological concerns regarding Jewish evangelism, there are sociological trends emerging in Judaism that are worth noting.

A Divisiveness in Mainstream Judaism

We see an increased polarization between the various streams of Judaism today, particularly between Orthodox Jews and those who are Reform, and between Reform Jews and those who would consider themselves secular or cultural Jews.

Rabbi Eric Yoffe, president emeritus of the Union for Reform Judaism, in a *Huffington Post* blog entitled, 'The Self-Delusions of Secular Jews,' argued that while he is

> … not without sympathy for those who see themselves as secular. They distance themselves from religion because they reject the intellectual certainty and the extremism with which it is too often associated: as a liberal religious Jew, I reject these things as well. At the same time, I know that Judaism properly understood is not about either certainty or extremism; it is about hope, rooted in a commitment to sacred community and to God. In short, 'secular Jews' and 'cultural Jews' may think that they can wring the holiness out of their Jewish identity and practice, but they cannot.'[14]

Leonard Fein, a professor of political science at Massachusetts Institute of Technology and professor of Jewish Studies at Brandeis University, in a rebuttal blog on the *Huffington Post* site, 'Are Secular Jews Really Self-Deluded?', pointed out that in his opinion, while 'among those who define themselves as secular Jews, some indeterminate number are militantly anti-religious – or more precisely, anti-God … his own experience in secular circles strongly suggests that most secularists are basically indifferent to the God question'.[15]

To further underline the differences, in the August/September 2013 issue of *First Things* magazine, Eric Cohen, Adjunct Fellow at the Ethics and Public Policy Center and editor-at-large of *The New Atlantis*, offers his

---

[13] Richard Harvey, *Mapping Messianic Jewish Theology: A Constructive Approach* (Milton Keynes, UK: Paternoster, 2009), 182.

[14] www.huffingtonpost.com/rabbi-eric-h-yoffie/the-self-delusions-of-secular-jews_b_2479888.html.

[15] http://forward.com/articles/170761/are-secular-jews-really-self-deluded.

view on theological liberalism in the Reform and Conservative movements of Judaism:

> In the two largest movements by numbers, Reform and Conservative, theological liberalism has won decisively. Gay marriage and gay rabbis have been embraced. Adherence to *halakha* (Jewish religious law) has been abandoned or twisted beyond recognition. Judaism is essentially modern liberalism in a (sometimes) Hebraic key, with the twin gods of the self and social justice at the center. And even Jewish nationalism – pride and support for the miraculous re-founding of the modern Jewish state – has weakened, replaced by a theology of Jewish guilt, at worst, or sophisticated ambivalence, at best, over Israel's morally imperfect yet ultimately heroic effort to survive and flourish in a region gripped by anti-Jewish and anti-Western madness. This hardly looks like victory for religious orthodoxy to me. And I think if one looked at the mainline Protestant churches, one would find a similar story.
>
> While theological liberalism has won in the hearts and minds of the liberal Jewish seminaries, the liberal movements are in steady – or in some cases steep – decline. When religion redefines itself as liberalism, it turns out that many people are perfectly happy just being unaffiliated liberals – or Nones.[16]

This divisiveness can be seen in Israel as well. There is a high degree of tension between the religious (*haredim*) and the secular Israelis. The secular Israelis don't find that the synagogue or the religious establishment has much to offer them. When it comes to convenience, it's certainly easier to be married by an Orthodox rabbi, to get a divorce by an Orthodox rabbi and a burial as well. But that is as far as it goes. They see Israel as a democracy, not a religious entity.

The resentment comes into play when the religious minority seeks to impose restrictions on the non-religious majority. For example, on the Sabbath, Israel is, for the most part, closed down. If one does not use the day to worship in the synagogue, the options are very limited. Businesses are closed; the national airline doesn't fly, etc.

In addition, most *haredim* have received exemption from military service, which is compulsory for all other Israeli men and women after high school. The religious also get special subsidies for religious studies. This has engendered much resentment from the secular Israelis who pay high taxes and do their service in the Israeli Army at great personal risk.

Theodore Herzl, the father of Modern Zionism, dreamt of a secular state where the religious authorities extended no influence beyond the walls of the synagogue. On the other hand, Rav Kook, when he established the chief rabbinate in Jerusalem in 1921, intended that to be preparatory for the re-establishment of a Sanhedrin in Jerusalem. The coming clash between the secular courts and the religious courts in Israel seems inevitable.

Tensions also exist between the religious in Israel. "To understand why members of the Orthodox establishment refuse to sit in the same room as

---

[16] www.firstthings.com/article/2013/08/passion-and-prudence.

Reform representatives, don't bother asking a theologian," says Michael Marmur, dean of the Hebrew Union College–Jewish Institute of Religion in Jerusalem. He goes on to say, "A psychiatrist may help, but not as much as the real expert on Jewish unity: a patient lawyer. Ultimately, the frenzied struggle to keep Reform and Conservative Jews out of the picture is about holy protectionism."[17]

The increasing fragmentation within the Jewish community calls for increasing energy and creativity on the part of those who engage in Jewish evangelism. Perhaps we even need to think about more specialization within the specialized ministry of Jewish evangelism. All this ferment in the Jewish community means that the face of the Jewish people differs markedly from what it was in the past. Therefore our approaches to Jewish evangelism, our apologetics, the structure into which we invite Jewish seekers, need to be re-thought in order for us to remain relevant and effective.

Looking Forward to the Future

In recent times, the church, under pressure from rabbis, has come to question the validity of Jewish evangelism. Those committed to evangelism remain uncertain as to the best way to relate to the changing climate within Judaism today. One thing, however, cannot be ignored – more and more Jews today are coming to faith in Christ and stepping forward to take their place within the body of Christ. What is the common thread for all these conversions?

Perhaps a good way to put this in perspective is to recognize that all evangelism must speak to, direct and find its openness in a person's quest for spirituality. Most people who become Christians or convert to other world religions are not seeking to affirm their ethnic identity. Rather they are hoping to touch something that is spiritual in nature; particularly they desire to realize that which is eternal or God. Much of mission methodology overlooks the fact that most people are on a spiritual quest.

Among the Jewish people and certain tribal people, spirituality is bound up with ethnic identity. In most cases the myths surrounding ethnicity tend to lead a person away from the one true God. The Jewish people are an exception because for us such 'myths' are not myths but Scripture. Our ethnic reality is a sense of being chosen by the Creator of the Universe, a fact that Christians affirm.

The other two major world religions – Christianity and Islam – affirm the historicity of Abraham and build important doctrine on his personhood. That affirmation communicates to Jewish people the validity of their Jewishness.

---

[17] Michael Marmar, 'Copyright Infringement', in *The Jerusalem Post* 22nd Jan 1999, 9.

How does spirituality for a Jew differ from that of a Christian or a Muslim or even a New Ager? To a Christian, spirituality means being filled with the Spirit and enabled by the Holy Spirit to commune with God. To the Muslim, spirituality is wrapped up in being submitted to the will of Allah. Submission brings insight and joy. New Age or Animist spirituality means communing with the creation, becoming one with 'the all'. However, Jewish spirituality has to do with becoming a better Jew, a more knowledgeable Jew. To the Jewish person, spirituality is seeking the meaning of one's roots or simply working out the concept of 'chosenness'. The quest is always constrained by one's Jewishness.

Susan Handelman is a Jew who teaches English at a secular university. She also teaches in adult Jewish education programmes. She retells a story about one of her students, a 45-year-old Jewish attorney, in a Jewish education class in which she was analyzing the creation account. This student, who was an outspoken feminist and anti-traditionalist, exclaimed: "I am tired of analyzing all this from a literary and historical and feminist point of view. I want to know what I can personally believe, and how it helps me relate to God, and what I can teach my kids and how it affects me spiritually ... They are always teaching us about 'What Jews believe'. But I need to know what I believe."[18]

This attorney's questions are true for Jews worldwide. If we can get a handle on how to answer her questions, in what Handelman calls an era of post-secularism for Jews, we will have come far.

We have a spiritual path to offer, but for the most part our Jewish people are still guarding their hearts against believing anything they fear is contrary to their identity as Jews.

They need to see that what they need and want is more than a practice or a poultice to help them feel more spiritually grounded. They need more than bits of truth to show them that they are developing their spiritual side. They need to see the outworking of what is true: how Jesus is not only true, but also how a relationship with him is pragmatic. They need to see Jewish belief in Jesus as the normal consummation of a spiritual journey.

In his foreword to Joy Davidman's book, *Smoke on the Mountain*, C.S. Lewis had this to say about Jewish people, and perhaps his summation gives us that proper perspective to move forward:

> In a sense, the converted Jew is the only normal human being in the world. To him, in the first instance, the promises were made, and he has availed himself of them. He calls Abraham his father by hereditary right as well as by divine courtesy. He has taken the whole syllabus in order, as it was set; eaten

---

[18] Susan Handelman, 'Crossing the Void: A Postmodern Jewish Theology', in Bernard Lightman and Michael Brown (eds), *Creating the Jewish Future* (Walnut Creek, CA: Alta Mira Press, 1999), 46.

the dinner according to the menu. Everyone else is, from one point of view, a special case, dealt with under emergency regulations.[19]

[19] C.S. Lewis, 'Foreword,' in Joy Davidman, *Smoke on the Mountain: An Interpretation of the Ten Commandments* (Philadelphia, PA: The Westminster Press, 1954), 7-8.

A CASE STUDY: THE INFLUENCE OF THE LAUSANNE MOVEMENT ON YOUNGER KOREAN CHRISTIAN LEADERS

Chulho Han

Introduction

The greatest beneficiaries of the *Lausanne Covenant* in the Korean Church were the Christian young adults and college students. Although the *Lausanne Covenant* was published in 1974, it had no immediate influence on the Korean Church. Even with 65 Koreans present at the Lausanne Congress in 1974, the Lausanne Movement was seen merely as a theological agenda among a few theologians in Korea.[1] The Lausanne Movement and the *Lausanne Covenant* remained largely unknown to the Korean Church until 1990 when Dr Chongnahm Cho, then Chairman of the Asia Lausanne Committee, published a booklet which included the translation of the *Lausanne Covenant* into Korean.[2] Those who participated in the 1974 Lausanne Congress were mostly evangelical or conservative church leaders, and the content of the *Lausanne Covenant* was seen as being too radical for it to be introduced to the Korean Church at that time. Instead, the *Lausanne Covenant* was introduced to the Korean Church in a more wholesome manner by younger workers within the InterVarsity Christian Fellowship (IVF), Korea.

Korean Society and Church in the 1980s

Korean society in the early 1980s experienced much despair which caused college students to engage in desperate movements. The young people of the country had already lost much hope as a result of a strong militant dictatorship which continued on from the 1960s. Although some Christians did fight against such military dictatorship, most conservative evangelical churches and pastors were either uninterested in the current affairs of the country or aided the military regime in order to maintain their positions. As

---

[1] Chongnahm Cho, 'Lausanne Congress and Evangelical Missiology', in Jong Yun Lee (cd), *Lausanne Movement for World Evangelization* (Seoul: Korea LCWE, 2009), 10.

[2] Chongnahm Cho, History and Spirit of Lausanne Movement (Seoul: IVP Korea, 1990).

a result, the conservative evangelical churches failed to be light and salt of the world. Against such a background, Christian young adults were even more anxious. The lessons they learned from the Bible, on the one hand, and from the reality of their lives, on the other, were simply too different from each other. The gospel they believed in had little effect on their colleges or on reality. This 'gospel' was a powerless echo within the church, with no transformative effect in the world. Although preachers continued to claim that the Gospel was the way and the power, young adults found that the Christian faith did not result in transformation.

Some college students organized themselves into democratization movements and proclaimed justice and righteousness in anti-government demonstrations. Although it seemed like they had power to change the world, Christian college students found themselves caught in between, as they could neither participate in anti-government demonstrations stained with much violence, nor let injustice and anti-democratic practices continue.

At the same time, the churches continued to preach a one-sided gospel without showing any response to the pains of the world. As the Korean Church continued growing, congregations became larger and the church buildings rose taller. But the truth and the power of the Gospel remained hidden and prosperity theology became rampant.

In colleges, internationally connected campus ministries such as the InterVarsity Christian Fellowship (IVF), Campus Crusade for Christ (CCC), Navigators, and Youth With A Mission (YWAM), and Korean indigenous campus ministries such as the University Bible Fellowship (UBF), Evangelical Student Fellowship (ESF), and Students For Christ (SFC), emerged and began to take on more active roles in evangelization. They focused their work on reaching the non-Christians on campuses, and in the 1970s they concentrated on evangelization of students and of the whole nation through large-scale conferences. Most campus ministries had specific goals for discipleship training, Bible studies, and overseas missions. As a result, they did convert many college students, but had little effect in changing society.

Then some groups became interested in a publishing ministry and began introducing Christian books written in the west. As more western Christian books and resources became available in Korea, younger Christians in the country began to recognize their responsibility in the church and in society. With more reading came the ability to analyze the issues of society from a Christian perspective and the need to view the world with a Christian perspective of history and of society. In particular, the Gwangju Democratization Movement in 1980 played a crucial role. In May 1980, many young adults and citizens of Gwangju Metropolitan City lost their lives as they protested against the dictatorship of the country. In this process, young adults with a Christian conscience began to understand that being ignorant of the oppression of human rights and liberty was neither biblical nor evangelical.

However, younger Christians could not join those college students in the mainstream political movement based on the radical Marxist worldview because of the fundamental difference between Christian faith and the Marxist worldview. Although some Christian students did participate in the anti-government student movement based on the Marxist worldview, most Christian students believed that participating in violence-driven protests was not in line with their faith. Then in the early 1980s, some college students and graduates began forming study groups. They pursued answers for questions of their identity as evangelical Bible-believing Christians, such as, 'What does it take to live in the world as Christians believing in the authority and power of the Bible?' and 'How can we carry out the evangelical faith in the reality of our world today?' And in their pursuit, they found the *Lausanne Covenant*. It was like a ray of light for them. The *Lausanne Covenant* showed that their pursuit was not only just but also biblical. This idea became even more widespread as several Christian campus ministry leaders such as Jikhan Kho, Byoungryoung Hong, Inho Kim, and Chulho Han participated in Lausanne II in Manila in 1989. They were greatly challenged as they shared ideas with evangelical leaders from around the world at the Congress. And upon their return to Korea, they actively started introducing the *Lausanne Covenant* to young Korean Christians.

As a result, young Christian leaders believed that the *Lausanne Covenant* and the *Manila Manifesto* – published at Lausanne II in Manila in 1989 – would provide a theological basis for younger Christians in Korea to respond to the practical issues of society while adhering to the traditional evangelical faith. The *Lausanne Covenant* not only emphasized the theology of the Triune God, the authority of Bible, and Jesus Christ as Saviour, but also asserted that "evangelism and social responsibility are both the duty of Christians", and that "the Gospel we proclaim must be holistic and should be witnessed to in word, deed, and power". This gave them hope, vision and encouragement. The challenge to Christians to pay attention to issues of peace, justice and freedom around the world, and the call for 'the Whole Church to take the Whole Gospel to the World' became a new theological standard for them. Moreover, the *Lausanne Occasional Papers*, published as a result of various follow-up conferences of the 1974 Lausanne Congress, and presenting biblical principles and solutions on wide-ranging topics, served as excellent guides for them in dealing with the issues they were facing. Subsequently, in the mid- and late 1980s, many Christian organizations, based on the biblical principles they found in the theology of Lausanne, became strongly active. This served as the dawn of the so-called revival era of the evangelical intellect in Korea.

Influence of Lausanne Movement on Younger Christians

Christian Campus Movements

As various campus ministries like IVF Korea began adopting the *Lausanne Covenant* as their statement of faith, the paradigm of evangelization among college students began to change as well. No longer seeing conversion as the end of evangelization, they started viewing various issues in colleges and in society from a biblical perspective. Since they did not view evangelism as something separate from campus culture, they started transforming the campuses with the power of the Gospel and began to see significant changes take place. Colleges at that time were heavily influenced by hardliners who subscribed to the Marxist theory of change. But these Christian college students, challenged by the *Lausanne Covenant*, started sharing in colleges a message of peace, justice and love without using violence, and started a movement of mutual forgiveness and reconciliation. Young evangelical adults also began participating actively in the Democratization Movement. One example of such social participation was the hundreds of evangelical college students who organized fair-election monitoring groups nationwide for the 1987 presidential election, and campaigned for the election to be held in fairness according to democratic procedures. This kind of movement gained popularity among Christian and non-Christian students alike. As a result, evangelical campus ministries grew rapidly from the end of the 1980s to the mid-1990s. This campus movement continued to experience exponential growth up until the turn of the millennium.

Publications and Their Influence

Lausanne documents such as the *Lausanne Occasional Papers* gave rise to various study groups. At the same time, books by leaders of the Lausanne Movement such as John Stott were translated and published in Korean, building an intellectual foundation for the evangelical movement after the 1980s. Thus, the *Lausanne Covenant* served as the *Magna Carta* of Korean evangelical theology.

With increased reading of Lausanne documents, young evangelical intellectuals of Korea also began to produce publications with biblical perspective on various issues in Korea at that time. And those publications began to slowly influence younger Christians in Korea. Younger evangelicals in Korea found it a pure joy to master the *Lausanne Covenant* and other related documents, and to use the lessons learned to come up with solutions for the issues they were faced with. This gave rise to many study groups such as Christian Worldview Studies in 1981 and the Korea

Institute for Christian Studies in 1987.[3] These groups adopted the *Lausanne Covenant* as their statement of faith and published many works concerning faith, academics and the Christian worldview..

Perhaps the greatest distributor of the Lausanne spirit and theology was InterVarsity Press Korea (IVP). IVP translated and distributed many books by the leaders of the Lausanne Movement as well as the *Lausanne Covenant,* the *Manila Manifesto* and *Lausanne Occasional Papers* such as the *Willowbank Report – Consultation on Gospel and Culture.* IVP introduced books by John Stott, Samuel Escobar, Christopher Wright, Ronald J. Sider and others. Other publishers also introduced Lausanne-related documents and books. Such publications greatly influenced young Christians and intellectuals in Korea. They equipped younger Christians to view politics, economics, society, culture, arts and so on in a Christian perspective. Subsequently, as they graduated from college, they began to exercise significant Christian influence in all aspects of society. Having been influenced by the *Lausanne Covenant*, young graduates began to live out their Christian thinking and practice in the workplace. As a result, the end of the 1980s through to the beginning of 1990s saw the rise of a Christian movement in every major career path such as the TCF (Teachers Christian Fellowship), NCF (Nurses Christian Fellowship), CMF (Christian Medical Fellowship), and CLF (Christian Lawyers Fellowship). Members of these groups genuinely asked themselves what it meant to live as Christians, seeking answers to this question in the Bible, and endeavouring to practise the lessons learned. Some of those organizations evolved into large movements of Christian professionals. For example, the TCF has become the GTM (Good Teachers Movement) and continues to hold a large conference of over 3,000 Christian teachers every other year. The GTM also develops curriculums for schools according to the Christian worldview, and asserts significant influence on the government concerning national education policy.

Emergence of Organizations Based on the Lausanne Covenant

Gospel and Context

A monthly publication that expressed the Lausanne spirit well was the magazine called *Gospel and Context*, first published in 1991. This magazine attempted to analyze the context of the Korean Church and Korean society in the light of the Gospel and present solutions. *Gospel and Context* adopted the *Lausanne Covenant* as its statement of faith, and aimed at providing Christian answers to many of life's questions that younger

---

[3] Today, these organizations have been merged into the Christian Worldview Studies Association of Korea: http://worldview.or.kr.

Christians at that time had, based on the premise of Lausanne theology that 'evangelism and social responsibility are both the duty of Christians'. Several young pastors and campus ministry leaders who had been influenced by the *Lausanne Covenant* participated in this magazine project. Across the bottom of the cover of the first issue of *Gospel and Context* appeared: '*Gospel and Context* is a Christian magazine that sheds the light of the Gospel on history and society based on the confession of faith expressed in the *Lausanne Covenant*'. The magazine carried many articles analyzing societal and ecclesiastical issues of the time and proposed biblical solutions.

In the twentieth anniversary edition of *Gospel and Context*, Prof. Man-Youl Lee, the inaugural editor of the magazine, recalled the impact of the Lausanne Movement: "Many young evangelical students at that time were simply watching radical Christians actively participate in democratization and unification, and had many regrets over the fact that praying without taking any action was unworthy of evangelical Christians, but the introduction of the *Lausanne Covenant* in Korea provided an ideological basis for Korean evangelical Christians to actively participate in social issues."[4] In particular, Section 5 (Christian Social Responsibility) and Section 9 (The Urgency of the Evangelistic Task) of the *Lausanne Covenant* clearly stated the social responsibility of Christians, providing a solid reason for the existence of the magazine. Since then, *Gospel and Context* has continued to handle evangelism and social responsibility in a holistic manner, challenging many in evangelical circles. For a time, *Gospel and Context* was also the best-selling Christian magazine in Korea.

Joint Christian Student Movement

'Co-operation in evangelism',[5] emphasized in the *Lausanne Covenant*, challenged campus ministries, steeped as they were in division and self-centeredness, to co-operate with one another for evangelization. Each campus ministry was engrossed in itself and different ministries working on one and the same campus hardly met together or co-operated. But as a result of the efforts made by some campus ministry leaders for 'a deeper unity in truth' through overcoming 'a sinful individualism and needless duplication', as emphasized in the *Lausanne Covenant*, campus ministries on each campus began to join hands. Campus ministry leaders additionally worked with local churches in evangelizing colleges. This spirit of unity provided a platform for the Korea Campus Evangelization Network (KCEN) to emerge in 1989 for the evangelization of college students.

---

[4] Man-Youl Lee, 'Twenty-year history of Gospel and Context', in *Gospel and Context,* Vol 243, 18.

[5] Lausanne Covenant, Section 7.

Today, 19 campus ministries and 400 churches are working together for the evangelization of college students under the banner of KCEN.

The Mission Korea Movement

Another effect the *Lausanne Covenant* had on the younger Christians of Korea was joint movements for missions. The *Lausanne Covenant* not only awakened younger Christians to evangelism and social responsibility within Korea but also challenged them with 'the urgency of the evangelistic task of the world'. As younger Christians started responding to this call in the late 1980s, their interest in overseas mission grew rapidly. As a result, a joint movement for mission mobilization among university students called *Mission Korea* emerged in 1988. *Mission Korea* began as a collaboration between campus ministries and overseas mission agencies based on the theology and vision of the *Lausanne Covenant* that "the gospel must be preached to all nations to fulfil the promise of his coming".

Leaders of *Mission Korea* worked together to teach, encourage and challenge the young adults and college students of Korea to rise and take up the call to global evangelization in their generation. Their goal was to see a new generation of overseas missionaries arise from among young adults and college students. Another intended outcome of the *Mission Korea* movement was that young adults and students would return to their churches and communities, and start their own local prayer movement and collaborative mission conferences, transforming their churches into missional churches and paving the way for another wave of awakening.

Mission Korea conferences have been held biennially since 1988. Campus ministry leaders saw much fruit through these conferences. First, the most noticeable fruit was that younger Christians were mobilized for overseas missions in huge numbers. Present at the first *Mission Korea* conference in 1988 were 500 young adults. The number grew to 1,500 in the second conference in 1990, and to 3,000 in the 1992 conference. Since then, each *Mission Korea* conference has been attended by about 4-5,000 young adults and is today the largest mission conference in Asia. To date, over 50,000 university students have attended *Mission Korea* conferences with over 26,000 attendees making decisions to be long- or short-term missionaries for services lasting at least one year each. There are about 25,000 Korean missionaries around the world today, and it is believed that a great number of them made the decision to be missionaries through *Mission Korea* conferences.

Second, the *Mission Korea* movement had a positive influence on the mission movement of the Korean Church. After attending conferences, many young adults started their own mission and prayer movements in their respective churches and communities. Mission training programmes emerged in many churches. Many got involved in prayer meetings for mission. As a result, even more young people dedicated their lives for mission, and this in turn challenged older Christians in the churches to be involved in mission. Prior to the *Mission Korea* conferences, mission was believed to be for pastors and full-time Christian workers only. But as many young adults and college students began to get involved in mission through the *Mission Korea* conferences, it became clear that mission was God's great commission for all members of the church.

Third, *Mission Korea* conferences had a great influence on the strategies and direction of Korean missions. Many new missionary strategies and directions were introduced to churches across the country through *Mission Korea* conferences. Frontier mission movement for reaching unreached people groups, lay missions movements, tentmaking missions movements, mission trips, short-term missions and other strategic concepts were introduced and developed. In particular, as Ralph Winter's challenge of the unreached people movement – first published at the 1974 Lausanne Congress – was introduced to the Korean Church through *Mission Korea* conferences, the direction of the mission movement of the Korean Church started shifting toward reaching unreached peoples.

Fourth, the *Mission Korea* movement sparked off an urge for greater unity. The model of unity seen in the *Mission Korea* movement had a positive impact on the evangelization of campuses, and various campus ministries in each university began to work in close unity. The *Mission Korea* movement also contributed to unity between overseas mission agencies and campus ministries, and unity between campus ministries and churches for mission. A total of 11 campus ministries and 25 overseas mission agencies are currently working together under the banner of *Mission Korea*. This kind of unity for mission was never seen before in the history of the Korean Church.

Fifth, *Mission Korea* conferences presented a new model of non-western mission mobilization movements. Today we are seeing the emergence of various mission mobilization movements among young adults and students not only in America and Europe, but also in Asia, Latin America and Africa. The model of unity of *Mission Korea* is becoming an important model for these new movements. For instance, delegates have been sent from Indonesia, Nagaland in India, Bangladesh and the Philippines to *Mission Korea* conferences and have then spearheaded unity-focused mission conferences in their own countries based on the *Mission Korea* model. Similar unity-driven mission movements are currently under preparation in Mongolia and other countries.

Recently, the *Mission Korea* movement took on a new structure to mobilize young Korean adults for mission even more effectively. Named 'Mission Korea Partners', this new arm aims to provide better mobilization, training, and preparation of younger Christians for mission with lasting results.

Lausanne Study Groups

As seminary students voluntarily study the *Lausanne Covenant* and Lausanne documents, the Lausanne Movement is taking root within seminaries in Korea. This adoption has been encouraged by growing numbers of younger professors who have accepted Lausanne theology and, more recently, the emergence of Lausanne study groups among students. To date, these groups can be found in twelve major seminaries including the Presbyterian Theological College and Seminary. Professors with a keen interest in the Lausanne Movement are studying Lausanne-related documents with students and are helping them build their theology. In addition to weekly meetings, all of these study groups meet together twice every year for retreats. Seminary students of different denominations are coming together in unity and fellowship in the Lausanne spirit. A similar unity remains relatively rare in the Korean churches as denominations generally hold to their own theological doctrines and often refuse to converse with other denominations. However, with the formation of Lausanne study groups in major Korean seminaries, the theology and spirit of Lausanne are expected to become more widely accepted among future pastors of the Korean Church. The *Lausanne Covenant* might therefore help bring unity to the Korean Church as a whole.

Christian Art and Culture Groups

The theology of Lausanne has also had a great impact on Christian artists. The *Lausanne Covenant*'s call that "churches must seek to transform and enrich culture, all for the glory of God" served as a great encouragement for young Christian artists. Traditionally, the Korean Church tended to view culture and art as being anti-Christian. As a result, the artistic talents of Christian artists were hardly expressed. But as Christian artists were encouraged by the *Lausanne Covenant*, they began to express their Christian creativity in various forms of art including music, paintings, sculptures, writings and movies. Such changes were also evident in worship services. Artistic talents have been embraced in worship, sometimes through the usage of Korean traditional music and art in Christian expressions. Christians in mainstream art also became more confident in revealing God's truth through their creative works. Younger Christians learned that the Gospel should not be confined to the issues of spiritual salvation but that it must be clearly expressed that God reigns in all aspects of their lives and culture.

The Future of the Lausanne Movement in Korea

With the new millennium, the Korean Church is faced with a serious crisis. The churches are becoming highly secular. Young people are leaving churches and are not responding to the Gospel. Society has little respect for the churches. Although the Korean Church grew rapidly and has sent many missionaries overseas in the last thirty years, it has failed to be light and salt within Korean society and is now becoming weak. Pastors often find themselves at the centre of societal criticism. Although there are churches on practically every street, they are becoming more detached from the world. With God's abundant blessing, the Korean Church grew large, and Korean Christians have become the rich and the powerful of Korean society. But now the church is seen as a group of self-seeking people rather than a neighbour-serving community.

The Korean Church today is perhaps in a more serious situation than in the despairing Korean society of thirty years ago. Back then, the church was seen as a community of hope in a country oppressed by military dictatorship. Many younger Christians at that time studied ways of fighting the injustice and unfairness of the time. But today, younger Christians have become secularized, and they have little expectation of the church showing them the way. Young people are no longer thinking of their neighbours and the world but are focused on their practical needs. Colleges are no longer places for advancing academics and preparing minds for changing the world but have become venues of competition for job training and employment. Secularism has engulfed the colleges. The number of young people participating in Christian groups in colleges is also decreasing. The same is happening in local churches. Except for a few mega-churches, the number of young adults in most churches is decreasing. Young people do not find churches attractive any more and see no hope in them.

Change is necessary in the Korean Church. The essence of the Gospel must be restored and the Church must recognize the full authority of the Bible and start living in full obedience to the Word. Christians must start living lives worthy of Scripture and show the change in word and action. For Christians to live as the light and salt of the world and lead the world to the feet of the Lord, a new spiritual awakening is required through theological reflection and the resulting response. Younger Christians must be shown that hope is in Christ. It must be proclaimed that the power of the Gospel can strengthen and empower them from despair into new hope. The hope in Christ that the *Lausanne Covenant* presented to young Korean Christians thirty years ago must be stirred in the hearts of younger Korean Christians again today.

In this regard, the direction and challenges expressed in the *Cape Town Commitment* of 2010 are expected to provide yet another turning-point for the Korean Church and her younger Christians to be salt and light once more. The *Cape Town Commitment* includes a detailed listing of contexts and needs around the world today, and proposes the actual practice of Christian love in this world. The *Cape Town Commitment* also challenges Christians to take on certain attitudes in practising such love. Today's complex and diversified world has many more problems and requires detailed solutions to these problems. The same is true for the Korean

Church and for younger Christians in Korea. Younger Christians today are lethargic because they are unable to identify, let alone handle, the issues at hand. They are also unsure how such issues are connected to their faith. In this regard, the issues and solutions prescribed in the *Cape Town Commitment* will pose a new challenge to younger Christians in Korea.

Among the over 130 Korean delegates at the Cape Town 2010 Congress were more than thirty younger leaders. When selecting younger leaders for Cape Town 2010, young people of various fields were intentionally nominated. They were not only seminarians and pastors but also young Christians actively involved in the economy, medicine, politics, culture, art and many other fields. As they participated in discussing various issues in their line of interest, they realized that answers to these issues could be found in the Bible, and that these issues could be dealt with by working together within the Christian community.

Korean society has been greatly influenced by Confucianist customs, and the Korean Church has been no exception. While it is important to respect good traditions, it is also important to reject unjust authoritarianism and let younger Christians experience the power of the Gospel so that they might be nurtured as leaders of the Church. The Korean Lausanne Committee recently became active again, and it was decided that the Committee should increase its support for younger leaders. The Lausanne leaders are visiting seminaries to introduce the Movement to young pastors, and plans are underway for actively supporting campus ministries. The Korean Lausanne Committee will also actively find lay leaders in various fields, help them discover their true Christian identity in their respective fields, and encourage them to transform their worlds with Christian values. This will help restore the reputation of the Korean Church and provide an effective platform for further and deeper evangelization. When the Korean Church stops acting as a religious group isolated from society and starts embracing the pains and sufferings of Korean society for its healing, the Korean Church and her Christians will be able to bring transformation to the world.

Conclusion

In this article, I have examined the influence of the Lausanne Movement on younger Korean Christians. Just as the *Lausanne Covenant* provided a ray of hope thirty years ago when Korean society was in a desperate situation and the church was ignorant of it, we hope that the Lausanne Movement will shed new light on the Korean Church and her younger Christians who are faced with another kind of despair today. We must encourage these young people to be the cornerstones of a new transformation and revival of the Korean Church. Those who learned about the *Lausanne Covenant* and were challenged by it thirty years ago are leaders of the Korean Church today. The future of the Korean Church lies with its young people today. It is important to help them to stand righteous before God in order to see today's crisis of the Korean Church turn into tomorrow's revival. We are in need of younger Christians who are biblically learned, historically founded, and culturally engaged. And we believe that the calling of the Lausanne Movement is to help the younger Christians of Korea towards this goal.

STRATEGY IN MISSION – TWENTY-FIRST CENTURY STYLE

Roy Peterson and Gilles Gravelle

> We urge the development of regional and functional cooperation for the furtherance of the Church's mission, for strategic planning, for mutual encouragement, and for the sharing of resources and experience. 1974 – The *Lausanne Covenant*, Section 7: 'Cooperation in Evangelism'.[1]

Lausanne I, the 1974 International Congress On World Evangelization, was attended by 2,300 leaders from 150 countries. The Movement was global from the start: together leaders from so many countries drafted and signed the *Lausanne Covenant* which would define for decades to come 'the necessity, responsibilities, and goals of spreading the Gospel'. Section 7 of the *Lausanne Covenant* outlines at least five macro-strategies in mission. The strategies describe partnership co-operation, strategic planning, mutuality, resource-sharing, and knowledge-sharing.

Soon after the closing of Lausanne I, the first Strategy Working Group was formed. It was chaired by Peter Wagner (1976-81), followed by Ed Dayton (1981-93), Bryant Myers (1993-96), and Paul Eshleman (1996-2012). Each working group focused on advancing mission research and knowledge. Their collective work helped shape themes of subsequent Lausanne Movement global gatherings, such as Pattaya, Thailand, in 1980, Lausanne II in Manila 1989, and Lausanne III in Cape Town 2010, as well as issue-based gatherings in the intervening years.

Strategic mission research and planning was not born out of Lausanne I. In fact, however, Lausanne I was a return to it. Ed Dayton and David Fraser reminded us that applying research in planning missionary enterprises typified mission planning in the 1890s through to the 1920s.[2] Even so, mission scholars, such as Samuel Escobar and Mark Knoll, cautioned evangelical mission leaders to not see mission simply as managerial missiology or managerial theology.[3] Indeed, Escobar's warnings and concerns expressed in 'A Movement Divided' (1991) began a lively debate

---

[1] www.lausanne.org/en/documents/lausanne-covenant.html.

[2] E. R. Dayton and D. A. Fraser, *Planning Strategies for World Evangelization* (Grand Rapids, MI: Eerdmans, 1980), 9.

[3] M. A. Knoll, 'Common Sense Tradition and American Evangelical Thought', in *American Quarterly* 37 (1985), 216-38.

with Ralph Winter, who wrote a rejoinder to Escobar's article.[4] Certainly, awareness of cultural context is important, as are appropriate strategy models.[5] Dayton and Fraser also reminded readers that the ideas they discussed needed to be applied in culturally sensitive and appropriate ways. However, they did not suggest that strategic planning should only be something the west brought to global mission.

Today, global evangelical mission still places much emphasis on good research and planning. Majority World strategists, like Paul Opoku-Mensah of Ghana and Musa Dube of Botswana, are producing insightful studies in the area of mission strategy in general and Bible translation strategy in particular. But there is an increasing level of accountability brought to mission planning and execution these days. Global conversations on what constitutes effective strategies are still needed to maintain balance.

These days, more Majority World leaders understand the importance of vision casting, sound planning, with clear benchmarks, and accounting for results. Focus on these things will only increase in the 21st century. This may be a result of globalization, as ideas and standards spread more quickly because of the internet, among other things. In the globalized period of mission, partnership, teamwork and mutual assistance will not go far without a clear understanding of what success is for any co-operative endeavour. Success cannot be understood unless the steps to achieving it are mapped out between the planners and those affected by such plans from the start.

This article discusses how the five macro-strategies first devised as a result of Lausanne I, and moved forward by each subsequent strategy working group, are taking on new life in 21st century mission. This builds on the assumption that research and planning is understood from a trans-disciplinary view developed through local, regional and global agency collaboration. This should be a safeguard, albeit an imperfect one, against foreign or local dominance that threatens the ultimate aim of mission – people saved and freed from the impoverishments that keep them down.

Trends in 21st Century Mission

Since the first gathering at Lausanne, we have witnessed a mission shift. Now in the period of global Christianity, more local believers are capable of leading mission efforts. However, how they lead may look different from place to place. After all, global Christianity does not mean homogeneity. Global Christianity is universalizing in our understanding of Christ, but diverse in its expressions.

---

4 G. Gravelle, www.wciujournal.org/blog/post/on-social-transformation-and-unreached-peoples (2012).

5 S. Escobar, 'A Movement Divided: Three approaches to world evangelism in tension with one another', in *Transformation*, (1991) 8:4.

Mission strategy, 21st century-style, requires an understanding of the times. The following section describes five key trends, according to scholars.

Globalizing of Theology

In the introduction to *Globalizing of Theology*, editors Craig Ott and Harold Netland assert, "Globalizing means local Christian communities enabled to do theology within their own local contexts but in conversation with other Christians globally."[6] Missiologist Darrel Whitman claims, "Self-theologizing recognizes the necessity of every community of believers to connect the gospel to their own worldview and to address the problems in which they struggle."[7] Hwa Yung believes, "Indigenous theology more effectively empowers Christians for mission. A mature church is not just self-governing, self-supporting and self-propagating, it must also be self-theologizing."[8]

This understanding of theology, especially from a practical or missional point of view, requires mission strategists to evaluate plans based on such diversity. Planning cannot be a top-down process, but rather something worked out according to local theological sensibilities.

Contextualizing Hermeneutics

Globalized theology is concomitant with localized hermeneutics. This notion is particularly challenging for western trained mission workers who have understood a more monolithic hermeneutic formed in the west. As theologian Kevin Vanhoozer said, western mission, at times, "assumed right procedures for knowing the exegetical pretense to objectivity and universality ... (However) the hermeneutical principle is attention to lived experience, especially that of the poor, as the medium in which biblical interpretation takes place".[9]

Expressing an Asian dimension, religion professor Moonjang Lee claims, "It is now widely recognized that culture plays the role of a hermeneutical filter, and what we bring to the biblical text is bound to affect the way we read, understand, and interpret text."[10] Missiologists

---

[6] C. Ott and H. A. Netland (eds), *Globalizing Theology* (Grand Rapids, MI: Baker, 2006), 29ff.

[7] D. Whiteman, 'Anthropological Reflections', in Ott and Netland (eds), *Globalizing Theology*, 60.

[8] H. Yung, *Mangoes or Bananas?* (Oxford, UK: Regnum, 1997), 10.

[9] K. Vanhoozer, 'Theological Method in an Era of World Christianity', in Ott and Netland, *Globalizing Theology*, 92ff.

[10] M. Lee, 'Reading the Bible in the Non-Western Church: An Asian Dimension', in A. Walls and C. Ross (eds), *Mission in the 21st Century: Exploring the Five Marks of Global Mission* (Maryknoll, NY: Orbis, 2008), 148.

David and Cynthia Strong agree. “Different cultures may use different hermeneutics while fully recognizing scriptural authority.”[11]

How will mission strategists plan for and evaluate programme effectiveness, given this understanding of hermeneutics? Good results of a project may not be recognizable to people if they interpret results through a different cultural filter. Knowing what success could look like in unique settings is part of good planning. Indeed, Paul Hiebert’s (among others) notion of self-theologizing suggests positive change could present itself in unique ways from one location to another, at least in the way a cultural outsider might view such change.[12]

Indigenizing Bible Translation

Simon Crisp, Co-ordinator for Translation Standards and Scholarly Editions with the United Bible Societies, expressed how strategies for training need to be refreshed now in the indigenous period of translation: “Training and capacity building … have not always taken sufficient account of local cultures and sensibilities in its construction and delivery … A more culturally appropriate model of empowerment would be to privilege the choices, traditions and solutions of local communities, with the expectation that outside direction and guidance would over time become less necessary.”[13]

Diversifying Training

Theological educator Lois Douglas is concerned that formal academic training in the west may not align well with today’s training need, especially in some regions of the world: “Education requires culturally appropriate and theologically appropriate models that are as diverse as the contexts in which they occur … Far too many programs are being driven by pragmatic concerns related to accreditation, funding, recruiting, and the expectation of constituencies. If we are ever to break out of this pattern of business as usual, creativity and intentionality are needed.”[14]

---

[11] D. Strong and C. Strong, ‘The Globalizing Hermeneutics of the Jerusalem Council’, in Ott and Netland (eds), *Globalizing Theology*, 133.

[12] Hiebert, Anthropological Insights for Missionaries (Grand Rapids, MI: Baker Book House, 1985).

[13] S. Crisp, ‘Translation Consultancy: Set in stone or historically conditioned?’, paper given at *BT 2011 Conference,* SIL, Dallas, TX, 18th Oct 2011.

[14] L. Douglas, ‘Globalizing Theology and Theological Education’, in Ott and Netland (eds), *Globalizing Theology*, 277.

Emphasizing Ethics

Simply stated, how do mission strategists understand the power and influence certain practices exert on the people they serve? Ethical behaviour builds trust. Unethical behaviour builds walls. In doing Bible translation, United Bible Societies consultant, Esteban Voth, reminds us that "a small group of experts can exert a lot of power and translators are not above suspicion. They bring certain ideology to their work based on traditional conformity inherited from others."[15] These ethical concerns apply to other mission sectors as well. For example, the use of position, funding methods, the use of designated funds and financial reporting. The *Lausanne Covenant* called for a high standard in ethical and moral behaviour as part of its framework (1974, Articles 12 and 13). Even so, greater attention to ethics in 21st century mission is a significant trend.

Strategies in the 21st Century

Together, these five trends inform how these macro-strategies will continue to take shape in the 21st century. In this section, each strategy will be explored using examples from mission today.

Building Strategic Partnerships Based on Mutuality

> "The supremacy and centrality of Christ in our mission must be more than a confession of faith; it must also govern our strategy, practice and unity."[16]

Participants at Lausanne II in Manila 1989 made a significant step forward in recognizing that mission has become a global endeavour. Now many of the traditional missionary receiving countries have more Christians than the western nations who sent them. That reality would affect mission strategies and planning in the third millennium, especially in the area of partnership.[17] Lausanne III in Cape Town built on this understanding.

Now, in the globalized period of Christianity, people from nearly every region of the world are connecting with cellular phone technology and over the internet, and not in negligible ways. Social media platforms provide constant multi-media interaction. Video conferencing makes face-to-face meetings possible. There are no excuses for not working together closely because collaboration is now more possible than ever.

Indeed, there are calls in the religious and social sectors for greater partnership co-ordination in project planning and implementation. This is for the simple reason that partnership alliances can mobilize more resources and ultimately achieve greater sustainable impact in the long run. In fact,

---

[15] E. Voth, 'Towards an Ethic of Liberation for Bible Translation; Part 1: Ideology', in *SBL Forum*, http://sbl-site.org/publications/article.aspx?articleId=754.

[16] *CTC*, IIF.2b.

[17] *Manila Manifesto*, Section B9.

donors rightly look to partnership as a condition for funding for these reasons.

Before specific plans are made, it is important that project planners find out who else is working with the people or the task they desire to serve. They could be other mission agencies, a local or national church body or a non-governmental organization. In other words, they could be any other expression of the church among the people. Through dialogue, the partners begin to understand what each ministry seeks to accomplish. Then they consider together how each ministry could help the people whom their ministry serves to achieve greater impact.

Partnership alliances are not necessarily easy to form. As one expert said, "It is critical for an organization to assess its own contributions as an alliance partner in order to identify potential partners. Each organization must be clear on its own focus, competencies and capabilities in order to identify what roles alliance partners can play in moving closer toward the vision."[18]

This is mutuality, where each partner, regardless of social, educational or economic status, is able to contribute resources (funds, skills, materials, knowledge, etc.) according to their abilities to do so. It also expresses the notion of interdependency, because in order to achieve a mutually desired outcome, the partners need to understand that they need each other.

The globalized period of mission requires some strategic adjustments when it comes to partnership development and planning. Although the majority of Christians live in non-western countries, financial and educational resources needed to carry out mission work are certainly not equally available. Equality, however, is not necessarily the point. Mutuality and generosity are perhaps better operating terms for mission strategy – 21st century style. Former bishop Hwa Yung addressed this topic well when he asked:

> To address adequately the issue of partnership would require us to seriously deal with a whole range of questions. For example, in terms of finance and trained personnel, how and what can the West contribute to augment the meager resources of many non-Western churches? At the same time, how can this be done without giving rise to a dependency mentality on the one hand, and the perpetuation of missionary control on the other. With respect to developing leadership for non-Western churches up to the highest levels, what can we learn from John Stott's work through the Langham Trust of training national scholars with PhDs? And would international agencies, traditionally under Western control, dare to incorporate non-westerners fully into their leadership on the basis of genuine mutuality?[19]

---

[18] J. Wei-Skillern et al., *Entrepreneurship in the Social Sector* (London: Sage Publications, 2007), 198.

[19] H. Yung, 'Strategic Issues in Missions – An Asian Perspective', in *Evangelical Missions Quarterly*, Jan 2004.

Example: Assessment of the Task through Partnership

Evangelical research organizations have worked hard for years trying to develop a strategic assessment of remaining evangelism needs in the world. Joshua Project, Global Mapping International, IMB, Wycliffe Center for the Study of Global Christianity at Gordon-Conwell Theological Seminary, the U.S. Center for World Mission, Table 71's Finishing the Task, and many others have focused their individual attention on answering this question.

Now researchers from these organizations are asking with one unified voice: How can more people living in places still needing evangelism help provide the data themselves? How can social media and community collaboration methods enable greater participation by people everywhere?[20] Web 1.0 technology provided access to data. Now media-rich Web 2.0 technology allows for live interaction with the very people we long to know and serve. New efforts to improve evangelism data are now underway. Importantly, this is increasingly happening through broad, dedicated partnership rather than individually.

Example: Partnerships That Accelerate Bible Translation

> Hasten the translation of the Bible into the languages of peoples who do not yet have any portion of God's Word in their mother tongue. [21]

At one time, Bible translation agencies worked rather independently. Geographical isolation, different translation practices and especially organizational legacies naturally contributed to this separation of effort. Even so, significant gains were made in providing access to Scripture in thousands of languages. Now globalization is fuelling people's desire for more and better Scripture translations.

Additionally, internet growth, social media, smartphones and PC tablets provide an amazing array of options for how Scripture is translated and communicated. More people can actively participate in translation work for their people group. And besides reading their new translation, people can also listen to it, sing it, tell it, view it, tweet it and act it out, sometimes all at the same time!

The urgent need for understanding and hope in difficult situations coupled with the increasing desire for Scripture in one's own language requires greater collaboration among translation agencies. This is what leaders from several major Bible translation agencies recently concluded, and they are changing their practices because of it.

---

[20] Inter-agency Webinars: *Crowdsourcing for UUPG Research*, March 21st 2012 and June 11th 2012, hosted by the U.S. Center for World Mission and The Seed Company.

[21] *CTC*, IID, 1C.

These agencies are working together to develop better web-based translation training for anyone, anywhere. They are developing ways for far more people to participate more directly in Bible translation work through web-based crowdsourcing. To spread translated Scripture faster, they are developing digital just-in-time publishing.

All of this is being done through translation agency collaboration. It involves knowledge-sharing and cost-sharing. Bible translation work today is simply too large and too accelerated for any one agency to develop and maintain alone. It takes a larger team working together to achieve the vision of every person in the world having access to God's Word in their own language.

Access to Strategic Resources

> … our missional calling includes responsible stewardship of God's creation and its resources.[22]

Certainly, taking care of God's physical creation must improve, but an extended notion of God's creation and its resources also includes material and cognitive resources that God provides, such as finances, goods, knowledge, experience and capabilities (James 1:16).

Mission strategy in the 21st century requires a shift in the use of finances. Western mission agencies see a global Christianity shift occurring, and they say it's time for the church in these countries to take over leadership in evangelism, church planting and Bible translation. However, Lois Douglas wonders what we have left them to lead with?[23] Douglas asks this question because the resources and methods brought by western mission agencies to foreign countries are fast losing practical usefulness and relevancy. This means most of the western mission funds spent annually on sending workers to the mission field are not creating sufficient sustainable growth and impact in the places the missionaries serve. This is particularly true for Bible translation work. Much of the corpus of translation resources was developed by western scholars for western workers. Some resources have been translated into national languages and fewer have been localized. Yet Majority World believers are launching the bulk of new translations and revising earlier ones. Focusing finances on the development of new localized resources can improve the situation.

Moreover, the majority of western missionaries are working in traditional missionary receiving countries or regions that now have significant Christian populations. This means, about 85% of western Christian mission work is aimed at Christians in these places, while there is almost no interaction with followers of other major world religions in non-

---

[22] *CTC*, IIB.

[23] See L. Douglas, 'Globalizing Theology and Theological Education', in Ott and Netland (eds), *Globalizing Theology*, 231-249.

Christian countries. And it costs several billion dollars annually to maintain these western workers.

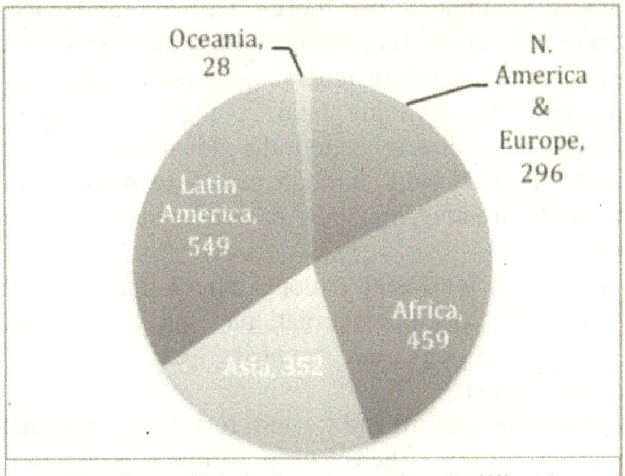

Number of Christians by region (Millions)

Additionally, several billion dollars are also spent annually on sending new western missionaries overseas, mostly to Christian nations.[24]

Annual Cost of Western Foreign Mission Sending as of 2010		
Foreign sending to Christian nations	306,000 (73.1% of workforce)	$13 billion
Foreign sending to unreached nations	10,200	$250 million

In comparison, unreached nations receive significantly less missionaries, resulting in a lower use of mission funds. This is not surprising given the closed or limited access to these nations. Even less is spent on equipping and supporting the minority church presence in those unreached places. This concern is not about western business efficiency. Rather, it is about stewardship; the strategic use of funds entrusted by God to his church for the greatest effects.

[24] T. M. Johnson and K. R. Ross (eds), *The Atlas of Global Christianity and Bible translation, distribution and use* (Boston: Gordon-Conwell Theological Seminary, 2010).

Some Strategic Uses of Mission Finances

1. Funding national and western mission agencies that focus primarily on training national church partners could accelerate capacity building so that those Christians can launch, nurture and sustain missionary movements within their own countries and the countries of their close neighbours, especially unreached groups.
2. Changing the spending ratio so that the majority of western mission funds directly benefit the global south churches' ability to carry out their work through access to more relevant resource materials, training methods, project management and expansion work.
3. Significantly increasing national church mission funding provides more funds to empower national and local church efforts in unreached regions and countries (e.g. Buddhist, Hindu and Muslim regions).

Mission funding in general and western funding in particular have a long and complicated history. There is no shortage of missiology articles pointing out the negative effects funding has had on missionary endeavours. *The Lausanne Standards* ('Affirmations and Agreements for Giving and Receiving Money in Mission')[25] affirm the important role that funding and the people who provide the funds have in 21st century missions. It addresses the problems of the past and provides guidance for the giving, receiving and wise use of funds during these times. Mutual accountability in giving and receiving funds can help build lasting and effective partnerships.[26]

Access to Strategic Information

There is an abundance of strategic mission knowledge. It consists of discipleship training, leadership training, strategic planning, missiology, guides to fund-raising and financial reporting, Bible translation, pastor training, church planting, practical theology and much more. As the old saying goes, 'Knowledge is power'. But a majority of the global church is not feeling empowered this way because a vast amount of that knowledge is still inaccessible to them, making the information scarce. Does the age of the internet change this? As one author put it, "The rise of computers and digital technology paved the way for the monumental shift form a "scarcity" mentality to one of 'abundance'".[27] So, one might wonder why information scarcity exists in the age of the internet.

---

[25] See www.lausanne.org/en/documents/lausanne-standards.html.

[26] Movingmissions.org, see esp. http://movingmissions.org/missions-and-money.

[27] T. Jore, *The Christian Commons: Ending the spiritual famine of the global church*, https://distantshoresmedia.org/thechristiancommons/introduction (2012), 106-108.

Certainly, the internet is a vast repository of information, but there is still a lot of information that is inaccessible to people serving in church missions. For one reason, much of the information is in English, thus making it inaccessible to church workers who do not speak English. Another reason is much of the information is protected by intellectual property rights, therefore only licensees have access. Finally, the cost of published material can be prohibitively expensive in many parts of the world. Not all of this expensive, proprietary knowledge is applicable in new times. Some of the material produced by the west for western workers is not necessarily relevant to people in other places. However, much of it still is. What is available and still useful is blocked by language, copyright and cost barriers.

Author Tim Jore claims, "It is when adequate 'unlocked' discipleship resources do not exist that the spiritual growth of the global church is hindered. The 'walling off' of the garden (the sum total of discipleship resources in a given language) tends to segment the church. This, in turn, tends to keep the various elements of the 'team' disconnected and, effectively, in competition against each other." Jore's solution is to consider the sum total of the aforementioned resources that exist in all languages to be released under an open licence known as the Creative Commons Attribution – Share Alike licence. This would allow much of the materials to be adapted, translated and further developed where they are most needed.[28]

Knowledge for developing expertise and leadership in places where it is more urgently needed demonstrates the mutuality Hwa Yung recommended.

Strategic Planning – How is Your S-Curve?

Perhaps one of the most important considerations in 21st century mission strategy is ensuring that an organization remains maximally effective and responsive to change. Smart business leaders know that certain ways of doing things have a limited life span. Some people view such a life span following an S-curve, as illustrated here. At first new ideas, methods or processes create a surge in effectiveness because they are well-aligned with the times. However, as time goes on, methods become less effective because the world has changed.

A typical business cycle S-curve is about five years. Some mission agencies have effectively used this analytical planning tool and time frame to keep pace with rapid change in the world. A mission agency that is unwilling to deal with poor or declining results will generally become less

---

[28] For more on the concept of a Christian commons, see Tim Jore (2012), 250-276. https://distantshoresmedia.org/thechristiancommons/introduction.

relevant in a changing world. Today, willingness to change is valued over the more traditional values of consistency and stability.[29]

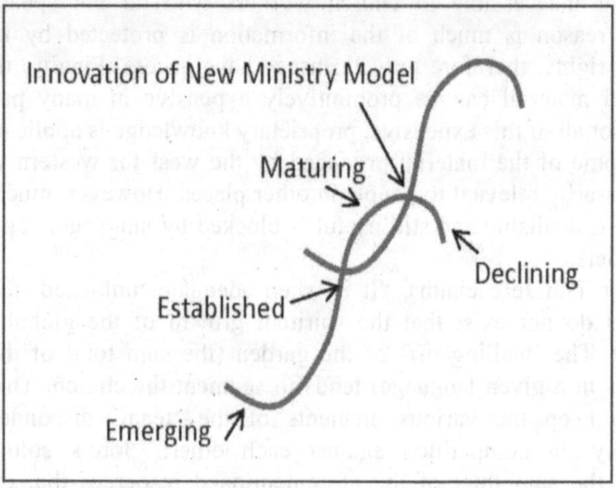

Now more mission agency leaders understand the importance of reinvention to keep pace with change and to be more effective. What are they doing differently? They are building partnership alliances with more organizations, even those outside traditional circles. Change is also affecting recruiting. They want to be more international, so they no longer assume western people shoulder leadership roles on the field. Instead, they are recruiting local talent to fill those roles. Finally, they view legacy practices as less important in comparison to finding new ways to fulfil their legacy mission. This means old practices can be replaced with new ones if that is what it takes to achieve the sort of impact they have always wanted.[31]

Conclusion

Mission strategy in the 21st century continues on the wise path established by the framers of the 1974 *Lausanne Covenant*. This article has addressed macro-strategies expressed in that Covenant. There are numerous books and articles written by mission scholars from every continent, excluding perhaps Antarctica. They have produced comprehensive work on micro-strategies designed for more focused activities, such as engaging unreached people groups, understanding major world religions, practising business as

---

[29] G. Gravelle, *The Age of Global Giving, a Guide for the Donors and Recipients of Our Time* (Forthcoming, Pasadena: William Carey Library).

[31] MovingMissions.org, see esp. http://movingmissions.org/mission-reinvention-why-some-leaders-think-it-is-urgent.

mission, effective cross-cultural missions, medical missions, indigenous missions and much more.

Our recommendation is to apply the macro-strategies described in this article to any of these micro-strategies. The macro-strategies provide a sound framework for any ministry effort these days: that is, working through close partnership, sharing resources, using financial resources where they are needed most, making copyright information freely available, and working to ensure mission practices remain relevant and effective.

Globalization of theology reveals a shift to local theologies that are practical and relevant. Global Christianity applies a universal understanding of Christ, but it is lived out through multiple expressions within each unique language and cultural context. Therefore, understanding the times and the contexts will help a mission worker understand how to apply these five strategies more successfully.

Calling the Church of Christ Back to Humility, Integrity and Simplicity[1]

Chris Wright

The Mission of God

About 4,000 years ago, God launched his global mission, with the first Great Commission, to Abraham, telling him to "Go … be a blessing … and through you all nations on the earth will be blessed" (Gen 12:1-3). That is God's great mission. That, says Paul, is the Gospel that the Scriptures announced in advance to Abraham (Gal 3:8-9) – God will bless the nations!

How would that happen? God's plan was that it should happen by God first creating a people, his own people, a people chosen in Abraham, redeemed through Christ, *and* (as God reminded himself in conversation with Abraham after lunch one day in Genesis 18), a people called to "walk in the way of the Lord by doing righteousness and justice", so that God could keep his promise to Abraham and bless all nations through him (Gen 18:19). That's why I chose Abraham, God says. The whole purpose of our election is ethical and missional (as Paul observed when he calls us to live out the fruit of our predestination by living to the praise of God's glory (Eph 1:4, 6, 11-12).

And God has been keeping that promise to bless the nations. Some foreigners came to faith in the living God and experienced his blessing in the Old Testament, e.g. Rahab, Ruth, Naaman. Many more in the New Testament, such as the woman of Syro-Phoenicia, the Roman centurion, the Ethiopian eunuch, Cornelius – and multitudes, of course, through the missionary work of Paul and his team. And of course, at the Cape Town Congress we celebrated, visibly and tangibly, that the people of God are now to be found among many nations, tribes and peoples all over the earth. That's God's great mission.[2]

---

[1] This article is the slightly edited text of the address given on Day 5 of the Third Lausanne Congress on World Evangelism, Cape Town, Oct 2010.

[2] I have explored these themes of biblical mission in much greater depth in several books: *The Mission of God: Unlocking the Bible's Grand Narrative* (IVP: 2006); *Salvation Belongs to Our God: Celebrating the Bible's Central Story* (IVP: 2008); and *The Mission of God's People: A Biblical Theology of the Church's Mission* (Zondervan: 2010).

Obstacles to God's Mission

But there were, and still are, many obstacles; many things that keep frustrating and hindering that great, loving, saving, mission of God. The Cape Town Congress considered many of them. Which might we consider to be the greatest of those obstacles to God's desire for the evangelization of the world?

I would suggest that it is *not*: other religions, persecution, post-modernity, or resistant cultures. The overwhelming witness of the Bible is that the greatest problem for God in his redemptive mission for the world is ... *his own people*. What hurts God most, it seems, is not just the sin of the world, but the failure, disobedience and rebellion of those whom God has redeemed and called to be his people, his holy people, his distinctive people.

In the Old Testament, the vast bulk of the words of the prophets were addressed to God's own people – Israel, and only a few chapters to 'oracles against the nations'. By contrast, we tend to spend all our time attacking and complaining about the world and ignoring our own failures. God's calling on Old Testament Israel was very clear, as it is for us:

- God called them to be 'a light to the nations'. But according to Ezekiel (5:6; 16:44-52), Israel sank even lower than the nations, including Sodom and Gomorrah. They were hardly a shining light in that condition!
- God called them to know him, to love and worship him alone, as the one true living God. But they constantly went after other gods, falling into repeated idolatry. This was a tragic squandering of the greatest privilege and blessing they had – the fact that they were his redeemed, covenant people, chosen for the sake of bringing God's blessing to the rest of the nations.

Idolatry

I believe that idolatry is the biggest single obstacle to world mission. For if God's mission is to bring people into the blessing of knowing and worshipping him alone as Creator and redeemer, then the greatest threat to that is the worship of other gods, false gods, no gods. But the problem, as we see in the Old Testament very clearly, is *not* just the idolatry of the foreign nations and their false gods, but the idolatry that is rampant among God's own people.

There are many false gods and idols, of course, that entice us away from the living God alone, but three in particular seem especially seductive, just as much for evangelical Christians today as for Israel of old:

- the idol of power and pride;
- the idol of popularity and success;
- the idol of wealth and greed.

The wise writer of Proverbs 11:2-4 puts all three together in three successive verses

2 When pride comes, then comes disgrace,
but with humility comes wisdom.
3 The integrity of the upright guides them,
but the unfaithful are destroyed by their duplicity.
4 Wealth is worthless in the day of wrath,
but righteousness delivers from death.

Those verses are wise warnings, but the prophets, Jesus, and the apostles all challenge us with powerful, prophetic condemnation of these three destructive idols that pollute and pervert the mission of God's people.

Power and Pride

Listen to the word of the Lord, through Isaiah:

> The LORD Almighty has a day in store for all the proud and lofty, for all that is exalted (and they will be humbled) … The arrogance of man will be brought low and the pride of men humbled; the LORD alone will be exalted in that day … and the idols will totally disappear. (Isa 1:12-18)

Listen to the God's great requirement, through Micah:

> What does the LORD require of you? To act justly and to love mercy and to walk humbly with your God. (Mic 6:8)

Listen to the Lord Jesus Christ himself:

> Jesus said to them, "The kings of the Gentiles lord it over them …. But you are **not** to be like that. Instead, the greatest among you should be like the youngest, and the one who rules like the one who serves … I am among you as one who serves. (Luke 22:24-27)

Listen to the apostle Paul. When he talks about the life that is worthy of our calling in the Gospel, the very first thing he says is this:

> Be completely humble and gentle; be patient, bearing with one another in love. (Eph 4:2)

Sisters and brothers, to be obsessed with power and status in Christian work is sheer disobedience to Christ and the Bible. It destroys the very thing we are trying to accomplish.

We are called back in repentance to *Humility*.

Popularity and Success

Obsession with these idols leads us into manipulation, dishonesty, distortion, duplicity. We can end up like the false prophets, who claimed to speak the word of God but were really acting in their own self-interest. They claimed to be 'men of God', but they were really only giving the people whatever they most wanted to hear or see at the time. They were popular and successful – but they were false prophets in the grip of a false god.

Listen to the word of God through Micah:

> As for the prophets who lead my people astray, if one feeds them, they proclaim 'peace'; if he does not, they prepare to wage war against him … Yet they lean upon the LORD and say, "Is not the LORD among us? No disaster will come upon us." (Mic 3:5-11)

Or listen to the word of God through Jeremiah:

> From the least to the greatest, all are greedy for gain; prophets and priests alike, all practice deceit. They dress the wound of my people as though it were not serious. 'Peace, peace,' they say, when there is no peace. Are they ashamed of their loathsome conduct? No, they have no shame at all; they do not even know how to blush. (Jer 6:13-15)

You don't need to feel ashamed, or blush, when you're popular and successful, when you've got thousands of followers, mega-everything, and a lifestyle to match. But you can still be a false prophet, with all of that.

And even in the early church, Paul warned against those who "peddle the word of God for profit", those who "use deception and distortion" (2 Cor 2:17, 4:2). The church in Corinth was dazzled by these 'super apostles' as he called them. They loved to boast about their credentials, their impressive speaking, their great popularity. *They* were the kind of leaders the church at Corinth wanted; because when a church has leaders like that, it makes them proud of their own image. 'Look at us, *we* have [BIG NAME] as *our* pastor!'

But listen to Paul:

> Such men are false apostles, deceitful workmen, masquerading as apostles of Christ. And no wonder, for Satan himself masquerades as an angel of light. It is not surprising, then, if his servants masquerade as servants of righteousness. Their end will be what their actions deserve. (2 Cor 11:13-15)

Sisters and brothers, we cannot build the kingdom of the God of truth on foundations of dishonesty. Telling lies about our success, or accepting what we know to be very questionable statistics, in order to get, or to grant, funding for our projects, is nothing short of bowing down to the idols of manipulated success. The pressures are sometimes very great. We can justify all kinds of questionable practices on the grounds of 'doing God's work'. But God's work cannot be done by using the tools of Satan (lies) to boost the statistics of our own success.

We are called back in repentance to *Integrity.*

Wealth and Greed

The idolatry of greed infected the religious leaders of Israel too.

Listen again to the word of the Lord through Micah:

> Her leaders judge for a bribe, her priests teach for a price, and her prophets tell fortunes for money. Yet they lean upon the LORD and say, "Is not the LORD among us? No disaster will come upon us." (Mic 3:11)

Isaiah saw in his day, as ours, a whole culture of greed, accumulation, and covetousness – which Paul reminds us *is* idolatry.

> Woe to you who add house to house and join field to field till no space is left and you live alone in the land. (Isa 5:8)

Of course, we know that God provides abundantly for his people. But Moses, who rejoiced in that expectation, also warned against the danger:

> When you eat and are satisfied, when you build fine houses and settle down, and when your herds and flocks grow large and your silver and gold increase and all you have is multiplied, then your heart will become proud and you will forget the LORD your God, who brought you out of Egypt, out of the land of slavery. (Deut 8:10-18)

Jesus gave the same stern warning: "Watch out! Be on your guard against all kinds of greed; a person's life does not consist in the abundance of his possessions." (Luke 12:15) And neither, he could have added, does a person's ministry. And yet it seems that some Christians actually rate great leaders and mega-pastors by how wealthy they are.

We are called back in repentance to *Simplicity.*

The Temptations of Jesus

It is interesting to notice that Jesus himself, in fact, faced the same three fundamental temptations (Satan has no originality).

- The devil offered him *power and status* over all nations, from a high mountain. Jesus refused it, choosing to worship God alone. Jesus chose the path of *humility*.
- The devil suggested he *manipulate* the crowds by a spectacular death-defying miracle. Jesus recognized the way Satan was twisting Scripture to get him to achieve success. He chose the path of *integrity* in his trust in God.
- The devil dangled before him the *lucrative prospect* of abundant food for himself and the hungry masses – turn stones into bread! Why, you could make a fortune for yourself with such a miracle! Jesus resisted with the scriptural truth that God could supply bread, but human beings need greater food for life than that. He chose the path of *simplicity* in dependence on the promises of God.

So Jesus resisted these temptations to give in to the false gods. But tragically, it seems that so many Christian leaders (including mission leaders) blatantly *fail* these tests at precisely the points that Jesus overcame them. They cannot resist the temptations of elevated status, manipulated success and selfish greed. And then the whole church pays the cost of their failure, in the loss of integrity and credibility. So whenever we point a finger of criticism at the sin of the world, we are told, bluntly and rightly – 'Clean up your own back yard'. We are, in short, a scandal, a stumbling-block, to the mission of God.

The Need for Reformation

In the pre-Reformation medieval church in Europe, we see these same three idols masquerading in the corrupt ecclesiastical system. There were powerful bishops, wielding enormous wealth and power. There were highly popular and successful cults of saints and shrines, making all kinds of false claims about their relics and miracles. There were people making their fortune from selling indulgences – exploiting the poor with promises of good things in the life to come.

Meanwhile, the ordinary people lived in ignorance of the Bible, which was neither available in their language nor preached from the pulpits. Reformation was the desperate need of the hour.

Surely the same desperate need is with us now. And, I dare to propose, it needs to begin in the worldwide evangelical community. For there are parts of the so-called evangelical church today where the same three idols are rampant.

- There are self-appointed 'super apostles' and other mighty and elevated leaders, unaccountable to anybody, popular with thousands of followers, exploiting the flock of Christ, unconcerned for the weak and poor, showing none of the marks of an apostle as described by Paul, and with no resemblance to the crucified Christ. That is nothing less than the idolatry of pride and power
- There is a craze for 'success', for 'results', to win the largest number in the shortest time. There is obsession with statistics and outcomes, leading to wild claims, unsubstantiated numbers, untrue reports – blatant manipulation and collusion in falsehood, all for the sake of funding, and ministry success and growth. That is the idolatry of success.
- There is the so-called prosperity gospel. Now, we should certainly affirm what the Bible says about God's blessing, about the power of God's Spirit and the victory of God over all that crushes and curses human life. But many promoters of this teaching distort the Bible (if they use it at all). They appeal to human greed or exploit human need. They have no place for the Bible's teaching on suffering and taking up the cross. They succeed only in enriching themselves to a lifestyle utterly contrary to the teaching and example of Christ. This is surely the idolatry of greed.

And meanwhile, just as in the pre-Reformation church, so today, the ordinary people of God in many churches around the world live in ignorance of the Bible. They have pastors who neither know the Bible themselves nor have the willingness or ability to preach and teach it clearly and faithfully. So we have the matching scandals of material obesity and biblical starvation – even in churches that claim the name evangelical.

Reformation, a 21st century reformation, is once again the desperate need. And it needs to start with us.

What Then Must We Do?

We need a radical return to the Lord. We need to take heed to the prophetic word, from the prophets and apostles of God, and from the Lord Jesus Christ himself: 'Repent, and believe the gospel …' Remember, Jesus preached that message, made that command, *not* to pagan unbelievers, Gentile outsiders, people of other faiths, but to those who already claimed to be God's covenant people. The command to repent comes first to the people of God – in the Old and New Testament. So,

- Before we go out to the world, we must come back to the Lord.
- If we want to change the world, we must first change our own hearts and our ways. (Jer 7:3-8)
- As we take the words of the Gospel to the world, we must also take with us words of confession to God. (Hos 14:1-2)
- Before we get off our seats to seek the lost, we must get on our knees to seek the Lord.

At the Cape Town Congress, this message was followed by a short time of confession, repentance and prayer for God's forgiveness, calling upon ourselves in the following terms:

- Where we have revelled in our status or squabbled over honours, or abused power, let us walk humbly with our God, for the Lord gives grace to the humble but puts down the proud.
- Where we have manipulated and distorted, exaggerated and boasted, let us walk in the light and truth of God, for the Lord looks on the heart and is pleased with integrity.
- Where we have sought to enrich ourselves, or have been envious of those who do so, let us walk in the simplicity of Jesus, for we cannot serve God and mammon.

Humility, Integrity, Simplicity.

H.I.S.

HIS People. Let us be what we are, for God's sake, for our mission's sake, for the world's sake.

POVERTY, PROSPERITY AND THE GOSPEL

Daniel Bourdanné

Participants at the Cape Town Congress in 2010 considered the impact of the prosperity gospel on the global church, recognising that this is an issue that cannot be ignored. Indeed the *Cape Town Commitment* refers specifically to the prosperity gospel in its call to action: calling the church of Christ back to humility, integrity and simplicity. Readers may find it helpful to read my paper[1] written in advance of the Congress, outlining in detail the theology of the prosperity gospel. In this paper, I shall also consider how the church can respond to the teaching of the prosperity gospel, especially in the context of poverty and suffering.

On a recent visit to Kenya, a friend took me to Kibera. Situated to the south of Nairobi, it is one of the largest slums in Africa. We went by car. As we made our way into the district, the streets became ever narrower. In this unhealthy environment, greenish puddles gave off odours of urine and decay. Children played in the streets, laughing loudly. Their joy and the smiles on their faces contrasted with the despair conveyed by the bad smells. They waved at us, clearly used to white visitors who would give them money as they went by.

The road narrowed and became completely impassable by car. We decided to park by a maize seller's stall and she readily agreed to keep watch over our car. We gave her some Kenyan shillings in exchange.

We completed our journey on foot, making our way through the maze of slum dwellings. In this part of Kibera there is no road map. Eventually we reached our destination. Entering a courtyard, we were led to a building that was scarcely three metres wide, made of rusty recycled sheets of metal. The shed of rusty metal sheets gave the whole place an air of ruin and evoked a sense of precariousness. Children were learning to read and write in the shed which was about two metres high. The volunteer teacher explained that this shed served as a church on Sunday and was used as a primary school during the rest of the week.

I admit that I was shocked and greatly taken aback by this level of poverty. I myself grew up in an African village. But I have never seen this

---

[1] Daniel Bourdanné, *All that Glitters is not Gold,* Cape Town Advance Paper 2010, published at http://conversation.lausanne.org/en/pages/advance-papers. See also Chris Wright's chapter in this volume on 'Calling the Church of Christ Back to Humility, Integrity and Simplicity'.

face of poverty. In my parents' home, and indeed in my village in general, apart from some lean periods when people faced food shortages while we waited for the harvest, we always had food to eat. We lived in clean and airy houses. We were poor but we did not live in the chaotic deprivation I saw in Kibera.

It is true that in Kibera urbanisation and the rapid expansion of urban population due to an exodus from the countryside have contributed to an increase in poverty and have given it a particularly ugly face. With modernisation and the industrialisation of society, the villages have become poorer and a move from the countryside to the cities has become a widespread phenomenon. Whole communities are leaving the countryside to seek work in the city. As in Kibera, millions of human beings live in unbearable and sometimes dehumanising misery. They do not have enough to eat, they do not have access to drinking water; living in an insanitary environment and at risk of all sorts of diseases, they cannot provide for themselves.

The United Nations has tried to define poverty levels according to income.[2] The World Bank has adopted the threshold of extreme poverty as being US$1.25 per person per day. According to this criterion, around 1.3 billion people still live below the poverty line around the world. Extreme poverty is concentrated in three large regions: East Asia, South Asia and sub-Saharan Africa.

But there are limits to a definition of prosperity and poverty based primarily on a monetary evaluation of income and consumption. Indeed, in some cultures, poverty is defined not just in terms of financial income, but even more in terms of social and spiritual values and autonomy. Poverty is a concept which is difficult to grasp fully or to measure. To do so, we must take into account elements such as social exclusion and other types of deprivation which undermine human dignity.

The Bible addresses two types of poverty: material or physical poverty, and spiritual poverty. Material poverty, which is what we are discussing in this article, may be voluntary, the result of a choice made by an individual or a group of individuals. For example, our Lord Jesus Christ left his celestial glory to live a simple life on earth. He became materially poor in order to bring spiritual riches. The apostle Paul also chose to become poor. Even today many people sacrifice their careers and lucrative professions in order to serve God and others. These people make a choice to embrace material poverty and, accepting the consequences, joyfully live out their lives for the glory of God.

Material poverty can, however, also be a bad thing, expressed in dehumanising misery and leading to suffering and alienation. It can have many different causes: injustice and exploitation (women abandoned with

---

[2] Tim Allen and Alan Thomas; *Poverty and Development into the 21st Century,* The Open University in Association with OUP, 2000.

no means to care for their children, unfair dismissal, mineral exploitation of land where the farmers have been expelled with no compensation, indigenous peoples suppressed by more powerful societies), diseases, and natural events such as drought and climate change. It can also be caused by laziness (Proverbs 6:9-11), ignorance, waste and bad management of God's gifts to us. People who are capable but unwilling to work live from and abuse the generosity of others. For this reason, we will always have the poor among us.

The figures and statistics from international organizations such as the World Bank or the United Nations are alarming. The statistics may give a global overview of poverty in the world and its geographic spread, but they often do not reveal much about the reality of poverty on the ground. The figures are no more than academic information which does not touch people's hearts, especially those who have never been exposed to severe poverty. In developed countries I often meet people who have never travelled beyond the closed circle of their own community. Even in their own country, they may have lost all contact with poor people. Their knowledge comes from the selective information supplied by the local or international media. Although they may feel compassion when they see images of poor people and poor countries, it is difficult for such people to understand just how degrading and dehumanising poverty is. If you have not encountered poverty lived out in the lives of women and children, or had the opportunity to meet poor people in the slums of Kibera, Kolkata in India, Rio de Janeiro in Brazil, or in the backstreets of New York or Dubai, it is hard to fully comprehend the deeply dehumanising effect of poverty on a human being. Even in Africa where physical poverty is common, those who live in their mansions and wealthy social silos are often unaware of the real poverty.

Today we live in a world of great contrasts. Extreme poverty exists side by side with extreme affluence. A minority enjoys material prosperity, owning more than 90% of the world's wealth. Sadly, this wealthy minority is not always ready to share in order to alleviate the situation of the poor. Throughout history our world has never known such disparity between rich and poor as we see today. Poverty rages unchecked. It not only harms the dignity of people created in the image of God, but it is also a source of much family and social instability. It poses a risk to world peace and freedom, including religious freedom.

World Christianity Cares About Poverty

As believers in Jesus Christ, we cannot remain indifferent and ignore the issue of poverty. Following the example of Jesus Christ, our response to poverty must be the expression of a loving and compassionate heart, leading to engagement on our part. A gospel which is not concerned with the poor and which does not encourage believers to consciously show compassion is an incomplete gospel. “Religion that God our Father accepts as pure and faultless is this: to look after orphans and widows in their distress and to keep oneself from being polluted by the world” (James 1:27).

The shift in the centre of gravity of Christianity from the west to the global south has not occurred without raising questions about the relationship between poverty, prosperity and the Gospel. Indeed many countries of the global south where Christianity is advancing demographically at a breath-taking speed are those countries where the largest majority of poor people is to be found (in Africa, Latin America and Asia). In these countries, Christians and non-Christians daily face the challenges of physical deprivation and disease. Whether in Africa or Latin America, we cannot help but be struck by the co-existence of two realities which appear to some as contradictory: exceptional religious fervour and immeasurable poverty.

The prosperity gospel, Spontaneous Theology with an Attractive Message

Particularly in Africa, living conditions are very harsh for poor people. Whole communities suffer from lack of food, medicine, drinking water and housing. Some of these conditions are aggravated by insufficient rainfall or floods, and chronic political instability gives rise to wars and massive displacement of peoples. A doctor working in a West African hospital recently told me: “Where I work, many relatives abandon their sick family members in the hospital because they do not have money to pay for the medicines. Others take their patients away to traditional healers or to preachers who promise miraculous healing through prayer.”

In this sort of environment, we should not be surprised by the appeal of such preachers and healers to the masses. They cover public billboards, use megaphones and TV and radio channels, mobile phones, internet and social networks to promise healing to the sick, abundance to the hungry, conception to the infertile woman, marriage partners to the single person, work to the unemployed and easy wealth to the poor. Spiritual success, they say, consists of immediate healing and acquisition of material wealth. Book, tapes and fiery sermons offer immediate wealth and success. For many people struggling under the weight of physical poverty and ignorance, they offer ‘spiritual keys’ which will open the door to prosperity and to the miracles that they seek in vain.

These preachers of a quick solution often present an image of those who have become materially prosperous. They are always well-dressed in suits from leading fashion houses, have the latest mobile phones, drive large cars, live in mansions or reside in the most expensive hotels when they travel; they will be dripping in jewellery, travel first class or in private jets.

They present the 'health and wealth gospel' as a divine solution to the problems of the desperate, the poor and the sick.

In this environment, the poor do not approach the Gospel as something to be analysed rationally. They accept it in a spontaneous spiritual, emotional and existential response to the problems of daily life. And for the middle and upper classes in societies where outward appearances count above all, and where power, social status and influence are seen as important, the prosperity gospel offers even more influence. In other words, this 'gospel' is seen through a utilitarian rather than a theological lens.

In the light of all kinds of structural crises, people know instinctively that they are right to hope for something better than their daily experience. Dissatisfied with their situation, living sometimes in a state of deep existential crisis, they turn to a theology that will give instant answers to some of the questions they face: where is God in my suffering, poverty, misery and sickness? If God exists, why do I still live in my daily misery with no obvious way out? And for those who have a strongly developed religious conscience such as amongst many Africans where it is virtually impossible to disconnect religion from daily life, they conclude that they are responsible for their situation because of their own sin or some curse on them, their family or their people.

The preachers of the prosperity gospel respond to the difficult and complex questions raised by this spontaneous theology with a simplistic message which quickly draws adherents. Their message often relies on easily understood slogans that can be memorised and internalised. The people who preach this message are generally very charismatic and able to lead the crowd with their rhetoric. Some of the slogans they use: 'No more suffering!' 'If you have failed, come to Jesus!' 'If you want to be successful, come to Jesus!' 'Have faith!' 'Our God is a rich God; all gold and money belong to Him!' '"The silver is mine and the gold is mine," declares the Lord Almighty' (Haggai 2:8), 'Take your blessing', 'Receive your anointing', 'You are to be the head and not the tail'. This last phrase is particularly popular amongst students at exam times, or amongst managers who are seeking professional advancement in their careers. Students expect success in their exams even if they have not studied hard and done their homework. Those who fail prefer to blame themselves, telling themselves that they doubted and did not exercise positive faith. In his book, Femi Adeleye[3] tells stories of students being manipulated to claim their success, based on Deuteronomy 28:13.

The Theological Basis of the Health and Wealth Gospel

This 'gospel' teaches that believers are entitled to receive material blessing and good health: they can access these by faith, by positive confession and

[3] Femi Adeleye, *Preachers of a Different Gospel*, Hippobooks, 2011, 61.

by obeying the law of sowing. According to Kenneth Hagin,[4] one of the champions of this teaching, the power of faith expressed by the words of Jesus in Mark 11:23-24 is valuable as a formula. Hagin goes further when he affirms that Jesus appeared to him and said: "Anyone, anywhere, who puts into practice these four principles, will receive from me or from God the Father all that he desires: 1. Say, 2. Do, 3. Receive, 4. Tell." Anyone can then use these rules for his own benefit to access prosperity and healing. It is a spiritual law which, in some way, becomes like the law of gravity which is bound to work.

Following Hagin, Kenneth Copland[5] takes a universal principle from the text of Mark 10:29-30: "No one who has left home or brothers or sisters or mother or father or children or fields for me and the gospel will fail to receive a hundred times as much in this present age: homes, brothers, sisters, mothers, children and fields – along with persecutions – and in the age to come eternal life." This principle is simple and effective: give $1 for the Gospel and you will receive $100. Such a blueprint for success cannot fail to be attractive to an investor, drawing many people from all ranks of society. For example, a father having heard the message, gives his house to the preacher without consulting his family, expecting to receive back 100 houses; officials empty their bank accounts; others give a large part of their salary expecting to receive it back one hundredfold, but leaving their families to suffer while they wait to see the return on their investment.

During a visit to West Africa, I attended a church service where the preacher asked the believers to present their offerings to him ordered into several categories, ranging from the highest to lowest value. He personally took it upon himself to pray for those who gave a larger amount – he himself had set the minimum level – asking them to come forward and to hold their envelope up towards heaven to be sure of receiving their hundredfold return. In contrast, those who gave smaller amounts were not entitled to his prayers.

Such teaching supports the view that a Christian should not be poor. If the Christian remains poor, it is because he has not exercised sufficient faith. Even if money is invested for God by those who give in order to receive the hundredfold blessing, in practice we find that it is generally 'the man or woman of God' to whom it is given. A pastor who manages to persuade his flock to follow this practice is going to be well provided for. It doesn't take an expert to see that in less than a year a pastor can become rich if he is leading a local church of 1,000 members where each of them can give $100 or more per month or per term.

The theology also teaches that the Christian will not suffer illness. Why? Because Jesus took all our infirmities and diseases (Isa 43:4-5; Matt 8:17; 1 Peter 2:24-25). According to this teaching, a Christian will only get sick

---

[4] Quoted by McConnell, *A Different Gospel*, Hendrickson, 1991.
[5] Ibid.

if he does not positively claim his healing. How does this work? When he feels pain, he must claim healing in Christ and say: "I am healed in the name of Jesus." If he is paralysed, he must get up and walk in faith that he has been healed in the name of Jesus. Kenneth Hagin goes even further in saying that a Christian should not die before the age of 70. For him, to die before an age of between 70 and 120 is to choose to die before one's time. And what about children who are stillborn and do not have a chance to exercise their own faith? Hagin answers that it is the fault of their parents who have not exercised positive faith as they should have. Some proponents of this theology even refuse to go to hospital when they are ill as this would indicate a lack of faith.

This 'gospel' also advocates 'knowledge through revelation' which means receiving things directly from God even if they are directly in contradiction to his written Word. We can see the influence of this teaching in the language frequently used by Christians who have signed up to this 'gospel': they say "God told me ..." and hardly ever "the Bible says that ..." Effectively, without openly saying so, they place direct revelation above the authority of the Bible. In my book *L'évangile de la prospérité, une menace pour l'église africaine* (the prosperity gospel, a threat to the African Church), I give the example of a Christian who declared that he no longer needed to study the Bible as he was receiving guidance directly from God. Such actions lead to the authority of the Bible being limited and replaced by that of the individual.[6]

At first glance, this 'gospel' is shiny and attractive. Some of the selected Bible passages seem to make sense when they are taken out of context and others when they are taken literally. However, when examined in the light of the Word of God, it becomes clear that while this is a different gospel which may glitter brightly, all that glitters is not gold. The doctrine of health and wealth is made up of partial truths and we know that half-truths are seductive and therefore dangerous. Moreover, is it not a strategy of the devil to mislead Christians by half-truths? We must be vigilant against false teachers who, by using half-truths, dress themselves in sheep's clothing to hide the fact that they are really wolves.

As an example, these false teachers will say that the Bible clearly and literally says that Jesus came to take our suffering and disease on himself. But to stop at this point is only to see part of the truth. For the Bible also says that when the Lord returns in glory, all his promises will be accomplished. The biblical truth which encompasses both of these statements is this: when Jesus returns, there will be no more sickness or death. This means that as they wait with patience and perseverance for Jesus' return, some believers will continue to suffer from malaria, to die of hepatitis and cancer, and to live with the daily experience of physical

---

[6] Bourdanné, D.; *L'évangile de la prospérité, une menace pour l'église africaine*, PBA, 2011.

poverty and natural catastrophes such as tsunamis and earthquakes which affect both Christians and non-Christians alike. Suffering caused by poverty can even be a consequence of belonging to Christ.

The prosperity gospel Contradicts the Gospel of the Cross

The Cross of Jesus is a sign and manifestation of self-denial. The true Gospel only becomes reality in a person's life when they are able to give up their life. Jesus says: Whoever wants to be my disciple must deny themselves and take up their cross daily and follow me (Luke 9:23). He advises the rich young ruler: "Go, sell everything you have and give to the poor … then come, follow me" (Mark 10: 21-23).

The prosperity gospel contradicts the cross in that God, instead of being the ultimate object of our praise and worship, is reduced to being the means to satisfy our desire for wealth. For those who advocate this theology, their life with God is reduced to the search for social status. Their prosperity is reduced to possessions: money, cars, houses and jewels. These are not God-seekers but rather treasure-hunters that are using God merely as a kind of good luck charm. They limit God to being the source of wealth instead of being the sovereign God to whom all our wealth is to be offered.

According to these teachers, material wealth is a sign of God's approval. They justify this as follows: I am rich, therefore I have faith; I have been blessed, therefore God approves of me; I am poor or sick, so God is punishing me for my sin. However the Bible is full of passages that talk of wealthy people who do bad things. Some people even become rich because of their behaviour – employers who exploit their workers, drug dealers, traffickers, speculators.

Material wealth is not necessarily a sign of God's approval. In the Scriptures we read of servants of God who died in poverty as in the situation described in 2 Kings 4:1-7. The widow who came to the prophet Elisha was a servant of God: "Your servant my husband is dead, and you know that he revered the Lord. But now his creditor is coming to take my two boys as his slaves." Is it not strange that a man who believed in God should have accumulated such debts? It appears that he probably led a sacrificial life, dedicated to the service of God. The widow had nothing in her house except for a jar of oil. This reminds me of the life led by so many widows and orphans, servants of God in developing countries. They find themselves without money or support because their husbands or fathers have been unable to leave them any pension or inheritance.

Instead of bringing freedom, the 'health and wealth gospel' heaps guilt and depression onto the poor and sick. The poor believe that they are poor because they have done something displeasing to God. The sick say the same thing. I have met many people in Africa who have fallen into depression and even mental illness because they have been unable to reconcile the contradiction between their faith and their physical circumstances.

One of the contradictions I have seen is that these preachers of a different gospel preach about things on high, but they are attached to things here on earth. At first sight, their teaching may appear to be spiritual. They speak of God, of Jesus, of his power and salvation. But they choose to fix their eyes on the things of this life: Scripture tells us, "If, therefore, you have been reborn in Christ, seek things on high where Christ is seated at the right hand of God" (Col 3:1). But many people refuse to lift their eyes to Christ, to fully align themselves with his priorities.

This 'gospel' goes against the biblical theology of grace. Everything we receive from God comes from the grace of God and is not something that we have somehow earned. Even our faith is a gift of God. The arrogance of some proponents of this 'gospel' shows just how far removed they are from biblical thinking which emphasises values such as humility, service, compassion and a simple life. These values are of greater worth than material riches.

With regard to healing, we should reaffirm that even today God still continues to show his power in healing the sick whether they are Christians or not. For Christians, the grace of God seen in miraculous healings should bring those who are healed, and those around them, to praise and worship God as the author of the healing. But God does not heal all his children of their sickness and infirmity. To suggest that God must heal all Christians who are sick is to deny biblical truth. We know of many respected Christians who have died of illness. The Apostle Paul lived for years with his affliction. Yet who could doubt the faith and the deep and intense spiritual experience of this man who encountered Christ in such an extraordinary way, who carried the message of the Gospel across borders, and who submitted to all sorts of humiliations in the name of his faith? It is, however, this man of faith who, having prayed for healing, accepted and lived with God's message: my grace is sufficient for you. Paul's spiritual son, Timothy, also suffered from a stomach illness. Timothy certainly prayed for healing and Paul surely prayed for him. But when he was not healed, Paul advised him to take a little wine to help his condition.

Preaching a Holistic Gospel to Stand Against the Prosperity Gospel

Thousands of believers allow themselves to be manipulated by prosperity teaching because they have never been given the chance to hear a holistic and balanced presentation of the Gospel. They have been presented with a limited version of the Gospel which has no room for social concern. By presenting them with a holistic view of the world, believers are encouraged to integrate the physical and spiritual aspects of life and to live these out concretely in the sphere of their Christian life.

It is important to teach people how they can get to heaven. But it is also useful to teach them how to wait for heaven as they live on earth, taking into account their social condition. The message of the Gospel must, in contexts such as those of extreme poverty in Africa, encompass biblical compassion in order to counter the prosperity gospel. Our teaching must empathetically address questions of justice and of sustainable development.

The church could invest more in training young people and helping them to have a biblical view of work, of creativity and to understand how to integrate their work lives with their faith instead of leaving them to live in a dichotomy which hinders them from developing a holistic worldview. Thankfully, some mission initiatives have incorporated social action as an integral part of their evangelistic activity. Christians who have been raised with such a holistic view of the Gospel are generally less vulnerable to the ravages of the prosperity gospel.

In contexts of extreme physical poverty such as are found in Africa, we must of course go further than simply criticising the prosperity gospel. As we criticise, we must at the same time seek, in ongoing dialogue and in prayer, to see how we can offer practical responses to the poverty of our brothers and sisters living in destitution so that they do not go looking for prosperity anywhere other than in the true God. There are some communities in Africa today who give serious attention to the social plight of their members. Women work together to set up groups that engage in income-generating activities. These groups also provide a place for Bible study. In this way, they can teach their children, dress and feed themselves and meet their daily needs. By this means they transform their living situation and regain their dignity within the community. They know that their salvation does not come from an illusory gospel of prosperity, but from God working through their own creativity. Initiatives to encourage such projects in local churches, to organise young people into interest groups, and to give them training can help them to better resist the prosperity gospel.

In order to reduce the impact of the 'health and wealth gospel', the church, beyond its role as keeper of sound doctrine, must play its social role in educating its members to live as a truly different community. Education must play an important part in discipleship, raising awareness of the practical implications of the Gospel in areas such as work, creativity, stewardship, solidarity and social justice.

The Rightful Place of Material Wealth

In criticising the prosperity gospel, we run the risk of demonising material wealth, but we must not preach either a gospel of prosperity or a gospel of poverty. Neither is the true Gospel.

The Bible does not present poverty as a doctrinal ideal, and to misread Scripture in such a way can lead Christians to deny their responsibility as stewards of this world. It can cause people to accept the status quo, not because they are living in contentment, but because they end up with a deterministic view of the relationship between their poverty and their spirituality. That can even lead to a form of disengagement amongst Christians in the face of human suffering and the dehumanising misery caused by extreme poverty. It can also spill over into a fatalistic view of life and the devaluing of work.

However, the Bible continually warns about riches: Luke 6:24: "But woe to you rich people, for you have your consolation." Jesus, without actually condemning material prosperity, constantly seeks to warn the rich who face the danger of depending on their wealth and not on God. When the rich become the centre of attention because of their wealth, they can not only forget about God, but also about the poor people with whom they live. They are concerned only with their own interests and do not share their wealth with the needy. Jesus did not ask the rich young man to throw away his wealth or even to burn his possessions, but to go and sell them, and distribute the proceeds to the poor, and then to follow him (Luke 18:22). In this way he would be storing up 'treasure in heaven'.

Material wealth must serve to do good. Paul exhorts Timothy in 1 Tim 6:17-19: "Command those who are rich in this present world not to be arrogant nor to put their hope in wealth, which is so uncertain, but to put their hope in God, who richly provides us with everything for our enjoyment. Command them to do good, to be rich in good deeds, and to be generous and willing to share. In this way they will lay up treasure for themselves as a firm foundation for the coming age, so that they may take hold of the life that is truly life."

It is a privilege and a blessing to be rich but the rich person must recognize that there are values which are much more important that material wealth. He must seek justice, for wealth acquired by violence and injustice is a source of bitterness and indignity. The rich person must constantly turn to God, the true source of his wealth, and give glory to God through his wealth.

Christians must be helped to understand that God is not against the improvement of the physical conditions in which men and women live in this world. God, in his mercy, can grant material prosperity to individuals. The Bible gives examples of people to whom God has given such physical wealth: David, Solomon and others. Men and women who believe in God and have material wealth can contribute to the work of God through their assets, supporting God's work, helping widows and orphans and alleviating the terrible effects of poverty.

But it is also necessary to say that God has given us a guideline for prosperity. It is that of conscientious work, with integrity and often with sacrifice. A person often has to make sacrifices in order to establish his work, sometimes working long hours to start up a business and to run it with care and attention. And even if the business prospers, he must manage it with wisdom and self-sacrifice. In the countryside, the farmer has to work hard, sowing, weeding, and then waiting patiently for the harvest. There is no room for idleness, easy gain, or exploiting the generosity of others to gratify a person's desire for wealth.

Material wealth acquired legitimately can also be an excellent means of expressing solidarity with the community of men and women created in the image of God. God has given us individual and collective responsibility: those who have are invited to give to those who don't have, maintaining human dignity as a gift of God and a sacred value. We must stand together against dehumanising poverty and against the things that cause it.

Conclusion

In the face of the consumer society that tells us we will only find happiness as we acquire more belongings, we are invited to adopt the attitude of the wise man in Proverbs 30:8-9: "Give me neither poverty nor riches, but give me only my daily bread. Otherwise, I may have too much and disown you and say, 'Who is the Lord?' Or I may become poor and steal, and so dishonour the name of my God." We should teach neither the gospel of prosperity nor the gospel of poverty. Both are distorted versions of the Word of God. Rich and poor are created by God and loved by him. God knows the condition of the rich person just as he knows that of the poor (Proverbs 22:2). In his priestly prayer, Jesus demonstrates that he cares for both rich and poor. In teaching men and women, rich and poor, to pray, asking God the Father to give us our daily bread, he invites all to turn to God and not to become caught up in dangerous physical temptation or in degrading despair.

The 'health and wealth gospel' leads people to ignore the principles of dependence on God and of contentment. It encourages greed with its focus on material wealth. It leads believers to ignore the depth of values and of spiritual riches. Those who are spiritually rich are in fact those who, whether they are materially poor or rich, know that everything comes from God, in an attitude of humility and submission to him and his sovereignty. The rich know that their wealth comes from God, and the poor know that they can count on God for their daily bread, and that they can have hope. They do not try to manipulate God for their own ends but they lift their eyes daily to him in an attitude of complete dependence and contentment. They understand and live according to the revolutionary words of Jesus: "Blessed are the poor in spirit, for the Kingdom of God belongs to them" (Matthew 5:3).

THE CHURCH AND THE MESSAGE OF RECONCILIATION

Antoine Rutayisire

Introduction: Reconciliation in the Lausanne Movement

Reconciliation has always been one of the major concerns in the Lausanne Movement and its different conferences and consultation. This article, an expanded version of the talk I gave in the Cape Town Congress on World Evangelization,[1] is another contribution to a conversation that has been going on for years. The call to social responsibility in The *Lausanne Covenant* in 1974 with its emphasis on intrinsic human dignity "regardless of race, religion, colour, culture, class, sex or age" was already then a commitment to social reconciliation alongside with reconciliation with God, self and nature. The *Manila Manifesto* takes the issue to another level when it calls all who "claim to be members of the Body of Christ to transcend within our fellowship the barriers of race, gender and class". But nowhere is it better expressed than in the *Cape Town Commitment* that raises the issue of reconciliation at different levels and consecrates a whole Section (IIB) to the issue of building peace in our broken world. In a world devastated by sin, reconciliation will remain at the heart of the Good News as sin will always bring with it different levels of alienation. Reconciliation cannot be separated from the proclamation of the Gospel; even so, some of the worst divisions and consequent atrocities against human life have been committed in some of those areas with a high percentage of Christian churches. As we think of and plan how to take the Gospel to the ends of the earth, it is imperative to look closely at the issue of reconciliation if our witness to the Gospel is to be a convincing testimony.

---

[1] See A. Rutayisire, 'Our Gospel of Reconciliation', in J.E.M. Cameron (ed.), *Christ Our Reconciler: Gospel / Church / World. The Third Lausanne Congress on World Evangelization* (Nottingham: Inter-Varsity Press, 2012), 64-69.

Flourishing Churches in Broken Communities

Missiologists[2] affirm, with numbers as proof, that the epicentre of Christianity has moved to the southern hemisphere – but the same hemisphere turns out to be fertile ground for tribal wars, ethnic clashes and genocides, poverty, killer pandemics and other ills that contradict the presence of the Kingdom of God. The contrast between the religious fervour of the people and their barbaric killing of their neighbours has been vividly captured by this description given by the Canadian General Romeo Dallaire, Chief Commander of the UN forces in Rwanda during the time of the 1994 genocide against the Tutsis:

> On April 3, Easter Sunday, I flew to Byumba to review the bulk of my forces in the demilitarized zone … It looked like all the villagers in the country were dressed in their finest, walking in near-procession toward their places of worship. Here is what my experience in Rwanda has done: I am unable to remember the serenity, order and beauty of that scene without it being overlaid with vivid scenes of horror. Extremists, moderates, simple villagers and fervent worshippers were all in church that day, singing the message of Christ's resurrection. One week later, the same devout Christians would become murderers and victims, and the churches the sites of calculated butchery.[3]

How do we explain this discrepancy between the presence of flourishing churches and the manifest explosion of destruction in our communities? What has gone wrong with our evangelization and Christian discipleship? What can the church of Christ do to regain its call to be "ambassadors of reconciliation" (2 Cor 5:16-21)? The plea in this paper is that we need to rediscover 'the Gospel of reconciliation' and preach it with intentionality and consistency to heal our broken world.

In his book, *The Wounded Healer*, Henri Nouwen speaks of ministry in a wounded, dislocated world, populated by a rootless generation made up of 'desperate men', ministered to by 'a wounded healer'. In the chapter on 'Ministry by a Lonely Minister', Nouwen writes: "Since it is his task to make visible the first vestiges of liberation for others, he must bind his own wounds carefully in anticipation of the moment when he will be needed. He is called to be the wounded healer, the one who must look after his own wounds but at the same time be prepared to heal the wounds of others. He is both the wounded minister and the healing minister …" In every nation where reconciliation is needed, the 'healing ministers' are part of the population and they too are wounded. And it is only when they are healed that they can minister healing to others through sharing with them the experience of a healed life. That is what I will try to show in this paper. The

---

[2] Philip Jenkins, *The Next Christendom: The Coming of Global Christianity* (Oxford: OUP, 2002); Jonathan Bonk, *Africa Unbound*: www.christianitytoday.com/ct/2007/ november/37.46.html.

[3] Lt-Gen Romeo Dallaire *Shake Hands with the Devil: The Failure of Humanity in Rwanda* (Toronto: Random House Canada, 2003).

content of this paper is not an academic[4] or theoretical[5] analysis, but the presentation of experience distilled from twenty years of active participation in the healing of a broken nation, as a Christian and preacher and as a member of the Rwanda National Unity and Reconciliation Commission in the aftermath of the 1994 genocide against the Tutsi. The main thesis of this paper is that reconciliation is at the heart of the Gospel we preach, hence the necessity to relearn how to preach 'Christ and Him crucified' with a clear focus on restoring and healing a divided and wounded world. I will first look at where and why the church has failed in its reconciling mission, using Rwanda as an example (which could be extrapolated to other situations of open conflict), and then look at the content of the message of reconciliation.

Success and Failure in Evangelization and Discipleship: Rwanda as a Case Study

The general population census of 1991 showed that Rwanda was 89.6% Christian, with a large proportion of Roman Catholics (62.6%), followed by the different Protestant denominations (27%), with 8% traditionalists, 1.5% Muslims and 0.5% other religions. This dominance of Christian denominations is explained by the strategic implantation of the Catholic Church and the divine visitation of the 'Eastern African Revival' that started in the Anglican mission station of Gahini.

The White Fathers, the first Christian missionaries to set their feet in the 'Land of a Thousand Hills', arrived in Rwanda fired by the dream of Cardinal Lavigerie, the founder of their Order, to see the establishment of 'a Christian Kingdom in the heart of Africa'.[6] His recommended strategy was to convert the leadership and, through them, to conquer the whole population. This was not a novel approach (it worked with Constantine and other emperors after him), and it worked again. Christianity arrived in Rwanda in 1901, and by 1941 the king of Rwanda was baptized, bringing behind him the cortège of chiefs and influential personalities, and consequently the majority of the population, thus turning Rwanda into a model of a quickly fulfilled dream.

The Protestant missionaries were slow in their progress, blocked by the Catholics who had cut out a lion's share for themselves with the open support from the Belgian colonial administration. However, this hostile opposition did not prevent the explosion of the mighty Revival that started

[4] I wrote a more academic paper on repentance and forgiveness as pillars of reconciliation in Kalayjian and Raymond F. Paloutzian, *Forgiveness and Reconciliation: Psychological Pathways to Conflict Transformation and Peace Building (*New York: Springer, 2009).

[5] A longer French version of this article is presented in Daniel Bourdanné, *Le Tribalisme en Afrique* (Abidjan: PBA, 2002).

[6] Louis De Lacger, *Rwanda.*(Kabgayi: Imprimerie de Kabgayi, 1961).

in the Anglican Mission of Gahini in 1929, in the eastern part of Rwanda, and swept through the whole country before impacting the neighbouring countries of Uganda, Tanzania, Kenya, Burundi and beyond. There was reason to celebrate.

But between 1959 and 1963 the bloody overthrow of the Tutsi monarchy, accompanied by lootings and massacres of innocent Tutsis, sent a large number of refugees (mainly Tutsi) on the same routes the Revival missionaries had taken spreading the Gospel into the neighbouring countries. In the following years, the church kept growing, working hand-in-hand with the Government. The refugees who had left the country were never allowed the peaceful return they were asking for; discriminatory policies against the Tutsis were put in place and implemented inside the country with the connivance and compliance of the churches. No one ever raised a prophetic voice against the practices and no one spoke about reconciliation! The church was growing, populated by people who were wounded by those past events and the ongoing unjust ethnic policies. Then a spark touched the ethnic powder keg! The Tutsi refugees, who had lived all those years in refugee settlements in the neighbouring countries, finally tired of fruitless verbal pleading and took things in their own hands, 'repatriating' themselves by war. In this 90% Christian nation, ethnic hatred was fuelled through open hate propaganda and culminated in the 1994 genocide against Tutsis where approximately 1,000,000 people were brutally massacred, often inside church buildings and in many cases with the participation of clergy members. What was it that had gone wrong with our Christianity?

An Autopsy of the Church Failure

There are many reasons that may explain the situation but I will try to stick to the most obvious before drawing lessons for the future. First, the message of the Gospel that was presented was not contextualized to respond to the social needs and problems of the nation. When the missionaries arrived, they found a unified nation with three groups: Hutus, Tutsis and Twas, the power being in the hands of the Tutsi monarchy. The three groups were more like social classes than ethnic groups but there were already some seeds of future evil in their relationships. Social stereotypes pitted the noble Tutsis against the rabble Hutus; the political system favoured a given class of élite over those who were not economically favoured with cattle possessions; and the Hutus and Tutsis despised and held in contempt the small Twa group. The missionaries overlooked all these shortcomings and many others in their zeal to convert and civilize the country. Instead of using the Gospel and their newly introduced school education to eradicate the negative social stereotypes, the colonial authorities and the missionaries built on them, favoring the Tutsi over the other two groups. The Gospel that was presented did not respond to any of the relational ills and it came without any prophetic punch for a change in social relations. The end-result was a Christianity running at the surface while deep down the blood of ethnicity was still thicker than the water of baptism! This produced Christians who at heart were still 'Hutus, Tutsis and Twas' and not one race under Christ. And this fact was true not only for Rwanda but for many other countries that have suffered from racism, ethnocentrism, tribalism and other group-related problems.

The second weakness was in the methods of presentation. While African spirituality in general, and Rwandan spirituality in particular, are experiential, always linked to personal, family and national life, the missionaries brought a religion based on the intellect, very propositional and dependent on memorization. This would in the long run prove ineffective in a place where everything is linked, where the living and the dead are still together, where the animal kingdom and the inanimate world also play a role in spirituality. In the traditional African worldview, the world is one, and not split between the material, physical and visible and the spiritual and invisible.[7] The way Christianity was presented did not take into consideration that reality, and the consequence was that many people turned to Christianity but kept finding answers to their daily problems in their ancestral religion. In this kind of syncretistic situation, people kept relying on their traditional perceptions to define their ethnic, racial and tribal identities and relationships, and it is then no wonder that in times of conflict, people did not rely on their Christian faith but rather on 'what their fathers have told them'.

The third level of failure was with the messengers themselves: they were not a good role model of brotherly relationships. When the Germans lost the First World War, the Lutheran missionaries were chased out of Rwanda at the instigation of the Catholic missionaries who kept blocking the advance of other Christian denominations in the country. This created more divisions and animosities[8] among the people who did not see Christianity as a unifying factor, but rather as another colonial source of conflict and confrontation. Although we did not have such a thing as Hutu, Tutsi or Twa churches, Christianity did not in any way model that spirit of unity, reconciliation and love that is expected from disciples of Jesus Christ. Unfortunately this is a reality that is still prevalent in our Christian communities, characterized by denominational divisions.

Lastly, it has been well said that 'politics is like fire: when you get too close you run the risk of getting burnt, but when you stay too far away you get cold'. This could apply to the relationships between the church and the political leadership in Rwanda from the colonial days up to the genocide against the Tutsis. The Roman Catholic Church worked hand-in-hand with

---

[7] John Mbiti, *African Religions and Philosophies* (Oxford, UK: Heinemann, 1961).

[8] For a detailed analysis of the animosities, see H. H. Osborn, *Fire in the Hills: The Revival which Spread from Rwanda.* (Crowborough: Highland Books, 1991).

the government, often influencing their decisions but never taking a safe distance to raise a prophetic voice against their misdeeds, while the Protestant churches took a more distant stance out of timidity rather than courage and they too never raised a prophetic voice against the ethnic injustices and cruelties.[9]

This analysis of the Rwanda situation, although limited in scope, should serve as an eye-opener to the church everywhere. Our missiology has often been flawed by those blind spots about social issues and the relationships to the national political systems. If the church is to become a healing agent in society, it needs to make the right diagnosis of the inter-group relationships, their past and their present, and develop messages that will align the inter-group relationships with the truth of the Gospel.

Rediscovering the Gospel of Reconciliation

After the genocide of 1994, the church was covered in shame and sat on the bench of the accused for not having done anything to stop or at least denounce the mass killings. How could such a thing happen in a country that was 90% Christian? Isn't Christianity an obsolete practice to be deleted? The amazing thing is that, despite such questioning, Christianity is still growing. Just eight years after the genocide, the population census (2002) showed that Christians encompassed 94% while Muslims had grown to almost 2%[10] and the other religions share the rest of the 4%. And the question today is: Has anything changed? Yes and no! 'Yes', because we now know the message we should preach to heal the wounds of our nation. 'No', because not many churches are preaching it, and those who preach it are not doing it with intentionality – that is, preaching the message until we see change!

Preaching the Message of Reconciliation

Why are so many people finding it difficult to preach reconciliation? Our experience in Rwanda has shown that many have this shallow view that ethnic and racial reconciliation is a political agenda and are afraid to be accused of participating in politics when they raise their voices to preach reconciliation. This story from my testimony is worth thousands of lines of analysis. Some months after repenting from the hatred I had been harbouring against the Hutus for killing my father,[11] I gave my testimony in

---

[9] Tharcisse Gatwa, *Victim or Guilty: The Church and Ethnic Ideology in Rwanda 1900-1994* (Oxford, UK: Regnum, 2005).

[10] Some statistics put the number at 8% but what is presented here is taken from the official document of the population census of 2002 and only the publication of the 2012 general census will give more correct figures.

[11] My father was massacred with many other Tutsis in the first wave of massacres against the Tutsis in Rwanda between 1959 and1963.

a message I was preaching on the Cross. Everybody in the church was shocked, and when we came out, friends approached me and reminded me not to mix the Gospel with politics. Since then I have heard this kind of comment so many times that I could write a book on the issue! Others find the biblical message on reconciliation very confusing because the New Testament speaks of forgiveness while the Old Testament condones and even orders revenge. However, this is a misreading of the Bible. First, reconciliation, even ethnic and racial, is not just a political issue; it is the very heart of the Gospel. Second, God has never allowed for revenge; even where the Bible speaks of the avenger of blood, it was more about justice than about personal vindication. It was 'an eye for an eye, a tooth for a tooth, a life for a life' to limit the abuse that goes with revenge as human nature tends to 'double the damage': you gouge my eye out and I cut your neck! The proof of this is the number of stories of forgiveness found in the Old Testament (e.g. Joseph and his brothers, and David and Saul); even the first call to do good to your enemy is found in the Old Testament (Proverbs 24:17-18). How then shall we preach the message of reconciliation? What is its content? Preaching reconciliation becomes easy when we understand that sin is the root of all evils, including divisions.

A New Perspective on Sin and Alienation: Genesis 3

When sin entered the world, it brought with it four consequent levels of alienation reflected in different problems the world has always been faced with: alienation from God (spiritual problems); alienation from self (psycho-emotional problems); alienation from the others (social problems); and alienation from nature (ecological problems). Spiritual emptiness and many other spiritual problems that sprang from the separation of man from his Creator came with a plethora of other ills such as psychological disorders and all types of phobias, social problems such as wars and mass/individual violence as well as ecological issues (environmental degradation and pollution). Simply stated, the Gospel is God's mission to remedy those four types of problems ('The Bad News') through the Good News of Jesus Christ and his Cross. A complete, full Gospel will be a Gospel that will continually analyse the situation of each community in terms of these levels of alienation, and craft a relevant message with a clear focus on transformation. This calls for a change in the way we preach 'Christ and Him crucified'.

A New Perspective on Preaching Christ Crucified: Isaiah 53:4-6

Most of the sermons in our evangelistic outreach focus on sin, and our altar calls are consequently a call to repent, to accept Jesus Christ as Saviour and Lord. As people respond to the call we get churches full of people. But it is rare to hear people preaching about the pains, the frustrations, the grief, the bitterness and the hatred caused by different social ills. A new look at the message of the cross, as presented in Isaiah 53:4-6, gives us a new perspective on presenting 'Christ Crucified' to a broken world. Isaiah first presents Jesus as our *pain bearer*, the one who shared in and 'carried our sorrows', and second as our *sin bearer,* the one who took on himself 'our sins and our iniquities'. Christ the pain-bearer appeals more to the offended while Christ the sin-bearer appeals to the offender; but it is only when both the offended and the offender meet at the foot of the Cross that real peace is restored and real reconciliation takes place. Preaching the 'full Gospel' can be equated with speaking about Christ our pain-bearer and our sin-bearer who consequently becomes our reconciler.

In our experience with the Rwandan community, we have seen real reconciliation taking place only when forgiveness on the side of the offended is met with repentance and confession from an offender.[12] When a survivor from the genocide who has committed his life to Christ, has offloaded his emotions on Jesus the pain-bearer, has been healed from his inner wounds and has forgiven, meets an offender who has met Christ, has repented from his evil doing and is ready to confess and ask for forgiveness, only then does real reconciliation take place. Christ reconciles us through his Cross because he deals with both parties, not just one. "He is our peace" and that is how he has "made the two one and has destroyed the barrier, the dividing wall of hostility" (Ephesians 2:14). Most of the studies on reconciliation and social restoration focus on forgiveness,[13] and much has been written on this topic without much reference to repentance and confession, but such a single-factor approach will never bring real reconciliation. A message of the Cross that stresses only Jesus as our sin-bearer without taking time to look at Jesus our pain-bearer, will not bring real healing to the nations, and that is probably why we have nations with a great percentage of Christians in their population but without real reconciliation and peace.

A New Perspective on Our Identity: 2 Cor. 5:17

In most of the conflict-ridden areas of the world, people – even Christians – tend to identify themselves in terms of their ethnic, racial, regional and even religious groups. Tensions and hatred against other groups are at times part of a legacy of past wounds and negative stereotypes transmitted from generation to generation, often going back into the night of times immemorial. One way of helping people out of this quagmire is to take them through a pilgrimage into their roots, first to rediscover the source of

---

[12] See some of the stories well documented in Meg Guillebaud, *Rwanda: the Land God Forgot? Revival, Genocide and Hope* (Oxford, UK: Monarch Books, 2002).

[13] See for instance most of the references in Ani Kalayjian and Raymond F. Paloutzian, *Forgiveness and Reconciliation: Psychological Pathways to Conflict Transformation and Peace Building* (New York: Springer, 2009).

their identity and then shift to their new identity in Christ. The old roots of our 'human belonging' (as human beings, members of a tribe, ethnic group or race) yield the bitter fruit of the flesh, but our new grafting into Christ helps us to bear the divine sweet fruit of the Spirit (Galatians 5:22). When we are in Christ we become a new creation, a new race, a new family unto God and we no longer consider anybody from a "worldly point of view" (2 Corinthians 5:16). However, this is often easier said than done as we keep considering other people through the lenses of ancestry and social stereotypes.

In his preaching, Paul frequently goes back to those racially divisive issues and reminds us that when we are in Christ, "there is neither Jew nor Greek, slave nor free, male nor female, for you are all one in Christ Jesus" (Galatians 3:28). Although Jesus never explicitly preached about breaking the dividing wall of race and ethnicity, he implicitly broke it when he ministered to foreigners, and even spent days among the despised Samaritans (John 4), and he left us the mission to make of all nations his disciples. You cannot preach to people you despise and hate, and you cannot be a true disciple without loving (John 13:34-35). Our new identity in Christ is incompatible with any type of division. Once in Christ, we are all brothers and sisters, there are no more "Greek or Jew, circumcised or uncircumcised, barbarian, Scythian, slave or free, but Christ is all and is in all" (Colossians 3:11). At the foot of the cross we are all equal, and brothers and sisters, one Holy Nation unto God (1 Peter 2:9).

A New Perspective on the Mission of the Church: 2 Cor. 5:18

Once the church has understood its real identity as the Holy Nation of God on earth, then it will start fulfilling holistically its mission as true "ambassadors of reconciliation" (2 Corinthians 5:18), not just between God and man but also between man and himself, between man and his neighbour, and even between man and nature. Our identity as the Holy Nation of God – in other words our ecclesiology – defines our missiology. This is probably where the greatest failure has been: the church has preached a truncated message, often focusing on parts of the Gospel rather than on the 'whole counsel of God'. The Good News of Jesus Christ should touch all those areas that have been affected by sin, restoring our vertical relation with God and our horizontal relations with one another and nature. This kind of harmony presented in Genesis 1 and 2 will be restored and even improved when Christ comes back, as described in Revelation 21 and 22. The Bible starts in a garden and ends in a city with an infrastructure that is beyond what the human heart has ever conceived, but the greatest difference is that "the throne of God and of the Lamb will be in the city … and they will see his face and his name will be written on their foreheads" (Revelation 22:3-4). That is the restoring message of transformation and hope that we have been given to preach.

It is when the church of Christ lives in love and unity that great things will happen in our nations. First, the unity of the church is a silent evangelistic proclamation, a testimony to the mission of God through Jesus Christ. In his final prayer before going to the Cross, our Lord prayed for unity and stated clearly that we must be one "so that the world may believe that you have sent me" (John 17:21). Second, when we love each other, our reconciliation will be a testimony to our true identity as disciples of Jesus Christ. In his last message, our Lord reminded his disciples that our love for each other is our testimony of true discipleship: "… by this all men will know that you are my disciples, if you love one another" (John 13:35). Finally, our unity will be the source of power for our witness to the world. Already in Genesis 11 God reveals that unity is the secret of power for achieving any purpose: "… if as one people speaking the same language they have begun to do this, then nothing they plan to do will be impossible for them" (11:5). One version puts it in even clearer terms: "The people are united, and they all speak the same language. After this, nothing they set out to do will be impossible for them." This is a principle that is repeated in different words throughout the Bible (Psalm 133:3; Matthew 18:18-19; 1 Peter 3:7), but the devil seems to have caught the message faster and uses it better than the people of God. We tend to cherish our divisions rather than the promise of power and blessing offered in the practice of our unity and reconciliation.

Conclusion: Preaching Reconciliation in Action

As stated earlier, all types of alienation are the consequence of sin. The practice of reconciliation calls for a holistic approach to the proclamation of the Gospel, and I would like to close this article by expanding the domain of our proclamation of reconciliation by giving a brief testimony on how to develop a strategy for national rebuilding and reconciliation. When we were developing the National Policy for Reconciliation,[14] it became obvious to us that reconciliation is about responding to human needs, and the Maslow scale of human needs served as a good framework for the final document. Real reconciliation happens when the physical needs of the people, their need for security, social belonging, self-actualization and shared values are answered. In our distribution of roles among national stakeholders, churches were singled out to be the best in rebuilding relationships, responding to the physical needs, advocating the rights to self-actualization and the propagation of positive and constructive values. But more than anything else, the church was singled out for healing of emotions and forgiveness, repentance and confession since, after all, there is no other institution that has a message that speaks of loving and blessing your enemy. As one government minister put it: "As a government we are

[14] The document can be read from the following website: www.nurc.gov.rw.

determined to make the Rwandans live together in peace. We can force them to live next to each other without attacking or insulting each other, but we cannot force them to love each other."

This holistic perception of reconciliation is more aligned to the mission Jesus Christ spelled out when he started this ministry (Luke 4:18): he set out to build peace by responding to every need in the community he was serving, and it is the same mission he has left to us. We are ambassadors of total reconciliation: with God, with self, with others and with nature.

History of the Partnership of Men and Women in the Lausanne Movement

Jane L. Crane

The contributions to world evangelization by the Lausanne Movement are well known, but its modelling of the partnership of men and women in ministry has also been significant. This essay provides a historical account of actions taken by leadership in the Lausanne Movement toward this partnership. Reviewed are Lausanne's three major congresses, resulting formal documents, and one of its forums that specifically addressed this partnership. The essay is organized according to acts before, during, and after the Cape Town Congress. I write as Lausanne's first Senior Associate for the Partnership of Men and Women, and Special Interest Committee Chair for the same topic (2007-12).

Women in Lausanne Prior to the Cape Town Congress

Lausanne, Switzerland

For the first World Congress in 1974, writes sociologist William Martin, Billy Graham suggested in a goal ahead of its time that 10% of the participants be women.[1] Reportedly, 7% of the actual participants were indeed women.[2] Vonette Bright, wife of Bill Bright, the founder of Campus

[1] William Martin, *A Prophet with Honor: the Billy Graham Story* (New York: William Morrow and Company, 1991), 442. He writes that this was a 'significant departure from the common evangelical practice of barring women from public roles.'

[2] Robyn Claydon cites a figure of about 100 women in 'The Contribution of Women to Lausanne's Ministry,' *Lausanne World Pulse,* Oct/Nov 2011. www.lausanneworldpulse.com/page_print.php. Accessed 22 Oct 2011. Douglas Birdsall provided the figure of 7% in an email communication to the author, 12th April 2013. If the final list of participants was 2,400, as Martin reports, then 7% would have been 168 women.

Crusade for Christ, was the only woman on the board for the gathering, and her responsibility was prayer.[3]

The *Lausanne Covenant* gave only brief but significant comments regarding women. These foreshadowed the later, fuller comments to come about women in future Lausanne documents:

> We should share God's 'concern for justice and reconciliation throughout human society and for the liberation of men and women from every kind of injustice. Because men and women are made in the image of God, every person, regardless of race, religion, colour, culture, class, sex or age, has an intrinsic dignity because of which he or she should be respected and served, not exploited.'[4]

Manila, Philippines

When the second Congress took place in Manila, in 1989, far more women were in attendance, participated from the platform, and were addressed in substance in the Congress document. Out of 4,300 delegates, nearly a quarter were women.[5] In addition, women gave about 10% of the plenary sessions and presented workshops and some of the Bible studies.[6] Robyn Claydon of Australia presented a plenary Bible exposition, the first time this was done by a woman at a Lausanne Congress.[7] A man presided over the communion service, but a woman preached at the service, which did garner some complaints because she was a woman.

Many of the women participants requested a women's network in Lausanne, so Leighton Ford, who was very involved with the leadership of the Manila Congress, asked Robyn Claydon to start one. For the next 25 years, she travelled around the world encouraging women leaders, including younger ones, and eventually became Vice-Chair of the Lausanne board. I had the privilege of learning from her sterling and joyful example when I reported to her as chair of a Lausanne Special Interest Committee.

The official document that came from the Manila Congress, the *Manila Manifesto*, addresses gender issues in two of its 21 Affirmations. Together, the two Affirmations build toward a call for the partnership of women and men in evangelization:

---

[3] Email communication from Robyn Claydon and Elke Werner, current Lausanne board member and overseer of the Lausanne Women's Network, to the author, 18th Feb 2013.

[4] *Lausanne Covenant*, '5. Christian Social Responsibility'. www.lausanne.org/en/documents/lausanne-covenant.html.

[5] Alan Nichols (ed), 'Gifts of Women,' in *The Whole Gospel for the Whole World* (Charlotte, NC and Ventura, CA: Regal Books/LCWE, 1989), 66.

[6] Alan Nichols, *The Whole Gospel for the Whole World,* 67.

[7] Email communication from Robyn Claydon to Jane Crane, 18th Feb 2013.

> Affirmation 13: We affirm that we who claim to be members of the Body of Christ must transcend within our fellowship the barriers of race, gender and class.
>
> Affirmation 14: We affirm that the gifts of the Spirit are distributed to all God's people, women and men, and that their partnership in evangelization must be welcomed for the common good.[8]

The *Manila Manifesto* also states that while there is not full agreement as to what forms the leadership of women should take, they must be given opportunities to exercise their gifts and callings for suitable training for both men and women.[9] The *Manila Manifesto* deplored 'the failures in Christian consistency', including sexual discrimination,[10] and affirmed that 'co-operation in evangelism is indispensable', with both sexes working together.[11] What the partnership between men and women would look like, however, was not fully defined. That partnership, within and outside the Lausanne Movement, would have to emerge in future events.

Pattaya, Thailand

In addition to the three major Congresses, Lausanne organized dozens of smaller gatherings through the years, and one of these specifically addressed the partnership of women. Lausanne's 2004 Forum for World Evangelization in Pattaya, Thailand, drew together 1,530 delegates from 130 countries.[12] It was organized into 31 'issue groups' for study and preparation of a *Lausanne Occasional Paper*, with the set eventually being published in three volumes.[13]

One of these issue groups was entitled 'Empowering Men and Women to Use their Gifts Together in Advancing the Gospel'. Nearly fifty men and women from a dozen countries participated in it. The issue group's presentation to the Forum and the *Lausanne Occasional Paper* declared:

> For the whole church to take the whole gospel to the whole world, more labourers, both men and women, must be released to exercise their God-given gifts for ministry and leadership. More than half of the body of Christ are

---

[8] *Manila Manifesto*, www.lausanne.org/en/documents/manila-manifesto.html.

[9] *Manila Manifesto*, 6, The Human Witness.'

[10] *Manila Manifesto,* 7, The Integrity of the Witness.'

[11] *Manila Manifesto*, 9, Cooperating in Evangelism.'

[12] David Claydon (ed), *A New Vision, A New Heart, A Renewed Call, Lausanne Occasional Papers from the 2004 Forum for World Evangelization hosted by the LCWE in Pattaya, Thailand, Sept 29-Oct 5, 2004.* Copyright © 2005 LCWE (Pasadena, CA: William Carey Library, 2005), Volume One, x.

[13] David Claydon, *A New Vision, A New Heart, A Renewed Call,* Volumes One-Three.

> women, who are the most undervalued and under-utilized resource of the Church.[14]

Summary Affirmations produced by the leadership of the Forum included the following:

> In this Forum we have experienced the partnership of men and women working together. We call on the church around the world to work towards full partnership of men and women in the work of world evangelization by maximizing the gifts of all.[15]

The Cape Town Congress

Lausanne's World Congress in Cape Town in 2010 was called 'the most representative gathering of Christians to date',[16] with more than 4,000 leaders from 198 countries. This section examines women's participation in that Congress.

Women as Delegates and in Leadership

Delegates for the Congress were proposed by national selection committees, and Congress leadership requested that these committees include at least 35% women among their delegates. Under the leadership of Bishop Hwa Yung of Malaysia, the International Participant Selection Committee for the Congress developed this figure to exceed participation by women at the two earlier Lausanne Congresses, as well as at many smaller gatherings of Christian leaders at that time.[17]

Also recommended to selection committees was a certain percentage of young men and women delegates under the age of 40. A 10% variance was allowed within the categories of women and younger leaders for the national selection committees to reach their total numbers. Most countries complied with the guidelines. National nominating committees who did not comply were respectfully asked to go back to the drawing board to nominate more women and youth, and most of them did.

---

[14] David Claydon, *A New Vision, A New Heart, A Renewed Call,* Volume Two, 636. The content referenced is also available online as *Lausanne Occasional Paper 53,* 'Empowering Men and Women to Use their Gifts Together in Advancing the Gospel,' at www.lausanne.org/en/documents/lops/869-lop-53.html.

[15] David Claydon, *A New Vision, A New Heart, A Renewed Call,* Volume One, xii.

[16] ChristianityToday.com, daily online missive from the Cape Town Congress, 20th Oct 2010. Also referenced in www.lausanne.org.

[17] According to an email from Douglas Birdsall to the author on 12th April 2013, the percentage of women's involvement in the third Congress was much higher than at most of the dozens of gatherings of Christian leaders from around the world that he attended between 2007 and 2010, though these would have been smaller than the third Congress.

Women were also in some of the central leadership positions for the Congress. Two women were officers of the board. Robyn Claydon, the founder of the women's network, was Vice-Chair, and Esme Bowers from South Africa was Secretary. Other female board members included Judy Mbugua of Kenya, also on the Congress Advisory Council; Elke Werner of Germany, who then headed up Lausanne's women's network; Sarah Plummer from Australia, Chair of the Intercessory Working Group; and Grace Mathews of India, Congress Programme Director. Lindsay Olesberg, author of *The Bible Study Handbook,*[18] was co-ordinator of the team of Congress plenary Bible expositors. Some of the Senior Associates and Special Interest Committee chairs for Lausanne were also women. In addition, women held several of the key administrative positions, including Julia Cameron as Director of External Relations, Naomi Frizzell as Director of Communications, and Kimberly Iannelli as Co-Director of Participant Selection.

Women were also some of the table leaders at the Congress when discussions took place each day among the 4,000 delegates seated at tables of six, with generally a mix of men, women, and of nationalities.

Women Speakers and Partnership Themes

At platform levels, women gave some of the main plenary talks at the Congress. They also delivered numerous briefer presentations at the plenary level, spoke in most of the workshops, and led some of them. Glenn Smith oversaw the workshops, called multiplexes and dialogues, and aimed for at least 35% women speakers in all of them. Some of the main workshops were also led by women, such as one on leadership with Jane Overstreet with an overflow crowd of men and women.[19]

A woman gave one of the six plenary Bible expositions. Ruth Padilla DeBorst, a theologian from Latin America and General Secretary for the Latin American Theological Fraternity, expounded on Ephesians 2 to the entire Congress. In examining the question, 'Where does God live?' she included a few mentions of women. She pointed out that Jesus affirmed the dignity of women, spoke to them, and called men to account regarding their treatment of them. She said Paul 'daringly preached mutual submission to all', particularly to the powerful of that day – men and fathers. She said Paul acknowledged 'the anointed leadership of women'.[20] She also

[18] Lindsay Olesberg, *The Bible Study Handbook: A Comprehensive Guide to an Essential Practice* (Downer's Grove, IL: InterVarsity Press, 2012).

[19] Jane Overstreet, 'How to Build A New Generation of Christ-Like Leaders', in multiplex, 22nd Oct 2010, Cape Town 2010: The Third World Congress. http://conversation.lausanne.org/en/resources/detail/11000.

[20] Ruth Padilla DeBorst, Ephesians 2, Plenary Biblical Exposition. Cape Town 2010: The Third World Congress, 19th Oct 2010. http://conversation.lausanne.org/en/resources/detail/11324. Her speech is also available in J. E. M. Cameron,

included the interaction of men and women in her answer to the question of where God lives:

> God lives in the new humanity created by God, reconciled by Christ, and indwelled and diversely gifted by the Holy Spirit for the building up of that community and for works of peace and justice far outside its bounds. God lives wherever women and men together allow the Community-of-love to imprint God's image on them, to speak reconciliation into being in their midst, to tear down all humanly constructed walls and spiritually bolstered exclusions so that unity becomes visible, to remind them that once we were all together in death and that our lives, our value and our purpose depend entirely on God's unmerited grace. God yearns to build the world church today into his earthly dwelling place![21]

On the partnership-themed day of the Congress, husband and wife Ramez and Rebecca Atallah spoke together for the plenary Bible exposition on Ephesians 6.[22] Ramez was Programme Chair for the Congress and is General Secretary of the Bible Society of Egypt. Rebecca has been called 'Mother Theresa' to the untouchables of a garbage city outside Cairo, where she has worked since 1982.[23] Rebecca shared how God's power has overcome the forces of evil in that garbage city, including the discovery of a cave there that has become the largest church in the Middle East.

In another plenary session, Elke Werner from Germany spoke on the topic of men and women in ministry. "When Christ died on the cross," she said, "he brought full redemption to men and women. Women are not second-class citizens in God's kingdom."[24] "God has created us," she said, "men and women, to work side by side." She also voiced these key statements:

> We have to admit that we have failed to voice our concern for justice for women.
> God calls us to be a prophetic voice, an advocate for the oppressed and weak.
> God calls us to release women into the full use of their spiritual gifts.
> God calls us to reach out to women around the world.
> God calls us to be reconciled to one another as men and women.
> Let us determine today to partner together for Christ's sake.[25]

Christ Our Reconciler (Nottingham, UK and Downers Grove, IL: IVP/Lausanne Library, 2012).

[21] Ruth Padilla DeBorst, Ephesians 2, Plenary Biblical Exposition.

[22] Ramez and Rebecca Atallah, Ephesians 6, Plenary Biblical Exposition. Cape Town 2010: The Third World Congress, 24th Oct 2010. http://conversation.lausanne.org/en/resources/detail/11643.

[23] Glenn Smith, 'Transforming Lives in Cairo's Garbage Villages' in *Lausanne World Pulse,* Feb 2008. www.lausanneworldpulse.com/urban.php/903?pg=all, accessed 12th Sept 2013.

[24] Elke Werner, 'Men and Women in Ministry', Plenary Presentation, Cape Town 2010: The Third World Congress, 23rd Oct 2010. http://conversation.lausanne.org/en/resources/detail/11560.

[25] Elke Werner, 'Men and Women in Ministry'.

Leslie and Chad Segraves, a thirty-something husband-and-wife team who co-founded and lead an international ministry together, delivered a plenary session on the partnership of men and women in ministry. Both hold doctorates in Missiology from Fuller Seminary, but unfortunately only Chad's doctorate was identified in their biographies in the Congress programme. Chad tried admirably on-stage to rectify the omission, and with humour, by referring to the fact that Leslie received her doctoral degree a whole two hours before he did! Leslie shared that she has been discriminated against at times as a woman, with people wanting to know just about Chad's spiritual gifts. Their ministry trains and empowers both women and men. As a result, they said, 41,000 people from forty different unreached people groups have come to Christ through women church planters trained by the Segraves in collaboration with some of the churches in Asia.[26]

Chad and Leslie each shared how they 'fight against the Fall'. Chad said he does this as a man when he seeks to empower his sisters in the body of Christ to use every gift they have been given – requiring him to be humble, teachable, and willing to die to self. Leslie shared that, as a woman, she works against the Fall when she uses every gift that God has given her, including the gift of leadership – requiring her to be humble and willing to step up in a church culture that often prefers her brothers.[27] The Segraves' presentation to the Congress was interrupted repeatedly by applause.

On the last evening of the Congress, communion was led by Archbishop Henry Orombi of Uganda, Chair of the Africa Host Committee for the Congress, and the Revd Douglas Birdsall, Executive Chair of the Congress, with Grace Mathews of India, the Congress Programme Director.[28]

Multiplex and Dialogues

One of the major multiplex workshops was called 'Men and Women – A Powerful Team for the Completion of the Great Commission'. It was organized by the global team that I chaired, Alliance 2.29,[29] and included multiple speakers. David Hamilton, co-author of a book about women in ministry leadership with the founder of Youth With A Mission,[30] explored Scripture regarding men and women working together as a team, the inclusive treatment of women by Jesus and Paul, and the main idea of

---

[26] Leslie and Chad Segraves, 'Partnership of Men and Women', Plenary Presentation, Cape Town 2010: The Third World Congress, 24th Oct 2010. http://conversation.lausanne.org/en/resources/detail/11609.

[27] Leslie and Chad Segraves, 'Partnership of Men and Women'.

[28] 'Cape Town 2010 Closing Ceremony,' 24th Oct, Cape Town 2010: The Third World Congress. http://conversation.lausanne.org/en/ resources/detail/11010.

[29] Alliance 2.29 is based on Joel 2.29, where both men and women prophesy.

[30] Loren Cunningham and David Hamilton, *Why Not Women: A Biblical Study on Women in Missions, Ministry and Leadership* (Seattle: YWAM Publishing, 2000).

passages sometimes used to limit women's ministry.[31] Edwin Fillies, who grew up during apartheid in a small, male-dominated village in South Africa, shared how impactful Christian women were in his life and likened the pain of apartheid to gender discrimination.[32] A couple from Australia and another from Croatia spoke about their teamwork in ministry and equality in marriage.[33] A professor of New Testament at the Assemblies of God Seminary in the USA, Deborah Gill, spoke on the inclusion of women in the early church and making room for female leaders today.[34] Maureen Menard of South Africa facilitated the multiplex and shared some of her experiences as a single woman missionary.

The partnership of men and women was also addressed in three dialogue sessions.[35] In one, the former chair of the Asia Theological Association, Ivan Satyavrata, spoke with Deborah Gill on integrity in male-female ministry interactions. Another dialogue addressed men and women in evangelization, but one of the scheduled female speakers, a top leader in China, was in the delegation held back from the Congress by her government.

In a third dialogue, I presented facts and theories regarding the three main debated Scriptures about women.[36] In 1 Corinthians 11:3-12, does man as the 'head' of woman imply 'authority' or 'source' in the Greek and context of the passage? In 1 Corinthians 14:34-36, is Paul silencing women in the churches, or correcting a misapplication of Jewish 'law' to the early church? In 1 Timothy 2:11-15, is Paul setting up a prohibition that women

---

[31] David Hamilton delivered two presentations (due to the illness of one speaker) in the multiplex on 'Men and Women – A Powerful Team for the Completion of the Great Commission,' 23rd Oct 2010, Cape Town 2010: The Third World Congress. http://conversation.lausanne.org/en/resources/detail/11632 and http://conversation.lausanne.org/en/resources/detail/11634. Hamilton did his Master's thesis on the three main scriptures sometimes used to limit the ministry of women.

[32] Edwin Fillies' talk can be found after David Hamilton's first presentation and may be viewed at http://conversation.lausanne.org/en/resources/detail/11632.

[33] Robyn and David Claydon and Eva and Danijel Mrsic 'Men and Women, Husband Wife Partnership,' in the multiplex on 'Men and Women – A Powerful Team for the Completion of the Great Commission', 23rd Oct 2010, Cape Town 2010: The Third World Congress.http://conversation.lausanne.org/en/resources/detail/11633.

[34] Deborah Gill, 'Men and Women: Making Room for Female Leaders in the Broader Body of Christ', in the multiplex on 'Men and Women – A Powerful Team for the Completion of the Great Commission,' 23 Oct 2010, Cape Town 2010: The Third World Congress. http://conversation. lausanne.org/en/resources/detail/ 11635.

[35] The Dialogues were facilitated by Ellen Duffield of Canada. Due to the extensive number of Dialogues at the Congress, these were not videotaped.

[36] The Dialogues were not recorded, but this teaching was from Jane L. Crane, 'Map for Gender Reconciliation'. Published in part in *A New Vision, A New Heart, A Renewed Call,* David Claydon (ed) (Pasadena, CA: William Carey Library, 2005), Volume Two, 659-669. The complete Map, DVD, and CD of 100+ Power Points for teaching the Map can be found at www.gendermap.org.

should not teach or have authority over men, or correcting a particular woman or a pagan teaching then prominent in Ephesus? Examined were key Greek words and idioms, cultural practices of the day, Paul's other statements about women, and theories about each passage from both sides of the argument. A conclusion was left to the listeners.

Testimonies

Two additional talks by women merit special mention here. Though neither discussed the partnership of men and women in ministry, nor advocated women as individuals in ministry, the words and role model of these two women resulted in perhaps the most inspirational moments of the Congress. Many attendees, including Doug Birdsall, the Executive Chair, cited these talks as among the most impactful.[37]

The first was by a young woman of 18 originally from North Korea, whose name was withheld for reasons that will become obvious. She told how her father, once a political leader in her native country, had escaped but then went back to share the Gospel of Jesus Christ. He never returned and was probably shot publicly, she said. Now she too wants to help the North Korean people and, through tears, asked her brothers and sisters in the Congress to pray for them. When she had finished, a strong applause continued unabated for quite a while, probably the longest of any at the Congress.[38]

Libby Little, the recent widow of a medical missionary in a very dangerous place in the world, also gave one of the most moving talks of the Congress. As part of what she shared, she read from blood-stained notes recovered from her husband's body that were apparently for his last talk on the mission field before he was killed.[39]

In the end, the balance of speakers at the Congress between male and female seemed good to me, and apparently to others. I heard of no complaints from women enquiring where the women speakers were. I heard of no complaints from men that there were too many women speakers, though there may have been some. It seemed that the Congress leadership had struck a good balance for the times.

A Place to Gather

As with any minority, the women delegates needed a place to gather to encourage one another. The Congress leadership gave place in the

---

[37] Mass email by Doug Birdsall, 22nd Nov 2010.

[38] Testimony by unnamed young woman from North Korea, 23rd Oct 2010, Cape Town 2010: The Third World Congress. http://conversation.lausanne.org/en/resources/ detail/11671.

[39] For security reasons, this testimony has not been made available for viewing.

convention hall for women to gather at board member Elke Werner's brainchild, the 'Women's Café'. Here women, and some men, congregated to talk, relax, network, and take some of their meals. Each afternoon, women leaders from various regions around the world made presentations that included the spoken word, music and drama, giving more opportunity for women leaders to share their work for the Gospel.

The Cape Town Commitment

The *Cape Town Commitment*, the Movement's formal document from the Congress, includes a Section specifically on 'Men and Women in Partnership'.[40]

Contrary to much of Christian history when the extensive work of women has been marginalised, or even credited to men, this Section of the *Commitment* acknowledges:

> The enormous and sacrificial contribution that women have made to world mission, ministering to both men and women, from biblical times to the present.[41]

The *Commitment* affirms that:

> Women and men are … equal in creation, in sin, in salvation, and in the Spirit. All of us, women and men, married and single, are responsible to employ God's gifts for the benefit of others, as stewards of God's grace, and for the praise and glory of Christ … We should not quench the Spirit by despising the ministry of any.[42]

Further, the *Commitment* encourages churches to:

> Acknowledge godly women who teach and model what is good … and to open wider doors of opportunity for women in education, service, and leadership, particularly in contexts where the gospel challenges unjust cultural traditions.[43]

The *Commitment* also recognizes that different views exist regarding women in ministry and calls for a careful study of Scripture together on this issue, with due regard for the context and culture of the original authors, and without condemnation toward one another.[44] Further:

> Where there is resistance to the manifest work of the Holy Spirit in any sister or brother we must repent [and] commit ourselves to a pattern of ministry, male and female, that reflects the servanthood of Jesus Christ, not worldly striving for power and status.[45]

---

[40] *The Cape Town Commitment: A Confession of Faith and a Call to Action*. The Lausanne Movement (Great Britain: 2011), IIF, 3.

[41] *Cape Town Commitment*, IIF, 3A.

[42] *Cape Town Commitment*, IIF, 3.

[43] *Cape Town Commitment*, IIF, 3C.

[44] *Cape Town Commitment*, IIF, 3B (1), (2).

[45] *Cape Town Commitment*, IIF, 3B (3), (4).

This Section in the *Commitment* concludes with the following strong statement:

> We long that women should not be hindered from exercising God's gifts or following God's call on their lives.[46]

Though not under the partnership Section, another part of the *Commitment* calls the church of Christ to humility, integrity, and simplicity. It raises a topic that can be applicable to the subject of men and women in partnership for the Gospel. Here, the *Commitment* encourages pastors to

> … help believers understand, honestly discuss, and practise the mutual submission that God requires of his children towards one another. In a world of greed, power and abuse, God is calling his Church to be the place of gentle humility and selfless love among its members.[47]

Apparently a good balance was struck overall in the *Commitment* on the language of the partnership of men and women. I received reports that both sides of the debate at this time are pleased with it.

Beyond the Congress

Since the third World Congress and the release of the *Cape Town Commitment*, various follow-up resources have been developed with reference to the partnership of men and women. These include curricula for teaching the *Commitment* in churches and seminaries,[48] an extensive annotated bibliography of topics covered in the *Commitment*,[49] and a book of selected talks from the Congress, with Ruth Padilla DeBorst's biblical exposition.[50] In addition, many of the talks from the Congress, including most referenced in this essay, can be found online.[51] The bibliography, published as a follow-on to the *Cape Town Commitment* lists sources for

---

[46] *Cape Town Commitment*, IIF, 3C.

[47] *Cape Town Commitment*, IIE, 3B.

[48] Rose Dowsett, *The Cape Town Commitment Study Edition* (Peabody, MA: Hendrickson/Lausanne Library, 2012). Provides study questions suitable for personal or group use.
Sara Singleton and Matt Ristuccia, *The Cape Town Commitment Study Pack DVD and Study Guide* (Peabody, MA: Hendrickson/Lausanne Library, 2013). Provides video clips of Congress teachings and testimonials, targeted spiritual practices related to Congress topics, and study questions.

[49] Darrell Bock, ed., *The Cape Town Commitment: A Confession of Faith, A Call to Action, Bibliographic Resources* (Eugene, OR: Wipf & Stock, 2013).

[50] J. E. M. Cameron (ed), *Christ Our Reconciler* (Nottingham, UK and Downers Grove, IL: IVP/Lausanne Library, 2012). Compilation of selected Congress addresses.

[51] Libby Little's talk is not available for security reasons. Dialogues were not recorded. Recorded Congress talks are available at www.lausanne.org/en/multimedia/videos/ct2010-session-videos.html.

study on both sides of the debate about the ministry of women, but also includes the following statement:

> The third Lausanne Congress itself was produced with women in some of the central leadership and platform roles.[52]

After the Congress, Lausanne board chair Ram Gimoodal championed an increase of the percentage of women on the board, which would help it grow toward the 35% women who were delegates to Cape Town.

Another significant gathering of Christians from around the world, Edinburgh 2010, in which the Lausanne Movement participated, had many women attendees in addition to men. Women were also some of the speakers and were on the leadership team.[53] In addition, the influential World Evangelical Alliance, founded in 1846, currently has significant participation by women on its main leadership structures.[54]

Further, more people are studying the pertinent Scriptures about women, as the *Cape Town Commitment* encourages, and gaining more understanding. A recent book chronicles this shift in leaders from various ethnicities as they have studied the Scriptures in more depth.[55]

Conclusion

Undoubtedly, the blessing of God has been on the Lausanne Movement, and as the participation of women has increased since the first World Congress, that blessing has remained strong. Key factors in women's growing participation in the Movement have evidently been:

- the advocacy of women's participation by many men from around the world,
- the involvement of many godly and gifted women leaders, and
- a fuller understanding of the relevant passages in Scripture.

While further progress can be made to empower women more fully for the spread of the Gospel, both on their own and in partnership with men, I believe the sum total of the related actions by the Lausanne Movement thus far can be seen as progressive for the cause of Christ, and for the men and women who proclaim it.

---

[52] Darrell Bock (ed), *The Cape Town Commitment: A Confession of Faith, A Call to Action, Bibliographic Resources,* 108.

[53] Julie C. Ma, Council Member and Executive Member for Edinburgh 2010. Phone conversation with the author, 5th June 2013. Also see Kirsteen Kim and Andrew Anderson (eds), *Edinburgh 2010: Mission Today and Tomorrow* (Oxford, UK: Regnum, 2011).

[54] WEA Central has three women out of a total of 10, while the International Council has four women out of a total of 12. www.worldea.org/whoweare/leadership; www.worldea.org/whoweare/ governance. Accessed 5 June 2013.

[55] Alan F. Johnson (ed), *How I Changed My Mind about Women in Leadership: Compelling Stories from Prominent Evangelicals* (Grand Rapids, MI: Zondervan, 2010).

Lessons for the future are:

- Include women on leadership teams in sufficient numbers for a representative voice,
- Plan and advocate for sufficient delegate and speaker invitations to women, and
- Shape conference themes, where appropriate, and formal documents to include references to the ministry of women and the partnership of men and women for the Gospel.

The 'Spirit of Lausanne' includes partnership.[56] This historical account has reviewed the actions of Lausanne leadership regarding the partnership of men and women in Lausanne's three major Congresses, one pertinent Forum, and accompanying documents, toward the goal of the *whole Church* taking the whole Gospel to the whole world.

[56] The 'Spirit of Lausanne' is defined as exemplified by prayer, study, partnership and hope, in a spirit of humility. www.lausanne.org/en/about.html, accessed 10th Sept 2013.

SECTION THREE

REVIEWING THE CAPE TOWN CONGRESS:

"... IN EVERY NATION, IN EVERY SPHERE OF SOCIETY, AND IN THE REALM OF IDEAS."

Mission in 3D: A Key Lausanne III Theme

Lars Dahle

Participating in the Cape Town Congress was in many ways an overwhelming experience, especially for those of us who were newcomers on the global evangelical congress arena. Highly rewarding, mind-stretching and heart-warming, but also challenging, humbling and sometimes bewildering, would be appropriate words to describe my own Congress experience. As responsible for one of the so-called multiplex sessions on the first day – on media and technology[1] – and the subsequent related dialogue sessions, my primary thematic focus during the Congress was on media-related issues.

This article has therefore provided me with a privileged opportunity to seek a bird's eye view on the Lausanne III congress – both thematically in terms of lasting impressions and key ideas, and missiologically in terms of significant reflections, contributions, and practices.[2]

In terms of lasting impressions from the plenary sessions, many of us who were present at the Congress will echo previous Executive Chairman Doug Birdsall's retrospective and engaging reflections when he revisited the site two years afterwards:

> In the main plenary hall, I was reminded again of the wonderful worship we shared together and the Ephesians Bible expositions by Ajith Fernando, John Piper, Ruth Padilla DeBorst, Vaughan Roberts, Ramez and Rebecca Atallah, and Calisto Odede. I remembered the moving testimony from Gyeong Ju Son, the young woman from North Korea, Os Guinness speaking on Truth, the moving video tributes to Billy Graham and John Stott, the Palestinian Christian and the Messianic Jew standing side by side, Libby Little sharing her story, Chris Wright on H.I.S. Church, the power of Princess Zulu

---

[1] Reference is made to Lars Dahle, 'Media Messages Matter: On global technologies, glocal trends, and gospel truth' [*CT2010 Advance Paper*], http://conversation.lausanne.org/en/conversations/detail/10514.

[2] This chapter is written from an insider's perspective as an analytical introduction to major themes at Lausanne III. It should thus be seen as having a supplementary function to the paper by L. Dahle and M. S. Dahle on 'Resourcing the Global Church: A Guide to Key Lausanne Resources 1974-2013' in this volume. For insightful critical perspectives on the Cape Town Congress, reference is made to a number of chapters in Sections Three and Four of this volume.

speaking on HIV/AIDS, and Tim Keller challenging us to reach our burgeoning global cities with the reconciling gospel of Jesus Christ. Who can forget our table groups – 700 "communities of six" – that enabled global friendships to form?[3]

In terms of key ideas, the following Congress summary provided by the Lausanne website seems fitting:

Cape Town 2010

- sounded a ringing affirmation of the truth of Jesus Christ;
- presented a clear statement on Christian witness among people of other faiths;
- provided a re-focused emphasis on evangelism and the integral mission of the Church;
- issued a clarion call to eradicate Bible poverty;
- called the Church back to humility, integrity and simplicity;
- and offered an earnest challenge to new collaborative initiatives and partnerships addressing the important issues facing the church and God's world.[4]

This concise summary relates to the six Congress themes which defined the Congress programme and also formed the framework for Part II in the *Cape Town Commitment*.[5] The focus in this summary is thus on central thematic challenges for world evangelization, as expressed and affirmed at the Congress.

But, in the midst of these lasting impressions and key ideas from the Congress, is there a unifying missiological Congress theme that can be identified? At one level, of course, a unifying theological *leitmotif* is found in the official Congress theme of *'God in Christ, reconciling the world to himself' (2 Cor 5:19)*. This fundamental biblical theme was clearly a decisive shaping factor both for the six morning Bible expositions during the congress and for Part I of the *Cape Town Commitment*. However, at another level a unifying missiological theme may be found in the mission statement included in the signed Foreword to the *Cape Town Commitment*,[6] where Doug Birdsall and International Director Lindsay Brown describe

---

[3] Doug Birdsall, Oct 25th 2012, www.lausanne.org/en/blog/1877-second-anniversary-cape-town-2010.html. See also the article by Knud Jørgensen on 'The Lausanne Movement in Critical Contemporary Dialogue with the Whole Church' in this volume.

[4] www.lausanne.org/en/gatherings/global-congress/event/8-cape-town-2010-the-third-lausanne-congress-on-world-evangelization.html.

[5] See the Appendix to this article for an overview of the six Congress themes and the related multiplex topics. For the global process preceding the Congress of identifying the six themes, see Blair Carlson's article on 'The Cape Town Congress: Process and Event' in this volume.

[6] The inclusion of this mission statement in the signed official foreword is indicative of its significance, even though 'it was not a matter [explicitly] discussed by the Lausanne Board or by the Congress leadership'. (Doug Birdsall in an email to the author on 30th Jan 2014)

the goal of the Congress: "Its goal? To bring a fresh challenge to the global Church to bear witness to Jesus Christ and all his teaching – in every nation, in every sphere of society, and in the realm of ideas."[7]

This carefully expressed sentence originated with Lindsay Brown at the 2010 Congress[8] and has since become an influential perspective in the ongoing shaping of the self-identity of the Lausanne Movement.[9]

The aim of this article is to show how this mission statement may be seen as a unifying missiological theme for the plenary and the multiplex sessions:

1. The statement describes integral Christian mission in three dimensions – i.e. "in every nation, in every sphere of society, and in the realm of ideas".
2. The theological and missiological foundation for this 'Mission in 3D' is articulated in the first part of this mission statement – i.e. "to bear witness to Jesus Christ and all his teaching".

The exposition in this article of this mission statement, as expressed and illustrated at the congress and in the *Cape Town Commitment*, functions as a thematic introduction to subsequent chapters on the Lausanne III congress in Section III.[10]

---

[7] 'Foreword', *The Cape Town Commitment: A Confession of Faith and a Call to Action* (Hendrickson: Peabody, MA, 2011; The Didasko Files), 4. (Often referred to as *CTC*.)

[8] 'The whole statement was my idea. It was not used in Lausanne communications before Cape Town' (Lindsay Brown in email to the author on 28th Jan 2014). Reference is especially made to Brown's final address which is included in this volume. It should also be mentioned that the press release on 16th Oct 2010 included a briefer version of the mission statement: 'The Congress theme is "God in Christ, reconciling the world to himself" (2 Cor 5:19) and how to bear witness to Jesus Christ and all his teaching in every region of the world and every sphere of society.' (www.lausanne.org/en/about/news-releases/1279-the-third-lausanne-congress-opens.html)

[9] Reference should here be made to FAQ at the Lausanne website: '*1. What is Lausanne?* Lausanne is a global movement that mobilizes evangelical leaders to collaborate for world evangelization. Together we seek to bear witness to Jesus Christ and all his teaching, in every part of the world – not only geographically, but in every sphere of society and in the realm of ideas.' (www.lausanne.org/en/about/faqs.html)

[10] The primary sources for this chapter are the following: *The Cape Town 2010 Congress Handbook* (Cape Town: The Lausanne Movement, 2010); *CTC*; J. E. M. Cameron (ed), *Christ Our Reconciler: Gospel / Church / World. The Third Lausanne Congress on World Evangelization* (Nottingham, UK: IVP, 2012), and www.lausanne.org/en/gatherings/global-congress/cape-town-2010.html.

Bearing Witness to Jesus Christ and All His Teaching

In his closing address to the Congress, Lindsay Brown made the following comment on the mission statement for the congress:

> The term *bearing witness* is carefully chosen. In many ways I think it is better than *evangelization*. It is often translated from the Greek word *martyria* in the English Bible to imply both speech and behaviour. We must be committed to the lordship of Christ in every area of human activity.[11]

It is evident from the biblical material that *bearing witness* is a rich concept, which "is central to the truth question in the New Testament, not the least in the Gospel of John".[12] However, the limited format of this article makes it impossible to explore fully this thematic field in the biblical sources.

This fundamental notion of *bearing witness to Jesus Christ and all his teaching* opens up at least five key emphases in the Lausanne resources, both in the specific material from the Cape Town Congress and in the wider Lausanne tradition.[13]

First, when seen together with the official Congress theme, the first part of the mission statement strongly points to *the Gospel of Jesus Christ as the theological focus of Christian mission.*[14] This is why Day One, with its theme "making the case for the truth of Christ in a pluralistic, globalized world", formed "the basis for our week of discussion. Everything rests on our clear grasp of Christ, eternal Son of God, Creator, unique Saviour, in whom all things find coherence".[15]

The Gospel of Jesus Christ forms the natural focus of the first part of the *Cape Town Commitment*, where this Gospel is situated within a biblical Trinitarian framework. The centrality of the Gospel is here highlighted through statements such as the following: "The core of our identity is our passion for the biblical news of the saving work of God through Jesus Christ."[16] Later in the same Section ("We love the Gospel of God"), this is expounded as a fourfold passion for the Gospel: "We love the good news in

---

[11] L. Brown's 'Closing address: We Have a Gospel to Proclaim' is published in this volume.

[12] L. Dahle, 'Truth, Christian Mission and Apologetics: A Response and A Proposal', in *Norwegian Journal of Missiology*, 67:1 (2013), 24. This article is also published at http://larsdahle.no/acts-17. See also A. A. Trites, *The New Testament Concept of Witness* (New York: Cambridge University Press, 1977).

[13] Reference should be made to *Lausanne Occasional Papers* (LOP) 5-19 and 22-23 which all include 'Christian Witness to …' in their titles; cf. www.lausanne.org/en/documents/lops.html.

[14] "We chose the phrase 'Jesus Christ and his teaching', because we wanted to be clearly and explicitly Christocentric. We wanted to focus both on the person of Christ, his egocentric claims, and the implications of his teaching for individuals and society." (L. Brown in email to the author on 28th Jan 2014).

[15] *The Cape Town 2010 Congress Handbook*, 30.

[16] *CTC*, 23.

a world of bad news … We love the story the gospel tells … We love the assurance the gospel brings… We love the transformation the gospel produces."[17]

This fourfold passion was communicated in a number of different ways throughout the Congress, whether in plenaries, multiplexes or dialogue sessions. The focus on the passion for the Gospel was especially evident from the major Bible expositions and the small table fellowships during the morning plenaries (called 'Celebrations of the Bible').[18]

It should also be mentioned that the passion for the Gospel of Jesus Christ permeated the greetings from the Lausanne founders Billy Graham and John Stott during the opening ceremony.[19] Due to Stott's foundational theological influence on the Lausanne Movement,[20] it is appropriate in this context to include his succinct summary of the apostolic *kerygma*, as recorded in Acts:

> Thus the apostles told the same story of Jesus at three levels – as historical event (witnessed by their own eyes), as having theological significance (interpreted by the Scriptures), and as contemporary message (confronting men and women with the necessity of decision). We have the same responsibility today to tell the story of Jesus as fact, doctrine and gospel.[21]

Second, the first part of the mission statement of the Congress has *a robust didactic emphasis on the teaching of Jesus Christ.* This is in clear continuity with 'The Great Commission' in Matthew 28:16-20,[22] with its emphasis on discipleship and teaching. This didactic emphasis is explicit in Part I of *The Cape Commitment*: '*Above all there is a great need for sustained biblical teaching and preaching …* '[23] This is later formulated as a challenging re-commitment: "We recommit ourselves, therefore, to the on-going task of translating, disseminating and teaching the Scriptures in every culture and language, including those that are predominantly oral or non-literary."[24]

---

[17] *CTC*, 23-24.

[18] The six Bible expositions on Ephesians were given by Ajith Fernando (Sri Lanka), Ruth Padilla DeBorst (Argentina/Costa Rica), John Piper (USA), Vaughan Roberts (UK), Callisto Odede (Kenya), and Ramez Atallah (Egypt). The expositions are published in J. E. M. Cameron (ed), *Christ Our Reconciler.*

[19] Both these greetings are published in J. E. M. Cameron (ed), *Christ Our Reconciler*, 14-16.

[20] Reference is made to Julia Cameron's paper on 'John Stott and the Lausanne Movement: A Formative Influence' in this volume.

[21] J. R. W. Stott, *The Message of Acts*, (Leicester, UK: IVP, 1990), 81.

[22] For an insightful exposition of the 'Great Commissions' of all the four gospels, see T. C. Tennant, *Invitation to World Missions: A Trinitarian Missiology for the Twenty-First Century* (Grand Rapids, MI: Regel Publications, 2010), 125-157.

[23] *CTC*, 16.

[24] *CTC*, 17.

It is also important to note, that in Part II of the *Cape Town Commitment*, which was shaped as a result of key input from all the plenaries and the multiplexes, teaching is emphasized in a number of significant contexts including the following:

- Section II.A on 'Truth' introduces the need for "teaching and guidance" in relation to media awareness issues.
- Section II.B on 'Reconciliation' emphasizes the need for extensive biblical teaching on poverty and justice, with a focus on "God's desire both for systemic economic justice and for personal compassion, respect and generosity towards the poor and needy".[25] The same Section warns against the false teaching which claims that disabilities are due to "personal sin, lack of faith or unwillingness to be healed".[26]
- Section II.C on 'World faiths' challenges Christians in all kinds of societies and cultures: "Let us conscientiously obey biblical teaching to be good citizens, to seek the welfare of the nation where we live, to honour and pray for those in authority, to pay taxes, to do good, and to seek to live peaceful and quiet lives."[27]
- Section II.D on 'Priorities' emphasizes the eradication of Bible ignorance in the church as a key aim: "We long to see a fresh conviction, gripping all God's Church, of the central necessity of Bible teaching for the Church's growth in ministry, unity and maturity."[28] This fundamental concern is later underlined in relation to the discipling of Christ-centred leaders: "Bible teaching is the paramount means of disciple-making and the most serious deficiency in contemporary Church leaders."[29]
- Section II.E on 'Integrity' highlights the need for biblical teaching over against the idolatries of disordered sexuality, power, success, and greed. This includes denouncing as "unbiblical the teaching that spiritual welfare can be measured in terms of material welfare or that wealth is always a sign of God's blessing".[30]
- Section II.F on 'Partnership' emphasizes the key role of theological education for mission, claiming that "above all theological education must serve to equip pastor-teachers for their prime responsibility of preaching and teaching the Bible".[31]

However, in view of this consistently strong emphasis on the importance of teaching, it seemed almost a contradiction in terms that the actual format

---

[25] *CTC*, 43.
[26] *CTC*, 44.
[27] *CTC*, 52.
[28] *CTC*, 54.
[29] *CTC*, 56.
[30] *CTC*, 64.
[31] *CTC*, 70.

of the Congress plenaries and multiplexes were consistently more dialogical than didactic. The chosen programme structure, the chosen technological formats, and the resulting time constraints created many understandable – but also some regrettable – limitations. It would probably have been more fruitful to give some key speakers in the programme – such as e.g. Os Guinness (Day One), Antoine Rutayisire (Day Two), Benjamin Kwashi (Day Three), Tim Keller (Day Four), Chris Wright (Day Five) and Patrick Fung (Day Six) – more time to develop and present their arguments.[32]

Thirdly, the fundamental first clause of the mission statement has *a clear apologetic emphasis on the truth of Jesus Christ*. As we saw above, this emphasis on truth is implicit in the very concept of *bearing witness*. At the same time, this was made explicit in the overall theme of the first day: 'Making the case for the truth of Christ in a pluralistic, globalized world':

> Worldviews interact and clash in the public arena with new intensity. In our globalized and pluralistic world, we need to equip Christians for their proclamation, demonstration and defence of truth – as found in Christ, the source and embodiment of truth. He is the sustainer of the universe, the one in whom all things hold together.[33]

The foundational plenary paper for this essential apologetic concern for truth was given by Os Guinness. In his paper, he introduced six reasons why 'a high view of truth' is absolutely essential, both for the global Lausanne community and beyond:

> Only a high view of truth
> - honours the God of truth,
> - reflects how we come to know and trust God,
> - empowers our best human enterprises,
> - can undergird our proclamation and defence of the faith,
> - is sufficient for resisting evil and hypocrisy,
> - will help our growth and transformation in Christ.[34]

This strong emphasis on truth, with its clear implications for the task of taking the whole Gospel to the whole world, has been a consistent Lausanne theme throughout its history.[35]

Fourthly, the foundational first part of the mission statement presupposes *a holistic perspective on the task of bearing witness 'to Jesus Christ and all his teaching'*. The above-mentioned emphasis on truth leads

---

[32] To be fair to the organizers, it should be emphasized that *The Cape Town 2010 Advance Papers* were intended to provide full didactic input beforehand in relation to the various multiplex topics.

[33] *The Cape Town 2010 Congress Handbook*, 30.

[34] 'Why we need a high view of truth', in J. E. M. Cameron (ed), *Christ Our Reconciler*, 34-37.

[35] See Stefan Gustavsson's paper on 'Faith and Truth in a Pluralistic, Globalized World' in this volume.

naturally to a holistic perspective, both related to the message of the Gospel (as a worldview) and the missional task of the global church (as integral mission). These holistic dimensions are expressed elsewhere in the *Cape Town Commitment*. In terms of our message, the overarching biblical narrative of "creation, fall, redemption in history, and new creation … provides our coherent biblical worldview and shapes our theology".[36] In terms of integral mission, "the salvation we proclaim should be transforming us in the totality of our personal and social responsibilities".[37]

It is helpful at this point to relate this holistic dimension of the missional task to the classical Christian concept of calling, as expressed in the rich tradition from the Protestant Reformation: "Calling is the truth that God calls us so decisively to himself that everything we are, everything we do, and everything we have is invested with a special devotion, dynamism, and direction lived out as a response to his summons and service."[38] This essential definition corresponds to a major thrust in the biblical expositions presented at the Congress. The definition also resonates with central concerns in Part I of the *Cape Town Commitment*:

- "Like Israel we need to hear the call of the prophets and of Jesus himself to repent, to forsake all such rivals, and to return to obedient love and worship of God alone."[39]
- "Jesus calls us to discipleship, to take up our cross and follow him in the path of self-denial, servanthood and obedience."[40]
- "God calls his people to share his mission."[41]

Fifthly, the first clause of the mission statement includes an implicit emphasis on *the integrity of the message and the messenger*.

"Bearing witness to Jesus Christ and all his teaching" means faithfully communicating an authentic biblical message, through both words and deeds.[42] This means safeguarding the integrity of the biblical Gospel, "especially on four things; (i) the exclusive claims of Christ; (ii) the meaning of Christ's death; (iii) the necessity of conversion; (iv) the lostness of humankind".[43] It also includes "building the peace of Christ in our divided and broken world" (Day Two) and "bearing witness to the love of Christ among people of other faiths" (Day Three).

---

[36] *CTC*, 17.
[37] *CTC*, 28, quoting the *Lausanne Covenant*, paragraph 5.
[38] O. Guinness, *The Call: Finding and Fulfilling the Central Purpose of Your Life* (Nashville, TN: Word Publishing, 1998), 29.
[39] *CTC*, 11.
[40] *CTC*, 14.
[41] *CTC*, 27.
[42] "I deliberately chose the phrase 'bearing witness' because it covers life and lip, word and lifestyle, allowing no separation between our words and our lifestyle, between what we say and how we live." (L. Brown in email to the author on 28th Jan 2014).
[43] L. Brown, 'Closing Address: We Have a Gospel to Proclaim'.

However, there is a corresponding need to focus on the integrity of the messenger. This raises the challenging question of personal obedience: "We commit ourselves afresh to bear witness to Jesus Christ and all his teaching, in all the world, knowing that we can bear such witness only if we are living in obedience to his teaching ourselves."[44] This was powerfully brought home to the whole Congress on Day Five, with the challenging emphasis on "calling the church of Christ back to humility, integrity, and simplicity".

The plenary message by Chris Wright, the major author of the *Cape Town Commitment* and at the time Chair of Lausanne Theology Working Group, was followed by a short time of confession, repentance and prayer for God's forgiveness, calling upon ourselves in the following terms:

- Where we have revelled in our status or squabbled over honours, or abused power, let us walk humbly with our God, for the Lord gives grace to the humble but puts down the proud.
- Where we have manipulated and distorted, exaggerated and boasted, let us walk in the light and truth of God, for the Lord looks on the heart and is pleased with integrity.
- Where we have sought to enrich ourselves, or have been envious of those who do so, let us walk in the simplicity of Jesus, for we cannot serve God and mammon.[45]

Thus, bearing witness to Jesus Christ and all his teaching is intimately linked to safeguarding both the integrity of the Gospel message and the integrity of the Gospel messenger.

Bearing Witness in Every Nation

The Cape Town Congress reaffirmed the strong historical emphasis in Lausanne on bearing witness to Jesus Christ in the whole world. Thus, 'bearing witness in every nation' should be seen as *the first dimension of mission.*[46]

The classical Lausanne emphasis on 'unreached peoples', was supplemented in Cape Town with the newer concept of 'unengaged peoples'. These two concepts were essential on Day Four, under the overall topic 'Discerning the will of God for evangelization in our century'. It is appropriate at this point to quote the *Cape Town Commitment in extenso*:

> The heart of God longs that *all* people should have access to the knowledge of God's love and of his saving work through Jesus Christ. We recognize with grief and shame that there are thousands of people groups around the

[44] *CTC*, 15.

[45] C. Wright, 'Calling the Church Back to Humility, Integrity, Simplicity'.

[46] 'The expression "in every nation" was chosen to emphasize and reaffirm the evangelical church's undiminished imperative to spread the Gospel geographically to the ends of the earth.' (L. Brown in an e-mail to the author on 28th Jan. 2014.)

> world for whom such access has not yet been made available through Christian witness. These are peoples who are *unreached*, in the sense that there are no known believers and no churches among them. Many of these peoples are also *unengaged*, in the sense that we currently know of no churches or agencies that are even trying to share the gospel with them. Indeed, only a tiny percentage of the Church's resources (human and material) is being directed to the least-reached peoples. By definition, these are peoples who will not invite us to come with the good news, since they know nothing about it. Yet their presence among us in our world 2,000 years after Jesus commanded us to make disciples of all nations, constitutes not only a rebuke to our disobedience, not only a form of spiritual injustice, but also a silent 'Macedonian Call'.[47]

This led to a focus on major contemporary challenges for world evangelization, including the following urgent needs:

- taking Bible poverty seriously[48]
- taking oral cultures seriously[49]
- taking children and young people seriously[50]
- taking urbanization seriously[51]
- taking migration seriously[52]
- taking disadvantaged people seriously[53]

In order to meet such demanding geographical, ethnical, cultural and demographic challenges, there is a growing need to "partnering in the body of Christ towards a new global equilibrium" (Day Six).

Bearing Witness in Every Sphere of Society

The second dimension of mission, as expressed in the overall aim for the Cape Town Congress, is bearing witness to Jesus Christ and all his teaching 'in every sphere of society'. This was highlighted on the final evening: "Our hope for this Congress is that we leave here (i) passionately committed to communicating the gospel to the ends of the earth and (ii) equally committed to demonstrating that the eternal truths of Scripture have application to the whole of life."[54]

---

[47] *CTC*, 52.
[48] *CTC*, 52-53.
[49] *CTC*, 54.
[50] *CTC*, 56-57.
[51] *CTC*, 56.
[52] *CTC*, 49-50.
[53] *CTC*, 44-45.
[54] L. Brown, 'Final Address: We Have a Gospel to Proclaim'. He expanded on this in an email to the author on 28th of Jan 2014: 'The expression "in every sphere of society" was chosen to emphasize that the application of the Lordship of Christ has no limits; to avoid the division of the so-called "spiritual" and "secular"; and to respond to those who maintain that evangelical spirituality should only relate to our

This second dimension was highlighted on the first day of the Congress, where Gospel truth, Christian mission and discipleship are related conceptually to 'every sphere of society' and thus to the whole of life. This includes the task of 'bearing witness to Jesus Christ and all his teaching' in the following significant areas: [55]

- the workplace
- the globalized media
- the arts
- the emerging technologies
- the public arenas[56]

Such a holistic perspective on mission presupposes that the biblical worldview at large, as well as the biblical Gospel of Jesus Christ specifically, is objectively true and ethically and existentially significant. Following on from that, a number of significant contemporary issues in society were highlighted on Day Two of the Congress ('reconciliation'). This included ethnicity, poverty and oppression, disabilities, and creation care,[57] areas and issues where the biblical Gospel of reconciliation may be seen as uniquely relevant.[58]

On a more personal level, this second dimension of mission relates to our various private and professional roles, relations and arenas. We are called to 'live the truth'.[59] We also need to be equipped 'with the courage and the tools to relate the truth with prophetic relevance to everyday public conversation, and so engage every aspect of the culture we live in'.[60] In line with the above-mentioned emphasis from Day Five of the Congress ('integrity'), this dimension calls for 'humility, integrity, and simplicity' across these different spheres of society.

Bearing Witness in the Realm of Ideas

The third dimension of mission relates to 'the realm of ideas'.[61] 'Cultural and religious plurality is a fact.'[62] Globally, the Christian church is

---

private world and has nothing to say to the public sphere, from which we are often told we should retreat.'

[55] *CTC*, 35-39.

[56] Unfortunately, the significant section on 'Truth and the public arena' (*CTC*, 38-39) has no reference to the influential role of the media.

[57] *CTC*, 45-46. See also the post-Congress resources at www.lausanne.org/creationcare.

[58] See *CTC*, 39-46.

[59] *CTC*, 33.

[60] *CTC*, 35.

[61] 'The expression "in the realm of ideas" was added because of the conviction that ideas influence and govern the direction of societies, institutions and individuals, so that if the Christian worldview does not capture the imagination of a culture, as it did in the European Reformation, then a culture will not be transformed. Our goal is

increasingly faced with the challenge of pluralism. This means, among other things, that the uniqueness, credibility and relevance of the biblical Gospel need to be justified over against secular and religious worldview alternatives. Therefore, "we need to see greater commitment to the hard work of robust apologetics".[63]

This includes analysing and confronting various influential current worldview ideas, whether they challenge (a) the reality of God's transcendence and immanence, (b) the reality of God's spiritual and moral authority, or (c) the reality of God's unique revelation and reconciliation in Jesus Christ.[64]

The *Cape Town Commitment* highlights relativism as one of the global contemporary challenges in 'the realm of ideas', first related to the absolute truth claims of the Bible and secondly related to the relativistic culture of *post-modern*ism.

> We live ... in a world full of lies and rejection of the truth. Many cultures display a dominant relativism that denies that any absolute truth exists or can be known. If we love the Bible, then we must rise to the defence of its truth claims. We must find fresh ways to articulate biblical authority in all cultures. We commit ourselves again to strive to defend the truth of God's revelation as part of our labour of love for God's Word.[65]

> Most will seek to respect competing truth claims of other faiths and live alongside them. However, postmodern, relativist pluralism is different. Its ideology allows for no absolute or universal truth. While tolerating truth claims, it views them as no more than cultural constructs. (This position is logically self-destroying for it affirms as a single absolute truth that there is no single absolute truth.) Such pluralism asserts 'tolerance' as an ultimate value, but it can take oppressive forms in countries where secularism or aggressive atheism govern the public arena.[66]

The global challenge of relativism illustrates the key task of bearing witness to Jesus Christ and all his teaching in the realm of ideas.

---

not simply that people experience forgiveness of sins, vital and central though that is, but that their mindset, worldview and lifestyle is turned upside down, from top to bottom, and is shaped and reshaped by the Gospel and Christ-centred imperatives; and in turn, that this transformation spills over into every area of society for the good of all and the glory of God.' (L. Brown in email to the author on 28th Jan 2014).

[62] *CTC*, 34.

[63] *CTC*, 34.

[64] Responding to this threefold apologetic challenge may be done with Paul's threefold argument in Acts 17:16-34 as a model; cf. L. Dahle, 'Truth, Christian Mission and Apologetics', 32-33.

[65] *CTC*, 18.

[66] *CTC*, 34.

Mission in 3D: Media Engagement as a Case Study[67]

The contemporary media are the primary means by which news, ideas, and stories spread. They affect every part of society in every part of the world. Therefore, if we are to 'bear witness to Jesus Christ and all his teaching in every nation, in every sphere of society, and in the realm of ideas', we cannot neglect the fascinating and complex world of the media. In order to engage with media holistically, we need to broaden our engagement to include both 'media awareness', 'media presence', and 'media ministries'.[68]

Media awareness relates to the need for *more faithful discipleship (including both personal holiness and disciple-making) when encountering media messages.* It may be seen as a combination of educational, evangelism and discipleship concerns, when faced globally with a dramatic increase in media technology and media messages. However, this whole area seems to be a forgotten dimension in Christian mission.

Media presence relates to the need *to enter mainstream media with professionalism and Christian integrity.* This is due to an increasing acknowledgment of the influential role of mainstream factual and fictional media both in expressing and shaping identities and ideas. This implies a calling to public witness and integrity.

Media ministries relate to the need *to use every kind of media technology (whether old or new) to communicate the Gospel of Christ in the context of a holistic biblical worldview.* This is a legitimate emphasis on specialist media ministries, whether in radio, television, print, internet or new (social) media, whereas at the same time (due to the democratization of the media) emphasising the media ministry of every believer.

Conclusion: A Missiological Contribution

We may conclude that the Cape Town Congress reaffirmed the legitimacy and urgency of the first dimension of mission, i.e. 'bearing witness among all nations'. This has remained a central Lausanne concern since the first congress in 1974. At the same time, the Congress and subsequently the *Cape Town Commitment,* broadened the explicit understanding of Christian mission to include 'every sphere of society' and 'the realm of ideas'. Whereas the formulation of the second dimension is a natural development of the increasing emphasis on tentmaking, the workplace and business as mission since Manila in 1989, the third dimension seems to be a

---

[67] Reference is made to L. Dahle, 'Media Engagement: A Global Missiological Task', in *Lausanne Global Analysis*, Jan 2014, Vol. 3 (1), 9-12 (www.lausanne.org/analysis). See also the forthcoming *Lausanne Occasional Paper 66* on 'The Gospel and Media as a Lausanne Theme: Historical, Missiological, and Strategic Perspectives'.

[68] These three categories were conceptualized in my Cape Town Advance Paper 'Media Messages Matter', and were later included in *CTC*, 36-37.

comparatively new and explicit emphasis in Lausanne history.[69] Thus, the whole three-dimensional understanding of mission is a significant, new missiological contribution from Lausanne III.

This significant contribution should be seen in the context of the concluding emphasis in the *Cape Town Commitment*:

> We sought to listen to the voice of the Lord Jesus Christ [in Cape Town]. And in his mercy, through his Holy Spirit, Christ spoke to his listening people. Through the many voices of Bible exposition, plenary addresses, and group discussion, two repeated themes were heard:
>
> - The need for radical obedient discipleship, leading to maturity, to growth in depth as well as growth in numbers;
> - The need for radical cross-centred reconciliation, leading to unity, to growth in love as well as growth in faith and hope.
>
> Discipleship and reconciliation are indispensable to our mission. We lament the scandal of our shallowness and lack of discipleship, and the scandal of our disunity and lack of love. For both seriously damage our witness to the gospel.[70]

As argued in this chapter, our witness to the Gospel of Jesus Christ must include the urgent task of 'Mission in 3D'. This continues to be an urgent and significant challenge from the Cape Town Congress to the global church.

Appendix: An Overview of the Six Lausanne III Congress Themes and the Related Multiplex Topics[71]

Congress theme 1: Truth
Making the case for the truth of Christ in our pluralistic and globalized world

- Topic 1: Marketplace Ministry

---

[69] 'The expression *the realm of ideas* really encapsulated what Lausanne had already committed to implicitly from the start, particularly through John Stott's influence and example. It was implicit in Billy Graham's and Stott's including the word "study" in what made up "the spirit of Lausanne".' (Email from Julia Cameron to the author on 30th Jan 2014.)

[70] *CTC*, 70. For further theological and missiological reflections, reference is also made to the following background document for Lausanne III: 'The Whole Church taking the Whole Gospel to the Whole World: Reflections of the Lausanne Theology Working Group' (www.lausanne.org/en/documents/all/twg/1177-twg-three-wholes.html).

[71] The six key Congress themes were addressed in the plenary sessions, whereas the multiplex sessions applied these key themes to central topics for evangelism and integral mission in the contemporary world. The foundational material in the multiplex sessions were presented on beforehand as 'Advance Papers', see http://conversation.lausanne.org/en/pages/advance-papers. The videos from all plenary and multiplex sessions are available at www.lausanne.org/en/multimedia/videos/ct2010-session-videos.html, including accompanying material.

- Topic 2: Media and Technology
- Topic 3: Personal Witness
- Topic 4: Truth and Pluralism

Congress theme 2: Reconciliation
Building the peace of Christ in our divided and broken world

- Topic 1: Environment
- Topic 2: Ethnicity
- Topic 3: Poverty and Wealth
- Topic 4: Reconciliation
- Topic 5: Resource Stewardship

Congress theme 3: World Faiths
Bearing witness to the love of Christ among people of other faiths

- Topic 1: Diaspora
- Topic 2: Globalization
- Topic 3: Unreached People Groups
- Topic 4: World Faiths

Congress theme 4: New Missions Priorities
Discerning the will of God for evangelization in our century

- Topic 1: Forming leaders
- Topic 2: Orality
- Topic 3: Urban Mission

Congress theme 5: Authenticity & Integrity
Calling the church of Christ back to humility, integrity and simplicity

- Topic 1: Sexuality
- Topic 2: Human Future
- Topic 3: Integrity & Humility
- Topic 4: The prosperity gospel
- Topic 5: Women and men

Congress theme 6: Partnership
Partnering in the body of Christ towards a new global equilibrium

- Topic 1: Children & Youth
- Topic 2: Indigenous Leadership
- Topic 3: Partnership
- Topic 4: Scripture in Mission

The Cape Town Congress as Process and Event

Blair T. Carlson

Introduction

Billy Graham, in his address at the first Lausanne Congress in July 1974 said: "This is a Congress on world evangelization. Now we are enthusiastic about all the many things churches properly do, from worship to social concern. But our calling is to a specific sector of the church's responsibility – Evangelism. We believe our point of view has not been adequately represented at some of the other world church gatherings. Therefore, we are meeting to pray, talk, plan and – please God – to advance the work of evangelism."[1]

This description of Lausanne's purpose was equalled in clarity by John Stott's keynote message defining evangelism: "Biblical evangelism … is spreading by any and every means the good news of Jesus, crucified, risen and reigning. It includes the kind of dialogue in which we listen humbly and sensitively … and it invites a total response of repentance and faith which is … the beginning of an altogether new life in Christ, in the church and in the world."[2]

'To advance the work of evangelism' and to define 'biblical evangelism' – these were established as the twofold calling of the Lausanne Movement, and provided a dual focus for the third Lausanne Congress. What follows is a brief synopsis of the *process* – how the third Lausanne Congress developed, and of the *event* – the Congress itself. It is a collection of snapshots of a journey, of a vision germinating and developing over years, covering countless miles and involving hundreds of people praying, thinking, speaking, connecting, giving and working around the globe.

Building on the Past

Berlin 1966, Singapore 1967 and Amsterdam 1971 all provided foundations for Lausanne 1974. Billy Graham's letters from the early

---

[1] *Why Lausanne?* International Congress on World Evangelization, Lausanne, Switzerland 1974.

[2] *The Nature of Biblical Evangelism,* International Congress on World Evangelization, Lausanne, Switzerland 1974.

1970s gave a glimpse into his heart-vision. We were most grateful for the service and efficiency of the Billy Graham Center archives staff, enabling us to benefit from the detailed records of Bishop Jack Dain's voluminous correspondence,[3] from documents on the selection of participants, and also from the Lausanne II (Manila, 1989) Congress Handbook. Archives from previous Congress Directors[4] and countless others provided a rich source of knowledge and counsel. We trust the files, reports and materials generated from Cape Town 2010 will be equally inspiring and helpful.

Part 1: The Process – Global and Local Preparations

It all started with a God-given vision to revive the Lausanne Movement. We held regional consultations to begin to paint a picture of major issues relating to evangelism. At an early meeting in the Cape Town International Convention Centre, Michael Cassidy put words to the forward momentum as he paraphrased Acts 15:28, "It seems right to the Holy Spirit and to us that we should proceed." In June 2006 I was asked to be Congress Director, and the planning – creative, invigorating and consultative in each of its stages – began.

Congress Structure

The first task was to design a structure on which the Congress could be built. The basic framework had to be broad enough and flexible enough to withstand wind and storm, and to house a world congress. It was built with the following advisory and working components:

- *Advisory functions*, fulfilled by the honorary leadership of Billy Graham, John Stott and others; an Advisory Council and Board of Reference; a Pan-African Host Committee chaired by Archbishop Henry Orombi.
- *South Africa Working Groups*, made up of a Cape Town Trust and Cape Town Host Committee.
- *Global Working Groups*, made up of:
  a. Congress Management Team comprising (i) the Congress Chair, (ii) the International Director, (iii) the Congress Director, (iv) Chairs of Programme and Participant Selection.
  b. Associate Directors, Committee Chairs and Directors covering the varied areas of Administration; Arrangements; Arts; GlobaLink; Chief Financial Officer / Finance; Communications; Fund-raising; Information Technology; Intercessory (Prayer); Mission Africa; Participant Selection; Participant Services; Programme.

---

[3] Bishop Jack Dain chaired the above Congress. This correspondence is archived in the Billy Graham Center, Wheaton, Illinois, USA.
[4] Don Hoke, Thomas Wang and Paul McKaughan.

By God's grace and with Lausanne's vast network of contacts, most senior positions were filled by October 2007. Committee members tended to be self-funded or seconded from their organizations. We aimed for a representation of men and women, young and old, from various denominations, in church ministry and in secular vocations, and coming from all continents. The full committee eventually totalled several hundred remarkably talented people. An organizational diagram, along with detailed job descriptions were crucial tools in building the team.

The Chairs were mainly honorific, giving oversight as well as strategic leadership. Directors provided day-to-day leadership and direction for extended teams. In broad terms, we had a monthly conference call with each Chair and Director, and a monthly Skype call, when all Committee Directors briefed each other on developments and discussed matters of mutual concern.[5]

Three groups within the Lausanne Movement brought significant influence. The Theology Working Group spoke into the *Cape Town Commitment* and the programme. The Strategy Working Group highlighted special priorities. The International Deputy Directors (IDDs) brought a broad range of experience and perspectives.

A collaborative partnership between the World Evangelical Alliance and Lausanne was formalized in Budapest 2007. While specificities of this collaboration were not clear at times, there was interaction at various levels between the two organizations.

Selected Structure Notes

Administration / Budget: Personnel and budget management both came under the umbrella of Administration. As for any major event, the budget was an ongoing work in process. The initial draft drew on the expertise of the Billy Graham Evangelistic Association (BGEA), with its ready access to financial information from past Congresses. This draft, projecting expenditures by committee, was presented to the Lausanne Board in Budapest in June 2007 (approximately US$12 million with a suggested increase to US$18 million). It proved to be remarkably accurate. The Cape Town-based chief financial officer managed expenses and budget for South Africa, while a ministry in California undertook day-to-day operations for the rest of the world.

---

[5] The original design included a committee for follow-up, part of the planning from the beginning, tasked with keeping the momentum of implementation after the Congress. Regrettably, this committee was not activated. The original committee structure also called for five Associate Directors, each representing a different part of the world and overseeing 2-3 committees. Part of the rationale was to invest and empower the next generation, but for various reasons, this was not activated to the fullest extent.

Arrangements: Site survey meetings (October 2008; October 2009; February 2010) organized by the Arrangements Committee, were important building blocks. The TV Director, Technical Director, and many international experts joined with the South African team and selected committees (Programme, Communications, IT and GlobaLink) to advance the technical requirements for the Congress, talk with potential vendors, and arrange contracts.

Communications: This team took responsibility for making the facts and message of the Congress known, and to mobilize involvement across the world, connecting primarily with Christian media networks across the continents. Together with the Programme team, Communications collaborated with *Christianity Today* magazine to produce major articles on the Congress themes, which were published in whole or in part in many languages in the twelve months before the Congress. For various reasons, we weren't able to produce a successful informational video, but one of the highlights was the launch of the *Didasko Files* booklets which continue to publish various Lausanne authors.

Fund-raising: Originally fund-raising was to have been led by a chairman, a director and three associate directors working to garner partnerships with foundations, churches and individuals. This structure would have been mirrored to a degree across the continents so Christians worldwide would share in the blessing of giving. However, a more centralized system prevailed. The fact that the majority of funds were raised prior to the Congress was testimony to God's grace and the hard work of a few committee leaders.

Information Technology (IT): When this group of talented believers from the world of technology were introduced to each other, they spent much of their first meeting sharing dreams of how IT could be used to reach the world for Christ. Such is the blessing of working with ideas-driven people with a genuine heart for the Gospel.

The IT group worked to make a global virtual committee functional, devising means of document sharing, registration and credentialling. In addition, they were responsible for internet access at the venue, and the complexities of the GlobaLink technology.

Intercessory / Prayer: Mobilizing and co-ordinating prayer on a number of levels (international networks, prayer diary, personal) was the primary focus of the Intercessory Committee. In the final year, they prayed through the prayers of Paul in Ephesians, with Eph 3:20 being of particular significance: "Now unto him who is able to do immeasurably more than all we ask or imagine according to his power that is at work within us."

Mission Africa: In Berlin 66 and Lausanne 74, Billy Graham held missions concurrent with the Congresses on world evangelization. Following that example, we sought to bring together African and international evangelists for a series of missions on the continent, leading up to the Congress. By God's grace, Mission Africa fostered 21 events in twelve countries, with more than 58,000 responding to the Gospel message.

Participant Selection: Our hope was that participants on-site would be more than 'delegates'. Their charge was to represent evangelicals in their country by speaking into the Congress, and then, on returning home, to speak into their region from all they had gleaned.

In an effort to gather a cross-section of the church – not just leaders – the Participant Selection Guide outlined specific criteria: (i) a commitment to the Lausanne vision; (ii) 60% to be under 50 years old; (iii) 35% to be women; (iv) 10% to come from secular vocations; (v) that each region draw on a diversity of geography, ethnicity, language and denominations. Representation would be proportional to the size of the evangelical constituency in each country. We appointed an International Selection Committee whose names were not made public, to which the individual regions submitted their proposed lists.

The selection process was primarily in the hands of national leadership, including the IDDs, and was most effectively carried out where Lausanne networks were strong. In some cases, weak networks combined with limited internet access added serious complications. In some regions, cultural dynamics, friendships, loyalties and seniorities prevailed, and our goals were not always achieved.

Programme: The process of regional consultations fostered a sense of ownership. However, the four-year stream of input made programme development somewhat cumbersome.

Congress speakers each drafted Advance Papers with the intention that participants would read them prior to Cape Town. These were made available on the website, which meant they were only accessible in some areas of the world.

The book of Ephesians became the biblical framework for both preparation and event. Participants were encouraged to read the epistle a year in advance, the expositors met at retreats to study together pre-Congress, and the Congress team also embraced the vision of 'marinating' in Ephesians.

Statement Working Group: This first met as an assembly of eighteen theologians, drawn from around the world, in Minneapolis, USA, in December 2009. From here, Chris Wright was asked to craft the first half of the proposed statement, *The Cape Town Confession of Faith*, in consultation with a smaller group, again representing different parts of the world. This was presented at the Congress.[6] See below for *The Cape Town Call to Action*.

[6] It was felt wise to construct this with a group of theologians before the Congress, each member having been nominated by the region he or she represented. To ensure everyone saw it in their own Congress language at the same time, the presentation was late in the Congress. Several minor amendments were made to its wording in the weeks following, on the basis of comments received.

Scholarships: The Participant Selection Committee drew up the criteria for scholarship selection, including such factors as per capita GNI and the number of participants from each country. But it was impossible to create a formula that would work across the board. The Participant Services team took care of the detail once selections had been made, in close consultation with IDDs. Every national committee was encouraged to raise money to help fund participants from their regions. (Funds were pooled on a regional basis rather than by country to allow flexibility within a region.) Scholarship allocation was complex, and at the end of the day we supplemented the systems with a dose of good judgement and prayer.

Planning Meetings: Our goal was to have the whole world represented at the event, and in the planning process. With most of our work done virtually and by email, it was essential that we occasionally meet face-to-face, and also relate across committee lines. By design, we met twice a year, in different parts of the world, with a pre-planned agenda covering where we had come from and where we were going. These meetings included various combinations of the Congress Committee, the Lausanne Board of Directors, IDDs and local leaders from across the continent. Since the Congress was based in Africa, the input from African leaders was particularly significant in learning, listening and shaping the plans. Full details are available in my final report. [7]

Timeline: An initial timeline was drafted to cover the period from January 2007 to October 2011. It was updated on a regular basis and later was maintained by the Administrative Committee with input from each respective committee.

Virtual Officing: A Congress of this magnitude with a world committee in multiple locations would have been impossible without virtual communication. As helpful as electronic tools were, they carried inherent challenges: isolation, loneliness, misunderstandings because of the lack of face-to-face communication, language barriers, no paper trail, and technological limitations in many parts of the world.

The Cape Town Office: From the very beginning, we planned a fully-functioning local office during the year of the Congress. The Cape Town office, which opened in February 2010, served as a galvanizing meeting place for the local church base and all committee meetings held during the year prior to the main event. It was also the co-ordinating hub for all the details of the event itself (such as design, production, printing, translation, technical aspects and local involvement on all levels).

God provided for many of our needs through local Christians: a downtown location in a modern office block at a hugely discounted rate, office furniture and equipment. Local leaders helped us identify staff and volunteers. Salaries for the few local staff we had were processed by sympathetic local ministry organizations.

---

[7] Archived in the Billy Graham Center, Wheaton.

The Cape Town Trust: Since its founding, LCWE (now the Lausanne Movement) has operated as a legal entity in the USA. However, to handle business affairs for the Congress, a non-profit, tax-exempt, South African Trust was required. This was established early and ably run by a local committee who oversaw the signing of local contracts. The corporation had a pre-set date for closure sometime between June and October 2011.

The Cape Town Host Committee: From January 2007 we engaged with local South African church leaders. Though not a public event, the Congress had great potential to bless the local churches. Cape Town church leaders pledged help to recruit stewards, staff and volunteers, and to welcome participants into churches. A wholehearted invitation signed by forty church leaders was presented to the Executive Chair in February 2007.

Part 2: The Event

In his closing remarks, Doug Birdsall said the Congress was perhaps "the widest and most diverse gathering of Christians ever held in the history of the Christian Church". Michael Cassidy, one of the main leaders inviting the Congress to Africa, declared, "It was unforgettable. It was hugely inspirational. It was deeply motivational. It was history-making … and it … set a benchmark of mega organizational excellence which I can't visualize being matched again anywhere for a long time to come."

In total we welcomed 4,200 participants from 198 countries, bearing in mind that the participants from China were hindered at the last minute from leaving their country.[8] In addition, the GlobaLink sites in 91 countries extended the Cape Town experience to about 100,000 virtual participants. It was a truly global event, the impact of which continues to unfold.

Host City: A number of cities around the world were recommended as potential hosts, but a resounding voice emerged – come to Africa. When choosing Cape Town, we knew the football World Cup was scheduled for South Africa in June/July 2010. We had no idea how powerfully this world sporting event would impact the Congress. But God did. With an infusion of World Cup money, South Africa's infrastructure was transformed. Internet capacity was bolstered to accommodate global communications, roads were improved, the airport was expanded, hotels built, security was improved. Perhaps also in one sense Cape Town 2010 was a fulfilment of William Carey's unmaterialized dream in 1810 that the city would be the site of a world conference on evangelism.

The Cape Town International Convention Centre (CTICC) Venue: The CTICC was another draw. It was sufficient for our space requirements, and it was aesthetically pleasing. We enjoyed a most positive working

[8] In June 2013 a special gathering was held in Seoul for the Chinese participants.

relationship with the entire CTICC staff, and after the event, they noted their appreciation for the dignity and respect with which they were treated.

Master Schedule: A three-week Master Schedule tracked in one document all meetings and details of each committee taking place at any given time during the Congress event. (This included meetings of outside organizations that looked to us for logistical support.) It was essential for the allocation of rooms, organizing catering, and for personnel assignments; further, it highlighted potential schedule conflicts.

Arts and Film Festival: One of our stated values was to integrate the arts into each aspect of the Congress – with an African feel. Local artists (primarily Christian) provided Fine Art pieces with a biblical connection for various displays throughout the facility. South African township artisans created beaded banners, which live on as a visual picture of the overall Congress theme (2 Corinthians 5:19) and of the six daily themes, illustrated using Old and New Testament stories.

With the desire to showcase another medium for evangelism, Christian films from around the world were shown each evening during the Film Festival. As part of this, WEA premiered the Narnia film.

Administration: This committee looked after both personnel and office administration. Special offices were constructed in one of the large Convention Centre halls to serve the Congress Team. They served 144 Congress staff, 459 Committee volunteers, 300 stewards from 39 countries and produced 90,000 photocopies during the Congress, a volume that highlighted the need to have on-site print facilities.

Translation was also part of the Administration Committee, with work done pre-Congress, during, and post-Congress in all of the eight Congress languages. Co-ordination between committees needed constant assessment and refining throughout the entire process.

Arrangements: The core group of the Arrangements Committee was local Capetonians who took responsibility for all the logistics relating to the Congress venue, including sound, lighting, security, stewards and catering. We tried to go 'green' in every area possible.

The Congress took over the entire CTICC space. One of our ongoing prayers for the venue was that God would fill it with his peace and a sense of order. One of the ways in which God answered this was in a number of the CTICC staff wanting to know more about the Gospel, and three making a decision for Christ. One centre manager commented at a debrief: 'Seeing the way you treated each other, we could understand what the message of the Congress was all about.'

Christian policemen from several countries gave their services to help with security. Approximately 300 **Stewards**, drawn from each region of the world, served for long hours. The passion with which they served is exemplified through the words of Bonginkosi Nhlapo, on his return home:

> Today I'm back at work and my hope is for us to continue to be stewards, no longer for Lausanne III but for all mankind. The one lesson learnt above all

others in Cape Town was that the only way to be Christ-like is to serve like he did and empty oneself and take the lowest position available and be prepared to suffer so that others may taste and see that the Lord is good. May we put on our steward uniforms and never put them off, the uniform of humility and self-sacrifice and love.

An on-site **Bookstore** was run by a local Christian book vendor, especially to serve participants from countries where Christian literature is scarce and difficult to obtain. Publishers around the world enthusiastically participated and discounts were very generous. A percentage of books left over were donated to Bible schools and seminaries in Africa.

An **African market** featuring goods made by local artisans exceeded all expectations. It sold souvenirs which benefited local industry, and provided income to many African Christian charities. Participants were pleased to have such a service on-site.

Exhibition tables displayed ministry information under thirteen general categories.

Catering: Breakfast was served in the hotels or in home placements. Boxed lunches and simple regionally-themed hot evening meals fed all the participants at the CTICC using multiple serving stations. Additionally, receptions were organized for many different groups and gatherings. Water coolers were stationed throughout the venue, and coffee or tea could be purchased from kiosks during breaks. The CTICC catering staff were exceptional, and the food was a great success.

The **Arrangements Committee** also oversaw all levels of the technical aspects of the Congress. Local vendors were used for the sound and equipment, while an international team of experts came to help with production and managing the larger technical aspects. We overestimated the demand for walkie-talkies, portable phones and internal phone systems. The TV crew noted a conflict of priorities between the live event and recording it for broadcast. But overall, Technical Director Dan Keeney commented, "The golden thread of meticulous planning and consistent communication was the hallmark."

There were many wonderful stories of God's special provision for the Congress, but one stands out. A large screen behind the platform and a top-of-the-line TV truck, designed for the World Cup, were substituted at the last minute by the vendor at no extra charge, immensely enhancing the production quality.

Communications was responsible for Press & Media operations, photography/video, and print/publishing. Daily, in all Congress languages, they produced a four-page, full colour newssheet; and on the last day, a 16-page full-colour commemorative paper. Afternoon press conferences were led by a team of international hosts. The 69 on-site credentialled press represented 28 countries from both secular and religious media; further off-site credentialled media had privileged access to news. Programs were broadcast over TV and radio in 44 countries. The UK BBC Radio 4 *Sunday*

Worship programme created a special edition from London and Cape Town, with a listenership of more than 1.5 million. Along with Facebook and Twitter audiences, more than 500,000 viewed videos posted on the website. The inability of the Chinese delegation to leave the country was the single biggest news item.

GlobaLink: The Congress had two audiences – on-site participants and those at 450 GlobaLink sites around the world. A further 200 sites met following the Congress. Bible schools, seminaries, and theological institutions made up the majority of the 657 pre-registered sites. Online primers about Lausanne (history and background) and *The Lausanne Covenant Study Guide* by John Stott were made available to each site. This committee faced three major challenges: 1) the cyber attack that delayed the release of sessions for about 24 hours. The crew went to endless efforts to find alternative ways of relaying the videos; 2) problems with the upload of videos and incompatible database systems; and 3) the CTICC broadband connection that was not according to agreed-upon specification.

The **IT** Committee serviced not only the Congress Team's needs, but also provided well-used cyber cafés for participants, and helped with electronic signage. It was a testimony to God's provision when two stewards from India stepped in with extraordinary expertise to solve the cyber attack issue.

Participants included 4,200 selected by the regional committees, day guests, spouses, exhibitors, and local dignitaries. Our number also included Observers (Orthodox, Vatican, WCC, leaders of world denominational bodies), shepherded by Andrew Norman, Principal of Ridley Hall, Cambridge, who brought experience in senior ecumenical circles. These Observers were integrated into every aspect of the Congress.

Participant Services was a local team with exceptional expertise in event management and good relationships with local industry (hotels, airlines, transport and tourism), and civic authorities. They handled pre-registration and on-site registration, with the majority of participants getting through the process in a matter of seconds. They were responsible for issuing visa letters, negotiating rates with hotels and airlines, organizing 200 beds in local Christian homes, local transportation, registration, airport hospitality, hotel hospitality, off-site security, and for the participants' day off, organizing local tours and visits to local Christian ministries for a glimpse of God's work in Cape Town.

This committee also apportioned scholarships. Forty-eight per cent of the Congress participants were able to attend as a result of receiving a scholarship; many who received scholarships willingly contributed at least a small sum towards their costs.

On **Sunday 17th October**, the opening day of the Congress, local churches in the townships, city and suburbs of Cape Town, welcomed participants to speak or give testimony. It was a mutual blessing to everyone who participated.

Intercessory Prayer: The Congress was infused with a culture of prayer through a designated prayer room, a spiritual care room, and with prayer cards and boxes throughout the CTICC. Local intercessors led a 24-hour prayer group, and a strategic prayer group provided opportunities to pray for the sixty least-reached nations. Prayer emails were sent twice daily to international intercessors and text messages were used to mobilize urgent prayer. A variety of denominational styles and prayer practices were integrated into the programme, and the table groups provided a wonderful opportunity for prayer in small groups.

On the final day of the Congress, we learned that the city's police department had noticed a dramatic statistical drop in crime for the ten days of the Congress. We believe that focused prayers from around the world made a tangible impact on the city.

Programme: The Congress had an overall theme verse: 2 Corinthians 5:19: "God in Christ reconciling the world to himself."[9] Daily themes were as follows:

- Making the case for the *Truth of Christ* in a pluralistic, globalized world
- Building the *Peace of Christ* in our divided and broken world
- Bearing witness to the *Love of Christ* with people of other faiths
- Discerning the *Will of Christ* for 21st century world evangelization
- Calling the *Church of Christ* back to humility, integrity and simplicity
- Partnering in the *Body of Christ* toward a new global equilibrium

As a Congress on world evangelization, we aimed to build a bridge between these issues and the passion, vision and strategies needed to take the Gospel message into the world.

The programme included a morning Bible exposition on Ephesians and a plenary session; afternoon multiplex and dialogue sessions; and an evening plenary with a regional focus.

The Ephesians study was led by six expositors from different regions of the world. Talks were short to allow time for table group discussion utilizing study questions in the Congress Handbook.

The morning plenary looked at a core issue, a truth, and a hoped-for outcome. Documents were drafted in advance for cohesiveness.

Four major multiplexes each day focused on key issues that could not be handled in detail in the plenary sessions. There were 24 multiplexes in total, with 85 presenters, 66% coming from the Majority World.

---

[9] In the opening plenary on 20th Oct, John Piper summed it up as follows: "When the Gospel takes root in our souls, it impels us outward to the alleviation of all unjust human suffering in this age. And there's another truth … when the Gospel takes root in our souls, it awakens us to the horrible reality of eternal suffering … Come, O nations. Come to Christ. That's our message. It is the most important news in the universe."

Microphones were made available to the audience in order to interact with presenters. It became clear that people attended to discuss issues – not because of big names.

The dialogue sessions focused on even narrower themes, allowing significant, meaningful interaction. There were 160 dialogue sessions in total, with over 200 presenters, 40% from the Majority World, and 25% being women.

The evening plenaries showed *God on the Move* with a different regional focus each night, designed to be inspirational and testimonial. From the beginning, we dreamed about having some undisclosed influential guests. God in his providence sent two relatively unknown women – Libby Little and a North Korean teenager – whose testimonies were profound.

The Opening Ceremony featured a 'Four-Part Symphony': Welcome to Africa; the History of the Church from Jerusalem to Edinburgh; the Growth of the Church in Asia, Latin America, and Africa; and a concluding Hope for the World. This Symphony incorporated a variety of means, touching all the senses, enhanced by the vibrancy of local musicians/artists, and set the tone for the week.

The Closing Ceremony featured the Kenyan Anglican Communion Service set to specially written music. The service was led by Archbishop Henry Orombi (Uganda), with communion served by participants, staff and stewards at multiple stations set up around the auditorium. Again, local musicians and artists led this powerful, moving time of worship. The inclusion of the arts (drama, music, visual arts, video) was an integral part of the overall programme.

To organize all of this, the Programme Committee set up a committee of co-ordinators and producers over each segment, whose administrative teams dealt with the myriad of details.

One of the most talked-about aspects of Cape Town 2010 was the use of table groups. It was a huge logistical challenge, requiring the plenary hall to be expanded significantly, and much thought went into how to allocate participants. The table group dynamic ensured that people attended sessions, and many significant friendships and collaborations were formed from these groups.

Translation and interpretation occurred in eight official languages: Arabic, Chinese, English, French, German, Spanish, Portuguese, Russian. Swahili, Hindi and Korean had been considered. Deaf signing was slow in coming but in the end was provided.

We wrestled with the question of having languages other than English spoken from the platform. Given the logistical problems of simultaneous translation for huge numbers, requiring multi-lingual interpreters from a range of languages, or lengthening the talks with consecutive interpretation, it became an impossibility.

Auxiliary Groups: The Global Working Groups were expanded during the Congress to include the following:

GELF – Global Executive Leadership Forum: The purpose was to bring American and international donors together with strategic ministry leaders for fellowship, discipleship, and learning. It was self-funded and, for many, the first time they had attended a gathering of this calibre.

GBA – Government, Business, Academia Think Tank: The GBA was a late addition to the planning. Its purpose was to gather participants from government, business, and academia around the 'How then shall we live?' questions. This group came together for selected times during the day.

Senior Statesmen were a listening group representing various ministries and regions of the world, strategically brought together to serve as advisors/mediators.

Statement Working Group: Having completed the Confession of Faith (Part I of the *Cape Town Commitment*) in advance of the Congress, Chris Wright's group met on-site in a suite overlooking the main Congress hall, listening to what was happening from the platform, and sat in on multiplex and dialogue sessions. Further, they reviewed material from the data-mining team, which was being fed in online. From this, they distilled what they sensed was the confluence of voices as they compiled material for Part II – *A Call to Action.* After post-Congress editing, the complete *Cape Town Commitment* was published in multiple languages. The name was purposefully chosen. It is a commitment taken by the Lausanne Movement before God and the church; and now forms a road map for the movement in the coming years: a prophetic call to work and to pray.

Crisis Management Team: This was to be activated in case of extreme weather, a pandemic, protests or riots, acts of terrorism, a worldwide disaster, death of a major South African leader, disabling or evacuation of the CTICC, or deleterious media reports. The team was engaged in two instances – when printed materials were not ready on time, and during an intentional disruption of the internet.

Part 3: Some Reflections

The following comments received following the Congress highlight the multi-faceted nature of the process and the event.

The most-praised elements of the Congress were (i) the table groups of six which met each morning to study Ephesians and to process material from the stage; (ii) the way the event reflected the host continent; and, from the Congress team, the blessing of a positive team spirit and the joy of working with people from all over the world.

The most 'hoped-for in future' aspects noted for Lausanne events were: greater diversity of format; more contributions of substance by women and younger leaders (i.e. not just chairing or introducing speakers); multi-directional language interpretation to enable a global conversation.

Some of the more challenging aspects: we tried to be prepared with back-up plans to handle any situation, but we were caught off-guard with the cyber attack and problems with the internet.[10] To economize, we rented the CTICC space only for the dates of the Congress, which meant we were forced to find venues elsewhere for pre-Congress meetings and rehearsal space for dance, music, and art groups. This, along with holding multiplexes and dialogue sessions off-site during the Congress was challenging.

In previous Lausanne Congresses, a critical component was the study of papers prior to the Congress, with responses from Participants. This did not work as we had hoped.

Ramez Atallah had the vision of leading a programme committee made up of younger leaders from around the world. However, he observed in his final report that "Lausanne had too many heavyweight stakeholders to make this plan realistic or useful. The Regional and National committees that were formed … ended up being the main designers of the programme."

Issues and topics were identified to deal with the magnitude of the subject of world evangelization. However, at times the connection between examining the issues and the end-goal of world evangelization was cloudy.

Finance and budget management was a challenge. Cash flow was unpredictable and funds were not always available when commitments had to be made. Contributing factors included the lack of an international fund-raising team, operating in multiple currencies and the reality of fluctuating exchange rates.

From the outset we tried to keep samples for future reference. We never finalized the issue of what was best for archival purposes: electronic or paper files. Fast-changing technologies will undoubtedly complicate access to electronic copies in the future.

Keeping up with the database of thousands of names was a major task. We needed a full-time database manager but our budget did not stretch to this. We were blessed with committed leadership and many skilled volunteers, but we were challenged by being understaffed throughout the time of preparation.

There were doubtless many unplanned, unrecorded highlights of a spiritual magnitude. One highlight was the spontaneous and godly apology offered by the Portuguese and Spanish Christian leaders to African leaders for the slavery their ancestors had imposed.

We tried to incorporate an international perspective, but at times there was a tension between this and western influence, often an unintentional tendency in cross-cultural situations. A greater representation from the global south on the core committee may have provided stronger balance.

One of the surprise outcomes of the Congress was the response following the Mission Africa report, which resulted in requests from 46

---

[10] See the formal published record of the Congress: J. E. M. Cameron (ed), *Christ our Reconciler* (Nottingham, UK and Downers Grove, IL: IVP, 2012). Day 6, Endnote 1.

countries asking for help in evangelism. Mission Africa II carries a particular focus on French- and Portuguese-speaking countries, and is providing vision for other regions of the world in proclamation evangelism. Lindsay Brown observed that "Mission Africa was perhaps Africa's greatest gift to the world".

Close

This chapter has looked at the Congress through the lens of structures and systems. Other reports, along with the archives, give a fuller perspective on how God took the corporate effort of many, and multiplied it.

Billy Graham has often observed that it takes at least twenty years for the fruit of an evangelistic event to become apparent. The same will no doubt be true of Cape Town 2010. Lindsay Brown's rousing closing address charged the audience with keeping the objective of evangelism before the world, bearing witness to Jesus Christ and all his teaching, and implementing all that they had learned and experienced. One of our staff summarized it this way: "God called this event for his purposes and his plan, to reconcile the world to himself in Christ." May God, by the power of the Holy Spirit, use Cape Town 2010 in helping to accomplish this.

Some months after the Congress, my wife Elizabeth and I were invited to visit Billy Graham in North Carolina, and to give a report on the Congress. After a few minutes, Mr Graham cut to the chase and asked, "Blair, tell me – what are the various regions around the world doing? Are they advancing the work of evangelism? Are they reaching out with the Gospel?"

CLOSING ADDRESS: WE HAVE A GOSPEL TO PROCLAIM

Lindsay Brown

Before this address, 2 Corinthians 4:1-7 was read to the Congress in Arabic, French and Spanish.[1]

The Gospel of Jesus Christ is unique, wonderful, powerful and true. It is the greatest message in the history of the world and we want to share it with others. That is why we've been meeting together. It has been a memorable occasion. What do we hope will be the legacy of this Congress? What will we say when we return home?

Over the last year, Chris Wright and a team of theologians from around the world have been working on the first part of the *Cape Town Commitment*.[2] Its two-part structure is based on our attempt to respond to Jesus' two commands: to love God and to love one another. It follows the style of Paul's letters where he first outlines a series of doctrinal convictions and then spells out the implications of these beliefs for our lifestyle. In summarising our doctrinal convictions, we are not attempting to be doctrinaire. In our judgement it is important that each generation of believers should reflect on and restate in a fresh way what it believes. I hope you will read the *Commitment* carefully and digest it. Our prayer is that it will be a help to many mission agencies, churches and Christian organizations around the world.

---

[1] This address was given in the context of The Closing Ceremony, and followed by a service of Holy Communion with a liturgy written by the Church in Kenya. This address has previously been published (without footnotes) in J. E. M. Cameron (ed) *Christ Our Reconciler*, 191-202. Whereas the whole Closing Ceremony may be viewed at http://conversation.lausanne. org/en/resources/detail/11010, Lindsay Brown's final address may be viewed at http://conversation.lausanne.org/en/resources/detail/11646.

[2] The first meeting of what was then called The Cape Town 2010 Statement Working Group, made up of leading evangelical theologians, pastors and missiologists from around the world, was hosted by John Piper in Bethlehem Church, Minneapolis, Minnesota. Sinclair B. Ferguson was in the Chair. Chris Wright was invited to draft the first part of the statement, *The Cape Town Confession of Faith*, which was distributed at the Congress. The second part, *The Cape Town Call to Action* issued out of discussions at the Congress, and was published early in 2011 in eight Congress languages. It has subsequently been translated into many more languages.

In the preamble, the authors list the legacy of the first and second Lausanne Congresses. Among the major gifts to the world church of the first Congress in 1974, were (i) the *Lausanne Covenant*,[3] (ii) a new awareness of unreached people groups and (iii) a fresh discovery of the holistic nature of the biblical Gospel and of Christian mission. The second Congress gave birth to the *Manila Manifesto*,[4] and to more than 300 strategic partnerships between nations in all parts of the globe.

What will be the legacy of this Congress? Only God knows – we don't, at this stage. But I can tell you the fourfold vision and the hope of the organisers.

First and paramountly, for a ringing reaffirmation of the uniqueness of Christ and the truth of the biblical Gospel, and a crystal-clear statement on the mission of the church – all rooted in Scripture. We cannot engage in mission unless we are clear on what we believe. Without a foundational commitment to truth, we have little to offer. The great missionary conference of Edinburgh 1910 set in motion huge missionary endeavour.[5] But it had one big flaw – the organisers sidelined doctrine. Recently John Stott told me he was ashamed that leaders in his own communion refused to discuss doctrinal issues for fear of division. As a result, the Congress launched a movement without biblical consensus. As Stott said, "You cannot speak of the Gospel of Christ and the mission of the church without reflecting on biblical truth." To do so is folly.

So we need to have clarity, especially on four things: (i) the exclusive claims of Christ; (ii) the meaning of Christ's death; (iii) the necessity of conversion; (iv) the lostness of humankind. The *Cape Town Commitment* seeks to give this clarity. It is effectively a statement of what evangelicals believe. There is no need for us to be ashamed of this word 'evangelical'. It simply means 'people of the Gospel'. It is not a new word; it is neither a western word, nor a Reformation word. Nor is evangelicalism a sect. It has its roots in Scripture (*euangelion*) and was used amongst church leaders as early as the second century; for example, Tertullian used it in his defence of biblical truth against the heresies of Marcion.[6] When we use the term, we are simply aspiring to articulate and communicate authentic and biblical Christianity. Lausanne is an unashamedly evangelical movement.

Did you hear this ringing affirmation, and do you agree with it?

Secondly, our vision and our hope were to identify key issues which the church needs to address seriously in the coming decade. The mission statement for this Congress was 'to seek to bring a fresh challenge to the

---

[3] John Stott wrote a study guide to the *Lausanne Covenant*, published in 1975, available now from Hendrickson in the *Didasko Files* series.

[4] Available at www.lausanne.org/en/documents/manila-manifesto.html.

[5] See Knud Jørgensen's chapter in this volume on "Edinburgh, Tokyo and Cape Town – comparing and contrasting on the way to 2110".

[6] Marcion was a second century teacher; Tertullian straddled the second and third centuries. Tertullian's firm refutation of Marcion's teaching is easily found online.

global church to bear witness to Jesus Christ and all his teaching, in every part of the world – not only geographically, but in every sphere of society, and in the realm of ideas'. The term 'bearing witness' is carefully chosen. In many ways I think it is better than 'evangelization'. It is often translated from the Greek word *martyria* in the English Bible to imply both speech and behaviour. We must be committed to the lordship of Christ in every area of human activity. I love the words of Abraham Kuyper,[7] the Dutch theologian and prime minister, who once said, "There is not one centimetre of human existence to which Christ, who is Lord of all, does not point and say 'that is mine'."

The evangelical church has rightly put an emphasis on reaching every nation and every people group with the Gospel of Jesus Christ. That must not be diminished. We have, however, perhaps been a little weaker in our attempts to apply biblical principles to every area of society – for example, to the media, business, government, public policy, the university ... Charles Malik, the Lebanese statesman who led the UN General Assembly and fashioned the UN Declaration on Human Rights, asked, "What does Jesus Christ think of the university?" What a question! He urged Christians to "try to recapture the university for Christ", for, he said, "Change the university, and you change the world."[8]

During this Congress, we have also been challenged to apply a Christian mind to ethical issues such as ethnicity and creation care, amongst others. We need to engage deeply with human endeavour and with the ideas which shape it. As Sir Fred Catherwood once said, "To wash your hands of society is not love, but worldliness; to engage in society is not worldliness, but love."[9]

Many secularists have tried to persuade us to retain our faith only as a private matter and to keep it out of the public domain. This would imply that the Christian message is relevant only in our homes and churches, but not in society. That is not the teaching of the Bible. Our hope for this Congress is that we leave here (i) passionately committed to communicating the Gospel to the ends of the earth, and (ii) equally committed to demonstrating that the eternal truths of Scripture have application to the whole of life. For Christ is Lord over the whole of creation. Affirming the lordship of Christ and attempting to develop a Christian mind will have three implications: it will (i) glorify our Creator, (ii) enrich our Christian lives and (iii) enhance our witness.

---

[7] Kuyper (1837-1920) served as Prime Minister of the Netherlands from 1901-1905.

[8] See Malik's Pascal lectures *A Christian Critique of the University* (Waterloo University, 1981).

[9] British industrialist; author of *inter alia* the then ground-breaking *A Christian in Industrial Society* (IVP, 1964) and *Light, Salt and the World of Business* (Hendrickson/Lausanne *Didasko Files* series, 2009). He chaired the UK National Economic Development Council (1963-71) and served as Vice-Chairman of the European Parliament (1989-92).

Are you committed to bearing witness to Christ in every area of life?

Thirdly, our vision and our hope was that many fruitful partnerships would issue from this Congress; to this end, great care was taken in the formation of the small groups, so that many fresh friendships and partnerships would come into existence. In a needy and broken world, we cannot afford to be driven by a spirit of competition; such a spirit must give way to a spirit of partnership where both men and women, and people of different ethnicities, join hands under Christ to communicate the Gospel of Christ to the ends of the earth.

Such partnerships must transcend denominational and organizational divides. Our prayer is that after the Congress, like-minded mission agencies working in the same field will partner together to avoid duplication, competition and wastage. We need a new generation of evangelical statesmen and women who are driven by their commitment to the cause of Christ above all, and who genuinely rejoice, like Paul in Philippians 1, when the Gospel goes forth, no matter who is leading the charge.

Are you thinking of fresh partnerships into which you can enter after this Congress?

Fourthly, our vision and hope has been that many new initiatives will issue out of this Congress. We maintain too much, and pioneer too little. How can we rest when millions have never heard the Gospel? In 1974, there was a great surge of interest in unreached people groups. What will come from this Congress? Perhaps fresh initiatives in reaching oral learners, young people, diaspora or the cities. Who knows what new ministries the Congress will spawn? Will we see fresh energy in communicating biblical truth in the public domain, in the media, in the world of the arts, in the university and government? These all shape the value systems in nations and require bold, clear and coherent Christian testimony.

What fresh initiatives will *you* take, coming out of this Congress?

Whatever God is pleased to do, I believe the Apostle Paul in 2 Corinthians 4:1-7 gives us three principles to take away. These principles have been rehearsed throughout the Congress.

Mission is Christocentric

Our ministry, or calling, at its core, is to present the deity, incarnation, death, resurrection and lordship of Jesus Christ.

At the press conference today a journalist asked me, "Bishop Stephen Neill says that when mission is everything, mission is nothing. What is *not* the mission of the church?" My answer was this: "When the church proclaims a message without the deity, incarnation, death, resurrection and lordship of Christ at its centre, that is not mission."

Look at the way Paul highlights the following:

- v 4 – the light of the Gospel of the glory of Christ who is the image of God
- v 5 – preaching Christ Jesus as Lord
- v 6 – the glory of God in the face of Christ

Our message is unashamedly Christocentric. When Sadhu Sundar Singh, the great Indian leader, was once asked what was so special about the Christian faith, his reply was, "Only Christ."[10] I once asked a Christian woman in north India, where the vast majority are Hindus and Muslims, "Why are you a Christian?" She responded, "It is only through Christ that I can know God as my Father; only through Christ can I know my sins forgiven; and only through Christ can I have the hope of eternal life." He is not just *a* Saviour – but *the unique* Saviour of the world. He is not just one among many, but the *only* Lord and Saviour. He does not bear comparison with any other religious leaders. He is incomparable. Our calling is by *all* means to communicate this message to the world. Some will do it by preaching and by proclamation, but all are called, according to the New Testament, to bear witness to him.

Some of us may engage in dialogue in the public sphere. It is amazing how creative the early evangelists were, speaking in local synagogues, and in neutral territory, as did Paul on Mars Hill. There is no substitute for engaging in Christ's commission to testify verbally to his lordship.

Our communion meal this evening focuses around John the Baptist's ecstatic claim when he saw Jesus and called him 'the Lamb of God who takes away the sin of the world'.[11] When I was a student in Oxford University in the 1970s, I studied in the same college where John Wesley had been a professor 250 years previously. It was a wonderful place to read the letters and sermons of Wesley. I took the opportunity to read through his journals in which he wrote every day during his itinerant ministry. One phrase struck me, repeated day after day in his journals: 'I offered Christ to the people ... today I offered Christ to the people.' That is our primary calling, to offer Christ to the peoples of the world.

The Need for Integrity

We are to watch our walk! Our words must come from godly lives. We are called to be a witness to Christ as fallen, fragile people, or as 'earthen vessels' (v 7). We should be careful about over-focusing on technique, or on clever approaches (v 2); the Gospel should be shared, not by craftiness or by adulterating the word of God, but out of our weakness, (v 7), focusing on the power of God.

---

[10] Sadhu Sundar Singh (1889-c1929), born into a Hindu family. Author of eight books, written in Urdu and published in translation. Indian Christian history cannot be grasped without studying Sadhu Sundar Singh.

[11] See John 1:29, 36.

There is no room for over-confidence or triumphalism. We dare not say we will accomplish this task because we have the money and the technology. Rather, the mission of taking the Gospel to the ends of the earth will be accomplished only because of the greatness of the Gospel, the power of God, the unique message of the saving Christ and the help and power of the Holy Spirit and the Word of God. As we go out, we are to focus on the truth of the Gospel (v 2), the Gospel of the glory of God (v 4), the lordship of Christ (v 5), the glory of God in the face of Christ (v 6). But this word of truth is to be backed up by authentic, transformed, joyful lives.

John Stott said in his last published sermon that the greatest hindrance to the advance of the Gospel worldwide is the failure of God's people to live like God's people.

The teaching of the whole of Scripture is that we are to demonstrate godly lives before a watching world: lives which issue not just in pious statements, but in compassion in a needy and broken world by caring for the underprivileged, the poor, those affected by pandemics, the broken-hearted. It is intriguing to remember the words of Adolph Harnack, the Lutheran writer and great German church historian, who said that the two reasons the primitive church grew were that they out-*argued* the pagans (articulating and defending Christian truth in public) and they out-*lived* them.[12] These two things must come together. Jesus himself brought them together in the feeding of the five thousand. So should we.

Our calling is to be morally distinct without being socially segregated. For those who are very word-centred, with a strong commitment to verbal communication of the Gospel, our challenge is to balance this with empathy and care for the needy and broken. We must be careful to avoid the failings of the disciples who wanted Jesus only to speak to the 5,000 and then send them away. He would not allow that; neither should we.

For those committed to ministries of compassion, empathy and care, our challenge may be to ensure that our expressions of compassion are supported by taking every opportunity – graciously, sensitively, compassionately and wisely – but also verbally – to communicate the Gospel of Christ. J. I. Packer is right when he says, "A dumb Christian is a disobedient Christian." So we must do both. Earlier this week, Antoine Rutayisire from Rwanda gave us a wonderful biblical framework for a ministry of reconciliation which brought these two things together. He did not have time to share his own experience – how he saw his own father killed in front of him when he was six years old, or how, in his mid-thirties, he lost all his co-workers in the IFES-related student ministry, killed in the 1994 genocide because of their determination to stand against ethnic violence and demonstrate their unity in Christ across the ethnic divide. Soon afterwards he was taken to a refugee camp with his pregnant wife,

---

[12] Harnack, Adolf (1851-1930). He taught at Leipzig (1874) before becoming professor at Giessen (1879), Marburg (1886), and Berlin (1889-1921).

where he spent several months. I wrote to him from my home in Wales, offering to pay for him to come out of the country for a year's sabbatical to recover from the trauma. I'll never forget his reply. I still have the letter. He wrote, "Thank you, Lindsay, for your kind invitation to come to Wales for a sabbatical. It is very attractive. However, when the way is open, I will return to Kigali. For if I do not share in my people's pain, neither can I share with them the joy of the gospel."[13]

A radical Christian lifestyle may require sacrificial commitment and service. Words may not be enough.

A Call to Perseverance

Finally, the Apostle exhorts us not to lose heart (v 1). In 1 Corinthians 15:58 he said, "Be steadfast, unmovable, always abounding in the work of the Lord, knowing that your work is not in vain." Many of us will return to difficult circumstances, and may even entertain the idea of giving up because the work is so hard. Such temptations can come more strongly when we return from the mountain-top experience of a Congress like this. Then we are to remember our calling to persevere to the end and not to lose heart. I well remember talking with the only person from Somalia at the last Lausanne Congress, in 1989. He was employed by the United Nations, and working in the capital, Mogadishu. He was the only Somali elder in the only evangelical church in the city, made up of seventy believers. He had received an invitation to go and work with the UN in New York, but turned it down so he could serve among his own people. As a consequence, he lost his life in 1990, one year later. Indeed, Luis Palau had said at the Congress that if we were to gather in ten years' time, some would be absent because they had lost their lives in the Lord's service. That may well be true of some of us here. Gospel service is costly, but we are to continue because of the glory of the Gospel and the commission of our Lord.

Samuel Escobar,[14] one of the grandfathers of the Lausanne Movement, has said the only thing twentieth century man discovered was speed! We must have it and have it quick! Christian ministry is rarely like that. We thank God for rapid growth when we see it, but often the Word of God takes root slowly. We are to take a long view, not give up, and fulfil the

---

[13] For more of Antoine Rutayisire's story, see Chapter 6, *Shining Like Stars*: *The power of the gospel in the world's universities* by Lindsay Brown (IVP, 2006). See also Rutayisire's chapter in this volume on "The Church and the Message of Reconciliation".

[14] With fellow Latin American René Padilla, Samuel Escobar made a significant contribution to the International Congress on World Evangelization (Lausanne, 1974). This was to urge the church to understand what is now known as 'Integral mission', i.e. the seeking of social justice as being part of our Christian mandate. Through the *Lausanne Covenant*, this view took root as responsible evangelical thinking about society.

ministry which God has given us. We are called, as Eugene Petersen said, to 'a long obedience in the same direction'.[15] Before I close, let me give two illustrations of people who have done that.

One is Professor Jerry Gana, a senior politician in Nigeria who has served five consecutive presidents, Muslim and Christian.[16] Jerry has a reputation for remaining free of corruption. I once asked him how, in over thirty years of political life, he had managed to retain his reputation as a man of integrity and fairness. He said there were three factors:

1. He learned as a young student what it meant to abide in Christ and keep short accounts. We need to teach that too.
2. He chose his colleagues and partners slowly because, he said, even some Christian politicians make foolish mistakes. When you identify with a particular policy and individual, if it all goes wrong, you have to face the consequences and it can damage your testimony.
3. He realised from early on the importance of legacy. He said, "God has given me the privilege of serving in public life for thirty years. I hope I will be able to continue for another twenty-five. During that time, I'd like to mentor and develop a generation of young evangelical politicians in Nigeria. My hope and prayer is that they will go on and multiply that influence in their own generation; and that God will impact the political life of this nation through evangelical Christian politicians over a 60-year period." That is a tremendous long-term vision and aspiration!

The second is Adoniram Judson, one of the early American missionaries. You may remember that he arrived in Burma, or Myanmar, in 1812, and died there 38 years later in 1850. During that time, he suffered much for the cause of the Gospel. He lost his first wife, Ann, to whom he was devoted, as well as several children. He was imprisoned, tortured and kept in shackles. Statistics are unclear, but there were only somewhere between 12-25 professing Christians in the country when he died; there were no churches to speak of, but he had completed the translation of the Bible just before he died.

Paul Borthwick spoke at the 150th anniversary of the translation of the Bible into the Burmese language.[17] Just before he got up to speak, he noticed in small print on the first page the words, 'Translated by Rev A. Judson'. So he turned to his interpreter Matthew Hla Win and asked him, "Matthew, what do you know of this man?" Matthew began to weep. "We

[15] The book title for Petersen's study of the Songs of Ascent, first published by IVP in 1980.

[16] For more on Professor Jerry Gana, and for further inspiring examples of Christians in public service, see Chapter 5 of *Shining like Stars*: *The power of the gospel in the world's universities* by Lindsay Brown (IVP, 2006).

[17] Finally completed in 1834 and published in 1835. There are several biographies of this remarkable American missionary pioneer.

know him – we know how he loved the Burmese people, how he suffered for the Gospel because of us, out of love for us. He died a pauper, but left the Bible for us. When he died, there were few believers, but today there are over 600,000 of us, and every single one of us traces our spiritual heritage to one man – the Rev Adoniram Judson." But he never saw it!

And that will be the case for some of us gathered here. We may be called to invest our lives in ministries for which we do not see much immediate fruit, trusting that the God of all grace who oversees our work will ensure that our labour is not in vain.

> Therefore, beloved brethren, be steadfast, immovable, always abounding in the work of the Lord, knowing that your toil is not in vain in the Lord. (1 Corinthians 15:58)

Let me leave you with the words of John Wesley. As you seek to bear witness to Christ – "With God's help: Do all the good you can, by all the means you can, in all the ways you can, in all the places you can, at all the times you can, to all the people you can, as long as ever you can"[18] until Christ returns or calls us home. Let us all press on to the end in serving Christ, our King. God bless you.

> Following the address, the Congress sang the hymn *Facing a Task Unfinished.*

> The Closing Ceremony took the form of a special musical setting of the Kenyan service of Holy Communion. This was presided over by The Right Revd. Henry Luke Orombi, Archbishop of Uganda and Honorary Chair of the Cape Town 2010 Africa Host Committee. The bread and wine were served around the hall using communion sets borrowed from a hundred local churches around the world, symbolizing the remembering of Christ's death in many nations.

---

[18] From *Rule of Conduct*, Letters of John Wesley, ed. George Eayrs, 423.

A Latin-American Evangelical Perspective on the Cape Town Congress

Valdir Steuernagel

Two Stories as a Parable

Early in 1976 a pioneer missionary congress gathered university students and young professionals from all over Brazil, in the southern city of Curitiba. The event was organized by the *Aliança Bíblica Universitária do Brasil*,[1] under the theme *Jesus Cristo, Senhorio, Propósito e Missão* (Jesus Christ: Lordship, Purpose and Mission).[2] The International Congress on World Evangelization (Lausanne I) had just happened in 1974. Its news had barely arrived in Brazil, yet the so-called 'spirit of Lausanne' was there among those of us organizing the Missionary Congress 1976. Even though most of us did not know much about the Lausanne Movement, Lausanne was there. Two Latin American leaders who had significantly influenced Lausanne 74 and its Covenant were there, and the young leaders present at Curitiba 76 would gladly submit to the teachings and life inspiration of Samuel Escobar and René Padilla. The agenda of integral mission was also and foundationally there, as well as the call for a mission experience that would completely mark our lives and challenge those young professionals to look at their professions as mission. There was even an attempt to create a covenant (*O Pacto de Curitiba*, The Curitiba Covenant),[3] and together with Escobar and Padilla I had the privilege to not only write it, but also produce an explanation of it, as John Stott had done with the *Lausanne Covenant*. In fact, and most of all, it was the spirit of Lausanne that helped shape that Brazilian Congress, a significant event inspired by an earlier and ground-breaking event and movement called Lausanne. Lausanne represented an evangelical *Zeitgeist* (spirit of this time) and we were in it, participating, as I said at another place, in what became 'one of the most

---

[1] A movement associated with the International Fellowship of Evangelical Students (IFES).

[2] The main adresses of the Congress were published in *Jesus Cristo: Senhorio, Propósito e Missão. Compêndio do Congresso Missionário* (São Paulo: ABU Editora, 1978).

[3] The "Pacto de Curitiba" was published in *Jesus Cristo: Senhorio, Propósito e Missão. Compêndio do Congresso Missionário* (São Paulo: ABU Editora, 1978).

representative points of reference of contemporary evangelicalism' and a key evangelical expression of the worldwide church of Christ.[4]

Years later, in 1983, the first *Congresso Brasileiro de Evangelização* (Brazilian Congress of Evangelization) happened, and the spirit of Lausanne was there again. While this event was organized in dialogue with the Lausanne Movement, not even the International Director of Lausanne was able to be there when it happened. In addition, even the U$5,000.00 provided by Lausanne to help the organizers during the preparatory period were given back to the Movement; the money was not necessary. However, this event also embraced the agenda of integral mission while being specifically concerned with the evangelization of Brazil. The very theme of the Congress shows the identification with Lausanne 74: *Que o Brasil e o mundo ouçam a voz de Deus* (Let Brazil and the world hear God's voice).[5] The *Lausanne Covenant* inspired the outline of the Congress and the Continuation Committee, which was established after the event and followed in the footsteps of Lausanne 74. Again, although the link with Lausanne was not institutional, the spirit of Lausanne established the link while the Covenant was establishing the foundation.

I learned from the Brazilian theologian Frei Betto that 'your head thinks where your feet stand'.[6] So I had to start this article by talking about the Brazilian experience; after all, a Brazilian I am and in Brazil I live. But I risk saying that the Latin American overall experience with Lausanne was very similar to ours. A similar story could be told in regard to the different Latin American congresses of evangelization and their relation with the Lausanne Movement: the spirit of Lausanne arrived early in our Continent. The *Lausanne Covenant* came hand in hand with it and had a mostly good but narrow influence in our churches, mission schools and theological seminaries. The Lausanne Movement, as a movement, had barely arrived in the continent, and sometimes was even seen as ambiguous by those who had embraced a school of integral mission.

Latin Americans Arriving in Cape Town

It is with this background that around 400 leaders from the continent arrived in Cape Town for the third Congress of World Evangelization. They arrived talkatively as Latinos usually do. They greeted and embraced each other as they met in the corridors of the huge Convention Centre,

---

[4] See Valdir Steuernagel, in *The Theology of Mission in its relation to social responsibility within the Lausanne Movement. A dissertation submitted to the Faculty of the LSTC* (Chicago, IL: May 1988, 132).

[5] The main addresses of the event were published in *A Evangelização do Brasil: Uma Tarefa Incabada*, ed Valdir Steuernagel. São Paulo: ABU Editora, 1985.

[6] The flow is much better in the Portuguese language: "A cabeça pensa onde estão os pés".

speaking in Spanish and Portuguese since it is always a struggle to communicate in the official English language.

Unlike the Lausanne I experienced in 1974, in 2010 they arrived in big numbers and almost with pride. The Latino noise that could be heard and seen now indicated a difference. It had to do with the number of people present, but it was also an emotional and even factual difference. During the 36 years from 1974 to 2010 the Latino evangelical churches had grown consistently and almost exponentially. While in 1974 the evangelicals were still a notable minority in the overwhelmingly Catholic countries, in 2010 they had reached big numbers, as seen in Guatemala where they represent over 30% of the population, or in Brazil where they count over 40 million spread out throughout the country. Therefore, the Latinos arrived with a significant experience of church growth with its consequences: managing huge churches, administering increasing resources, diversifying ministerial approaches, becoming experts in mass communication, experiencing a new power base which also means to vote 'evangelical associates' into the political systems – to mention some of the marks which have kept the evangelical family busy, excited, hopeful and committed. Besides, many of those arriving had been establishing and nurturing a new cross-cultural mission movement as well as developing many different projects and approaches to poor communities, street children, drug addicts, only to mention a few initiatives which were essential to the picture of the evangelical family in the continent. Therefore, when the Latinos entered the Convention Centre their way of walking, talking and relating to others took place within this background, made up of hope, willingness to share and even some presumption that says, 'we know how to play the game'.

But it did not take long for voices of grumbling and of complaint to emerge and get louder. Even though it is impossible to speak for all of them and to portray a unanimous voice, I would risk saying that there was a feeling of misplacement and under-representation that characterized the Latino delegation.[7] A feeling and perception that was fed, not only by the way the Continent was portrayed at the occasion of the regional presentations, but also by the absence of a good representation of the Latin American church and mission experience in the programme. A few elements should be mentioned in order to decipher those feelings, perceptions and understanding:

One difficulty was to understanding the Lausanne Movement, which has never really laid down strong roots in Latin America. While the voices of

---

[7] A personal word is in place here. As a Latin American who is a member of the international Board of the Lausanne Movement, I not only was a witness to the dissatisfaction of quite a number of the Latinos at the event but also recognize that I could have done more in order to see the presence of our leaders and our experience at the shaping of the programme. I must confess that I did not dedicate enough time to this and only too late woke up to it. I am sorry for this and know that I did not honour the heritage that René Padilla and Samuel Escobar handed over to us.

René Padilla's and Samuel Escobar's presentations in Lausanne 74 were significant, and the continent heard their voices amplified at the Latin American Congresses of Evangelization, they always represented a minority within the evangelical world and were even looked at with suspicion by many leaders who were becoming the champions of church growth. Those champions, in fact, knew very little about Lausanne and were not that keen to participate in it. In addition, the very development of the Lausanne Movement with its tension concerning the emphasis on verbal evangelization vis-à-vis the social dimension of the Gospel, as well as its 'ups and downs' throughout the years, did not help to portray an image of consistency and relevance that would invite many Latino leaders to participate and engage in it. Therefore, alongside with the recognition of the new moment of Lausanne, as Cape Town made so very evident, there was also the suspicion as to what Lausanne would say on this occasion and how people would walk out of the Convention Centre afterwards.

The global church and the evangelical agenda had changed substantially while the Latinos had hardly noticed it, to exaggerate a bit. They were so busy and enchanted with their successful church growth, with their ministerial and mission initiatives that they had barely noticed the changes taking place. Those changes pointed to growing interreligious realities and tensions, re-emerging ethnic conflicts, the emergence of China as a global player, a deep secularizing trend fed by a western understanding and practice of globalization that was eating up many expressions of the western churches and even redefining the public arena in regard to faith expression – all of this coming together and calling for a new conversation in regard to the evangelical identity and the way to talk about it, while also stressing the need to revisit the task of evangelization and church growth in a much more difficult and challenging environment.

The integral mission agenda, so important for sectors of the evangelical world in Latin America, was still there and was embraced as never before. Yet, it had to be unpacked in so many different directions, as seen throughout the program. A most historic and significant moment of its affirmation became reality when René Padilla and Samuel Escobar stood on the platform to talk about the history of Lausanne and their contribution to it. But to look to the past was only a small gesture compared to the desire to look into the future in the attempt to outline an understanding of mission committed to the "whole gospel to the whole world". As *The Cape Town Commitment* (CTC) moved, in its second part, into a "call to action", this complexity, challenge and opportunity emerged as a gigantic task. A task that was embraced by the drafting committee and taken home by all the participants. This "Call to Action" became, in fact, a working agenda that will keep the movement working missiologically for the coming years.

The fact that the *Cape Town Commitment*[9] was distributed but not openly discussed, by all the participants, at the Congress didn't go well with a participative and engaging culture such as the Latino one. For many Latinos to embrace and to own something they need to be directly engaged in it. Therefore, it was not easy for them to leave Cape Town with the CTC under their arms and say, "Look what we did. This is our 'new covenant'. It is ours and it is for our generation." Some further work was necessary for that ownership to emerge, but this is already a task for the "day after".

Three Cases and the Search for a Trend

Latin America is so vast, rich and diverse that you can hardly embrace it as one common reality. On the other side, the fact that most of the continent speaks Spanish, except for Brazil that speaks Portuguese, a similar language, gives the continent a sense of unity. From the outside the Continent is very often seen and dealt with as being this 'one common reality'. I bring three examples here.

The Ambiguity of Edinburgh 1910 and the Affirmation of Panama 1916

The World Missionary Conference, held in Edinburgh in 1910, was certainly a ground-breaking event through which Protestant forces and mission initiatives came together and focused on 'unity and evangelism'. For Latin Americans, however, it became an ambiguous event which unleashed a process that was certainly not planned for. The leading forces within the Edinburgh gathering considered Latin America a Christian continent and decided that it would not be included in the list of places in need of evangelization. This provoked a reaction by the minority Protestant groups that were facing, at the time, serious difficulties to exist, be recognized and expand in the continent. As a consequence, the Latinos gathered and decided that it was time for the Protestant forces to bring together Latin America itself, which resulted in the Pan American Protestant Congress held in Panama in 1916. What Edinburgh represented at a global level, this event represented for the continent; the mainline Protestant churches, which had decided not to consider Latin America a

---

[9] The Cape Town Commitment has two main sections, being the first one "A Confession of Faith" and the second one "A Call to Action". The first part was produced prior to the event and distributed there, while the second part was worked on during the event, by mostly the same drafting committee, and finalized afterwards. There had been an earlier discussion about the possibility of having the CTC openly discussed by the participants, at the Congress itself, with the decision that this would be very hard to manage in such a large event. A regionally representative working group was then established with the understanding that this committee would become a good listening group in regard to the program and the perception of it by the participants.

continent in need of evangelization, now needed to grasp this regional development. At the same time, the independent churches and evangelical mission forces from the USA capitalized on this development and concentrated their forces keenly on the Latin American continent 'in need of evangelization'.[10] This case shows that the Protestant churches, with an ecumenical and European flavour, and the evangelistic forces, mostly based in the USA, did not arrive in the continent together and with the same agenda. On the contrary, they brought their tensions and divisions to this part of the world. While the Protestant forces were more concerned with church unity, the more independent forces were concerned with evangelism and even regarded the search for unity as a wrong agenda and rejected it as having an 'ecumenical flavour'. However, all things considered, the Panama event gave the Protestants and some evangelical forces a sense of mutual belonging and an agenda that affirmed the need for those churches to grow numerically as well as go after their right to legitimately exist in the continent, and also look for avenues of influence in their respective societies, an example of which was the emphasis on the implementation of education centres. Yet, the development in the continent was not that different from what was taking place in other parts of the world.

The Seed of Berlin 1966 and CLADE I[11]

The days after Edinburgh 1910 stressed the need for church unity, public impact in society as well as mission engagement. During the decades following the event, however, it was difficult and even impossible to keep these different emphases and initiatives together as priorities. As ecumenical forces (keenly influenced by western Protestant churches and movements, with a more theological liberal mindset) gathered around the World Council of Churches and stressed the importance of the unity and public ministry of the church, the evangelical forces felt dispersed and frustrated while seeing the emphasis on evangelism neglected. Out of that frustration, the desire for a new encounter focused on evangelism emerged and the World Congress on Evangelism was called and took place in Berlin in 1966. Its priority was to re-emphasize evangelism, stress its urgency and look for the best strategies and methods to do it.[12] One of the decisions of this first specifically evangelical event was to arrange regional events. In

---

[10] See *The Panama Congress of 1916 and its Impact on Protestantism in Latin America*, by J. B. A. Kessler, *Evangelical Review of Theology* 2, 1 (1978), 42.

[11] CLADE stands for Congreso Latino Americano de Evangelización (Latin American Congress of Evangelization).

[12] *Good News for a World in Need*, in *Christianity Today* 11, No.1 (Oct 14th 1966), 34.

Latin America, such an event took place in 1969 in Bogota, Colombia, and became the first Latin American Congress of Evangelization – CLADE I.[13]

The same tension between ecumenical and evangelicals which was witnessed at the global level was also seen in Latin America, with the peculiarity that the historical Protestant groups and forces, which leaned toward a more ecumenical experience, faced serious difficulties in finding roots in the continent and experiencing significant church growth, while evangelical forces, surrounded by a strong North American missionary influx, stressed evangelistic activities, and experienced expansion; through the arrival of Pentecostal forces and their immediate growth, they started gaining people, presence, visibility and influence.

CLADE I was an expression of this development. Organized under the auspices of the Billy Graham Evangelistic Association, which had been the main force behind Berlin 66, it gathered mostly evangelical forces from all over the continent. As these forces came together, it was difficult to avoid seeing the urgent need for a new and local leadership as well as identifying the growing influence of the North American mission enterprise with its clear and propositional agenda. Two dimensions were clearly seen:

An emerging continental leadership wanted to see the Gospel entering the tissue of society and stressed the social consequences of the Gospel and the social responsibility of their churches. As an expression of this desire and tendency, the speech by Samuel Escobar entitled 'The Social Responsibility of the Church' was a highlight of the event and was received with a long, standing ovation. The seeds of what is today called 'integral mission' were clearly seen as well as nurtured at CLADE I.[14]

In the light of the strong presence and influence of an almost fundamentalist missionary force in the continent, a group wanted to highlight a concern for and practice of evangelism marked by verbal proclamation of the Gospel, establishment of new churches with no involvement whatsoever in social engagement and not taking part in political life.

Those two tendencies are part of the recent history of churches and mission organizations in Latin America. At an early stage, some of the tensions regarding those perceptions were brought to the continent from abroad but have then been localized, becoming part of a difficult and divisive evangelical debate. However, there was also a desire and effort to build bridges and recognize the heritage brought by the pioneers of mission in the continent while recognizing an emerging leadership and a new agenda. This was expressed at the 'The Evangelical Declaration of Bogotá' in this way:

---

[13] There have been, by now, five CLADEs in the continent, the last one being in Costa Rica in 2012.

[14] S. Escobar, *The Social Responsibility of the Church in Latin America*, in EMQ 6, No. 3 (1970), 129.

> The evangelical presence in Latin America is the fruit of the actions of God through an immense flow of Christian love, missionary vision, sacrificial spirit, work, effort, time, and money invested here by the foreign missions which have been labouring for more than a century, including the work of the Bible Societies. This glance at our history cannot less than awaken within us a spirit of gratitude for the work of the pioneers. At the same time, looking toward the future, we are conscious of new responsibilities, new tasks, and new structures which form a true challenge to Latin American believers and to the indigenous leadership in all dimensions of the ministry.[15]

The Declaration issued at CLADE I is a good expression of the emerging evangelical reality as well as an expression of the desire to embrace people, initiatives and resources coming from abroad, while at the same time recognizing, empowering and challenging a local leadership that must incarnate an evangelical response to their time and context. In this sense, the 'Declaration' of yesterday is still relevant today.

The Voice of Latin America at Lausanne 74 and the Tension of CLADE II in 1979

Only a few years after 1969, some of the emerging leaders within Latin America got involved in the preparations for Lausanne I. The outcome of this journey was seen through the presence and voices of René Padilla and Samuel Escobar. There is no need to detail that journey except for two remarks:

Lausanne I embraced the fruits of Berlin 66 and the regional events that took place thereafter. In this sense Lausanne wanted to have non-westerners as participants, also on the platform. It was successful in doing so.

Lausanne I wanted to move from evangelism to evangelization; in the words of Bishop Jack Dain, "We need not only to think of evangelism that is the proclamation of the Gospel, but the whole task given to us by the risen Christ."[16] In this sense, Lausanne was moving towards a more holistic understanding and practice of mission.

Against this background, the ground was prepared for receiving two Latino leaders who were ready and eager to share their understanding.

The context in which the Gospel is lived out and preached is very important. It has to be taken into account, understood and engaged with. The Gospel is incarnational. It speaks to the context, and does it prophetically, denouncing evil and injustice and calling for transformation through the good news of the Gospel.

The Gospel has not only social implications, encouraging and challenging churches to engage in society, and in helping and empowering the poor, but has also a clear commitment to justice. Justice needs to be

---

[15] *The Evangelical Declaration of Bogotá*, in EMQ 6, No.3 (1970), 172.

[16] An interview by Jack Dain, quoted in *The Lausanne Story*. LCWE, 1987, 13.

lived out in the churches and looked for and asked for in our respective societies.[17]

Padilla and Escobar were obviously only two voices among others who might even stress different notes. However, when their voices are linked with John Stott's presentation on the 'The Biblical Basis of Evangelism',[18] we have a substantial piece of the *Lausanne Covenant* emerging, as well as a key and distinctive message of Lausanne that was identified within Latin America. When it came to CLADE II in 1979, where both Escobar and Padilla were key leaders, this was the focus that shaped the organizing process and the event itself.

Looking back, it is quite comforting to know that the *Lausanne Covenant* represents so much of, and so uniquely, the Lausanne Movement. It is also refreshing to see that the 'Spirit of Lausanne' was and is free to call evangelicals together in many different places and different ways, as seen in Latin America itself. Yet, when looking at some developments that took place after Lausanne I, the picture is much more disturbing and conflicting. A struggle over the interpretation of the event and of the Covenant started very early after the Congress and became a key issue at the first meeting of the Lausanne Continuation Committee in Mexico in 1975. Leighton Ford interprets the tension as follows: "The major debate in Mexico City, however, centered on the mandate and focus of the Continuation Committee itself. In his opening remarks, Billy Graham had urged that the committee should limit itself to the specific task of evangelism. John Stott, on the other hand, argued that the mandate of the Lausanne Movement came from the *Lausanne Covenant*, and that the committee should seek to influence the whole wider vision of the church."[19]

The conflict over a narrow or broader understanding of evangelization was, in fact, an issue that kept Lausanne busy for quite some time. At times, a good balance was reached, as seen in the Covenant itself, while at other times the tension became strong and even judgemental. CLADE II was impacted by the consequences of this tension and was almost denied its right to understand itself in tune with Lausanne, in spite of having the Covenant as its faith basis and following the motto of Lausanne 74: 'That Latin America May Hear God's Voice'. In a letter, Peter Wagner, then the co-ordinator of the Strategy Working Group of Lausanne, expressed his concerns in the following language: "Those who are organizing CLADE II are not those who are known to be especially concerned with evangelism as

---

[17] Escobar's presentation at Lausanne was entitled "Evangelism and Man's Search for Freedom, Justice and Fulfillment" while Padilla's was "Evangelism and the World". See *Let the Earth Hear His Voice: International Congress on World Evangelization, Lausanne, Switzerland.* Official Reference Volume (Minneapolis, MN: World Wide Publications, 1975).

[18] In *Let the Earth Hear His Voice.*

[19] Leighton Ford, A Vision Pursued: The Lausanne Movement 1974-1986. Fuller Lectures. Nov 1986.

we in the LCWE are looking at it. Rather, they tend to accentuate socio-political issues and rationalize their activities as a kind of evangelism. I do not believe they are in synch with the other congresses on evangelism which we are supporting in other regions of the world. Their agenda is quite different."[20]

But CLADE II went ahead to voice its understanding of the Gospel and its relation with the context, even if gathering fewer people[21] and suffering some funding difficulties in light of their position which was understood to be too radical and dangerous to some of the more conservative funding agencies, especially from the USA. That position, however, had already been highlighted at CLADE I and pointed to the future of this school of thought that could be identified as 'integral mission'. The 'Letter from CLADE II' said: "We have heard the Word of God, who speaks to us and who also hears the cry of those who suffer. We have lifted up our eyes to our own continent and have seen the drama and the tragedy that our people are living through in this moment of spiritual unrest, religious confusion, moral corruption, and social and political convulsion."[22]

This could sound like an old story, and it is, but not without reverberations in the present chapter of Lausanne, as seen in the biblical expositions on Ephesians held at Cape Town. There the Latin American voice coming through Ruth Padilla DeBorst's exposition affirmed the holistic dimension of the Gospel, while the North American John Piper, in his exposition, made an effort to affirm the priority of evangelism as it refers to eternal salvation, vis-à-vis our engagement in more historic dimensions of life. The old difficulties were on stage again, calling back the divisions within the evangelical family while at the same time inviting a historic Lausanne position: to embrace the whole spectrum of the evangelical family while affirming the holistic dimension of mission as expressed in the *Lausanne Covenant*.

Do Latin American Churches Need Lausanne? Which Areas Do We Need Help to Look Into?

As we have seen, the relationship between the Lausanne Movement and churches and Christian organizations in Latin America is not linear; it should here be added that many churches and Christian leaders in the continent are quite unfamiliar with Lausanne. It should be stressed, though, that there have been Latin Americans in the Movement throughout its journey. It should also not be forgotten that Lausanne is a Movement and as

[20] Peter Wagner, LCWE – Strategy Working Group, Jan 31, 1979. Archives of the Billy Graham Center: F-5, B-2, C-46.

[21] CLADE II gathered 266 people. See *Carta de Clade II, O Presente, o Futuro e a Esperança Cristã*. São Paulo: ABU Editora, 181.

[22] *The Lima Letter, Latin America, Nov 1979*, in 'Texts on Evangelical Social Ethics'.

such is based very much on relationships and a common agenda. And both need to be nurtured and have their limitations, seen keenly at times of transition. But so is CLADE and both of them have had moments of affirmation and of crisis. Both have faced their limitations and given significant contributions. Both have had funding challenges and the need to find new generations to embrace anew the call: 'The Whole Church Taking the Whole Gospel to the Whole World.' This is not an easy task as can be so clearly seen in the journey of the Lausanne Movement itself. During the last years Lausanne has, however, experienced a renewed vigour, of which Lausanne III was the best expression.

At this time the Lausanne Movement is attempting to reposition itself globally in order to become a living answer to its own call. The Movement was clearly re-energized by the Cape Town Congress, reorganized its global leadership and its operational structure for a global evangelical presence, impact and partnership in today's environment. An expression of this would be the International Deputy Directors. As they are placed in their different geographic regions, they have a positive possibility to listen to the regional leaders and build up a strategy that will respond to contextually detected needs. They will also be able to learn from others and contribute to them in order for the vision of world evangelization to be matured and advanced. And not least, to have at hand the *Cape Town Commitment* is an important step towards the affirmation of Lausanne's confessional identity as well as an attempt to read our times, identify new realities, challenges and opportunities as the Movement deepens its commitment to world evangelization.

As this listening and sharing exercise takes place, I venture to point to a few areas which we need to pay attention to in Latin America. This is done in the hope of joining with partners globally and establishing a fellowship table where avenues of ministerial obedience can be shaped as we live out our call today in our respective environments.

From Church Planting to Church Impact

The experience with church growth has been consistent and widespread throughout Latin America. While in some places that growth is already slowing down, it is still taking place, and in several other places it is still consistently strong. The overwhelming challenge and task of this time is to help so that a new and grown church sees itself as the 'new normal'. This church needs a new generation of leaders that will help it to become strong, consistent and focused on impacting our society. At this point of our journey we need to concentrate on the formation of a cadre of leaders who are called and capacitated to lead the church from a 'growing paradigm' to an 'impact paradigm' – an impact that should be built around the values of the Kingdom of God and not merely on measurable numerical outcomes or institutional standards. We need leaders that aim at a transformational impact that helps our societies to have a deeper glimpse of the nature of the Gospel and experience patterns of justice, peace and joy in their own circles and environment. We need help as we walk toward this challenge.

From Church Splitting to Church Unity

The reality of the evangelical churches in the continent is profoundly divisive. According to some voices, this divisiveness even helps the church grow (viewed from a sociological viewpoint). Our tradition in church splitting, however, is mostly built upon issues of power and of ego conflict. Such factors are fertilized by a lack of solid church structures as well as a society that is also emotionally divisive and likes new ventures. We depart from each other very easily, disregard history quite a lot and enjoy starting our own business. That's why church planting has become, in some places, quite an enterprise and the slogan 'small churches, big businesses' is so popular among us. We have, throughout the continent, a big need to listen to the Gospel and be converted to Jesus' prayer towards unity. We need to realize that the unity of the church is not an option but a command that must be obeyed, even though we are resistant to such obedience and don't even know how to do it in our emotional, volatile and charismatic context. We need help as we try to walk this path to become witnesses of unity.

Why is the 'Mission Movement' Slowing Down?

One of the beautiful and significant developments in the last decades is the establishment of a Latin American mission movement, as best seen in the existence of COMIBAM (*Cooperación Misionera Iberoamericana*). Only a few decades ago, to be a missionary meant being a 'gringo' living among us. Today it means to send out women, men and families to witness to the Lord in many different places throughout the world. A true wave touched many different mission movements and churches all over Latin America, and people were called to serve the Lord far away and have been kept there, nurtured there and supported there. By now there are thousands, involved in many diverse shapes of ministries, witnessing to others about the power of the global Gospel. This movement, however, is losing speed and steam while many churches spend all their energy inwardly, and mission agencies and movements ask themselves 'why'? We need help in answering this question and respond to it positively.

The Integral Mission Movement Needs to Walk Alongside a Still Growing Church

The movement of integral mission has a strong 'Latino flavor'. Latino leaders helped to identify in the Gospel the message of God who called us to full obedience and to design models and projects of incarnational witness by which beautiful signs of God's Kingdom would emerge and become a testimony to Christ. This movement, however, does not come without challenges. It has never been able to enter in a substantial way into the tissue of the churches in this continent. It has remained micro, and while being lived out at that level, it hasn't succeeded in being lived out at the level of the mega-churches, or to become a factor to impact society even in places where evangelical churches have become a substantial percentage of the population. We need to recognize that it also has, in many cases, suffered the temptation to stay quite cerebral, even if put in action, not being able to develop a spirituality of prayer, joy and emotions. We need help to deepen and expand the holistic understanding of the mission of the church in order for it to become *integral*.

These are only a few areas that should be looked into, as I discern them. I outline them as a plea not to leave us alone but to partner with us, even in spite of us, if necessary. We need the global church around us, lest we become too comfortable in our own territory and keep busy building our own walls. The experience in Cape Town, where many Latinos felt estranged, made it evident that we have lost much contact with the global church and with some of the major developments in the world today, especially as it relates to the re-emergence of other world religions, particularly Islam, and the reality of churches facing hardship and even being persecuted in many places today. We certainly need help to open our eyes, widen our prayers and expand our ministerial frontiers.

To become familiar with and dive into the *Cape Town Commitment* is certainly a good avenue for the Latino leaders to walk. There the necessary links of identity, challenges and opportunities, as well as a call to humble and transparent fellowship, can be identified as an invitation to become a part of the global church with a serving attitude.

Two Signs of Hope to Nurture the Walk of Today and of Tomorrow

Latin America Needs HIS

It was at Lausanne II (Manila 89) that Africans, Portuguese and Brazilians came together in a room as the opportunity was provided for the Portuguese-speaking delegation to share about what was going on in regard to Christian work in their respective places. At one point, and I remember the scenario, a Portuguese leader took the microphone and said: "Please do not send us any more Brazilian missionaries without even telling us about it!" – only to explain that some unexpected Brazilian missionaries who go to Portugal show up saying that God sent them there, and do this with an arrogance that conveys the message that 'renewal' has come with them to the country. It was a hard yet important word for the Brazilians to swallow. It is my perception that during the last decades we, Latin American

Christians, have tended to get enchanted with our growth, arrogant in regard to the blessings God has given us, and self-sufficient in light of our own successes with church growth, multiplication of ministries and the gain of influence in our own societies. We need HIS: *Humility*, *Integrity* and *Simplicity*. Lausanne III told us that and showed us the way to go about it. As all participants were invited into a liturgy of repentance and a call towards a new commitment marked by HIS, we Latin Americans needed to stay in line in order not to miss this gracious opportunity. We had the opportunity, at Cape Town 2010, to look into our own mirror in order to conclude that, as part of the evangelical family, we have to face traits of arrogance, self-sufficiency and sophistication and, therefore, are called to repentance. We did not like what we saw but we also heard the call of the Gospel to come back to the Word and allow us to walk into the arms of Jesus. It is there, embraced by him, that we meet each other and recognize that we are all part of God's family.

It is not easy to partner with us, Latin Americans. But, please, don't give up on us. We need the global church of Christ around us and the Lausanne Movement is an expression and a tool of it.

The Letter of the Brazilian to the African Delegation

One of the most meaningful and moving events at Lausanne III happened in one of the regional gatherings, when a few representatives of the Brazilian delegation presented the African brothers and sisters with a letter of repentance and a plea for forgiveness that said as follows:

> After the discovery and for almost 400 years the Brazil colony and the independent Brazil relied on slave labor for the formation of plantations, for digging our mines, for building our houses, our cities and our nation. So we have committed the sin of kidnapping people, destroying families and villages; we have left behind plenty of orphans, destroyed homes, villages and harmed deeply your nations.
>
> We have committed the sin of assassination, of treating human beings made in the image of God as beasts, imposing on your people moral, psychological and physical violence, abuse and suppression – and sub-human conditions of life. We have committed the sin of destroying whenever possible their national, ethnic and familiar identity.[23]

As that letter was presented, a deep and mutual commotion took place as an expression of deep historical sinfulness and suffering but also of a relief that comes out of repentance and opens the door of reconciliation and the experience of new fellowship. This is exactly what happened at that event. And when an African delegation came to the Brazilians in order to offer their forgiveness to us and to pray for that circle, reconciliation was affirmed and experienced at that very time.

[23] Letter of Oct 24, 2010.

As I remember that afternoon, a Brazilian lady missionary working in Africa comes to my heart and my mind. She couldn't but sob deeply and continuously as if a heavy load had been lifted from her shoulders and a new horizon of forgiveness and even of ministry had taken its place.

As I refer to this experience, I know that many others certainly took place during those days at Lausanne III, as well as at other events before and in the future.

Conclusion

Many years have passed since Edinburgh 1910. Thanks to a leadership that protested the trends of that conference, evangelization was made a priority for many people, missions and churches, and today this continent knows the Gospel much better than yesterday.

Fewer but still many years passed since Samuel Escobar delivered at CLADE I that keynote address which stated clearly, for his and for the coming generations, that the Gospel is a gift from God to rescue, renew and promote all dimensions of life and the life of all.

Latin America is rich and diverse but has common aspects that we celebrate and suffer as well. While today many of our countries experience democracy and economic growth, only yesterday many were experiencing military dictatorships, being champions in unjust distribution of wealth, and being a field of experimentation for organizations like the International Monetary Fund.

In this beautiful, graceful and suffering continent, many missions and churches have found their place of vocation. Thus, today we celebrate a vital and strong evangelical church. Millions have been found by the Gospel of Jesus Christ and have been transformed by him. However, the impact of those experiences and of the presence of so many big and different churches in the continent has not substantially changed the patterns of unjust distribution of wealth and of corrupt structures in our societies. It has not avoided the explosion of violence, especially among young people, in so many places. Our churches are packed with young people, yet street children are too many, too lonely and still exploited and abandoned. Our churches are getting more and more sophisticated but the level of poverty is still excruciating in many of our countries, cities and villages. While our political parties receive more and more so-called 'evangelicals', the level of corrupt manoeuvering is not diminishing and the credibility of those politicians is not that different from others.

We need the Gospel to keep on calling us to conversion. We have and want no other vocation than the one that calls us to listen to and to embrace the whole Gospel – a Gospel for all people and for the whole person. This is a common vocation for the whole church, and the Lausanne Movement is a sign and an expression of it. Latin America needs to be part of this.

Moving What to Where and Why? Reflections on the Lausanne Movement from an Asian Perspective

Paul Joshua Bhakiaraj

Introduction

If 'Evangelical Christianity' can be described as 'an international and multicultural religion of great, if also complex, vitality,'[1] then could it perhaps be true to say that the Lausanne Movement has had a significant part to play in that intriguing development? Put together, this observation and perhaps even a cursory glance around the world would suggest that the evangelical movement is not a single or monochrome entity but is now a rather complex set of relationships, networks, sub-cultures and theological emphasises. It extends all across the world and, in addition to its presence within established and mainline churches, it is also represented by its own denominations, networks of churches and organizations. Across this spectrum its unique family resemblance is clearly evident, in that its central declaration seems to converge around a few salient theological affirmations; yet its diversity is also a striking feature; particular expressions of it around the world will differ in significant ways. Perhaps nowhere else does this core commonality and colourful diversity find as clear expression, or is afforded as much space to exist, as it does in the Lausanne Movement. If such a 'breadth within boundaries'[2] is what its leaders identified as one primary feature of its ethos, then perhaps the Lausanne Movement may stand out as a key shaper of the evangelical expression of Christianity in 20th and 21st century Christian history.

This chapter will focus on the Lausanne Movement's contribution to such commonality and diversity as may be found within the evangelical movement from the perspective of an Asian participant. Although I came to participate personally in the Lausanne Movement only in July 2006 at the Younger Leaders' Gathering held in Port Dickson, Malaysia, I was

---

[1] Mark Noll, 'What is Evangelical?' in Gerald R. McDermott (ed), *The Oxford Handbook of Evangelical Theology* (Oxford, UK: OUP, 2010), 19-34.

[2] Doug Birdsall & Lindsay Brown, 'Foreword', in Julia Cameron (ed), *Cape Town Commitment: A Confession of Faith and a Call to Action* (Lausanne Movement, 2011), 5.

introduced to the Movement in 1974 as a young child. My father was a participant at the historic 1974 gathering in Lausanne. At that time, all I was interested in were the Swiss chocolates that he brought back for us, but over time I learnt the significant impact that this gathering had had on him personally as well as on the thousands of participants and beyond. As I began to prepare formally for my own ministry, my studies introduced me to the many key people, processes and pronouncements of the Lausanne Movement. While my own theological sensitivities resonated with some of its emphasis, I did struggle with others. Nevertheless, I realise how significant the Lausanne Movement has become for the worldwide Christian community. So my participant's perspective is as one who has been encouraged and equipped by the Movement and also as one who has struggled with some emphases of Christian brothers and sisters within the Movement.

History

Ever since it began in 1974 at the World Congress on World Evangelization held at Lausanne, a colourful diversity has found expression in the Lausanne Movement.[3] From the participants, to the speakers and the issues discussed, it was, to a certain extent, a representation and expression of the spread and colourful vitality of the world evangelical movement. While clearly it was led by Billy Graham, Jack Dain, John Stott and others, it nevertheless had leaders from around the world as an important part of the Movement. Asians figured prominently there in the persons of Saphir Athyal and Billy Kim among many others. In 1989, when the second Congress was held in Manila, Philippines, the geographical location also added a sense of the worldwide scope of Church. This location in Asia also urgently reminded the participants of the broad range of needs that existed, which had to be addressed. The vision emanating from these two gatherings set for the Lausanne Movement the glorious yet challenging task of learning – and being gripped by – what the whole Gospel is, what the whole church represents, and what engaging the whole world with the whole Gospel would really entail. This historic agenda also came to represent the objective behind the convening of the third Lausanne Congress. So while the unity under the banner of the Gospel of Jesus Christ represents the core commonality of the Movement, the fact that it is spread among the world's nations, tribes, peoples and languages, expressing a colourful cultural collage, represents its diversity. Thus, the Lausanne Movement entered the 21st century with a renewed vigour.

---

[3] A brief historical account of the Lausanne Movement can be found in Robert Hunt, 'A History of the Lausanne Movement, 1974-2010' in *IBMR*, Vol. 35, No. 2, April 2011, 81-84.

Preparation for Cape Town 2010

Preparation for the third Congress began many years before 2010. The choice of Cape Town as the venue was an inspired one. Besides being situated in and representing the Majority World where the church is growing remarkably, it also possessed some historical interest of missiological import. In 1792, when William Carey travelled around the African continent on his way to India, he observed its beauty and later called for a world missions conference to be held there in 1810. It was now about two hundred years later that his dream was to become a reality. The Chairman of the Lausanne Movement Doug Birdsall quipped: "We believe the 200th anniversary of William Carey's vision and the centennial of its fulfilment is an appropriate time to, once again, encourage international leaders to come together to chart the course for the work of world evangelization in the 21st century."[4]

Consultations that drew in people from a range of backgrounds were held in a few places to enable a process of worldwide listening and discernment. As a member of the Theology Working Group, I was involved in its study process, from 2007 to 2009, which sought to provide background reflection and enable a direct theological feed into the planning and preparation. As a participant in another programme planning event held in Oxford, UK, in February 2008, it was my privilege to get to grips with some of the real issues that were being discussed by other groups and realise the wonderful resources that we possessed in the world church. Furthermore, I was a member of the team that represented the Lausanne Movement at the Edinburgh 2010 gathering. This provided more opportunities for interaction and reflection on the shaping of Cape Town 2010 by bringing insights and ideas from the interaction there. All this fed into asking pertinent questions: What were the big issues that the world faced and what were some of the trends that needed recognition and response? What were the resources that the world church possessed? How might we reaffirm the truth of the Gospel of Christ in this kind of a world? How might we shape the programme at Cape Town 2010 as we engaged with those issues and employed those resources? Given this as our backdrop, we were also encouraged to consider how we might make Cape Town 2010 truly global and representative of the worldwide church. Whether or not that was achieved in every way possible might be open to debate, even disagreement, but having been a part of this consultative process, it seems to me that there was a clear desire for that to be the case. Also, as a matter for the record, is the manner in which speakers were chosen and guided in their preparation for the Congress. This included the plenary sessions, as well as the multiplex and dialogue sessions that were held in between the plenaries. As one who was invited to lead such a

---

4 www.lausanne.org/en/about/news-releases/81-lausanne-iii-cape-town-2010-international-congress-on-world-evangelization.html Last accessed Oct 24th 2013.

session ('Local Leaders in the Global Church'), I had the privilege of getting to know that process from the inside.

Cape Town 2010

When October 2010 arrived, there was an air of expectancy that was palpable in many circles. Thousands of people were praying for the forthcoming Congress; some were writing on blogs, magazines and other publications; at many a site hundreds more were preparing for what was called GlobaLink, a virtual link to the Congress for those who were unable to participate in person. Come October 17th 2010, there were more than 4,000 participants from 198 countries who arrived expectantly at Cape Town. Besides this there were 650 virtual connections to the Congress from about ninety countries. The participants at Cape Town, in and of themselves, were thought to be the most representative Christian gathering in history – which is no small feat in itself!

The Congress opened with a bang! There were loud and enthusiastic African drumbeats, sounded by drummers in bright and colourful costumes, who invited participants to the main entrance. They then led them into the massive congress hall in dance and the waving of flags. This large hall was to be the venue for all the plenary sessions both in the morning and evening. The plenary sessions, including Bible expositions, more theologically oriented addresses, as well as strategic ones, provided a valuable opportunity for the Lausanne Movement to declare for itself and the watching world its theological convictions, analyse some of the urgent challenges that the world faces, and then seek to address them by setting priorities for world evangelization in the decades ahead. The depth of engagement with the Scriptures, the breadth of the issues dealt with, and the scope of the priorities affirmed, were most encouraging. One noteworthy focus of the Congress, and to my mind much overdue, was the attention paid to the marketplace and the potential of disciples of Christ to exert an influence in that realm. The empowering of all God's people for service, wherever they happen to live and work, is a biblically sound emphasis, and its recovery and emphasis at Cape Town 2010 was a step forward indeed for the evangelical movement. The other encouraging feature was the visible and active role that women played. Younger people and children were thankfully featured as a key priority as well, which bodes well for the inclusion of all God's people in our missionary vision.

The Bible expositions were a good start to the day. That we had a representative set of leaders from around the world brought both diversity and vitality to the pulpit. They represented differing positions on the evangelical theological spectrum, which was a commendable move on the part of the organisers, just as equally commendable were the expositions offered. Three other plenary sessions made a particularly powerful impression on me – and doubtless on thousands of others as well. The testimony of Gyeong Ju Son, the young Korean student whose love for the Lord and dedication to serve him, come what may, together with Libby Little's testimony of the martyrdom of her husband while on medical service in Afghanistan, and in a similar vein the testimony of Bishop Ben Kwashi from Nigeria, were all a vital reminder that Christian mission is costly and involves much suffering. Yet out of their suffering these brothers and sisters were able to impress on us the deep joy that is theirs who serve and suffer for their Lord. A second plenary session that remains fresh in my mind was the presentation made by Shadia Qubti, the young Arab lady, and the young Jewish man, Dan Sered. In a context where the two peoples are at war with each other, it was clearly challenging to hear how, because of the Gospel of Jesus Christ, they were able to work in partnership with each other for the benefit of society at large. God was certainly reconciling peoples in his name. All this and more were salutary reminders for the participants, that Christian discipleship is a costly pursuit, and serious is the commitment that will be necessary in serving the Lord in a world of promise and pain.

Gaps were nevertheless evident in the programme. Most conspicuous among them was a dedicated session/s for an in-depth engagement with world religions, including Hinduism, Islam, Buddhism and Traditional Religions. From an Asian perspective particularly, this was a rather glaring omission, for the contemporary world cannot be understood without reference to the world's religions. While some plenaries and other sessions may have alluded to them, the fact that there were none dedicated exclusively to this study and analysis was felt by many. This ought to be a key priority for the church, but unfortunately the Lausanne Movement lost out on a valuable and crucial opportunity to discuss and declare its own position vis-à-vis world religions.

While there were clear signs that old battles fought in the Lausanne Movement (e.g. the exact relationship between evangelism and social action) were for many a matter of history, there were nevertheless indications that all had not been settled for others. Various emphases made from the stage, and interactions during the Congress, revealed that this continued to remain an issue of contention. Akin to that were the remnants of a pragmatic approach to evangelism, defined primarily as verbal proclamation and numerical addition to the church. In fact, at one plenary we had a grand scheme for world evangelization, all with unreached people groups explained and tabulated neatly. Although history has proven this to be a faulty approach practically (theologically, of course, it was suspect from Day One), this kind of thinking, which hatched strategies that would reach the world within a certain time period and through the use of certain tools, were clearly visible. That, even after about forty years, such issues continue to remain, for some, points not of minor nuance but of major significance suggest that these issues will continue to remain a fault line within the Movement.

The Lausanne Movement in and from Asia

Asian Christians played an important role in the Cape Town Congress. To begin with, it was most gratifying to learn of the number of people who supported the Congress in prayer. There were churches and organizations that spent time praying especially for the Congress and the participants. This created anticipation for a work of God at, and even subsequent to, the Congress. Meetings to carry the emphases further afield were held across the continent, where many people that were not able to go to Cape Town were blessed. It was most encouraging to learn of the number who supported the Congress financially. From smaller gifts that came from individuals to larger gifts that individuals and churches gave, it was a significant development for the Lausanne Movement to be funded to that extent by Asian Christians. South Asians from the diaspora and from within the sub-continent gave sacrificially. Chinese businessmen and women provided for many other Asian leaders who otherwise would not have been able to participate in the Congress. In fact, one of them even sold his house and donated the funds so that his brothers and sisters from Asia could take part.

Despite such magnanimous acts, it was particularly sad that the large Chinese delegation were not able to participate in the Congress. The excitement they harboured as they met in the airport to travel to Cape Town was short-lived as they were refused permission to leave their country. Surely the Congress was that much poorer by their absence. To compensate in a small way, it was gratifying to learn that in June 2013 the Lausanne Movement organised the Asian Church Leaders Forum in Seoul, Korea. About 100 Chinese leaders, and about 200 leaders from around the world, gathered to celebrate and to reaffirm their commitment to the Lord, each other and to world mission. It was a time to also reflect on the challenges that Asian, particularly Chinese, Christians faced in that land of opportunity and obstacle.[5]

The importance of the continent of Asia for the Lausanne Movement was further stressed when the Global Leadership Forum (GLF) was held at Bangalore, India, in June 2013. "Drawing 350 participants from over sixty nations, selected from the public arenas, churches, agencies and the media, its main work was to assess progress in issues identified in the *Cape Town Commitment*, and to stimulate further collaborative action towards the goals of its *Call to Action.*'[6] As one who participated in planning, preparing and participating in the event, it was most rewarding to be involved in serving and blessing the leaders of the Lausanne Movement and through them the world church. Among the many results accruing from that meeting are

---

[5] See the report at: www.lausanne.org/en/connect/regions/east-asia/updates/2145-asian-church-leaders-forum-report.html. Last accessed 24th Oct 2013.

[6] www.lausanne.org/en/about/news-releases/2127-strides-for-lausanne-movement.html. Last accessed 24th Oct 2013.

global consultations that are being held on a number of topics identified at Cape Town and clarified at Bangalore.

Equally important at the Bangalore GLF was the inducting of an Asian leader, in the person of Michael Oh, as the new CEO of the Movement. After years of dedicated and tireless service, Doug Birdsall made way for younger and fresh leadership in a God-honouring manner. With such a leadership change came a notable shift, not least in the moving of the headquarters of the movement from USA to Japan, where Michael Oh lives and serves. This internationalizing of the movement, and the inclusion of younger people, augurs well for the movement in the 21st century. Within that larger process, all these are surely clear signs that Asia continues to be a continent in which the Lausanne Movement thrives and from which it is now poised to serve and bless the world church in a fresh and new way.

Studying the Evangelical Movement

The Cape Town 2010 Congress and the Bangalore Global Leadership Forum 2013 were valuable showcases to display the diversity and affirm the commonality that is characteristic of the evangelical movement worldwide. This is the present reality we unmistakably notice in our world today. Yet when one works through studies of the evangelical movement, some of which have helpfully emphasised its history and theology as constituting its core essence,[7] there is however a propensity to treat it as a purely western phenomenon. In its origins, its shape and character, the evangelical movement, for the most part, is seen as a reality stamped and moulded by its western experience. Many such studies betray an obvious Euro-centricity which does little justice to the already observed diversity and commonality. If such studies are to be believed, the evangelical movement remains a North Atlantic phenomenon moulded and shaped by those realities. If it is recognized at all as being present outside that region, then it remains just a localised expression of what is primarily a western reality and hence not weighty enough for detailed scrutiny and analysis.

For example, in an ambitiously titled book *Evangelical Futures: A Conversation on Theological Method*,[8] we find a group pondering on the shape of evangelical theological reflection. While the choice of the title asserts that this book speaks for all evangelicalism, little do we find within its pages on the evangelical movement around the world. Apart from one author who includes a sub-section, 'Challenges from Africa and Asia',[9]

---

[7] One well-known definition highlighted four central themes: biblicism, crucicentrism, conversionism and activism. See David Bebbington, *Evangelicalism in Modern Britain: A History from the 1730s to the 1980s* (London: Unwin Hyman, 1989), 2-17.

[8] John Stackhouse Jr (ed), (Grand Rapids, MI: Baker Books, 2000).

[9] Alister McGrath, 'Evangelical Theological Method: State of the Art', 15-37. The section I refer to is found on 35.

though without offering any real engagement with Africa or Asia, let alone citing a work or conversing with a scholar from that part of the world, the rest of the book follows that now well traversed North Atlantic road, which implicitly locks the evangelical movement into that particular region of the world. Similarly, in another ambitiously titled book, *The Futures of Evangelicalism: Issues and Prospects,*[10] which it must be noted makes a laudable effort to address some of the key issues western evangelicalism faces (including theology, church, biblical interpretation, mission, ethics, spirituality, philosophy and politics), we have a set of eleven essays representing a collaborative reflection on the state and prospects of the evangelical movement. Now, if the title of the book was qualified so as declare that it was an analysis of western evangelicalism, it would have been quite true to its contents. Instead what we have here are some respected authors displaying a rather distressing myopia vis-à-vis the very thing that they intend to analyse – the future of evangelicalism. Thankfully though, there is one redeeming chapter in that collection, and as it so happens, it is the one that deals with mission! Here the author, rather refreshingly but quite atypically for the book, focuses on the Majority World as a key factor in Christian mission. In fact, he even goes to the extent of closing his chapter with these words:

> And as we seek a more biblical understanding of what it means to live and relate in truly human ways as an expression of the gospel itself, we in the West will have a lot to learn from the less impoverished traditions of humanity in community found among Christians in the non-Western world. In this as in so much else, the strength of evangelicalism in the Two Thirds World will be a major asset to the world church in mission.[11]

Unfortunately, such a neglect, indeed even the silencing of the colourful and vibrant character of the evangelical movement around the world, is what we have come to expect in much scholarship on evangelicalism from the west. Indeed, it seems that it is a rare scholar who recognizes the vitality of the evangelical movement in the Majority World, and even rarer still to recognize it as being an asset to the world church.[12]

---

[10] Craig Bartholomew, Robin Parry and Andrew West (eds), (Leicester, UK: IVP, 2003).

[11] Chris Wright, 'Future Trends in Mission', 149-163.

[12] Of the few that exist, two books that affirm the role Majority World Christians play within the evangelical movement are: Mark Hutchinson and Ogbu Kalu (eds), *A Global Faith: Essays on Evangelicalism and Globalization* (Sydney, CSAC, 1998); Donald Lewis, *Christianity Reborn: The Global Expansion of Evangelicalism in the Twentieth Century* (Grand Rapids, MI: Eerdmans, 2004). In terms of evangelical theology and its engagement with the Majority World, one important book is Timothy C. Tennent, *Theology in the Context of World Christianity* (Grand Rapids, MI: MI: Zondervan, 2007).

The Evangelical Movement in and from the Majority World

From my Asian perspective, it seems that to facilitate a process of learning from each other (i.e. western evangelicalism learning from the evangelical movement in the Majority World and vice versa), the Lausanne Movement is a valuable platform and indeed a catalyst. In the remainder of this chapter I would like to demonstrate how that has and continues to be the case. Among the many one could choose from, I will attend to three issues that have attracted the attention of the Lausanne Movement, and in turn suggest that these are valuable examples of how the Lausanne Movement has been serving the world evangelical movement creatively and effectively.

The first issue pertains to the relationship, already alluded to, between evangelism and social action. The particular contribution of two Latin American theologian-evangelists is to be noted here. It was such a joy to see and hear both René Padilla and Samuel Escobar at Cape Town reminisce about their experiences at the first Lausanne Congress in 1974, and the struggles they subsequently faced in urging the evangelical community around the world to see, understand and practise this truth of the Gospel. We were reminded, in the persons of these two stalwarts and the others who worked alongside them, that it was the Latin American church, assisted by the African church and the Asian church, which urged the Lausanne Movement to grow in its appreciation of, mature in its practice of, and serve the world with, the holistic Gospel of Jesus Christ. The role that INFEMIT, the association which they along with other key leaders from around the world created, has played is a key factor in this development. The evangelical movement worldwide has a debt they owe to the Latin American church for the creative and constructive manner in which they led the world evangelical movement to greater maturity and greater efficiency in its missionary calling. It was the seeds that they sowed at Lausanne 74 that have over the years borne much fruit around the world.[13]

The second issue pertains to spiritual warfare. The African continent, though this is true of many other places as well, is a prime example of the urgency for and vital role that such a ministry plays within the larger missionary calling of the church worldwide. However, western theology that accompanied forms of Christianity brought to Africa from outside, though doubtless helpful in many ways, had its limits. Because as a noted scholar observes:

> Western theology is, in general, too small for Africa; it has been cut down to fit the small-scale universe demanded by the Enlightenment, which set and jealously guarded a frontier between the empirical world and the world of

[13] Of the many books that can be cited here, two stand out. René Padilla & Chris Sugden (eds), *How Evangelicals Endorsed Social Responsibility* (Cambridge: Grove Books, 1985); Al Tizon, *Transformation After Lausanne: Radical Evangelical Mission in Global-Local Perspective* (Oxford, UK: Regnum, 2008).

> spirit. Most Africans live in a larger, more populated universe in which the frontier is continually being crossed. It is a universe that comprehends what Paul calls the principalities and powers. Africans require a theology that brings Christ to bear on every part of the universe, making evident the victory over the principalities that Paul ascribes to Christ's triumphal chariot of the Cross.[14]

To recognize and engage with this expansive universe that many in the Majority World inhabit, the Lausanne Movement organised a consultation in Nairobi, Kenya, in August 2000 called *Deliver Us From Evil* (DUFE). A book consisting of the papers presented at that consultation was published later in the hope that the wider evangelical community would understand and engage with such realities.[15] Once again, one may recognize here an instance where the evangelical movement in the Majority World takes the lead in addressing urgent theological and missiological dilemmas that they face. Recognising that western theology had few answers, they worked collaboratively with scholars and practitioners from around the world to find answers. We find the African church urging the world Christian community to grow in its appreciation for the potent Gospel that animates her life, and grow in its appreciation for the efficacy of the Holy Spirit to empower Christians to live unbounded lives. The evangelical movement worldwide has a debt they owe to the African church for the creative and constructive manner in which they led the world evangelical movement to a greater maturity and greater efficiency in its missionary calling.

The third issue, as already alluded to, pertains to the persecution and suffering that Christians face around the world, but perhaps particularly in Asia. China and India stand out as noteworthy sites, where discipleship is marked by suffering for the sake of Christ. This was particularly highlighted at Cape Town both by the absence of the Chinese delegation and the powerful testimony of Gyeong Ju Son, the North Korean schoolgirl. Persecution that Christians suffer is not a theoretical problem that is to be argued away; on the contrary, it is an existential eventuality that many in Asia face. From more subtle forms within the family to blatant and violent action against them for meeting to pray, Christians live with the constant danger of losing their lives. One can never be sure that when one goes to church that it is free from bombs planted under the pews, or that violent mobs do not come charging into the building where the congregation is gathering, to tear their Bibles, beat up the Church leaders, and violently disrupt or break up the meetings. We have come to learn from

---

[14] Andrew Walls, 'The Great Commission 1910-2010', in W. Stephen Gunter and Elaine Robinson (eds), *Considering the Great Commission: Evangelism and Mission in the Wesleyan Spirit* (Nashville, TN: Abingdon Press, 2005), 19.

[15] Scott Moreau, Tokunboh Adeyemo, David G. Burnett, Bryant L. Myers and Hwa Yung (eds), *Deliver Us From Evil: An Uneasy Frontier in Christian Mission* (Monrovia, CA: MARC, 2002).

Christians in Asia that Christian discipleship is a costly matter; it may entail losing your family, your livelihood, and sometime even your life.

How does the Christian community cope with such volatile and dangerous situations? How does a pastor prepare his congregation for such an eventuality? What recourse do Christians have to the political machinery of their nations? What if the political machinery itself is anti-Christian, and aids and abets such acts of violence toward the Christian community? These and more are questions that Asian Christians live with constantly. These are realities that they face every day. It is from such a deep and vital spirituality that is forged in such a hazardous context that Asian Christianity has many lessons to teach the worldwide church. Asian Christianity grows, because the blood of its martyrs, both historic and contemporary, has been its seed.

Moving What and to Where and Why?

In all these cases (and there are clearly many more that I could cite but want of space and time forbids me), the evangelical Christian community from the Majority World has lived through and endured grave dilemmas and faced serious questions. Yet at the same time, as we have been reminded, it is growing at an astonishing rate. The churches are outstripping the number of Christians in other parts of the world. Clearly, in their ongoing journey of Christian discipleship, they have many significant lessons to teach the church around the world. They represent mature and deep resources that this worldwide community can draw from and indeed even model their lives upon. That is not to say that they encounter little failure, disappointments, scandals and other such crises. While that is surely true, the Majority World Christian community is nevertheless a valid and integral part of the worldwide evangelical movement and as such is worthy of inclusion in any representation of the evangelical movement. It would be a severely lopsided Christianity that is presented if the evangelical movement of the Majority World were not mentioned.

I would also like to suggest that perhaps equally important in any study of the evangelical movement of the 20th and 21st centuries will be the role played by the Lausanne Movement. It has by God's grace created a platform open to many from these regions of the world. From this platform, Majority World voices have had, and continue to have, the opportunity to share their experiences, their successes, their failures, their dilemmas, their questions. Equally, since it has been led by many leaders and statesmen/-women from the ranks of the Majority World church itself, the Lausanne Movement has been a genuine international effort. In that sense, the Lausanne Movement can be seen both as a key facilitator of the evangelical movement in the Majority World and as an able representative of that phenomenon. Though there surely will be times when that seemed less visible than at others, it can nevertheless legitimately lay claim to performing both those roles. To answer the question that forms the title of this chapter, based on the foregoing, I would like to submit that the Lausanne Movement has particularly helped move the worldwide evangelical movement toward a greater theological maturity, wider ecumenical sensitivity and deeper missionary efficacy. While such a legacy is something to be thankful to God for, it equally lays a great responsibility on current and future generations to live up to, and even climb to greater heights, for the glory of the Triune God whom we love, worship and serve.

A MIDDLE EASTERN EVANGELICAL PERSPECTIVE ON THE CAPE TOWN CONGRESS: FROM MINORITY MENTALITY TO ACTIVE PARTICIPATION

Andrea Zaki

This paper provides a critical reading of the discontinuity and communication in evangelical thought and its relationship to Middle Eastern society. This relationship is historic (more than 150 years); I will, however, focus on this communication and discontinuity after the Cape Town Congress, and its implications.

Participation in the Cape Town Congress was unique in that, for the first time in such a context, worldwide evangelicals were exposed to and discussed non-traditional issues such as evangelism, religious freedom, peaceful co-existence, tolerance, and pluralism. The spirit of the Congress, in terms of worship and theological reflection, helped us rethink the future of evangelicals in the region in a different way.

The Intellectual Challenges that Encourage Discontinuity

There are many intellectual challenges that have increased the gap within our society. These challenges include scepticism, which limits all forms of national identity to religious identity, and considers it to be the sole indicator of human identity. This contributes to the curb of pluralism and creates a single-loyalty attitude.

The challenge of questioning the doctrine of 'the other' creates a kind of bitterness leading to violence, withdrawal, and marginalization. This doubt cannot easily be removed; in some cases this negative mental image is amplified and turned into a contempt of 'the other' doctrine, evolving into rejection of 'the other', and in some cases even isolation. This doubt may take the form of pressuring 'the other' to change his religion and conform, either legitimately or illegitimately. All of this leads to rejection of 'the other', provoking sectarian strife and creating a huge gap in the community, isolating and confining some Christians in the Middle East to their own communities, rather than being open and integrating into society. This in return leads to intensified violent sectarianism, as experienced during the past year.

There is a problem in the social and cultural alienation that results from a sense of marginalization and exclusion over an extended time, often caused by unfair practices of some leaders and officials. It also results in evangelicals excluding themselves from culture and civilization. In the cultural reality of the Middle East there exists also a biased treatment of their heritage. Discrimination of history and heritage has formed misconceptions and contributed to making co-existence a relative aspect; this has made evangelicals value their own heritage. Some groups have called for a refusal to use the Arabic language and consider it alien, leading to further estrangement and alienation.

The Minority Mentality

Given the importance of the debate that took place in the Middle East in the 1990s on the concept of minority and the possibility of describing Christians in the Middle East as a minority, I use the term 'minority' as a numerical indicator. With a quick glance at characteristics of the minority mentality, we can summarize some of them as follows:

Divine Intervention and the Millennial Kingdom

The mentality of the minority tends to include apocalyptic dreams represented in the return of Christ and the Millennial Reign. The second coming of Christ will contribute to ending pressure, creating a new society with no religious minorities. Here I do not discuss the doctrine of 'millennialism' as a theological doctrine; rather I discuss the political, social and cultural dimensions of this doctrine. Christ reigning on earth for a thousand years, as some believe, will provide an ideal model for a new government, based on divine right, which does not practise discrimination but achieves equality. This visionary dream of the Millennial Kingdom reflects the vision of religious connotations of political, social and cultural significance. It represents escaping from the pressures of current reality to ideal future dreams. When the minority thought and life in this manner are transferred from the world itself to the other world at the celestial level, history stops completely and thought becomes limited and not subjected to analysis and study.

Miracles

The increasing pressure on the minority makes them perceive miracles as an affirmation of God's support for the group, interfering in their favour. When the minority is subjected to pressure and suspicion of its faith and doctrine, threatening it with extinction, belief in miracles provides certainty of divine protection for the minority. Perhaps the repeated talks in the

Middle East about individual and collective testimonies reflect this attribute.

It is important to note here that I am not discussing the theological perspective of miracles, but rather a sociological perspective. I believe miracles are God's divine intervention in human history.

Identity

One of the most important contradictions in the minority's mind is religious identity. At a time when minorities need to push the community towards national identity, they slip and resort to religious identity. This contradiction creates a sort of hypocrisy affecting credibility of national loyalty. At the same time, they always fear the danger of a national melting-pot which makes them uphold their religious identity. This is what has happened in the Middle East during the past few decades as evangelicals turned to isolation. This complex situation has caused confusion and in some cases caused people to affiliate with extremists to use religious identity for political reasons.

Cultural and Linguistic Isolation

Minorities resort to linguistic isolation, which represents a sub-culture. In the opinion of the minority, using a particular language is a kind of uniqueness, but many times this uniqueness leads to isolation and misunderstanding. Perhaps the best evidence of this linguistic isolation is the way evangelicals present the doctrine of the Trinity in an Islamic society. We know that this theological doctrine was clearly formulated in the fourth century AD with Greek expressions, such as *hypostasis*, to indicate that the Father, the Son and the Holy Spirit are three distinct *hypostases* in one God. While this vocabulary was significant at the time when it was used, and changed the cultural environment and the establishment of Arab-Islamic civilization, today the same ideas require a new theological vocabulary.

Language plays an important role in communication. Therefore evangelicals need to speak the language understood by the public. The creation of a closed culture leads to isolation, alienation and marginalization, and so we are now invited to review our linguistics in order to build bridges and have a creative presence.

Briefly, the above are attributes constituting a minority mentality, and now we should look deeply at the reality in which we live. We live in an Arab-Islamic civilization, and simultaneously constitute a religious numerical minority. These two factors represent an important basis in the formulation of the evangelical presence in the Middle East today. From the experience in the Lausanne Congress, with the presence of evangelicals from across the world, and by theological, devotional and social action, it has become evident for us to think and act differently. Below, I will present the theological foundations of spirituality as well as community-based initiatives as two models of evangelical presence in the Middle East.

Theological Foundation of Spirituality

Evangelists in the Middle East were affected by two trends that formed contemporary evangelical spirituality: the first was the arrival of the Puritans with some of the early missionaries, and the second is Egyptian Coptic monasticism. These two trends have contributed significantly to the formulation of spiritual isolationism that implies that only ascetics can be spiritual persons. This has increased, in one way or another, the isolation of Christians in the Middle East, and has even made this isolation and seclusion a positive aspect.

Spirituality is a partnership, comprised of participation. The word 'participation' here goes beyond the traditional and narrow concept of giving and means equality. Although the word 'equality' is used in many ways, I use it here as a synonym for partnership.

Christianity has a point of view in this matter. Christians believe that man was created in the image of God (Genesis 1:27) and that sin corrupted that divine image. However, through the death and resurrection of Christ, this image was restored. The Apostle Peter expressed this idea, saying, "We may be … (humans) partakers of the divine nature" (2 Peter 1:4) and sons of God (Romans 8:14, 16, 19, 21; 9:8, 26; Galatians 3:26), meaning we have regained the image in which we were created.

From here, we see the profound meaning of partnership – giving from the depth of the self. In this kind of giving, the donor and the recipient disappear, and this is the essence of the Christian faith. God has expressed himself in the incarnation, so generosity and the love of God meet with humanity in order for man to retrieve his first image that was clearly mentioned in Genesis.

Spirituality, I believe, is a partnership between God and man, a genuine partnership reflecting practical love. Perhaps the words of Jesus in the Gospel of Matthew reflect this vision clearly as he said:

> When the Son of Man comes in His glory, and all the holy angels with Him, then He will sit on the throne of His glory. All the nations will be gathered before Him, and He will separate them one from another, as a shepherd divides his sheep from the goats. And He will set the sheep on His right hand, but the goats on the left. Then the King will say to those on His right hand, 'Come, you blessed of My Father, inherit the kingdom prepared for you from the foundation of the world for I was hungry and you gave Me food; I was thirsty and you gave Me drink; I was a stranger and you took Me in; I was naked and you clothed Me; I was sick and you visited Me; I was in prison and you came to Me.' Then the righteous will answer Him, saying, 'Lord, when did we see You hungry and feed You, or thirsty and give You drink? When did we see you a stranger and take you in, or naked and clothe you? Or when

did we see you sick, or in prison, and come to you?' And the King will answer and say to them, 'Assuredly, I say to you, inasmuch as you did it to one of the least of these My brethren, you did it to Me.' "Then He will also say to those on the left hand, 'Depart from Me, you cursed, into the everlasting fire prepared for the devil and his angels' (Matthew 25: 31-41 NKJV).

Originally, spirituality is a partnership in which everyone is standing on the same earth that Jesus Christ made through his death and resurrection. There is no reason why Christians, to maintain spirituality, should close their doors to those who stand on the other side or create a closed society, whether culturally or socially, and live in isolation. Instead, they should strive towards active participation in society through the development and enlightenment of the world, not as strangers, but through partnership that is derived from the doctrine of the Incarnation.

Spirituality: A Collective Action

The insight of the New Testament clearly reflects the collective vision of the Christian faith. Christ chose teamwork through the training of his disciples. When he called for repentance, he explained that we repent from sin against others, and perhaps the Sermon on the Mount reflects this vision. He talked about the poor in spirit, those who mourn, those who hunger and thirst for righteousness, the merciful and the peacemakers. He prohibited adultery, murder, anger, and revenge and called for love of enemies. All these actions are related to human beings and society.

The teachings of Jesus confirmed that there can be no relationship with God away from the relationship with the group. The church confirmed this effect in the first Epistle of John, who explained that partnership with God requires partnership with the other. The apostle John says: "This is the message which we have heard from him and declare to you, that God is light and in him is no darkness at all. If we say that we have fellowship with him, and walk in darkness, we lie and do not practice the truth. But if we walk in the light as he is in the light, we have fellowship with one another, and the blood of Jesus Christ his son cleanses us from all sin." (1 John 1:5-7).

We emphasize that sin has two dimensions: individual and collective. Each of them leads to the other. True repentance is repentance for the individual and the community together.

If relationship with God cannot be separated from relationship with the community, teamwork becomes a necessity for change. Here, too, comes the role of evangelicals as a congregation, described by Jesus Christ as salt and light, with the ability to influence and to change. When evangelicals escape from their social role, they escape from their role as light and salt of the world as God desired.

Spirituality: A Creative Action

The New Testament emphasizes the importance of the work of the Holy Spirit in the individual and in the community. The spiritual gifts mentioned in the New Testament, such as healing and speaking in tongues, education and others, are considered obvious manifestations of the work of the Holy Spirit in the church. Here I do not discuss the issue of spiritual gifts as much as I highlight this unique relationship between God and the community through the work of the Holy Spirit. Looking closely at the early church, it clearly shows the people's need of a divine touch at the time, which emphasizes God's presence alongside his people. In fact, this did not stop with the early church; church history has affirmed that the absence of interaction between the Holy Spirit and the community led to dark periods in the church's history, and to rigidity and isolation.

The interaction between the Holy Spirit and the community of faith led to the creation of creative talents that contributed to spreading the message of the Christian faith. Talents mentioned in the New Testament are all linked to supporting the group, spreading the message, and the growth of the church through the service of each member to the others, using spiritual gifts.

Spiritual talents are not for conceit but for edification (1 Cor 12:31). But the question I ask here is: Are the Holy Spirit talents restricted to New Testament texts? Or is the Holy Spirit a creative God working within the community in ways corresponding to the needs of each group and the historical conditions?

Answering this question requires a lot of research, but I think God's Spirit has yet to cease work and that interaction between the Holy Spirit and a group is what leads to ongoing effectiveness of the church in the world.

Spirituality, represented in a clear relationship between God and the community, is reflected in creative actions that seek development of the group's mission and vision. Aside from the debate on spiritual gifts, I believe that Christianity's excellence derives from this unique experience of divine presence in the group's life reflected in new creative actions, which should put the Church on the road to community service. This spirituality has led evangelical missionaries in the Middle East to provide services to needy communities, without intending to attract them to the Gospel but rather to develop the communities themselves. As such, the establishment of schools and hospitals, community development, the realization of human dignity and improvement of the standard of living, are matters not less spiritual than worship, but instead are within the mission and calling of the church of God.

Towards Community-Based Initiatives

Continuation of the Model

The evangelical church, as mentioned at the beginning, has offered unique community models with outstanding education, health and social work, in general, for over a century and a half. The importance of these community-based initiatives lies in the model. In a society influenced by corruption, a good Christian model can create a different atmosphere, emphasize communication and support the building of bridges. At a time when many call on excluding the other, these community-based initiatives, with an enlightened model, can swim against the current and prove an effective presence.

Encouraging Civil Society

Although Arab civil society is weak, promotion of civil society will contribute significantly to the presence on the ground. An active civil society is one that promotes a pluralistic identity through diverse affiliations as it creates new common ground through volunteer work. It also contributes to democratic practices and provides the ability of promoting a civil state achieving diversity and citizenship; that is when the deepest meaning of presence comes in. Because the church is part of the community, it should take initiatives and work hard to consolidate values of democracy and volunteerism as well as emphasize the importance of the individual to be influential in his/her society.

Self-Realization through the Presence of the Other

With the discourse of exclusion, the Church must emphasize the importance of self-realization through the presence of the other and through new community-based initiatives that emphasize active participation in planning, implementation and evaluation.

New and non-traditional community initiatives in social, cultural, and political fields that ensure the presence of the other effectively are important in the formulation of the positive presence of everyone. While I am not proposing models for such initiatives, I desire to confirm the idea that non-traditional community-based initiatives seeking self-realization through the presence of the other play an important role in the formulation of new reactions that build bridges within the community.

A Western Evangelical Perspective on the Cape Town Congress

Rose Dowsett

Introduction

Put half a dozen Europeans from different countries – or even half a dozen from the same country – in a room together and you will be sure to have half a dozen different opinions and perspectives on almost anything. Stir in some North Americans and some Australians and New Zealanders, very roughly to fill out our rather out-dated terminology of 'western', and the different views multiply alarmingly. Even within the borders of the evangelical family, there is extensive diversity, including in many areas of Christian belief and practice, and in the understanding of mission. Making claims to establishing 'a western evangelical perspective' would be presumptuous folly.

So I begin with a disclaimer: I am one northern European woman, and my observations on the Cape Town Congress are limited and particular, personal rather than necessarily communal. Many of my northern and western brothers and sisters might have very different things to say. Further, I was involved in a particular way, as a member of the Theology Working Group in the years leading up to the Congress, and then as one of the team of eight who worked on the *Cape Town Commitment*. This meant that there were some parts of the whole process where I was fully immersed, and other parts that probably passed me by. Other 'western evangelicals' might well have had a very different experience, and would have a different perspective from mine. At the same time, I have tried to reflect the feedback I have received both formally and informally, at national and international consultations since Cape Town, and through wide-ranging correspondence.

A Meaningful Centenary?

Marking anniversaries has long been a way in which God's people pause and remember what he has done, with thanksgiving, and with opportunity for refreshed faith and dedication. A jubilee or centenary has special resonance.

It was inevitable that some within the missionary and global church community would wish to mark the centenary of the missionary conference held in Edinburgh, Scotland, in 1910. In the end, there were a number of different events, all claiming in different ways to be the appropriate commemoration. Perhaps we should regard them simply as complementary to one another. Yet it is probable that many of those who participated in those events had no very clear idea as to what was significant about the 1910 conference, and in that sense the centenary date was not especially relevant.[1] Even in Edinburgh itself, where an international 2010 conference was held, following on from a lengthy global study process, few people in the local community had any idea what is was all about. That was as true amongst church people as among people in the street.

Perhaps that is a sad indication of how marginalized the Christian faith has become in a once faith-vibrant country with a strong missionary heritage. But it does beg the question as to whether for most participants – apart from missiologists and church historians – this was a meaningful centenary or simply a year with a profusion of conferences. Cape Town offered the briefest of video introductions to 1910 at the start of the Congress, by way of explanation for choosing the year to hold Lausanne III, but did not offer any detail or evaluation of the strengths and weaknesses of 1910, or of how its legacy played out, or how it contributed to the shape of Christianity a hundred years later. Since many of the current problems in the world church, as well as vision to see it become global, can be traced at least in part to the omissions and achievements of 1910, it would have been helpful to give some substantive attention to this.

In particular, it would have been helpful to have explored carefully the *theological legacy,* the *ecclesiological legacy,* and the *legacy of imperialism,* since each of these has profoundly affected the development of the church in both global south/east and global north/west. We will come back to some of these later in this essay. For the moment, we need to recognize that the Christian faith is a deeply history-related faith, with God's actions of grace located firmly in real history. If we do not pay full attention to where we have come from under God's sovereign hand, and full attention to where history is heading in its final fulfilment in the new creation, we will make many mistakes in the present. It is possible to be so existentialist and wrapped up in the here-and-now that we ignore the

---

[1] The one notable exception to this was the very stimulating process, completed prior to all the 2010 conferences, instigated by the Scottish Towards 2010 Council. Academic institutions in Scotland, together with agencies and some churches, joined forces to revisit in turn, in annual or biannual consultations, each of the eight commission reports from Edinburgh 1910, International scholars and missiologists offered critique of the reports in context, and traced developments in the ensuing century around the theme. The papcrs given are published in Eds. David A. Kerr and Kenneth R. Ross, *Edinburgh 2010: Mission Then and Now* (Oxford, UK: Regnum, 2009).

important lessons of history. That is crucially true when we think about world mission, what it is and how to engage in it.

The study of the complex history of the twentieth century is inseparable from an informed understanding of how the global church developed, just as the study of 1910 with all its vision and all its blind spots and mistakes is important in understanding the development of beliefs about mission, what it is and how to do it, in a century which more than any other saw Christianity become a truly world faith. We recognize that facing history can be very painful, especially for those who have suffered under imperial abuse, or indeed for those ashamed of being part of a nation who may have perpetrated that abuse. Yet the ambiguities of imperialism were highly evident at the 1910 conference and have indeed affected much of the world church, for both good and ill. Christianity is still perceived by many non-Christians all over the world as a western religion, and much that has been said and done in world mission has served to reinforce that perception. It is hard to know why Cape Town ignored this fundamental dimension of the past century, and the struggles by many Christians today in both north/west and south to disentangle the Gospel from its cultural chains.

Preparation

As with Edinburgh 2010, Lausanne III had a significant process of consultation leading up to the Congress. In particular, a consultation in Hungary a few years in advance attempted to identify some of the most pressing issues facing the church in various parts of the world as she witnessed to Jesus Christ in her own contexts and as she engaged in ongoing world mission. Lausanne leaders later refined the list of suggestions to extrapolate six large umbrella themes, which became the themes for the six plenary days of the Congress: truth, reconciliation, world faiths, priorities, integrity, and partnership.

It is inevitable that some very important themes didn't make it to the final six, but it would be unreasonable to expect any one conference to cover all possible topics. Nonetheless, as those themes were developed, some important issues fell by the wayside. Some delegates from the global south, on several occasions in my hearing, expressed their surprise (and sometimes anger) that, in their view, the six themes were unduly influenced by northern concerns and addressed through northern plausibility structures. I don't personally think that that was quite a fair conclusion, but perhaps as a northerner I miss some important perspectives. Maybe in a global consultation it is simply not possible to prioritize everybody's concerns, and the Lausanne organizers simply could not have satisfied everybody. Certainly the chosen themes were big and important ones, and of course during each day many sub-themes were addressed.

Also in preparation, there was a well-developed website and process for online discussion, posting of papers and general interaction. Some topics fared better than others, and in some cases the discussion was accelerated because there was already in place a Lausanne-based working group. It was not very easy to break into some of these groups if you weren't already part of that particular conversation, and in some cases almost all the participating contributors were from the north and west, and/or from the English-speaking world. It remains very difficult to facilitate a truly multilingual online discussion, and to escape from the dominance of English as the most common medium of international communication. It could also be argued that the very process of online debate is much more the product of western history, academic traditions, and certain assumptions about democratic interaction. Many global south cultures are more at home in face-to-face discussion, and in grounded experience and practice. It was good that many fruitful discussions took place locally and in local languages, though it was hard to capture the richness of that into the online debates. Certainly, whatever may have been lost in the preparatory phase, Lausanne is to be commended for its hard work in trying to provide simultaneous translation into a number of languages during the Congress at plenaries and some smaller meetings, along with supporting translation of documents flowing from the Congress, such as the *Cape Town Commitment*. The scale of the Congress made it easier to achieve this than for some of the smaller events, but it was good to see such serious commitment to enabling participation way beyond the English-speaking world. Those chairing non-plenary meetings also worked hard to facilitate full participation by non-native English speakers.

Another conundrum relating to participation is the sophistication of technology, whose availability is not necessarily at the disposal of some of those who need to be heard. It could be argued that, at the Congress, laptops and mobile phones were firmly attached to an astonishing number of delegates. But the question remains whether in this kind of process those who got involved and those who came were in some measure self-selected on the grounds of access to technology. In the Lord's eyes, there are some very significant leaders among the poor and marginalized, who – despite generous scholarships – proved unable to participate. Money is still a divisive issue of power, and we have not yet figured out a good way of addressing the ramifications of it. This is not of course a problem for Lausanne alone, but we need to remain sensitive to it in all international Christian networks and events. Globalization excludes as well as includes, particularly when it operates on western assumptions and practices

The Theology Working Group

I had the privilege of being part of the Theology Working Group (TWG) for its three major consultations (between 2007 and 2010) leading up to the Congress, and also of the small eight-person team working on the *Cape Town Commitment*. In both cases, we worked under the inspired and inspiring chairmanship of Chris Wright of the Langham Foundation, London.

Lausanne has a strapline: 'The Whole Church Taking the Whole Gospel to the Whole World.' In three successive meetings, the TWG addressed each of those 'wholes' in turn, producing a key document from its studies. That document and some of the papers from each consultation were published in a series of special editions of *Evangelical Review of Theology*, the journal of the Theological Commission of the World Evangelical Alliance. This was a reflection of the fact that Lausanne and WEA were designed to be in full partnership for the Congress and the process leading up to it; we will return to this later. The document also appeared on the Lausanne website, though little reference was made to it in Lausanne mass emailings leading up to the Congress. Given that the strapline remains, and is intended to sum up what Lausanne stands for, it is troubling and rather astonishing that this piece of work did not achieve a higher profile.

Further, the TWG, and especially Chris Wright, worked before the Congress on the first half of what was to become the *Cape Town Commitment*, 'A Confession of Faith'. The TWG understood that the 'Three wholes' document,[2] and the 'Confession of Faith' were to provide a theological framework and undergirding for the deliberations of the Congress. As evangelicals, we aspire to be people living by the light of Scripture's revelation, and to seek that our beliefs and praxis stem from it. There has probably never been a generation in the history of the world church where it has been more important to assess what we believe and do in the light of what God says, and to ensure that our praxis is shaped by that rather than by the competing (significant but subsidiary) claims of the behavioural sciences or of our own cultural presuppositions.

In the event, I heard no reference from the platform to the 'Three Wholes' document at all, and the 'Confession of Faith' was distributed only on the penultimate evening of the Congress. The explanation later given was that other language editions had been delayed at the printers, and it was considered unfair to privilege English speakers over others. While I am sure the Lausanne leadership would vigorously and honestly dispute this in any way as an intention, the 'message' was that theology is not important in forming our praxis. It is hard to express too strongly the dismay some of us felt. For those of us familiar with the 1910 story, where theological discussion was ruled inadmissible because it would be divisive, the dismay was all the deeper; because it is arguable that many of the problems in the world church today flow precisely from the unwillingness in 1910 to dig deeply into Scripture and theology, and instead to focus purely on action. Action without deep theological roots is quite as dangerous, possibly even more so, as theological discussion that does not lead properly to mission

---

[2] This document is published online at www.lausanne.org/en/documents/all/twg/1177-twg-three-wholes.html.

and discipleship. Lausanne had a marvellous opportunity to insist that we keep truth and practice, theology and mission, together. I believe that that opportunity was largely bypassed.

There are numerous tensions among evangelicals, let alone with other parts of the world church, which profoundly impact world mission today: what we believe mission to be all about, as well as how to do it. There are deep presuppositional differences that cause difficulties, especially flowing from deep differences in eschatology, and more deeply still differences in how we set about theologizing in different cultures, and then living out the faith. Cape Town afforded a unique opportunity gently and lovingly to explore some of those, so that at the very least there should be greater mutual understanding and respect among evangelicals around the world. In large measure we missed it. It is unlikely that there will be another such opportunity for decades to come.

It could be argued that the high profile that has been given to the *Cape Town Commitment* subsequently has compensated for this. Possibly; perhaps not. Certainly, just as the *Lausanne Covenant* from 1974 has been such an influential document, the *Commitment* may have significant impact in years to come. It has been translated into many languages, and is being studied in many places and through a variety of methods. The Lausanne leadership are to be commended for their active promotion of the document, facilitating translation and distribution, and support for a variety of study guides. It may be more used by mission agencies and training colleges than by grassroots Christians in local churches, and it may still be too western in format, but it is too soon to tell. Anecdotally, there are local congregations who are reported to be using it as a training scheme in Christian belief and practice. A number of WEA's national alliances are also finding it a strategic resource. Lausanne as an organization is certainly taking it seriously, and using it as a road map for its priorities in the years ahead.

Partnership or Distant Friends?

In early discussion about the Congress and the process leading up to it, there was much promise that this would be a full partnership between Lausanne and the WEA. This would bring together the two great global networks of evangelicals, reinforcing world mission at the heart of the churches and not just as the preserve of mission agencies and individuals. Those of us in northern Europe cheered happily, because in a number of countries the two movements are so intertwined or even structurally integrated that this seemed a wonderful opportunity to demonstrate a deepened unity among evangelicals. The cause of the Gospel is larger and more central than either.

In the event, the message of partnership was largely lost, despite hugely impressive communications. Probably it was Lausanne personnel who raised the greater part of the very large budget – but, as was clearly expressed from the platform in a slightly different context, partnership should not be dependent on equality of financial resources, because different partners under God bring different gifts to the table. WEA certainly had plenty to bring, including established structures to deliver the message of Cape Town widely to churches. Perhaps, sadly, there were evangelical politics at work. Of course, not all the world's evangelicals subscribe to WEA: for some it is too conservative, for others too broad; for some it is too charismatic, for others not charismatic enough. But that should not have been a problem for Lausanne, whose umbrella cheerfully accommodated Pentecostals and conservatives, and all points in between, and the full range (and beyond) of WEA membership.

Many WEA people were of course involved. Indeed, some of the Lausanne leaders in various parts of the world are also deeply involved in their national Evangelical Alliances, national missionary movements, or in the WEA Theological Commission or Mission Commission. Many of us missed the acknowledgment of that, and encouragement to take the opportunity of strengthening co-operation into the future. At the Congress itself, after Geoff Tunnicliffe, the International Director of WEA, spoke at the opening, the name 'Lausanne' occurred constantly, 'WEA' not at all. It seemed a missed opportunity.

Happily, the TWG was able to model full partnership, with a joyous mix of people drawn from the previous forms of the Lausanne Theology Working Group, and people from both the WEA Theological Commission and the Mission Commission. Sadly and inexplicably, the Lausanne leadership declined to have that integrated group continue to work together following the Congress, and have reinstated an exclusively Lausanne TWG. Probably 'on the ground' in many places the distinction between the two groups – Lausanne and WEA – is ignored, and brothers and sisters in Christ work together regardless of labels. The Gospel needs that, and the Lord prayed for it.

The Congress

It is difficult to think of a more stunning setting than Cape Town for a Congress. It must be one of the most dramatic and beautiful backdrops in the world in terms of scenery. Further, following the World Cup held a little while beforehand, the infrastructure was good, and the total capacity for local accommodation all that could be desired. The facilities at the conference centre were excellent. The South African people were friendly and helpful. The South African Christians were marvellously and vibrantly welcoming and served us brilliantly. Their enthusiastic contribution to plenary worship was a joy to experience, and their practical service in numerous ways generous and exemplary.

The organization of such a complex event was masterly, the film clips and other visuals of superb quality, the plenary presentations of a consistently professional standard and clearly planned to the last minute of allotted time. The multiplexes and dialogue sessions were well equipped and helpfully stewarded. Many people found the table groups during the plenaries a great blessing; they probably helped many people cope with being in such a large gathering where one could easily feel completely anonymous. Undoubtedly new friendships across nationalities and backgrounds were forged as a result. The Bible studies each morning were a feast – each very different from the others, but a lovely example of the Word coming freshly from representatives of the different continents. I doubt whether anyone could have gone away without learning something new from the riches of the Scriptures.

There is something breathtakingly inspiring about worshipping alongside brothers and sisters in Christ from so many nations and language groups, and the final celebration of the Congress was unforgettable. To many it seemed as close as it is possible to experience here on earth to that amazing, glorious glimpse into eternity that we see in the book of Revelation, where those of every tribe and tongue gather round the throne of the Lamb and join in perfect worship. It was truly a communion of the saints of a kind that most of us will not experience more than once or twice in our lifetimes, and of the whole Congress was probably the most powerful immersion in what it means to be members of a worldwide family.

There were of course some more troubling aspects of the Congress, and without doubt different people, and those from different contexts, would name different things. For many, the professionalism and rigid time control of each element of the plenaries seemed to leave little space for the Holy Spirit to intervene at any point. Some felt it was at points like an expensive western TV programme, a rather slick baptized chat show, for which they were spectators. Despite people on the platform coming from many different ethnicities, the culture and style was very western/northern. Global events still follow a northern/western way of doing things, and, for some of those from the global south, that grated and felt as if the north has not yet learned the grace of humility and the abandonment of power. Probably we haven't.

Was the mood too celebratory and verging on the triumphalistic? There was not much space for repentance and sober reflection in relation to what has been or still is harmful in the way we have engaged in mission, or distorted the Gospel, or been content with shallow discipleship. It is undoubtedly difficult to set quite the right tone in such a large gathering, and clearly it is not the context in which spontaneity is easy to accommodate. All the same, sometimes it seemed a little too controlled and organized, too wedded to efficiency and detailed planning, too bound in western preoccupation with timekeeping, a little too close to entertainment, not quite enough of the balance of godly mourning for sin, and tears. It is dangerously easy to manipulate people along the lines of repentance that is emotional only, especially in a mass gathering, so perhaps the organisers felt this was not the arena in which to introduce them, but it left one feeling the note of triumphalism came across too strongly.

Despite a small number of observers from various other streams of the world church – Roman Catholics, Orthodox, WCC conciliar, and so on – the overall tendency was to present the evangelical and Pentecostal communities as being the whole sum of the Church. Clearly evangelicals in different parts of the world approach this differently, but for many from northern Europe – and indeed for many from certain parts of the global south – the issue is much more complicated. If you live in a culture that is overwhelmingly secular, as many Europeans do today, or in a setting where the Christians are a tiny minority in the face of another dominant faith, as is true in much of Asia or the Middle East, then affirming genuine believers far beyond the boundaries of evangelicalism is urgent. In my own country, for instance, it is normally the Roman Catholic Church that most consistently and boldly challenges secular pressure, especially in areas of ethics and of freedom of conscience – and often makes clearer statements of Gospel truths into public debate than anyone else with the exception of the Evangelical Alliance.

Since 1974, Lausanne has been officially committed to a holistic understanding of mission and of the Gospel. At the same time, there have continued to be those – mostly but not exclusively from the northern world – who have rejected that, and regarded anything other than the speediest possible oral proclamation of the Gospel to all people groups as a diversion from the core business of mission and of the church. This has without doubt contributed to one of the most frequently expressed challenges to the world church today: the shallowness of discipleship, and the lack of deep-level conversion. This ongoing fundamental divergence of understanding as to the very nature of mission was not tackled properly at the Congress, despite the fact that it continues to cause tension across the mission community. So there were those from the platform who espoused Lausanne's holistic commitment, and some who vociferously didn't, but no attempt to address this tension was made. Evangelism in the narrower sense, and holistic mission, belong together in the dominical commission to disciple-making.

I would suggest that the battles of 1974 need to be re-addressed in each generation. Few of those at Lausanne 1974 were present at 2010, and fewer still remain in leadership positions of influence (and rightly so after 36 years!). Many younger Christian leaders have never explored some of these seminal missiological issues for themselves. Evangelicalism is by nature activist, but it remains critical that we constantly refresh our theological foundations, and for each generation to assess its praxis in the light of Scripture. Like faith, we need to make it our own, not inherit it second-hand.

Further, evangelicalism is itself more diverse than it was even twenty years ago. That is in part a reflection of the growth of the world church and the maturity of contextualized theology and mission. For some at the Congress it was unsettling, even dismaying, to encounter those from different parts of the world with a very different understanding of various parts of Scripture, while all still deeply affirming its authority and inspiration. Because some of these deeper divergences were not explored (which they could have been, in a sensitive as well explicit way) some felt that many presentations, including some of the plenaries, remained on a disappointingly superficial level. There was also rather little attention to the rich store of theological reflection, and specifically missiological reflection, now emanating from the global south. Some of this emerged in some of the smaller gatherings, but rarely in the plenaries.

It is of course right to stress that no one gathering can cover all possible themes and issues, and in such a large Congress perhaps the note of celebration was rightly the dominant one. There is so much to celebrate in the grace of God! The organizers of the plenaries may very well have wanted to focus as strongly as possible on all that unites us, and to leave our differences and disagreements to one side. If the Congress was deemed the wrong forum in which to face them together, it is important for integrity's sake, and for our ongoing mutual understanding, that we acknowledge them, and in follow-up from the Congress explore ways of addressing them. The Congress was after all 'an event in a process'.

And After the Congress?

The cost of the Congress was enormous. The cost of attending it was also enormous, for any but those from the most affluent economies, and even when using the simplest accommodation available. The Lausanne leadership is to be commended for raising a very large amount of money, and being very generous in scholarships to enable those from poor economies to attend. Yet such large expenditure remains troubling to many. Amongst other 'unintended consequences', some fine Christian ministries found their income sharply dropping as giving was diverted. It seems ironic that some front-line mission ministries ceased because of a big mission Congress. It is of course very hard to balance the value of these different expressions of Christian mission, but I think a number of Europeans were hoping that no similar diversion of funds would happen again in the next decade.

Even after nearly three years, it is difficult to assess the lasting impact of the Congress. Follow-up in different countries has varied enormously. Probably missionary college students and mission agencies will pore over the *Commitment*, as in the past over the *Lausanne Covenant*. How much will it all influence what churches and agencies actually do? That will undoubtedly vary, too. The leadership of my own agency, Overseas

Missionary Fellowship International, is taking it very seriously, and to my knowledge some of the Asian churches. For how long? The Lord alone knows the answer to that, but the signs are good. Numerous publications, study syllabi and study guides, are already in circulation, and regional and international meetings are seeking to build on what has been achieved. As with the *Lausanne Covenant* following Lausanne I, the *Commitment* may prove to be a powerful tool in affirming evangelical identity, around which many gladly unite.

Following the Congress, the Lausanne leadership announced a strengthening of long-term structures and a bold programme of ongoing smaller conferences, building on some of the key findings of the Congress. Some of those themes are the focus of already established networks and agencies, so it is to be hoped that there will be full consultation rather than competition or repetition, and where possible a serving of what is already in place rather than setting up of a specifically Lausanne brand initiative. From a European perspective, co-operation and non-multiplication is often more important than it is in North America, where the strong entrepreneurship of Christian, as well as general, culture expects a group to stress its distinctives and uniqueness rather than its similarities to others, and where multiplication and competition are generally assumed to be good. That is not a view shared by much of northern Europe. Where Lausanne is able to bring something that is genuinely a distinctive contribution to the cause of the Gospel, then that is something to support and thank God for. In some countries, Lausanne leadership would be wise to seek a deeper liaison with WEA structures. In others, WEA may be weak or underdeveloped, and Lausanne may be able to provide a rallying-point for evangelicals to work better together in mission. Cape Town spoke strongly of the biblical nature of partnership, and of the destructive nature of competitiveness and duplication. Lausanne now needs to demonstrate that conviction itself.

Conclusion

Cape Town undoubtedly generated high interest through much of the evangelical world, and provided a platform for Christians from all over the world to gather together in worship, study and fellowship. That was very precious. In my lifetime the church has become global as never before, and to see that celebrated in physical presence gathered in one place left me revelling in the grace and majesty of our God. It could be argued that this alone, the testimony of many, constituted an outcome that fully justified all the years of preparation and the massive expenditure.

It is too soon to evaluate the long-term impact: how congregations will be motivated to greater commitment to the Great Commission, how nationals and expatriates will serve better side by side in equality in the family of God, how many corners of the world where as yet there is no

Gospel witness will soon be encountering the Gospel made visible and audible in all its transforming power, how disciples all over the world may be more deeply changed into the likeness of Jesus Christ. We pray that all of those will happen, not for the aggrandizement of the Lausanne Movement or any human reputation, but for the glory of God – Father, Son and Holy Spirit.

SECTION FOUR

CRITICAL REFLECTIOS AND DISCUSSIONS:

"CALLING THE WHOLE CHURCH TO TAKE THE WHOLE GOSPEL TO THE WHOLE WORLD."

Edinburgh, Tokyo And Cape Town: Comparing and Contrasting on the Way to 2110

Knud Jørgensen

The year 2010 was an eventful one for an old missionary like me. I carry in me the genes of both 'ecumenical' and 'evangelical'. It was therefore exciting to be allowed to play active roles both within the Edinburgh 2010 process and in Cape Town. Beginning in 2007, many of my hours and days were spent on these endeavours, particularly on the Edinburgh 2010 process, as chair of the group that monitored the progress of the nine study processes or commissions prior to 2010. I am still involved in this process as a member of the editorial team of the Regnum Edinburgh Centenary Series which the present volume is part of. My life with the Lausanne Movement goes back to 1974 when I as a young journalist of 32 years of age with fear and trembling signed the *Lausanne Covenant* at the first Congress on world evangelization. I have never had any regrets. Since then I have been involved with Lausanne at all conceivable levels from the international administrative committee and Theology Working Group to establishing an umbrella organization in Norway for Lausanne and the World Evangelical Alliance (WEA). In Cape Town I was a member of a group for 'senior (not senile) mission statesmen', a forum for the old-timers who were asked to monitor the progress of the Congress and give input to the leadership. Unfortunately, I was not in Tokyo, but I have tried as best I can to monitor and read what happened. One of the volumes in the Regnum Edinburgh Centenary Series contains a good amount of the material from and reflections on Tokyo 2010.[1]

In the following, I shall outline the purposes of the three events and show how I think they relate to three of the key concerns of Edinburgh 1910, world evangelization, discipleship/discipling, and mission and unity. Looking ahead to 2110, I shall then highlight two of our key challenges, the

[1] Beth Snodderly & A. Scott Moreau (eds), *Evangelical and Frontier Mission. Perspectives on the Global Progress of the Gospel* (Oxford, UK: Regnum, 2011).

call to rethink mission as ministry of reconciliation and to revisit spirituality as a source of mission.[2]

Purpose and Focus

Since the 1970s there has been a discussion about who is the legitimate child of Edinburgh 1910. The only real recommendation of Edinburgh 1910 was to establish a continuation committee to pursue the concern for unity in mission. This committee resulted in the creation of the International Missionary Council (IMC). The concern for unity resulted in the formation of conciliar movements for 'Life and Work' and 'Faith and Order'. In 1948 these two merged into the World Council of Churches (WCC), and in 1961 the IMC was integrated into the WCC as the Commission on World Mission and Evangelism (CWME). This development constitutes what we today call 'the ecumenical movement'. The primary focus of Edinburgh 1910 was however on 'the evangelization of the world in this generation'. The desire to lift up 'world evangelization' as a priority for mission led in 1974 to the creation of the Lausanne Committee on World Evangelization (LCWE), a movement of evangelical leaders who wanted a renewed impetus for evangelization.[3] Some would therefore claim that the broad Evangelical Alliance movement, including the World Evangelical Alliance (WEA), was the successor of the zeal for evangelism. To this may be added that most of the participants in 1910 were representing the mission agencies. In the course of the formation of the ecumenical movement, some would claim that the agencies or para-church organizations were squeezed out. A legitimate heir to Edinburgh 1910 should therefore give space and voice to what Ralph Winter called *the sodalities* (the go-structures) and not just *the modalities* (the come-structures) of the church.[4] The Tokyo 2010 Global Mission Consultation was a gathering of sodalities from around the world.

To draw the conclusion that Edinburgh 2010 was the conciliar heir to 1910, Cape Town the evangelism heir and Tokyo the para-church heir is, however, too easy and simplistic. Both the Lausanne Movement and the WEA were among the stakeholders in Edinburgh 2010, and a fair number of the para-church representatives in Tokyo 2010 are among the key actors

---

[2] Reference is made to Knud Jørgensen, "Inspiration and Challenges from Cape Town and Edinburgh to Church and Mission" in *Transformation* Vol 29, No 4, 2012 where some of the perspectives in the following are used.

[3] The desire to prioritise evangelization was part of an evangelical reaction to the critique of classical mission coming from the WCC Uppsala Assembly (1968) and the CWME meeting on 'Salvation Today' in Bangkok (1973).

[4] A reading of the relevant biblical texts will view the two structures as integral to what it means to be church; see e.g. Knud Jørgensen, 'Misjon og kirke' in Jan-Martin Berentsen, Tormod Engelsviken & Knud Jørgensen, *Missiologi I dag* (Oslo: Universitetsforlaget, 2004), 316ff.

within the Lausanne Movement and took part in Lausanne III in Cape Town.

This 'lack' of clear divisions is, in my view, a positive omen for the future of mission and evangelism. In this connection it is also enlightening and encouraging to note that the statements from the three events (*The Tokyo Declaration*,[5] *The Common Call*,[6] and the *Cape Town Commitment*[7]) are irenic documents without any polemic against one another. This does not mean that all the actors are ready to join in a common conciliar, evangelical, para-church boat. In the midst of growing convergence there are still significant areas of disagreement as regards theology, strategy and methodology. These questions must be dealt with in an open and honest manner if endeavours related to strategy were to be pursued.

The Edinburgh 2010 event came as a conclusion of a study process during which nine commissions or think-tanks had worked on nine themes identified as being key to mission in the 21st century.[8] The results of this process were presented and discussed at a conference in Edinburgh in June 2010. The event was a landmark event: it brought together a wide coalition of different Christian churches and confessions. The General Council of Edinburgh 2010 included representatives of all the main strands of Christianity: Protestant, Orthodox, Catholic, Evangelical, Pentecostals and independent churches (such as African independent/initiated churches). It was probably the most representative mission conference ever held. Even more remarkable was that these diverse strands of world Christianity agreed to issue *The Common Call* to mission on behalf of all of the participants.

Prior to the Edinburgh 2010 event, the Tokyo 2010 Global Mission Consultation was held in May with almost one thousand delegates from 73 countries.[9] The gathering was sponsored by a broad spectrum of national, regional and global mission networks and associations representing 100,000 cross-cultural missionaries. The purpose was 'to celebrate the progress made in missionary efforts since Edinburgh 1910, assess what remained to be done in making disciples of all peoples, and develop plans

[5] "Tokyo 2010 Declaration: Making Disciples of Every People in Our Generation", in Snodderly & Moreau, *Evangelical and Frontier Mission, 207-211.*

[6] "Edinburgh 2010 Common Call" in Kirsteen Kim & Andrew Anderson (eds), *Edinburgh 2010. Mission Today and Tomorrow* (Oxford, UK: Regnum, 2011), 1-2.

[7] The Lausanne Movement, *The Cape Town Commitment. A Confession of Faith and a Call to Action* (Great Britain, 2011).

[8] Daryl Balia & Kirsteen Kim (eds), *Edinburgh 2010. Witnessing to Christ Today* (Oxford, UK: Regnum, 2010).

[9] Yong Cho & David Taylor, "Making Disciples of Every People in Our Generation: The Vision, Purpose and Objectives of Tokyo 2010", in Snodderly & Moreau, *Evangelical and Frontier Mission*, 201-206.

for inter-mission co-operation to fully engage the remaining least-reached peoples in our generation'.[10]

The third Lausanne Congress on World Evangelization (Lausanne III) was held in Cape Town in October. The goal of the Congress was 'to re-stimulate the spirit of Lausanne, as represented in The *Lausanne Covenant*, and so to promote unity, humility in service, and a call to active global evangelization'.[11] The Congress brought together some 4,000 leaders from 198 countries as participants and observers; many more took part by joining the Cape Town GlobaLink. Many from small and isolated Christian communities and from countries where Christians are persecuted received here their first and overwhelming experience of the church universal in all its vitality and diversity. As described elsewhere in this book, Lausanne III became a major celebration across all sorts of borders.

Comparison, Convergence and Contrasts

The inheritance from Edinburgh 1910 is at least threefold: *World evangelization, making disciples, and a vision about mission and unity.* Before we look at how the three events handled this inheritance, it is however noteworthy that they all share the *missio Dei* paradigm: mission begins with God and belongs to God. It is at the very heart of the Trinity, it is at the centre of what it means to be Christian and church, it emphasizes that mission is one, and it affirms God's concern with the whole world and all life.[12] This paradigm was not on the agenda in 1910. Instead the conference marked the climax of a western belief in its own power to open up the rest of the world for mission efforts from the west to the rest. The *missio Dei* paradigm was inspired by the theology of Karl Barth, but it did not fully surface until the decline of church and mission in the west, the Maoist takeover in China, and the breakdown of colonialism. These events left mission empty-handed. It was in that situation that the *missio Dei* concept helped church and mission rethink and reinvent mission. In the course of the last decade or so it has been embraced by all churches and movements.[13] The fact that it undergirds all three events – Edinburgh, Tokyo and Cape Town – is a strong indication that the starting point for their understanding of mission is the same.

---

[10] Cho & Taylor, "Making Disciples of Every People in Our Generation: The Vision, Purpose and Objectives of Tokyo 2010", 202.

[11] Cape Town 2010: www.lausanne.org/about.html.

[12] Kirsteen Kim, "Mission in the Twenty-First Century" in Kirsteen Kim & Andrew Anderson (eds), *Edinburgh 2010. Mission Today and Tomorrow* (Oxford, UK: Regnum, 2011), 351ff.

[13] There will, however, be variations in how the concept is interpreted; see Tormod Engelsviken, 'Missio Dei: the understanding and misunderstanding of a theological concept in European churches and missiology' in *International Review of Mission,* 92, No. 4 (2003): 481-97.

The primary legacy from Edinburgh 1910 is world evangelization. All three movements and events lift up this legacy. There may be good reason for criticizing Edinburgh 1910 and its overly optimistic vision, but in the wake of 1910 the Christian faith has truly become a global religion. Would that have happened without God using Edinburgh 1910 as a torch-bearer and gate-opener? Is it not because of the impetus from Edinburgh 1910 that we have experienced the huge reversal and the shift of the centre of gravity of Christianity to the global south? It is this shift that marks the frame of reference for how all three movements talk about world evangelization. Lausanne III and the *Cape Town Commitment* (hereafter often CTC) are crystal-clear: "We are committed to world mission, because it is central to our understanding of God, the Bible, the Church, human history and the ultimate future."[14] This tone is the *leitmotif* for the entire *Commitment*: "God commands us to make known to all nations the truth of God's revelation and the gospel of God's saving grace through Jesus Christ, calling all people to repentance, faith, baptism and obedient discipleship."[15]

The Tokyo consultation uses the watchword 'Finishing the Task' when it talks about world evangelization. The specific focus was on the final frontiers of the Great Commission. In that sense the Tokyo movement may be viewed as an eschatological 'closure movement':[16] "We are closer now to finishing the task than at any time in modern history. God has entrusted this generation with more opportunities and resources to complete the task than any previous one ... God will require much of our generation."[17] Against this background the overall purpose of Tokyo 2010 was to build a global alliance of at least 2.000 mission agencies around the world working together to finish the task of reaching all the remaining frontier people groups.

Edinburgh 2010 has a different tone, but is equally clear when it talks about our challenge to witness and evangelism: "Hearing the call of Jesus to make disciples of all people – poor, wealthy, marginalised, ignored, powerful, living with disability, young, and old – we are called as communities of faith to mission from everywhere to everywhere."[18] At the same time the broader platform is viewed as a call to not only 'reach the unreached', but also to receive from one another in our witness by word and action. This focus on mission as 'witness' was strong in the Edinburgh 2010 conference and in the study processes prior to the 2010 event Edinburgh 2010 is therefore less preoccupied with 'the unengaged' (groups where we know of no churches or agencies that are even trying to share the

[14] *CTC*, 27.

[15] *CTC*, 29.

[16] Kevin S. Higgins, "Missiology and the Measurement of Engagement: Personal Reflections on Tokyo", in Snodderly & Moreau (eds), *Evangelical and Frontier Mission*, 212.

[17] *Tokyo 2010 Declaration*, 209

[18] *Common Call*, 2.

Gospel with them[19]) than with the different contexts and changing landscapes.

Migration and diaspora were not on the Edinburgh 1910 agenda for world evangelization even though western imperialism and colonialism constituted migration *par excellence*. Both Cape Town and Edinburgh 2010 were preoccupied with today's migration in the context of world evangelization. Unlike the migration movement of the 19th and 20th centuries which moved from the powerful nations of the west to the powerless in the south, migrants and refugees today often function as 'missionaries' who bring the faith from one place to another. *The Common Call* celebrates 'the renewal experienced through movements of migration and mission in all directions'.[20] One of the volumes in the Regnum Edinburgh Centenary Series will deal with the topic of diaspora and migration viewed within the framework of world evangelization. The CTC talks about migration as one of the great global realities of our era and encourages church and mission to recognize and respond to the missional opportunities presented by global migration and diaspora communities. This also and primarily implies encouraging "Christians who are themselves part of the diaspora communities to discern the hand of God … and to seek whatever opportunities God provides for bearing witness to Christ in their host community …".[21] One of the Tokyo leaders even talks about 'diaspora missiology' as a new paradigm, together with a 'relational paradigm'.[22] The migrants are on the move, and so are God's people: "As people move geographically and spiritually, the Church should follow the moving of the Spirit accordingly."[23] Today's migration from the global south to the north and the west represents a new dynamic witness in the midst of a faltering Christianity in Europe and North America. The routes of migration have always been pathways of mission, and migration has always been one of the most important factors in religious expansion and in the spread of the Christian faith, from the Jewish diaspora up till today's movements of people from the south to the north. Every Christian migrant is a potential missionary.[24] This positive missional perspective stands in contrast to the widespread fear in the west of migration and 'Islamization' from the south. A large proportion of the migrants coming to Europe are Christians.

---

[19] *CTC*, 52f.

[20] *Common Call*, 2.

[21] *CTC*, 50.

[22] Enoch Wan, "Celebration, Consultation and Congress: From Edinburgh 1910 to Tokyo 2010 and Cape Town 2010", in Snodderly & Moreau, *Evangelical and Frontier Mission*, 228f.

[23] Enoch Wan, 229.

[24] See Jehu J. Hanciles, *Beyond Christendom: Globalization, African Migration and the Transformation of the West* (Maryknoll, NY: Orbis Books, 2008).

'Making disciples and discipling' form another primary legacy from Edinburgh 1910. The primary focus was on 'Carrying the Gospel to all the non-Christian world', but parallel to this the conference discussed 'The Church in the Mission Field' as a community of disciples, and much emphasis was given to 'Education in Relation to the Christianization of National Life'.[25] The agencies and persons behind Tokyo 2010 have traditionally had a particular focus on the unreached; this focus is still there, but in such a way that the 'breadth' of the Great Commission goes hand in hand with attention to the 'depth' of the Great Commission: "... we acknowledge both the breadth of the unfinished task – *all peoples* – and the depth of the task – *making disciples* ..."[26] The depth of the task contains three essentials: Penetration ('go'), consolidation ('baptizing'), and transformation ('teaching to obey'). Transformation implies "teaching Christ-followers to observe his commands with the outcome of transformed lives. The new believers' worldview must be adjusted to a biblical worldview; his lifestyle changed to increasingly conform to the image of Christ; and his ethical conduct progressively marked by biblical morals ... As a consequence, whole communities, cultures and countries benefit from the transforming power of the gospel".[27]

The entire Edinburgh 2010 process has had a strong focus on discipling and discipleship. Even when the words are not mentioned, the focus is on "witness and evangelism in such a way that we are a living demonstration of the love, righteousness and justice that God intends for the whole world".[28] The model is Jesus' way of witness and service; this model we are called to follow "joyfully, inspired, anointed, sent and empowered by the Holy Spirit, and nurtured by Christian disciplines in community".[29]

This focus became the overriding focus of Cape Town. Lausanne III still talked quite a lot about strategies of outreach and evangelization, of the wise use of media and the need for integral service. But the backdrop was discipleship and a call to humility, integrity and simple lifestyle. As disciples, we are to walk in the light; we must be different from the divided and broken world in which we serve. The CTC was quite specific[30] in relating this to misuse of power, idolatry of success, wrong handling of resources and lack of faithfulness. Discipleship has to do with being a counter-culture, confronting a secular worldview that also is spreading in the global south. Nominalism is no longer just a western problem; it is also relevant in churches with great vitality, but lacking solid biblical teaching.

---

[25] Three of the topics dealt with by three of the eight commissions at Edinburgh1910.
[26] Tokyo 2010 Declaration, 208.
[27] Tokyo 2010 Declaration, 209.
[28] *Common Call,* 1.
[29] *Common Call,* 2.
[30] *CTC,* 58ff.

The *Cape Town Commitment* has the form of a declaration of love – 'For the Lord we love' because he loved us first. It is this love that defines and characterises the identity of the disciples. "We therefore commit ourselves afresh to come to the Father through Jesus the Son: to receive and respond to his fatherly love; to live in obedience under his Fatherly discipline; to reflect his Fatherly character in our behaviour and attitudes …"[31] The obedience is to Christ: "Jesus calls us to discipleship, to take up our cross and follow him in the path of self-denial, servanthood and obedience."[32] In the same way we are called to commit ourselves to the truth and the life which the Bible requires: "Nothing commends the gospel more eloquently than a transformed life, and nothing brings it into discredit so much as personal inconsistency … we recommit ourselves to prove our love for God's Word by believing and obeying it. There is no biblical mission without biblical living."[33]

Commitment to mission grows out of such a discipleship. God calls his people to share his mission: "Our mission is wholly derived from God's mission, addresses the whole of God's creation, and is grounded at its centre in the redeeming victory of the cross."[34] We should live the truth, be the face of Jesus, especially so among family and colleagues. Christian leaders are therefore challenged to train people in 'whole-life discipleship'. Cape Town is clearly inspiring and challenging us to radical obedient discipleship and to radical Cross-centred reconciliation.

A third important legacy from Edinburgh 1910 is the vision of mission and unity. A primary reason for calling the 1910 conference was a longing for more 'Co-operation and the Promotion of Unity'.[35] Closer co-operation would result in more effective evangelism. The conference was, however, not supposed to have on its agenda the question of uniting churches, but, even so, some of the delegates from Asia voiced their hope for the oneness of the church in the future. This set in motion a movement and a longing for the unity of the church which eventually led to the formation of WCC in 1948. One of the Edinburgh 2010 commissions dealt with the topic of 'Mission and unity – ecclesiology and mission', and *The Common Call* expresses commitment to that unity for which Christ lived and prayed:

> … we are called to ongoing co-operation, to deal with controversial issues and to work towards a common vision. We are challenged to welcome one another in our diversity, affirm our membership through baptism in the One Body of Christ, and recognize our need for mutuality, partnership, collaboration and networking in mission, so that the world might believe.[36]

[31] *CTC*, 13.
[32] *CTC*, 14.
[33] *CTC*, 18, quoting the *Manila Manifesto*.
[34] *CTC*, 28.
[35] The topic for one of the eight commissions in 1910.
[36] *Common Call*, 2.

Both mission and unity have their roots in the life of the Trinity and in God who sends the Son and his Spirit to bring salvation. It is not possible to be true to the New Testament and be unconcerned about the unity of the church.

This urge also has to do with building alliances and networks. The Tokyo 2010 Declaration concludes with a call to "effective cooperative efforts of the entire global body of believers. To facilitate cooperation and on-going cooperation between mission structures worldwide, we agree to the necessity of a global network of mission structures".[37] This call is, however, more guided by the need for action than for unity. The call is for pragmatic co-operation in a task-oriented manner and less an invitation to talk about ecclesiology and church unity.

The CTC opens by affirming that those who speak are 'members of the worldwide Church of Jesus Christ'.[38] Under the heading 'We love the people of God' the document emphasizes that this love calls for unity, a unity in love across the world's inveterate divisions: 'We urgently seek a new global partnership within the body of Christ across all continents, rooted in profound mutual love, mutual submission, and dramatic economic sharing without paternalism or unhealthy dependency'.[39] In a Section on the Unity of the Church we find lamentations over the dividedness and divisiveness of our churches and organizations and a call to make every effort to maintain the unity of the Spirit in the bond of peace.

> While we recognize that our deepest unity is spiritual, we long for greater recognition of the missional power of visible, practical, earthly unity. So we urge Christian sisters and brothers worldwide, for the sake of our common witness and mission, to resist the temptation to split the body of Christ, and to seek the paths of reconciliation and restored unity wherever possible.[40]

These are strong words of theology and ecclesiology. However, what happened on the floor and on the stage in Cape Town sometimes contradicted the ecumenical affirmation. The observers in Cape Town from the WCC Commission on World Mission and Evangelism had this to say about relations with other Christians:

- We are concerned about the way relations with other Christians were represented – and not represented, especially on the opening evening.
- We appreciated the invitation to the General Secretary of the World Council of Churches to address the Congress. Even though this was before the conference was officially opened, it was significant in being the first such invitation.

---

[37] Tokyo 2010 Declaration, 210.
[38] *CTC*, 6.
[39] *CTC*, 26f.
[40] *CTC*, 65f.

- We are worried about claims that were made on the opening evening about this being the most diverse Christian gathering ever, and that it represents all the world's Christians. We do not believe this to be the case.
- We did not see ourselves clearly in the portrayal of Christian history to 1910, and we were puzzled as to why there was a sudden jump from 1910 to 2010 with no attention to mission movements and mission thinking in the last one hundred years.
- We were disappointed that the opportunity was lost on the first evening to affirm Edinburgh 2010, in which both Lausanne and WEA were stakeholders, along with WCC … the Catholic Church, many global communions, and so on.[41]

So how does one reconcile the Lausanne focus on 'the whole church' with the sad fact that WCC and Lausanne's participation in Edinburgh 2010 were made invisible on the stage in Cape Town?

There are still different views among Conciliars and Evangelicals on some key theological and ecclesiological issues. Most important among these issues are the uniqueness of Christ, the view of revelation in other living faiths, the understanding of Scripture as the sole source of and norm for faith and praxis, the radical nature of sin, and the role of the *magisterium* (pastoral office) vis-à-vis the priesthood of all believers. This fact makes it even more important that the conversation between these theologies of mission continues – and that Lausanne and WEA participate actively and wholeheartedly. The call for unity, as expressed in the *Cape Town Commitment*, is clear but may be interpreted as if it is an internal unity among evangelicals that is called for. Lausanne has been clear on what is meant by 'gospel' and 'world' (in its motto 'Calling the Whole Church Taking the Whole Gospel to the Whole World'), but what is meant by 'the whole church'? It is urgent and vital for mission in the 21st century that evangelicals understand and acknowledge positively the larger ecumenical context. This does not ignore the biblical call to guard the good deposit, the faith of the apostles and the Gospel of truth.

On the Way to 2110

Some of the topics and concerns dealt with at the conferences in 2010 will remain on the agenda for church and mission on the way to 2110.[42] The West will increasingly be a mission field – and a difficult mission field with "a cold contempt for the Gospel which is harder to face than

[41] *Feedback of observers from the Commission on World Mission and Evangelism of the World Council of Churches to the organisers of Cape Town 2010.*

[42] Kenneth R. Ross, *Edinburgh 2010. Springboard for Mission* (Edinburgh 2010, 2009), 53ff.

opposition ..."[43] Migration as a massive movement from the non-western world to the western world will continue. Concern for the poor will be with us, but even more so the missionary activity in which the poor, as primary agents of mission, take the Gospel to the rich. Post-modernity will be a new cultural frontier for the Gospel calling for the creation of new languages, in the same way as mission always has been a translation project. The 21st century will be marked by the growing Pentecostal-Charismatic movement, bringing new vitality to Christian witness and causing havoc in terms of dogma and order. Plurality of religions and a pluralistic society will challenge us to get involved in constructive dialogue without losing sight of the uniqueness of Christ. Responsibility for creation and the environment will increasingly be on the mission agenda and will question our lifestyles. And we shall have to deal afresh with the matter of unity in new ways as southern Christianity takes the lead and jumps over the traditional confessional fences.

Criss-crossing these concerns and challenges will be, I believe, *a call to rethink mission as ministry of reconciliation and to revisit spirituality as a source of mission.* The global war on terrorism, the growing gap between rich and poor, conflicting truth claims, the jagged borders of ethnicity, and the suppression of women are some of the challenges to churches to come up with different tools for reconciliation. Reconciliation with God and with my fellow human beings is the heart of the Gospel.

Cape Town 2010 had as its watchword 'God in Christ, reconciling the world to himself'. In a similar way, the WCC Commission on World Mission and Evangelism gathered in 2005 under the theme 'Come, Holy Spirit, Heal and Reconcile'.[44] And Edinburgh 2010 has recently published a whole volume on 'Mission as Ministry of Reconciliation'.[45] These various streams converge in an understanding of reconciliation as a new paradigm on mission – not just any type of reconciliation, but a 'radical Cross-centered reconciliation, leading to unity, to growth in love as well as growth in faith and hope.'[46] There are many reasons (inside and outside the Christian community) why reconciliation, together with discipleship, is so central. Chris Rice[47] calls our attention to what might be termed God's 'triple reconciliation' for individual persons, society, and creation.

The Bible declares God's redemptive purpose for creation itself. Integral mission means discerning, proclaiming and living out the biblical truth that

---

[43] Leslie Newbigin, *Unfinished Agenda: An Autobiography* (Grand Rapids, MI: Eerdmans, 1985).

[44] Jacques Matthey, "Athens 2005: Reconciliation and Healing as an Imperative for Mission", in Robert Schreiter, Tormod Engelsviken & Knud Jørgensen (eds), *Mission as Ministry of Reconciliation* (Oxford, UK: Regnum, 2013).

[45] Schreiter, Engelsviken & Jørgensen (eds), *Mission as Ministry of Reconciliation.*

[46] CTC, 70.

[47] Chris Rice, "Cape Town 2010: Reconciliation and Discipleship", in Schreiter, Engelsviken & Jørgensen (eds), *Mission as Ministry of Reconciliation.*

the Gospel is God's good news, through the cross and resurrection of Jesus Christ, for individual persons, and for society, and for creation. All three are broken and suffering because of sin; all three are included in the redeeming love and mission of God; all three must be part of the comprehensive mission of God's people. Christian unity is the creation of God, based on our reconciliation with God and with one another.[48]

Against this background, I believe the following perspectives[49] are essential on our way towards 2110:

- Mission needs witnesses deeply rooted 'in Christ' (2 Cor 5:14-21). The manner Paul talks about baptism in Romans 6 describes 'in Christ' as being included in the historical death and resurrection of Christ himself. Therefore, and only therefore, am I a new creation. What happened to Christ, happened to me. When Christ was mocked, ridiculed and spat on, I was mocked, ridiculed and spat on. When Christ was crucified, I was crucified and died with him. When Christ was raised to life, I was raised to life. Why is this so important? Because it is the story of how God in Christ reconciled me, and therefore, and only therefore, the story he has sent me as his ambassador to share with others: 'Be reconciled with God!' – let God change you, as he changed me.
- Any model of reconciliation is embedded within a particular culture and structure. Awareness of this structure is essential for understanding what reconciliation in this case is all about. Reconciliation is an action, a praxis, a struggle and a movement before it becomes a theory or a general principle. Reconciliation is never ahistorical. It can only be grasped and understood as a process in which we become engaged.
- Reconciliation is concrete: It is about building bridges, about allowing conflicting stories to interact and collide in ways that create meeting space, build relationships and help restructure power relations. But for reconciliation to be genuine, it must be *tangible, visible* and *concrete*. There are concrete steps to be taken – leaving my gift at the altar as I hurry to be reconciled to my brother, stretching out a hand as a sign of forgiveness.
- Mission as ministry of reconciliation is vulnerable mission in the midst of a world of fear. Vulnerability is in my view an enabling condition for mission. In the Bible's image of a reconciling God, we meet his vulnerability, and in Christ God makes God self-vulnerable, to the extent that Jesus is God's 'wound in the world' (K. Koyama). The vulnerable God calls us to be vulnerable if we want to be 'wounded healers' in his service.

---

[48] *CTC*, 20.

[49] These perspectives are based on the eighteen case studies on reconciliation found in Schreiter, Engelsviken & Jørgensen (eds), *Mission as Ministry of Reconciliation*.

A second overriding concern on the way to 2110 will be *spirituality as a source of mission.* In several of the documents and statements from 2010 spirituality is highlighted,[50] a spirituality that encompasses prayer, worship, Scripture, and the call to live as witnesses in our daily life. A central component in the Norwegian centenary celebration in 2010 was the visit of a team with members from the global south. While Edinburgh 1910 was the west making strategies for the south, we wanted the team from the south to challenge church and mission in Norway. The topic was 'Transforming Mission'. Rather than presenting us with a set of strategies, the team said loud and strongly: "Transforming mission is about spirituality." It is the Holy Spirit who makes dead bones live again. The life of church and mission is the life of God's Spirit in the world. The sources for this life are to be found in Word and Sacrament. The means of grace transform us into new human beings. This spirituality finds many expressions: adoration, prayer, meditation, contemplation, spiritual guidance, and equipping God's people with spiritual gifts. And pay attention to the spiritual yearning among many. Note such signs as the retreat movement, the interest in pilgrimage, the Taizé movement, the Sant'Egidio movement, *lectio divina* – and don't forget to monitor what happens on the borders of Christian communities in the form of new religious movements and a secular spirituality. The team then challenged us to live within the triangle of 'word', 'prayer', and 'everyday life'. Many among us live a superficial spiritual life. God's people need to wake up to God's power. When he acts, the renewal comes, as Christians in the global south experience. Learn from them how to live out spirituality in everyday life outside the walls of the church, in a life of incarnation. 'If the Word does not become flesh (*sarx*) it becomes the sarcophagus (the coffin) of the gospel'.[51]

Edinburgh 1910 talked about 'advancing the kingdom of Christ'. Today we should rather talk about mission as 'joining in with the Spirit', a movement from below, less a task than a spirituality.[52] The spiritual life is the context which creates and gives form to mission. And this spirituality encompasses both communion with God (*contemplatio*) and action in the world (*praxis*). The two should not be divided. Contemplation without praxis is escape from reality; praxis without contemplation is activism that lacks transcendent meaning. *A Common Call* describes such a holistic spirituality in the following way:

> Knowing the Holy Spirit who blows over the world at will, reconnecting creation and bringing authentic life, we are called to become communities of compassion and healing, where young people are actively participating in

---

[50] See e.g. *CTC*, 15-16, 58-64; *Common Call*, 1.

[51] Knud Jørgensen, "Misjon til forandring – transforming mission", in *Norwegian Journal of Missiology*, No 1-2, Vol 65, 2011, 76-86.

[52] Kirsteen Kim, "Mission in the Twenty-First Century" in Kirsteen Kim & Andrew Anderson (eds), *Edinburgh 2010. Mission Today and Tomorrow* (Oxford, UK: Regnum, 2011), 360f.

> mission, and women and men share power and responsibilities fairly, where there is a new zeal for justice, peace and the protection of the environment, and renewed liturgy reflecting the beauties of the Creator and creation.[53]

Conclusion

Under the banner and heading of 'God Is on the Move', Cape Town took us every night on a tour around the world to see and celebrate what the Triune God is doing. God is on the move. 'Joining in with the Spirit' is another way of calling us to move in step with God. On the way we must never lose sight of the vision of Edinburgh 1910 'The Evangelization of the World in this Generation'. Unless 'this generation' is evangelized, there will be no church in the next generation. As my father often said to me, "Remember, God has no grandchildren!" Faithfulness to Edinburgh 1910 challenges us to carry with us the vision of world evangelization, of discipleship and discipling, and of mission and unity.

As God is on the move, so we must be on the move – not primarily in terms of strategies and new methods of evangelization and church growth, but by being 'wounded healers' in a broken world and by demonstrating a true spirituality of contemplation and praxis.

[53] *Common Call,* 1.

DIALOGUE AND MISSION IN A GLOBALIZED WORLD DEVELOPMENTS IN THE WORLD COUNCIL OF CHURCHES AND THE LAUSANNE MOVEMENT

Øyvind Økland

'Dialogue' has become a frequently used term in Christian mission theology. It is a very recent concept though, and was introduced only about fifty years ago. What was the background for its introduction, and how has the understanding of it been shaped to what it is today? Literature tends to talk about 'liberal' and 'conservative' understandings of dialogue, without a specific definition of where it comes from and the different nuanced interpretations of the concept. And how do these 'liberal' and 'conservative' positions understand the meaning of dialogue in a globalized world, where the religions increasingly meet and have to relate closely to each other's? Have there been developments in the viewpoints, and what are the similarities and differences? And how do the different positions relate to culture and the plurality of cultures? The aim of this article is to show how the development of the dialogue concept in the ecumenical movement has played a role in the evangelical movement's understanding of mission in a changing and globalized world. At the same time, the developments in the evangelical movement have also had consequences for the ecumenical understanding of mission.

To show this, I have looked at some ecumenical and evangelical conference papers from 1961 till 2010 as the basis of the analysis. Ecumenicals are here defined as persons oriented toward the World Council of Churches (WCC), and evangelicals are defined as those who today prefer to support the Lausanne Movement. It must, however, be emphasized that there is a substantial overlap between the two, and it is impossible to have clear-cut dividing lines between them.

The 1960s: Identity Formation

Dialogue was first used in an official WCC document in 1961, at the WCC General Assembly in New Delhi. It was mentioned together with other missionary methods, such as group dynamics, and study groups without giving any further definition.[1] That year the WCC and the International Missionary Council (IMC) merged and became the Division (later Commission) for World Mission and Evangelism (CWME). This symbolized that mission was now understood as an integrated part of church life. The objective of this commission was "to further the proclamation to the whole world of the Gospel of Jesus Christ, to the end that all men may believe in him and be saved".[2]

An urgent issue for CWME was to respond to cultural and religious pluralism in the world.[3] Many non-western churches joined the WCC, among them eleven African, two Latin American and a larger number of Orthodox churches,[4] and WCC had an increasing contingent of persons from the third world in the leadership of WCC, especially from India, such as Paul David Devandan, M. M. Thomas, and Stanley J. Samartha.[5]

CWME's first meeting in Mexico in 1963 dealt more fully with the dialogue concept, and gave it a deeper meaning.[6] A true dialogue was not only having a listening attitude, but being willing to learn what God was revealing in the dialogue, and, consequently, a willingness to change: "Faithfulness to this task of witness to men of other faiths will assuredly increase the Christian's own understanding of the Gospel and devotion to his Savior."[7] The most fundamental new perspective coming from the Mexico meeting was the understanding that mission no longer was from the western churches to the rest of the world. Mission took place by people from all continents in all continents.

The ecumenical interpretation of dialogue provoked the evangelicals, especially after the report from 1966, called *The Church for Others* (CFO), which viewed 'humanization' and *shalom* as the goal of mission. This report was answering the challenges from secularized society. Secularism as an ideology was distinguished from secularization which was a God-willed process.[8] Therefore, God was seen as being active in the world, and not only within the church. The church could even prevent the proclamation of the Gospel to humanity. The church was not supposed to

---

[1] Willliam A. Visser't Hooft (ed), *The New Delhi Report: The Third Assembly of the World Council of Churches, 1961* (New York: SCM Press, 1962).

[2] Willliam A. Visser't Hooft, *The New Delhi Report*, 421.

[3] Visser't Hooft, *The New Delhi Report*, 250.

[4] Roger C. Bassham, *Mission Theology: 1948:1975. Years of Worldwide Creative Tension, Evangelical and Roman Catholic* (Pasadena: William Carey Library, 1979), 61.

[5] J. Verkuyl, *Contemporary Missiology. An Introduction* (Grand Rapids, MI: Eerdmans, 1978), 75-76.

[6] R. K. Orchard (ed), *Witness in Six Continents. Records of the Meeting of the Commission on World Mission and Evangelism* (London: Edinburgh House Press, 1964), 146-147.

[7] Orchard, *Contemporary Missiology*, 19, 148.

[8] *The Church for Others and the Church for the World (CFO)* (Geneva: WCC Publications, 1967), 9-10.

proclaim to an audience who was just listening passively. Dialogue was therefore self-evident, and not monologue. The relationship between human experience and the Gospel should be the most important point in all dialogues.[9] These new viewpoints were very much seen in the WCC conference on Church and Society in Geneva in 1966; it stated *inter alia* that the churches should work for the transformation of society.[10]

In 1967 WCC arranged a meeting of Orthodox, Roman Catholics and Protestant Christians in Kandy, Sri Lanka (then Ceylon). The conference was particularly devoted to discuss the dialogue concept. A fundamental principle for dialogue was the fact that Christ is active in the hearts of all human beings. The genuine willingness to listen was the most fundamental basis for the dialogue. When a Christian enters into dialogue with another human being, Christ is present, and Christ can speak to the Christian through the non-Christian. Dialogue is a positive effort to get a deeper understanding of the truth through a common discovery of the other's convictions and witness. And in the dialogue something new happens: if it is genuine, a new and unknown dimension is introduced.[11]

At the general assembly in Uppsala in 1968[12] dialogue was described as a natural consequence of a meeting between religions, "a genuinely Christian approach to others must be human, personal, relevant and humble".[13] The Uppsala document stated that Christ speaks in this dialogue. The focus was not on conversion, but on the revelation of Christ in the dialogue. Proclamation and dialogue were not the same, but they complemented each other in a total witness.

Karl Barth's and Hendrik Kraemer's[14] 'theology of discontinuity' had been dominant within WCC until 1961, but now a 'theology of continuity' became more and more important, also called 'theology of dialogue'.[15] Dialogue went from being a more sensitive missionary method, to becoming a concept filled with theological content.[16]

Against the background of these developments, the evangelicals both within and outside WCC felt the need to respond. An evangelical conference in Wheaton in April 1966 expressed its scepticism towards

---

[9] *CFO*, 27.

[10] *World Conference on Church and Society* (official report) (Geneva: WCC Publications, 1967), 49.

[11] "Christians in Dialogue with Men of Other Faiths: The Kandy Report", *Religion and Society*, 14, No. 2 (1967): 64-69.

[12] N. Goodall (ed), *The Uppsala Report 1968: Official Report of the Fourth Assembly of the World Council of Churches, Uppsala July 4th-20th 1968* (Geneva: WCC Publications, 1968), 28.

[13] Goodall, *The Uppsala Report 1968*, 29.

[14] Hendrik Kraemer, *The Christian Message in a Non-Christian world* (London: Edinburgh House, 1938).

[15] Olav G. Myklebust, *Misjonskunnskap* (Oslo: Gyldendal, 1976), 157-60.

[16] Visser't Hooft, *The New Delhi Report*, 78, 83, 84.

WCC on several points. Billy Graham, known for his evangelistic campaigns, using proclamation leading to conversion as a method, was a prominent figure here. The integration of IMC and WCC was especially criticized.[17] At the conference WCC was judged as universalistic and syncretistic.[18] The slogan from the Student Volunteer Movement from 1910 was an important background for the conference: 'The evangelization of the world in this generation.' Dialogue was not mentioned in the final document from the Congress, but it emphasized the need to study social sciences in order to communicate the Gospel in the most effective way.[19] In this way dialogue was just defined as a useful method which did not alter the foundation of the Christian Gospel.

Some months later *Christianity Today* sponsored another large evangelical conference in Berlin. Donald McGavran and Peter Beyerhaus reacted especially to the 'depreciation' of the church and the 'appreciation' of the world, as presented in the new model: 'God-world-church',[20] and not as before: 'God-church-world'.[21] Apparently, the primary goal of mission was no longer to win new members to the church,[22] but 'Christian presence' – to be a part of and show solidarity with the oppressed peoples' struggle against the oppressor. For evangelicals, it was important to emphasize that they were not willing to compromise the content of the Gospel. New methodologies were welcomed, and *Christian presence* and dialogue were approved of as long as they functioned as missionary methods only, and not as a new mission theology. *Proclamation* was, however, still the primary method, and the viewpoints of the WCC were regarded as posing a fundamental crisis in mission.[23]

The result of changes in the WCC and the evangelical polemics against it resulted in a growing identity formation among evangelicals, to find their own foundations, and to react against ecumenical theology and its understanding of mission. The 1960s was therefore characterized by a mutual influence between the two groups, but in a polarizing manner.

---

[17] Bassham, *Mission Theology: 1948:1975. Years of Worldwide Creative Tension, Evangelical and Roman Catholic,* 210.

[18] Harold Lindsell (ed), *The Church's Worldwide Mission: Proceedings of the Congress on the Church's Worldwide Mission, 4-16 April, 1966, at Wheaton College* (Waco, TX: Word Books, 1966), 89

[19] Lindsell, *The Church's Worldwide Mission,* 232-233.

[20] *CFO,* 18.

[21] E. Persson (ed), *Allting nytt? En bok om Uppsala 68* (Stockholm: Verbum, 1968), 30.

[22] *CFO,* 19.

[23] Peter Beyerhaus, *Krise i misjonen. Med Frankfurt-erklæringen om grunnlagskrisen i misjonen* (Oslo: Lunde, 1970).

The 1970s: Coming of Age

The beginning of the 70s marked a climax in the opposition against the WCC among evangelicals. In a meeting of independent university lecturers and theologians, among others, in Frankfurt 1970, the 'fundamental crisis' within modern missions was discussed. The Frankfurt Declaration stated that proclamation leading to salvation of the individual was the basic foundation in mission. Dialogue was accepted as a method, but only as a 'good point of contact' to mission.[24]

Within the WCC dialogue was by the early 70s an integrated part of its missionary thinking, as an independent sub-division of Faith and Witness, with Stanley Samartha as the first director. The Central Committee meeting in Addis Ababa in 1971 discussed the concept more thoroughly than before. It was stated that dialogue was not a replacement of traditional mission. At the same time it was recognized that in dialogue, mission could lose its real content on the one hand, and on the other be accused of using dialogue as just another method for proselytizing. There was a disagreement in the meeting as to whether dialogue would 'blunt the cutting edge' of mission, or whether the community of human and spiritual discourse created by dialogue would further it.[25]

CWME's second meeting in Bangkok in 1973 brought to light many differences vis-à-vis the evangelicals. The resistance among some towards traditional mission was evident, especially from Third World churches at this conference. The call to dialogue was seen to 'arise out of our faith'.[26] It was considered important to see what God was doing among people from other religions and ideologies, and on the other hand, adherents of other religions should be enabled to tell about their experiences in dialogue. One must listen carefully to their insights, which meant that they have a mission too. They have a mission because one in dialogue shares common human aspirations and responsibilities, and such a dialogue is therefore a meeting between people from different cultural and religious traditions who, on both sides, claim to have an 'authentic relationship with the Ultimate'.[27] The relationship between dialogue and mission was discussed, and the conclusion was that there was not necessarily any tension between the two. Dialogue would lead to a deeper understanding, and would clear away

---

[24] Peter Beyerhaus, *Missions: which Way? Humanization Or Redemption. Contemporary evangelical perspectives* (Grand Rapids, MI.: Zondervan Publishing House, 1971), 112.

[25] Stanley J. Samartha (ed), *Living Faiths and the Ecumenical Movement* (Geneva: WCC Publications, 1971), 51-52.

[26] Bangkok Assembly, 1973, *Minutes and Report of the Assembly of the Commission on World Mission an Evangelism of the World Council of Churches, Dec 31, 1972 and Jan 9-12, 1973* (Geneva: WCC Publications, 1973), 78.

[27] *Bangkok Assembly*, 79.

misunderstandings.[28] And there was appreciation of the fact that mission was increasingly carried out in the spirit of dialogue.

The evangelical Congress in Lausanne in 1974 laid the ground for a viable and constructive connection between evangelicals worldwide. Following Lausanne, both Manila in 1989 and Cape Town in 2010 dealt with fundamental issues in the Christian faith, including how to communicate it to others.

The Lausanne Congress contributed significantly to an evangelical identity and solidarity. It was attended by approximately 2,500 delegates from 150 countries, with half of them from the Majority World.[29] John Stott was the architect behind the formation of the *Lausanne Covenant* and his thinking would also be decisive in the coming years.

Three methods of communicating the Gospel were especially mentioned in the *Lausanne Covenant*: presence, dialogue and proclamation. Christian presence meant a physical presence of Christians to witness about Christ through their deeds, and dialogue was to listen attentively in order to understand the other part better.[30] Proclamation was understood as persuading people to be 'reconciled with God' on a personal level.[31]

When the *Lausanne Covenant* mentioned the necessity of social action and its important place in mission, many saw this as an influence from the WCC.[32] So far, mission had been interpreted basically as the proclamation of the Gospel. Evangelicals had reacted against the Social Gospel movement at the beginning of the twentieth century and consequently not defined social work as a central part of mission, although *diakonia* had always been central to the church's part in mission.[33] The *Church for Others* report and the Uppsala meeting's emphasis of social action had, however, not passed unnoticed, and now this concern were taken up by the evangelicals as well.

The same openness from the ecumenicals towards the evangelicals was found in the WCC's General Assembly in Nairobi in 1975. It was more open to the evangelical focus on world evangelization, although there was a considerable concern among some of the participants. The confrontation line was especially obvious between some north European (Scandinavian?)

---

[28] *Bangkok Assembly*, 79.

[29] James D. Douglas (ed), *Let the Earth Hear His Voice: International Congress on World Evangelisation, Lausanne, Switzerland. Official Reference Volume: Papers and Responses* (Minneapolis, MI.: World Wide Publications, 1975).

[30] John Stott, *The Lausanne Covenant. An exposition and Commentary* (Lausanne: LCWE, 1978), 20.

[31] Stott, *The Lausanne Covenant. An exposition and Commentary,* 20

[32] Stott, *The Lausanne Covenant. An exposition and Commentary,* 25.

[33] Al Tizon, *Transformation after Lausanne. Radical Evangelical Mission in Global-Local Perspective* (Oxford, UK: Regnum, 2008), 23.

theologians and theologians from Asia.[34] John Stott was among the participants who managed to make the conference include an introduction that focused more on evangelization.[35] Furthermore, the evangelical fear of syncretistic tendencies within WCC was said to be without any foundation. A statement was made against any form of syncretism, in spite of M. M. Thomas' slogan from the opening address of 'Christ-centered syncretism'.[36] The Nairobi meeting may be regarded as a reaction to the documents from the Uppsala meeting, which had provoked strong feelings also within the WCC. When dialogue got its own section at the conference, the north European theologians[37] regarded it as their duty to fight for the necessity of evangelization and conversion.[38]

In April 1977 another WCC dialogue conference was held in Chiang Mai, Thailand. The objective was to discuss dialogue in the Christian community and in society generally. It resulted in a report that mentioned two basic reasons for the necessity of dialogue. The first reason for dialogue was the closeness we experience with people from other religions and ideologies, therefore as neighbours we should develop "mutual human care and searching for mutual human understanding".[39] And secondly, one should engage in a dialogue in order to realize an extended community where peace and justice were predominant. The vision was to create a world community based on all local societies. Dialogue had to be described, experienced and developed as a lifestyle, and should be seen as a tool to get rid of all possibly distorted pictures we might have of other religions and ideologies. Dialogue was therefore a concrete expression of loving one's neighbour as oneself, according to the Chiang Mai report.[40]

In 1979 the Central Committee of WCC debated and agreed on a statement called 'Guidelines on Dialogue'. This was the first statement by WCC that took an official stand on dialogue. The statement was a modified version of the Chiang Mai statement on dialogue from 1977.[41] The emphasis was, as in Chiang Mai, on a dialogue between different religious communities, and not on scholarly discussion among the religious elite. It was described as a lifestyle more than a philosophical exchange of ideas.

---

[34] Carl F. Hallencreutz, *Dialogue and Community. Ecumenical Issues in Interreligious Relationships* (Uppsala: 1977), 100.

[35] Åge Holter, "Misjonen I Nairobi", in *Norsk Tidsskrift for Misjon*, 30, No. 2 (1976): 65-72.

[36] Holter, "Misjonen I Nairobi", 71.

[37] Hallencreutz, *Dialogue and Community*, 100.

[38] Holter, "Misjonen I Nairobi", 72.

[39] Stanley J. Samartha (ed), *Faith in the Midst of Faiths. Reflections on* Dialogue *in Community* (Geneva: WCC Publications, 1977), 143.

[40] Samartha, *Faith in the Midst of Faiths,* 144.

[41] James A. Scherer and S. B. Bevans (eds), *New Directions in Mission and Evangelization I: Basic Statements 1974-1991* (Maryknoll, NY: Orbis Books, 1992), 12.

Dialogue was regarded as a tool to eliminate wrong perceptions of other religions. The Bible should give the guidelines, but there would always be a danger of syncretism, according to the Chiang Mai report.[42]

The 1980s and 1990s: Convergence?

As seen from the previous periods, the main division lines had been on the view of the relation between evangelization and dialogue. Is an individual conversion necessary as a consequence of salvation, or is dialogue with people of other faiths a goal in itself, to further understanding between peoples of different faiths? WCC had appeared to be more open to a willingness to negotiate one's position. God is at work within other religions too, and one should therefore acknowledge truth elements in them. The evangelicals had reacted against this. They gave their own definitions to dialogue and its relation to mission.

In many ways, the next decades showed signs of increased mutual understanding. In 1980, CMWE had its third meeting in Melbourne and reiterated the proclamation concept and the importance of the church in proclaiming the Gospel to those who have not heard. A starting point for dialogue could be solidarity with the oppressed, and dialogue is not in opposition to mission, but the proclamation of the Gospel should be performed in God's spirit and not aggressively and in a crusading manner, according to the statement from the meeting.[43]

In 1982, the Central Committee of WCC approved an important document, *Mission and Evangelism: an Ecumenical Affirmation.* Some characterized it as 'the single most important ecumenical statement on mission in this period', and it was the only official WCC statement on mission until 2012.[44] Its importance was based on the way it was received in evangelical circles, as well as in ecumenical ones.[45]

The document was characterized by the above-mentioned signs of convergence. It stressed the importance of the church in the proclamation of the Gospel in a manner that had not been done in previous WCC documents.[46] In the Section called 'Witness among people of living faiths', it started out with the need to bring the "message of God's salvation in

---

[42] Samartha, *Faith in the Midst of Faiths,* 144.

[43] *Your Kingdom Come. Mission Perspectives. Report on the World Conference on Mission and Evangelism, Melbourne, Australia, 12-25 May 1980* (WCC: Geneva, 1980), 188.

[44] Scherer & Bevans, *New Directions in Mission and Evangelization I: Basic Statements 1974-1991*, 36.

[45] Alan J. Bailyes, "Evangelical and Ecumenical Understanding of Mission", in *International Review of Mission*, 85, No. 339 (1996): 485-503.

[46] Scherer & Bevans, *New Directions,* 39.

Jesus Christ to every person and to every people".[47] On the other hand, since God is at work among other people, dialogue is necessary to owe them full respect. Witness is always a two-way process, it states.[48] In this way it included both evangelical and ecumenical viewpoints.

This was followed up at the Fifth Assembly of WCC in Vancouver in 1983. The conference had a significant representation of evangelicals "a milestone in ecumenical – evangelical relationships".[49] In 1989, CWME held its fourth meeting in San Antonio, only six weeks before the LCWE's Lausanne II meeting in Manila. A group of evangelicals attended both.[50] Many sections of the San Antonio document were based on *Mission and Evangelism: an Ecumenical Affirmation* from 1982.[51] The shift from the emphasis of the *Church for Others* report on God's action in the world was obvious. Evangelism and mission were now central parts of the church's mission, and the model was again, 'God-church-world'.[52] Dialogue was mentioned towards the end of Section One, which recognizes the complex relationship and the debate about the relationship between witness and dialogue.[53] At the same time, it is recognized that one might meet God through the other person in this dialogue. The tension between the belief that God is present in people from other religions and the fact that salvation is through Jesus Christ is recognized, "at the same time we cannot set limits to God's saving power ... We appreciate this tension, and do not attempt to solve it."[54]

> We do not water down our own commitment if we engage in dialogue; as a matter of fact, dialogue between people of different faiths is spurious unless it proceeds from the acceptance and expression of faith commitment".

Statements such as these were well received among the evangelicals.[55] Also in 1989, over 3,000 persons from 170 countries gathered in Manila for the Lausanne II meeting. They came together on the basis of the *Lausanne Covenant*. The *Manila Manifesto* was a follow-up of Lausanne,

---

[47] Scherer & Bevans, *New Directions in Mission and Evangelization I: Basic Statements 1974-1991,* 50.

[48] Scherer & Bevans, *New Directions in Mission and Evangelization I: Basic Statements 1974-1991,* 50.

[49] Bailyes, "Evangelical and Ecumenical Understanding of Mission", 495.

[50] Bailyes, "Evangelical and Ecumenical Understanding of Mission", 495-496.

[51] Scherer & Bevans, *New Directions in Mission and Evangelization I: Basic Statements 1974-1991,* 73.

[52] Priscilla Pope-Levison, "Evangelism in the WCC", in *IRM*, 81, no. 321 (1992): 121.

[53] Scherer & Bevans, *New Directions in Mission and Evangelization I: Basic Statements 1974-1991,* 79

[54] Scherer & Bevans, *New Directions in Mission and Evangelization I: Basic Statements 1974-1991,* 79.

[55] Norman E. Thomas, "Ecumenical Directions in Mission: Melbourne to San Antonio", in *Missiology: An International Review*, 18, no. 2 (1990:) 149-161.

emphasizing the authority of the Bible and evangelism as "the proclamation of the historical, biblical Christ as Saviour and Lord".[56] As in the *Lausanne Covenant*, the priority was given to traditional mission. The WCC meeting in San Antonio the same year highlighted the importance of evangelism; the evangelicals and the ecumenicals should look more at what they had in common than the differences.[57]

In 1991 the organization of the WCC was restructured. Twenty years after placing dialogue as a sub-unit, apart from the Missions and Evangelism department where it had been before, it was no longer a specific unit or office, but the concern for dialogue became part of different units. The theological questions of dialogue were placed in Unit 2, Mission, Education & Witness, while general inter-religious matters and practical dialogue belonged to the General Secretariat.[58] By this restructuring, the difficult and hot issue of the theological meaning of dialogue was lifted away from the commonly accepted perception of the need for a witness that should be carried out in a dialogical spirit of mutual respect and understanding.

We conclude from this period that these two main streams within the Protestant mission movement in a way were interdependent, and that they were listening to the other part when forming their views, either in complete opposition to it or by appreciating some aspects of it. These developments were most clearly seen from 1974 onwards. According to van Butselaar in 1985, there were signs of convergence as well as signs to the contrary,[59] although some claimed that WCC in its eagerness to dialogue with people from other religions had been more willing to listen and learn from these than from their own 'brothers' within the evangelical movement.[60]

2000 and Beyond: Adjusting to New Global Challenges

From the 1990s and onwards, the world has seen a rapid growth in technology and migration, making the world even more interconnected. Globalization, as well as *post-modern*ism, has become a concept widely used in academia as well as in popular culture. A common way of understanding globalization has been to regard it as an increasing

[56] www.lausanne.org/en/documents/manila-manifesto.html.

[57] Alan Neely & James A. Scherer, "San Antonio and Manila 1989: ... Like Ships in the Night?", in *Missiology: An International Review*, 18, no. 2 (1990):139.

[58] S. Wesley Ariarajah, *The Bible and People of Other Faiths* (Geneva: WCC, 1991), 2-5.

[59] Jan van Butselaar, "Dialogue and Witness" in *The Ecumenical Review*, 37, no. 4 (1985): 119-125.

[60] David J. Hesselgrave, "Interreligious Dialogue: Biblical and Contemporary Perspectives" in David Hesselgrave (ed), *Theology and Mission. Papers given at Trinity Consultation. No. 1* (Grand Rapids, MI: Baker, 1978), 236.

consciousness of being part of the same world.[61] The ecumenicals as well as the evangelicals have realized the need for a taking this new world situation into account.

In Christian mission the consequences of globalization need to be taken into consideration as well.[62] In the Lausanne Movement the challenges of globalization and *post-modern*ity were given special attention in two papers from working groups. Globalization illustrates the diversity we live in as human beings and as Christians; there are different perceptions of reality, and the challenge is to realize that we are on the same global road.[63] The papers are of importance because they recognize a new globalized and *post-modern* reality, and discuss the challenges.[64]

The year 2010 marked the centenary anniversary of the ecumenical gathering in Edinburgh 1910. A large network of organizations and Catholic, Orthodox, Pentecostal, African indigeneous, evangelical and Protestant churches co-operated in and came together for this conference. An outcome was a statement where dialogue was not mentioned explicitly. It acknowledged the need for rethinking missions in a plural world, for instance, through migration.[65] The Lausanne Movement was part of this endeavour and event.

The third gathering of the Lausanne Movement took place in Cape Town in 2010. Here *post-modern*ism and relativist pluralism were recognized explicitly as a challenge to mission. Jesus Christ as the ultimate truth was emphasized, as opposed to secular relativism. Truth was also stressed as an ultimate value and goal in all aspects of life, such as in the workplace, in the globalized media, in mission, in science and emerging technologies, and public arenas.[66] Dialogue was mentioned in the document by using Paul's engagement with Jews and Gentiles. In relation to people of other faiths, in Section IIA, the truth aspect runs through repetitively, emphasizing the exclusivist, rather than a relativistic approach to mission and dialogue. The document could be read as having a more negative view of dialogue and

---

[61] See e.g. the definition in Roland Robertson, *Globalization. Social Theory and Global Action* (London: Sage, 1992), 9.

[62] See an analysis of the trends and consequences in Kirsteen Kim, "Mission's Changing Landscape: Global Flows and Christian Movements", in *IRM*, 100, No. 2 (2011): 244-267.

[63] Lausanne Occasional Paper 30, *Globalization and the Gospel: Rethinking mission in the contemporary world* (Lausanne: LCWE, 2004).

[64] Lausanne Occasional Paper 31, *The Uniqueness of Christ in a Postmodern World and the Challenge of World Religions* (Lausanne: LCWE, 2004).

[65] www.edinburgh2010.org/fileadmin/Edinburgh_2010_Common_Call_with_explanation.pdf

[66] *Cape Town Commitment*, www.lausanne.org/en/documents/ ctcommitment.html

not seeing the work that God already is doing among people of other faiths, as we can read from Acts 17.[67]

It therefore seems that the similarities and differences between ecumenicals and evangelicals remain the same in this period. WCC had more focus on dialogue. The Lausanne Movement stressed the existence of an ultimate truth, and dialogue as a means of evangelizing with humility and respect. Both movements were very clear in their condemnation of proselytism as a form of conversion based on force and unethical methods.

Dialogue and Mission in a Globalized World

What are the conclusions that we can draw from this short outline of some of the developments?

If we go back to the 1960s, dialogue emerged as a response to some of the challenges of this period. At this time the colonies had gained their independence and there was a growing awareness of a world that had changed from a north-south division to a world where migration took place in many directions. Another feature of the 60s was the secularization and the secularization theories.[68] In the 80s and 90s and onwards globalization and *post-modern*ism, as well as the resurgence of religions, emerged as dominant trends and theories. The world, through technology and migration, had become a smaller place, and the grand theories and belief in universal truth were questioned and for many regarded as out-dated.

Pressing questions in this new reality are how to relate to the variety of religions and the variety of cultures. The first focus here will be to see what the statements say about the truth question and consequently the need for conversion from other religions to Christianity. Is it possible to claim that there is one truth, or is dialogue a method to search for this truth together, and thus having the goal of bringing people from different cultures and religions closer?

A common way of describing the different theology of religions is to categorize them as exclusivist, inclusivist or pluralist.[69] Scott Appleby and Lederach have a slightly different categorization: conversion, witness, solidarity and dialogue.[70] According to them, the conversion mode has

---

[67] Knud Jørgensen, "Kristus til mennesker av annen tro", in Rolf Ekenes, Tormod Engelsviken, Knud Jørgensen, Rolf Kjøde (eds), *Misjon til forandring: Refleksjoner og visjoner fra Lausanne III* (Skjetten: Hermon, 2011) 106f.

[68] An important contribution was Harvey Cox, *The Secular City* (New York: Collier books, 1965).

[69] See e.g. Timothy C. Tennent, *Christianity at the Religious Roundtable: Evangelicalism in Conversation with Hinduism, Buddhism, and Islam* (Grand Rapids, Michigan: Baker Academic, 2002) 16-22.

[70] R. Scott Appleby & Angela J. Lederach, "Conversion, Witness, Solidarity, Dialogue: Modes of the Evangelizing Church in Tension", in *The Review of Faith & International Affairs*, 7, no. 1 (2010): 11-19.

exclusive truth claims and preaches the need for an immediate and personal conversion. The witness mode has exclusive truth claims as well, but here the socio-political and economic issues are also emphasized and thus offer a more holistic paradigm. The solidarity mode differs quite radically from the conversion and witness mode. These Christians are uncomfortable with the truth claims as well as the term 'evangelism'. The focus is on transforming corrupt socio-political systems. Finally, Scott Appleby and Lederach mention the dialogue mode. This mode sees proselytism to be antithetical to the Gospel. The goal is not conversion but to create peaceful relationships, humanly and religiously. In its most extreme form, dialogue is the new paradigm for mission, thus rejecting evangelism and traditional mission.[71]

From the presentation above, it is not possible to place either the ecumenicals or the evangelicals within any of these modes completely. It might, however, be shown that the ecumenicals have tended to lean more towards the dialogue mode and the solidarity mode. Evangelicals have, as we have seen, leaned more towards the conversion and witness mode, but also the dialogue mode. Dialogue can therefore be seen both as a divergent term as well as a possible uniting term, where the ecumenicals and the evangelicals can find common ground. It is all a matter of understanding the content of dialogue and its relation to traditional mission and evangelization.

As we have seen, WCC has on several occasions expressed that there is a tension between dialogue and missions.[72] By giving dialogue increased significance, one can see that a traditional understanding of the proclamation of the Gospel has become weaker within the ecumenical movement. Dialogue should be acknowledged as a completely new attitude towards people with other beliefs, an attitude where it would be impossible to be accused of imperialism.

In WCC's most radical statements it was discipling and the significance of conversion on the horizontal level that were in focus.[73] Ecumenical documents regard the dialogue and what happens in the dialogue as an end in itself, and of importance to the Christian's own understanding of his/her faith. Especially the two Indians M.M. Thomas and Stanley Samartha have had great influence on this way of thinking. They came out of a South Asian context, with a demand of tolerance between the religions, and where the meaning of dialogue was not a personal conversion but, according to Thomas, a revolutionary ferment for a fuller and richer human life. It is within the context of such a dialogue that proclamation of Christ becomes meaningful.[74]

---

[71] Scott Appleby & Lederach, "Conversion, Witness, Solidarity, Dialogue: Modes of the Evangelizing Church in Tension", 18.

[72] Samartha, *Faith in the Midst of Faiths,* 36, 52.

[73] *Bangkok Assembly,* 76.

[74] M. M. Thomas, *Salvation and Humanization*, Madras, CLS, 1971, 4.

In the evangelical conferences, conversion was understood as a personal conversion from sin and to God. Social consequences of the conversion were also recognized, but it was the vertical dimension that had the priority.[75]

The evangelicals used the term dialogue more carefully and did not define it in the same way. The emphasis was therefore still on proclamation, but this proclamation contained both dialogue and communication. The evangelicals emphasize very passionately the fact that there is an absolute truth that can never be changed.

A second *leitmotif* in the statements in the ecumenical-evangelical developments has been the relation between Christianity and the variety of cultures. In colonial times Christianity was closely related to western civilization and other cultures were regarded as pagan or non-Christian. From the 50s and 60s this changes and a more positive view of the pluralism in cultures emerges,[76] and the focus changes to "mission in six continents".[77] This marked a radical shift in the understanding of mission. It was no longer a one-way traffic from the west to the rest, but all parts of the world were involved, and the different cultures deserved respect. The Gospel should be presented differently in the different contexts.

The term 'contextualization' was first introduced by Shoki Coe[78] in 1972 as a response to the need for a new approach to presenting the Gospel within non-western cultures.[79] It was rooted in Latin American liberation theologies of the time and stated that there was a need for "an anthropocentric orientation of theology".[80]

The same anthropocentric and worldly-oriented focus is seen in the *shalom* and humanization concepts found in the *Church for Others* report in 1966. This should be seen in light of the secularization theories[81] of the time and J. C. Hoekendijk's critique of a church-centered approach to mission.[82] God's mission is to the world, and the church is a church only as

---

[75] John R. W. Stott, *Christian Mission in the Modern World* (Downers Grove, IL: IVP, 1975) 25.

[76] Paul Hiebert, "Gospel and Culture: the WCC Project", in *Missiology: An International Review,* 25, No. 2 (1997), 202.

[77] Orchard, *Contemporary Missiology.*

[78] Coe was attached to the Theological Educational Fund (TEF) which was under WCC.

[79] Shoki Coe, "Contextualizing Theology", in Gerhard H. Anderson and T. F. Stranski (eds), *Mission Trends No. 3: Third World Theologies* (New York/Grand Rapids, MI: Paulist Press/Eerdmans, 1976), 19-24.

[80] *B. C. Fleming, Contextualization of Theology: An Evangelical Assessment* (Pasadena, CA: William Carey, 1980), 17.

[81] E.g. Harvey Cox, The Secular City: Secularization and Urbanization in Theological Perspective (New York: Collier Books, 1965).

[82] J.C. Hoekendijk, *The Church Inside Out* (London: Westminster Press, 1966).

far as it is a part of that mission.[83] Dialogue then, according to this view, was a dialogue not primarily with the religions, but with the peoples of these faiths.

As a method of understanding the secular society, the social sciences were important, especially sociology which concentrated mostly on western societies. One should enter a dialogue with sociology to understand the changes in the world as a part of God's mission. A ministry in the world requires an engagement not only led by 'a sociology of change' but also a 'theology of change'.[84] According to this, dialogue and contextualization should take place as 'praxis' between the church and the world, in doing God's mission. Bevans categorizes this contextualization as a praxis model, since the social change and the struggle for human justice are the primary goals of mission.[85]

The evangelicals acknowledged in the same way the need for a mission with a deeper understanding and respect of local cultures, and contextualization was embraced as a useful concept on how this dialogue with local cultures should be practised.[86] The evangelicals operate with a 'contextual indigenization' which means all that was implied in the traditional concept of 'indigenization',[87] but goes deeper, by using the insights from anthropology and the Scriptures.[88]

WCC has been the front-runner in exploring what dialogue might mean. The evangelicals went from being sceptical about dialogue, to accepting it, but giving it its own meaning. A conclusion is therefore that both WCC and the evangelicals have kept proclamation and witness as basic concepts in their view of mission. The understanding of the concept, however, differs. Within WCC the concept is increasingly given dialogical content. The evangelicals have developed it more towards a communicative content. For the evangelicals the changes in this period have primarily taken place at the methodological level, while in WCC there has been development at the theological level. For WCC dialogue was not only a missionary methodology, it was a goal in itself, a goal towards world community and world reconciliation. It was therefore important to speak about a 'theology of dialogue', and dialogue as a part of God's mission.[89]

---

[83] J.C. Hoekendijk, "The Church in Missionary Thinking", in *IRM*, 41, No. 3 (1952) 324-336.

[84] See *CFO,* 27, 49-50; Samartha, 135; Orchard, 126.

[85] Stephen Bevans, *Models of Contextual Theologies* (Maryknoll, NY: Orbis Books, 1992).

[86] John Stott and R. T. Coote (eds), *Gospel and Culture. The Papers of a Consultation on the Gospel and Cuiture, convened by the Lausanne Committee's Theology and Education Group* (Wheaton, IL: William Carey Library, 1979).

[87] David Bosch, *Transforming Mission: Paradigm Shifts in Theology of Mission* (Maryknoll, NY: Orbis, 1991), 301.

[88] Fleming, *Contextualization of Theology: An Evangelical Assessment,* 53.

[89] Samartha, *Faith in the Midst of Faiths,* 22.

The change in the goal of mission in WCC led, as we have seen, to the fact that the evangelicals became opponents to WCC, but from there they developed to be an alternative with their own integrity, and included some of the thinking of WCC. At the same time, WCC came closer to some of the evangelical viewpoints without eliminating the clear dividing lines that had developed since 1961 and seeing dialogue as a goal in itself.[90]

An important lesson should be to regard dialogue in our global and pluralistic society as a dialogue with people of other living religions. Dialogue should take place with consistency between methods and goals, as well as allowing the context to determine the form of witness.[91] Likewise, effective communication of the Christian message is fundamental, but it should contain an authentic concern and respect for the other person, and not regard him or her as objects of conversion, but in a true interpersonal and intercultural spirit.[92] Having said this, eventually the basic question is whether one has a conviction of Christianity as the ultimate truth or not. Then mission can be carried out in a true dialogical spirit.

---

[90] Samartha, *Faith in the Midst of Faiths,* 38.

[91] See Terry Muck & Frances S. Adeney, *Christianity Encountering World Religions. The Practice of Mission in the Twenty-first Century* (Grand Rapids, Michigan: Baker Academic, 2009).

[92] Øyvind Økland, "Intercultural Communication: A tool or a goal? Missionary methodology in view of development in intercultural communication" in *Mission to the World: Communication the Gospel in 21st Century* (Oxford, UK: Regnum, 2008), 163-177.

BEYOND DICHOTOMY: TOWARDS A CONVERGENCE BETWEEN THE ECUMENICAL AND EVANGELICAL UNDERSTANDING OF MISSION IN CHANGING LANDSCAPES

Jooseop Keum

Introduction

In an international symposium to celebrate the centenary of the Edinburgh 1910 World Missionary Conference, Jong Yun Lee claimed, "There is an urgent need for us to reformulate the paradigm, strategy, programme, and even the slogan of mission, in order to pro-actively and effectively respond to the changes in today's world."[1] It is true that both ecumenical and evangelical endeavours in world mission have been losing their dynamism while keeping a dichotomy and even tensions in our mission thinking and practice inherited from ancestors. In the Edinburgh 2010 study process, an interesting statistics was reported: "It can be noted that the percentage of Christians in the world population has not changed significantly for the last hundred years, holding steady at around 33%."[2] Considering that we are still at about the same percentage of Christians in the world as a century ago, in spite of all the efforts we have made for world evangelization, it is urgent to re-imagine mission and evangelism today, as Lee insists.

However, there was a radical change in the internal statistics in the midst of stagnation. In 1910, over 70% of Christians in the world were living in the so-called Christian west, the global north, and less than 30% were living in the south. In 2010, we are facing a reversed reality: more than 70% live in the south and less than 30% in the north.[3] The new WCC

---

[1] Jong Yun Lee, "Can Lausanne Work with WCC as Partner in Mission?" in Kook Il Han (ed), *Centenary of 1910 Edinburgh World Missionary Conference: Retrospect and Prospect of Mission and Ecumenism* (Seoul: Mission Academy, 2009), 307.

[2] CWME Working Group on Mission and Ecclesiology, "The Church as Mission in Its Very Life: Towards Common Witness to Christ and Visible Unity of the Church" in *IRM*, 101.1 (394), April 2012, 109; cited, Ernst Pulsfort (ed), *Herders neuer Atlas der Religionen* (Herder, Freiburg i. Br., 2010), 75.

[3] Cf. Todd M. Johnson, Kenneth R. Ross (eds), *Atlas of Global Christianity* (Edinburgh: Edinburgh University Press), 2009.

Ecumenical Affirmation on Mission and Evangelism approved by the central committee in 2012 raises missiological questions regarding this reality:

> The history of Christian mission has been characterized by conceptions of geographical expansion from a Christian centre to the "un-reached territories", to the ends of the earth. But today we are facing a radically changing ecclesial landscape described as "world Christianity" where the majority of Christians are either living, or have their origins in the global South and East ... What are the insights for mission and evangelism – theologies, agendas and practices – of this "shift of the centre of gravity of Christianity"?[4]

Another phenomenon that merits our attention is the emergence, in the last century, of a strong Pentecostal movement. In the time of Edinburgh 1910, the Pentecostal movement, which had just started burgeoning, was considered a very marginal phenomenon in world Christianity. Today Pentecostal churches have become the second largest after the Roman Catholic Church. In a contemporary ecclesial landscape, approximately half the Christians in the world are Roman Catholic and a quarter are so-called mainline Protestant and Orthodox. The remainder quarter are Pentecostal![5] The exponentially growing Pentecostal churches show a strong missionary fervour. While most of the traditional churches worldwide, regardless of whether they are ecumenical or evangelical, have been stagnant or decreasing in terms of numerical growth; the Pentecostal churches are almost the only ones growing today.

In this new demographic landscape of Christianity, even before considering thematic issues, it is questionable whether the dichotomy of ecumenical and evangelical perspectives is still relevant for envisioning the future of world Christianity. One could even ask whether it is rather a hindrance to 're-formulating' the future of mission. Is it not imperative to articulate a new approach to revitalize mission? What are the emerging issues and main themes? How could we reformulate our mission theology, agenda and programme beyond dichotomy? Where is the dynamism to articulate fresh concepts and to encourage a renewed commitment to mission? In this paper we shall seek a way to overcome the missiological confrontations of the last century and attempt to develop a new synergy between the two approaches, ecumenical and evangelical. It will be argued that one of the most significant missiological developments in the 21st century is a convergence between the ecumenical and evangelical understandings of mission. We shall also examine how this convergence can be nurtured to heal the wounds of divisions and lead to a new

---

[4] *Together towards Life: Mission and Evangelism in Changing Landscape, A New WCC Affirmation on Mission and Evangelism* (hereafter *TTL*), (WCC Central Committee, Crete, Greece), 5th Sept 2012, 1.

[5] Allen Anderson, *An Introduction to Pentecostalism: Global Charismatic Christianity* (Cambridge, CUP, 2004), 1.

opportunity of common witness to the good news of Jesus Christ in a world where the credibility of the Christian faith has been seriously challenged.

Division and Dialogue: A Historical Re-Examination

Looking back to the history of tensions is painful. However, talking about a rosy dream without a critical assessment of history may cause us to repeat the mistakes of the past. Therefore, to better understand the two different perspectives, we will revisit some of the moments of division and re-examine the root causes of missiological misunderstandings.

Kingdom of God vs. World Evangelization

The world mission conference in Edinburgh in 1910 with its watchword of 'the evangelization of the world in this generation' is considered the symbolic starting point of the modern ecumenical movement. There had been earlier major mission conferences, but at Edinburgh, steps were taken towards a certain institutionalization of the co-operation between Protestant mission councils.[6] Edinburgh cannot be considered 'ecumenical' in the actual sense of the word, since there were no Roman Catholic or Orthodox delegates present. Out of the 1400 participants, 17 came from the 'third world'; all of them, in fact, from Asia. Edinburgh had been very carefully prepared in thematic commissions. Despite quite 'progressive' debates in some of those commissions, Edinburgh 1910 reflected in general a traditional conservative and optimistic approach to mission, linking the proclamation of the Gospel to the heathens with the spread of western civilization.

The mood at the second world mission conference, held in Jerusalem in 1928, was quite different. The First World War provoked by 'Christian' countries had profoundly challenged the ideal of western civilization as the embodiment of the Gospel.[7] Edinburgh believed that the evangelization task had already been fulfilled in the west. The missionary obligation was to go out to the unreached territories and teach the good news of Jesus Christ in the non-western world. However, after the experience of Christians killing each other, the limits of the geographical and quantitative understanding of mission to fully explain what Christian mission means were realized. Furthermore, the communist revolution of 1917 had made

---

[6] See *World Missionary Conference 1910 – Report of Commission VIII: Co operation and the Promotion of Unity* (Edinburgh/London: Oliphant, Anderson & Ferrier; New York/Chicago/Toronto: Fleming H. Revell Company), 1910.

[7] "He (Jesus Christ) stands before men as plainly greater than Western civilization, greater than the Christianity that the world has come to know." International Missionary Council, *The World Mission of Christianity: Messages and Recommendations of the Enlarged Meeting of the International Missionary Council held at Jerusalem, March 24th-April 8th, 1928* (IMC, London/New York, 1928), 7.

the dream of evangelizing the whole world within one generation unrealistic.

Therefore, in Jerusalem, a new qualitative concept of mission emerged and was strongly debated. Two major questions came up on which no real consensus was reached: World Evangelization versus Kingdom of God. For one, they were not able to give up the task of evangelizing the whole world but still believed that they could achieve it during their lifetime. It was a non-negotiable mission for them to send out more missionaries to the non-western world. Others revisited the aim of mission – whether the Edinburgh concept of world mission in a geographical and quantitative sense was really what Jesus meant. In sight of Calvary, the representatives of missionaries laid down their own expectations and focused on the mission of Christ, namely the Kingdom of God.[8] Since Jerusalem, the two different approaches, the quantitative and the qualitative concept of mission, have become a missiological backbone of the division between ecumenical and evangelical perspectives in mission. J. Lee evaluates the dichotomy between the above two concepts as follows:

> During the past one hundred years the worldwide Protestant Church has, on the one hand, focused too excessively on "social ethics" and "human liberation" as a consequence of its traumatic experience of the First and Second World Wars and the ideological division of East and West which were the consequences of imperialistic ambitions. On the other hand, the Protestant Church has neglected "humanism" and "preservation of life" while narrowly focusing on "evangelization for the growth of my own church." However, the "evangelization" of the world and "human liberation," which is the liberation of the suffering people who suffer because of the evil powers of this world are like the two inseparable pillars of mission.[9]

"God is love" (1 John 4:8). "For God so loved the world that he gave his son, that whoever believes in him shall not perish but have eternal life. For God did not send his Son into the world to condemn the world, but to save the world through him" (John 3:16-17): Mission is a response to God's urging love shown in creation and redemption. 'God's love invites us' (*Caritas Christi urget nos*) to his mission to give life to suffering humanity and creation. Living in that love of God, the church is called to become good news for all. "The Triune God's overflowing sharing of love is the source of all mission and evangelism."[10] Therefore, the ultimate foundation of mission is sharing the love of God and the proclamation of the good news of God's Kingdom revealed by Jesus Christ. Therefore, the Kingdom of God is the content of mission, and world evangelization is a method of mission. One is not enough without having the other. There is no room for a missiological dichotomy if we are authentically faithful to God's mission.

---

[8] Ibid. 7-16.

[9] Jong Yun Lee, "Can Lausanne Work with WCC as Partner in Mission?" op. cit., 307-8.

[10] *TTL*, §55.

Missio Dei vs. Missio Ecclesiae

The third world mission conference took place in 1938 in Tambaram, India. In a world context where peace was increasingly threatened by fascist-type regimes in Germany, Italy, Portugal, Spain and Japan, the discussions focused on the importance and centrality of the church in mission in order to fight against the evil of fascism. Ever since Edinburgh 1910, churches and missionary societies struggled how to relate to each other. Still there was a strong dominance of missions without direct relationship with the church in the International Missionary Council (IMC). Therefore, there was an intentional emphasis on the centrality of the church in mission to overcome the dichotomy between mission and church. Tambaram affirmed that the essence of the church is mission.

At Tambaram representatives from the so-called 'younger' churches were already in the majority. Tambaram also defended the ultimate truth of the Christian message vis-à-vis other religions, while advising missionaries to show a listening and dialoguing approach in practice.[11] It is important to note that the importance of interfaith dialogue in world mission was discussed even before the sharp division between the evangelical and ecumenical approaches on this issue, also before the establishment of the WCC.

While Tambaram was focused on the mission of the church, the fifth world mission conference in Willingen, Germany, in 1952 shifted to a new concept of mission. Under the threat of events in China to the traditional mission enterprise, the delegates rediscovered that mission depended first and foremost on God's own activity. Mission is the purpose and action of the Triune God. The Willingen Conference declared that:

> The missionary movement of which we are a part has its source in the Triune God Himself. Out of depth of God's love for us, the Father has sent forth his own beloved Son to reconcile all things to himself, that we and all men might, through the Spirit, be made one in Him with the Father in that perfect love which is the very nature of God.[12]

Willingen is rightly considered as one of the conferences that have had the most lasting influence on ecumenical mission theology. Indeed, the idea of *missio Dei,*[13] which was taken up in the follow-up to Willingen, proved

---

[11] See *The World Mission of the Church: Findings and Recommendations of the Meeting of the International Missionary Council, Tambaram, Madras, India, Dec. 12-29, 1938* (IMC, London/New York, 1939).

[12] *Willingen 1952: The Missionary Obligation of the Church* (IMC, London: Edinburgh House Press, 1953), 2.

[13] Missiologists agree that the notion of *missio Dei* originated in Karl Barth's address at the Brandenburg Mission Conference in 1932. It was Karl Hartenstein who actually coined this terminology in 1934. The concept of *missio Dei* was more substantially conceptualized at the Willingen IMC in 1952. See Karl Barth, "Die Theologie und die Mission in der Gegenwart", *Theologische Fragen und Antworten*, Zollikon, Theologischer Verlag Zürich, 1957, 100-184; Karl

to be most creative. Karl Hartenstein coined the phrase in 1952: "... participation in the sending of the Son, in the *missio Dei*, with an inclusive aim of establishing the lordship of Christ over the whole redeemed creation."[14] The strong emphasis on the centrality of the church in mission since Tambaram was replaced by an enlarged perspective which allowed interpreting events in the world as determining factors for mission.[15]

According to Tormod Engelsviken, in post-war missiological thought, there was a dynamic triangle encounter of three concepts: *missio Dei*, the Kingdom of God, and the Church. In Willingen, there was a shift from "a more anthropocentric understanding of mission to a more theocentric and from a more ecclesiocentric perspective to a more cosmocentric".[16] The world became the centre of attention, and God's economy in the world became a subject of mission. There was not a unanimous agreement on this new concept at Willingen. Rather, evangelicals were uncomfortable with the change of focus from missionaries' work to God's economy, from the church to the world. However, Willingen worked hard to keep a balance between *missio Dei* and *missio Ecclesiae.*

There is some misunderstanding of *missio Dei.* First, *missio Dei* was understood as a missiology of the 'social gospel', only focused on an ethical aspect rather than a theological one. Second, it was perceived as if *missio Dei* totally rejected *missio Ecclesiae.* In my own view, it is highly important to fully reflect the theological aspects of *missio Dei* to avoid unnecessary misunderstandings. In the original meaning at Willingen, there were two main theological foci of *missio Dei*: The Trinitarian understanding of mission, and the incarnation and *Kenosis* of Christ for Mission, i.e. divine sending.

Missionary Church or Special Agent?

Although there were tensions in Jerusalem and Willingen, the debates on the Kingdom of God and *missio Dei* did not result in a visible division of

---

Hartenstein, *Die Mission als theologisches Problem. Beiträge zum grundsätzlichen Verständnis der Mission* (Berlin: Furche Verlag, 1933), 31; "A Statement on the Missionary Calling of the Church", *Minutes of the Enlarged Meeting and the Committee of the International Missionary Council, Willingen, Germany, July 5th-21st 1952* (London/New York: IMC, 1952), Appendix A, 53-56.

14 W. Freytag, K. Hartenstein and A. Lehmann, *Mission zwischen Gestern und Morgen* (Stuttgart: Evangelischer Missionsverlag, 1952), 54.

15 See IMC, *Minutes of the Enlarged Meeting and the Committee of the International Missionary Council, Willingen, Germany, July 5th to 21st, 1952* (IMC, London/New York), 1952.

16 Tormod Engelsviken, "*Misso Dei*: The Understanding and Misunderstanding of a Theological Concept in European Churches and Missiology", *IRM*, Vol. XCII, No.367, Oct 2003, 481.

mission. However, this happened for the first time in history since Edinburgh when IMC met in Achimota, Ghana, in 1958. The proposal to unite IMC with the WCC, with which the IMC shared several programmes and had intensive relations, was debated. The proposal was accepted by a great majority, while some theologically more conservative mission councils refused the idea of an integration of mission and church. They wanted to preserve the missionary freedom and not become dependent on ecclesiastical authorities and agendas.[17] The evangelical missions were afraid that, if the missionary movement came under the hierarchy of the church, it might lose the dynamism of the movement. Paradoxically, the conservative missionary councils, that had supported the mission of the church at Willingen, now opposed integration between mission and church. After a long debate, eventually only two national mission councils, the Congolese and Norwegian, did not join the WCC. At grassroots level, however, more evangelical mission agencies were uncomfortable with the integration.

In 1961, the 'integration' of church and mission, in practice of the IMC with the WCC, became effective at the assemblies of New Delhi. The mission councils affiliated to the IMC became affiliated to the CWME (Commission on World Mission and Evangelism) of the WCC. From now on, the world mission conferences could really be called 'ecumenical' because of the much larger denominational participation, including Orthodox churches and soon after Vatican II also Roman Catholic observers.

The missiological concept underlying the integration was 'the church as the primary agent of mission'. There was reconciliation between the Tambaram and Willingen mission concepts, i.e. *missio Ecclesiae* and *missio Dei*. With the integration, CWME launched an ambitious project, 'Structures for Missionary Congregations',[18] to transform the Church into a missionary church.

In 1963, the first CWME met in Mexico City under the theme of 'mission in six continents'. The perspective of mission was enlarged to encompass every continent and not only those of the 'south'. Meeting during the first development decade, the conference dealt intensively with witness in a world understood as the place where God was active, inviting the churches to join in *missio Dei*. However, not all missions were ready to accept the idea of mission as a multi-directional movement, 'from everywhere to everywhere'. The evangelical mission agencies in Europe

---

[17] See R. K. Orchard (ed), *The Ghana Assembly of the International Missionary Council, 28th Dec, 1957 to 8th Jan, 1958* (London: Edinburgh House Press, 1958).

[18] See "The Church for Others and The Church for the World", A Quest for Structures for Missionary Congregations, Two Reports on the Missionary Structure of the Congregation, Final Report of the Western European Working Group and North American Working Group of the Department on Studies in Evangelism (Geneva, Switzerland: WCC, 1968).

and North America still held the view that mission is a movement from the north to the south, from the west to the east. At the time of Mexico City, it was too early to accept the reality that the north and west were becoming an urgent mission field.[19]

At least up to this stage, the tensions between these two different expressions of missiological thinking were not at their highest tide. Whether ecumenical or evangelical, their missiological understanding was largely conservative with a strong influence of neo-orthodox theology, particularly the mission theology of Karl Barth. The situation dramatically changed in the 1970s.

Contextualization, Holistic Salvation and Moratorium: A Moment of Farewell

The world mission conference in Bangkok, at the turn of the years 1972-73, became famous for its holistic approach to the theme 'Salvation Today, encompassing its spiritual as well as socio-political aspects, without giving priority to one over the other. Bangkok acknowledged the need for contextual theologies and the recognition of cultural identity as shaping the voice of those answering and following Christ. The delegates struggled with the situation of exploitation and injustice also in relations between churches. In order to enable local churches in Africa, Asia, Latin America and the Pacific to set their own priorities in mission, the proposal was made of a temporary 'moratorium' of sending money and missionaries from the north. An alternative proposal for more justice in mission relations was seen in the transformation of the Paris Mission Society into a Community of Churches in Mission (CEVAA), the London Missionary Society to the Council for World Mission (CWM).[20]

The three key controversial issues in Bangkok were contextualization, holistic understanding of mission, and missionary moratorium. The two different circles of mission thinking were facing a fundamental difference of their mission understandings. Some evangelicals[21] and some ecumenicals would seem to endorse a universal theology as an authentic interpretation of the Gospel, and one truth relevant to all contexts. They were anxious that the truth in Jesus Christ was compromised or replaced by local cultures in

---

[19] See Ronald K. Orchard (ed), *Witness in Six Continents: Records of the Meeting of the Commission on World Mission and Evangelism of the World Council of Churches held in Mexico City, Dec 8th to 19th, 1963* (London: Edinburgh House Press, 1964).

[20] See *Bangkok Assembly 1973: Minutes and Report of the Assembly of the Commission on World Mission and Evangelism of the World Council of Churches, Dec 31, 1972 and Jan 9-12, 1973* (Geneva: WCC, 1973).

[21] Most evangelicals, like most ecumenicals, did not hold this view. Rather they were concerned that the Christological core of the Gospel be preserved when contextualising. Thus Paul Hiebert talked about 'critical contextualisation'.

the process of contextualization while theologians and missiologists from Asia and Africa tried to enroot the Gospel in their own soils. However, the issues, challenges and worldviews of their daily context in the global south were largely different to the mission thinking and agenda shaped by the western schools. For the people in the south, the Gospel was not only food for their souls but bread for all aspects of life. As CWME affirms, "God did not send the Son for the salvation of humanity alone or give us a partial salvation. Rather the Gospel is the good news for every part of creation and every aspect of our life and society."[22] However, the evangelicals in Bangkok were suspicious of the notion of holistic salvation as an attempt to replace mission as social justice, human liberation and inculturation. And they were concerned that 'salvation' could become replaced by 'solutions'.

The demand for a missionary moratorium poured oil on the controversial debates in Bangkok.[23] It was a shock for both the evangelicals and ecumenicals. It was understood as a slogan: 'Missionaries go home!' For missionaries who had experienced being expelled from China by the Communist regime, it was an unforgivable demand. However, the demand for a moratorium can be understood in a different way. In the context of the Korean Presbyterian Church in 1973, if the stipends for the Korean pastors totally relied on mission funds from the American Presbyterian Mission Board, if our moderator and most of the church leaders were Americans and if more than half of the ordained ministers of the Korean church were foreigners, what should we say? I am not talking of the context of Edinburgh 1910 but of Bangkok 1973. We have to remember that as early as Edinburgh 1910, Chi Ho Yun dared to claim that in the deciding how to spend mission funds, the local leaders and missionaries have to decide together because the indigenous leaders know their context and the needs of people better. He therefore asserted that missionaries should prepare to hand over their leadership to Koreans.[24]

In some circles, the moratorium request led to the situation that evangelicals could no longer stay together with ecumenicals.[25] For the

---

[22] *TTL*, §4.

[23] John Gatu, general secretary of the Presbyterian Church in East Africa, said that their continuing sense of dependence on and domination by foreign church groups inhibits many churches in Asia, Africa and Latin America from development in response to God's mission. He explained, "Our problems … can only be solved if all missionaries can be withdrawn in order to allow a period of not less than five years for each side to rethink and formulate what is going to be their future relationship … The churches of the Third World must be allowed to find their own identity, and the continuation of the present missionary movement is a hindrance to this selfhood of the church." Cited from M. E. Uka, *Missionaries Go Home?* (New York: Peter Lang, 1987), 191.

[24] See *World Missionary Conference, 1910: Report of Commission II* (Edinburgh and London: Oliphant, Anderson & Ferrier, 1910), 358-9.

[25] The moratorium request was, however, not the primary issue. Thus professors at Fuller's School of World Mission were in support of moratorium. The divisive issue

evangelicals, Bangkok meant giving up the uniqueness of Christ and the urgency of world evangelization, which they recognized as priorities of mission more than any other mission thinking or agenda. Many of them gathered in Lausanne, in 1974 and launched the Lausanne Committee for World Evangelization. At first, there was a strong dominance by the American evangelicals led by Billy Graham. However, there were radical and moderate evangelicals too, e.g. Andrew Kirk, Samuel Escobar and Jim Wallace, led by John Stott. Remarkably, Stott and many European evangelicals have kept their relationship with CWME and raised the evangelical voice within WCC as well. As we know, the final version of the *Lausanne Covenant* was drafted by John Stott based on a more holistic view of mission. Philip Potter, WCC General Secretary, was invited to deliver a speech at Lausanne. Although the division was a regrettable event, CWME and Lausanne stayed in contact and maintained a dialogical relationship. But for the first time since the unity of Edinburgh, world mission was visibly divided into two groups.

After the division, WCC considered it necessary to affirm its mission understanding. Therefore, WCC central committee adapted the mission statement, *Mission and Evangelism: An Ecumenical Affirmation* in 1982, which remained the fundamental text on mission for the WCC until 2012. It is a landmark document which draws on insights from Protestant, evangelical, Orthodox and Roman Catholic mission theologies. After the tensions experienced during the 1970s with the creation of the Lausanne Committee for World Evangelization in 1974, the 1982 document can be seen as an attempt by CWME at re-centering ecumenical mission theology by finding a balance between a clear commitment to the proclamation of the Gospel without losing the prophetic voice.

Interfaith Dialogue and Inculturation

Many evangelicals nurture the misconception that WCC has accepted pluralism and thus recognizes salvation in other religions in its mission policy. Interfaith dialogue is an important agenda of mission, particularly for those churches who are living as a minority, or are in a conflict situation between different religions. The world mission conference at San Antonio, USA, in 1989 became famous for the consensus statement on the relation between Christianity and other religions: "We cannot point to any other way of salvation than Jesus Christ; at the same time we cannot put any limit to God's saving power."[26] There is a tension between these affirmations

---

was primarily the understanding of sin, salvation and the uniqueness of Christ. The major debate about moratorium came after the Bangkok meeting and was to some extent caused by journalists who reported on this issue.

[26] Frederick R. Wilson (ed), *The San Antonio Report* (Geneva: WCC, 1990), 32.

which we acknowledge and cannot resolve. This statement remains the official position of WCC with regard to interfaith dialogue and mission.

The last WCC conference on mission in the twentieth century took place in Salvador de Bahía, Brazil, in 1996 and was fully dedicated to the relationship between Gospel and culture. After the change in world politics of 1989, and the increased influence of cultural and ethnic identities on violent conflicts, a renewed missiological reflection on culture was needed. Reaffirming Bangkok's position on inculturation, Salvador insisted on the richness of cultural diversity as God's gift, but also on the Gospel imperative to link the affirmation of one's cultural identity with openness to other identities. Salvador recognized the fundamental, equal value of all cultures, but also their ambiguity. In its relation with cultures, the Gospel may be illuminated, but also obscured. Churches in mission may have to confirm elements of their culture but also challenge others. In the face of the situation, particularly in the Eastern part of Europe, Salvador reaffirmed the WCC's opposition to proselytism and the need for co-operation in mission and common witness.[27]

Up to Salvador, the previous tension between the Kingdom of God and World Evangelization was somehow resolved. In the *Manila Manifesto*, evangelicals accepted social justice as an integral part of mission. A holistic understanding of mission has been widely recognized.[28] In fact, the social Gospel was also rooted in the neo-orthodox paradigm of mission. Therefore, it should not be difficult to reconcile this with the concept of world evangelization because both are based on the notion of the sovereignty of God. However, inculturation, contextualization and interfaith dialogue belong to different dimensions. The claim of an eminent evangelical missiologist and historian, Andrew F. Walls, is notable:

> Christian faith is serial, rooted first in one place, then in another. Christianity has no equivalent of Mecca, no single permanent centre. Christian communities often wither in their heartlands, their areas of seeming strength, and then flower anew at or beyond the periphery. No one country, no one culture, owns the Christian faith. There's no permanently Christian country, no one form of Christian civilization, no single Christian culture. At different periods, different areas of the world have taken leadership in the Christian mission and then the baton was passed on to others.[29]

With regard to the dialogue between Gospel, culture and indigenous religions, Walls cites examples of the doctrine of the Trinity and the Incarnation, which the church at large confesses in its creeds now, being constructed from the concepts and ideas of the middle period of Platonism, converted to handle the material of the Christian tradition. When Greek-

---

[27] Andrew F. Walls, "Demographics, Power and the Gospel in the 21st Century", SIL International Conference and WBTI Convention, 6th June 2002, 2.

[28] See *The Manila Manifesto*, LCWE, 1989.

[29] Andrew. F. Walls, *The Cross-Cultural Process in Christian History* (Edinburgh: T. & T. Clark), 32-3.

speaking pagans accepted the Gospel, they called Jesus *Kyrios*, the name they used for their cult divinities. He asks, "Shouldn't the Gentile converts learn about the Messiah as Israel's national Saviour?" He concludes that in fact the use of the term was enriching. It made people think about Christ in a different way because they now thought of him in indigenous categories,[30] as their own Saviour and not a foreign one.

One of the characteristics of Christianity is its openness to cultures. For instance, the Bible has been translated into vernacular languages wherever it goes while the Koran remains only in Arabic. The Gospel takes root in different contexts through engagement with specific cultural, political and religious realities. Respect for people and their cultural and symbolic life-worlds are necessary if the Gospel is to take root in those different realities. In this way it must begin with engagement and dialogue with the wider context in order to discern how Christ is already present and where God's Spirit is already at work. A plurality of cultures is a gift of the Spirit to deepen our understanding of our faith and one another. As such, intercultural communities of faith, where diverse cultural communities worship together, is one way in which cultures can engage with one another authentically, and where culture can enrich Gospel.[31] 'Christianity lives by crossing the boundaries of language and culture.'[32] Here are issues where WCC and Lausanne agreed almost from the very outset. The question of Gospel and culture was dealt with in depth in the Lausanne Willowbank report from 1978.[33] On the whole, Lausanne has over the years been just as preoccupied with Gospel and culture as the CWME (Paul Hiebert, Charles Kraft, David Hesselgrave, etc.).

Search for Healing

Athens 2005

In May 2005, the Conference on World Mission and Evangelism met in Athens, Greece, for the first time in a majority Orthodox context, and also for the first time with representatives from the Roman Catholic Church and from evangelical (of both WEA and LCWE) and Pentecostal churches as delegates with full rights. The theme was 'Come, Holy Spirit, Heal and Reconcile: Called in Christ to be reconciling and healing communities'. This allowed for a more humble approach to mission, reminding ourselves of the priority of God the Holy Spirit's mission in the world, the only one able to really bring healing and reconciliation in the full sense of the term. Within that overall dynamic of God in the world, the churches have a

---

[30] Ibid.

[31] *TTL*, 94, 100.

[32] Andrew F. Walls, "Demographics, Power and the Gospel in the 21st Century", 5.

[33] www.lausanne.org/en/documents/lops/73-lop-2.html

specific calling, which is to be ambassadors of reconciliation, and in particular to build, renew, and multiply spaces where humans can experience something of God's healing and reconciling grace.[34]

The conference thus allowed for an approach which linked *missio Dei* and *missio Ecclesiae.* And while focusing on pneumatology, the CWME resisted the tendency to separate the Spirit from Christ, and intentionally remained within a Trinitarian framework. The emphasis on healing allowed for an opening to the Pentecostal tradition and experience while affirming the intrinsic link between mission, the healing ministry and Christian health services. Reconciliation allowed for both taking stock of the experiences made in post-conflict reconstruction and challenged the churches to continue their search for visible unity. A period of missiological *détente* was opened.

Edinburgh 2010

In June 2010, 300 delegates from 200 churches and Christian organizations, 115 different church backgrounds, and 77 nationalities celebrated together the centenary anniversary of the 1910 Edinburgh mission conference. Several books containing contributions from the Edinburgh study process had been published. One in particular was the basis for the conference's deliberations.[35] In 300 pages, the nine international and interdenominational teams co-ordinating reflection on the main mission themes had summarized the results of the work done worldwide by academic institutions and mission bodies. For the first time in mission history, representatives from all traditions of Christianity and global mission actors gathered together to celebrate the centenary anniversary.[36] Among the stakeholders were both LCWE and WEA. As an outcome, the conference issued a 'Common Call'.[37]

---

[34] See Jacques Matthey (ed), *Come Holy Spirit, Heal and Reconcile: Report of the WCC Conference on World Mission and Evangelism, Athens, Greece, May, 2005* (Geneva: WCC, 2008).

[35] See Daryl Balia and Kirsteen Kim (eds), *Edinburgh 2010 – Witnessing to Christ Today* (Oxford, UK: Regnum, 2010).

[36] Among others who participated in the Edinburgh conference were the presidents or moderators and/or the general secretaries of the WCC and its mission commission (CWME), of the LCWE, the WEA and also its mission commission, the PCPCU, WARC, WSCF, IFES, Orthodox delegates led by Metropolitan Nifon, well-known Pentecostal theologians including Young Hoon Lee, the senior pastor of Yoido Full Gospel Church and other important Christian leaders from the Anglican communion, Baptist, Methodist, Lutheran and Sevevnth Day Adventist traditions. Among the mission bodies represented, Areopagos, the Council for World Mission, also representing UEM and Cevaa, and the Evangelisches Missionswerk in Hamburg played key roles, as did individual churches.

[37] See "The Common Call" in Kirsteen Kim and Andrew Anderson (eds), *Edinburgh 2010: Mission Today and Tomorrow* (Oxford: Regnum, 2011), 1-2.

Edinburgh 2010 has enlarged the fellowship and led to reconciliation among different mission streams. It has increased confidence among partners involved, allowed for sharing of power and provided space for each other. Its final aim was *relational*, reaching in the long term a form of *koinonia* in mission. WCC intentionally remained in a more supporting role for Edinburgh 2010 to nurture the fellowship. WCC was open in Edinburgh for constant updates, modifications and reformulations of its own positions on mission and evangelism, in the search for a new consensus on the matter.

An analysis of *The Common Call* produced at the Edinburgh conference shows that positions defended over decades by WCC have now become somewhat common ground: *missio Dei,* empowerment and humility, creation as the scope of mission, holistic content of Gospel, mission from everywhere to everywhere, unity and mission. There has also been a particular emphasis on pneumatology, where one can discern an influence of Pentecostal traditions. Indeed, Edinburgh 2010 was a moment of celebration, healing and convergence of the missionary movement. At the same time, *The Common Call* highlighted the evangelical concern for 'the uniqueness of Christ' and for conversion.

From Convergence to Co-operation

Recommendations for Conducts

'Christian Witness in a Multi-Religious World: Recommendations for Conduct', regarding respectful actions on the part of missionaries, evangelists and other witnesses when sharing the Christian faith were issued following a five-year series of consultations among the WCC, WEA, and the Pontifical Council for Inter-religious Dialogue (PCID) of the Roman Catholic Church in 2011. The three bodies include a combined membership of some two billion people representing nearly 90% of the world's Christians. Geoff Tunnicliffe, general secretary of the WEA, said that the document represents formal agreement on 'the essence of Christian mission' while also demonstrating that diverse Christian bodies 'are able to work together and to speak together'. In this sense, the release of the text was 'a historic moment' in the quest for Christian unity.[38] It was an unimaginable achievement that the three major global Christian bodies reached a consensus on ethical principles when mission engages in conversion of other faiths. In the text, the Trinitarian understanding of mission, the Kingdom of God and inter-religious and inter-cultural dialogue are emphasized.

---

[38] www.oikoumene.org/en/news/news-management/eng/a/article/1634/christians-reach-broad-co.html?tx_ttnews%5Bswords%5D=recommendations%20of%20 conduct&cHash=3545519941ec53351a5a853c7757fced

New Ecumenical Affirmation

A new ecumenical affirmation on mission and evangelism, *Together Towards Life: Mission and Evangelism in Changing Landscapes,* was unanimously approved as an official statement of the World Council of Churches (WCC) by the central committee held in Crete, Greece on 5th September 2012.

The statement is in its essence *Trinito-centric and Life-centric*. In this sense, it is *missio Trinity.* It affirms that the Triune God is a God of Life and that we are called to participate in the life-affirming mission of the Holy Trinity (*missio Spiritus*). The statement affirms that "the purpose of God's mission is fullness of life and this is the criterion for discernment in mission".[39]

The statement is *Creation-centred.* It articulates a missiology that begins with Creation. Creation, in other words, is at the heart of the missiology that is expounded here. Mission is to turn to the Triune God in creation. God celebrates creation and Life, and this celebration is deemed a mission activity of God. In this new statement, creation is not simply deemed an object of human concern, but also an agent of God's mission where creation becomes a channel of divine grace and blessing. The Statement affirms that "Mission begins with God's act of creation and continues in re-creation".[40]

The statement conveys a *prophetic missiology*. One of the distinct features of the new statement is the affirmation of the agency and subjecthood of the marginalized in mission. It is mission from the margins, not mission to or even at the margins, where the poor and the marginalized are treated as objects of charity. It further claims that the marginalized have a special gift to distinguish life-affirming forces from life-negating ones.[41] The prophetic dimension of the new mission statement is also brought out forcefully in its outright rejection of the idolatry of mammon in the free market economy.[42]

The statement affirms that *evangelism is at the centre of Christian mission.*[43] The new mission statement has four main chapters on spirituality, margins, church and evangelism. It is important to note that the entire section on evangelism was drafted jointly by the WEA mission commission and the WCC evangelism desk. The co-operation between WCC and WEA in the work of the 'Recommendations for Conduct' and the new mission statement is a remarkable achievement which we could not have dreamt of during the last century, and was a sign of overcoming the

---

[39] *TTL*, 102.
[40] *TTL*, 103.
[41] *TTL*, 107.
[42] *TTL*, 108.
[43] *TTL*, 109.

dichotomy and bringing about synergies in mission.[44] In this connection it is also timely to refer to the Cape Town Commitment and its strong focus on mission as reconciliation – a focus and concern which evangelicals and ecumenicals share.

Conclusion

I would like to conclude that the studies of the history of divisions and dialogue in mission between ecumenical and evangelical understandings of mission indicate that significant missiological convergences have been developed in recent history.

First, *missio Dei* is a common foundation of mission. Nowadays, whether evangelical or ecumenical, whether mission thinker or practitioner, almost every mission actor and school has accepted the notion of *missio Dei* as their theological basis of mission.

Second, the Kingdom of God is a common goal of mission. Paradoxically, we can listen more often to the Kingdom message in evangelical circles today, while ecumenicals are a bit hesitant because of the accusations in the past. It is certain that there is no more tension on this notion.

Third, the holistic understanding and practice of mission is a common method of mission. There is no longer an argument regarding the hierarchy of mission priorities. The purpose of God's mission is to save life and give fullness of life (John 10:10) and this is the criterion for discernment in mission. Any mission practice to save life is participation in the sacred mission of God.

Fourth, contextualization is a common theological task. For both ecumenical and evangelical circles, there is still the domination of the theological agenda, resources, and leadership by the western churches and mission bodies. However, it is only a matter of time before churches in the global south will have taken full responsibility to lead the global ecumenical and evangelical movement. Therefore, the development of contextual ecumenism and evangelicalism is an urgent task. Western missions which distinguished between churches in the global south as ecumenical or evangelical, are no longer teaching us how to achieve unity. The missions which do not know how to do evangelism in their home countries will no longer be able to teach others evangelism.

Lastly, we can say that the missiological tensions during the last century have to a large extent been overcome. More dialogue is still needed on many remaining issues. But for the future of Christianity, it is time to shift gears from convergence to co-operation.

---

44 The full text of the new mission statement can be downloaded from www.oikoumene.org/fileadmin/files/wcc-main/2012pdfs/Mission_statement_approved_10_09_2012_final.pdf.

The Lausanne Movement and the World Evangelical Alliance

Rose Dowsett

The First Bridges across Evangelical Divides

In 1846, 900 delegates, from 52 'bodies of Christians' and drawn from eleven countries, met in London, England. For thirteen days they prayed and discussed, grappling with complex issues, but with the overwhelming desire to find a way to express the unity in Christ that they believed to be more fundamental than their differences.[1]

Their meeting was the culmination of several years of correspondence and meetings, of small initiatives but far larger dreams. The great evangelical revivals and awakenings of the eighteenth century, on either side of the Atlantic, had produced under God's good hand huge energy for the Gospel. Yet, paradoxically, with the new century two completely opposite phenomena became apparent. On the one hand, Protestant Christianity was fracturing at an alarming rate, with more and more denominations and groups being formed, often acrimoniously. On the other hand, there was a growing swell of desire to find ways to work together in unity. Surely brothers and sisters in Christ ought to be able to bridge denominational distinctives, preferences and convictions, and to live out the profound reality of being one Body in the Lord?

Many of those distinctives and convictions were by no means trivial, and many Christians bore scars from painful separation from a former church. To be in reconciled fellowship across divisions was often costly. In particular, there were literal and historical war wounds dividing 'churchmen' (those of state churches, usually Episcopal in structure, though some state churches were Presbyterian or Reformed) and 'Dissenters' (in turn to be known as Free Church, those who followed the Anabaptist tradition, and who were independent of state ties). Such wounds of body, mind and heart went deep, and were not easily healed.

---

[1] The story of the founding of the World Evangelical Alliance may be found in numerous volumes, among them Ian Randall and David Hilborn, *One Body in Christ: The History and Significance of the Evangelical Alliance* (Paternoster, 2001); W. Harold Fuller, *People of the Mandate: the story of the World Evangelical Fellowship* (Baker Book House/WEF, 1996).

Yet, by the end of their time together, those 900 delegates had agreed on a doctrinal statement of shared evangelical faith, drawn up a series of practical resolutions about how to conduct relationships across denominations,[2] established commonality and mutual love and respect, inaugurated three national Evangelical Alliances with eight more following within a few short years, and determined to foster ongoing friendship and meeting together.

Challenges and Advances

Sadly, the hoped-for world structure foundered not over doctrinal differences but over disagreement over the issue of slavery. The North American contingent were themselves opposed to owning slaves, but were not willing to turn their backs on believers in the southern States who ran their plantations with slave labour, at a time of delicate negotiations. In 1884, once again it was the Americans who blocked the establishing of an international committee, this time on the grounds that small Alliances should not have power to influence their own American decisions. History would repeat itself once more, in 1951, at the birth of the World Evangelical Fellowship, when the American delegation once again were not able to become fully identified, this time over the failure to include the term 'infallible' in relation to Scripture. This history probably lies behind the rather chequered profile of the Evangelical Alliance in the USA and, sadly, a certain level of suspicion relating to the WEA.

Nonetheless, following 1846 a fully functioning network of national alliances kept in close touch with one another, and met every few years for extensive international consultations. (Here, America played a fuller part, at least till the 1890s, for instance attending conferences in Europe, and in 1873 hosting the sixth general conference, held in New York.) In this, the networking and conferences established the practice we take for granted today that Christians of different cultures and denominations can work together in close harmony in common cause. It is impossible to express too strongly what a remarkable achievement this was, overcoming historic and theological divisions.

It is also important to note that many of the international consultations were deeply exercised by the need to engage in world mission as well as local mission, and the national alliances were fully involved. This was fostered by the international conferences meeting in different countries each year or two, but also by contributing strongly to the international mission conferences in 1878, 1888 and 1900 as expressions of evangelical co-operation. Further, the European countries where the national EAs were at their strongest were also countries with Empire and colonial links to

---

[2] The full text of the Basis of Faith and of the Practical Resolutions may be found in Randall and Hilborn, 358-365.

much of the unevangelised world. Whatever the ambiguities of imperialism, Christians in those European countries often had a strong interest in what was happening around the world, and contributed hugely to world mission.

It is arguable that without the proven track record of national evangelical alliances, and their international co-operation through the informal links of the World Evangelical Alliance, long before the formal establishment of the World Evangelical Fellowship (WEF) in 1951, the Lausanne Movement could not have been born. Nor for that matter would many of the great interdenominational mission agencies of the mid-nineteenth century onwards have been possible.[3] Lausanne built on a century of evangelical interdenominationalism and international relationships pioneered and modeled by WEA.

The Establishing of WEF with International Structures

The years following the Second World War saw many global bodies formed, both because of increasing globalization and also because the appalling experiences of the two world wars had convinced many people that only commitment to global structures could prevent further massive wars. So in 1945 the United Nations was established, in 1947 the International Fellowship of Evangelical Students,[4] in 1948 the World Council of Churches, and in 1951 the World Evangelical Fellowship (the latter following renewed consultation from 1946 onwards). While the UN was concerned primarily with political affairs, the three Christian bodies were all in different ways seeking to bring together Christian people from different parts of the world, in shared understanding and shared enterprise.

This was not entirely without precedent, not only because of the history of the national evangelical alliances, but also because of the great Missionary Conference held in Edinburgh in 1910.[5] Many of the delegates there were active in their respective national evangelical alliances as well as in their own denominations, or mirrored EA principles in working together with those of other denominations or agencies in their mission fields. For

---

[3] In particular, the Faith Missions which began in the nineteenth century, such as the China Inland Mission, drew together evangelicals from across various denominations, in shared mission enterprise. This was distinct from the denominational mission agencies, and allowed for more flexible ecclesiology when pioneering. This model of mission agency has been a strong contributor to the Lausanne Movement.

[4] The IFES has produced many leaders both for EAs and for Lausanne. The story of IFES is found in Douglas Johnson *A Brief History of the International Fellowship of Evangelical Students* (IFES, 1964) and Lindsay Brown *Shining Like Stars* (IVP, 2006).

[5] For a full study of the Edinburgh 1910 conference, see Brian Stanley *The World Missionary Conference, Edinburgh 1910* (Eerdmans, 2009).

instance, in the great mission field of China, the leaders of many agencies, denominational and interdenominational, had for years met annually to agree patterns of working and to deal with problems. Edinburgh 1910 was concerned to see mature churches all over the world, and the Gospel taken to every corner of the globe. Further, the Edinburgh delegates believed that the world could only be evangelized if Christians worked together in harmony and united purpose. Again, it is hard to see how this way of looking at things could have been taken for granted had it not been for the pattern demonstrated through the WEA.

Two world wars smashed much of the optimism (and arguably, wrong triumphalism) of Edinburgh 1910, and post-war initiatives were both more cautious and more realistic. Nonetheless, evangelicals worked hard at reconciliation with those from countries with whom so recently their own nations had been at war, and there were fresh commitments to world mission from both Europe and North America. At the same time and understandably, European national EAs were often fully occupied in contributing to the reconstruction of their own countries so devastated by war. Some of the formerly active alliances, both in Europe and in Asia, disappeared (or at least went underground) under the iron fist of Communism.

In 1951, more than 90 delegates from 21 countries and national EAs gathered in Holland, and informal fellowship moved on into a global administrative body, the World Evangelical Fellowship (later named the World Evangelical Alliance). They adopted a Statement of Faith closely based on that of 1846, and defined WEF's purpose as threefold: (a) the furtherance of the Gospel (Phil 1:12); (b) the defence and confirmation of the Gospel (Phil 1:7); and (c) fellowship in the Gospel (Phil 1:5). Since 1861, the national EAs together had held an annual week of prayer, not only linking themselves but also focusing on the whole world and its needs, so that world mission was always a strong element of the alliances' commitment.

Among the delegates were Jack Dain, later Bishop, and the young Anglican minister John Stott, both of whom were deeply involved in their national EA, and who later – especially John Stott – would also be key to the Lausanne Movement. Stott said later that the meeting in Holland was his first experience of worldwide evangelicalism, to which he would go on to contribute so much in his lifetime. It was also through WEF and the British EA that his friendship with Billy Graham would blossom, when Graham was invited through EA (on whose Council Stott served) to conduct a mission in London in 1954.

From the beginning, it was understood that WEF's structures would be 'light touch', serving to support and develop national EAs and then regional groupings of EAs, not seeking to set the agenda for them or to be strongly directive. With a small budget, and very small staff team, WEF/WEA has not always had high visibility, preferring that that role should be taken primarily by national EAs, each working in their different religious, ecclesiastical, cultural and historical contexts. This has not always been understood or appreciated by those more accustomed to equating effectiveness with high budgets, uniformity, and dominant leadership. Nonetheless, with some 130 national and regional alliances today, representing some 600 million Christians worldwide, there are frequently times when the international leadership of WEA has been able to speak to global issues, or to governments where Christians are oppressed, for instance, in a way not so effective when done by an individual EA or a single denomination. There have also been times when lack of funds, or a clear sense of distinct purpose, has left WEA with a weaker voice than it should have.

The Birth of Lausanne

The initiative for the international consultation in Lausanne in 1974 came from the Billy Graham Evangelistic Association, but the planning committee included several who were leaders in, or active in, their national EA. The Executive Chairman was Bishop Jack Dain from Australia, who in 1951 had been a founding member of WEF and who was still closely involved. The specific purpose of the gathering, to which 2,400 delegates from 150 countries came as well as about 1,300 observers, guests and journalists, was to consider world evangelization: what remained to be done and how to do it. This echoed Edinburgh 1910, but in a different world context after sixty turbulent years. The church had been birthed in many places where there had been no known Gospel witness in 1910, and the church was indeed more truly global than ever before. God had done marvellous things! But there were still too many places where Christ remained unknown.

What in retrospect came to be known as Lausanne I undoubtedly brought fresh impetus to world mission. That story has been frequently told elsewhere, and deservedly so. It was probably the first time that some leaders from the global south had had the opportunity of speaking so clearly and with authority into a community still dominated by northerners and westerners.[6] It demonstrated that the 'young churches' of the global south had come of age, and indeed were often more vigorous than many of the older churches of the north and west. It introduced some very different ways of thinking about the unevangelised world, focusing on people groups rather than nations or sharply demarcated geographic areas.[7] It produced the *Lausanne Covenant*, a document which takes its place among the great

---

[6] Especially influential were the contributions of Samuel Escobar and René Padilla, both Latin Americans with an IFES background. There were other delegates, too, who were leaders in IFES movements, many of them invited to Lausanne by John Stott who by now had a significant worldwide ministry among IFES movements.

[7] Significantly through the input of North American Ralph Winter.

statements of the church down through the centuries. It remains to this day a formative event for much of the world church, and impacted generations of mission leaders.

There is however another side to the story that is not so well acknowledged, perhaps symbolized by the fact that 400 of the 2,400 official delegates chose not to sign or affirm the Covenant. There was a deep-seated disagreement over the nature of mission, and the adequacy or otherwise of evangelism more narrowly defined. Some of the tensions WEF had already struggled with over the generations were inevitably present in this new context too. There were different assumptions about the role of the churches, and of relating to already established ministries in any given context. And there was disagreement about creating a new global structure following on from the consultation.[8]

In 1974, Billy Graham was at the height of his ministry. His passion was evangelism, and God gifted him for that. Only the Lord knows how many men, women and children came to faith through Graham's preaching. That is beyond dispute. But Graham was heavily dependent on being invited to a place, and having national churches fully involved in every part of a campaign. He did not pioneer into a vacuum. Almost always it was the national EA that acted as catalyst, both for the invitation and then for all the practicalities of making the campaign work. Graham's role was one part of a much bigger picture and process, not just practically but also in terms of a much more complex praxis of evangelism. Further, in the greatest majority of cases, Graham was preaching in a context where there was a significant Christian history, so that a simple revivalist style of evangelism was effective and appropriate, and the local churches – usually co-ordinated by the EA – could follow through on discipling those who professed faith or who indicated some level of interest. Graham's understanding of what evangelism is, and how to set about it, did not seem to grasp fully that in fact there were many crucial ingredients beyond a simple conversionist message. There were many at Lausanne I who saw evangelism in similar terms: proclamation (and at that, proclamation that was simply a transposition of the message and style that was used in the west), looking for a decision for Christ, and anything else being a distraction from the essential business, or, even worse, a sell-out to liberalism with its socio-political concerns.

The problem was that equally many understood evangelism rather differently. In his opening address, John Stott, himself a greatly gifted evangelist, insisted that making disciples cannot be separated from loving one's neighbor: the two are intertwined, and the Great Commission and Great Commandment belong together. The appeal of the Gospel by proclamation must be complemented by the appeal of the Gospel through

---

[8] See chapter 7, 'World Evangelization: The Lausanne Vision', in Timothy Dudley-Smith, *John Stott: A Global Ministry* (IVP, 2001)

loving service, and concern for the whole person in his whole context. Words alone lacked credibility, and true conversion to God must involve transformation of life in all dimensions. The Gospel is more comprehensive and more radical than urging a person to seek personal salvation.

Simplistic evangelism does not produce deep-level conversion or radical disciples, nor does it lead to a demonstration of the Kingdom – reign – of God. Many of the Lausanne delegates knew that superficial evangelism had left them with shallow churches and shallow Christians, more in tune with their culture than with God. In fact, that was a problem for the west quite as much as for the rest of the world, but was often masked by the impact of centuries of Christendom.

For many of the Latin Americans, evangelism divorced from seeking justice and changed lives for the poor and hungry, for instance, was a parody of what the good news in Christ is all about. Further, while highly individualistic western cultures saw evangelism as focusing on individuals, with rather less attention to the communal life of the Christian community, the church (or indeed of family and community dynamics), those with a stronger ecclesiology or from the more communal cultures of the global south could not separate authentic evangelism from the corporate life of believers. Equally, evangelism needed to be addressed to groups – families, communities according to structures in context – not just to individuals. Lastly, those from the context of another world faith, or from the increasingly post-Christian parts of the west, knew that evangelism must much more patiently lay deeper foundations before making an appeal. This longer task depended on the church, where it was established, and long-term commitment from expatriate missionaries where it was not.

The *Lausanne Covenant* sought to capture these major concerns, and expressed the essential partnership between evangelism by proclamation and social action, amongst other statements. In theory, the Lausanne Movement ever since has been committed to holistic or integral mission, as it came to be called. The *Lausanne Covenant*, the *Manila Manifesto*, and the *Cape Town Commitment*, all 'official position documents' of the Lausanne Movement, all state clearly the commitment to a holistic understanding of evangelism and mission. Nonetheless, in practice there remain many within its ranks who still hold fast to a narrower agenda for evangelism, and for whom the primary concern is ensuring that everyone 'hears the Gospel once' in the shortest possible time, and with limited focus on the more complex task of seeing strong, mature churches established, an abiding concern of WEA.

Two Global Evangelical Organizations or One?

The other major area of disagreement before and after Lausanne was over whether or not to establish another global organization in addition to the WEF. Many people, including John Stott and Jack Dain, pleaded that there should not be another evangelical global structure, and WEF made a formal plea to the same effect. The WEF leadership, and leaders of national EAs, were willing to take forward the agenda from Lausanne, and indeed many of the delegates were already active in their EAs. However, there was pressure from some to establish a new entity, perhaps because of some of the differing views suggested above, and perhaps because some came from cultures where multiple competing organizations was simply an expression of entrepreneurship and perfectly acceptable. Billy Graham was in favour of a new organization, with the sole focus of evangelism. In the event, a Continuation Committee was established, a form of compromise; but in the way of such groups, it was not long before the committee set up to facilitate certain gatherings gained a complete life of its own, and became the separate organization with which we are familiar today.

There have been several occasions since when a merger between Lausanne and WEA has been sought, and to the end of his long life Stott continued to pray for a closer relationship, if not merger, between the two organizations. As for many, separateness seemed to him to be a denial of unity as it should be expressed between evangelicals. So, for instance, with Stott's encouragement, WEF in 1980 made a formal appeal to Lausanne for a merger. The irony has been that many of those who have served Lausanne over the years have also been EA people, and that Lausanne continues to be heavily dependent on leaders and networks fostered through EAs, and frequently overlaps with WEA ministries, including the WEA Commissions. In 2011 there was a request that one of Lausanne's working groups should integrate with a parallel Commission of WEA, but the request was turned down by Lausanne leaders.

The practical relationship between Lausanne and WEA has differed at different periods and in different places. For instance, in several northern European countries, there is simply one body, the national manifestation of the Mission Commission of the WEA, and no differentiation as to whether a person is involved in a theoretically Lausanne project or a WEA one, while in some countries it seems that the profile of the two organizations is much more distinct. Most Associates of the WEA Mission Commission and a high proportion of those who have attended recent conferences of the Mission Commission, were also present at the Cape Town Congress, and many were involved in some of the preparatory consultations and activities. The Theology Working Group of Lausanne has had a long history of quietly incorporating serving members of both the WEA Mission Commission and the WEA Theological Commission. This practice was established by John Stott, who initially chaired the Lausanne group. It was wisely and graciously continued under the chairmanship of Chris Wright. This combined group met several times preparing a theological framework leading up to the Congress in Cape Town, and issuing a document expounding the *Lausanne Covenant's* phrase: 'The Whole Church Taking the Whole Gospel to the Whole World'. In addition, the team of eight tasked with drawing up the *Cape Town Commitment*, again under the leadership of Chris Wright, were almost all men and women active in both Lausanne and WEA, including their national EA movements, and WEA's Mission and Theological Commissions.

It was widely stated that the Cape Town Congress would be a partnership between Lausanne and WEA. In some ways it was, in some ways it wasn't. There was undoubtedly a warm friendship between many leaders of both organizations, including the respective chief Executives. As described above, there was wide overlap between people operating happily under both Lausanne and WEA umbrellas. All the same, 'WEA' appeared on publicity only after repeated requests and some protests, and then usually in small letters somewhere on the document. There was no agreed protocol drawn up between the organizations, and little consultation over key decisions and little invitation to WEA structures to be involved. The WEA Mission Commission was invited to present a plenary, and then after considerable work found almost by accident that the invitation had been extended to someone else instead. Perhaps different parts of the necessarily complex Lausanne planning structure were not entirely co-ordinated, but it led to some unhappy results. At the Congress, the name 'Lausanne' was referred to frequently from every platform, but WEA was rarely mentioned. Few delegates understood that this was intended to be a partnership. It was even only after considerable negotiation that WEA was allowed to have a stall in the concourse.

Perhaps it would be more godly to say that neither organization should be in the business of raising profile in any kind of competitive way. Nobody should be empire-building; the Kingdom of God is far more crucial than any organization. Yet it seemed to many delegates that a great opportunity had been missed to model a far more robust kind of partnership, and in particular an equal partnership that did not depend on equal finances (a huge issue in developing healthy partnerships in the mission world, especially between global north and south). Others concluded that since Lausanne leaders had raised most of the enormous cost of the project, and employed a large team to deliver it all (with huge efficiency and brilliance, it should be said), they should be entitled to quietly sideline WEA whose resources are of a very different order. Some concluded that some major donors have reservations about WEA. Others thought there were doctrinal politics at work. Perhaps there were as many conclusions, true and false, as there were delegates, but it was sad that an opportunity that probably will not come again, and certainly not for a generation, did not fulfil its potential to live out the deepest kind of evangelical unity. Will the Lord hold us all responsible?

Where Do We Go Next?

What of the future? Lausanne has an ambitious range of plans for the next decade at least. The Continuation Committee of 1974 has morphed into a complex organizational structure with worldwide involvement, though still (many would say) observably western in culture. Many of its working groups and networks will provide valuable resources and consultations. The commitment and integrity of its senior leadership is beyond question.

There remain some questions. Is it really right to have such duplication in many areas that we continue to find ourselves with? Many of the current Lausanne working groups and networks, and the consultations they plan, duplicate the WEA Commissions and working groups that have been steadily at work for decades. Is there not an element of 'I belong to Apollos, I belong to Paul' about all this, which the apostle so roundly condemned? What does this say to the watching world? That evangelicals are incapable of working together? Duplication is also financially draining. Many Christian agencies, including some national EAs, found that the Cape Town Congress, together with the complicated processes leading up to it, diverted scarce resources from other ministries, sometimes with devastating effect.

It is undoubtedly sometimes easier to bypass the churches and 'do our own thing' in mission. That doesn't make it right. How will the good work that Lausanne does through its groups and networks be accountable to, and serve, the churches? WEA's structures seek to stimulate local churches and denominations to engage in every dimension of mission, discipleship and holistic Christian witness locally, nationally and globally. Strengthening Gospel churches to fulfil their God-given calling, including evangelism, in other words full-orbed disciple-making and forming, seems a fundamental New Testament pattern.

This is all the more urgent now that in the goodness of God there are indeed Gospel churches all over the world, and ongoing expatriate missionary work needs increasingly to work alongside and under national leadership rather than engaging in independent initiatives. Even where the churches are not evangelical, and especially where they have maintained a Christian witness for centuries, even under persecution, we need to work hard at building relationships, in humility. 'The whole church' of Lausanne's slogan comprises more than evangelicals, as Lausanne's own documents testify. It takes patience to mobilise local congregations, but it is crucial in God's economy, not least to conserve those who make professions of faith and to develop them as lifelong disciples. This does not by any means rule out the role of agencies and individuals, but it does set that role in a biblical context.

The WEA, through its Mission Commission, has for a long time supported the new mission movements of the global south and of Eastern Europe. Sometimes Mission Commission staff and Associates have served as midwives, facilitating the birth of such movements and assisting them in getting established. This is a huge contribution to ongoing world evangelization, representing new energy and vision, but also enabling easier entry into pioneer situations where westerners may no longer be welcome. In many instances, the new mission movements are more fully integrated into the churches than was the pattern often set by agencies in the past. Also, WEA's pattern of light-touch structure, and the considerable measure of freedom of each national alliance (apart from subscribing to a shared Basis of Faith), means that it is simple for local alliances and mission movements to emerge which are financially and culturally contextualized and viable. This respects diversity and indigeneity, both essential for long-term health, and for sustained and sustainable involvement in cross-cultural mission.

In his brief speech of greetings at the start of the Cape Town Congress, Geoff Tunnicliffe referred to some of the unprecedented challenges facing today's world – and the church within it – and then went on to say: "Our commitment to seeking to fulfil God's purposes demands greater levels of partnership between all of us than ever before: between North and South, as well as between South and South and North and North. Our God, and the needs of our world, demand a deeper humility and deeper commitment to being God's agents of reconciliation and justice together, in a broken and oftentimes harsh world."

Since the Lausanne III (Cape Town) Congress, WEA senior staff and Lausanne senior staff have made a mutual commitment to some simple guidelines designed to strengthen global Gospel and Kingdom efforts, and to help avoid misunderstandings or duplication.[9] The WEA remains very committed to doing all in its power to foster evangelical unity. It is to be hoped that those guidelines will be adopted throughout both organizations, and indeed that partnership will be strengthened and duplication avoided.

Our Shared Goal

The WEA's founding purpose, implicit from 1846 and explicitly stated and adopted in 1951, is the furtherance of the Gospel, the defence and confirmation of the Gospel, and fellowship in the Gospel, in the context of the whole world and the worldwide church. Lausanne's purpose is expressed as 'the Whole Gospel, from the Whole Church, to the Whole World'. It is hard to see how these differ from one another in any meaningful way. Both organizations draw together those with shared doctrinal convictions in all primary matters, and with freedom for diversity in secondary matters. Both revolve around love for the Lord Jesus Christ, and commitment to be the human agents that carry out his mission in every generation and in every corner of God's world. Both are committed to making disciples of all peoples, and to do that in fellowship across

[9] The full text of the agreement is included in the Appendix below.

denominations and ethnic distinctives. Both are committed to Scripture as a governing authority, both preach the Cross and Resurrection of Christ, both foster active discipleship.

With so much in common, it is to be hoped that WEA and Lausanne will find many ways in which to live out our shared calling, for our good but most of all for God's glory.

Appendix

Personal and corporate relationships between leaders of Lausanne and World Evangelical Alliance:

Recognising that close relationships of mutual trust are an essential foundation for strong relationships between the two movements, the leaders of Lausanne Movement for World Evangelization and the WEA nevertheless recognize that a framework is also needed for the relationship between the two movements.

They have therefore agreed a process designed to maximize partnership opportunities and minimize conflicts or misunderstandings. They agreed to:

1. Meet regularly to strengthen their relationship with one another.
2. Share news with one another about their respective activities.
3. Review events and structures to discern areas of common concern.
4. Connect people in the two movements already active in areas of common concern.
5. Clarify the language used about each other's movements and describe each other with the terminology preferred by their respective movements.
6. Discuss ways to communicate with one another about people asked to carry senior responsibilities in the movements.

Review and adjust these simple guidelines as necessary.

FROM THE LAUSANNE COVENANT TO THE CAPE TOWN COMMITMENT: A THEOLOGICAL ASSESSMENT[1]

Robert Schreiter

The third Lausanne Congress on World Evangelization convened in Cape Town, South Africa, in October, 2010. It brought together over four thousand evangelical leaders, plus guests from other Christian traditions, to ponder where faithful Christians are called today in God's mission. The Lausanne Movement, inaugurated in Lausanne in 1974, has been one of the most important voices in Christian mission over the past thirty-five years, with its Congresses, working groups, and forums. Given its importance, it would be worthwhile to trace how its theology has developed through the course of its three international Congresses: at Lausanne (1974), Manila (1989) and now Cape Town (2010). Can changes be signalled or trends detected? As one observer has put it: Is there movement in the Movement?

This article is an attempt to assess the directions of its theology from the perspective of a non-evangelical: in this case, a Roman Catholic who has great sympathy and respect for so much of what evangelical mission has achieved, but is nonetheless willing to cast a critical eye as needed upon its developments. I did not participate in the Cape Town Congress or in any of its predecessors, so my reading of the theological statements reflects more the final form of those statements rather than how they were produced. I am familiar, however, with a good number of the *Lausanne Occasional Papers*, a number of which have been influential in my own work.

This assessment is in four parts. The first part looks at the theological significance of the stated genre of the three statements: as 'Covenant' (Lausanne), as 'Manifesto' (Manila), and as 'Commitment' (Cape Town). What might these choices of genre be saying about the theological self-understanding of those who produced these statements? The second and third parts look at the theological understandings of mission and at the world in which mission is undertaken, respectively. What do these theological 'frames' tell us of the theological assumptions that have shaped and are shaping the Movement? The fourth and final part looks at a number

[1] This article has been published in the Jan 2011 issue of IBMR (IBMR). It is included here with the permission of the author and the editor of IBMR.

of individual theological themes that are found in the three documents that have developed (or disappeared) in the course of these Congresses.

Needless to say, this will be an assessment in very broad strokes, given the space allotted. It is intended to track some of the larger or more salient developments in evangelical mission over these past three and a half decades. But in so doing, it is hoped that this will contribute to a greater understanding of what directions evangelical mission is taking – at least from the perspective of an interested outsider.

Covenant – Manifesto – Commitment

What might the genre chosen for each of these documents tell us about the theological self-understanding of those who wrote them and, albeit obliquely, the dynamics of the Congresses themselves? The fact that evangelical Christianity is a very diverse phenomenon – even as it holds firmly to certain biblical and theological tenets – makes any generalization at once hazardous and intriguing. They are hazardous because one can unduly see it as a monolith because of its shared convictions, overlooking its considerable diversity. But it is also intriguing because of how it manages this very pluralism in light of its biblical faith. To use the phrase of the preamble to the Cape Town document, it seeks 'breadth within boundaries'.

Secondly, these documents are consensus documents, i.e. they were intended to give a shared expression to the outcome of meetings in which thousands of people were involved. Their consensus nature is most evident in the careful wording found at certain points to articulate central but sometimes contested points, such as the Bible as the infallible word of God, the place of spiritual warfare, or the role of women in evangelism.

These two caveats about the diversity of those gathered and the nature of their consensus documents are important to keep in mind as one reads what follows here. Not knowing the intricacies of the dynamics of the meetings themselves, as well as the contents of the drafts that preceded the final forms of these statements, can qualify or even nullify some of the conclusions made here. At the same time, how the documents get read by an interested outsider remind us that texts take on a life of their own once they leave the hands of their authors.

But what of the genres themselves? For Lausanne, the choice was 'covenant'. Covenant of course has deep biblical resonance, as well as being an important concept in Reformed theology. It should be remembered that this was the final document at the first of these Congresses. Besides its biblical basis, the concept of covenant served another purpose as well: it marked the point where people from more than 150 nations, together for the first time, could make a common confession of their faith. Inasmuch as it was the final statement of a first gathering, 'covenant' also held the biblical implication of a chosen people setting out on a journey together with their

God (cf. Exodus 24). Such an idea of a covenanted people may well reveal the understanding of the theological significance of the event for the participants.

With covenant as the frame for Lausanne, we see that the document therefore speaks more to the participants (and, of course, to God) than to the general public. It is a document aimed at their self-understanding and self-motivation for mission. And like the covenants in the Hebrew Scriptures, it tends toward dichotomous language about what should and should not be believed or done. This preference for dichotomous language has a long history in evangelicalism, with its emphasis on personal conversion and total commitment to Jesus Christ. It also can function as a kind of shorthand or indicator to an in-group about its most deeply held tenets.

Manila produced a 'manifesto'. It is not a biblical term, although at the time of the Manila meeting Luke 4:16-20 was often referred to as the 'Nazareth Manifesto' in theological circles. The *Oxford English Dictionary* defines 'manifesto' as a public proclamation of a group to explain its past actions and give its intentions for future action. The *Manila Manifesto* certainly does that. As such, it moves beyond the more in-group approach of Lausanne to an outward-oriented message. It begins with twenty-one 'Affirmations' followed by its intentions to bring the 'whole Gospel proclaimed by the whole Church to the whole world'. In its outward orientation, it bespeaks a group that has now consolidated itself and can speak more confidently to an external audience. While manifesto may not be a biblical term, the proclamatory nature of this genre has the resonance of preaching the Good News. Here the theological self-understanding is the discipleship embodied in the Great Commission of Matthew 28:19-20.

Cape Town produced a 'commitment'. It is in two parts: a confession of faith and a commitment to action. A much more extensive document than its two predecessors, it moves away from the preference for dichotomous expression and public proclamation to a more essay-like mode. In so doing, it leaves a more prepositional approach behind to embrace a more nuanced presentation of its confession and commitments. It sees this very approach as building a link from belief to 'praxis' reminiscent of Paul in his letters to the Christian communities (Foreword). One sees echoed here theologically the model of discipleship and, with Paul, a concern for the extensiveness and the diversity of the peoples and communities to be served.

'Commitment' may not be a prominent biblical term, but it is certainly biblical in that it is a response to the call of Jesus Christ. It connotes a long-term investment in the peoples to whom the missionary is sent, and an ongoing accompaniment of them. As such, it carries a sense that those who make this commitment are not coming together for the first time (as at Lausanne); nor are they making an initial proclamation to outsiders (as Manila could be read). There is a certain matured quality here that reflects a movement that has become much more self-assured.

Theological Understandings of Mission

What theologies of mission arise from these three documents? Lausanne sees mission as participating in the "purpose of God", who "has been calling out from the world a people for himself, and sending his people back into the world to be his servants and witnesses, for the extension of his kingdom, the building up of Christ's body, and the glory of his name" (Affirmation 1). A strong sense of being servants and witnesses to God's plan and of being sent 'into the world' comes through quite clearly here. The mode of carrying this plan is by proclamation, but also by witness of life and "that kind of dialogue whose purpose is to listen sensitively in order to understand" (Affirmation 3). This leads to "obedience to Christ, incorporation into his Church, and responsible service in the world" (ibid.). The theology of mission here is quite straightforward: God has a plan for the world, to which we are called in order that it might be brought to completion. This conforms with the centrality of the Great Commission, that by going out, preaching, teaching, and baptizing, the world might be brought to Christ. Indeed, the Great Commission forms the theological basis for mission here.

The *Manila Manifesto* begins by reaffirming the *Lausanne Covenant*. In its twenty-one Affirmations, it sets out the task of mission in single-sentence form, building a narrative of creation, the fall, and the atonement, followed by distinct modes of action for mission (the role of other religions, the importance of pursuing justice and peace, spiritual warfare, etc.), ending with an Affirmation of the whole church being called to bring the whole world. This final Affirmation is reflected in Affirmations 7-20. Perhaps because it presumes what was said at Lausanne, it focuses more on the manifold issues of what is entailed in mission. Here one hears echoes of the 'Nazareth Manifesto' of Luke 4, with a concern for justice and for the poor. This had come into widespread use in the 1980s in missiological circles as a theological motivation for mission alongside the Great Commission, so it is not surprising to see it included in Manila document. The Nazareth Manifesto might be seen as the distinctive theological understanding of mission here. The emphasis on holism (the importance of the study of culture, the coupling of social action with traditional evangelism, inclusiveness) in preaching the whole Gospel to the whole world is evidence of an expanding view of mission that occurred in mainline Protestantism and Roman Catholicism at this time, albeit here with a distinctively evangelical accent.

Cape Town does not use propositions or affirmations in either its confession of faith or its commitment to action. The confession of faith includes a narrative of God's action in the world, but it is all consciously framed by two theological concepts: love and reconciliation. The theme of love echoes the Johannine writings in the New Testament, and reconciliation, the Pauline writings. Whereas Matthew and Luke provide distinctive frameworks for the two previous documents, here John and Paul prevail. The theme of God's love for the world and our response in love frames the entire confession of faith. For Paul, it is especially the image of cosmic reconciliation of all things in Christ (cf. Col 1:15-20) that stands out. Indeed, the Cape Town document speaks of "the cosmic integration is God's plan" (II.1) The salience of reconciliation reflects a larger interest in reconciliation that developed across the Christian church in the 1990s into the first decade of the new century. The 2004 *Lausanne Occasional Paper* 51 was devoted to the topic, and it was the principal theme of the 2005 Congress on World Evangelism and Mission of the World Council of Churches.

The second part of the Cape Town document addresses the various modalities of mission such themes as truth, peace, love, and the will of Christ. These are each put in the context of mission, such as living in a pluralist and globalized world, the problems of war and of poverty, other religions, challenges to evangelization today, and so on.

With its affirmation of the two preceding Congresses, Cape Town brings together a more complete biblical basis for Christian mission together. What is striking is how much more there is of a conscious *theological* basis for the entire document. The extensive use of John and Paul lend themselves to a more comprehensive theology than the selected quotations from Matthew and Luke. Moreover, this more comprehensive theology allows for a more nuanced engagement with the world.

Mission and the World

What are the implications of such a more nuanced engagement with the world? In the Lausanne document, the church is seen as set over against the world. The quotes given above about Christians being called 'out of the world' and then sent back 'into the world' are evidence of this God-world and church-world dichotomy. This 'over against' stance flows from its interpretation of the fall of humankind in Genesis 3. Manila maintains something of this stance in its fourth Affirmation, but strikes a more positive view of the importance of engaging the world. Cape Town takes a different approach by framing the biblical narrative of God's action in the world with the theme of love. It does not deny sinfulness by any means (cf. "Unchanged Realities", Preamble), but placing the emphasis on loving the world as God does is striking. We humans do not love sin, but we love the whole of creation and the world that exists within it.

The stance toward the world, especially as it is manifested in the Lausanne and Manila documents, is shaped by a Reformed theology of the fall of Adam and Eve that emphasizes the utter separation between God and the world because of their sin, and our helplessness before God. This theology developed at the time of the Reformation in order to emphasize the overwhelming power of God's justification of us in Jesus Christ, and that we are saved by faith and not by our own works. What is striking about the view of radical separation and human helplessness is that it says more about God's power and mercy than it does about humanity and the world: we see our world only as refracted through this affirmation of God's action in Christ. Roman Catholics take a more measured position, believing that human nature is damaged but not totally destroyed by sin; God can be discerned in the world and that there is a natural law ordained by God that can be known with unaided human reason. This stands over against the 'utter depravity of humankind' of the Synod of Dordt and the belief that humankind is, in its unredeemed condition, not capable of doing any good. It is this possibility of a 'natural theology' against which the Reformed Karl Barth protested so strongly in his exchanges with Roman Catholic theologians.

The question I want to raise here is this: does Cape Town represent a fundamental shift in an evangelical theology of mission? Does its warm embrace of the world create a dissonance with its Reformed reading of the radical character of the fall of Adam and Eve that has been at the basis of its theology of mission? Its wanting to overcome the 'sacred-secular' divide (I.3) could be read as a move away from traditional Reformed thinking about sin. To be sure, in the place where Cape Town mentions this, it is concerned about separating the workplace from Christian life. But the divide between the sacred and the secular is also sustained by a sense of the utter fallenness of the world in light of God's grace.

The Johannine writings, so central to Cape Town's theological concept of love, also have an ambivalence about the 'world'. The world is seen at once as utterly alienated from God but also the object of God's great love (cf. John 3:16). Perhaps that ambivalence, using Johannine texts, might have clarified this matter somewhat, at least from the point of the Scriptures. At any rate, the apparent dissonance between the Reformed theological anthropology heretofore so prominent in evangelical missiology and Cape Town's reading of the world bears further thought and discussion.

Individual Theological Themes

The second and third parts of this article looked at some overarching theological frameworks that have shaped the three documents. This final part looks at some individual theological themes that have appeared in the documents, and also themes that have become increasingly muted. Some of these have to do with basic tenets of evangelical faith, whereas others have to do with the relative salience of issues within the contexts in which mission is being carried out.

The Bible as the Word of God. This is of course a fundamental article of faith for all Christians, but has held a more specific meaning among evangelicals. Because of the disputes about its exact nature in the first half of the twentieth century, how this article comes to be worded can reflect continuing tensions.

Article 2 of the *Lausanne Covenant* affirms "the divine inspiration, truthfulness and authority of both Old and New Testament Scriptures in their entirety as the only written word of God, without error in all that it affirms, and the only infallible rule of faith and practice". Affirmation 2 of the *Manila Manifesto* states "that in the Scriptures of the Old and New Testament God has given us an authoritative disclosure of his character and will, his redemptive acts and their meaning, and his mandate for mission". Cape Town affirms "... the whole Bible as the Word of God, inspired by God's spirit, spoken and written through human authors. We submit to it as supremely and uniquely authoritative". (I.6) It goes on to say that the Scriptures can "speak in fresh ways" to people of every culture.

There are no contradictions between these statements. But it is obvious that Cape Town wants to situate its evangelical belief within a pluralist, multi-religious society.

Christ and Other Religions. As Christians come into closer social contact with people of other faiths, the relation of the unique and definitive salvation brought by Christ amid other religions has become an increasingly neuralgic point for all the churches. Both Lausanne and Manila reaffirm traditional doctrine here – although Manila goes further affirming that "the religions which have arisen do sometimes contain elements of truth and beauty" (Affirmation 3). Cape Town does not deny this doctrine, but circumvents the issue somewhat by placing its discussion under the challenge of pluralism and notes that Asian Christians "seek to respect competing truth claims of other faiths and live alongside them" (I.3). It does not address the question of the truth of Christ and other religions directly. The document at this point seems more concerned with the ideology of *post-modern*ism and its relativizing of all truth claims. Later, a whole Section (III) is devoted to loving people of other faiths. It is preoccupied especially with tolerance and respect of peoples of other faiths. Indeed, love is seen as the entry point of dealing with people of other faiths.

Spiritual Warfare. Spiritual warfare or combat has been a contentious topic in evangelicalism. Both Lausanne (No. 12) and Manila (Affirmation 11; No. 6) address its necessity in evangelism. Cape Town only mentions it in passing (5C, regarding the casting out of demons). Does this represent the fading of a once prominent point of contention?

Human Rights and Religious Freedom. Lausanne took up the question of human rights and religious freedom in the context of persecution and imprisonment (No. 13), looking perhaps especially to the persecution of Christians for their beliefs. Manila explicitly mentions the abuse of human rights (No. 4). Cape Town makes a careful statement about defending human rights, including the religious freedom of others (III.6). The statement affirms that defending the right to religious freedom of people of other faiths does not mean endorsing their faith by Christians, and makes distinctions between proselytizing and evangelizing. Here no doubt the experience of Asian Christians played a role in these careful formulations.

The Arts and Mission. The arts are not mentioned explicitly in the *Lausanne Covenant,* although it notes that cultures can be "rich in beauty and in goodness. Because they are fallen, all of it is tainted with sin and some of it is demonic" (No. 10). Cape Town, on the other hand, devotes a whole Section to the arts (I.5), which begins with: "We possess the gift of creativity because we bear the image of God. Art is an integral part of what we do as humans and in its many forms can reflect something of the beauty and truth of God." Here one can see the contrast of attitudes toward the world discussed above.

There are so many other themes that could be explored, such as co-operation with other traditions within Christianity, abuses of evangelization (the prosperity gospel), and attention to specific issues and topics (such as persons with disabilities, human trafficking, care for creation, and many others). But these five stand out especially. For this person's reading what stands as theological 'movement' in the Lausanne Movement from Lausanne to Cape Town is its more comprehensive theology of mission, a potential inconsistency between its embrace of the world and a Reformed view of the fallenness of creation, and above all, its willingness to listen and consider the many voices within evangelical Christianity (and even beyond) today.

A PENTECOSTAL PERSPECTIVE ON THE LAUSANNE MOVEMENT

Opoku Onyinah

Introduction

The Lausanne Movement operates under a memorable mission statement: 'The Whole Church Taking the Whole Gospel to the Whole World'. Since its initial meeting in 1974, the movement has convened large and small gatherings on a wide range of issues – all related to its mission statement regarding world evangelization.[1]

The first Congress convened by Billy Graham was held in Lausanne, and approximately 2,700 Christian leaders from over 150 countries gathered for the ten-day programme. It produced the *Lausanne Covenant*, one of the most profound and influential writings in recent church history. The *Lausanne Covenant* affirmed the necessity of reaching the world with the Gospel, the uniqueness of Christ, the authority of the Bible, the importance of social action, the value of cultural sensitivity, the richness of co-operation, and sorrow for having failed to complete the task of world evangelization. That Congress also produced immediate impact. Ralph Winter transformed mission strategy by emphasising the need to reach every people group within all the nations of the world. He helped us understand that having a church in a nation did not mean we had reached that nation. What about all the other ethnic groups within that country that spoke other languages and lived quite a distance from that church? To reach them would require intentional cross-cultural efforts that targeted those who had never heard the Gospel. This emphasis on 'unreached people groups' became the new frontier in missions.

Faithful to this clarion call, the Lausanne Movement has organised numerous regional and global conferences since 1974 to constantly urge the church to hasten the task of world evangelization. Prominent among them were the Second Lausanne Congress, convened in Manila, in 1989, and the third Lausanne Congress in Cape Town, South Africa, in 2010. The Manila Congress focused on the progress, resources, and methods of evangelising the world. It produced the *Manila Manifesto*, which is an elaboration of the

[1] 'Lausanne Gatherings'. Available at: www.lausanne.org/en/gatherings. Accessed 25th Aug 2012.

Lausanne Covenant.[2] Significant in the Manila Congress and its manifesto was the work of the Christian mission strategist Luis Bush, who first highlighted the need for a major focus of evangelism in the 'Resistant Belt', covering the middle of the eastern hemisphere: the 10/40 window.[3]

The third Congress produced the *Cape Town Commitment* (CTC), which sought to build upon the previous documents. The CTC strongly advocates that "we must respond in Christian mission to the realities of our own generation".[4]

In all three Congresses – Lausanne, Manila, and Cape Town – some attention was given to one of the most notable movements within the worldwide church in the last century: the rise of Pentecostalism.[5] The empowering of the Holy Spirit was reflected in all three global Lausanne Congresses and in each of the publications, although less in 1974, a bit more in 1989, and fully in 2010. The Pentecostal perspective is critical in any major global discourse on Christianity. It is from this viewpoint that I examine the third Lausanne Congress on World Evangelization (Cape Town 2010).

Representation and Participation

The third Lausanne Congress on World Evangelization brought together 4,200 evangelical leaders from 198 countries, and thousands more participated online. Cape Town 2010 is considered one of the most diverse gatherings of Christians in history.[6] Participants reflected the worldwide church in its global, ethnic, denominational,[7] age and gender diversity. This broad representation signalled an 'all-hands-on-deck' approach to reaching

---

[2] R. A. Hunt, 'The History of the Lausanne Movement, 1974-2010', *IBMR* 35 (2): (April 2011), 81-85.

[3] 'Second International Congress on World Evangelization', available at: http://en.wikipedia.org/wiki/Second_International_Congress_on_World_Evangelization. This article states, "Further research in the mid-1990s led to the '10/40 Window' concept, which contrasts the major needs and few resources devoted to this part of the world."

[4] The Third Lausanne Congress, *Cape Town Commitment* (Lausanne, 2011), 8. Accessed at: www.lausanne.org/en/documents/ctcommitment.html

[5] W. Hollenweger, *Pentecostalism: Origins and Developments Worldwide* (Peabody, MA: Hendrickson, 1997), 6-17; E. K. Larbi, *Pentecostalism: the Eddies of Ghanaian Christianity* (Accra: SAPC, 2001), 1-11; A. Paul, *Signs and Wonders: Why Pentecostalism is the World's Fastest Growing Faith* (San Francisco, CA: Jossey-Bass, 2009), 4-17.

[6] John W. Kennedy, 'The Most Diverse Gathering Ever', in *Christianity Today* (Sept 29th 2010). Available at: www.christianitytoday.com/ct/2010/september/34.66.html

[7] However, the Catholics, who are about 1.2 billion, and the Orthodox were not there. It was possible that other churches affiliated with the World Council of Churches were also not there.

a lost world. It was also a way of de-emphasising denominational individualism and strengthening co-operation, as the Lausanne Movement has always sought to do. The diversity also re-echoed the need to focus on what binds Christians together as we renew all efforts to complete the Great Commission.

Pentecostals were broadly represented among the participants, but unlike the Lausanne II Congress in Manila where Pentecostals fully contributed in the Congress, in Cape Town the Pentecostal voice was lacking on the podium. Commenting about the Manila Congress, Peter Wagner wrote:

> In dramatic contrast to Lausanne I, held in Switzerland in 1974, Lausanne II embraced leaders of the Pentecostal/charismatic movements at all levels from the Lausanne Committee itself through the plenary sessions and workshops to the thousands of participants who regularly worshiped with raised hands. Remarkably, the three most attended workshop tracks (of 48 offered) were on the Holy Spirit, spiritual warfare and prayer. Speakers such as Paul Yonggi Cho, Jack Hayford, Omar Cabrera, Dick Eastman, William Kumuyi and many others like them reflected the lowering of the barriers between evangelicals and Charismatics over the 15 years between the two congresses".[8]

It was thought the trend in Manila would continue but that was not so in Cape Town. The issue of Spiritual Warfare, for example which was prominent in the late twentieth century could have been discussed to find out progress so far.[9] Pentecostals strongly believe in the imminent coming of Christ and thus embark on aggressive evangelism. Since Pentecostals and Charismatics are perhaps the driving force in mission today, they should have been featured in a plenary session. It is hoped that in future Congress this 'Christian traditional' balance will be considered. The worldwide church needs to learn from each tradition's experiences. In addition, a strong challenge from a Pentecostal for the infilling of the Holy Spirit would have been appropriate at such a strategic gathering.

Cape Town 2010 was on African soil, and Africa is home to some of the emerging largest churches in the world, such as the Church of Pentecost with its headquarters in Ghana, and the Redeemed Christian Church of God headed by Bishop E.A. Adeboye, which has become a city of its own in Nigeria. Though Africa was featured geographically, it was not featured theologically, and some participants were disappointed that none of the African 'mega-voices' had the opportunity to speak. It was felt that the Congress organisers distanced themselves from these ministries, most of which are Pentecostal/Charismatic and are major agents of worldwide Christian transformation.

---

[8] Cited at www.seekgod.ca/darkangels.htm. Accessed Oct 11th 2012.

[9] See for examples, Opoku Onyinah, *Pentecostal Exorcism: Witchcraft and Exorcism in Ghana* (Blandford: Deo Publishers, 2012); and Opoku Onyinah, *Spiritual Warfare* (Cleveland, TN: CPT, 2012).

Opening Celebration

The opening celebration at Cape Town 2010 was colourful, historical and educative. A two-part video presentation entitled 'Turning Points in Church History: From Pentecost to Edinburgh' traced the growth of the church in the face of many obstacles. In addition to the video, dramatic presentations highlighted the expansion of Christianity in China, Latin America, and Africa.

As a result of the impact of the Pentecostal renewal on Christianity since the beginning of the twentieth century, Pentecostals expected the Azusa Street revival that led to the worldwide Pentecostal movement to have been highlighted in such presentations. Instead it was conspicuously absent. Neither was there any mention of the charismatic renewal in the last century. The video documentary of the history of the Christian church and its development over time stopped at the year 1900. As a result, nothing at all was said about the impact of Pentecostalism in the last 100 years. The impression was that Pentecostalism was being marginalised, and that we had been invited as observers and not participants. Although that was disappointing, everyone could appreciate the central message of the opening ceremony: that from its small beginnings, the church has grown to encompass the world.

The Role of the Holy Spirit in Christian Living and Global Missions

Pentecostalism places much emphasis on the work of the third person of the Godhead, the Holy Spirit, and we believe strongly in a direct personal experience of God through the baptism of the Holy Spirit. One of our central messages is that the Holy Spirit enables believers to live the Christian life and to effectively perform the tasks assigned to each believer. The Spirit gives supernatural ability to Christians to witness, preach, cast out evil spirits, heal the sick, and defend themselves against unseen evil forces. Likewise, the Spirit is seen as the motivating force behind all Christian mission activities.[10]

The Cape Town 2010 Congress was celebrated as a gathering to re-energise worldwide Christian leaders to complete the evangelization of the entire world. Pentecostals wish there had been a greater emphasis on the necessity of the empowerment of the Holy Spirit in accomplishing this great task.

[10] A. Pomerville, *Introduction to Missions: An Independent-Study Textbook* (Irving: ICI University Press, 1987), 100. Cf. W. Hollenweger, *The Pentecostals: The Charismatic Movement in the Churches* (Minneapolis, MN: Augsburg Publishing House, 1972), 7-21.

The Gospel is about Jesus Christ

Pentecostals believe in the preaching of the Lord Jesus as the Saviour, the Baptizer of the Spirit, the Healer, and the soon-coming King. Though we extend emergency humanitarian assistance and social welfare to needy people, we do not believe these should be the central focus of ministry. Pentecostals maintain that the preaching of the Gospel must undergird all social action, such as establishing schools, healthcare, recreation, involvement in politics and commerce.[11] In other words, Pentecostals hold that confronting the needs of society demonstrates the reality of the Gospel but does not replace the necessity for its preaching.

Cape Town 2010 prioritised the preaching of the Gospel in the same manner, though there was a certain level of tension about this. Some participants felt the emphasis on social problems was too great. Dr John Piper tried to address this in his exposition of Ephesians 3 when he said that "for Christ's sake, we Christians care about all suffering, especially eternal suffering". He said very poignantly that if we are not concerned about the world's suffering, we have a defective heart; if we are not concerned about people's eternal suffering, we have a defective view of hell.

No doubt, presentation after presentation brought us face-to-face with many of the world's problems, such as relativism and pluralism, yet the Gospel which is the power of God was consistently presented as the answer. The Congress affirmed belief in absolute truth, and particularly in Jesus Christ as the Truth. Christians, therefore, were called to live and proclaim the truth in the workplace, in the media, in government, and in academia. Cape Town 2010 encouraged Christians to respond to *post-modern* relativism and pluralism with sound and healthy apologetics. In this regard, Cape Town 2010 was on focus, pointing the church to the commission of its Master, Jesus Christ.

Unreached and Unengaged Groups

The concept of 'unreached people groups' is one of Lausanne's greatest legacies. However, it was a surprise that it was not given enough attention in the plenary sessions. Only Paul Eshleman spoke directly on this topic and provided participants with lists of the unreached people groups in their respective countries. This subject had deserved more attention.

Nevertheless, academic work, literature and video clips on unreached areas were helpful. Thus the Congress helped set participants on course. This focus is vital, because co-ordination, co-operation and progress of mission activities remain slow in unreached areas. Much work remains to

[11] Grant McClung, "Beyond Basic Evangelism: Pentecostals and a Broadened Lausanne Evangelistic Agenda", Part Two, June/July 2010, Available at: www.lausanneworldpulse.com/perspectives.php.../06-2010?p. Accessed Oct 18th, 2012.

be done in Central and North Africa, Central America, Asia, the Middle East, and the Arabian Peninsula.

Ironically, the label 'unreached' may soon include portions of the west, which is another evangelistic concern that deserved more attention. This area needs renewed ecumenical attention because the west still has a powerful voice in the directing of world Christianity.

From a Pentecostal perspective, the decline of Christianity in the west and the challenge of the unreached areas are important issues that should constantly inform our prayers. We praise God for every strategy that is being marshalled to stem the tide of secularism in the west and to shine God's light among the unreached. However, prayer is one of our most powerful weapons, and little attention or teaching was heard on this great subject and its importance in carrying out the Great Commission. A concerted time to pray for the unreached would have been welcome.

Worship

Generally the worship before the main services was warming, but the Pentecostal bones cried out for some prayers within the plenary sessions to address the challenges that were brought to our attention day by day (even hour by hour). We heard much talk on living the Christian life. Perhaps what was lacking was fervent prayer to energise our ability to live the talk.

The *Cape Town Commitment*

The central aim of Lausanne III was to "bring a fresh challenge to the global Church to bear witness to Jesus Christ and all his teachings in every nation, in every sphere of society, and in the realm of ideas".[12] The *Cape Town Commitment* is an enduring expression of those goals.

The *Commitment* is in two parts. Part I establishes the boundaries of the evangelical faith, passed down to us in the Scriptures. Here, writers tried to distinguish primary truths (upon which the church must be united), from secondary issues (upon which Christians can thoughtfully disagree). Part II is a call to action with regard to world evangelization. It is hoped that the *Commitment* will serve as the road map for the Lausanne Movement in the coming decade.[13]

The *Cape Town Commitment* is a remarkable document, and I was pleased to chair a recent nationwide congress in Ghana that revolved around its teachings. As a Pentecostal, I was immediately drawn to the section in Part I, 'We Love God the Holy Spirit'. It spoke urgently of the need for the Spirit's empowering presence and said our engagement in mission is "pointless and fruitless without the presence, guidance and

---

[12] *CTC*, 4.
[13] *CTC*, 5.

power of the Holy Spirit". I think all Pentecostals will say a hearty 'Amen!' to that. The caution in that section about charlatans who distort the ministry of the Holy Spirit is in order.

Implementation

In Cape Town 2010, a good attempt was made to translate ideas and strategies into implementable realities. This was evident in the regional meetings. However, in some places, for instance in Africa, such strategies work better when sub-regional groups have a voice in regional planning and implementation. Perhaps this could have been accomplished with specific tasks-and-expectation modules, as well as specific input-output frameworks. In self-supporting Christian ventures, it appears that in Africa the Pentecostal and the Charismatic movements are in better shape to achieve more than the other traditions, which often remain tied to outside funding.

Conclusion

The task of completing world evangelization requires the joint effort of all Christian traditions. The Lausanne Movement has sought to address this. Islamic militancy and renewed fundamentalism in the Middle East and North Africa, as well as recent Buddhist uprisings in South East Asia and Central Asia, should inform the Christian world that theoretical affirmations at well-advertised conferences are not enough.[14] Recent expressions of Nigerian Christianity have shown a certain level of militant resistance in the face of Islam's aggression. Although the posture of the Nigerian church is one of self-defence, the ecumenical reality to push for more civil and political space to evangelise the world has become necessary.

This study has attempted to show that although the Lausanne Movement has achieved a lot, there is still the need to adopt the strengths of all Christian faith traditions to reach the unreached areas. These include the Pentecostal distinctive of emphasising the work of the Holy Spirit in missions and fervent prayers in the life of Christians.

---

[14] J. MacArthur, *Hard to Believe: The High Cost and Infinite Value of Following Jesus* (Nashville, TN: Thomas Nelson, 2003).

THE CAPE TOWN COMMITMENT: CONTINUITY AND CHANGE

Harold Netland

One of the enduring contributions of the International Congress on World Evangelization in Lausanne in 1974 is the *Lausanne Covenant*. This concise document has served not only as a clarion call for world evangelization but also as a marker of evangelical identity, uniting otherwise disparate groups of Christians around the world in a common commitment to Christian mission.

Lausanne 1974 did not result in a new denomination or ecumenical institution as such but rather in a *movement* united around the theological framework of the *Lausanne Covenant* and the task of world evangelization. Movements, while perhaps lacking the stability and clear definition of a denomination or institution, have the advantage of flexibility in adjusting to changing conditions. At its best, this has been part of the genius of the Lausanne Movement. For it has combined an unchanging commitment to the theological foundations expressed in the *Lausanne Covenant* and the task of world evangelization with an increasing sensitivity to the ever changing contexts within which such evangelization occurs.

Thirty-six years after Lausanne I the third Lausanne Congress on World Evangelization was held in Cape Town in October, 2010. The Cape Town Congress produced the *Cape Town Commitment*, a much longer document than the Covenant, comprising two parts:. a confession of faith and a commitment to action. The *Cape Town Commitment* is to be read in conjunction with the earlier *Lausanne Covenant* and *Manila Manifesto*.[1] The 2010 Commitment is a theologically and missiologically rich statement which includes a concise summary of key evangelical theological themes as well as a keen awareness of the many challenges facing the church today. It issues a forthright call to bring the unchanging Gospel to our troubled world in a winsome and compelling manner.

As such, the Commitment could be assessed on a variety of grounds. In this essay I will first note some areas of continuity between the *Cape Town Commitment* and the earlier *Lausanne Covenant*, and then suggest some

---

[1] The Second International Congress on World Evangelization was held in Manila in July, 1989, and produced the *Manila Manifesto*. While the Manifesto is significant, it will not be discussed in this essay due to space limitations.

ways in which the Commitment goes beyond the Covenant in addressing fresh issues which are especially urgent in the early 21st century. A comprehensive analysis is impossible here, but two issues in particular will be highlighted -- Christian witness in contexts of religious pluralism and the need for an appropriate apologetic for the Christian Gospel today. Both issues receive explicit and implicit treatment in the Commitment, and in order to appreciate the significance of these issues it will be necessary to comment briefly on the changing social and intellectual conditions throughout the world in the decades since 1974.

These observations come from someone who self-identifies as an evangelical but has not been particularly active in the Lausanne Movement. Nevertheless I have followed the Lausanne Movement with appreciation and I am largely in agreement with the substance and tone of the Commitment. I have been active in missions and theological education in Asia and North America since 1983. Although I was present at Lausanne II in Manila, I was not at Lausanne I or Lausanne III, nor was I involved in any of the preliminary discussions leading to the drafting of the *Cape Town Commitment*. So I read and respond to the Commitment as a written text, apart from the activities and concerns leading to its composition.

Foundational Commitments

The *Commitment* begins with a twofold commitment to "the living God and his saving purposes through the Lord Jesus Christ" and to "the vision and goals of the Lausanne Movement." As such, it articulates a renewed commitment to "the task of bearing worldwide witness to Jesus Christ and his teaching" and "to the primary documents of the Movement – the *Lausanne Covenant* (1974), and the *Manila Manifesto* (1989)."[2] In other words, the *Cape Town Commitment* is intended as an expression of continuity with what has been foundational to the Lausanne Movement from its inception.

The 1974 *Lausanne Covenant* affirms clearly a number of core theological convictions which in turn form the basis for the call to co-operation in the task of world evangelization. The Covenant, for example, affirms belief in the Triune God, the divine inspiration and full authority of the Old and New Testaments, the uniqueness of Jesus Christ as the one Lord and Savior for all humankind, the lostness of humankind due to sin, and the necessity of evangelism.[3]

The *Cape Town Commitment* accepts and reaffirms these core theological convictions. Although the Commitment is different from the *Lausanne Covenant* in length, structure and tone, the same basic

---

[2] *The Cape Town Commitment: A Confession of Faith and a Call to Action*, Preamble (Peabody, MA: Hendrickson / The Lausanne Movement, 2011) 6.

[3] See Sections 1-5 of the Lausanne Covenant.

theological convictions are evident. Part I of the Commitment expresses the theological foundations, while Part II builds upon this with specific calls to action on the part of believers. The theological convictions in Part I are not articulated simply as assertions but rather as affirmations expressed in the language of our love for God, the world and others. For example, the Commitment begins by expressing our love for the Triune God and acknowledging that we love because God first loved us. Moreover, Christian mission – which is the underlying concern throughout the document -- is rooted in the nature of the loving God and our own love for God. "The mission of God flows from the love of God. The mission of God's people flows from our love for God and all that God loves."[4]

The preamble bases the church's mission upon certain unchanging biblical truths, including the conviction that human beings "stand under the just judgement of God in our sin and rebellion, and without Christ we are without hope". In response to the human predicament, the Gospel is portrayed as "the unchanged story of what God has done to save the world, supremely in the historical events of the life, death, resurrection, and reign of Jesus Christ."[5] The *Commitment* echoes the 1974 Covenant in its emphasis upon evangelism and disciple making. "God commands us to make known to all nations the truth of God's revelation and the gospel of God's saving grace through Jesus Christ, calling all people to repentance, faith, baptism and obedient discipleship."[6] The Commitment explicitly reaffirms the *Lausanne Covenant's* call for 'the Whole Church to take the Whole Gospel to the Whole World', and the entire document can be understood as an attempt to tease out the implications of this within the context of our love for God, for the Gospel, and for the world in the early 21st century.[7]

The *Lausanne Covenant* was written at a time when soteriological universalism and more pluralistic perspectives on the religions were becoming influential within some sectors of the church. Accordingly, Section 3 of the Covenant is a clear affirmation of the uniqueness of Jesus Christ as the only Lord and Savior for all humankind and rejection of universalism.

The issues of pluralism and soteriology were even more pressing in 2010 and thus the *Cape Town Commitment* is unequivocal on the uniqueness of Jesus Christ. "God commanded Israel to love the LORD God with exclusive loyalty. Likewise for us, loving the Lord Jesus Christ means that we steadfastly affirm that he alone is Saviour, Lord, and God… We proclaim Christ. In Christ alone God has fully and finally revealed himself,

---

[4] *Cape Town Commitment*, I.1, 9.

[5] *Cape Town Commitment*, Preamble, 7.

[6] *Cape Town Commitment*, I.10.B, 29.

[7] *Cape Town Commitment*, Preamble, 8. The quote is from Section 6 of The Lausanne Covenant.

and through Christ alone God has achieved salvation for the world."[8] Not all will be saved. "Those who refuse to repent and 'do not obey the gospel of our Lord Jesus Christ will be punished with eternal destruction and shut out from the presence of God.'"[9]

Although there is clear continuity between the *Lausanne Covenant* and the *Cape Town Commitment* in many respects, there are some differences as well. We might begin by considering a question raised by the Roman Catholic theologian Robert Schreiter in his thoughtful analysis of the Commitment. Schreiter calls attention to what he perceives as a possible shift in the Commitment away from traditional evangelical commitments on sin. "Does Cape Town represent a fundamental shift in an evangelical theology of mission? Does its warm embrace of the world create a dissonance with its Reformed reading of the radical character of the fall of Adam and Eve that has been the basis of its theology of mission? Its wanting to overcome any 'sacred-secular divide' (II.I.3) could be read as a move away from traditional Reformed thinking about sin."[10]

Schreiter's question is perceptive and deserves a more substantial response than can be given here. Although the Commitment has a somewhat different tone and often shows greater nuance in expression than the Covenant, I do not think that this indicates a fundamental move away from classical evangelical commitments on sin. The *Commitment* does adopt a more affirming posture toward the world, including human cultures and the physical creation, than is sometimes heard in evangelical circles. Thus, "We share God's passion for his world, loving all that God has made, rejoicing in God's providence and justice throughout his creation, proclaiming the good news to all creation and all nations..."[11] Christ's followers are challenged to bring the Gospel of truth and peace to the various domains of culture and to act responsibly with respect to the earth's resources. "Creation care is thus a gospel issue within the Lordship of Christ."[12]

This might suggest a less dualistic understanding of the relation between the church and the world, but two considerations should temper claims about a theological shift here. First, although the language in the *Lausanne Covenant* is terse and tends toward binary opposition between the Gospel and the world, it too has positive things to say about culture (see Sections 5 and 10). Second, despite its more positive tone, the *Cape Town Commitment* also speaks clearly about sin and evil in the world. "The world of God's good creation has become the world of human and satanic

---

[8] *Cape Town Commitment*, I.4, 13 and 15.

[9] *Cape Town Commitment*, I.8.A, 23. The embedded quotation is from 2 Thess. 1:8-9.

[10] Robert J. Schreiter, 'From the Lausanne Covenant to the Cape Town Commitment: A Theological Assessment', in *IBMR*, 35:2 (April 2011) 90.

[11] *Cape Town Commitment*, I.7, 19.

[12] *Cape Town Commitment*, I.7.A, 19.

rebellion against God. We are commanded not to love that world of sinful desire, greed, and human pride."[13]

Schreiter's comment might be prompted by the more comprehensive understanding of the Gospel and Christian mission operative in the Commitment when compared with the earlier *Lausanne Covenant*. Lausanne 1974 had stimulated a vigorous debate among evangelicals on the meaning of the Gospel and the relation between overt evangelism and social justice or compassion ministries. There is no need to rehearse that story here but, largely due to the influence of the Lausanne Movement, by Lausanne II in 1989 it was widely accepted by evangelicals that the Gospel includes both evangelism and social justice / compassion ministries and this consensus is reflected in the 2010 Commitment with its call for meeting the varied needs of people as well as caring for creation. But I do not see this development as inconsistent with the 1974 Covenant but rather as a healthy maturing of evangelical understandings of the Gospel and mission. The danger, of course, is that with a more comprehensive definition of mission explicit evangelism will be neglected. The *Commitment* itself does not ignore evangelism, but church and mission leaders will need to be vigilant in keeping evangelism central to Christian engagement with the world's many problems.

I do, however, see the *Cape Town Commitment* moving beyond the *Lausanne Covenant* in addressing Christian witness in contexts of religious diversity and the need for an appropriate apologetic for the Christian Gospel today. The prominence of these issues in the Commitment is due, in part, to the changes in our world since 1974. In many ways the world was a very different place in 2010 from what it had been in 1974, something acknowledged by the Commitment: "Almost everything about the way we live, think and relate to one another is changing at an accelerating pace."[14] We will highlight briefly some changes that make the claim that Jesus Christ alone is Lord and Savior for all humankind – which is foundational to the Commitment -- increasingly implausible for many today.

Changing Religious Patterns

One way to get at the changes in the past four decades is to consider the different ways in which scholars think of secularization and globalization today. Not that long ago there was general acceptance of the idea that modernization (inevitably?) results in the decline of religion, it social marginalization and insignificance. Steve Bruce, a vigorous current defender of this model, argues that secularization includes three interrelated changes: the decline of popular involvement with the churches; the decline in scope and influence of religious institutions; and the decline in the

[13] *Cape Town Commitment*, I.7.E, 22.
[14] *Cape Town Commitment*, Preamble, 6.

popularity and influence of religious beliefs.[15] This version of the secularization thesis was dominant among observers of religion in the 1960s and 70s. Sociologist Peter Berger, for example, writing in 1968 – just six years prior to Lausanne I -- predicted that by "the 21st century, religious believers are likely to be found only in small sects, huddled together to resist a worldwide secular culture".[16]

But since the 1980s the traditional secularization thesis has come under withering criticism, with most social theorists now either abandoning it entirely or modifying it considerably. In a remarkable about-face, Peter Berger changed his mind, stating in 2002, "It is fair to say that the majority of sociologists dealing with religion today no longer adhere to the equation of modernity and secularization."[17] Critics not only call into question the evidence alleged to support the traditional thesis but produce impressive counter-evidence from around the world suggesting that, far from being the norm, the decline of religion in parts of western Europe might be an anomaly.[18] Berger observes, "The world today is massively religious, is *anything but* the secularized world that has been predicted (whether joyfully or despondently) by so many analysts of modernity".[19] We are familiar with the dramatic growth of Christianity throughout Asia, Latin America and Africa in recent decades.[20] Less acknowledged by evangelicals, however, is the resurgence of traditional religions such as Hinduism, Buddhism and Islam throughout the world, along with the emergence of thousands of new religious movements and alternative spiritualities, often in modernized, technologically advanced societies.[21] We are reminded on a daily basis of the global impact of radical Islamist

---

[15] Steve Bruce, *Religion in the Modern World: From Cathedrals to Cults* (Oxford, UK: OUP, 1996) 26; see also Bruce, *Secularization* (New York: OUP, 2011).

[16] Peter Berger, "A Bleak Outlook Is Seen for Religion", *New York Times*, Feb 25, 1968, 3; as cited in Monica Duffy Toft, Daniel Philpott, and Timothy Samuel Shah, *God's Century: Resurgent Religion and Global Politics* (New York: W.W. Norton, 2011) 1.

[17] Peter Berger, "Secularization and De-secularization", in *Religions in the Modern World*, eds. Linda Woodhead, Paul Fletcher, Hiroko Kawanami and David Smith (London: Routledge, 2002) 291.

[18] See Rob Warner, *Secularization and Its Discontents* (New York: Continuum, 2010).

[19] Peter Berger, *The Desecularization of the World* (Grand Rapids, MI: Eerdmans, 1999) 9.

[20] Mark Hutchinson and John Wolffe, *A Short History of Global Evangelicalism* (New York: Cambridge University Press, 2012) chapters 8 and 9.

[21] See for example, *Religions in the Modern World: Traditions and Transformations*, 2nd ed., eds. Linda Woodhead, Hiroko Kawakami, and Christopher Partridge (New York: Routledge, 2009); *The Cambridge Guide to New Religious Movements*, eds. Olav Hammer and Mikael Rothstein (New York: Cambridge University Press, 2012); and *The Oxford Handbook of Global Religions*, ed. Mark Juergensmeyer (New York: OUP, 2006).

movements as well as violence instigated in part by militant Hindu, Buddhist, Sikh, and Christian groups.[22]

Yet the idea of secularization is not so easily dismissed. Clearly there are significant differences in religion in modern societies at the beginning of the 21st century when compared with, for example, premodern societies of the thirteenth century. In parts of western Europe involvement with traditional Christian institutions has declined dramatically and there is a marked increase in the numbers of those rejecting traditional Christian beliefs. Rejection of traditional religious beliefs and practices is also evident in parts of Latin America and Asia, notably China. Religious scepticism is rampant in many parts of the world. Religious statistics are notoriously problematic, but certain trends worldwide are discernible. Thus, Johnson and Grim report that between 1910 and 2010 the numbers of atheists and agnostics worldwide "grew more than four times faster than the world's population".[23] Whereas in 1910 the five countries with the highest percentage of atheists were the Netherlands (0.2%), Belgium, Hungary, Argentina and Uruguay, in 2010 the top five were North Korea (15.6%), Sweden, China, Viet Nam and Uruguay. The five countries with the highest percentage of agnostics today are North Korea (56.1%) followed by Estonia (50.9), Czech Republic (39.4), China (32.6), and New Zealand (30.6).[24] Religious pluralism, the view that all the major religions are roughly equally legitimate and effective responses to an ultimate divine reality, feeds off of a general attitude of scepticism toward the particular claims of any single religion. The ethos of religious pluralism is increasingly influential in popular culture as well as in the academy.

But rather than mapping these changes simply in terms of *the decline of religion*, as did classic secularization theory, many scholars today consider these to be indicators of significant shifts in *how people are religious today*. In his massive and rich study, *A Secular Age*, Charles Taylor considers secularization in the west as a process of change which is reflected in in the following question: "[W]hy was it virtually impossible not to believe in God in, say, 1500 in our western society, while in 2000 many of us find this not only easy, but even inescapable?"[25] For Taylor, the transition to a secular age involves three changes in society at large and in individual consciousness.[26] First, there are the changes in public institutions and practices, so that "whereas the political organization of all pre-modern societies was in some way connected to, based on, guaranteed by some

---

[22] Mark Juergensmeyer, *Global Rebellion: Religious Challenges to the Secular State, From Christian Militias to Al Qaeda* (Berkeley, CA: University of California Press, 2008).

[23] Todd M. Johnson and Brian J. Grim, *The World's Religions in Figures* (Oxford, UK: Wiley-Blackwell, 2013) 11.

[24] Johnson and Grim, *The World's Religions*, 43.

[25] Charles Taylor, *A Secular Age* (Cambridge: Harvard University Press, 2007) 26.

[26] Taylor, *A Secular Age*, 1-3.

faith in, or adherence to God, or some notion of ultimate reality, the modern western state is free from this connection". The second is the decline in the numbers of those who continue to embrace traditional religious beliefs and participate in traditional religious practices. Despite the resurgence of interest in religions in much of the world, there is strong evidential support for such decline in some parts of Europe. In parts of Asia, Latin America and North America there is also a significant rise in the numbers of those who claim to be non-religious, including growing numbers of explicit atheists. Ian Reader, for example, has produced impressive data showing a clear decline in religious belief and activity in Japan in the past several decades and China includes evidence of both religious resurgence and widespread agnosticism and atheism.[27]

But the third transformation Taylor speaks of acknowledges that religion continues to be significant for many people in modern societies, although the way in which they "are religious" is different. The shift here "consists, among other things, of a move from a society where belief in God is unchallenged and indeed unproblematic, to one in which it is understood to be one option among others, and frequently not the easiest to embrace". Secularization involves the change "which takes us from a society in which it was virtually impossible not to believe in God, to one in which faith, even for the staunchest believer is one human possibility among others.... Belief in God is no longer axiomatic. There are alternatives."[28]

Secularization in this third sense is a reality in many societies worldwide which are becoming increasingly globalized and diverse. Through globalization and the pluralization of societies people are aware of religious diversity to an unprecedented degree and this often has destabilizing effects on traditional commitments. Christian claims about a unique Gospel for all people in all cultures are especially problematic for many. This produces a major issue for Christian missions. As Peter Berger puts it, "If our situation forces us to choose between the gods, since no god can any longer be taken for granted, why should we choose the Biblical God?"[29]

Religious scepticism has been a significant force in the west since the seventeenth century, and it is today often reinforced through the modern research university. With globalization, the influences of the western university culture reach worldwide. Thus Berger speaks of the globalizing effects of the "faculty club culture", which involves the "internationalization of the western intelligentsia, its values and

---

[27] Ian Reader, "Secularisation, R.I.P.? Nonsense! The 'Rush Hour Away from the Gods' and the Decline of Religion in Contemporary Japan", in *Journal of Religion in Japan*, 1, (2012) 7-36. For religious patterns in China see Fenggang Yang, *Religion in China: Survival and Revival Under Communist Rule* (New York: OUP, 2012).

[28] Ibid., 3.

[29] Peter Berger, *Questions of Faith: A Skeptical Affirmation of Christianity* (Oxford, UK: Blackwell, 2004), 20.

ideologies". This class of international intellectuals "spreads its beliefs and values through the educational system, the legal system, various therapeutic institutions, think tanks, and at least some of the media of mass communication".[30] Influences from western academia and the media thus shape the educational elite in other parts of the world, spreading secular values and assumptions. This is the world that the *Cape Town Commitment* addresses, and it is to be commended for taking religious scepticism and religious pluralism seriously. It is not enough just to proclaim the Gospel. Those with sincere questions need to be helped to understand why they should accept the Gospel of Jesus Christ, rather than other alternatives available, as true.

Apologetics in a Sceptical, Pluralistic World

It is interesting that already in 1995, as he reflected back upon the twenty years since Lausanne 1974, John Stott, architect of the *Lausanne Covenant*, recognized the need for a responsible apologetic in Christian witness.

> We evangelical people need to repent of every occasion on which we have divorced evangelism from apologetics, as the apostles never did. We have to argue the Gospel we proclaim. We need to be able to say confidently to our hearers what Paul said to Festus: "What I am saying is true and reasonable" (Acts 26:25). We cannot possibly surrender to the current understanding of "pluralism" as an ideology that affirms the independent validity of every religion. Our task, rather, is to establish the criteria by which truth claims can be evaluated and then to demonstrate the uniqueness and finality of Jesus Christ.[31]

The first theme in Part II of the *Cape Town Commitment* is "Bearing Witness to the Truth of Christ in a Pluralistic, Globalized World." The *Commitment* states, "We long to see greater commitment to the hard work of robust apologetics." Responsible apologetics must involve both "those who can engage at the highest intellectual and public level in arguing for and defending biblical truth in the public arena" and pastors and other Christian leaders who can equip ordinary believers so that they are confident in their faith and able to share it intelligently with others.[32]

This is a refreshing and significant statement. For too long evangelical approaches to Christian witness have been dominated by a pervasive pragmatism and even anti-intellectualism which has ignored difficult issues about the plausibility of the Christian faith. Difficult and disturbing questions cannot be ignored and the Commitment is right in identifying this as an urgent issue for the church. There are encouraging signs that the

---

[30] Peter Berger, "Four Faces of Global Culture", *National Interest*, 49, (Fall 1997), 24-25.

[31] John Stott, "Twenty Years After Lausanne: Some Personal Reflections", *IBMR* 19:2 (April 1995), 54.

[32] *Cape Town Commitment*, II.A.2.A, 34.

church is taking seriously the need to engage in responsible apologetics, although too often apologists focus just upon traditional issues and methods.[33]

Traditional issues that Christian apologists have been addressing for years in the west are important and will continue to demand thoughtful response. How can we know that an eternal creator God exists? Can one really believe in an all good and all powerful God given the nature and extent of evil and suffering in the world? Why should one believe that Jesus of Nazareth was in fact God incarnate? And so on.

But globalization and awareness of religious diversity place the traditional issues in a broader context and also introduce some difficult new issues. Christian apologetics in the days ahead must contend with some fresh questions, including sophisticated challenges from adherents of other religions and a pluralistic ethos which rejects any particular religion as distinctively true. With the many religious and non-religious worldviews available today, why should one become or remain a Christian? Given the widespread disagreement among religions, can one reasonably suppose that his own particular religious tradition is true and all others are false? How is one to know which, if any, sacred scriptures are indeed divinely inspired? Why accept the Bible as God's Word but not the Qur'an or Gita? Many religions include miracle claims. Are they all to be accepted as true? If not, why should we accept the miracle claims in the Bible but not those in other religious texts? Do certain mystical states provide direct access to ultimate reality? If not, why not? And so on. Christian apologetics in the post-Christendom, globalizing, and religiously pluralistic world of the 21st century must not only be biblically faithful and intellectually responsible. It must also be appropriately humble, gracious, and sensitive to the diverse social and cultural contexts in which we offer a reason for the hope that is in us (1 Pet. 3:15-16).[34]

Christian Witness Among Religious Others

Not surprisingly, the *Cape Town Commitment* gives much greater attention to issues concerning witness in contexts or religious diversity and pluralism

---

[33] See the helpful essay by Lars Dahle, "Truth, Christian Mission and Apologetics: A Response and Proposal", http://larsdahle.no/acts-17.

[34] For my own work in this area see Harold Netland, "Interreligious Apologetics", in *Christian Apologetics: An Anthology of Primary Sources*, eds. Khaldoun A. Sweis and Chad V. Meister (Grand Rapids, MI: Zondervan, 2012) 39-45; *Can Only One Religion be True? Paul Knitter and Harold Netland in Dialogue*, eds. Robert B. Stewart (Minneapolis, Fortress, 2013); Harold Netland, "Jesus Is the Only Way to God", in *Debating Christian Theism*, eds. J. Moreland, Chad Meister, and Khaldoun A. Sweis (New York: OUP, 2013) 497-508. See also Keith Yandell and Harold Netland, *Buddhism: A Christian Exploration and Appraisal* (Downers Grove, IL: InterVarsity Press, 2009).

than did the *Lausanne Covenant*. Questions about other religious others were not particularly pressing for evangelicals in the 1960s and 70s and so the *Lausanne Covenant* has only two sentences mentioning non-Christian religions. "We also reject as derogatory to Christ and the gospel every kind of syncretism and dialogue which implies that Christ speaks equally through all religions and ideologies.... To proclaim Jesus as 'the Saviour of the world' (John 4:42) is not to affirm that all people are either automatically or ultimately saved, still less to affirm that all religions offer salvation in Christ."[35]

By 2010, however, questions about religious diversity and pluralism were inescapable. Asian Christian leaders in particular were insisting that theologians and missiologists give more careful thought to issues of Christian faith and other religions. The *Commitment* acknowledges the attraction of pluralism, observing that "[w]e are tempted to compromise our belief in the uniqueness of Christ under the pressures of religious pluralism".[36] But the *Commitment*, like the earlier Covenant, clearly rejects the idea that other religions are to be regarded as equally acceptable alternatives to the Christian faith. "The one true God is replaced or distorted in the practice of world religions".[37] There is no ambiguity in the *Commitment* concerning the distinctive truth of the Christian Gospel, Jesus Christ as the only Lord and Savior for all peoples, and the need for Christian witness to Christ among all peoples, including sincere adherents of other religions.

Section C of Part II is devoted to issues concerning Christian witness to Jesus Christ among people of other faiths. The amount of space devoted to the subject, the variety of issues addressed, and the carefully nuanced wording all speak to the maturing of evangelical thinking about these questions. Although the *Commitment* follows earlier statements in its insistence upon the uniqueness of Jesus Christ as the only Savior and the ongoing need for evangelism, it introduces several important fresh themes. First, the call to witness in interreligious contexts is framed in terms of love, that is, Christians living out the love of Christ through our interactions with people of other faiths. The section begins with the recognition that "'Love your neighbour as yourself' includes persons of other faiths", and proceeds to distinguish evangelism from proselytizing, calling for humble, respectful evangelism that is "scrupulously ethical".

> We are called to share good news in evangelism, but not to engage in unworthy proselytizing. *Evangelism*, which includes persuasive rational argument following the example of the Apostle Paul, is 'to make an honest and open statement of the gospel which leaves the hearers entirely free to

---

[35] "The Lausanne Covenant", Section 3, in *New Direction in Mission and Evangelization 1: Basic Statements 1974-1991*, eds. James A. Scherer and Stephen B. Bevans (Maryknoll, NY: Orbis, 1992), 254-55.

[36] *Cape Town Commitment*, Part I.2.A, 11.

[37] *Cape Town Commitment*, Part I .2.B, 11.

> make up their own minds about it. We wish to be sensitive to those of other faiths, and we reject any approach that seeks to force conversion on them.' *Proselytizing*, by contrast, is the attempt to compel others to become 'one of us', to 'accept our religion', or indeed to 'join our denomination'.[38]

There is a humble spirit throughout the section, with candid acknowledgement of past failures in Christian witness. "In the name of the God of love, we repent of our failure to seek friendships with people of Muslim, Hindu, Buddhist and other religious backgrounds. In the spirit of Jesus we will take initiatives to show love, goodwill and hospitality to them".[39] Christian witness is also placed within an ethical framework that demands honestly, integrity, and respect for the other.[40] The *Commitment* denounces false depictions or caricatures of other faiths, prejudice and the incitement of fear of religious others. It calls for "the proper place of dialogue with people of other faiths", a dialogue which "combines confidence in the uniqueness of Christ and in the truth of the gospel with respectful listening to others".[41]

These are welcome and important emphases that must be taken seriously by evangelicals. The world of the early 21st century is a fragile one marked by deep tensions and animosities. Religious resurgence has not resulted in a more peaceful world; religious tensions are widespread and acts of violence by religious extremists are increasingly common. The language of the *Commitment* is very much in line with another significant document produced in 2011 by representatives from the Roman Catholic Pontifical Council for Interreligious Dialogue, the World Council of Churches, and the World Evangelical Alliance -- *Christian Witness in a Multi-Religious World: Recommendations for Conduct.*[42]

As we conclude it is important to note a final theme in the *Cape Town Commitment* which should accompany the call for a more robust apologetic and Christian witness among religious others. This is the reminder that how Christians live can be more significant than what they say. The plausibility of Christian apologetics and interreligious witness is directly related to the moral integrity and Christ-likeness manifest in Christians. "The evangelization of the world and the recognition of Christ's deity are helped or hindered by whether or not we obey him in practice."[43] Sadly, our witness is often undermined by the lack of Christ-likeness in how we live and treat others. The following statement from the *Commitment* provides a

---

[38] *Cape Town Commitment*, II.C.1, 47.

[39] Ibid., II.C.1.B, 48.

[40] Although my comments here concern Christian witness among adherents of other religions the basic principles apply also to witness among nominal Christians or secularists.

[41] Ibid. Part II C.1, c and e, 72.

[42] www.oikumene.org/fileadmin/files/wcc-main/2011pdfs/ChristianWitness recommendations.pdf.

[43] *Cape Town Commitment*, Conclusion, 71.

helpful summary for what Christian witness today should include: "Loving God in the midst of a world that rejects or distorts him, calls for bold but humble witness to our God; robust but gracious defence of the truth of the gospel of Christ, God's Son; and a prayerful trust in the convicting and convincing work of his Holy Spirit."[44]

[44] *Cape Town Commitment*, I. 2.B, 12.

A Dialogue With the Whole World and the Whole Church

Knud Jørgensen

This is a chapter about a friend of mine, Doug Birdsall, the former Executive Chair of the Lausanne Movement. Or more correctly: about his dialogue with family and friends of Lausanne, with the ecumenical world, with north and south, with men and women, with established and emerging leaders, with the whole world and the whole church.

The first time I met him was in Helsinki in 2004. He had recently taken over the Lausanne chair and was now travelling the globe to get acquainted with the Movement and to bring new wind into the sails. To that end, he had asked leaders from the Nordic countries to come and meet him. At the outset I was rather apprehensive. Was this another of these American evangelicals with limited knowledge of the European situation or of the need for relating to evangelicals within established churches as well as new, so-called free churches? Was he a prototype of the para-church model that I had met within evangelical mission agencies and Christian organizations? Had he come to teach us or to listen? The man I met was better than expected, in fact, much better. He listened and tried to understand; he had integrity and made us relax. True, he was also rather 'eloquent' for my Scandinavian taste, but OK; I was probably much too arrogant for his taste.

He gave me a glimmer of hope in the Movement. Later the same year he visited Norway and spent time with some of the older and younger Lausanne supporters in this region – a small group in the office of one of our mission organizations and a group of Lausanne seniors around a dinner table. He got us on board. We decided to give him and Lausanne a new chance.

Regularly I kept telling him that at least in Europe and Scandinavia there were probably more evangelicals within established churches than outside, and that he therefore ought to build bridges and enter into dialogue with the larger ecumenical movement. A year later he asked me if I would take him on a guided tour to the Ecumenical Centre in Geneva, Switzerland. In the course of two brief days we met with leaders from the World Council of Churches (WCC), the Lutheran World Federation, the Conference of European Churches, and the World Association of Reformed Churches. Doug Birdsall listened and learned. And he presented the visions of the

Lausanne Movement in an atmosphere of dialogue. I am not sure of his prejudices prior to the visits, but I do remember his delightful surprise when the WCC General Secretary, Dr Sam Kobia, at the close of our meeting asked if could pray together.

Throughout his tenure, Doug kept this dialogue with the ecumenical movement alive,[1] also evidenced by his increasing contacts with Orthodox churches and with the Vatican,[2] and of course, with the World Pentecostal Fellowship[3] and the World Evangelical Fellowship.[4] Several years earlier the WCC had taken the initiative to form a Global Forum with broader participation than the WCC constituency. Lausanne people have been part of this since the beginning. When a new person, Dr Olav Fykse Tveit, took over as WCC General Secretary, Doug Birdsall understood the importance of personal relations and paid a second visit to Geneva and invited him to come to Cape Town. Fykse Tveit accepted the invitation and came to the Lausanne Congress in October 2010 where he was given an opportunity to greet the Congress from the platform. In this greeting he stretched out a hand of dialogue and offered closer ties between Lausanne and Geneva. I am sure that Birdsall grasped the importance of this gesture, but far from all Lausanne leaders understood that they were witnesses to a historic moment. Here Birdsall could, in my opinion, have played a stronger role among his peers and made clearer his own views on a continued theological and relational dialogue.

When, in the spring of 2012, the WCC Commission on World Mission and Evangelism (CWME) invited Lausanne to take part in the work on a new mission document 'Together Towards Life', Doug Birdsall went to Manila and took me along. There were parts of the document that made us uneasy or with which we downright disagreed, but we spoke up, loud and clear, and the final version of the document showed that the editors had heard quite a bit of our concerns – not so that the 'Lausanne theology' was now included in or converged with a CWME missiology, but we experienced a genuine desire on both sides to relate, to reflect and listen to the Spirit and to one another.

For several years Birdsall pursued doctoral studies at the Oxford Centre for Mission Studies (OCMS). His dissertation proved to be a major attempt to view the contemporary missiological agenda in a broader perspective

[1] See Jooseop Keum's chapter in this volume 'Beyond Dichotomy: Towards a Convergence between the Evangelical and Ecumenical Understanding of Mission in Changing Landscapes'.

[2] See Robert Schreiter's chapter in this volume on 'From the Lausanne Covenant to the Cape Town Commitment: A Theological Assessment'.

[3] See Opoku Onyinah's chapter in this volume on 'A Pentecostal Perspective on the Lausanne Movement'.

[4] See Rose Dowsett's chapter in this volume on 'The Lausanne Movement and the World Evangelical Alliance'.

than just Lausanne. This was the focus of his PhD dissertation.[5] The juxtaposition of 'conflict and collaboration' in the title is characteristic of Birdsall's way of thinking, with a major focus on 'collaboration' and a minor one on 'conflict'. Birdsall is an irenic person, and as a missiologist he is looking for bridges and stepping stones, primarily between evangelicals – as exemplified in the very title of his PhD dissertation which brought together Lausanne, World Evangelical Alliance (WEA), AD 2000 Movement, and International Fellowship of Evangelical Mission Theologians (now called International Fellowship for Mission as Transformation) – but as a missiologist and missional strategist he is also concerned about finding and creating bridges beyond the evangelical camp.

In the introductory chapter to this book[6] we have listed certain interconnected levels of the Lausanne story; Birdsall combines in his thinking and praxis what we have called the *catalyst* and the *relational* levels of Lausanne. *Catalyst* in his desire to influence the wider Christian world with foundational evangelical theological and missiological convictions; *relational* in his success in creating formal and informal networks.

In the following I will let Doug Birdsall speak. I have perused some of his Lausanne writings since 2010 – his article in 'The Commemorative Newspaper' from Cape Town 2010 and his contributions to the Lausanne blog until the news of his resignation in late 2012. I have selected relevant portions from this material. An essential perspective in my selection grid has been 'dialogue with the whole world and the whole church'. In addition, the extracts are 'windows' into the Lausanne Movement – windows through which Birdsall wanted both to draw us and others into the movement and to spread the Lausanne Spirit to the world and the church.[7] At the same time, they shed light on Birdsall's sense of being called and his ability to relate and build networks.

---

[5] Doug Birdsall, *Conflict and Collaboration: A Narrative History of Four Global Movements that have Shaped the Contemporary Missions Agenda (LCWE, World Evangelical Alliance, AD 2000 Movement, The International Fellowship of Evangelical Mission Theologians)* (Middlesex University, 2013).

[6] 'Evangelical Perspectives on Mission: From Lausanne to Cape Town'.

[7] A note of caution: this material contains shorthand information and illustrations that are probably better understood if the reader has read some of the preceding chapters in this volume. I have changed neither Birdsall's style nor the format.

Why Cape Town 2010?[8]

In preparing for Cape Town, Birdsall went globetrotting around the world to challenge and inspire leaders and churches to discern the times and catch the vision of Cape Town. Here is an illustration.

We are living in a time of enormous threat and amazing opportunity for the church. The life and witness of the church around the world is being assailed by external pressures while simultaneously being weakened by internal troubles. Yet the church also faces unprecedented global opportunities for the spread of the Gospel and open doors for ministry in regions traditionally closed to the witness of Christ. Unfortunately, a concerted and well-reasoned response to these global issues and opportunities has been difficult because the church, and evangelicalism in particular, is highly fragmented.

Together the leaders (coming together in Cape Town 2010) will wrestle with six issues that are of paramount importance for the future of the church and world evangelization, in terms of profound theological reflection and strategic action. The church is the most thoroughly global entity in the world, with the majority of Christians now in Africa, Latin America and Asia. Together, we must establish a new global equilibrium for the church whereby we relate to one another on the basis of our shared vision, our shared calling, our shared wealth, and our shared poverty, and come together to address these issues:

1. The Challenge of the New Atheism. World evangelization is based on foundational truth claims about the uniqueness of Christ, the centrality of the Cross and the authority of Scripture. In light of the aggressive attacks on truth by the New Atheism, we must make a compelling case for TRUTH. We cannot afford to lose the battle for the minds of this generation or the next.

2. The Impact of Hedonism. We are bombarded every day with images and messages that serve to undermine our moral and biblical foundations. The church is being impacted by nominalism, superficiality and the troubling consequences of the prosperity gospel. We must respond with a prophetic critique of the church which calls us to AUTHENTICITY and INTEGRITY. We must call Christians to a deeper level of repentance, renewal and discipleship.

3. The Reality of Islam. Islam is a missionary faith with a global vision. With a very deliberate strategy, Islam's mission and impact has spread beyond the Arab world to significantly influence universities and governments in Africa, Europe, Asia and the Americas. The church must develop an equally deliberate strategy that enables us to live in fidelity to

[8] Doug Birdsall, Spring 2010, A Case Statement for the Third Lausanne Congress: www.lausanne.org/en/gatherings/global-congress/cape-town-2010/why-cape-town-2010.html. See also Lars Dahle's chapter on 'Mission in 3D: A Key Lausanne Theme' in this volume.

the Gospel, influence public institutions and faithfully witness to men and women in all WORLD FAITHS.

4. The Globalized World. Mega-cities, diaspora, new technologies, social networking, political corruption and uncertain futures for the next generation, are only a sample of the challenges and opportunities of a Globalized World that require us to establish NEW PRIORITIES for world evangelization.

5. The Brokenness of Our World. If our witness is to be prophetic, we must identify with the pain and suffering in the lives of individuals, families, communities and nations. Not only must we connect with the brokenness but we must also be people of hope and peace as agents of RECONCILIATION, emphasizing the core theme of Cape Town 2010, 'God in Christ Reconciling the World to Himself'.

6. Seismic Shifts in Global Christianity. Global PARTNERSHIPS for world evangelization, unlike anything possible in the previous twenty centuries, are now attainable as we develop relationships that are based on mutual respect – acknowledging that God has called us to be one in him. These new partnerships, increasingly led by visionary leaders from the Majority World, will also involve more lay people who comprise the vast majority of those who bear witness to Christ in this century. By sharing the best available resources and best practices, together 'the whole church (will) take the whole Gospel to the whole world'.

Global Impact[9]

Cape Town 2010 (Lausanne III) will build on the historic influence of the first two Lausanne Congresses and subsequent smaller regional and topical gatherings. The first Lausanne Congress convened by Billy Graham, Bishop Jack Dain and John Stott (Lausanne, 1974) gave three major gifts to the global church:

- The *Lausanne Covenant,* deemed to be one of the most influential evangelical theological documents in recent memory.
- A New Paradigm for understanding 'nations' as People Groups from Dr Ralph Winter.
- The Rediscovery of Holistic Mission from Dr Samuel Escobar and Dr René Padilla.

Lausanne II (Manila, 1989), served to bring Pentecostals and Charismatics together in dialogue and partnership with those of other evangelical traditions, while the *Manila Manifesto* re-emphasized the importance of holistic evangelism. Lausanne II participants also received fresh inspiration and vision on networking and partnerships, and in the ten

[9] See also in this volume Tormod Engelsviken, 'The Role of the Lausanne Movement in Modern Christian Mission', and Timothy Tennent, 'Lausanne and Global Evangelicalism – Theological Distinctives and Missiological Impact'.

years following the Congress, participants established more than 300 new partnerships and organizations for world evangelization, to the glory of God.

Cape Town 2010 will be an unprecedented gathering of thousands of global Christian leaders – those on-site in Cape Town and those participating through the Lausanne Global Conversation and Cape Town GlobaLink. We trust that it will be said of the participants of this Congress as it was said of the men of Issachar, "They understood the times and they knew what to do."

Cape Town and the Future[10]

The following article was written by Birdsall on the last day of the Cape Town Congress while he was caught up in the whirl of activities and conflicting demands on him and his attention. In the midst of this vortex, he managed to overcome the temptation to be overly short-sighted; instead he draws up a vision for the future based on five imperatives.

What a week this has been! Over the past seven days the unity, diversity, and vitality of the worldwide Church have been on dramatic display in Cape Town. We gathered from 198 countries, the most globally representative assembly of evangelicals in history. Representing a broad spectrum of denominations, organizations, academic institutions, and the worlds of business, government and the arts, we engaged the most pressing issues of our day through the prism of 'God in Christ, reconciling the world to himself' (2 Corinthians 5:19). I want to extend my heartfelt thanks to our host committee for graciously welcoming us to the beautiful city of Cape Town in the dynamic country of South Africa on a continent where the church of Jesus Christ is vibrant and growing. This Congress has been decidedly global in scope and yet distinctly African in flavour. The warmth and generosity of our hosts have been a tremendous blessing to all of us, and I pray that God would pour out his blessing on our African brothers and sisters.

Now that the Congress is over, what's next? Reflecting on Lausanne 1974, John Stott said, "Many a conference has resembled a firework display. What is exciting about Lausanne, however, is that its fire continues to spark off other fires." In 2010 we have once again brought together thousands of the church's best leaders, and this time, through new technology, we have broadcast the Congress to viewers around the world via our website and hundreds of GlobaLink venues. My hope is that God would use Cape Town 2010 as a fire that sparks more fires. As we look to the future, we recognize that Lausanne is not an institution but simply a

[10] Doug Birdsall, "Cape Town and the Future", in *Cape Town 2010. News and Insights from The Third Lausanne Congress on World Evangelization* (Cape Town 2010). www.lausanne.org/docs/capetown2010/commemorative/English_comm.pdf.

movement of volunteers – men and women, scholars and practitioners, clergy and laymen – all drawn from the four corners of the earth for the common purpose of world evangelization. Like any movement, Lausanne is by its nature creative, generative, organic, and unpredictable.[11]

Moving forward from Cape Town, I see five imperatives for the movement. First, Lausanne must stay light on its feet, remaining agile in its ability to respond to new challenges and opportunities. Second, the movement must be strong theologically, being firmly rooted in Scripture and nourished by the best reflection on how we take the Word to the world. Third, we must provide a reliable and credible contribution to Christian discussion and mission. Fourth, Lausanne must keep a focus on identifying and developing younger leaders. And fifth, we must continue to be strategic in gathering the right people at the right times in the right places.

Lausanne gatherings in the days ahead will breathe oxygen into the fire that sparks more fires and track the progress made on the priorities established in Cape Town. Future consultations will be national, regional or international, depending on the nature of the issues to be discussed. The Lausanne Committee's various working groups will continue their important initiatives, and the Lausanne Biennial International Leadership meeting will take place in 2012. The Lausanne Global Conversation continues as well, so please stay connected through our website. And as a dynamic movement, Lausanne will give rise to many more catalytic conferences and partnerships than we can foresee now. We put our trust in God, and as the great missionary Adoniram Judson said, "The future is as bright as the promises of God."

I thank each and every one of you for coming to Cape Town. And I want to express my profound gratitude to all our stewards, volunteers, staff, and donors who made Cape Town 2010 a success. The Lord has blessed us all and I trust that we return home to extend this blessing, with new insights and renewed passion for working as the whole church to take the whole Gospel to the whole world.

The Movement in Motion[12]

The following extract illustrates the difficult, but necessary, transition from 'event' to 'movement'. It also illustrates Birdsall's agenda for today and tomorrow.

In June (2011), many Lausanne leaders will gather for our Lausanne Annual Leadership Meetings here in Boston. I want to share with you the five primary objectives for our meeting this year:

---

[11] See also the concluding chapter of this volume: 'Moving on from Cape Town – Beyond the 40th Lausanne Anniversary'.

[12] 4th April 2011 by Doug Birdsall: www.lausanne.org/en/blog/1548-the-movement-in-motion-boston-and-other-upcoming-activities.html.

1. Celebration and Doxology: We want to praise God for his tremendous blessings on Cape Town 2010 and we want to express gratitude to those who worked so hard to make the Congress a reality.

2. Vision and Direction: The challenge before us is to translate ten days of discussion and ideas at Cape Town 2010 into ten years of solid progress in the work of world evangelization. It is important that we have clarity of vision and are aligned with one another as we develop more specific objectives, calendars and budgets for the coming years.

3. Roles and Responsibilities: We want to ensure that every person in Lausanne has clarity with respect to their role. Additionally, we will share advancements in our communications resources and structure, decision-making processes in Lausanne, and the responsibilities of working together in a Movement.

4. Training and Team Development: Together we will focus on the post-Congress message of Lausanne so that we can share the vision, mission and history of the Movement, as well as the significance of Cape Town 2010, in a way that is consistent and compelling.

5. *Cape Town Commitment*: This beautifully crafted document will be our road map for the decade to come. We will review it and discuss ways in which each person involved in Lausanne can find their place in the outworking of the *Commitment.*

Summary Report on Boston 2011 Biennial Meeting[13]

How may a restructured movement meet the challenges of a globalized world and the opportunities for witnessing to Christ? As the following shows, this calls for a minimum of vehicles and structures, but even more it calls for a missiological vision and commitment.

I am writing to provide you with a report on the recent Lausanne Biennial Leadership Meeting. In my opinion, this was the most productive and gratifying meeting that we have had since I began serving as the Chairman for Lausanne in 2004.

I believe the most significant accomplishment of the week is that we successfully transitioned from Event Mode to Movement Mentality and came away with a clear sense of unity, vision and direction, strong leadership and growing momentum. Three factors made this possible:

- Gaining clarity on our vision and message for the future;
- Restructuring Lausanne's leadership to serve the needs of a global Movement and;
- Aligning the entire Lausanne Movement with the *Cape Town Commitment.*

---

[13] 2nd Aug 2011 by Doug Birdsall: www.lausanne.org/en/blog/1607-summary-report-on-boston-2011-biennial-meeting.html.

Additionally, we officially launched the Global Executive Leadership Forum. Approval was given for the development of the monthly *Lausanne Global Analysis*. Support was also given to proceed with plans for the first 'Davos-like' Lausanne Global Briefing in 2013 for 350 of the world's leading pastors, scholars, mission leaders and business executives. At those biennial global consultations we will assess progress in world evangelization with respect to the *Cape Town Commitment*. We also began the initial planning for the Younger Leaders' Gathering in 2015.

I am particularly pleased to announce that Ram Gidoomal has agreed to serve as the Board Chairman. Ram is a man of great distinction with experience in business, government, higher education and mission. He is the prototypical 21st century global Christian leader, a convert to Christ from Hinduism, a Diaspora man of South Asian heritage who was raised in Africa, who then helped build a global enterprise while based in Geneva and London. He leads mission movements in the United Kingdom and South Asia and serves on a number of prominent boards in England, India and the USA.

Our team of twelve International Deputy Directors (IDDs), working under the leadership of International Director Lindsay Brown, has been further strengthened and reconfigured with seven new members. Lausanne IDDs provide global presence and regional advocacy for the Movement. They will be convening regional consultations in the next 18 months with the next two major consultations in Moscow (Eurasia) and in Cairo (Middle East/North Africa region).

To ensure that we are making solid progress in the priorities articulated in the CTC, 30-35 Lausanne Senior Associates will be appointed who will each take responsibility for one of the Commitments. They will be supported by mission organizations and networks who will serve as resource partners. These Senior Associates will work to convene consultations and catalyze new initiatives in their area of specialized responsibility over the next three years.

As an expression of Lausanne's historic commitment to the development of younger leaders, plans were initiated for the next Younger Leaders' Gathering in 2015. In the years leading up to that global gathering, younger leaders will be identified, developed and connected to mentors and to one another in each of the twelve Lausanne regions. Interestingly, many of the leaders for Cape Town 2010 first came into Lausanne through the 1987 Lausanne Younger Leaders' Conference in Singapore.

At a moment in history when we are dealing with unanticipated global challenges and with unprecedented opportunity for bearing witness to the power of the Gospel, it is a sign of hope to see fresh vision, new expressions of unity and a rising generation of leaders come together with renewed passion for 'the whole church to take the whole Gospel to the whole world'.

Developing Momentum[14]

Birdsall is an astute missiologist, but his platform is not academia but concrete steps to be taken on the road to the whole world. 'Developing momentum' he calls it; do we detect a glimpse of the American spirit of entrepreneurship?

The year 2011 has been one of listening, reflecting, and transition for the Lausanne Movement as we have shifted from event mentality to movement mode. Daily I hear how God has used Lausanne and Cape Town 2010 as a catalyst in the development of new or renewed mission and evangelism initiatives. We give thanks to God.

The momentum I see developing in Lausanne for 2012 and beyond energizes me. Our infrastructure of Working Groups, Senior Associates and Special Interest Committees is being fine-tuned to reflect our Movement focus on the *Cape Town Commitment*. Our IDDs are developing Regional Advisory Councils as they work with younger leaders and Communications Managers to plan regional consultations and make preparations to host issue-focused consultations over the next two years. Eurasia IDD Anatole Glukhovski has just hosted a consultation with several hundred Christian leaders in Moscow where Lindsay Brown and Blair Carlson were also present. Grace and Rajan Mathews provided leadership for a consultation on Corruption in Church and Society in India.

We will soon announce the 2012-13 Lausanne Global Calendar which includes consultations on Islam, Mega-Cities, Truth in the Public Sphere, the prosperity gospel, Nominalism and more. Curriculum is being developed to provide resources to seminaries, Bible colleges and adult Bible study groups on the *Cape Town Commitment*. Our communications strategy, including website and social media, has been enhanced to provide greater connection and information for the global church.

Plans are developing nicely for our first 'Davos-like' World Evangelization Forum to be convened in India in June 2013 with 350 participants to assess progress and to chart the course for the future with respect to priorities articulated in the *Cape Town Commitment*. Relatedly, we are also moving forward with plans for an '*Oxford Analytica*-like' briefing on world evangelization.

Now, as we come to the end of the year, I would ask for your prayers … for Egypt and the entire Middle East. The 'Arab Spring' has signalled rising hopes but also growing frustrations. In consultation with our colleagues in Egypt, Lausanne Vice-Chair Ramez Atallah, and IDD Andrea Zaki, we will be sending more information soon on a global call to prayer for Egypt and the Middle East on the first Sunday of the New Year, 7th January, which is also the day Coptic Orthodox Christians in Egypt celebrate Christmas.

---

[14] Doug Birdsall, Dec 2011 Update: www.lausanne.org/en/blog/1744-december-update-from-doug-birdsall.html.

Portrait of a Christian leader John Stott[15]

One of the fathers of Lausanne passed away in July 2011. It did not come unexpectedly; Stott had been weakening for quite some time. This article appeared in The Times (London, 14th January 2012), the day after his memorial service.

I travelled to London this week from my home in Boston, USA, for the memorial service for John Stott. The Apostle Paul was his mentor, through the pages of Scripture, so St Paul's Cathedral had a symbolic ring as a choice of venue. Stott shared with the apostle both a sharp intellect and a deep and driven passion for the Christian Gospel.

John Stott, who died on July 27, 2011, was a winsome figure, urbane, perceptive; he served as Chaplain to the Queen, wrote fifty books (translated into sixty languages), was appointed CBE, and named by *Time* magazine in 2005 as one of the world's 100 most influential people. He received honorary doctorates, and became the subject of doctoral theses. In addition, he was an expert in ornithology. Although the media gave wide coverage of his death, he barely featured in the news.

Stott served the congregation of All Souls', Langham Place, London, as Rector from the age of 29. He did not spare himself in reading, study, writing and in urging the church to a holistic faith. In 1970 he handed over leadership of the church to Michael Baughen, as he was becoming widely used around the world as a gifted university evangelist.

The son of a Harley Street consultant, and educated at Rugby School, John Stott lived simply. In 1970 he moved into a small, two-roomed flat. He could have lived comfortably on his royalties alone – his books sold in their millions – but he used that money for the work of what became Langham Partnership International, which he set up to help to strengthen the church in the developing world.

In 1981, aged 60, he declined a See, which would have given him a seat in the Lords. It was not in order to retire. That year he founded the London Institute for Contemporary Christianity, to bring Christ's presence robustly into every sphere of society.

How did this urbane, humble, mild-mannered man come to be regarded globally as perhaps the most noble Christian leader of the twentieth century? I offer two suggestions. First, John built genuine friendships. The sense of friendship was tangible yesterday as his old friends gathered to thank God for his life. He worked and he networked through friendship, which was 'embedded in his character'.

Second, he believed that effective leaders are those who are dissatisfied with what is, and who strive always for what could be.

---

[15] 19th Jan 2012 by Doug Birdsall: www.lausanne.org/en/blog/1757-portrait-of-a-christian-leader.html. Reference is also made to Julia Cameron's article in this volume on 'John Stott and the Lausanne Movement: A Formative Influence'.

The singer Paul Simon spoke in an interview published in *Religion and Ethics* last week of a long conversation with Stott, evidently enjoyed by both of them. Whether talking with the Royal Family, senior academics, singers or the poor in the world's mega-cities, Stott gave them his full attention. His authority was won through sheer authenticity. Eidi Cruz from Mexico grew up knowing 'Tío Juan' (Uncle John), as her parents were among his close friends. In a poem she wrote: "He taught me about humility / that listens to others / with the devotion with which we listen to a nightingale."

In what did this 'fifteen-talent man' (as the theologian J. I. Packer called him) take most pride? His writing? His glitterati friends? His CBE? No. He loved to tell the story of how, at Rugby, he listened to the public schools' evangelist Eric Nash (better known as Bash) and was pointed to the beautiful depiction of Christ in Revelation, standing at the door, as painted by Holman Hunt.

One February afternoon, aged 16, Stott grasped his need to invite Christ into his life, and to trust in Christ's death on the cross, in his place, for forgiveness of sin. Like the apostle Paul, here was his only ground for his boasting.

His biographer and friend from student days, Bishop Timothy Dudley-Smith, preached at yesterday's service, directing our eyes to the risen and glorified Christ. He posed the question often used by John to conclude an address. It was a universal question, simple and profound; the temporal intersecting with the eternal.

I could imagine John addressing a hall of students in Europe, the Americas, Africa, Asia, Oceania: Bible on the podium, left hand in his pocket, authoritative and engaging. The historicity of the Gospel had been clearly argued, a persuasive apologetic for Christ's claims laid out.

But an acquiescence of mind is not sufficient. "How is it between you and Jesus Christ?" he would ask. The wording may now sound slightly archaic, but the force of the question is as immediate as ever.

Not "What's Next?" but "What's Now?"[16]

'God is on the move!' was a catchword at Cape Town 2010, probably inspired by C.S. Lewis's Narnia stories about Aslan, the lion on the move. Birdsall had recently emerged after a sabbatical where he (at long last) brought to completion his PhD dissertation.

During my first full month back to work following sabbatical, the most frequently asked question I hear is, "What's next?" I always answer by saying, "There are many exciting things on the horizon but the most compelling thing is, 'What's Now!'"

---

[16] Doug Birdsall, Feb 16 2012: www.lausanne.org/en/blog/1766-doug-birdsall-february-update.html

As evangelicals, we must resist the temptation to always be looking forward to the next big event. Instead, we should discipline ourselves with a sustained and intensive commitment to the work of world evangelization that has been entrusted to us.

Cape Town 2010 ushered in a century of Global Partnership. Every week I learn of new initiatives under way as a result of connections that were made, and the ideas that were shared, in Cape Town. African leaders are building on the Congress as they encourage unity, bring hope, and strengthen the witness of the church. Next month, Lausanne leaders in the Middle East and North Africa will meet in Cairo for the same purpose. Last month, several of us met with Orthodox bishops and missionaries who want to be more involved in the Lausanne Movement for missiological and doxological purposes. Last week, leaders from South East Asia and East Asia met in Seoul, Korea. Younger leaders in the western world are meeting together to share vision and ideas they have received from leaders in the Majority World. God is on the move!

Currently we have leaders working on new mission partnerships and consultations on the following issues: Islam, Theological Education in the 21st Century, Nominalism, the prosperity gospel, Ethnicity and Identity, Gospel and Media, Theology of Work, Creation Care, Global Executive Leadership Forum (GELF), and Scripture Engagement.

The Power of Clear Vision: the *Cape Town Commitment* is gaining ownership around the world. Great progress is being made on two curriculum projects. The first is being developed for seminary and graduate school levels. The second will be for local churches and adult study groups. They will provide an amazingly rich resource of videos, papers, study guides and bibliographies for studying and engaging in world evangelization priorities for the coming decade.

Great Ideas Attract Exceptional People: In the year following Cape Town 2010, one of the most encouraging developments I have witnessed is the calibre of people who have been drawn to work with one another in the Movement. The 22 men and women who serve on the Lausanne Movement Board of Directors represent a virtual 'Council of Elders' for global evangelicalism. These leaders represent influence for the cause of Christ from every region of the world and from the major streams of world mission, the church, and academia.

Next June (2013), Lausanne will convene a meeting of 350 world evangelism innovators, scholars, and strategists for five days in Bangalore, India. The purpose will be to assess progress in world evangelization with respect to the *Cape Town Commitment*. This select global gathering represents our commitment to hold ourselves accountable for priorities and goals articulated at Cape Town 2010. It also acknowledges our need to continually identify emerging leaders, discover new resources, and learn from each other as we wrestle with new challenges in a world of dynamic change.

Celebrating the Second Anniversary of Cape Town 2010[17]

It was inevitable that the prime mover of the Cape Town Congress would reminisce about it. In the following, Birdsall takes us on a guided tour of the past to remind us of what lies ahead.

It was just two years ago on a Sunday evening, 24th October, that the third Lausanne Congress on World Evangelization came to a close. I have been here in Cape Town to celebrate with our friends and to thank those colleagues who helped to make the vision for the third Lausanne Congress a reality …

Last Saturday, Miles Giljam drove me to the Cape Town International Convention Centre. For nearly an hour, we walked the halls of that great facility and reflected upon what God did during those ten days as 4,200 participants and 1,200 staff, volunteers, media, and stewards met together. I walked up to the third floor veranda to get a view of Table Mountain, and remembered the joy and the energy of the many meetings that took place. Down the long hallways, I could hear the beautiful sound of various languages as multiplied thousands of conversations took place among participants from 198 nations.

Outside the Convention Centre, I remembered the production facilities with the most sophisticated media truck in Africa surrounded by 24 trailers that served as home for ten days for several hundred volunteers. The trailers were packed with high-tech equipment and talented people who were editing every presentation into 18-minute bundles for distribution to over 600 GlobaLink sites around the world. These teams also helped us understand what the participants, and other global leaders not in Cape Town, were saying through the Lausanne Global Conversation, while other teams were preparing video and audio reports for media outlets around the world. Never in history has a global Christian gathering been so meticulously planned and effectively executed.

In the main plenary hall, I was reminded again of the wonderful worship we shared together and the Ephesians Bible expositions by Ajith Fernando, John Piper, Ruth Padilla DeBorst, Vaughan Roberts, Ramez and Rebecca Atallah, and Calisto Odede. I remembered the moving testimony from Gyeong Ju Son, the young woman from North Korea, Os Guinness speaking on Truth, the moving video tributes to Billy Graham and John Stott, the Palestinian Christian and the Messianic Jew standing side by side, Libby Little sharing her story, Chris Wright on H.I.S. Church, the power of Princess Zulu speaking on HIV/AIDS, and Tim Keller challenging us to reach our burgeoning global cities with the reconciling Gospel of Jesus Christ. Who can forget our table groups – 700 'communities of six' – that enabled global friendships to form?

---

[17] Doug Birdsall, Oct 25th 2012: www.lausanne.org/en/blog/1877-second-anniversary-cape-town-2010.html.

As I stood in the hall, the memory of the glorious Closing Ceremonies was poignant. I pictured the Archbishop of Uganda, Henry Orombi, leading the recessional march with banners waving as God's pilgrim people left the hall for the four corners of the earth. As the symphony played and the choir sang, we all joined in lifting our hearts and voices towards Heaven. The words and music of the closing hymn, 'Crown Him with Many Crowns', rang joyfully in my ears and reverberated deeply in my soul. We praise and give God thanks that truly this Congress was a testimony to the truth of Christ and the reconciling Gospel of peace.

We are still discovering and discerning what God was doing in our midst in and through the Congress. It is too soon to fully assess the impact of the Congress, and only time and eternity will tell. However, I frequently hear people talk about the impact of the Congress in terms of:

> "A strong reaffirmation of Truth, moving from ambivalence to confidence."
>
> "Strength for what lies ahead through the articulation of a theology of suffering."
>
> "Returning the Bible to its proper centre in the work of world evangelization."
>
> "The introduction of a new century of global partnership."
>
> "Connecting and empowering a new generation of younger leaders."
>
> "A movement towards humility and unity, and a call to integrity and authenticity."
>
> "The Congress provided a shared experience and a historic point of reference."

This is what Chris Wright wrote about the *Commitment*:

> The *Cape Town Commitment* is not the memorial of a moment. It is the conviction of a Movement and the voice of multitude. It distills a vast quantity of input from the global Church. We profoundly hope and pray that we are hearing not just the voice of Cape Town 2010, but the voice of our Lord Jesus Christ who walked among us there.

Some people ask, "How can we be involved?" Lausanne is not an organization to join. It is a global Movement, a thought leader for world evangelization, and a catalyst for new initiatives and partnerships. The most effective means for involvement is to implement the vision and priorities of the *Cape Town Commitment* into your immediate ministry context. ....

We are propelled forward with the vision to be a part of God's redemptive work. Our heart's desire is to be obedient to his call to 'the whole church to take the whole Gospel to the whole world'. Please pray that God would bless the Lausanne Movement. Pray that God would provide for all that is needed by way of financial provision. Pray that he would give wisdom to our leaders. Pray that we might experience greater unity in the global church, greater courage and conviction. Pray that we will be a people of hope and a reconciling influence for peace with God through Jesus Christ, our one and only Saviour who came to bring 'peace on earth, goodwill among men with whom he is pleased'.

Lausanne Movement Leadership Transition Underway[18]

> For many it was unexpected that Birdsall would move on from Lausanne. He had almost become the wallpaper of the movement. Announcing his change of direction, he remains the challenger and the 'positive thinker': "These are great days for Lausanne." Sometimes I miss the vulnerable Birdsall and the vulnerability of mission; 'great days', yes, but we are to serve, not with a crusading mind, but with a crucified mind, as the Japanese missionary and theologian Kosuke Koyama has reminded us.

I am writing to let you know, as a friend and supporter of the Lausanne Movement, that I will be leaving my position next year as Lausanne CEO and Executive Chair…

These are encouraging days for the Lausanne Movement, as we see the momentum from Cape Town 2010 continue. Let me tell you why I am bullish on Lausanne, why I believe it should command the respect of Christian leaders around the world, and why I believe the Lausanne Movement should attract the generous investment and financial support of churches, foundations, ministries, and individual donors:

1. Legacy of Truth and Trust: Billy Graham and John Stott. They have been two of the greatest evangelical leaders of our time. They shaped the Lausanne Movement and have personified its vision and values. They summon us to be our best selves.

2. Authoritative Documents that Provide Wisdom for the Global Church: the *Lausanne Covenant, Manila Manifesto,* and the *Cape Town Commitment.*

3. Grandeur of Vision: 'The Whole Church Taking the Whole Gospel to the Whole World.'

4. Spirit of Lausanne: Humility, Study, Prayer, Partnership, and Hope.

5. Cape Town 2010 – Breadth of Impact: a. "The most representative gathering of Christian leaders in church history" *(Christianity Today)*; b. The *Cape Town Commitment* in 25 languages; c. Five major publications in the last year based upon the *Commitment*; d. 35 Lausanne Senior Associates, each with a global network, taking responsibility for one of the Calls to Action in the *Commitment*; e. The Lausanne website (www.lausanne.org) which hosts online conversations about each of these issues.

6. Depth of Global Leadership: a. Board of Directors – Chaired by Ram Gidoomal, comprised of 21 thought-leaders of global influence; b. International Deputy Directors – twelve exceptionally capable people

---

[18] Doug Birdsall, 27th Nov 2012: www.lausanne.org/en/blog/1885-lausanne-movement-leadership-transition-underway.html. See also Michael Oh's Foreword to this volume.

who advocate the cause and lead the Movement; c. Working Groups – Theology, Strategy, Communications and Intercession, each comprised of leaders of missions, seminaries, churches, and businesses.

7. Strength of Thought-Leadership: Launch this month of a new publication, called *Lausanne Global Analysis*. This is patterned after *Oxford Analytica* and is edited by David Taylor, senior editor at *Oxford Analytica* and former diplomat with the British Foreign Service.

8. Convening Power: When Lausanne leaders call a meeting, you can expect that the leaders in any given field will be there, that they will come with information that is invaluable, and they will leave with vision and strategies to make a difference in the world.

9. Younger Leaders: One of the fundamentals that causes me to be most bullish on Lausanne is the fact that it is blessed with a deep reservoir of talent and energy from younger leaders. Lausanne has a history of younger leader development. Just six years ago we convened a gathering of 550 younger leaders from 115 countries. That investment is producing very significant dividends for the cause of world evangelization as they have brought of surge of energy and creativity into the Movement.

10. Compelling Nature of the Lausanne Global Leadership Forum: The Forum that will be convened next June is fully subscribed with 350 global leaders. We will come together to assess global developments since Cape Town 2010, progress and obstacles in world evangelization, and to refine our priorities as we move forward.

Many people compared Cape Town 2010 with the Olympics. Such a gathering creates great excitement, visibility, impact, and inspiration. The athletes come together for competition for only two weeks. Then they return to their homes around the world to train, to coach, and to move ahead with the benefits of having been an Olympian. The levels of global visibility and excitement are adjusted to proper levels, but the global impact continues.

The same is true with Lausanne. The Congress was a once-in-a-lifetime experience for most of us who were there. But the real work is now taking place through relationships, partnerships, ideas, resources, and inspiration generated by ten days at a Lausanne Congress: Cape Town 2010.

These are great days for Lausanne. The best is yet to be. Be certain that I am praying for the Movement and continue to be involved in the work of Lausanne. It is a Movement and a global community of friends that I love so much.

Twenty-five years ago I came into Lausanne through the Younger Leaders' Conference: Singapore 87. I thank God that my life has been wonderfully enriched throughout the course of these years of involvement in Lausanne.

Now it is time to entrust the Movement to a new leader who will be able to take the Movement higher and further, to the glory of God. I look forward to being part of it and urge you to continue your involvement in the Movement as well.

Looking through the Rear Mirror

To many of us, Doug Birdsall has impersonated and revitalized what Billy Graham already in 1974 called 'The Spirit of Lausanne'. This spirit does not rhyme with what some call 'a bounded set', i.e. a territory with borders where people are either in or out. A bounded set is closed and has the focus on itself. The spirit of Lausanne rather reflects 'a fuzzy set' where the borders are 'fuzzy' and where relations dominate. It is not a club for 'members only' but 'an organic body of personal relations and responses, a living and evolving community of creativity and compassion', as the evangelical anthropologist Paul Hiebert has defined the fuzzy set.[19]

In word and deed Birdsall has mirrored and actualised the Lausanne inheritance from Billy Graham and John Stott. His missiology is based on a biblical understanding of evangelism, the urgency of 'completing' the task of world evangelization, an integral view of evangelism and social responsibility, and a stubborn attempt to move forward an expanding fellowship among evangelicals of all persuasions. It is not exaggerating to say that Birdsall has revitalized Lausanne as a unique global community. In the same manner one will find in Birdsall's thinking distinct echoes of Stott's Trinitarian emphasis on the Word, the Cross and the Spirit as essentials to which evangelicals – and indeed ecumenicals – are called to bear witness. The centre, also for Birdsall, has been God the Father's initiative in revealing himself, in redeeming us through Christ crucified, and in transforming us through the indwelling Spirit.[20]

In all of this, the spirit of Lausanne has been a *leitmotif* in Doug Birdsall's view of Lausanne – a 'place' where people are drawn into personal response and accountability in learning to know one another and to co-operate with one another across boundaries and borders. Purposely or not, he has, in my view, developed Lausanne as a 'fuzzy set'. A fuzzy set has a clear centre and core; this provides for boldness in relating to and dialoguing with others. When the central core is clear, one does not have to fight for borders and boundaries. Rather than using energy on building fences, one may spend maximum energy on strengthening the centre – the Christocentric core of incarnation, life, cross and resurrection. The South African missiologist David Bosch often talked about 'bold humility' and

---

[19] Paul Hiebert, *Transforming Worldviews. An Anthropological Understanding of how People Change*, (Grand Rapids, MI: Baker Academic, 2008), 36ff.

[20] See to this both the introductory chapter 'Evangelical Perspectives on Mission: From Lausanne to Cape Town' and the concluding chapter 'Moving on from Cape Town – Beyond the 40th Lausanne Anniversary'.

'humble boldness'[21] – 'humble' because we serve a crucified God and 'bold' because we know the power of his resurrection. Birdsall's modelling of the spirit of Lausanne has illustrated this double-bladed perspective of boldness and humility.

This modelling continues to be a dynamic and future-oriented contribution to the global church and the global task of evangelization. The Lausanne Movement does not live for itself; it must constantly try to discern where and how God is on the move so that the spirit of Lausanne listens to and obeys the Spirit of the Triune God.

---

[21] David J. Bosch, *Transforming Mission: Paradigm Shifts in Theology of Mission* (Maryknoll, NY: Orbis Books, 1991).

CONCLUSION

Moving On From Cape Town – Beyond The 40th Lausanne Anniversary

Lars Dahle, Margunn Serigstad Dahle
and Knud Jørgensen

This volume in the Regnum Edinburgh Centenary Series has presented documentations of and reflections on key missiological concerns, strategies and developments within the Lausanne Movement. The contributions have ranged from historical and theological analysis of key Lausanne events, publications, resources, networks and initiatives since the beginning in 1974, through engagement with key themes at Lausanne III in Cape Town in 2010, to critical discussions, strategic proposals and personal perspectives from both insiders and outsiders.

This concluding chapter seeks to summarize key contributions from Lausanne to the wider world of Christian missiology and mission. This is followed first by a section on how the Lausanne leadership describes the essential Lausanne identity as the Movement moves on from Cape Town, and secondly, by a summary of significant current developments, initiatives, and strategies within the movement since Cape Town and beyond the 40th Lausanne anniversary in 2014. The chapter finally includes some editorial reflections on the future of the Movement.

Missiological Contributions from Lausanne

In his opening speech at Lausanne I in 1974, Congress host Billy Graham expressed four hopes for this event:

> 1. *I would like to see the Congress frame a biblical declaration on evangelism.* The time has come again for the evangelical world to speak with a strong clear voice as to the biblical definition of evangelism.
> 2. *I would like to see the church challenged to complete the task of world evangelization.* Never has the church been stronger, more deeply entrenched in more countries, more truly a world church, and more able to evangelize than it is today.
> 3. *I trust we can state what the relationship is between evangelism and social responsibility.* Let us rejoice in social action, and yet insist that it alone is not evangelism and cannot be substituted for evangelism. This relationship disturbs many believers. Perhaps Lausanne can help clarify it.

> 4. *I hope that a new 'koinonia' or fellowship among evangelicals of all persuasions will be developed throughout the world.* I hope there will develop here what I like to call 'The Spirit of Lausanne'. The time has come for evangelicals to move forward, to encourage, challenge and bring hope to the World Church.[1]

This key quote is shaped by Graham's own personality and ministry, as well as by the theological and cultural context at the time. At the same time, it captures much of the theology, strategy and mentality of the Lausanne I Congress, as well as some of the central defining features of the subsequent Movement. It is therefore appropriate to use this fourfold perspective when seeking to summarize significant missiological contributions from Lausanne to the wider missional community.[2]

First, Lausanne has reintroduced a classical evangelical theology of evangelism and mission as a significant and vibrant tradition into contemporary missiology and missions. This has included expressing, expounding and emphasizing such essential evangelical tenets as the uniqueness of Christ as Lord and Saviour, Scripture as the sole source of and norm for faith and praxis, the radical nature of sin, the need for conversion, the priesthood of all believers, and the urgency of evangelism. The Lausanne Movement has thus contributed to increasing theological clarity and missiological confidence for many evangelical leaders, missions and churches. This is clearly a continued central concern behind the first part of the *Cape Town Commitment* (i.e. 'A Confession of Faith'). Key evangelical theological concerns were originally upheld in clear conflict with dominant ecumenical theological emphases, as they were expressed in influential WCC meetings and documents in the 1960s and onwards. However, as documented in various contributions in this volume, the current evangelical-ecumenical climate is characterized more in terms of an ongoing open, sympathetic but also critical dialogue with significant tensions, especially related to the unresolved central theological themes mentioned above.

Secondly, Lausanne has consistently communicated the urgent task of world evangelization to the global evangelical church and beyond. This task has been communicated with a dual emphasis. First, evangelization should be seen as having a clear focus on sharing the Gospel of Jesus Christ within the task of integral mission. As expressed in the *Cape Town Commitment,* the global church is called 'to bear witness to Jesus Christ and all his teaching – in every nation, in every sphere of society, and in the

---

[1] Billy Graham, 'Why Lausanne?', in J. D. Douglas (ed), *Let the Earth Hear His Voice. International Congress on World Evangelization* (Minneapolis, MN: World Wide Publications, 1975), 34.

[2] It should be noted that the following summary should be seen in the context of the richer overall picture provided by this volume as a whole.

realm of ideas'.[3] Secondly, evangelization involves the constant task of identifying and reaching out to unreached and unengaged people groups. According to Part II of the *Cape Town Commitment* ('A Call to Action'), such groups are found in religious and secular 'faith communities' all over the world, as well as increasingly among unprivileged groups, in migrated people groups, in oral cultures, in urban contexts, and among the increasing number of children and youth.

Thirdly, Lausanne has gradually formulated a significant and influential theology of integral mission. This has resulted in seeing social responsibility and action both as a consequence of evangelism, as a bridge to evangelism, and as a partner of evangelism. It has also resulted in an increasing emphasis on the ministry of lay people and in the workplace (based on the priesthood of all believers) and on a recurring emphasis on personal integrity, prayer, and spiritual warfare. Again, it is worth emphasizing the prominence of 'every sphere of society' and 'the realm of ideas' in the *Cape Town Commitment.*

Fourthly, throughout its history, Lausanne has provided a unique global community context for evangelical leaders, whether mission or church leaders, influential marketplace leaders or key reflective practitioners. This is particularly evident in many of the contributions in this volume, through the open sharing of how formative key Lausanne events, resources and networks have contributed towards the personal development of many leaders, as well as to the development of their respective ministry contexts.

Keeping Identity as Lausanne Moves Forward

The Cape Town Congress and the *Cape Town Commitment* have in many ways revitalized, energized and mobilized the Lausanne Movement. In view of the above-mentioned missiological contributions, the key questions of identity, purpose and strategy become essential when moving forward as a movement from Lausanne III in 2010 and moving beyond the Lausanne 40th anniversary in 2014.

It is appropriate at this point to include the following concise statement on these key issues from Doug Birdsall's article on 'Cape Town and the Future'. This article was published in the commemorative newspaper from the Congress and was distributed to all Lausanne III participants immediately after the final ceremony:

> As we look to the future we recognize that Lausanne is not an institution but simply a movement of volunteers – men and women, scholars and practitioners, clergy and laymen – all drawn from the four corners of the earth

[3] D. Birdsall and L. Brown, 'Foreword', in the *Cape Town Commitment. A Confession of Faith and a Call to Action [CTC]* (Peabody, MA: Hendrisckson Publishers, 2011), xi.

> for the common purpose of world evangelization. Like any movement, Lausanne is by its nature creative, generative, organic, and unpredictable.
>
> Moving forward from Cape Town, I see five imperatives for the movement. *First*, Lausanne must stay light on its feet, remaining agile in its ability to respond to new challenges and opportunities. *Second*, the movement must be strong theologically, being firmly rooted in Scripture and nourished by the best reflection on how to take the Word to the world. *Third*, we must provide a reliable and credible contribution to Christian discussion and mission. *Fourth*, Lausanne must keep a focus on identifying and developing younger leaders. And *fifth*, we must continue to be strategic in gathering the right people at the right times in the right places.[4]

In February 2013, Doug Birdsall was succeeded as Executive Chair and CEO of the Lausanne Movement by the younger Michael Oh. The above quote from Birdsall should therefore be complemented with Oh's 'Foreword' to this volume, where he encourages the readers to look to the future:

> As we look forward, we have much to celebrate as we participate in the mission of God, for we are Christ's ambassadors, entrusted with the message of reconciliation (2 Corinthians 5:18-20)... It is our calling, as the people of God, to engage our world in ways that are paradoxical and powerful, courageous and creative, yet marked by humility, integrity, and simplicity.

Thus, both Doug Birdsall (now Honorary Chairman) and Michael Oh (as the new CEO) emphasize the dynamic nature of the Lausanne Movement, with solid evangelical theological foundations combined with vigorous engagement in the missiological issues of today and the future.

It should also be added, that with the appointment of Michael Oh, the headquarters of the Lausanne Movement has shifted to Japan. This is seen by the Lausanne leadership as a symbolic statement as well as a strategic move to develop more Lausanne relationships as well as more Lausanne resources beyond North America and Europe.

Moving on from Cape Town

It is now possible – in view of the preceding summary of its missiological contributions and its essential identity as a movement – to outline how the Lausanne Movement moves forward from Cape Town and beyond the 40th anniversary in 2014.[5]

---

[4] D. Birdsall, 'Cape Town and the Future', in *Cape Town 2010: News and Insight from The Third Lausanne Congress on World Evangelization* (Cape Town: The Lausanne Movement, 2010), 7. This commemorative newspaper is published at www.lausanne.org/docs/capetown2010/commemorative/English_comm.pdf.

[5] It is appropriate at this point to acknowledge valuable information on current Lausanne developments, initiatives and strategies from the following: Executive Chair / CEO, Michael Oh; Chief Collaboration Officer and Teaching Pastor, David

The Cape Town Commitment as the Road Map

When seeking to understand the current concerns, developments, and strategies of the Lausanne Movement and its leadership, it is crucial to understand the key role of the *Cape Town Commitment* for the way forward. This is clearly expressed in the Foreword:

> The *Cape Town Commitment* will now act as a blueprint for the Lausanne Movement over the next ten years. Its prophetic call to work and to pray will, we hope, draw churches, mission agencies, seminaries, Christians in the workplace, and student fellowships on campus to embrace it and to find their part in its outworking.
>
> Many doctrinal statements affirm what the Church believes. We wished to go further and to link belief with praxis.
>
> We have worked here to model Lausanne's principle of "breadth within boundaries", and in Part I those boundaries are clearly defined.
>
> While we speak and write from the evangelical tradition in the Lausanne Movement, we trust the *Cape Town Commitment* may be helpful to churches of all traditions. We offer it in a humble spirit.
>
> What are our hopes for the *Cape Town Commitment*? We trust that it will be talked about, discussed, and afforded weight as a united statement from evangelicals globally; that it will shape agendas in Christian ministry; that it will strengthen thought-leaders in the public arena; and that bold initiatives and partnerships will issue from it.[6]

This excerpt clearly communicates the pivotal role of the *Cape Town Commitment* for the future global, regional and national initiatives, strategies and activities of the Lausanne Movement.

An Overview of the Upcoming Series of Lausanne Global Consultations

Central to the ongoing strategic communication, implementation and application of the *Cape Town Commitment* is a series of planned global consultations. This is in line with the history of the movement where global consultations have played a key role throughout. The Lausanne leadership has identified a number of significant issues for such global consultations in the second part of the *Cape Town Commitment*, which they consider to be of strategic importance and where there are few or no other global evangelical initiatives.

At the time of writing, the tentative list of future global consultations exploring such thematic areas includes the following topics:

- The Gospel and Creation Care.[7] This consultation was held in the Caribbean in October-November 2012.

Bennett; Director of Global Consultations, Daniel Willis; Director of Publishing, Julia Cameron; and Director of Communications, Andrew Brumme.

[6] Birdsall and Brown, xi-xii.

[7] *CTC*, Sections I7(A), IIB 6, and IID 6.

- The Gospel and Media.[8] This consultation will be arranged in the USA in November 2013, based on an advisory regional consultation in Norway in November 2012.
- The Gospel and Prosperity Theology.[9] This consultation was held in Brazil in April 2014.
- The Gospel and the Challenge of Islam.[10] This consultation was held in West Africa in April 2014.
- Truth in the Public Sphere.[11]
- The Gospel and Identity & Ethnicity.[12]
- The Gospel and Nominalism.[13]
- The Gospel and Work.[14]
- The Gospel and Megacities.[15]
- The Gospel and the Image of Man.[16]
- The Gospel and Partnership.[17]
- The Gospel and Globalisation.[18]
- The Gospel and Human Sexuality.[19]

This tentative list gives an overall picture of central missiological issues which the Lausanne Movement will focus on through global consultations when moving forward. However, other topics may arise where a global conversation will be required and the above list should therefore be seen as indicative and flexible.

A Sample Overview of Current Issue Networks

The Lausanne Movement is by nature a dynamic global network of global networks. This is clearly the case with the so-called Lausanne Senior Associates (SA). The individual SA is responsible for missiological leadership, strategic initiatives and networking within the designated area of missiological importance. These areas can often be linked to key issues in 'A Call to Action' (Part II of the *Cape Town Commitment*).[20] The full list

[8] *CTC*, Sections IIA 4 and IID 6.
[9] *CTC*, Sections IIB 3, IIE 5, and IID 6.
[10] *CTC*, Sections IIC 1, 6, and IID 6.
[11] *CTC*, Sections IIA 7 and IID 6.
[12] *CTC*, Sections IIB 1-2, IIF, and IID 6.
[13] *CTC*, Sections IIA 1-2 and IID 6.
[14] *CTC*, Sections IIA 3 and IID 6.
[15] *CTC*, Sections IID 4 and IID 6.
[16] *CTC*, Sections IIA 6 and IID 6.
[17] *CTC*, Sections IIF and IID 6.
[18] *CTC*, Sections IIA 4 and IID 6.
[19] *CTC*, Sections IIE 2 and IID 6.
[20] Since the publication of *CTC* in 2011, each of the Senior Associates (whether previously or recently appointed) have been required to reference specific Sections of CTC in their formulation of goals for the next few years.

of the current SAs is found at the Lausanne website. It is not possible to include the work and the Issue Networks of all the SAs in this overview.[21]

We have therefore chosen to include a sample list of some of the SAs with the currently most active Lausanne-related Issue Networks:

- Byron Spradlin is the SA for Arts. He recently organized major gatherings on Arts in Mission in Eurasia, Dallas (USA) and Japan and is currently building a global network of Lausanne Arts Catalysts.[22]
- Joy Tira leads the Global Diaspora Network as the SA for Diasporas,[23] and is currently preparing for a major global gathering on Diaspora in Manila in March 2015.
- Samuel Chiang is the SA for Orality. He leads the International Orality Network, which was birthed out of the Lausanne Global Forum in Pattaya, Thailand, in 2004.[24]
- John Azumah is the SA for Islam. Having formed an international steering committee of evangelical experts in Islam, he is now laying the foundation for Lausanne Global Consultation on Islam in Ghana in April 2014.
- Mats Tunehag is the SA for Business as Mission. He was responsible for the second Business as Mission Think Tank which was held in Thailand in April 2013. This gathering was an indication of the accelerating global awareness of this strategy for world evangelization.[25]
- Ed Brown is the SA for Creation Care. He led the first Lausanne Global Consultation on Creation Care. As mentioned above, this consultation was held in Jamaica in October 2012, with representatives from nine of the twelve Lausanne regions.[26]
- Bradford M. Smith is the SA for Care and Counsel as Mission, with an increasing global network called Care & Counsel International.[27]
- Lindsay Olesberg is the SA for Scripture Engagement, with the task of modelling Bible study and providing essential study material for the global Lausanne community. Together with the small group

---

[21] See www.lausanne.org/en/about/leadership/issue-based-leadership.html. Some of the other SAs and their Issue Networks are mentioned in Section 2 of this volume, including Jewish Evangelism and Partnership of Men and Women.

[22] The videos from the Lausanne / WEA Consultation on Arts in Mission in Dallas in May 2013 are published at www.lausanne.org/en/multimedia/videos/arts-in-mission-videos.html. See also *CTC*, Section IIA 5.

[23] See www.globaldiaspora.org and *CTC*, Section IIC 5.

[24] See www.orality.net and *CTC*, Section IID 2.

[25] See http://bamthinktank.org and *CTC*, Sections IIA 3, 5.

[26] See *www*.lausanne.org/creationcare *and CTC,* Section IIB 6.

[27] See http://careandcounsel.org/ and *The Cape Town Declaration on Care and Counsel as Mission* (www.lausanne.org/en/documents/cape-town-2010/1792-care-and-counsel-as-mission.html).

architect Ole Magnus Olafsrud, she has had a central role in shaping the format of biblical expositions at such key Lausanne events as the Cape Town Congress (2010) and the Global Leadership Forum in Bangalore (2013).[28]

The Bangalore Forum also provided a launch pad for several new Senior Associates and their Issue Networks. This list includes Ashish Chrispal (as SA for Hinduism), Kang-San Tan (as SA for Buddhism), Blair Carlson (as SA for Proclamation Evangelism, a new international network of proclamation evangelists), and Bishop Efraim Tendero (as SA for Integrity and Anti-Corruption).

It should also be mentioned that the Interaction Sessions at the Bangalore Forum were built around turning the calls to action in Part II of the *Cape Town Commitment* into measurable goals for the next two to three years within each Issue Network.

A Sample Overview of Current Strategic Initiatives

A number of current strategic initiatives can also be identified. These are often related to – but usually distinct from – the work of individual SAs and their Issue Networks.

The Lausanne leadership expresses the need for an ongoing broadening of the global Lausanne network and its leadership. This intention is especially evident in the following areas: The board of directors represents the breadth of the twelve Lausanne regions; an increasing proportion of the Senior Associates live in or have roots in the Majority World; each of the Issue Networks is intentionally pursuing relationships in all the Lausanne regions; and there is a continuing search for women to lead in these areas, as well as an intentional cultivation and inclusion of younger leaders.[29]

There is ongoing strategic networking among evangelists and missions within the Lausanne Movement related to the significant task of identifying and reaching out in partnership to 'unreached and unengaged peoples'.[30] It should be mentioned in this context that Paul Eshleman, as previous chair

---

[28] See especially L. Olesberg, *The Bible Study Handbook* (Downers Grove, IL: IVP, 2012) and *Ephesians: Studying with the Global Church* (2013). The latter DVD and study-guide resource grew out of the plenary Bible expositions at Lausanne III.

[29] The current senior Lausanne leadership emphasizes the prominence of the need to enlist new generations of younger leaders for the Lausanne Movement. This is seen symbolically in the appointment of the younger Michael Oh as CEO, and in having an upcoming global Younger Leaders' Gathering (currently proposed for Kiev in 2015) as a focal point for this emphasis. See also *CTC*.

[30] See *CTC*, Section IID 1. This has been a central emphasis of the Lausanne Movement throughout its history, especially as expressed in the *Lausanne Covenant* (Section 9): "We are convinced that this is the time for churches and para-church agencies to pray earnestly for the salvation of the unreached, and to launch new efforts to achieve world evangelization."

of the Strategy Working Group, had a key role in launching the *Issachar Initiative*.[31] Informed by influential research initiatives and databases such as the Joshua Project, World Christian Database and Operation World, such Lausanne-inspired mission partnerships continue to focus on this central Lausanne concern for world evangelization.[32]

There are a number of current strategic initiatives related to networking across the various Issue Networks. Lausanne Workplace Network is a key example, which includes Business as Mission Network, The Tent Makers Network, and The Marketplace Ministry Network. These shared strategic workplace initiatives resulted in the Global Executive Leadership Forum at the Cape Town Congress and in the workplace emphasis of the Lausanne Global Forum 2013 in Bangalore programme.

Other significant current strategic Lausanne initiatives include the following:

- *Lausanne Global Analysis* was launched in late 2012 as a bi-monthly new service for the global community of evangelical leaders linked to the Lausanne Movement. The purpose is 'to deliver strategic and credible information and insight from an international network of evangelical analysts so that Christian leaders will be equipped for the task of world evangelization'.[33]
- Global Generosity Network has been launched (together with WEA), in order to stimulate giving in general and to facilitate and encourage transparency and partnership among and between major donors.[34]
- Mission Africa was launched in connection with the third Lausanne Congress in Cape Town. This is continuing to be a significant partnership initiative in evangelism, both in terms of resource mobilization on the African continent and as an inspiring model for other Lausanne events and regions.
- There are a number of significant ongoing dialogue initiatives, which the Lausanne Movement has initiated and/or where the movement is involved at senior leadership level, both with other Christian communities and with other faith communities.

---

[31] See http://issacharinitiative.org. This initiative is linked to the wider networking platform called Table 71 (www.table71.org/) which was formed in 2000 at the Billy Graham Conference on Evangelism in Amsterdam.

[32] See http://joshuaproject.net/, http://worldchristiandatabase.org/wcd/, www.operationworld.org/ and the paper on 'Strategy in Mission – 21st Century Style' in this volume; see also T.C. Tennent, 'Access and Reproducibility in Missions Strategy', in his *Invitation to World Missions: A Trinitarian Missiology for the Twenty-first Century* (Grand Rapids, MI: Kregel, 2010), 354-386.

[33] See www.lausanne.org/en/analysis.

[34] See http://generositymovement.org.

A Sample Overview of Current Lausanne Working Groups Initiatives

The so-called 'working groups' have played a key role in the history of Lausanne since the early days. True to the nature of Lausanne as a Movement, with a flexible structure and a constant turnover of people, there have been a number of changes related to numbers, names and functions of the working groups throughout the years. It is likely that this will be a dynamic area also in the future.[35]

For the purpose of this concluding chapter, it is sufficient to note that the four classical working groups currently mentioned on the Lausanne website[36] have been active with various strategic initiatives since Cape Town 2010. This includes the following key activities:

- The Theology Working Group (TWG) has worked on completing a theological commentary on Part I of the *Cape Town Commitment*.[37]
- The Strategy Working Group (SWG) has continued to work on shaping global strategies for evangelism in the 21st century.[38]
- The Intercession Working Group had a key role in the development of the material for the Lausanne Global Prayer Focus during the month of May 2013. This special prayer focus was initiated in connection with the shift in leadership from Doug Birdsall to Michael Oh.[39]
- The Communication Working Group has been involved in the further development of strategic communications in Lausanne, as well as in the strategic planning of the global consultation on the Gospel and media in Los Angeles (USA) in November 2013.[40]

---

[35] In 1975, four Working Groups were appointed by the LCWE – Communications, Intercession, Strategy, and Theology and Education (later 'and Education' was dropped) – each headed by a member of the Executive Committee. At one point there was a Nominations Working Group and a Statistics Working Group, neither of which have continued. In earlier years, Senior Associates were related to the Working Groups. Sometime prior to 2001, a Leadership Development Working Group was added. Additional Working Groups added in recent years include Resource Mobilization and BGEMM (Business, Government, Education, Media and Marketplace).

[36] See www.lausanne.org/en/about/leadership/issue-based-leadership.html.

[37] See also the paper in this volume by the TWG Chair Timothy Tennent on 'Lausanne and Global Evangelicalism – Theological Distinctives and Missiological Impact'.

[38] This is also evident from the paper in this volume by SWG chair Roy Peterson and SWG member Gilles Gravelle on 'Strategy in Mission – 21st Century Style'.

[39] See www.lausanne.org/en/about/prayer.html.

[40] See also the paper in this volume by CWG members Julia Cameron and Lars Dahle on 'Communicating Lausanne – Yesterday, Today and Tomorrow'.

Concluding Reflections

As we conclude this volume on the Lausanne Movement, we consider it appropriate to present what we as editors consider to be the most significant tasks for the movement as it moves beyond the 40th anniversary in 2014.

First, the Lausanne Movement needs to continue to have firm evangelical foundations, as most recently expressed in Part I of the *Cape Town Commitment*. This confession of faith ('For The Lord We Love') presents 'the heart of the Christian gospel, i.e. primary truths on which we must have unity'. This confession is simultaneously intended (as mentioned above) to define the boundaries of evangelical faith and thus model the Lausanne principle of 'breadth within boundaries'.[41]

Secondly, the Lausanne Movement continues to play a key role in shaping how established and emerging evangelical leaders understand evangelization in the context of integral mission. This is why the emphasis in the *Cape Town Commitment* on 'bearing witness to Jesus Christ and all his teaching – in every nation, in every sphere of society, and in the realm of ideas' is so significant. This is also why the threefold foci in the Bangalore 2013 programme was so significant – emphasizing (a) implementation through the local church, (b) much greater inclusion in the movement of people whose primary roles are in the workplace, and (c) heightened awareness of the importance of reaching cultural influencers.

Thirdly, the Lausanne Movement continues – and needs to be further strengthened – in its key role as catalyst and bridge-builder. This means being in dialogue with 'the whole church', which includes being open and committed towards building bridges in the following relations:

- Lausanne in dialogue with north and south, with men and women, with established leaders and emerging leaders, with the church/ churches in China, and with theologians and evangelists.
- Lausanne in dialogue with the WCC, the Vatican, the Orthodox churches, the World Pentecostal Fellowship, and the WEF.

Fourthly, we consider it appropriate to consider the future of the Lausanne Movement through the challenging lens provided by John Stott in the final fivefold call in his *Evangelical Truth: A Personal Plea for Unity*:

The call for evangelical integrity
The call for evangelical stability
The call for evangelical truth
The call for evangelical unity
The call for evangelical endurance[42]

Stott formulated this fivefold call as a result of an exposition of Philippians 1:27-30. He summarizes this call as follows:

---

[41] Birdsall and Brown, 'Foreword', *CTC*, 5.
[42] Stott, (Leicester, UK: IVP, 1999), 135-146.

> We can hardly fail to be stirred by the apostle's summons at the end of Philippians 1, as it comes to us across the centuries. He calls us to live a life that is worthy of the gospel, to stand firm in it, to contend for it earnestly, to struggle for it together, and to be willing to suffer for it. All this is involved in the challenge to maintain the evangelical faith today.[43]

We observe that this fivefold call is identical to some of the key concerns expressed in the *Cape Town Commitment* as the current road map for the Lausanne Movement.

The Lausanne Movement is still on the move as a global evangelical movement for world evangelization. It will continue to be so, provided it keeps its solid evangelical foundations, its focus on evangelism within the context of integral mission, and its dynamic identity as a movement.

[43] Stott, *Evangelical Truth*, 146.

APPENDIX
SUMMARY OF THE CAPE TOWN COMMITMENT[1]

Part I
For the Lord We Love: The Cape Town Confession of Faith

The opening sentences set the framework, 'The mission of God flows from the love of God. The mission of God's people flows from our love for God and for all that God loves.'

The first five points deal with our love for God himself. We love the living God, above all rivals and with a passion for his glory. We love the Triune God: Father, Son, and Holy Spirit. With respect to the Father, the CTC calls for a renewed appreciation of God's fatherhood. Concerning the Son, it highlights our duty to trust, obey, and proclaim Christ. Of the Spirit, it says, 'Our engagement in mission, then, is pointless and fruitless without the presence, guidance and power of the Holy Spirit … There is no true or whole gospel, and no authentic biblical mission, without the Person, work and power of the Holy Spirit.'

The last five points cover our love for God's Word, world, Gospel, people, and missions. (a) We reaffirm our submission to the Bible as God's final revelation, and affirm our love for the Person it reveals, the story it tells, the truth it teaches, and the life it requires (while admitting we often confess to love the Bible without loving the life it teaches, a life of costly practical discipleship). (b) We love God's world, all that he has made and loves. This includes caring for creation, loving all peoples and valuing ethnic diversity, longing to see the Gospel embedded in all cultures, loving the world's poor and suffering people, and loving our neighbours as we love ourselves. It does not mean loving or being like 'the world' (i.e. worldliness). (c) We love the Gospel – the story it tells, the assurance it gives, and the transformation it produces. (d) We love all God's people, recognising that such love calls for unity, honesty, and solidarity. (e) We love the mission of God. 'We are committed to world mission, because it is central to our understanding of God, the Bible, the Church, human history and the ultimate future … The Church exists to worship and glorify God for all eternity and to participate in the transforming mission of God within history. Our mission is wholly derived from God's mission, addresses the whole of God's creation, and is grounded at its centre in the redeeming victory of the cross.' We are called to integral mission, which is the proclamation and demonstration of the Gospel.

---

[1] This summary of *The Cape Town Commitment* was prepared by Kevin Smith. It is published at http://www.lausanne.org/en/documents/ctcommitment/ctc-summary.html and reprinted here with permission.

Part II
For the World We Serve: The Cape Town Call to Action

The call to action uses the six Congress themes, which are linked to the six expositions of Ephesians.

A. Bearing witness to the truth of Christ in a pluralistic, globalized world. The Congress affirmed belief in absolute truth, and particularly in Jesus Christ as the Truth. Christians, therefore, are called to be people of truth, to live and proclaim the truth. We must face the threat of *post-modern* relativistic pluralism with robust apologetics. We must promote truth in the workplace and the global media. We must harness the arts for mission, promote authentically-Christian responses to emerging technologies, and actively engage the public arenas of government, business, and academia with biblical truth.

B. Building the peace of Christ in our divided and broken world. Christ has reconciled believers to God and to one another; the unity of God's people is both a fact and a mandate. The Church, therefore, has a responsibility to live out its reconciliation and to engage in biblical peace-making in the name of Christ. This includes bringing Christ's truth and peace to bear on racism and ethnic diversity, slavery and human trafficking, poverty, and minority groups such as people with disabilities. It also means our missional calling includes responsible stewardship of God's creation and its resources.

C. Living the love of Christ among people of other faiths. Our 'neighbours' include people of other faiths. We must learn to see them as neighbours and be neighbours to them. We seek to share the good news in ethical evangelism, and we reject unworthy proselytizing. We accept that our commission includes a willingness to suffer and die for Christ in reaching out to people of other faiths. We are called to embody and commend the Gospel of grace in loving action, in all cultures. We need to respect 'diversity in discipleship', and encourage one another to exercise cultural discernment. We recognize global diaspora as strategic for evangelization: scattered peoples can be both recipients and agents of Christ's mission. While being willing to sacrifice our own rights for the sake of Christ, we commit to uphold and defend the human rights of others, including the right to religious freedom.

D. Discerning the will of Christ for world evangelization. Six key areas are identified as strategically important for the next decade: (a) unreached and unengaged people groups; (b) oral cultures; (c) Christ-centred leaders; (d) cities; (e) children; all with (f) prayer. The focus on Christian leaders is to prioritize discipleship and address the problems that arise from 'generations of reductionist evangelism'. Within this, key priorities are Bible translation, the preparation of oral story Bibles and other oral methodologies, as well as eradicating biblical illiteracy in the Church. Cities are home to four strategic groups: future leaders, migrant unreached peoples, culture shapers, and the poorest of the poor. All children are at risk; children represent both a mission field and a mission force.

E. Calling the Church of Christ back to humility, integrity and simplicity. The integrity of our mission in the world depends on our own integrity. The Congress called Christ-followers back to humble, sacrificial discipleship, simple living, and moral integrity. We need to be separate and distinct from the world (morally). Four 'idolatries' were singled out: disordered sexuality, power, success, and greed. Disciples of Christ must reject these. (The prosperity gospel is rejected under the banner of 'greed'.)

F. Partnering in the body of Christ for unity in mission. Paul teaches us that Christian unity is a creation of God, based on our reconciliation with God and with one another. We lament the divisiveness of our churches and organizations, because a divided Church has no message for a divided world. Our failure to live in reconciled unity is a major obstacle to authenticity and effectiveness in mission. We commit to partnership in global mission. No one ethnic group, nation or continent can claim the exclusive privilege of being the ones to complete the Great Commission. Two specific aspects of unity in mission are the partnership of women and men and the recognition of the missional nature of theological education.

BIBLIOGRAPHY

1. Primary Sources[1]

a) Lausanne 1974

Douglas, J. D. (ed) *Let the Earth Hear His Voice. Official Reference Volume, Papers and Responses. International Congress on World Evangelization* (Minneapolis, MN: World Wide Publications, 1975).

Stott, J. R. W. *The Lausanne Covenant: An Exposition and Commentary* (Charlotte, NC: LCWE, 1975). Available online as LOP 3: www.lausanne.org/en/documents/lops/69-lop-3.html.

The Lausanne Movement. *The Lausanne Covenant: complete text with study guide* (Peabody, MA: Hendrickson, 2012). The Didasko Files. Also available online: www.lausanne.org/en/documents/lausanne-covenant.html. Also published in *New Direction in Mission and Evangelization 1: Basic Statements 1974-1991*, James A. Scherer & Stephen B. Bevans (eds), (Maryknoll, NY: Orbis Books, 1992), 254-55.

The Lausanne Movement: www.lausanne.org/en/gatherings/global-congress/event/10-lausanne-i-the-international-congress-on-world-evangelization.html.

b) Manila 1989

Douglas, J. D. (ed) *Proclaim Christ until He Comes. Calling the Whole Church to Take the Whole Gospel to the Whole World. Lausanne II in Manila. International Congress on World Evangelization* (Minneapolis, MN: World Wide Publications, 1990).

Nichols, A. (ed) *The Whole Gospel for the Whole World* (Charlotte, NC: LCWE & Regal Books, 1989).

The Lausanne Movement: *The Manila Manifesto: an elaboration of the Lausanne Covenant 15 years later.* 'Making Christ Known: Historic Mission Documents from the Lausanne Movement 1974-1989', J. R. W. Stott (ed) (Carlisle: LCWE and Paternoster Press, 1996), 225-249. Also available online: www.lausanne.org/en/documents/manila-manifesto.html.

The Lausanne Movement: www.lausanne.org/en/gatherings/global-congress/manila-1989.html.

c) Cape Town 2010

Bock, D. (ed) *Bibliographical Resources for the Cape Town Commitment: A Confession of Faith, A Call to Action* (Eugene, OR: Wipf & Stock, 2013). Also

[1] See also the chapter by L. Dahle and M. S. Dahle on 'Resourcing the global church: A guide to key Lausanne resources 1974-2013' in this volume.

available online: www.lausanne.org/en/documents/ctcommitment/bibliographic-resources.html.

Cameron, J. E. M. (ed) *Christ Our Reconciler: Gospel / Church / World: The Third Lausanne Congress on World Evangelization* (Nottingham, and Downers Grove, IL: IVP, 2012).

Dowsett, R. *The Cape Town Commitment: Study Edition. A Confession of Faith and a Call to Action* (Peabody, MA: Hendrickson Publishers, 2012).

Lausanne Theology Working Group. *LOP 63. The Whole Gospel* (2008 Chiang Mai Consultation, Thailand). Statement and papers published in *Evangelical Review of Theology* 33:1 (Jan 2009). Available online: www.lausanne.org/en/documents/lops/1236-lop-63.html.

Lausanne Theology Working Group. *LOP 64. The Whole Church* (2009 Panama City, Panama Consultation). Statement and papers published in *Evangelical Review of Theology* 34:1 (Jan 2010). Available online: www.lausanne.org/en/documents/lops/1237-lop-64.html.

Lausanne Theology Working Group. *LOP 65. The Whole World* (2010 Beirut Consultation, Lebanon). Statement and papers published in *Evangelical Review of Theology* 34:3 (July 2010). Available online: www.lausanne.org/en/documents/lops/1238-lop-65.html.

Lausanne Theology Working Group. 'The Whole Church Taking the Whole Gospel to the Whole World: Reflections of the Lausanne Theology Working Group' (www.lausanne.org/en/documents/all/twg/1177-twg-three-wholes.html).

Olesberg, L. *Ephesians: Studying with the Global Church* [DVD / Study Guide] (Peabody, MA: Hendrickson Publishers, 2014).

Singleton, S. & M. Ristuccia (eds) *The Cape Town Commitment: A Call to Action. A Study Guide for Small Groups* (Peabody, MA: Hendrickson Publishers, 2013).

The Cape Town Commitment: A Confession of Faith and a Call to Action (Peabody, MA: Hendrickson, 2011). The Didasko Files. Also available online: www.lausanne.org/en/documents/ctcommitment.html.

The Lausanne Movement: www.lausanne.org/en/gatherings/global-congress/event/8-cape-town-2010-the-third-lausanne-congress-on-world-evangelization.html.

The Lausanne Movement *Cape Town 2010: News and Insight from The Third Lausanne Congress on World Evangelization* (Cape Town: The Lausanne Movement, 2010). Commemorative newspaper; published at: www.lausanne.org/docs/capetown2010/commemorative/English_comm.pdf

d) Other primary sources

Birdsall, J. (ed) *Living & leading like Jesus: Plenary Addresses from the 2006 Younger Leaders' Gathering* (Pasadena, CA: William Carey Library, 2007).

Claydon, D. (ed) *A New Vision, A New Heart, A Renewed Call. Lausanne Occasional Papers from the 2004 Forum of World Evangelization hosted by the LCWE in Pattaya, Thailand, September 29th-October 5th 2004.* 3 vols (Pasadena, CA: William Carey Library, 2005).

Lausanne Committee for World Evangelization. *Evangelism and Social Responsibility. An Evangelical Commitment* (Exeter: Paternoster Press, 1982).

Stott, J. R. W. (ed) *Making Christ Known: Historic Mission Documents from the Lausanne Movement 1974-1989* (Carlisle: LCWE / Paternoster Press, 1996).

The Lausanne Movement. *Lausanne World Pulse:* www.lausanneworldpulse.com.

The Lausanne Movement: www.lausanne.org/en/documents/all.html. These online resources include the following:

- Most of *The Lausanne Occasional Papers* (LOP) (www.lausanne.org/en/documents/lops.html).
- Many *Lausanne Consultation Statements* (www.lausanne.org/en/documents/all/consultation-statements.html)
- *Lausanne Global Analysis* (www.lausanne.org/analysis)
- Overview of Lausanne Congresses, Consultations, Conferences etc. (www.lausanne.org/en/gatherings.html)

2. Secondary Sources

Adeleye, F. *Preachers of a Different Gospel* (Nairobi: Hippobooks / Word Alive Publishers, 2011).

Alexander, P. *Signs and Wonders: Why Pentecostalism is the World's Fastest Growing Faith* (San Francisco, CA: Jossey-Bass, 2009).

Allen, T. & A. Thomas. *Poverty and Development into the 21st Century* (Oxford: OUP / The Open University, 2000).

Anderson, A. *An Introduction to Pentecostalism: Global Charismatic Christianity* (Cambridge: CUP, 2004).

Ariarajah, S. Wesley. *The Bible and People of Other Faiths* (Geneva: WCC, 1991).

Ariel, Y. *Evangelising the Chosen People: Missions to the Jews in America 1880-2000* (Chapel Hill, NC: University of North Carolina Press, 2000).

Balia, D. & K. Kim (eds) *Edinburgh 2010. Witnessing to Christ Today* (Oxford: Regnum, 2010).

Bartholomew, C., R. Parry & A. West (eds) *The Futures of Evangelicalism: Issues and Prospects* (Leicester: IVP, 2003).

Bassham, R. C. *Mission Theology: 1948-1975. Years of Worldwide Creative Tension, Ecumenical, Evangelical and Roman Catholic* (Pasadena, CA: William Carey Library, 1979).

Bebbington, D. W. *Evangelicalism in Modern Britain: A History from the 1930s to the 1980s* (London: Unwin Hyman, 1989).

Beidelman, T. O. *Colonial Evangelism: A Socio-Historical Study of an East Africa Mission at the Grassroots* (Bloomington, IN: Indiana University Press, 1982).

Berentsen, J. M., T. Engelsviken & K. Jørgensen (eds) *Missiologi i dag* (Oslo: Universitetsforlaget, 1994 & 2004).

Berger, P. *The Desecularization of the World* (Grand Rapids, MI: Eerdmans, 1999).

Berger, P. 'Four Faces of Global Culture', *National Interest*, 49 (Fall 1997), 24-25.

Berger, P. *Questions of Faith: A Skeptical Affirmation of Christianity* (Oxford: Blackwell, 2004).

Bevans, S. *Models of Contextual Theologies* (Maryknoll, NY: Orbis Books, 1992).

Beyerhaus, P. *Krise i misjonen. Med Frankfurt-erklæringen om grunnlagskrisen i misjonen* (Oslo: Lunde, 1970).

Beyerhaus, P. *Missions: which Way? Humanization Or Redemption. Contemporary evangelical perspectives* (Grand Rapids, MI: Zondervan Publishing House, 1971).

Biema, D. 'Missionaries under cover'. *Time*, 4th August 2003.

Bock, D. L. & M. Glaser (eds) *To the Jew First: The Case for Jewish Evangelism in Scripture and History* (Grand Rapids, MI: Kregel, 2008).

Bockmühl, K. *Evangelicals and Social Ethics*. Trans. D. T. Priestly (Downers Grove, IL: IVP, 1979).

Bonk, J. J. 2007. *Africa Unbound.* www.christianitytoday.com/ct/2007/November/37.46.html.

Bosch, D. J. *Transforming Missions. Paradigm Shifts in Theology of Mission* (New York: Orbis Books, 1991).

Bourdanné, D. *Le Tribalisme en Afrique* (Abidjan: PBA, 2002).

Bourdanné, D. *L'évangile de la prospérité, une menace pour l'église africaine* (Abidjan: PBA, 2011).

Bowen, J. W. E. *Africa and the American Negro: Addresses and Proceedings of the Congress on Africa* (Atlanta, GA: Gammon Theological Seminary, 1896).

Bright, V. & B. A. Jennings (eds) *Unleashing the Power of Prayer* (Chicago, IL: Moody Press, 1989).

Bruce, S. *Religion in the Modern World: From Cathedrals to Cults* (Oxford: OUP, 1996).

Buswell III, J. O. "Contextualization: Is It Only a New Word for Indigenization?" *Evangelical Missions Quarterly* 14:1 (1978), 13-20.

Chan, S. *Liturgical Theology. The Church as Worshiping Community* (Downers Grove, IL: IVP, 2006).

Church, J. E. *Quest for the Highest: An Autobiographical Account of the Eastern Africa Revival* (Eastbourne: Apologia Publications, 1981).

Coe, S. 'Contextualizing Theology'. *Mission Trends* No.3 Third World Theologies (eds) G. H. Anderson & T. F. Stransky (New York: Paulist Press, 1976), 19-24.

Conn, H. M. *Eternal Word and Changing Worlds: Theology, Anthropology, and Mission in Trialogue* (Grand Rapids, MI: Academic Books, 1984).

Crisp, S. Translation Consultancy: set in stone or historically conditioned? Paper given at *BT2011 Conference,* SIL, Dallas, TX, *18th October 2011.*

Cunningham, L. & D. Hamilton. *Why Not Women: A Biblical Study on Women in Missions, Ministry and Leadership* (Seattle, WA: YWAM Publishing, 2000).

Dahle, L. '*Acts 17:16–34. An Apologetic Model Then and Now?* [Dissertation Summary]' *Tyndale Bulletin* 53:2 (2002), 313-316.

Dahle, L. 'Truth, Christian Mission and Apologetics: A Response and A Proposal'. *Norwegian Journal of Missiology*, 67:1 (2013), 21-38.

Dallaire, Lt-Gen. R. *Shake Hands with the Devil: The Failure of Humanity in Rwanda* (Toronto: Random House Canada, 2003).

De Lacger, L. *Rwanda* (Kabgayi: Imprimerie de Kabgayi, 1961).

Della P. S. *World Jewish Population 2000. Vol. 100* (New York: Division of Jewish Demography and Statistics, American Jewish Year Book, 2000). http://ajcarchives.org/AJC_data/files/2000_13_wjp.pdf

Dias, E. '¡Evangélicos!' *Time*, 15th April 2013.

Dudley-Smith, T. *John Stott: The Making of a Leader, Volume 1* (Leicester: IVP, 1999).

Dudley-Smith, T. *John Stott: A Global Ministry, Volume 2* (Leicester: IVP, 2001).

Døving, C. A. & S. E. Kraft. *Religion i pressen* (Oslo: Universitetsforlaget, 2013).

Eagleton, T. *After Theory* (London: Basic Books, 2003).

Ekenes, R. & T. Engelsviken, K. Jørgensen, R. Kjøde (eds) *Misjon til forandring: Refleksjoner og visjoner fra Lausanne III* (Skjetten: Hermon, 2011).

Engelsviken, T. "Convergence or divergence? The relationship between recent ecumenical and evangelical mission documents". *Swedish Missiological Themes,* Vol. 89, No. 2, 2001, 197-220.

Engelsviken, T. "Missio Dei: The Understanding and Misunderstanding of a Theological Concept in European Churches and Missiology". *International Review of Mission,* Vol. XCVII, No. 367, October 2003, 481-97.

Engelsviken, T. *Spiritual Conflict in Today's Mission*: *Lausanne Occasional Paper* 29 (Monrovia, CA: MARC Publications, 2001).

Engelsviken, T., E. Harbakk, Rolv Olsen & Thor Strandenæs (eds) *Mission to the World: Communicating the Gospel in the 21st Century. Essays in Honour of Knud Jørgensen* (Oxford: Regnum, 2008).

Escobar, S. 'A Movement Divided'. *Transformation,* 8.4 (October 1991), 11-13.

Escobar, S. 'Evangelical Missiology: Peering into the Future at the Turn of the Century'. *Global Missiology for the 21st Century,* William Taylor (ed) (Grand Rapids, MI: Baker Academic, 2000), 109-112.

Fernando, A. "Evangelism: An Extension of Colonialism?" *World Evangelization* 35 (1984), 1-3.

Fleming, B.C. *Contextualization of Theology*: *An Evangelical Assessment* (Pasadena, CA: William Carey, 1980).

Freytag, W., K. Hartenstein & A. Lehmann. *Mission zwischen Gestern und Morgen* (Stuttgart: Evangelischer Missionsverlag, 1952).

Fuller, W. H. *People of the Mandate. The Story of the World Evangelical Fellowship* (Grand Rapids, MI: Baker Book House / WEF, 1996).

Gairdner, W. H. T. *"Edinburgh 1910": An Account and Interpretation of the World Missionary Conference* (Edinburgh & London: Oliphant, Anderson & Ferrier, 1910).

Gatwa, T. *The Churches and Ethnic Ideology in the Rwandan Crises 1900-1994* (Oxford: Regnum, 2005).

Gilliland, D. S. (ed) *The Word Among Us: Contextualizing Theology for Mission Today* (Dallas, TX: Word Publishing, 1989).

'Gospel Contextualization Revisited'. *MARC Newsletter 97:3* (1997), 6.

Gravelle, G. *The Age of Global Giving, a Guide for the Donors and Recipients of Our Tim*e (Pasadena, CA: William Cary Library, forthcoming).

Green, M. *The Message of Matthew.* The Bible Speaks Today (Leicester: IVP, 2001).

Gross, E. N. *Is Charles Kraft an Evangelical? A Critique of Christianity in Culture* (Elkins Park, PA: Christian Beacon Press, 1985).

Guillebaud, M. *Rwanda, the Land God Forgot? Revival, Genocide and Hope* (Oxford: Monarch Books, 2002).

Guillebaud, M. *After the Locusts: How Costly Forgiveness is Restoring Rwanda's Stolen Years* (Oxford: Monarch Books, 2005).

Guinness, O. *The Call: Finding and Fulfilling the Central Purpose of Your Life* (Nashville, TN: Word Publishing, 1998).

Guinness, O. 'Found Faithful: Standing Fast in Faith in the Advanced Modern Era'. *Renewing the Evangelical Mission,* R. Lints (ed) (Grand Rapids, MI: Eerdmans, 2013).

Hallencreutz, C. F. *Dialogue and Community. Ecumenical Issues in Interreligious Relationships* (Uppsala: Studia Missionalia Upsaliensia XXXI , 1977).

Hammar, K G & A. Lönnroth. *Jag har inte sanningen, jag söker den* (Ordfront: Stockholm, 2004).

Hanciles, J. J. *Beyond Christendom: Globalization, African Migration and the Transformation of the West* (Maryknoll, NY: Orbis Books, 2008).

Harmelink, B. "Ethical Dimensions of Bible Translation Strategies". Paper presented at the annual meeting of the SBL, Atlanta, GA, 23rd November 2010.

Harvey, R. *Mapping Messianic Jewish Theology: A Constructive Approach* (Milton Keynes: Paternoster, 2009).

Heinlein, R. A. *Job: A Comedy of Justice* (New York, NY: Del Rey/Ballantine, 1985).

Henry, C. F. H. "Review Article: The Cultural Relativizing of Revelation". *Trinity Journal* 1 (Fall 1980), 153-164.

Hesselgrave, D. J. & E. Rommen. *Contextualization: Meanings, Methods and Models* (Grand Rapids, MI: Baker Book House, 1989).

Hesselgrave, D. J. *Paradigms in Conflict* (Grand Rapids, MI: Kregel Publications, 2005).

Hiebert, P. G. *Anthropological Insights for Missionaries* (Grand Rapids, MI: Baker Book House, 1985).

Hiebert, P. G. 'Critical Contextualization'. *International Bulletin of Missionary Research* 11:3 (1987), 104-112.

Hiebert, P. G. *Transforming Worldviews: An Anthropological Understanding of How People Change* (Grand Rapids, MI: Baker Academic, 2008).

Hoekendijk, J.C. *The Church Inside Out* (London: Westminster Press, 1966).

Hollenweger, W. *Pentecostalism: Origins and Developments Worldwide* (Peabody, MA: Hendrickson Publishers, 1997).

House, H. W. (ed) *Israel, The Land and the People: An Evangelical Affirmation of God's Promises* (San Francisco, CA: Jews for Jesus, 1998).

Hunt, R.A. 'The History of the Lausanne Movement, 1974-2010'. *International Bulletin of Missionary Research* 35:2 (April 2011), 81-85.

Hutchinson, M. & O. Kalu (eds) *A Global Faith: Essays on Evangelicalism and Globalization* (Sydney, CSAC, 1998).

Høyland, K. H. & J. W. Nielsen (eds) *Chosen to Follow: Jewish Believers through History and Today* (Jerusalem: Caspari Center for Biblical and Jewish Studies, 2012).

Jenkins, P. *The Next Christendom: The Coming of Global Christianity* (Oxford: OUP, 2002)

Johnson, A. F. (ed) *How I Changed My Mind about Women in Leadership: Compelling Stories from Prominent Evangelicals* (Grand Rapids, MI: Zondervan, 2009).

Johnson, T. & K. R. Ross (eds) *Atlas of Global Christianity* (Edinburgh: Edinburgh University Press, 2010).

Johnson, T. M. & B. J. Grim. *The World's Religions in Figures* (Oxford: Wiley-Blackwell, 2013).

Jong Yun Lee. "Can Lausanne Work with WCC as Partner in Mission?" *Centenary of 1910 Edinburgh World Missionary Conference: Retrospect and Prospect of Mission and Ecumenism,* Kook Il Han (ed) (Seoul: Mission Academy, 2009).

Jore, T. *The Christian Commons. Ending the spiritual famine of the global church.* Available online: https://distantshoresmedia.org/thechristiancommons/introduction, 2012, 106-108.

Jørgensen, K. 'Misjon til forandring – transforming mission'. *Norwegian Journal of Missiology*, Nos. 1-2, Vol. 65 (2011), 76-86.

Kalayjian, A. & R. F. Paloutzian. *Forgiveness and Reconciliation: Psychological Pathways to Conflict Transformation and Peace Building* (New York: Springer, 2009).

Kerr, D. A. & K. R. Ross (eds) *Edinburgh 2010: Mission Then and Now* (Oxford: Regnum, 2009).

Kim, K. & A. Anderson (eds) *Edinburgh 2010. Mission Today and Tomorrow* (Oxford: Regnum, 2011).

Knapp, S. C. "Introducing 'Gospel in Context'". *Gospel in Context* 1:1 (1978).

Kpobi, D. "The PCG, a Church in Mission in the 21st Century: Renewal and Reformation". *Akrofi-Christaller Centre News* 25 (1999), 8-12.

Kraemer, H. *The Christian Message in a Non-Christian World* (London: Edinburgh House, 1938).

Kraft, C. H. "The Contextualization of Theology". *Evangelical Missions Quarterly* 14:1 (1978), 31-36.

Kraft, C. H. *Christianity in Culture: A Study in Dynamic Biblical Theologizing in Cross-Cultural Perspective* (Maryknoll, NY: Orbis Books, 1979).

Kraft, C. H. 'The Development of Contextualization Theory in Euro-American Missiology'. *Appropriate Christianity,* C. H. Kraft (ed) (Pasadena, CA: William Carey Library, 2005), 15-34.

Larkin, W. J. *Culture and Biblical Hermeneutics: Interpreting and Applying the Authoritative Word in a Relativistic Age* (Grand Rapids, MI: Baker Book House, 1988).

Lewis, D. *Christianity Reborn: The Global Expansion of Evangelicalism in the Twentieth Century* (Grand Rapids, MI: Eerdmans, 2004).

Lienemann-Perrin, C. *Training for a Relevant Ministry* (Madras: Christian Literature Society, 1981).

Lindsell, H. (ed) *The Church's Worldwide Mission: Proceedings of the Congress on the Church's Worldwide Mission, 4th-16th April 1966, at Wheaton College* (Waco, TX: Word Books, 1966).

Lundström, K. *Gospel and Culture in the World Council of Churches and the Lausanne Movement* (Uppsala: Studia Missionalia Svecana CIII, 2006).

MacArthur, J. *Hard to Believe: The High Cost and Infinite Value of Following Jesus* (Nashville, TN: Thomas Nelson, 2003).

Marquez, W. D. "Let's Contextualize, But ..." *Global Church Growth Bulletin* 17:3 (1980), 32.

Matthey, J. "Athens 2005: Reconciliation and Healing as an Imperative for Mission". *Mission as Ministry of Reconciliation* (eds) R. Schreiter & K. Jørgensen (Oxford: Regnum, 2013), 37-51.

Mackey, L. 'Participants discuss charismatic question'. *LCWE press release*, July 1989.

Marshall, P., L. Gilbert & R. Green-Ahmanson (eds) *Blind Spot: When Journalists Don't Get Religion* (New York, OUP, 2009).

Martin, W. *A Prophet with Honor: the Billy Graham Story* (New York: William Morrow & Co, 1991).

Mbiti, J. S. *African Religions and Philosophies* (Oxford: Heinemann, 1969).

Mbiti, J. S. "Theological Impotence and the Universality of the Church". *Third World Theologies, Mission Trends No. 3* (eds) G. H. Anderson & T. F. Stransky (New York: Paulist Press, 1976), 6-18.

McConnell, D.R. *A Different Gospel: A Historical and Biblical Analysis of the Modern Faith Movement* (Peabody, MA: Hendrickson, 1991).

McGrath, A. E. *Evangelicalism and the Future Christianity* (London: Hodder & Stoughton, 1988).
Meeking, B. & J. R. W. Stott (eds) *The Evangelical-Roman Catholic Dialogue on Mission 1977-1984: A Report* (Grand Rapids, MI: Eerdmans, 1986).
Melhus, K. 'John Stott. The listener'. *LCWE press release*, July, 1989.
Moreau, A. S. et al (eds) *Deliver Us From Evil: An Uneasy Frontier in Christian Mission* (Monrovia, CA: MARC, 2002).
Moreau, A. S. *Contextualization in World Missions: Mapping and Assessing Evangelical Models* (Grand Rapids, MI: Kregel Academic & Professional, 2011).
Muck, T. & F. S. Adeney. *Christianity Encountering World Religions. The Practice of Mission in the Twenty-first Century* (Grand Rapids, MI: Baker Academic, 2009).
Mumper, S. 'Gift of women considered at congress'. *LCWE press release,* July, 1989.
Muvala, F. *Aperçu Historique de l'Evangélisation du Rwanda* (Kigali: Pallotti Presse, 1990).
Myers, B. "Research? What for?" *MARC Newsletter* 97:3 (September 1997), 3-4.
Neill, S. *A History of Christian Missions* (Harmondsworth: Penguin Books, 1964).
Netland, H. 'Interreligious Apologetics'. *Christian Apologetics: An Anthology of Primary Sources* (eds) K. A. Sweis & C. V. Meister (Grand Rapids, MI: Zondervan, 2012), 39-45.
Netland, H. 'Jesus Is the Only Way to God'. *Debating Christian Theism* (eds) Moreland, J.P., Meister, Chad & Sweis, Khaldoun, A. (New York: OUP, 2013), 497-508.
Newbigin, L. *Unfinished Agenda: An Autobiography* (Grand Rapids, MI: Eerdmans, 1985).
Nicholls, B. J. *Contextualization: A Theology of Gospel and Culture* (Downers Grove: IVP, 1979).
Nicholls, B. J. (ed) *Word and Deed: Evangelism and Social Responsibility* (Grand Rapids, MI: Eerdmans, 1986).
Noll, M. 'What is Evangelical?' *The Oxford Handbook of Evangelical Theology*, Gerald R. McDermott (ed) (Oxford: OUP, 2010), 19-34.
Olesberg, L. *The Bible Study Handbook* (Downers Grove, IL: IVP, 2012).
Onyinah, O. *Pentecostal Exorcism: Witchcraft and Exorcism in Ghana* (Blandford: Deo Publishers, 2012).
Onyinah, O. *Spiritual Warfare* (Cleveland, TN: CPT Press, 2012).
Orchard, R. K. (ed) *Witness in Six Continents: Records of the Meeting of the Commission on World Mission and Evangelism of the World Council of Churches held in Mexico City, 8th to 19th December 1963* (London: WCC, 1962).
Osborn, H. H. *Fire in the Hills: The Revival Which Spread from Rwanda* (Crowborough: Highland Books, 1991).
Ott, C. & H. A. Netland (eds) *Globalizing Theology: Belief and Practice in an Era of World Christianity* (Grand Rapids, MI: Baker, 2006).
Ott, C., S. J. Strauss & T. C. Tennent. *Encountering Theology of Mission: Biblical Foundations, Historical Developments, and Contemporary Issues* (Grand Rapids, MI: Baker Academic, 2010).
Padilla, C. R. & C. Sugden (eds) *Texts on Evangelical Social Ethics* (Nottingham: Grove Books, 1985).

Padilla, R. & C. Sugden (eds) *How Evangelicals Endorsed Social Responsibility* (Cambridge: Grove Books, 1985).
Padilla, C. R. *Mission between the Times* (Grand Rapids, MI: Eerdmans, 1985).
Parker, D. (ed) *Jesus, Salvation and the Jewish People: The Uniqueness of Jesus and Jewish Evangelism* (Milton Keynes: Paternoster, 2011).
Persson, P. E. (ed) *Allting nytt? En bok om Uppsala 68* (Stockholm: Verbum, 1968).
Philips, J. M., & R. T. Coote (eds) *Toward the 21st Century in Christian Mission* (Grand Rapids, MI: Eerdmans, 1993).
Pierard, R. V. "The World Missionary Conference, Edinburgh, 1910: Its Shortcomings and Historical Significance". *Missiongeschichte als Geschichte der Globalisierung von Wissen.* Edited by U. van der Heyden & A. Feldtkeller (Stuttgart: Franz Steiner Verlag, 2012), 299-306.
Pomerville, P. A. *Introduction to Missions: An Independent-Study Textbook* (Irving, TX: ICI University Press, 1987).
Randall, I. & D. Hilborn. *One Body in Christ: The History and Significance of the Evangelical Alliance* (Milton Keynes: Paternoster, 2001).
Reader, I. 'Secularisation, R.I.P.? Nonsense! The "Rush Hour Away from the Gods" and the Decline of Religion in Contemporary Japan'. *Journal of Religion in Japan*, 1 (2012), 7-36.
Robinson, R. A. (ed) *God, Torah, Messiah: The Messianic Jewish Theology of Dr Louis Goldberg* (San Francisco, CA: Purple Pomegranate Productions, 2009).
Rosen, M. & C. Rosen. *Witnessing to Jews: Practical Ways to Relate the Love of Jesus* (San Francisco, CA: Purple Pomegranate Productions, 1998).
Rosen, R. *Called to Controversy: The Unlikely Story of Moishe Rosen and the Founding of Jews for Jesus* (Nashville, TN: Thomas Nelson, 2012).
Ross, K. R. *Edinburgh 2010. Springboard for Mission* (Pasadena, CA: William Carey International University Press, 2009).
Ross, K. R. & D. A. Kerr (eds) *Edinburgh 2010: Mission Then and Now* (Oxford: Regnum, 2009).
Rouse, R. "Voluntary Movements and the changing ecumenical climate". *A History of the Ecumenical Movement. 1517-1948* (2nd ed) (eds) Ruth Rouse & Stephen C. Neill (London: SPCK, 1967), 309-349.
Salvaing, B. *Les missionnaires à la rencontre de l'Afrique au XIXe siècle* (Paris: Editions l'Harmattan) 1994.
Samartha, S. J. (ed) *Living Faiths and the Ecumenical Movement* (Geneva: WCC, 1971).
Sampson, P., V. Samuel & C. Sugden (eds) *Faith and Modernity* (Oxford: Regnum, 1994).
Samuel, V. & C. Sugden (eds) *The Church in Response to Human Need* (Oxford: Regnum and Grand Rapids, MI: Eerdmans, 1987).
Samuel, V. & C. Sugden (eds) *Mission as Transformation* (Oxford: Regnum, 1999).
Sanneh, L. "Missionary Enterprise". *Encyclopedia of Africa South of the Sahara,* J. Middleton (ed) (New York: C. Scribner's Sons, 1997), 288-297.
Scherer, J. A. *Gospel, Church, and Kingdom* (Minneapolis, MN: Augsburg Publishing House, 1987).
Scherer, J. A. & S. B. Bevans (eds) *New Directions in Mission and Evangelization I: Basic Statements 1974-1991* (Maryknoll, NY: Orbis Books, 1992).
Schnabel, E. J. *Paul the Missionary – Realities, Strategies and Methods* (Leicester: IVP, 2008).

Schreiter, R. J. *Constructing Local Theologies* (Maryknoll, NY: Orbis Books, 1985).

Schreiter, R. J. 'Faith and Cultures: Challenges to a World Church'. *Theological Studies* 50 (1989), 744-760.

Shenk, W. R. 'The Missionary Encounter with Culture Since the Seventeenth Century'. *Appropriate Christianity,* Charles H. Kraft (ed) (Pasadena, CA: William Carey Library 2005), 35-48.

Shorter, A. *Inculturation in Africa: The Way Forward* (Chicago, IL: CCGM Publications, 2005).

Sider, R. J., 'Evangelizing the World: Reflections on Lausanne III'. *Prism* (Jan/Feb 2011), 48.

Sire, J. W. *The Universe Next Door: A Basic Worldview Catalog* (Downers Grove, IL: IVP, 2005; 5th ed.).

Smith, E. L. *Mandate for Mission* (New York, NY: Friendship Press, 1968).

Snodderly, B. & A. S. Moreau (eds) *Evangelical and Frontier Mission. Perspectives on the Global Progress of the Gospel* (Oxford: Regnum, 2011).

Spieckermann, H. & R. Feldmeier. *God of the Living.* Trans. M. E. Biddle (Waco, TX: Baylor University Press, 2011).

Stackhouse, J. Jr (ed) *Evangelical Futures: A Conversation on Theological Method* (Grand Rapids, MI: Baker Books, 2000).

Staff writer. 'Chinese Christians barred from conference'. *New York Times*, 15th October 2010.

Staff writer. 'House churches insist on end to travel ban'. *South China Morning Post*, 17th October 2010.

Stanley, B. *The World Missionary Conference. Edinburgh 1910* (Grand Rapids, MI: Eerdmans, 2009).

Stanley, B. *The Global Diffusion of Evangelicalism: The Age of Billy Graham and John Stott* [A History of Evangelicalism, Vol. 5 (1940s-1990s)] (Nottingham: IVP, 2013).

Steer, R. *Inside Story: The Life of John Stott* (Nottingham: IVP, 2009).

Steuernagel, V. *The Theology of Mission in its relation to social responsibility within the Lausanne Movement.* PhD dissertation submitted to the Faculty of the Lutheran School of Theology at Chicago. 1988.

Steuernagel, V. (ed) *A Evangelização do Brasil: Uma Tarefa Incabada* (São Paulo: ABU Editora, 1985).

Stott, J. R. W. *Christian Mission in the Modern World* (Downers Grove: IVP, 1975).

Stott, J. R. W. & R. T. Coote (eds) *Gospel and Culture. The Papers of a Consultation on the Gospel and Cuiture, convened by the Lausanne Committee's Theology and Education Group* (Pasadena, CA: William Carey Library, 1979).

Stott, J. R. W. *The Message of Acts.* The Bible Speaks Today (Leicester: IVP, 1990).

Stott, J. R. W. 'Twenty Years After Lausanne: Some Personal Reflections'. *International Bulletin of Missionary Research* 19:2 (April 1995), 50-55.

Stott, J. R. W. *Evangelical Truth* (Downers Grove: IVP, 1999).

Stott, J. R. W. *The Authority of the Bible* (Downers Grove, IL: IVP, 1999).

Stott, J. R. W. *The Cross of Christ*, 20th Anniversary Edition (Downers Grove, IL: IVP, 2006).

Taylor, C. *A Secular Age* (Cambridge: Harvard University Press, 2007).

Tennent, T. C. *Christianity at the Religious Roundtable: Evangelicalism in Conversation with Hinduism, Buddhism, and Islam* (Grand Rapids, MI: Baker Academic, 2002).

Tennent, T. C. *Theology in the Context of World Christianity* (Grand Rapids, MI: Zondervan, 2007).

Tennent, T. C. *Invitation to World Missions: A Trinitarian Missiology for the 21st Century* (Grand Rapids, MI: Kregel, 2009).

Tiénou, T. "Christianity and African Culture: A Review Article". *Evangelical Review of Theology* 3:2 (1979), 198-205.

Tizon, A. *Transformation after Lausanne: Radical Evangelical Mission in Global-Local Perspective* (Oxford: Regnum and Eugene, OR: Wipf & Stock, 2008).

Tozer, A. W. *Let My People Go: The Life of Robert A. Jaffray* (Harrisburg, PA: Christian Publications, 1947).

Trites, A. A. *The New Testament Concept of Witness* (New York: CUP, 1977).

Verkuyl, J. *Contemporary Missiology: An Introduction* (Grand Rapids, MI: Eerdmans, 1978).

Vicedom, G. *The Mission of God: An Introduction to the Theology of Mission.* Trans. G. A. Thiele & D. Hilgendorf (Saint Louis, MO: Concordia Publishing House, 1965).

Visser't Hooft, W. A. (ed) *The New Delhi Report: The Third Assembly of the World Council of Churches, 1961* (New York: SCM Press, 1962).

Volf, M. "When Gospel and Culture Intersect: Notes on the Nature of Christian Difference". *Pentecostalism in Context: Essays in Honor of William W. Menzies,* W. Ma & R. P. Menzies (eds) (Sheffield: Sheffield Academic Press, 1997), 223-236.

Voth, E. 'Towards an Ethic of Liberation for Bible Translation, Part 1: *Ideology*', SBL. Forum, http://sbl-site.org/publications/article.aspx?articleId=754, 2008.

Walls, A. F. *The Missionary Movement in Christian History: Studies in the Transmission of Faith* (Maryknoll, NY: Orbis Books and Edinburgh: T&T Clark, 1996).

Walls, A. F. *The Cross-Cultural Process in Christian History* (Maryknoll, NY: Orbis Books & Edinburgh: T&T Clark, 2002).

Walls, A. F. "Demographics, Power and the Gospel in the 21st Century", *SIL International Conference and WBTI Convention.* 6th June 2002.

Walls, W. 'The Great Commission 1910-2010'. *Considering the Great Commission: Evangelism and Mission in the Wesleyan Spirit,* W. S. Gunter & E. Robinson (eds) (Nashville, TN: Abingdon Press, 2005).

Walls, A. & C. Ross (eds) *Mission in the 21st Century: Exploring the Five Marks of Global Mission* (Maryknoll, NY: Orbis Books, 2008).

Wan, E. & T. Zaretsky. *Jewish-Gentile Couples: Trends, Challenges and Hopes* (Pasadena, CA: William Carey Library, 2004).

Wei-Skillern, J. et al. *Entrepreneurship in the Social Sector* (London: Sage Publications, 2007).

Wells, D. F. *God the Evangelist: How the Holy Spirit Works to Bring Men and Women to Faith* (Grand Rapids, MI: Eerdmans, 1987).

Wells, D. F. *Turning to God: Biblical Conversion in the Modern World* (Grand Rapids, MI: Baker Book House, 1989).

Wilson, F. R. (ed) *The San Antonio Report* (Geneva: WCC, 1990).

Woodworth, S. 'Lausanne Communication Working Group Report'. 29th December 2010. Archived in the BGC Archives, Wheaton College.

Woolnough, B. & W. Ma (eds) *Holistic Mission: God's Plan for God's People* (Oxford: Regnum, 2010).

World Council of Churches. *The Church for Others and the Church for the World. A Quest for Structures of Missionary Congregations* (Geneva: WCC, 1968).

World Council of Churches. *The Church for Others and The Church for the World, A Quest for Structures for Missionary Congregations*. Two Reports on the Missionary Structure of the Congregation, Final Report of the Western European Working Group and North American Working Group of the Department on Studies in Evangelism (Geneva: WCC, 1968).

World Council of Churches. *The Uppsala Report 1968: The Official Report of the Fourth Assembly of the World Council of Churches, Uppsala July 4-20, 1968* (Geneva: WCC, 1968).

World Council of Churches. *Bangkok Assembly 1973. Minutes and Report of the Assembly of the Commission on World Mission an Evangelism of the World Council of Churches, December 31, 1972 and January 9-12, 1973* (Geneva: WCC, 1973).

World Council of Churches. "Mission and Evangelism: An Ecumenical Affirmation". *You are the Light of the World. Statements on Mission by the World Council of Churches 1980-2005* (Geneva: WCC Publications, 2005), 1-38.

World Council of Churches. "Mission as Ministry of Reconciliation". *You are the Light of the World. Statements on Mission by the World Council of Churches 1980-2005* (Geneva: WCC Publications, 2005), 90-126.

WCC Central Committee. *Together towards Life: Mission and Evangelism in Changing Landscape, A New WCC Affirmation on Mission and Evangelism* (Crete, 5th September 2012).

World Council of Churches et al. 'Christian Witness in a Multi-Religious World: Recommendations for Conduct', www.oikumene.org/fileadmin/files/wcc-main/2011pdfs/christianwitnessrecommendations.pdf (2011).

Wright, C. et al. *John Stott: Pastor, Leader and Friend: A man who embodied 'the spirit of Lausanne'* (Peabody, MA: Hendrickson Publishers, 2012). The Didasko Files.

Wright, C. J. H. *The Mission of God: Unlocking the Bible's Grand Narrative* (Downers Grove, IL: IVP, 2006).

Wright, C. J. H. *Salvation Belongs to Our God: Celebrating the Bible's Central Story* (Downers Grove, IL: IVP, 2008).

Wright, C. J. H. *The Mission of God's People: A Biblical Theology of the Church's Mission* (Grand Rapids, MI: Zondervan, 2010).

Wright, T. *Acts for Everyone, Part 2* (London: SPCK, 2008).

Yang, F. *Religion in China: Survival and Revival under Communist Rule* (New York: OUP, 2012).

Yung, H. *Mangoes or Bananas? The Quest for an Authentic Asian Christian Theology* (Oxford: Regnum, 1997).

Yung, H. 'Strategic Issues in Missions – An Asian Perspective'. *Evangelical Missions Quarterly* (Jan 2004), 26-34.

Zacharias, R. *Can Man Live Without God?* (Dallas, TX: Word Publishing, 1994).

Zorn, H. M. *Viability in Context: A Study of the Financial Viability of Theological Education in the Third World, Seedbed or Sheltered Garden?* Bromley: Theological Education Fund, 1975).

LIST OF CONTRIBUTORS

The Editors

Lars Dahle, b. 1961. Cand. Theol. from MF Norwegian School of Theology, PhD in Religious Studies, Open University, UK. Theologian, apologist and educator, has from 1991 served in various academic, administrative and leadership roles at Gimlekollen School of Journalism and Communication, Norway. Currently Vice Rector of External Relations at Gimlekollen / NLA University College, Vice Rector and Associate Professor in Systematic Theology and Apologetics at NLA Gimlekollen, and Lausanne Senior Associate for Media Engagement. Published various academic and popular articles, primarily on media and apologetics. Founding Editor of the Nordic apologetic journal *Theofilos*. Steering Committee Member, European Leadership Forum.

Margunn Serigstad Dahle, b. 1960. BA in Religious Studies and English, BA in Education (teacher training college), MA in Religious Education. Practised as teacher at various levels, and from 1991 served in various academic roles at Gimlekollen School of Journalism and Communication, Norway. Currently Director for and Associate Professor in the Bachelor Programme in Communication and Worldviews at Gimlekollen / NLA University College, also serving as Director for Team and Production in Damaris Norway. Editor of two books, author of academic and popular articles on analyzing and engaging media and popular culture, and also a regular columnist.

Knud Jørgensen, b. 1942. MTh from University of Copenhagen, Denmark, PhD in Missiology, Fuller Theological Seminary, USA. Journalist and theologian, served with Radio Voice of the Gospel, Addis Ababa, Ethiopia, the Lutheran World Federation, Geneva, Switzerland, the International Mass Media Institute, Kristiansand, Go out Centre, Hurdal, Norway, Norwegian Church Aid, the Mekane Yesus Seminary, Addis Ababa, Ethiopia, and the mission foundation Areopagos. Dean of Tao Fong Shan, Hong Kong until 2010. Adjunct Professor at the MF Norwegian School of Theology and the Lutheran Theological Seminary, Hong Kong. Published several books and articles on journalism, communication, leadership and mission. One of the editors of the Regnum Edinburgh 2010 Series. Involvement in the Lausanne Movement since 1974 (Communication Working Group, Theology Working Group, administrative committee, Lausanne Journal). Has served on various boards and international councils.

The Contributors

Ramez Atallah, b. 1946. BSc (1966) and MSW (1968), McGill University, Montreal, Canada. MDiv (1972) and DD (2011), Gordon-Conwell Theological Seminary, USA. After serving with IFES in Canada and Egypt, since 1990 General Secretary of Bible Society of Egypt. Seminar presenter at first Lausanne Congress (1974) and appointed as a youth representative on the Lausanne Committee in 1975. Served on the Committee 1975-94 while also assisting the Chairman of the Committee, Dr Leighton Ford, eventually becoming himself one of the Deputy Chairs in 1986. Program Chairman for Lausanne Cape Town 2010, and in 2011 again appointed a Deputy Chair of Lausanne.

Daniel K. Bourdanné, b. 1959. PhD in Animal Ecology, University of Abidjan, Côte d'Ivoire. Served as Literature and Training Secretary IFES in Francophone Africa where he led training initiatives including the Forum de Théologie pour l'Eglise, the Centre Africain du Christianisme Contemporain and the Tyrannus Biblical Preaching Initiative. Various publications. Currently serves as International General Secretary of IFES. Member-At-Large, Board of Directors, the Lausanne Movement.

Lindsay Brown, b. 1953. MA in Modern History (University of Oxford), studies in theology (Free Faculty of Theology, Paris), and DD (Hon.) from Caribbean Graduate School of Theology (Jamaica). Served for many years as General Secretary of IFES. Currently International Director of the Lausanne Movement and IFES Evangelist-at-Large. Has recently established Fellowship of Evangelists in the Universities of Europe (FEUER). Author of *Shining Like Stars: The Power of the Gospel in the World's Universities* (2007). International speaker and preacher.

Julia E. M. Cameron, b. 1954. MA University of Aberdeen. Publisher, writer, editor, and obituarist for UK broadsheets. Served with UCCF, UK, in ministry and administrative capacities, then in communication and publishing roles with OMF International and IFES. Co-Director of Communications for Cape Town 2010. Lausanne Movement Director of Publishing since 2011. Editor of *Christ Our Reconciler: Gospel / Church / World. The Third Lausanne Congress on World Evangelization* (2012); series editor of *The Didasko Files*.

Blair T. Carlson, b. 1952. BA Art & Anthropology from Wheaton College, USA. Diploma in Theology and Ministry from University of Durham, UK. Ordained Anglican minister. Served the Billy Graham Evangelistic Association for 26 years in a variety of capacities, primarily as Mission Director for many of the world's largest cities. Congress Director for Cape Town 2010. Serves on boards for PULSE, Lazarus Trust, Greenhouse Paris. Chairman of the Lausanne Proclamation Evangelism

Network. Founder and Director of GoodWORD Partnership, and indigenous evangelists worldwide.

Robyn Claydon, b. 1935. MA from Sydney University. Diploma in Education from London University. ThL from the Australian College of Theology. Fellow of the Australian College of Education. Vice-Principal Abbotsleigh Girls' School. Sydney, Lausanne Senior Associate for Women. Vice-Chair Lausanne. Member of the Lausanne Planning Committee for Manila 89. Chair Australian Lausanne Committee, Program Chair 2004 Forum. Mentor Younger Leaders' Gathering 2006, Malaysia. Advisor Lausanne III Cape Town 2010. Published books and journals on education and Christian faith.

Jane L. Crane, b. 1951. MA in Peace and Justice from the University of San Diego, USA. PhD student, Oxford Centre for Mission Studies, UK. Founder/President of Adopt A Widow, advocating for assistance for widows in Africa. Lausanne Senior Associate for the Partnership of Men and Women/Special Interest Committee Chair, 2007-12. Board officer for Billy Graham San Diego Crusade 2003. County Chair for National Day of Prayer San Diego, 2001-04. Author on Scriptures related to women in ministry and book of interviews with over 60 widows in seven African countries. Contributor to the *Cape Town Commitment* bibliography for the partnership of men and women.

Rose(mary) Dowsett, b.1943. BA Bristol University, UK. Since 1969, member of OMF International. Seconded 1970-77 to InterVarsity Christian Fellowship, Philippines; staff training, student discipling and church planting. Since 1978 based in Scotland. Lecturer in Church History and Missiology at Glasgow Bible College (1980-98). WEA Mission Commission since 1999, co-leading Global Missiology Task Force. Lausanne Theology Working Group; member of *Cape Town Commitment* Writing Group. Visiting lecturer/Bible teacher and convention speaker in many countries. WEA Representative on Edinburgh 2010 Council and Executive. Author, editor, and contributor to numerous books and journals, especially on missiological issues.

Tormod Engelsviken, b. 1943. Cand. Theol. MF Norwegian School of Theology, PhD 1981, Aquinas Institute of Theology, USA. Teacher at Mekane Yesus Theological Seminary, Ethiopia, studies in USA, teacher at Fjellhaug School of Mission, Norway, Adjunct Professor at Gimlekollen School of Journalism and Communication, Norway, Associate Professor and Professor in Missiology at MF Norwegian School of Theology until 2013, member and Chairman of the Norwegian Lausanne Committee, member of the Lausanne Theology Working Group 1985-2000, Moderator of the Church of Norway Council for Ecumenical and Foreign relations

1999-2003, member of the Commission on World Mission and Evangelism in the World Council of Churches 1999-2005, member of the Mission Commission of the World Evangelical Alliance, Editor of the Norwegian Journal of Missiology 2006-12. Written several books and articles on the Bible, mission, religion, the Holy Spirit, the Pentecostal/Charismatic movement and spiritual conflict.-

Gilles Gravelle, b. 1953. PhD in Linguistics from Vrije University Amsterdam, Netherlands, MA in Applied Linguistics from Darwin University, Australia, and BA in Environmental Planning from California State University, USA. Adjunct faculty member at William Cary International University, Pasadena, USA. Currently, Director of Research & Innovation with the Seed Company, USA. Practises a trans-disciplinary approach to research, writing, and speaking with a focus on language and linguistics, translation, theology, missiology, internet technology, strategic planning and evaluation. Has published a monograph, papers and blog articles on mission strategy.

Stefan Gustavsson, b. 1960. MDiv from University of Lund, Sweden. Theologian, apologist and writer; served with L'Abri Fellowship and IFES Sweden (Credo). Currently Director of the Credo Academy, General Secretary of The Swedish Evangelical Alliance, and Associate Professor in Christian Apologetics, Gimlekollen / NLA University College, Norway. Member of the Executive Committee of IFES International and of the Steering Committee of the European Leadership Forum. Published books and articles, primarily on issues related to Christian apologetics. Columnist, public speaker and debater.

Chulho Han, b. 1956. Studied at London School of Theology and at Asian Theological Seminary in the Philippines. MDiv from Hapdong Theological Seminary, Seoul, Korea. Served with Korea InterVarsity Fellowship for a long time, with the IFES (International Fellowship of Evangelical Students) East Asia Regional Team, and as Director of the Mission Korea Movement since 2000. Currently Director of Mission Korea Partners. Has served on Korea Lausanne Committee since 1989 and is currently Deputy Chair of the Lausanne Intercession Working Group. Adjunct Professor at Westminster Theological Seminary, Seoul. Published several books and articles on student ministry and mission.

Paul Joshua Bhakiaraj, b. 1967. PhD from Vrije Universitiet, Amsterdam, Netherlands. Lives in Bangalore, India, where he is Commended Worker from and Elder at Tamil Brethren Church and serves as Professor of Theology at South Asia Institute of Advanced Christian Studies (SAIACS). Member of the Theology Working Group and of the Editorial Board of the *Lausanne Global Analysis*. Associate of the Missions

Commission of the World Evangelical Alliance and member of the International Networking Team of the International Fellowship of Mission as Transformation (INFEMIT). Publications include chapters in *Atlas of Global Christianity* (Edinburgh 2010) and *Oxford Handbook of Christianity in Asia* (forthcoming); Co-editor, *Missiology for the 21st Century: South Asian Perspectives* (2005); *Indian & Christian: Changing Identities in Modern India* (2011). Itinerant preaching teaching ministry in churches, para- church agencies and conferences.

Jooseop Keum, b. 1967. Missiologist from the Presbyterian Church of Korea. Served the Council for World Mission in London as Executive Secretary for mission programme 2003-07. Joined WCC as Director of Commission on World Mission and Evangelism (CWME) and Editor of the International Review of Mission in 2007. Co-ordinated development of the new WCC mission statement *Together towards Life: Mission and Evangelism in Changing Landscapes*. Has written extensively on mission and evangelism.

Kåre Melhus, b. 1948. BA in Sociology, Trinity College, Deerfield, USA. MA in Journalism, University of Missouri, USA. Served as reporter and editor with Norwegian Broadcasting Corporation; Press Officer with African Evangelistic Enterprise, Kenya and Zimbabwe; Consultant with International Mass Media Institute, Kristiansand, Norway; Press Centre Manager at Lausanne II, Manila, and at Lausanne III, Cape Town; Project Manager for Kosovo Institute of Journalism and Communications, Pristina; Academic Co-ordinator for Faculty of Journalism and Communication, Addis Ababa University, Ethiopia. Associate Professor in Journalism, Gimlekollen / NLA University College, Norway.

Scott Moreau, b. 1955. MDiv (Missions) and DMiss from Trinity International Divinity School, USA. Served ten years with Cru Africa, teaching science at Ntonjeni Swazi National High School and missions at the Nairobi International School of Theology (NIST), Kenya. In 1991, he joined the Intercultural Studies department at Wheaton College, USA, where he is Professor of Intercultural Studies and Missions and Acting Associate Dean of Wheaton College Graduate School. He edits *Evangelical Missions Quarterly* and the *Encountering Mission* series (Baker), and serves on several agency and other boards. Has written or edited eighteen books and many articles in journals, magazines, dictionaries and websites.

Harold Netland. b. 1955. MA, PhD from Claremont Graduate University, USA. Served as missionary educator in Japan 1984-93. Professor of Philosophy of Religion and Intercultural Studies at Trinity Evangelical Divinity School, Deerfield, USA. Publications include *Dissonant Voices: Religious Pluralism and the Question of Truth* (Eerdmans, 1991);

Encountering Religious Pluralism (IVP, 2001); (with Keith Yandell) *Buddhism: A Christian Exploration and Appraisal* (IVP, 2009); and co-edited with Craig Ott, *Globalizing Theology: Belief and Practice in an Era of World Christianity* (Bake, 2006).

Opoku Onyinah, b. 1954. PhD in Theology, University of Birmingham, UK. Pastor and theologian. Currently, Chairman of The Church of Pentecost, a Pentecostal denomination with its headquarters in Ghana and with branches in 85 nations worldwide. A Commissioner of World Missions and Evangelism of the World Council of Churches (WCC). Co-Chairman of Empowered21, African Cabinet. Published several books and articles. His research and writing interests focus on witchcraft/demonology, exorcism, healing, Pentecostalism and pastoral books for the church.

Susan Perlman, b. 1950. Communications major, Hunter College, New York City, USA. Practitioner, mission strategist, communication specialist, conference speaker. Associate Executive Director, Jews for Jesus, since 1973. Member of Jews for Jesus US and European Boards of Directors, Member of Board of Regents, Dallas Theological Seminary, USA, Executive Committee Member, MissioNexus, Member of Editorial Boards of *Evangelical Missions Quarterly* and *The Messianic Times*. Member of the Lausanne Committee for World Evangelization, 1980-90. One of the Founders and Steering Committee Members, Lausanne Consultation on Jewish Evangelism. Writer and editor of Jewish-oriented evangelistic literature and apologetics essays.

Roy L. Peterson, b. 1954. BSc in business administration from Roger Williams University, and MA in social sciences and leadership studies from Azusa Pacific University, USA. Former President and CEO of The Seed Company (a Wycliffe Bible Translators affiliate) since 2003, and President CEO of Wycliffe Bible Translators USA 1997-2003. Prior to that served in Ecuador and Guatemala, also for Wycliffe organizations. He completed the Executive Program for Nonprofit Leaders at Stanford Graduate School of Business and has an honorary doctorate from Taylor University, USA, for his work in Bible Translation. Chair, Lausanne Strategy Working Group.

Antoine Rutayisire, b. 1958. BA in Modern Literature and Linguistics from the National University of Rwanda, MA in Applied Linguistics from University College of North Wales (Bangor), UK, and MA in Global Leadership from Fuller Theological Seminary. Currently working on a Doctorate of Missiology (leadership development). Formerly lecturer at the National University of Rwanda, secondary school teacher and headmaster, General Secretary with IFES for Rwanda, Team Leader of African

Evangelistic Enterprise-Rwanda and currently Senior Pastor of St Peter's Remera Anglican Church and Principal of Kigali Anglican Theological Seminary. Formerly Commissioner and Vice-President of the Rwanda National Unity and Reconciliation Commission and sits on the Boards of many Christian organizations in Rwanda. Has written many articles and spoken extensively on reconciliation, has published four books, one in English and three in Kinyarwanda.

Robert J. Schreiter, b. 1947. Theol.dr., University of Nijmegen, Netherlands, 1974. Teaching at Catholic Theological Union in Chicago, USA, since 1974. Guest professorships in Germany and Netherlands. Past President of American Society of Missiology and the Catholic Theological Society of America. Publications: *Constructing Local Theologies* (1985); *The New Catholicity: Theology between the Global and the Local* (1997); *Reconciliation: Mission and Ministry in a Changing Social Order* (1992); *The Ministry of Reconciliation: Spirituality and Strategies* (1998); ed. *Mission in the New Millennium* (2001); edited, with Frans Wijsen, *Global Christianity: Contested Claims*; edited, with Knud Jorgensen, *Mission as Ministry of Reconciliation* (2013).

Valdir Steuernagel, b. 1950. Lutheran pastor and theologian. MTh and PhD from the Lutheran School of Theology in Chicago, USA. Served with the Aliança Bíblica Universitária do Brasil (IFES – Brazil), Latin American Theological Fraternity, and World Vision International. Co-founder and Director of the *Center for Pastoral Missions* and currently pastoring at the Comunidade do Redentor of the Evangelical Church of Lutheran Confession in Curitiba, Brazil. Board member of the Lausanne Movement and the World Evangelical Alliance, and heading the Aliança Cristã Evangélica Brasileira (Brazilian Evangelical Christian Alliance). Published books and articles in the area of integral mission in Portuguese, Spanish, English and German.

Timothy C. Tennent, b. 1959. MDiv from Gordon-Conwell, ThM from Princeton Theological Seminary, USA, and PhD in missiology from University of Edinburgh, UK. Pastor, theologian and author, ordained in the United Methodist Church, pastored churches, taught at New Theological College in Dehra Dun, India, Toccoa Falls College, USA and taught and directed the missions programme at Gordon-Conwell Theological Seminary. Since 2009, President and Professor of World Christianity at Asbury Theological Seminary, USA. Chair, Theology Working Group of Lausanne. Author of *Christianity at the Religious Roundtable*, *Theology in the Context of World Christianity*, *Invitation to World Missions: A 21st Trinitarian Missiology for the 21st Century*, plus dozens of missiological articles as well as a three-volume catechesis series for the church.

Tite Tiénou, b. 1949. MTh from Faculté Libre de Théologie Evangélique, Vaux-sur-Seine, France, MA in Missiology and PhD in Intercultural Studies, Fuller Theological Seminary, USA. Theologian with cross-cultural interests. Served as Founding Director and Professor, Maranatha Institute, Bobo-Dioulasso, Burkina Faso; Pastor, Central Church of the Christian Alliance Church, Bobo-Dioulasso, Burkina Faso; Professor of Theology and Missiology, Alliance Theological Seminary, USA; President and Dean, Faculté de Théologie Evangélique de l'Alliance Chrétienne, Abidjan, Côte d'Ivoire; Dean and Senior Vice President of Education, Professor of Theology of Mission, Trinity Evangelical Divinity School, USA. Published books and articles on mission, African theology, and academic leadership.

Al Tizon, b. 1962. MA in Church Leadership Studies from Vanguard University of Southern California, USA; PhD in Missiology, Graduate Theological Union, USA. As a missionary, served with Action International Ministries in the Philippines, founding a Filipino community development organization called LIGHT Ministries. As a pastor, provided leadership for a church plant among the poor in Olongapo City, Philippines, as well as an established church in Berkeley, California. Ordained in the Evangelical Covenant Church. Co-president of Evangelicals for Social Action and Ronald J. Sider Associate Professor of Holistic Ministry at Palmer Theological Seminary of Eastern University Philadelphia, USA. Published several books and articles on holistic mission, cross-cultural partnerships, missional preaching, discipleship, and Asian-American theology and ministry.

David Wells, b. 1939. Distinguished Research Professor at Gordon-Conwell Theological Seminary, USA. Born in Bulawayo, Rhodesia (now Zimbabwe). Studied architecture at the University of Cape Town, South Africa, then earned BD (University of London), ThM (Trinity Evangelical Divinity School), PhD in Theology (University of Manchester). Appointed post-doctoral research fellow at Yale Divinity School. Author and editor of numerous books and articles, including *The Courage To Be Protestant: Truth-lovers, Marketers, and Emergents in the Postmodern World* (2008), and the Lausanne volumes *God the Evangelist: How the Holy Spirit Brings Men and Women to Faith* (1987) and *Turning to God: Biblical Conversion in the Modern World* (1989). Served on the Lausanne Committee for World Evangelization and the Theology Working Group. In 1985 appointed a Distinguished Lecturer for the London Institute for Contemporary Christianity in London.

Christopher J. H. Wright, b. 1947. PhD in Theology from Cambridge University. Served as Anglican minister in the UK, theological teacher at Union Theological Seminary, India, and as Academic Dean and Principal at

All Nations Christian College, UK. Currently International Ministries Director for Langham Partnership. Chair of the Lausanne Theology Working Group 2005-11. Attended Cape Town Congress, Chair of the Statement Committee, and chief architect of the resulting *Cape Town Commitment.* Has written several books on the Old Testament, mission and ethics, including *Old Testament Ethics for the People of God, The Mission of God,* and *The Mission of God's People.* Member-At-Large, Board of Directors, the Lausanne Movement.

Øyvind Økland, b. 1956. Cand. Philol. from University of Bergen, PhD in Intercultural Studies, Trinity International University, USA. Teacher at Nordborg High School, Norway; director of Wycliffe Bible Translators, Norway; Principal at Danvik Folk High School, Drammen; Associate Professor at Gimlekollen / NLA University College and University of Agder, Kristiansand, Norway. Co-founder of Norwegian Forum for Bible Translation, Norwegian Association for Intercultural competence (NOFIK) and *Agder for alle* (an organization for immigration and integration issues). Has written on intercultural communication and journalism issues, and is currently working on immigration research in Norway.

Andrea Zaki Stephanous, b. 1960. BTh (Cairo), Dip of Soc Dev (Nova Scotia), MA in Theology (Eastern University), and PhD in Religions and Politics (Manchester). General Director of the Coptic Evangelical Organization for Social Services (CEOSS). Currently serving as Vice-President of the Protestant Community of Egypt, President of the Fellowship of Middle East Evangelical Churches, and International Deputy Director for Middle East and North Africa (MENA) in the Lausanne Movement. Part-time Lecturer at the Evangelical Theological Seminary in Cairo. Author of *Political Islam, Citizenship, and Minorities*, as well as of two books in Arabic.

REGNUM EDINBURGH CENTENARY SERIES

David A. Kerr, Kenneth R. Ross (Eds)
Mission Then and Now
2009 / 978-1-870345-73-6 / 343pp (paperback)
2009 / 978-1-870345-76-7 / 343pp (hardback)

No one can hope to fully understand the modern Christian missionary movement without engaging substantially with the World Missionary Conference, held at Edinburgh in 1910. This book is the first to systematically examine the eight Commissions which reported to Edinburgh 1910 and gave the conference much of its substance and enduring value. It will deepen and extend the reflection being stimulated by the upcoming centenary and will kindle the missionary imagination for 2010 and beyond.

Daryl M. Balia, Kirsteen Kim (Eds)
Witnessing to Christ Today
2010 / 978-1-870345-77-4 / 301pp (hardback)

This volume, the second in the Edinburgh 2010 series, includes reports of the nine main study groups working on different themes for the celebration of the centenary of the World Missionary Conference, Edinburgh 1910. Their collaborative work brings together perspectives that are as inclusive as possible of contemporary world Christianity and helps readers to grasp what it means in different contexts to be 'witnessing to Christ today'.

Claudia Währisch-Oblau, Fidon Mwombeki (Eds)
Mission Continues
Global Impulses for the 21st Century
2010 / 978-1-870345-82-8 / 271pp (hardback)

In May 2009, 35 theologians from Asia, Africa and Europe met in Wuppertal, Germany, for a consultation on mission theology organized by the United Evangelical Mission: Communion of 35 Churches in Three Continents. The aim was to participate in the 100th anniversary of the Edinburgh conference through a study process and reflect on the challenges for mission in the 21st century. This book brings together these papers written by experienced practitioners from around the world.

Brian Woolnough and Wonsuk Ma (Eds)
Holistic Mission
God's Plan for God's People
2010 / 978-1-870345-85-9 / 268pp (hardback)

Holistic mission, or integral mission, implies God is concerned with the whole person, the whole community, body, mind and spirit. This book discusses the meaning of the holistic gospel, how it has developed, and implications for the church. It takes a global, eclectic approach, with 19 writers, all of whom have much experience in, and commitment to, holistic mission. It addresses critically and honestly one of the most exciting, and challenging, issues facing the church today. To be part of God's plan for God's people, the church must take holistic mission to the world.

Kirsteen Kim and Andrew Anderson (Eds)
Mission Today and Tomorrow
2010 / 978-1-870345-91-0 / 450pp (hardback)

There are moments in our lives when we come to realise that we are participating in the triune God's mission. If we believe the church to be as sign and symbol of the reign of God in the world, then we are called to witness to Christ today by sharing in God's mission of love through the transforming power of the Holy Spirit. We can all participate in God's transforming and reconciling mission of love to the whole creation.

Tormod Engelsviken, Erling Lundeby and Dagfinn Solheim (Eds)
The Church Going Glocal
Mission and Globalisation
2011 / 978-1-870345-93-4 / 262pp (hardback)

The New Testament church is… universal and local at the same time. The universal, one and holy apostolic church appears in local manifestations. Missiologically speaking… the church can take courage as she faces the increasing impact of globalisation on local communities today. Being universal and concrete, the church is geared for the simultaneous challenges of the glocal and local.

Marina Ngurusangzeli Behera (Ed)
Interfaith Relations after One Hundred Years
Christian Mission among Other Faiths
2011 / 978-1-870345-96-5 / 338pp (hardback)

The essays of this book reflect not only the acceptance and celebration of pluralism within India but also by extension an acceptance as well as a need for unity among Indian Christians of different denominations. The essays were presented and studied at a preparatory consultation on Study Theme II: Christian Mission Among Other Faiths at the United Theological College, India July 2009.

Lalsangkima Pachuau and Knud Jørgensen (Eds)
Witnessing to Christ in a Pluralistic Age
Christian Mission among Other Faiths
2011 / 978-1-870345-95-8 / 277pp (hardback)

In a world where plurality of faiths is increasingly becoming a norm of life, insights on the theology of religious plurality are needed to strengthen our understanding of our own faith and the faith of others. Even though religious diversity is not new, we are seeing an upsurge in interest on the theologies of religion among all Christian confessional traditions. It can be claimed that no other issue in Christian mission is more important and more difficult than the theologies of religions.

Beth Snodderly and A Scott Moreau (Eds)
Evangelical Frontier Mission
Perspectives on the Global Progress of the Gospel
2011 / 978-1-870345-98-9 / 312pp (hardback)

This important volume demonstrates that 100 years after the World Missionary Conference in Edinburgh, Evangelism has become truly global. Twenty-first-century Evangelism continues to focus on frontier mission, but significantly, and in the spirit of Edinburgh 1910, it also has re-engaged social action.

Rolv Olsen (Ed)
Mission and Postmodernities
2011 / 978-1-870345-97-2 / 279pp (hardback)

This volume takes on meaning because its authors honestly struggle with and debate how we should relate to postmodernities. Should our response be accommodation, relativizing or counter-culture? How do we strike a balance between listening and understanding, and at the same time exploring how postmodernities influence the interpretation and application of the Bible as the normative story of God's mission in the world?

Cathy Ross (Ed)
Life-Widening Mission
2012 / 978-1-908355-00-3 / 163pp (hardback)

It is clear from the essays collected here that the experience of the 2010 World Mission Conference in Edinburgh was both affirming and frustrating for those taking part - affirming because of its recognition of how the centre of gravity has moved in global Christianity; frustrating because of the relative slowness of so many global Christian bodies to catch up with this and to embody it in the way they do business and in the way they represent themselves. These reflections will - or should - provide plenty of food for thought in the various councils of the Communion in the coming years.

Beate Fagerli, Knud Jørgensen, Rolv Olsen, Kari Storstein Haug and Knut Tveitereid (Eds)
A Learning Missional Church
Reflections from Young Missiologists
2012 / 978-1-908355-01-0 / 218pp (hardback)

Cross-cultural mission has always been a primary learning experience for the church. It pulls us out of a mono-cultural understanding and helps us discover a legitimate theological pluralism which opens up for new perspectives in the Gospel. Translating the Gospel into new languages and cultures is a human and divine means of making us learn new 'incarnations' of the Good News.

Emma Wild-Wood & Peniel Rajkumar (Eds)
Foundations for Mission
2012 / 978-1-908355-12-6 / 309pp (hardback)

This volume provides an important resource for those wishing to gain an overview of significant issues in contemporary missiology whilst understanding how they are applied in particular contexts.

Wonsuk Ma & Kenneth R Ross (Eds)
Mission Spirituality and Authentic Discipleship
2013 / 978-1-908355-24-9 / 248pp (hardback)

This book argues for the primacy of spirituality in the practice of mission. Since God is the primary agent of mission and God works through the power of the Holy Spirit, it is through openness to the Spirit that mission finds its true character and has its authentic impact.

Stephen B Bevans (Ed)
A Century of Catholic Mission
2013 / 978-1-908355-14-0 / 337pp (hardback)

A Century of Catholic Mission surveys the complex and rich history and theology of Roman Catholic Mission in the one hundred years since the 1910 Edinburgh World Mission Conference. Essays written by an international team of Catholic mission scholars focus on Catholic Mission in every region of the world, summarize church teaching on mission before and after the watershed event of the Second Vatican Council, and reflect on a wide variety of theological issues.

Robert Schreiter & Knud Jørgensen (Eds)
Mission as Ministry of Reconcilation
2013 / 978-1-908355-26-3 / 382pp (hardback)

There is hope – even if it is "Hope in a Fragile World", as the concluding chapter of Mission as Ministry of Reconciliation puts it. At the very heart of the gospel of Jesus Christ is a message of hope and reconciliation. Nothing could be more relevant and more necessary in a broken world than this Christian message of hope and reconciliation. ... I would like to congratulate the editors of Mission as Ministry of Reconciliation, for they listened carefully and planned with farsightedness. ... This rich book offers a valuable elucidation of the importance and the understanding of mission as ministry of reconciliation.

Petros Vassiliadis, Editor
Orthodox Perspectives on Mission
2013 / 978-1908355-25-6 / 262pp (hardback)

Orthodox Perspectives on Mission is both a humble tribute to some great Orthodox theologians, who in the past have provided substantial contribution to contemporary missiological and ecumenical discussions, and an Orthodox input to the upcoming 2013 Busan WCC General Assembly. The collected volume is divided into two parts: Part I: The Orthodox Heritage consists of Orthodox missiological contributions of the past, whereas Part II includes all the papers presented in the Plenary of the recent Edinburgh 2010 conference, as well as the short studies and contributions prepared, during the Edinburgh 2010 on going study process.

Pauline Hoggarth, Fergus MacDonald,
Bill Mitchell & Knud Jørgensen, Editors
Bible in Mission
2013 / 978-1908355-42-3 / 317pp (hardback)

To the authors of Bible in Mission, the Bible is the book of life, and mission is life in the Word. This core reality cuts across the diversity of contexts and hermeneutical strategies represented in these essays. The authors are committed to the boundary-crossings that characterize contemporary mission – and each sees the Bible as foundational to the missio Dei, to God's work in the world.

Wonsuk Ma, Veli-Matti Kärkkäinnen
& J Kwabena Asamoah
Pentecostal Mission and Global Christianity
*2014 / 978-1908355-43-0 / 397pp (*hardback)

Although Pentecostalism worldwide represent the most rapidly growing missionary movement in Christian history, only recently scholars from within and outside the movement have begun academic reflection on the mission. This volume represents the coming of age of emerging scholarship of various aspects of the Pentecostal mission, including theological, historical, strategic, and practical aspects.

Afe Adogame, Janice McLean & Anderson Jeremiah, Editors
Engaging the World
Christian Communities in Contemporary Global Societies
*2014 / 978-1908355-21-8 / 235pp (*hardback)

Engaging the World deals with the lived experiences and expressions of Christians in diverse communities across the globe. Christian communities do not live in a vacuum but in complex, diverse social-cultural contexts; within wider communities of different faith and social realities. Power, identity and community are key issues in considering Christian communities in contemporary contexts.

Peniel Jesudason Rufus Rajkumar, Joseph Prabhakar Dayam
& IP Asheervadham, Editors
Mission At and From the Margins
Patterns, Protagonists and Perspectives
2014 / 978-1908355-13-3 / 283pp (hardback)

Mission At and From the Margins: Patterns, Protagonists and Perspectives revisits the 'hi-stories' of Mission from the 'bottom up' paying critical attention to people, perspectives and patterns that have often been elided in the construction of mission history. Focusing on the mission story of Christian churches in the South Indian state of Abdhra Pradesh this collection of essays ushers its readers to re-shape their understanding of the landscape of mission history by drawing their attention to the silences and absences within pre-dominant historical accounts.

REGNUM STUDIES IN GLOBAL CHRISTIANITY

David Emmanuel Singh (Ed)
Jesus and the Cross
Reflections of Christians from Islamic Contexts
2008 / 978-1-870345-65-1 / 226pp

The Cross reminds us that the sins of the world are not borne through the exercise of power but through Jesus Christ's submission to the will of the Father. The papers in this volume are organised in three parts: scriptural, contextual and theological. The central question being addressed is: how do Christians living in contexts, where Islam is a majority or minority religion, experience, express or think of the Cross?

Sung-wook Hong
Naming God in Korea
The Case of Protestant Christianity
2008 / 978-1-870345-66-8 / 170pp (hardback)

Since Christianity was introduced to Korea more than a century ago, one of the most controversial issues has been the Korean term for the Christian 'God'. This issue is not merely about naming the Christian God in Korean language, but it relates to the question of theological contextualization - the relationship between the gospel and culture - and the question of Korean Christian identity. This book demonstrates the nature of the gospel in relation to cultures, i.e., the universality of the gospel expressed in all human cultures.

Hubert van Beek (Ed)
Revisioning Christian Unity
The Global Christian Forum
2009 / 978-1-870345-74-3 / 288pp (hardback)

This book contains the records of the Global Christian Forum gathering held in Limuru near Nairobi, Kenya, on 6 – 9 November 2007 as well as the papers presented at that historic event. Also included are a summary of the Global Christian Forum process from its inception until the 2007 gathering and the reports of the evaluation of the process that was carried out in 2008.

Young-hoon Lee

The Holy Spirit Movement in Korea

Its Historical and Theological Development

2009 / 978-1-870345-67-5 / 174pp (hardback)

This book traces the historical and theological development of the Holy Spirit Movement in Korea through six successive periods (from 1900 to the present time). These periods are characterized by repentance and revival (1900-20), persecution and suffering under Japanese occupation (1920-40), confusion and division (1940-60), explosive revival in which the Pentecostal movement played a major role in the rapid growth of Korean churches (1960-80), the movement reaching out to all denominations (1980-2000), and the new context demanding the Holy Spirit movement to open new horizons in its mission engagement (2000-).

Paul Hang-Sik Cho

Eschatology and Ecology

Experiences of the Korean Church

2010 / 978-1-870345-75-0 / 260pp (hardback)

This book raises the question of why Korean people, and Korean Protestant Christians in particular, pay so little attention to ecological issues. The author argues that there is an important connection (or elective affinity) between this lack of attention and the other-worldly eschatology that is so dominant within Korean Protestant Christianity.

Dietrich Werner, David Esterline, Namsoon Kang, Joshva Raja (Eds)

The Handbook of Theological Education in World Christianity

Theological Perspectives, Ecumenical Trends, Regional Surveys

2010 / 978-1-870345-80-0 / 759pp

This major reference work is the first ever comprehensive study of Theological Education in Christianity of its kind. With contributions from over 90 international scholars and church leaders, it aims to be easily accessible across denominational, cultural, educational, and geographic boundaries. The Handbook will aid international dialogue and networking among theological educators, institutions, and agencies.

David Emmanuel Singh & Bernard C Farr (Eds)

Christianity and Education

Shaping of Christian Context in Thinking

2010 / 978-1-870345-81-1 / 374pp

Christianity and Education is a collection of papers published in *Transformation: An International Journal of Holistic Mission Studies* over a period of 15 years. The articles represent a spectrum of Christian thinking addressing issues of institutional development for theological education, theological studies in the context of global mission, contextually aware/informed education, and academies which deliver such education, methodologies and personal reflections.

J.Andrew Kirk

Civilisations in Conflict?

Islam, the West and Christian Faith

2011 / 978-1-870345-87-3 / 205pp

Samuel Huntington's thesis, which argues that there appear to be aspects of Islam that could be on a collision course with the politics and values of Western societies, has provoked much controversy. The purpose of this study is to offer a particular response to Huntington's thesis by making a comparison between the origins of Islam and Christianity.

David Emmanuel Singh (Ed)

Jesus and the Incarnation

Reflections of Christians from Islamic Contexts

2011 / 978-1-870345-90-3 / 245pp

In the dialogues of Christians with Muslims nothing is more fundamental than the Cross, the Incarnation and the Resurrection of Jesus. Building on the *Jesus and the Cross*, this book contains voices of Christians living in various 'Islamic contexts' and reflecting on the Incarnation of Jesus. The aim and hope of these reflections is that the papers weaved around the notion of 'the Word' will not only promote dialogue among Christians on the roles of the Person and the Book but, also, create a positive environment for their conversations with Muslim neighbours.

Ivan M Satyavrata

God Has Not left Himself Without Witness

2011 / 978-1-870345-79-8 / 264pp

Since its earliest inception the Christian Church has had to address the question of what common ground exits between Christian faiths and other religions. This issue is not merely of academic interest but one with critical existential and socio-political consequences. This study presents a case for the revitalization of the fulfillment tradition based on a recovery and assessment of the fulfillment approaches of Indian Christian converts in the pre-independence period.

Bal Krishna Sharma

From this World to the Next

Christian Identity and Funerary Rites in Nepal

2013 / 978-1-908355-08-9 / 238pp

This book explores and analyses funerary rite struggles in a nation where Christianity is a comparatively recent phenomenon, and many families have multi-faith, who go through traumatic experiences at the death of their family members. The author has used an applied theological approach to explore and analyse the findings in order to address the issue of funerary rites with which the Nepalese church is struggling.

J Kwabena Asamoah-Gyada

Contemporary Pentecostal Christianity

Interpretations from an African Context

2013 / 978-1-908355-07-2 / 194pp

Pentecostalism is the fastest growing stream of Christianity in the world. The real evidence for the significance of Pentecostalism lies in the actual churches they have built and the numbers they attract. This work interprets key theological and missiological themes in African Pentecostalism by using material from the live experiences of the movement itself.

David Emmanuel Singh and Bernard C Farr (Eds)

The Bible and Christian Ethics

2013 / 978-1-908355-20-1 / 217pp

This book contains papers from the Oxford Centre for Mission Studies' quarterly journal, Transformation, on the topic of Christian Ethics. Here, Mission Studies is understood in its widest sense to also encompass Christian Ethics. At the very hearts of it lies the Family as the basic unit of society. All the papers together seek to contribute to understanding how Christian thought is shaped in contexts each of which poses its own challenge to Christian living in family and in broader society.

Martin Allaby
Inequality, Corruption and the Church
Challenges & Opportunities in the Global Church
2013 / 978-1-908355-16-4 / 228pp

Why are economic inequalities greatest in the southern countries where most people are Christians? This book teases out the influences that have created this situation, and concludes that Christians could help reduce economic inequalities by opposing corruption. Interviews in the Philippines, Kenya, Zambia and Peru reveal opportunities and challenges for Christians as they face up to corruption.

Paul Alexander and Al Tizon (Eds)
Following Jesus
Journeys in Radical Discipleship – Essays in Honor of Ronald J Sider
2013 / 978-1-908355-27-0 / 228pp

Ronald J. Sider and the organization that he founded, *Evangelicals for Social Action*, are most respected for their pioneering work in the area of evangelical social concern. However, Sider's great contribution to social justice is but a part of a larger vision – namely, biblical discipleship. His works, which span more than four decades, have guided the faithful to be authentic gospel-bearers in ecclesial, cultural and political arenas. This book honors Ron Sider, by bringing together a group of scholar-activists, old and young, to reflect upon the gospel and its radical implications for the 21st century.

Cawley Bolt
Reluctant or Radical Revolutionaries?
Evangelical Missionaries and Afro-Jamaican Character, 1834-1870
2013 / 978-1-908355-18-8 / 287pp

This study is based on extensive research that challenges traditional ways of understanding some evangelical missionaries of nineteenth century Jamaica and calls for revision of those views. It highlights the strength and character of persons facing various challenges of life in their effort to be faithful to the guiding principles of their existence.

Isabel Apawo Phiri & Dietrich Werner (Eds)
Handbook of Theological Education in Africa
2013 / 978-1-908355-45-4 / 1110pp

The *Handbook of Theological Education in Africa* is a wake-up call for African churches to give proper prominence to theological education institutions and their programmes which serve them. It is unique, comprehensive and ambitious in its aim and scope.

Hope Antone, Wati Longchar, Hyunju Bae, Huang Po Ho, Dietrich Werner (Eds)
Asian Handbook for Theological Education and Ecumenism
2013 / 978-1-908355-30-0 / 675pp (hardback)

This impressive and comprehensive book focuses on key resources for teaching Christian unity and common witness in Asian contexts. It is a collection of articles that reflects the ongoing 'double wrestle' with the texts of biblical tradition as well as with contemporary contexts. It signals an investment towards the future of the ecumenical movement in Asia.

Bernhard Reitsma
The God of My Enemy
The Middle East and the Nature of God
2014 / 978-1-908355-50-8 / 206pp

The establishment of the State of Israel in 1948 for the Church in the West has been the starting point of a rediscovery of its own roots. In the Middle East the effect has been exactly the opposite: Christians have become estranged from their Old Testament roots, because they have been expelled from their land exactly because of an appeal to the Old Testament. The concept of Israel changed from a nation in the Bible, with which they could associate, to an economic, political and military power that was against them

REGNUM STUDIES IN MISSION

Kwame Bediako
Theology and Identity
The Impact of Culture upon Christian Thought in the Second Century and in Modern Africa
1992 / 978-1870345-10-1 / 507pp

The author examines the question of Christian identity in the context of the Graeco–Roman culture of the early Roman Empire. He then addresses the modern African predicament of quests for identity and integration.

Christopher Sugden
Seeking the Asian Face of Jesus
The Practice and Theology of Christian Social Witness in Indonesia and India 1974–1996
1997 / 1-870345-26-6 / 496pp

This study focuses on contemporary holistic mission with the poor in India and Indonesia combined with the call to transformation of all life in Christ with micro-credit enterprise schemes. 'The literature on contextual theology now has a new standard to rise to' – Lamin Sanneh (Yale University, USA).

Hwa Yung
Mangoes or Bananas?
The Quest for an Authentic Asian Christian Theology
1997 / 1-870345-25-5 / 274pp

Asian Christian thought remains largely captive to Greek dualism and Enlightenment rationalism because of the overwhelming dominance of Western culture. Authentic contextual Christian theologies will emerge within Asian Christianity with a dual recovery of confidence in culture and the gospel.

Keith E. Eitel
Paradigm Wars
The Southern Baptist International Mission Board Faces the Third Millennium
1999 / 1-870345-12-6 / 140pp

The International Mission Board of the Southern Baptist Convention is the largest denominational mission agency in North America. This volume chronicles the historic and contemporary forces that led to the IMB's recent extensive reorganization, providing the most comprehensive case study to date of a historic mission agency restructuring to continue its mission purpose into the twenty-first century more effectively.

Samuel Jayakumar

Dalit Consciousness and Christian Conversion

Historical Resources for a Contemporary Debate

1999 / 81-7214-497-0 / 434pp

(Published jointly with ISPCK)

The main focus of this historical study is social change and transformation among the Dalit Christian communities in India. Historiography tests the evidence in the light of the conclusions of the modern Dalit liberation theologians.

Vinay Samuel and Christopher Sugden (Eds)

Mission as Transformation

A Theology of the Whole Gospel

1999 / 978-18703455-13-2 / 522pp

This book brings together in one volume twenty five years of biblical reflection on mission practice with the poor from around the world. This volume helps anyone understand how evangelicals, struggling to unite evangelism and social action, found their way in the last twenty five years to the biblical view of mission in which God calls all human beings to love God and their neighbour; never creating a separation between the two.

Christopher Sugden

Gospel, Culture and Transformation

2000 / 1-870345-32-3 / 152pp

A Reprint, with a New Introduction, of Part Two of Seeking the Asian Face of Jesus

Gospel, Culture and Transformation explores the practice of mission especially in relation to transforming cultures and communities. - 'Transformation is to enable God's vision of society to be actualised in all relationships: social, economic and spiritual, so that God's will may be reflected in human society and his love experienced by all communities, especially the poor.'

Bernhard Ott

Beyond Fragmentation: Integrating Mission and Theological Education

A Critical Assessment of some Recent Developments in Evangelical Theological Education

2001 / 1-870345-14-9 / 382pp

Beyond Fragmentation is an enquiry into the development of Mission Studies in evangelical theological education in Germany and German-speaking Switzerland between 1960 and 1995. The author undertakes a detailed examination of the paradigm shifts which have taken place in recent years in both the theology of mission and the understanding of theological education.

Gideon Githiga

The Church as the Bulwark against Authoritarianism

Development of Church and State Relations in Kenya, with Particular Reference to the Years after Political Independence 1963-1992

2002 / 1-870345-38-x / 218pp

'All who care for love, peace and unity in Kenyan society will want to read this careful history by Bishop Githiga of how Kenyan Christians, drawing on the Bible, have sought to share the love of God, bring his peace and build up the unity of the nation, often in the face of great difficulties and opposition.' Canon Dr Chris Sugden, Oxford Centre for Mission Studies.

Myung Sung-Hoon, Hong Young-Gi (Eds)

Charis and Charisma

David Yonggi Cho and the Growth of Yoido Full Gospel Church

2003 / 978-1870345-45-3 / 218pp

This book discusses the factors responsible for the growth of the world's largest church. It expounds the role of the Holy Spirit, the leadership, prayer, preaching, cell groups and creativity in promoting church growth. It focuses on God's grace (charis) and inspiring leadership (charisma) as the two essential factors and the book's purpose is to present a model for church growth worldwide.

Samuel Jayakumar

Mission Reader

Historical Models for Wholistic Mission in the Indian Context

2003 / 1-870345-42-8 / 250pp

(Published jointly with ISPCK)

This book is written from an evangelical point of view revalidating and reaffirming the Christian commitment to wholistic mission. The roots of the 'wholistic mission' combining 'evangelism and social concerns' are to be located in the history and tradition of Christian evangelism in the past; and the civilizing purpose of evangelism is compatible with modernity as an instrument in nation building.

Bob Robinson

Christians Meeting Hindus

An Analysis and Theological Critique of the Hindu-Christian Encounter in India

2004 / 987-1870345-39-2 / 392pp

This book focuses on the Hindu-Christian encounter, especially the intentional meeting called dialogue, mainly during the last four decades of the twentieth century, and specifically in India itself.

Gene Early

Leadership Expectations

How Executive Expectations are Created and Used in a Non-Profit Setting

2005 / 1-870345-30-9 / 276pp

The author creates an Expectation Enactment Analysis to study the role of the Chancellor of the University of the Nations-Kona, Hawaii. This study is grounded in the field of managerial work, jobs, and behaviour and draws on symbolic interactionism, role theory, role identity theory and enactment theory. The result is a conceptual framework for developing an understanding of managerial roles.

Tharcisse Gatwa

The Churches and Ethnic Ideology in the Rwandan Crises 1900-1994

2005 / 978-1870345-24-8 / 300pp

(Reprinted 2011)

Since the early years of the twentieth century Christianity has become a new factor in Rwandan society. This book investigates the role Christian churches played in the formulation and development of the racial ideology that culminated in the 1994 genocide.

Julie Ma

Mission Possible

Biblical Strategies for Reaching the Lost

2005 / 978-1870345-37-8 / 142pp

This is a missiology book for the church which liberates missiology from the specialists for the benefit of every believer. It also serves as a textbook that is simple and friendly, and yet solid in biblical interpretation. This book links the biblical teaching to the actual and contemporary missiological settings with examples, making the Bible come alive to the reader..

I. Mark Beaumont

Christology in Dialogue with Muslims

A Critical Analysis of Christian Presentations of Christ for Muslims from the Ninth and Twentieth Centuries

2005 / 978-1870345-46-0 / 227pp

This book analyses Christian presentations of Christ for Muslims in the most creative periods of Christian-Muslim dialogue, the first half of the ninth century and the second half of the twentieth century. In these two periods, Christians made serious attempts to present their faith in Christ in terms that take into account Muslim perceptions of him, with a view to bridging the gap between Muslim and Christian convictions.

Thomas Czövek,

Three Seasons of Charismatic Leadership

A Literary-Critical and Theological Interpretation of the Narrative of Saul, David and Solomon

2006 / 978-1870345-48-4 / 272pp

This book investigates the charismatic leadership of Saul, David and Solomon. It suggests that charismatic leaders emerge in crisis situations in order to resolve the crisis by the charisma granted by God. Czovek argues that Saul proved himself as a charismatic leader as long as he acted resolutely and independently from his mentor Samuel. In the author's eyes, Saul's failure to establish himself as a charismatic leader is caused by his inability to step out from Samuel's shadow.

Richard Burgess

Nigeria's Christian Revolution

The Civil War Revival and Its Pentecostal Progeny (1967-2006)

2008 / 978-1-870345-63-7 / 347pp

This book describes the revival that occurred among the Igbo people of Eastern Nigeria and the new Pentecostal churches it generated, and documents the changes that have occurred as the movement has responded to global flows and local demands. As such, it explores the nature of revivalist and Pentecostal experience, but does so against the backdrop of local socio-political and economic developments, such as decolonisation and civil war, as well as broader processes, such as modernisation and globalisation.

David Emmanuel Singh & Bernard C Farr (Eds)

Christianity and Cultures

Shaping Christian Thinking in Context

2008 / 978-1-870345-69-9 / 271pp

This volume marks an important milestone, the 25th anniversary of the Oxford Centre for Mission Studies (OCMS). The papers here have been exclusively sourced from Transformation, a quarterly journal of OCMS, and seek to provide a tripartite view of

Christianity's engagement with cultures by focusing on the question: how is Christian thinking being formed or reformed through its interaction with the varied contexts it encounters? The subject matters include different strands of theological-missiological thinking, socio-political engagements and forms of family relationships in interaction with the host cultures.

Tormod Engelsviken, Ernst Harbakk, Rolv Olsen, Thor Strandenæs (Eds)
Mission to the World
Communicating the Gospel in the 21st Century:
Essays in Honour of Knud Jørgensen
2008 / 978-1-870345-64-4 / 472pp (hardback)

Knud Jørgensen is Director of Areopagos and Associate Professor of Missiology at MF Norwegian School of Theology. This book reflects on the main areas of Jørgensen's commitment to mission. At the same time it focuses on the main frontier of mission, the world, the content of mission, the Gospel, the fact that the Gospel has to be communicated, and the context of contemporary mission in the 21st century.

Al Tizon
Transformation after Lausanne
Radical Evangelical Mission in Global-Local Perspective
2008 / 978-1-870345-68-2 / 281pp

After Lausanne '74, a worldwide network of radical evangelical mission theologians and practitioners use the notion of "Mission as Transformation" to integrate evangelism and social concern together, thus lifting theological voices from the Two Thirds World to places of prominence. This book documents the definitive gatherings, theological tensions, and social forces within and without evangelicalism that led up to Mission as Transformation. And it does so through a global-local grid that points the way toward greater holistic mission in the 21st century.

Bambang Budijanto
Values and Participation
Development in Rural Indonesia
2009 / 978-1-870345-70-4 / 237pp

Socio-religious values and socio-economic development are inter-dependant, inter-related and are constantly changing in the context of macro political structures, economic policy, religious organizations and globalization; and micro influences such as local affinities, identity, politics, leadership and beliefs. The book argues that the comprehensive approach in understanding the socio-religious values of each of the three local Lopait communities in Central Java is essential to accurately describing their respective identity.

Alan R. Johnson
Leadership in a Slum
A Bangkok Case Study
2009 / 978-1-870345-71-2 / 238pp

This book looks at leadership in the social context of a slum in Bangkok from a different perspective than traditional studies which measure well educated Thais on leadership scales derived in the West. Using both systematic data collection and participant observation, it develops a culturally preferred model as well as a set of models based in Thai concepts that reflect on-the-ground realities. It concludes by looking at the implications of the anthropological approach for those who are involved in leadership training in Thai settings and beyond.

Titre Ande

Leadership and Authority

Bula Matari and Life - Community Ecclesiology in Congo

2010 / 978-1-870345-72-9 / 189pp

Christian theology in Africa can make significant development if a critical understanding of the socio-political context in contemporary Africa is taken seriously, particularly as Africa's post-colonial Christian leadership based its understanding and use of authority on the Bula Matari model. This has caused many problems and Titre proposes a Life-Community ecclesiology for liberating authority, here leadership is a function, not a status, and 'apostolic succession' belongs to all people of God.

Frank Kwesi Adams

Odwira and the Gospel

A Study of the Asante Odwira Festival and its Significance for Christianity in Ghana

2010 /978-1-870345-59-0 / 232pp

The study of the Odwira festival is the key to the understanding of Asante religious and political life in Ghana. The book explores the nature of the Odwira festival longitudinally - in pre-colonial, colonial and post-independence Ghana - and examines the Odwira ideology and its implications for understanding the Asante self-identity. Also discussed is how some elements of faith portrayed in the Odwira festival can provide a framework for Christianity to engage with Asante culture at a greater depth.

Bruce Carlton

Strategy Coordinator

Changing the Course of Southern Baptist Missions

2010 / 978-1-870345-78-1 / 273pp

This is an outstanding, one-of-a-kind work addressing the influence of the non-residential missionary/strategy coordinator's role in Southern Baptist missions. This scholarly text examines the twentieth century global missiological currents that influenced the leadership of the International Mission Board, resulting in a new paradigm to assist in taking the gospel to the nations.

Julie Ma & Wonsuk Ma

Mission in the Spirit:

Towards a Pentecostal/Charismatic Missiology

2010 / 978-1-870345-84-2 / 312pp

The book explores the unique contribution of Pentecostal/Charismatic mission from the beginning of the twentieth century. The first part considers the theological basis of Pentecostal/Charismatic mission thinking and practice. Special attention is paid to the Old Testament, which has been regularly overlooked by the modern Pentecostal/Charismatic movements. The second part discusses major mission topics with contributions and challenges unique to Pentecostal/Charismatic mission. The book concludes with a reflection on the future of this powerful missionary movement. As the authors served as Korean missionaries in Asia, often their missionary experiences in Asia are reflected in their discussions.

Allan Anderson, Edmond Tang (Eds)

Asian and Pentecostal

The Charismatic Face of Christianity in Asia

2011 / 978-1870345-94-1 / 500pp

(Revised Edition)

This book provides a thematic discussion and pioneering case studies on the history and development of Pentecostal and Charismatic churches in the countries of South Asia, South East Asia and East Asia.

S. Hun Kim & Wonsuk Ma (Eds)
Korean Diaspora and Christian Mission
2011 / 978-1-870345-89-7 / 301pp (hardback)

As a 'divine conspiracy' for Missio Dei, the global phenomenon of people on the move has shown itself to be invaluable. In 2004 two significant documents concerning Diaspora were introduced, one by the Filipino International Network and the other by the Lausanne Committee for World Evangelization. These have created awareness of the importance of people on the move for Christian mission. Since then, Korean Diaspora has conducted similar research among Korean missions, resulting in this book

Jin Huat Tan
Planting an Indigenous Church
The Case of the Borneo Evangelical Mission
2011 / 978-1-870345-99-6 / 343pp

Dr Jin Huat Tan has written a pioneering study of the origins and development of Malaysia's most significant indigenous church. This is an amazing story of revival, renewal and transformation of the entire region chronicling the powerful effect of it evident to date! What can we learn from this extensive and careful study of the Borneo Revival, so the global Christianity will become ever more dynamic?

Bill Prevette
Child, Church and Compassion
Towards Child Theology in Romania
2012 / 978-1-908355-03-4 / 382pp

Bill Prevett comments that "children are like 'canaries in a mine shaft'; they provide a focal point for discovery and encounter of perilous aspects of our world that are often ignored." True, but miners also carried a lamp to see into the subterranean darkness. This book is such a lamp. It lights up the subterranean world of children and youth in danger of exploitation, and as it does so travels deep into their lives and also into the activities of those who seek to help them.

Samuel Cyuma
Picking up the Pieces
The Church and Conflict Resolution in South Africa and Rwanda
2012 / 978-1-908355-02-7 / 373pp

In the last ten years of the 20th century, the world was twice confronted with unbelievable news from Africa. First, there was the end of Apartheid in South Africa, without bloodshed, due to responsible political and Church leaders. The second was the mass killings in Rwanda, which soon escalated into real genocide. Political and Church leaders had been unable to prevents this crime against humanity. In this book, the question is raised: can we compare the situation in South Africa with that in Rwanda? Can Rwandan leaders draw lessons from the peace process in South Africa?

Peter Rowan
Proclaiming the Peacemaker
The Malaysian Church as an Agent of Reconciliation in a Multicultural Society
2012 / 978-1-908355-05-8 / 268pp

With a history of racial violence and in recent years, low-level ethnic tensions, the themes of peaceful coexistence and social harmony are recurring ones in the discourse of Malaysian society. In such a context, this book looks at the role of the church as a reconciling agent, arguing that a reconciling presence within a divided society necessitates an ethos of peacemaking.

Edward Ontita

Resources and Opportunity

The Architecture of Livelihoods in Rural Kenya

2012 / 978-1-908355-04-1 / 328pp

Poor people in most rural areas of developing countries often improvise resources in unique ways to enable them make a living. Resources and Opportunity takes the view that resources are dynamic and fluid, arguing that villagers co-produce them through redefinition and renaming in everyday practice and use them in diverse ways. The book focuses on ordinary social activities to bring out people's creativity in locating, redesigning and embracing livelihood opportunities in processes.

Kathryn Kraft

Searching for Heaven in the Real World

A Sociological Discussion of Conversion in the Arab World

2012 / 978-1-908355-15-7 / 142pp

Kathryn Kraft explores the breadth of psychological and social issues faced by Arab Muslims after making a decision to adopt a faith in Christ or Christianity, investigating some of the most surprising and significant challenges new believers face.

Wessley Lukose

Contextual Missiology of the Spirit

Pentecostalism in Rajasthan, India

2013 / 978-1-908355-09-6 / 256pp

This book explores the identity, context and features of Pentecostalism in Rajasthan, India as well as the internal and external issues facing Pentecostals. It aims to suggest 'a contextual missiology of the Spirit,' as a new model of contextual missiology from a Pentecostal perspective. It is presented as a glocal, ecumenical, transformational, and public missiology.

Paul M Miller

Evangelical Mission in Co-operation with Catholics

A Study of Evangelical Tensions

2013 / 978-1-908355-17-1 / 291pp

This book brings the first thorough examination of the discussions going on within Evangelicalism about the viability of a good conscience dialogue with Roman Catholics. Those who are interested in evangelical world missions and Roman Catholic views of world missions will find this informative.

Alemayehu Mekonnen

Culture Change in Ethiopia

An Evangelical Perspective

2013 / 978-1-908355-39-3 / 199pp

This book addresses the causes and consequences of culture change in Ethiopia, from Haile Selassie to the present, based on thorough academic research. Although written from an evangelical perspective, this book invites Ethiopians from all religions, ideological, and ethnic backgrounds to reflect on their past, to analyse their present and to engage in unity with diversity to face the future.

Godwin Lekundayo
The Cosmic Christ
Towards Effective Mission Among the Maasai
2013 / 978-1-908355-28- 7 / 259 pp

This book reveals a complex interaction between the Christian gospel brought by western missionaries and the nomadic Massai culture of Tanzania … an important insider's voice courageously questioning the approach to condemn some critical Maasai practices, particularly polygamy, and its missionary consequences. This is a rare study from a Maasai Christian leader.

Philippe Ouedraogo
Female Education and Mission
A Burkina Faso Experience
2014 / 978-1-908355-11-9 / 263pp

This volume is the result of six years research in 'Overcoming Obstacles to Female Education in Burkina Faso'. It narrates how Christians and religious groups can speed up female education and contribute to the socio-economic growth of Burkina Faso. Religious culture and traditions were seen as a problem to female education. However, the evidence from this research shows that Christianity is also part of the solution to a quality female education, thus a key factor of socio economic growth
of the country.

Haw Yung
Mangoes or Bananas?
The Quest for an Authentic Asian Christian Theology
(Second Edition)
2014 / 978-1-908355-47-8 / 232pp

Over the past few decades there has been a growing awareness of the need for contextual theologies throughout Asia. But how genuinely contextual are these? Based on the premise that theology and mission are inseparable, the author applies four missiological criteria to representative examples of Protestant Asian writings to assess their adequacy or otherwise as contextual theologies.

Daniel Taichoul Yang
Called Out for Witness
The Missionary Journey of Grace Korean Church
2014 / 978-1-908355-49-2 / 167pp

This book investigates the theological motivation for GKC's missions: Reformed theology, Presbyterian theology, and mission theology. The book also shows the extent of the church's mission engagement by continents. Finally, the book turns its attention to the future with an evaluation of the church's missionary journey.

REGNUM RESOURCES FOR MISSION

Knud Jørgensen
Equipping for Service
Christian Leadership in Church and Society
2012 / 978-1-908355-06-5 / 150pp

This book is written out of decades of experience of leading churches and missions in Ethiopia, Geneva, Norway and Hong Kong. Combining the teaching of Scripture with the insights of contemporary management philosophy, Jørgensen writes in a way which is practical and applicable to anyone in Christian service. "The intention has been to challenge towards a leadership relevant for work in church and mission, and in public and civil society, with special attention to leadership in Church and organisation."

Mary Miller
What does Love have to do with Leadership?
2013 / 978-1-908355-10-2 / 100pp

Leadership is a performing art, not a science. It is the art of influencing others, not just to accomplish something together, but to want to accomplish great things together. Mary Miller captures the art of servant leadership in her powerful book. She understands that servant leaders challenge existing processes without manipulating or overpowering people.

Mary Miller (Ed)
Faces of Holistic Mission
Stories of the OCMS Family
2013 / 978-1-908355-32-4 / 104pp

There is a popular worship song that begins with the refrain, 'look what the Lord has done, look what the Lord has done'. This book does exactly that; it seeks to show what the Lord has done. Fifteen authors from five different continents identify what the Lord has indeed been doing, and continues to do, in their lives. These are their stories.

David Cranston and Ruth Padilla DeBorst (Eds)
Mission as Transformation
Learning from Catalysts
2013 / 978-1-908355-34-8 / 77pp

This book is the product of the first Stott-Bediako Forum, held in 2012 with the title *Portraits of Catalysts*. Its aim was to learn from the stories of Christian leaders whose lives and work have served as catalysts for transformation as each, in his or her particular way, facilitated the intersection between the Good News of Jesus Christ and the context in which they lived, in particular amongst people who are suffering.

Brian Woolnough (Ed)
Good News from Africa
Community Transformation Through the Church
2013 / 978-1-908355-33-1 / 123pp

This book discusses how sustainable, holistic, community development can be, and is being, achieved through the work of the local church. Leading African development practitioners describe different aspects of development through their own experience.

Makonen Getu (Ed)
Transforming Microfinance
A Christian Approach
2013 / 978-1-908355-31-7 / 264pp

"This book highlights the important role that Christian-based organisations bring to the delivery of financial services for the poor. It is times, significant and important and deserves a wide circulation".

Lord Carey of Clifton, former Archbishop of Canterbury

Jonathan Ingleby, Tan Kand San, Tan Loun Ling, (Eds)
Contextualisation & Mission Training
Engaging Asia's Religious Worlds
2013 / 978-1-908355-40-9 / 109pp

Contextualisation & Mission Training, offers "contextual frameworks" and "explorations" in order to enhance deeper engagement with the complexity of Asian social, cultural and religious systems.

On Eagle's Wings
Models in Mentoring
2013 / 978-1-908355-46-1 / 105pp

David Cranston writes unashamedly as a Christian for whom no account of mentoring would be complete without placing it in the biggest context of all – that of the relationship between humans and God.

John Lennox, Professor of Mathematics, University of Oxford
Fellow in Mathematics and Philosophy of Science

GENERAL REGNUM TITLES

Vinay Samuel, Chris Sugden (Eds)
The Church in Response to Human Need
1987 / 1870345045 / xii+268pp

Philip Sampson, Vinay Samuel, Chris Sugden (Eds)
Faith and Modernity
Essays in modernity and post-modernity
1994 / 1870345177 / 352pp

Klaus Fiedler
The Story of Faith Missions
1994 / 0745926878 / 428pp

Douglas Peterson
Not by Might nor by Power
A Pentecostal Theology of Social Concern in Latin America
1996 / 1870345207 / xvi+260pp

David Gitari
In Season and Out of Season
Sermons to a Nation
1996 / 1870345118 / 155pp

David. W. Virtue
A Vision of Hope
The Story of Samuel Habib
1996 / 1870345169 / xiv+137pp

Everett A Wilson
Strategy of the Spirit

J.Philip Hogan and the Growth of the Assemblies of God Worldwide, 1960 - 1990
1997 /1870345231/214

Murray Dempster, Byron Klaus, Douglas Petersen (Eds)
The Globalization of Pentecostalism
A Religion Made to Travel
1999 / 1870345290 / xvii+406pp

Peter Johnson, Chris Sugden (Eds)
Markets, Fair Trade and the Kingdom of God
Essays to Celebrate Traidcraft's 21st Birthday
2001 / 1870345193 / xii+155pp

Robert Hillman, Coral Chamberlain, Linda Harding
Healing & Wholeness
Reflections on the Healing Ministry
2002 / 978-1- 870345-35- 4 / xvii+283pp

David Bussau, Russell Mask
Christian Microenterprise Development
An Introduction
2003 / 1870345282 / xiii+142pp

David Singh
Sainthood and Revelatory Discourse
An Examination of the Basis for the Authority of Bayan in Mahdawi Islam
2003 / 8172147285 / xxiv+485pp

REGNUM AFRICA TITLES

Kwame Bediako
Jesus in Africa, The Christian Gospel in African History and Experience
(2000) (Theological Reflections from the South series)
SECOND EDITION FORTHCOMING 2013

Mercy Amba Oduyoye
Beads and Strands, Reflections of an African Woman on Christianity in Africa
(Theological Reflections from the South series)
2002 / 1-870345-41-X / 114pp

Kä Mana
Christians and Churches of Africa Envisioning the Future, Salvation in Christ and the Building of a new African Society
(Theological Reflections from the South series)
2002 / 1-870345-27-4 / 119pp

Ype Schaaf
On Their Way Rejoicing, The History and Role of the Bible in Africa
2002 / 1-870345-35-9 / 252pp

E.A.W. Engmann
Kpawo-Kpawo Toi Kpawo – Vol. 1, Adesai, Oboade, Lalai, Ajenui ke Shwemoi (Folklore of the Ga People)
(Gbotsui Series - Indigenous Sources of Knowledge in Ghanaian Languages)
2009 / 978-9988-1-2296-6 / 70pp

Philip Tetteh Laryea
Yesu Homowo Nuntso (Jesus, Lord of Homowo)
(Nyamedua series in Mother-tongue Theology)
(reprinted 2011) / 1-870345-54-1 / 176pp

E.A.W. Engmann
Kpawo-Kpawo Toi Kpawo – Vol. 2, Kusumii (Folklore of the Ga People)
(Gbotsui Series - Indigenous Sources of Knowledge in Ghanaian Languages)
2012 / 978-9988-1-2294-2, 186pp

Philip T. Laryea
Ephraim Amu: Nationalist, Poet and Theologian (1899–1995)
2012 / 978-9988-1-2293-5, 425pp

Jon P. Kirby
The Power and the Glory, Popular Christianity in Northern Ghana
(Trends in African Christianity Series)
2012 / 978-9988-1-2295-9, 350pp

For the up-to-date listing of the Regnum books visit www.ocms.ac.uk/regnum

Regnum Books International
Regnum is an Imprint of The Oxford Centre for Mission Studies
St. Philip and St. James Church
Woodstock Road
Oxford, OX2 6HR

regnum